A HISTORY OF THE
SOVIET UNION

SECOND EDITION

A HISTORY OF THE SOVIET UNION

David MacKenzie

The University of North Carolina at Greensboro

Michael W. Curran

The Ohio State University

Wadsworth Publishing Company
Belmont, California
A Division of Wadsworth, Inc.

History Editor: *Peggy Adams*
Editorial Assistant: *Cathie Fields*
Production Editor: *Angela Mann*
Designer: *Carolyn Deacy*
Print Buyer: *Barbara Britton*
Art Editor: *Bobbie Broyer*
Permissions Editor: *Bob Kauser*
Copy Editor: *Pat Tompkins*
Photo Researcher: *Judy Mason*
Compositor: *GGS*
Cover: *Carolyn Deacy*

Printed in the United States of America   50

3 4 5 6 7 8 9 10   95 94 93

Library of Congress Cataloging-in-Publication Data

MacKenzie, David.
   A history of the Soviet Union/David MacKenzie. Michael W.
Curran.—2nd ed.
      p.   cm.
   Includes bibliographical references and index.
   ISBN 0-534-14910-3
   1. Soviet Union—History—1917–   I. Curran, Michael W.
II. Title.
DK266.M22   1991   90-44832
947.84—dc20

To Bruce, Bryan, and Brendan MacKenzie;
To Sara and Elizabeth Curran;
and
In memory of Peter F. Curran

CONTENTS

2

REFORM AND REACTION, 1855 – 1904

3

OPPOSITION TO TSARISM

6

WAR AND REVOLUTION, 1914 – 1917

7

FROM MARCH TO NOVEMBER 1917

8

WAR COMMUNISM, 1917–1921

9

THE NEW ECONOMIC POLICY AND POWER STRUGGLE, 1921–1927

10

THE POLITICS OF STALINISM, 1928 – 1941

11

THE GREAT TRANSFORMATION

18

THE BREZHNEV ERA, 1964–1982

PREFACE TO THE SECOND EDITION

In this volume we provide a succinct, up-to-date history from the last years of the imperial tsarist regime to the current Soviet Union of Mikhail Gorbachev. We have attempted to balance the treatment of the Great Russian people, centering in Moscow, with that of the numerous national minorities of the Soviet Union, now emerging from a lengthy subordination to the Russian core.

The theories of Marxism-Leninism, presently being sharply questioned in the USSR and eastern Europe, cannot explain the history of 20th-century Russia and the Soviet Union, although they have sometimes produced useful insights and interpretations. Rejecting the tendency of Marxist-Leninists to force facts and trends into preconceived and rigid patterns, we question whether socioeconomic change necessarily precedes or determines political change. Many Western textbooks on Soviet history have slighted Soviet viewpoints and scholarship, but we have included such interpretations throughout this volume. Indeed, recent Soviet views often differ sharply from what was accepted doctrine only a few years ago. To introduce college and university students to major controversies among various historical schools, notably between Soviet and Western historians, and recently among Soviet scholars, we have included here a series of problems that present contrasting views and interpretations of key events. We hope that these problems will stimulate students to think about major historical issues, to probe further on their own, and to reach their own conclusions based on examination of the evidence. History, after all, is not primarily about memorizing facts and dates but analyzing and arranging specific data into general and meaningful patterns.

In *A History of the Soviet Union* we have tried to present a balanced overall view of modern and contemporary Russia and the USSR. Besides political, socioeconomic, military, and diplomatic history—written entirely by David MacKenzie—are several chapters written mainly by Michael W. Curran on Russian and Soviet culture. Our aim has been to write directly and straightforwardly for the present college generation, including material on recent cataclysmic events. We hope that this volume will also attract other readers interested in learning about the Russian and Soviet past. We welcome suggestions for improvement and modification.

David MacKenzie
Michael W. Curran

ACKNOWLEDGMENTS

To all those who kindly introduced me to the study of Russian history, language, and culture, profound thanks; without their inspiration I could not have written this book. To Boris Miller of Stuttgart in the German Federal Republic, my first teacher in the Russian language and history, who encouraged me to devote myself to lifelong study of the Russian and Slavic experience, heartfelt thanks. At the Russian Institute of Columbia University I had the good fortune to study under professors Philip E. Mosely, Geroid T. Robinson, Henry L. Roberts, and John Hazard, all of whom contributed greatly to my training in the field of Slavic studies. Extended visits to the USSR in 1958–59 and 1966 under the auspices of the Inter-University Committee on Travel Grants, and shorter sojourns in the Soviet Union in 1969 and 1974, provided me with essential firsthand exposure to Russia and the opportunity to travel widely and to conduct research in Soviet libraries and archives. At Moscow State University, I received valuable advice and encouragement from the eminent Soviet historians S. A. Nikitin and P. A. Zaionchkovskii. During these sojourns, I visited historic cities in the USSR and took photographs, some of which are contained in this book. Contributing expert advice and suggestions on individual chapters were professors Samuel Baron and John Keep, who, of course, are not responsible for errors this volume may contain. I wish to thank my graduate assistant, Susan Starnes, for her help in preparing the bibliography and putting together the manuscript for this book. This text derives, in part, from lectures for my students at the University of North Carolina at Greensboro; let me thank them for their interest and support. Without the patience and self-sacrifice of my wife, Patricia, I could neither have traveled to the Soviet Union nor had the time needed to complete this volume.

DM

While it is not possible to acknowledge all those who have contributed to this endeavor, I do wish to recognize some of the most important. I owe a very special debt of gratitude to those who first introduced me to Russia and Russian history: the late Michael B. Petrovich of the University of Wisconsin, and Werner Philipp of the Free University of Berlin. Their knowledge of Russia and their scholarly enthusiasm have been a source of inspiration over many years. My brief association with the late George C. Soules did much to shape my views of Russian history. Special thanks are due my colleagues at The Ohio State University: Arthur E. Adams, Charles Morley, Allan Wildman, and Eve Levin. Their criticisms, helpful suggestions, encouragement, and constant intellectual stimulation are reflected in this volume. I am particularly indebted to my graduate students whose enthusiasm and intellectual curiosity have contributed significantly to the evolution of this book. I hasten to add, however, that any shortcomings and errors contained in this study are entirely my own. I also wish to express my thanks to the Inter-University Committee on Travel Grants and to the Ministry of Higher and Specialized Secondary Education of the USSR, which together provided me with two periods of extended study and research in the USSR in 1962–63 and 1966. The Ohio State University has supported a number of additional trips to the Soviet Union, the most recent in 1988. The contributions of my two daughters, Sara and Elizabeth, who are just discovering the powerful magnetic qualities of Russian history and the Soviet Union, are too numerous to recount as are the contributions of my wife, Ann M. Salimbene; suffice it to say that without their support and encouragement and their understanding patience this work would never have been completed.

MWC

We would both like to thank reviewers Kathy Carter, High Point College; Benedict V. Maciuika, University of Connecticut; Thomas S. Noonan, University of Minnesota; Norman E. Saul, University of Kansas; and John Treadway, University of Richmond, for their helpful comments.

DM
MWC

A NOTE ON RUSSIAN DATES, NAMES, MEASURES, AND MONEY

Dating Russian events has been complicated by the use in Russia until 1918 of "Old Style" dates of the Julian calendar, which in the 18th century were 11 days behind those of the Gregorian calendar employed in the West. In the 19th century the lag was 12 days, and in the 20th 13 days. Early in 1918 the Soviet regime adopted the "New Style" Gregorian calendar. Generally, dates have been rendered here according to the calendar used in Russia at the time, except that we have shifted to "New Style" dates beginning with 1917.

Transliterating Russian names into English likewise presents some peculiar problems. We have adhered largely to the Library of Congress system, but have omitted diacritical marks for the sake of simplicity. Most Russian first names have been replaced with English equivalents, such as Peter, Nicholas, and Catherine, but not John and Basil instead of Ivan and Vasili.

Russian weights, measures, and distances have been rendered in their English equivalents for the convenience of English-speaking readers. However, Russian rubles have been retained with indications of their dollar value. The ruble, containing 100 kopeks, was worth about 50 cents in 1914. The official value of the Soviet ruble in 1990 was about $1.60 but foreign tourists were receiving 6 rubles to the dollar.

LIST OF FIGURES

LIST OF TABLES

LIST OF MAPS

CHAPTER ONE

BACKGROUND AND EARLY HISTORY

Is the Soviet Union, despite its numerous contemporary problems, still expansionist? Is Soviet Communism as a system still viable, or is it a disintegrating economic failure? Will the Soviet Union remain unified, or will it dissolve into its component national parts? If free emigration were permitted from the USSR, how many people would choose to leave? Such questions are being asked currently about the USSR and have been for some years. They cannot, of course, be answered definitively or even satisfactorily. However, we can uncover clues to the answers by examining the Soviet past and Soviet institutions.

This volume seeks to introduce the serious reader to 20th-century Russia and the Soviet Union through a factual survey of events and a number of problems that suggest the widely divergent views held both inside and outside about the Soviet Union. This Soviet history text, based on the last portion of our *A History of Russia and the Soviet Union*, includes a summary of major themes and developments in Russian history down to about 1900 for those who have not studied those earlier periods. We have sought to steer the perilous passage between excessive factual detail and facile generalization.

A history of the Soviet Union cannot properly begin in November 1917 if it hopes to explain the Bolshevik Revolution or the institutions and policies established by the Soviet regime thereafter. Rather, we need to look first at a few basic factors and controversies in Russian history and then summarize historical developments to 1855. In Chapter 2, we will examine major political, economic, social, cultural, and diplomatic developments from 1855 to 1904 at somewhat greater length. Chapter 3 will describe oppositionist and revolutionary movements in Russia from 1600 to 1904. Chapter 4 explores political developments from the Revolution of 1905 until World War I, and Chapter 5 will assess cultural trends before 1917. These chapters provide some background for studying the Soviet Russian experience since 1917. While concentrating on the Great Russian core of the Soviet Empire, we have sought also to indicate the role of some of the numerous national, ethnic, and religious groups that compose the Union of Soviet Socialist Republics.

A basic controversy between Soviet and non-Soviet scholars[1] in all periods of Russian history is whether external or internal factors and influences have predominated in shaping the course followed by the Russian and Soviet peoples. Generally speaking, Soviet scholars—those living and working in Soviet Russia since November 1917—basing their views necessarily upon the Marxist-Leninist scheme, have argued the primacy of *internal* factors in Russia's historical development from the formation of the first significant Russian state to the present. Internal socioeconomic change, they argue, has produced political change in an evolution from primitive communism through feudalism and capitalism to the present socialist Soviet system. External factors such as migrations of peoples, wars, conquest, and alien rule, they agree, have at times had a significant impact, but invariably have remained subsidiary to the inexorable laws of internal development and the maturation and decline of institutions.

Among non-Soviet historians, Normanist and Eurasian scholars especially have asserted that *external* influences upon Russia have been preeminent in influencing the development of its peculiar institutions,

---

[1]The latter may be subdivided into "Western" scholars of non-Russian nationality living in various parts of the world, prerevolutionary Russian historians who lived in Imperial Russia, and émigré Russian scholars who have left Soviet Russia since 1917. Each of these groups has its own peculiar ax or axes to grind in assessing Russian history; the dates and places of publication of their works often provide clues to their biases.

attitudes, and the character of its people since the dawn of history.[2] Thus, the Normanists—chiefly Scandinavian and German scholars—have asserted that the Varangians, or Vikings, allegedly invited into Russia by its Slavic tribes about A.D. 850 to rule over them, created the first cohesive Russian state and a basis for Russian civilization. These claims have been rejected vehemently by Soviet and some Western scholars. Nonetheless, it seems clear that the Varangian impact on early Russian development, as on western Europe, was significant, although by no means as great as the Normanists have affirmed. Less questionable, though also controversial, are Byzantine influences upon Kievan and subsequent Muscovite Russia. The late British historian B. H. Sumner described as Byzantine "gifts" to nascent Kievan Rus religion, the alphabet, the arts, and law, suggesting Russia's profound debt to Constantinople, or Tsargrad (the imperial city), as Russians called it. Thus some Byzantinists and Western scholars consider Kievan Rus a political and economic satellite of the Byzantine Empire. The Soviet view, on the other hand, emphasizes that Kievan Rus, described as a powerful and independent feudal Slavic state, was a native product evolving from previous tribal confederations living under primitive communism. Agriculture, they affirm, predominated over foreign trade in the Kievan era, suggesting independence from external influences.

Likewise, there is a wide divergence of interpretations over Asiatic impact on Russia, notably over the great Mongol invasion (1237–1241) that destroyed Kievan Rus and established Asiatic control over most parts of the Russian land for 200 to 250 years. The Eurasian school, taking a generally positive view of this cataclysmic event, regards Moscow as the political successor of the Golden Horde, stresses the growth and advantages of Eurasian trade, and considers the Mongol era as vital to an emergent Russian autocracy and empire. Soviet views of the Mongol conquest, however, resembling ancient Russian chronicle accounts, emphasize its terrible destructiveness and claim that the Mongol yoke was primarily responsible for centuries of Russian backwardness relative to a more fortunate western Europe. Furthermore, Soviet historians fail to discern major Mongol influence on Russia's institutional development.

Over the past three centuries the chief and most pervasive influence upon Russia and the Soviet Union unquestionably has been western European and still more recently American. Nonetheless, there is major disagreement between Western and Soviet scholars over its extent and impact on Russian institutions. The outstanding Russian historian V. O.

---

[2]On Normanism see *A History of Russia and the Soviet Union* (Homewood, Ill., 1987). pp. 23–26, and on the Eurasian school, pp. 97–98.

Kliuchevskii (1841–1911) discerned even in 17th-century Muscovy a profound cultural conflict between Greco-Byzantine traditional elements and values in Russian life associated with the Orthodox Church and Latin-Western values introduced into Muscovy by European travelers, merchants, and officers. What had been in Kliuchevskii's view merely casual contacts with the West prior to 1600 became subsequently genuine influence (*vliianie*) upon Russian institutions, beginning with the army.[3] Under Peter I, "the Great" (1672–1725), this Western influence deepened and broadened. Most Western scholars agree that western Europe served as the chief model for the partial modernization of Russian institutions under Peter I, Catherine II, and Alexander I and II, from roughly 1700 to 1881. However, Soviet scholars, while granting that Western influences were undoubtedly present, affirm that the reforms instituted by those monarchs originated primarily in Russian needs and were derived from the Russian past. Similarly, Western economic historians argue whether Russia represented a backward European land following belatedly in western Europe's footsteps or a unique entity between Europe and Asia pursuing its own distinctive development. Did Russia, after 1860, undergo "modernization" (C. E. Black)—a process faced by all modern societies, or "Westernization" (T. von Laue), that is, adapting its institutions to a west European model? Finally, since World War II, especially since Stalin's death in 1953, American influences, notably cultural and economic, have become significant despite stubborn Soviet efforts until recently to block their entry or application.

To place Soviet history in proper context, underlying geographical, climatic, and ethnic factors must also be understood. The peoples of the USSR, commonly called the Soviet Union, shaped by their natural environment, have responded in distinctive ways to its multiple challenges, thus making Imperial Russia and the Soviet Union significantly different from both the United States and the countries of western Europe.

GEOGRAPHY

The Soviet Union, of which Russia comprises about three fourths the area and about half the population, is a huge country almost three times the size of the United States and about equal in area to all of North America. Spanning most of eastern Europe and northern Asia, it extends about 6,000 miles east to west and over 3,000 miles north to south to include

---

[3]Kluchevsky, *Course of Russian History* (New York, 1911–1931) III.

about one sixth the land area of the globe. By its vastness and location the Soviet Union is in a position to dominate the combined land mass of Europe and Asia called Eurasia.

Most of the USSR is a huge plain extending eastward from Poland almost to the Pacific Ocean. Narrowing as one moves across Siberia, it runs out in the plateau and mountainous terrain of eastern Siberia. This expanse is barely interrupted by the low, worn Ural Mountains (maximum height 6,214 feet), which divide Europe from Asia only in part. Between the Urals and the Caspian Sea to the southwest is a gap some 800 miles wide through which successive waves of Asiatic invaders poured into Europe until the 13th century. Impressive mountain ranges are limited to the frontiers: the Carpathians in the southwest, the Caucasus to the south, and the Pamir, Tien-Shan, and Altai mountains on the borders of Afghanistan, India, and China. European Russia, where the main drama of Russian history has been played, is mostly flat and low. The Valdai Hills, a plateau in the northwest where the great European Russian rivers rise, reaches a maximum elevation of only 1,000 feet above sea level.

Flowing slowly through the European Russian plain, the rivers have served throughout history as arteries of communication and commerce. The Northern Dvina and Pechora flow northward into the Arctic basin; most of the others southward: the Dniester, Bug, Dnieper, and Don into the Black Sea and the Sea of Azov, and the majestic "mother" Volga, comparable in breadth and importance to the Mississippi, into the Caspian Sea. These rivers and their tributaries form an excellent water communications system, greatly improved in modern times by connecting canals. In Siberia (the region east of the Urals and north of Central Asia) the Ob, Lena, Enisei, and Kolyma rivers, moving northward into the frozen Arctic, are of limited commercial value. Only the Amur, part of the modern boundary with China, moves eastward into the Pacific.

The climate of the Soviet Union is continental, that is, marked by extremes of heat and cold. Most of Russia lies in the latitudes of Canada and Alaska. The Gulf Stream, which moderates the climate of the east coast of the United States and the northwest coast of western Europe, affects only the western part of the north Russian coast from Murmansk to Archangel. Extremes of temperature generally increase as one moves eastward, but even in European Russia there are no internal mountain barriers to keep icy winds from sweeping to the Black Sea. Northeast Siberia is one of the world's coldest regions: temperatures as low as −90° F have been recorded in Verkhoiansk region. However, heat waves occur in European Russia, and even Siberia, during the summer. In the Central Asian deserts temperatures of 120° F are not uncommon. Precipitation in the USSR, partly because of the continental climate, is generally moderate or light and often greatest in summer.

There are five major soil and vegetation zones in the USSR, stretching generally northeast to southwest. About 15 percent of the country in the extreme north is level or undulating treeless plain, called tundra, and 47 percent of it has permanently frozen subsoil. (See Map 1.1.) The tundra, a virtually uninhabited wasteland, has many lakes and swamps, with moss and low shrubs the only vegetation. South of it lies the taiga, or coniferous forest in the north and mixed coniferous and deciduous forest farther south. This vast forest belt, the largest in the world, extends across all Russia and covers over half its territory. The poor ashy soils, called *podzol,* of the boggy coniferous forest with their low acid content are mostly unfit for crops. Agriculture is possible only in cleared portions of the southern forest region. The mixed forest zone to the south, the heart of Muscovite Russia, has richer gray and brown soils. Below this the forest shades into wooded steppe or meadow, mostly with very fertile black soil (*chernozem*), excellent for grains wherever there is sufficient rainfall. Still farther south is mostly treeless prairie like the American Great Plains, extending monotonously for hundreds and hundreds of miles, also a fertile black soil region. East of the Caspian Sea this black soil shades into semidesert, then true desert to the south and east. In the Crimea and along the Caucasian shore of the Black Sea lies a small subtropical region, Russia's Riviera. Early frosts, a short growing season, and barren or frozen soil mean that only about 10 percent of the Soviet Union is under cultivation, although one third is potentially arable. In some regions with rich soil rainfall is often insufficient for crops. Even the black soil region of the southern steppe has a shorter growing season than the American plains.

How has geography affected Russia's history? Until the late 19th century, chiefly European Russia should be considered. Siberia remained sparsely populated, its great resources unexploited; Central Asia and the Caucasus were acquired only in the 19th century. European Russia's flat plains fostered colonization and expansion, persistent themes in Russian history for almost 1,000 years. Unworried by waste, Russians cleared forest glades and ploughed up virgin steppe lands. In the 19th century, a continental colonialism developed as the Russians occupied areas next to their borders.

Geography has provided the USSR with natural ocean frontiers on the north and east and mountain boundaries in the south and southwest. These frontiers were attained after centuries of struggle with Asian invaders and by Russian expansion. In the west such natural barriers were lacking. In modern history foreign invasions of Russia have come from the west, and Russian efforts at expansion have focused there. Until

Map 1.1 *Vegetation Zones*

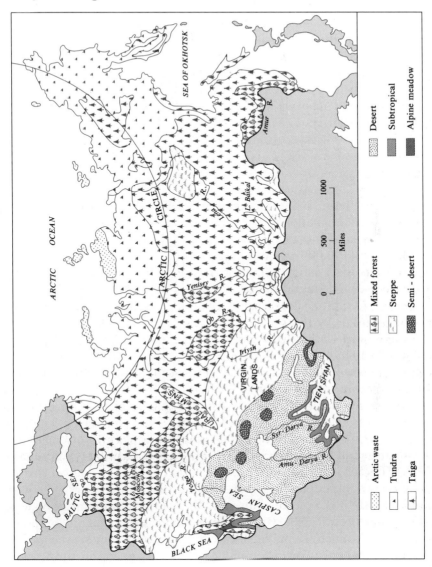

recently, Russia was largely landlocked without ready access to warm-water ports or to foreign markets. Some historians, such as R. J. Kerner, have interpreted Russian expansion as a drive to secure such ports and unfettered access to the Pacific Ocean and Baltic, Black, and Mediterranean seas. Vast distances, while contributing to the eventual defeat or absorption of invaders, have complicated the achievement or maintenance of unity and perhaps have promoted highly centralized, authoritarian regimes. The severe climate of the north and Siberia contributed to sparse population and easy Russian conquest.

THE PEOPLES

The Soviet Union, a multinational and multiethnic country, contains almost 180 distinct nationalities and tribes, speaking about 125 languages and dialects, and practicing 40 different religions. Ninety-five groups number over 100,000 persons each; 54 have their own national territories. About three fourths of the Soviet population are eastern Slavs who began as a single people, then separated after the Mongol invasion of 1237–1241 into three major groups: Russians, Ukrainians, and Byelorussians.

Russians, or Great Russians, the most numerous Soviet people, number about 145 million or 51 percent of the USSR's population. (See Map 1.2.) They have played a dominant historical and political role in both the Russian Empire and the Soviet Union. About five sixths of ethnic Russians reside in the RSFSR (Russian Republic), which occupies almost three fourths of the entire Soviet Union. The remaining 25 million Russians live in other union republics, mostly in large cities, often holding key political and economic positions. The almost 45 million Ukrainians, the USSR's second most numerous national group, are descended directly from the people of Kievan Rus. In the 17th century they were reunited with the Great Russians, initially received autonomy, then were subjected to direct Russian rule. Presently about 85 percent of Ukrainians live in the Ukrainian Republic, where they compose about three fourths of the population. Over 3.5 million Ukrainians reside in the Russian Republic. Byelorussians, or "White Russians," number over 10 million and compose about 80 percent of the people of the Byelorussian Republic; some 1.6 million live elsewhere. Byelorussia was absorbed into the Russian Empire in the 17th and 18th centuries. Most of the Soviet Union's approximately one million Poles, the fourth largest Slavic group, entered the USSR involuntarily in 1939 after Soviet annexation of eastern Poland.

Map 1.2 *Chief Soviet Ethnic Groups**

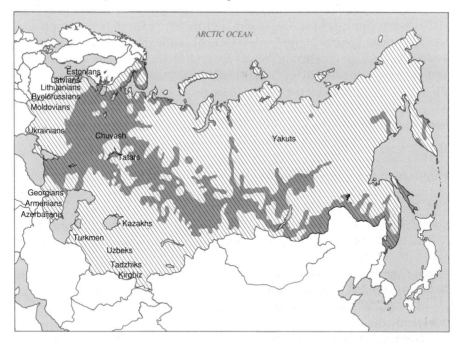

*Predominantly Russian areas are shown in gray.
Source: Joe LeMonnier *NYT Magazine* Jan. 28, 1990. Copyright 1990 by The New York Times Company. Reprinted by permission.

The Baltic peoples—some 5.5 million—mostly inhabit the republics of Latvia, Lithuania, and Estonia in the extreme western USSR. After enjoying independence from 1919 to 1940, they were forcibly annexed to the USSR under the Nazi-Soviet Pact of 1939. The 3 million Lithuanians had a proud heritage of independence as a Grand Duchy, then were linked with Poland until annexed to the Russian Empire in 1795. Latvian and Lithuanian are Baltic Indo-European languages; Estonian is a Uralic tongue closely related to Finnish. All three peoples use the Latin alphabet, are strongly European in outlook, and are mostly Catholic or Lutheran.

The leading peoples of the Caucasus are Armenians, Georgians, and Azerbaijani, and their three republics contain about 15 million people. Many of the 4.4 million Armenians live outside the Armenian Republic within which they represent almost 90 percent of the population. Armenians, like Georgians and Azerbaijani, are heirs of an ancient and proud civilization; their language is Indo-European. Annexed to the Russian Empire in 1828, Armenia enjoyed brief independence from 1918 to 1920, as did Georgia and Azerbaijan, before being forcibly incorporated into the Soviet Union. Neighboring Georgia with about 5 million people, two thirds Georgians who are mostly Eastern Orthodox, have an alphabet and language totally different from Russian. Georgia was annexed to Russia in 1801. Unlike their Christian neighbors, most of the Muslim Azerbaijani, who speak a Turkic language, live in Soviet Azerbaijan; many live in neighboring Iran. The mountainous Caucasus region also contains many smaller groups, some possessing autonomous status.

Muslims, numbering over 50 million persons, are the second largest religious group in the USSR after the Orthodox. In the Volga River basin live smaller Turko-Tatar peoples including the Kazan Tatars, Bashkirs, and Chuvash; the Crimean Tatars are only now returning to their homeland. All are descendants of the Mongol and Turkic warriors who conquered Russia in the 13th century only to be overrun in the subsequent Russian eastward and southward expansion. Further east lies Soviet Central Asia with some 45 million people, comprising five union republics established arbitrarily early in the Soviet era: the Uzbek, Kazakh, Turkmen, Tajik, and Kirghiz republics. Their inhabitants are chiefly Muslim with Turkic languages written in Cyrillic, except for the Iranian Tajiks. Between 1730 and 1885 Russian armies conquered Central Asia and renamed it Russian Turkestan. It was absorbed into the Soviet Union by the early 1920s.

Two other significant minorities in the Soviet Union that lack union republics of their own recently have left the USSR in large numbers. Germans (about 1.5 million) who mostly settled along the Volga River in the 18th century were scattered during World War II; many have emigrated to West Germany. Jews (some 1.8 million) reside chiefly in large cities of European Russia and the Ukraine; since 1970 emigration has sharply reduced their numbers.

Russian remains the official language of the Soviet government and army and is spoken natively by about 60 percent of its inhabitants, studied as a second language in all non-Russian schools, and spoken by a majority of other Soviet citizens. Ukrainian, the second most widespread language of the USSR, is related closely to Russian, and Byelorussian is even closer; all three share a common Cyrillic alphabet. Until 1985 there was a strong trend toward linguistic Russification, which was reversed under Gorbachev. Unlike the United States—a melting pot for diverse national and racial elements—the Soviet Union has preserved distinct national territories and languages. There have been disquieting recent trends toward ethnic violence.

CHALLENGE AND RESPONSE

Location, climate, and topography have confronted the Russian people with severe challenges during a difficult, turbulent history. Until recently Russia, and the USSR, was a poor country where most people extracted a precarious living from the soil. Poverty, vulnerability to attack, and poor interior communications helped produce responses distinguishing Russian history and culture in important ways from those of western Europe and the United States. The chief responses to peculiar Russian conditions and problems seem to have been autocracy, collectivism, and mysticism; these may provide keys to unlock the complex Russian past. The first two, especially, have persisted regardless of regime or ideology as vital elements of the Russian experience.

Autocracy, or statism, conspicuously absent during early Russian history, began to develop during the unification of Great Russia about 1500. It has persisted ever since as a centralized monarchical or Communist state with a virtual monopoly of power, except for a few brief "times of trouble" (1598–1613, 1725–1730, and 1917–1921). During the 16th and 17th centuries autocracy grew as limitations on the tsar's powers, such as an independent hereditary aristocracy, representative institutions like the assembly of the lands, and an autonomous church, withered. Although of Greek origin, autocracy in Russia derived more from the practice of the Mongol Golden Horde than from Byzantine political theory. Russian tsars, such as Ivan IV, "the Terrible," Peter the Great, and Nicholas I, wielded awesome authority that resembled Oriental despotism more closely than west European monarchy.

Unlike western Europe, Russia did not experience prolonged or complete feudalism and fell increasingly under strong, centralized monarchical power. People and property became possessions of the Muscovite state, as they had been in the Mongol Golden Horde. Institutions that challenged state authority were gradually stripped of influence. Autocracy grew more powerful and pervasive over time, mobilized Russia's natural and human resources in order to resist external invasions, and conquered contiguous areas; in the Soviet period it created formidable industrial and military power. Absorbing parts of the Byzantine and Mongol political traditions, autocracy used the principle of service to the state to subordinate to its dictates both the bodies and minds of individuals, not protected as in western Europe by corporate groups with inherent rights.

Collectivism, which contrasts with the individualism of western Europe and the United States, has been another peculiar Russian response linked closely with autocracy. For centuries, under tsars and commissars alike, most land in Russia has been held and worked in common, and taxes were gathered and paid collectively by village communities, long after these practices died out in western Europe. Collectivism aided Muscovy, the Russian Empire, and finally Soviet Russia, to mobilize resources to combat severe external and internal challenges. The collectivism inherent in the Great Russian repartitional commune of the 18th and 19th centuries foreshadowed that of Soviet collective and state farms in our own era. About 1600, autocracy subjected a semifree Russian peasantry to the collective bondage of serfdom, a degrading but vital feature of Russian life until the 1860s.

Finally, the prevalent mysticism of the Russian Orthodox tradition, increasing subordination of the Church to the state, and the relative lack of intellectual inquiry within the Church differed greatly from the rationalism and questioning in western Catholic and Protestant faiths. In Muscovite Russia, matters such as the spelling of the name of Jesus and elements of ritual and tradition acquired vast significance for an unsophisticated populace. The prevalent belief that Russia was the center of the only true faith tended to intensify suspicion of foreigners and their institutions. In a sense Soviet Communism, despite a theoretically antithetical ideology, continued this mystical tradition. Until World War II, Soviet spokesmen reiterated that the USSR was the only land of socialism and center of the true Marxist-Leninist faith. Xenophobia, extreme fear of foreigners and suspicion of their motives, persisted and was reinforced deliberately by the Soviet regime. Like Russian Orthodoxy under tsarism, with the passing years Soviet Marxist-Leninist ideology also has tended to degenerate into a sterile dogmatism incapable of inspiring or convincing the young.

To be sure, the roles and personalities of rulers, both tsarist and Soviet, have been important in shaping Russian history, providing a convenient, if not always revealing, method of dividing it into periods. Such major figures as Ivan IV, Peter, and Catherine the Great in the tsarist era, and Lenin, Stalin, Khrushchev, and perhaps Gorbachev in the Soviet period stand out above the flood of events. But unless one accepts the "great man" (or woman) theory of history, to view an era through the career and character of the ruler exaggerates the importance of individual leadership and oversimplifies complex and continuing trends. Instead, tracing such themes as autocracy, collectivism, and mysticism through history may prove more effective in clarifying how Russia and its peoples have evolved.

SUMMARY OF RUSSIAN HISTORY TO 1855
Ancient Rus[4] (to about A.D. 850)

Because of the lack of written Russian sources, the era prior to the mid-9th century, often called ancient or prehistoric Russia, remains obscure despite numerous archeological discoveries in the 20th century. Where the Slavs originated and when they settled the western portion of today's USSR, remains disputed. No central political, military, or economic organizations existed among these rather primitive pagan people, who lacked a written alphabet and worshipped local or regional deities often associated with nature. The early Slavs were constantly exposed to incursions by new waves of invaders sweeping across the steppes out of Asia. Following the Marxian scheme, Soviet historians designate this period primitive communism with most land and goods held collectively. The Slavs gradually prevailed over non-Slavic Asiatic intruders. The first Russian state, affirm Soviet scholars, arose in what is today the western Ukraine in the 6th or 7th century A.D.; by the mid-9th century feudalism had triumphed in both eastern and western Europe.

Kievan Rus (about 850–1240)

Controversy persists over the formation of Kievan Rus in the mid-9th century among Soviet, Normanist, and Western scholars,[5] but the results are evident. During the late 9th century, a federation emerged of about a dozen Slav-Varangian principalities, ruled by princes belonging to a single dynasty, generally called the House of Riurik, and centered in Kiev in the south and Novgorod in the north. Unity was forged partly by several Varangian-Slav attacks upon the Byzantine capital, Constantinople. Normally, the prince of Kiev was senior in the ruling family, exercising limited and uncertain control over other principalities. Politically, Kievan Rus comprised a federation, later a confederation, decentralized and lacking a single army or administration. According to Soviet scholars, it constituted a powerful feudal state with a definite sense of national purpose. Within Kievan Rus political power was divided among ruling princes, noble advisory councils (*boyar duma*), and town councils (*vieche*), reflecting respectively monarchical, aristocratic, and democratic principles. At its peak in the 10th and 11th centuries, Kievan

---

[4]The term *Rus* refers to much of the territory that would later become Russia. We will use *Rus* until about 1300, when the process of unification of Great Russia under the aegis of Moscow began.

[5]See MacKenzie and Curran, *A History of Russia and the Soviet Union*, pp. 23–29.

Rus traded extensively with nearby Byzantium, although most of its population engaged in subsistence agriculture. Kievan society was diverse and mobile: middle-class freemen *(liudi)* were significant, its peasantry was mostly free, although there were indentured groups and slaves. Thus it does not appear to fit the feudal patterns of contemporary western Europe.

Internationally, Kievan Rus's chief relations were with the Byzantine Empire, and some scholars even consider it a Byzantine satellite. Following a series of attacks from Kievan Rus upon Constantinople, regular commercial relations were established as well as close links between Kievan and Byzantine rulers. During the 12th century Kievan Rus's commercial and political ties with central and western Europe increased. There was little contact between Kievan Rus and the Arab world to the south.

Culturally, Kievan Rus relied heavily on Byzantium, deriving its alphabet, religion, art, church architecture, and iconography (paintings on wood portraying religious themes) from Constantinople. Thus the Greek brothers Saints Cyril and Methodius created a written alphabet for the Slavs, fostering the translation of Greco-Byzantine religious works into Church Slavonic. In 988, Kievan Rus converted to Orthodox Christianity under Prince Vladimir I, though paganism survived for centuries in remote areas. Greco-Byzantine clergy dominated an Orthodox Church directly subordinate to the Patriarchate of Constantinople. The cultural traditions that emerged during Kievan times—notably those of the Orthodox Church—would play a very significant role in the development of Russian culture into the 18th century and beyond.

Both internal and external factors contributed to the decline and fall of the Kievan Rus federation: political disintegration, rising civil strife, economic decline, vulnerability to nomadic attacks from the east, and inability to resist the great Mongol onslaught of the mid-13th century. Nonetheless, the Kievan epoch represented a diversified, relatively free, and prosperous beginning to Russian history.

Appanage or Mongol Era (1240 to about 1450)

Relative unity of the early Kievan era yielded to disunity and fragmentation after 1139, accelerated a century later by the Mongol conquest. Kiev's politicoeconomic decline was accompanied by outward migration and emergence of three separate centers of life in Rus, all subject to much foreign control of influence between 1200 and 1450. The southwestern principalities of Galicia and Volhynia retained former Kievan culture and prosperity until falling victim first to Mongol conquest, then Lithuanian and Polish rule. In the 12th and early 13th

centuries, the cities of Suzdal and Vladimir, in the northeastern mesopotamia formed by the Volga and Oka rivers, flourished briefly before
succumbing to Mongol conquest. From 1157 to 1240, Vladimir served as
unofficial capital of all Rus, replacing declining Kiev. In the northwest,
the virtually independent commercial city-republics of Novgorod and
Pskov, resembling by their institutions the German Hansa towns, continued Kievan traditions of diversity and freedom well into the 15th century.
Developing an extensive empire to the north and east, Novgorod in the
13th century under Prince Alexander Nevskii repelled invaders from the
west (Teutonic Knights, Swedes, and Lithuanians), but felt compelled to
submit to Mongol overlordship.

In the midst of this fragmentation of Rus came the devastating
Mongol invasion (1237–1241), the final Asiatic assault on Rus. The
triumphant Mongols, under Khan Batu, grandson of Chingis-khan,
established the Golden Horde, a separate state centered at Sarai on the
Volga. From there they administered the conquered country through
Rus vassal princes who supplied their Mongol overlords with tribute
money and army recruits. The khans of the Golden Horde were Oriental
despots claiming total authority and ownership of all land; they were
emulated subsequently by their faithful servitors and tax collectors, the
princes of Moscow.

Moscow's initial rise occurred during this Mongol or appanage era.
Founded in the mid-12th century in the northeastern mesopotamia,
Moscow enjoyed a favorable location for trade, settlement, and colonization. In the early 14th century, the Golden Horde bestowed the grand
princely title on Moscow; it also became the seat of the Orthodox Church,
which the Mongols generally did not persecute. In 1380, Moscow's Prince
Dmitri "Donskoi" (of the Don), heading an army of Russian princely
contingents, inflicted the first serious defeat on the Horde. By the mid-
15th century, as the Horde fragmented into several warring khanates, an
expanded Moscow, or Muscovy, constituted one of several major Russian
principalities contending for territory and power in central Russia.

The culture of Rus under Mongol rule, cut off from most outside
contacts, was forced inward. Byzantine forms in art and architecture
adopted during the Kievan era were internalized, and in the process
much of the refined Byzantine subtlety and sophistication was lost. Many
skilled crafts, such as pottery making, elaborate enamel work, and intricate gold and silver work, practiced in the towns declined or disappeared altogether. However, Orthodox Byzantine Christianity helped
preserve the national identity and the nucleus for a national Russian
culture.

Muscovite Era (1450–1689)

During the 15th century Mongol disintegration yielded to increasing integration and unification of Great Russia under Muscovite princes. Ivan III, "the Great" (1462–1505), defeated and incorporated Novgorod, Tver, and lesser rivals, then established diplomatic relations with leading European states. Ivan III set for Moscow the aim of securing control over all territories that once had belonged to Kievan Russia. After marrying the niece of the last Byzantine emperor whose remaining domains had fallen to the Ottoman Turks, he asserted that Moscow was the true successor to Byzantine imperial traditions, claimed equality with European rulers, and refused further subservience or tribute to the fragmented Mongol Golden Horde. Internally, he undermined the power of his brothers and other appanage princes, built a more centralized army, issued a national law code, and increased church dependence on the crown. The centralizing policies and military victories of this so-called gatherer of the Russian lands created a powerful but primitive Muscovite monarchical state.

Ivan III's grandson, Ivan IV, "the Terrible" (ruled 1533–1584), was crowned as the first Muscovite tsar (Caesar) in 1547. Conquering the Mongol khanates along the Volga River in the 1550s, he inaugurated an eastward expansion across the Urals, which by 1640 had brought Russian Cossacks (frontiersmen) and fur trappers to the forbidding shores of the northern Pacific. Claiming full autocratic powers, Ivan IV launched a reign of terror—the Oprichnina (1564–1572)—against titled boyars, churchmen, and other domestic opponents. Defeated in the lengthy Livonian War by a western coalition of Sweden, Lithuania, and Poland, and driven from the shores of the Baltic Sea, Ivan created near chaos at home with his unbridled Oprichnina and then murdered his eldest son, Ivan Ivanovich. In 1598 the death of Fedor, his imbecile second son, ended the old Muscovite dynasty and helped produce a "time of troubles" (1598–1613) involving a struggle for the throne, a social revolt of the southern frontier against the Moscow elite, and foreign intervention by Sweden and Poland. This bloody, confused era ended with expulsion of foreign invaders and restoration of unity under the new Romanov dynasty (ruled 1613–1917), elected by a representative assembly of the land (*zemskii sobor*).

Early Romanov tsars (1613–1689) were mediocre and physically weak, but royal power, supported by a growing central bureaucracy, prevailed over the hereditary aristocracy (*boyars*), the church, and poorly organized representative bodies. Serfdom and a virtual caste system enslaved over 90 percent of the Russian people and bound them to their residences and occupations. By mid-century serfs on private estates were under the absolute power of noble landowners who controlled their lives and exacted increasing rents and forced labor services. There developed a profound schism in the Russian Orthodox Church with millions of Russian peasants remaining "Old Believers," worshipping from traditional Muscovite church books; they were anathematized by the official Church and persecuted by the state. Under the early Romanovs was completed the conquest of Siberia and incorporation of the eastern Ukraine after lengthy warfare with a disorganized and disintegrating Poland.

The cultural traditions of northeast Russia received a powerful impetus from Moscow's emergence in the 15th century as a major political, economic, and cultural center with the support of the Orthodox Church. A sense of religious superiority emerged, especially after Constantinople's fall to the Ottoman Turks in 1453, which fostered the subsequent concept of Moscow as "the Third Rome," that is, as the successor of Rome and Constantinople as the center of "true" Christianity. Russians now viewed Moscow as the capital of an independent Muscovite state and the spiritual capital of Orthodox Christendom. Historical chronicles and cultural attitudes began to reflect the enhanced stature of an independent Muscovy. However, the progressive centralization of Russian political and economic institutions under Moscow produced a rigid, immobile, and Church-dominated culture that severely restricted individual initiative and creativity. The unfortunate results were cultural stagnation and a very defensive attitude toward non-Russian cultures. The monolithic Byzantine cultural tradition of the Orthodox Church was finally shattered during its 17th-century struggle with the tsarist state over liturgy and ritual. The triumph of the state prepared the way for a reorientation and secularization of Russian culture.

Early Imperial Era (about 1700–1855)

The first energetic Romanov ruler and unchallenged Russian autocrat was huge and dynamic Peter I, "the Great" (ruled 1689–1725). During a turbulent youth, Peter developed a passionate interest in the army, navy, and European technology. After almost a year studying technology and recruiting experts in western Europe, Peter returned home, crushed opposition of the conservative palace guard (*streltsi*), and launched the Great Northern War (1699–1721) against imperial Sweden. Eventual victory in that conflict ended Russia's virtual isolation from Europe, gave it control of the eastern Baltic shores (his "window to the West"), and enabled Peter to construct a new capital—St. Petersburg—near the Baltic Sea. (See Map 1.3.) During that war Peter transformed an ill-disciplined,

Map 1.3 *Expansion of Russia—1462 to 1815*

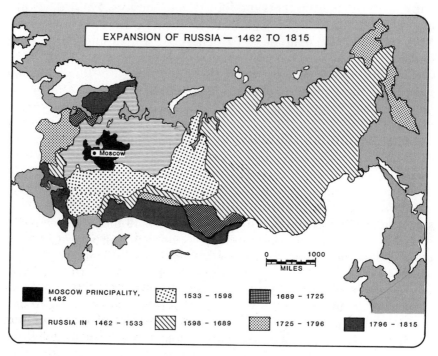

EXPANSION OF RUSSIA — 1462 TO 1815

Moscow

0   1000
MILES

MOSCOW PRINCIPALITY, 1462

RUSSIA IN 1462 – 1533

1533 – 1598

1598 – 1689

1689 – 1725

1725 – 1796

1796 – 1815

inefficient armed force into a large regular standing army of conscripts. By now a vast Eurasian multinational empire, Russia became a great European power, recognized as such by the others: Great Britain, France, the Austrian Empire, and a rising Prussia. Requirements for war underlay most of Peter I's far-reaching domestic reforms: a centralized administration, headed by a Senate and organized by a Table of Ranks into parallel hierarchies for the military, civil service, and the court; a more efficient and onerous system of taxation of the masses; and a superficially educated and westernized upper-class elite. The Petrine reforms harnessed all elements of a highly stratified Russian society, resting on a bonded peasantry paying the poll tax and a nobility pressed into lifelong service to the state. Peter's mercantilistic economic policies laid foundations for Russian heavy industry, but did little to promote the growth of towns or an urban middle class so important for economic development in western Europe. Russia remained overwhelmingly rural, peasant, and illiterate, scarcely affected by Petrine reforms of dress and beard shaving. In 1725, Peter I died suddenly without designating a successor.

2nd wife
Catherine I
1725-7

Following an interlude often called the "Era of Palace Revolutions" because a series of minors and women were enthroned and manipulated by the nobility in Peter's Guard's regiments, a remarkable German woman married to the immature ruler, Peter III, usurped power as Catherine II, "the Great" (ruled 1762–1796). She ruled through a series of official favorites who shared her bed but rarely her power. Posing as a legitimate, enlightened despot like Frederick II of emergent Prussia, the superbly educated Catherine continued Peter the Great's expansion at the expense of Poland—thrice partitioned—and the Ottoman Empire—twice defeated. By the end of her reign Russia had solved the Swedish, Polish, and Turkish "problems." Millions of Poles and Jews had been subjected involuntarily to Russian rule, which now extended over the entire Baltic region, Byelorussia, the entire Ukraine, and the northern shores of the Black Sea. Initially aligned with Prussia in a northern bloc, later Russia allied with Austria; they were opposed by France especially because of their partitions of Catholic Poland. Russia began to exert influence over Christian peoples in the Balkans, subject to a corrupt and disintegrating Ottoman Empire. At home, Catherine reformed provincial and local government, crushed the massive Pugachev Revolt of peasants and Cossacks, and rewarded her loyal nobility with rights and privileges. Catherine continued the Petrine policies of westernization and cultural and economic development. Exploiting a freer intellectual atmosphere, liberal noblemen like Nikolai Novikov and Alexander Radishchev criticized serfdom and autocracy, only to be imprisoned when the aging empress grew fearful that the ideas of the French Revolution would prove contagious.

The last period of an old regime resting on serfdom and autocracy (1796–1855) was an age of bureaucratic monarchy as rulers and their ministers gradually reasserted control over the nobility. The autocratic Paul I (ruled 1796–1801), Catherine's disgruntled son, stressed Prussian-style discipline even over the nobility and Guards. Predictably, he was murdered by a palace conspiracy, which placed in power his enigmatic son, Alexander I (ruled 1801–1825). Aided by the able Mikhail Speranskii, Alexander partially reformed the central administration (replacing Petrine administrative colleges with European-style ministries) and restricted serfdom, avoiding fundamental political and social change for fear it might undermine his autocratic powers. Thus he refused to implement Speranskii's reform plan of 1809, proposing a monarchy based on law with strict separation of functions and several levels of elected assemblies culminating in a national assembly (State Duma). Drawn into abortive coalition wars against Napoleon (1805–1807), Alexander felt compelled to conclude an unpopular alliance with the French emperor and join his Continental System directed against Britain. In 1812, Napoleon launched a massive invasion of Russia and reached Moscow only to be defeated by Russian national resistance, a severe climate, and bad roads. Russia then joined the other European great powers to destroy the Napoleonic empire. The Congress of Vienna (1814–1815), ending the Napoleonic wars, confirmed Russia's predominance in eastern Europe and its annexation of most of Poland, Finland, and Bessarabia, adding millions more non-Russians to its empire. For the next 40 years a conservative and satiated Russian Empire aligned itself with equally conservative and legitimist Prussian and Austrian monarchies. All three feared liberal ideas emanating from western Europe, notably Britain and France, and national feeling of subject peoples.

Alexander I's reign ended in political reaction, public disillusionment, and revolt by liberal noblemen. Forming secret societies that spread across Europe after 1815, the so-called Decembrists mostly favored constitutional monarchy, liberal reforms, and abolition of serfdom. However, Pavel Pestel, leader of their Southern Society, whom some consider Russia's first professional revolutionary, advocated a Jacobin-type unitary republic and confiscation of much noble land. After Alexander I's sudden death (1825), the Northern Society tried to seize power with the slogan: "Constantine and Constitution!" Constantine, Alexander's younger brother, ordinarily would have become tsar, but had in a secret letter renounced his claims in favor of his younger brother Nicholas. Some soldiers in regiments supporting Constantine apparently believed "constitution," which has a feminine ending in Russian, was Constantine's wife! In any case, Nicholas quickly quelled the poorly planned Decembrist Revolt, hung the ringleaders, and sent many more to Siberia, creating martyrs for the incipient revolutionary movement.

Assuming power was Nicholas I (ruled 1825–1855), dubbed the "Iron Tsar" for his stern military image and conservative, repressive policies. Nicholas viewed Russia as a vast fortress, which under his determined command would withstand winds of change sweeping eastward from Paris across Europe. Wrote a French visitor, Marquis de Custine: "The Emperor of Russia is a military commander and each one of his days is a day of battle." The official ideology of Nicholas's regime, announced by his Minister of Education, Count Uvarov, in 1833 was autocracy, orthodoxy, and nationality—one emperor, one faith, and one dominant language and people (Russian). To supplement the regular state machinery, Nicholas elaborated a powerful personal chancellery whose Third Section, or political police, exercised surveillance over foreigners, dissidents, and suspected persons and reported on public moods and opinions. Although Nicholas's system became synonymous with despotism, repression, censorship, rampant bureaucracy, and brutal punishments, it employed some capable, dedicated ministers who

Tsar Nicholas I, 1825–1855. (*John Massey Stewart*)

sought to improve efficiency and reform abuses. Thus his Second Section under Count Speranskii codified Russian civil and military law; the Fifth Section led by the able Count P. D. Kiselev reformed and improved conditions of the state peasantry.

The so-called marvelous decade (1838–1848) began a great debate between Slavophiles and Westernizers, small groups of intellectuals, over Russia's past and future, which has persisted ever since. The Slavophiles were Russia-firsters, mostly conservative nationalists who idealized pre-Petrine Orthodoxy and traditional Muscovite institutions like the Assembly of the Land and the peasant commune as distinctly Russian and superior. The Westernizers, mostly liberal or radical critics like V. G. Belinskii, castigated the Orthodox Church and were ardent individualists. With a strong faith in civil liberties, science, and education, Westernizers believed Russian development should follow west European paths and methods, as under Peter I. The European revolutions of 1848 cut short this promising intellectual evolution as the fearful Nicholas responded to its ideas of liberalism and nationalism with iron-fisted repression and censorship.

Nicholas's despotism rested on the powerful pillars of bureaucracy, church, police, and army. Upon his beloved army Nicholas lavished resources and attention. Suspicious after the Decembrist Revolt of innovative, educated officers, Nicholas relied instead on harsh discipline, seniority, the bayonet, and precise parade-ground drill. The Russian army was Europe's largest (some 860,000 men in peacetime) but also the least literate and the poorest equipped and prepared for battle. After easy victories over Persians, Turks, Poles, and Hungarians, its commanders were overconfident and complacent, believing in Russian omnipotence. When severely tested in the Crimean War (1853–1856), Nicholas's army, the product of a backward agrarian economy based upon serfdom, failed even to defend Russian soil. The Crimean conflict, fueled by deep suspicions in western Europe about Russian intentions and grave miscalculations by both Nicholas and the western powers, pitted an isolated Russia against the declining Ottoman Empire backed by Britain, France, and Piedmont-Sardinia. In the midst of that bloody and futile war, Nicholas I died a broken, discouraged man. After the fall of Sevastopol, his son and successor, Alexander II, wisely accepted the Treaty of Paris (1856), which prescribed the demilitarization of Russia's Black Sea coast and naval bases, restored Bessarabia to Turkish control, and ended Russia's vague protectorate over the Balkan Christians. This marked the demise of the old regime in imperial Russia.

In the realm of culture Peter the Great's Western-influenced reforms initiated a totally new direction. At first affecting only the noble elite, this cultural change became institutionalized as the Russian Empire mastered Western cultural forms much as Kievan artisans and scholars had absorbed Byzantine forms earlier. The culture that emerged from the 17th-century Church-state conflict was largely emancipated from Orthodox religious traditions and became secularized. Art, literature, music, and architecture, at first imitated Western cultural forms, then gained a confidence and originality by drawing on native Russian traditions.

Symbolic of Russia's cultural reorientation was the city of Sankt Peterburg (St. Petersburg), founded by Peter the Great as his new capital on the Gulf of Finland with easy access to the West. Peter's famous "window on Europe," St. Petersburg was the antithesis of traditionalist, clerical, and obscurantist Moscow. Carefully planned and contemporary, St. Petersburg epitomized Russia's cultural integration into Europe. Its broad avenues and thoroughfares, its neoclassical and rococo buildings, glittering palaces, bustling commercial activity, and foreign languages gave it a cosmopolitan atmosphere in sharp contrast with other Russian towns. St. Petersburg welcomed foreigners of all kinds who helped reshape Russian culture. During the early imperial period, the magnificent imperial court at St. Petersburg came to resemble closely other European royal courts, and in some ways it outshone its Western rivals.

This "Westernization" process symbolized by St. Petersburg drove a deep cultural wedge between upper and lower classes, divided now by profound political and socioeconomic differences. The "Westernized" noble elite, speaking mostly French and German, created a vast cultural gulf between itself and lower classes speaking only Russian; this gulf deepened thereafter, contributing to a growing impasse between state and society.

From the late 18th century, Western values and education, theories of the Enlightenment and the French Revolution, and gradual socioeconomic change all contributed to a growing disillusionment with autocracy and serfdom, the pillars of the Russian old regime. Well-educated Westernized Russian aristocrats, beginning with Nicholai Novikov and Alexander Radishchev, began to expose the basic injustices of a system that granted almost unlimited power to the few and virtually enslaved the many.

Meanwhile Russian culture in the early 19th century was emancipating itself from slavish dependence on Western models. In literature the age was dominated by giants such as Alexander Pushkin, Mikhail Lermontov, and Nicholas Gogol. In music the chief innovators were Mikhail Glinka and Alexander Dargomyzhskii, who established bases for a Russian national school with their operas. In painting Karl Briullov and Alexander Ivanov were original artists who placed their personal stamps on a developing Russian school of art. By the mid-19th century Russian culture was bursting forth in a flurry of creative activity that propelled it into the forefront of European culture.

Suggested Additional Reading

Geography and Geopolitics

ADAMS, ARTHUR, et al. *An Atlas of Russian and East European History* (New York, 1967).

CHEW, ALLEN. *An Atlas of Russian History* (New Haven, Conn., 1970).

DEWDNEY, JOHN C. *A Geography of the Soviet Union*, 2d ed. (New York, 1971).

GILBERT, MARTIN. *Russian History Atlas* (New York, 1972).

LYDOLPH, PAUL E. *Geography of the USSR*, 3d ed. (New York, 1977).

PARKER, W. H. *An Historical Geography of Russia* (London, 1968).

SUMNER, B. H. "The Frontier," in *A Short History of Russia* (New York, 1949).

TREADGOLD, DONALD. "Russian Expansion in the Light of Turner's Study of the American Frontier," *Agricultural History, 26*, pp. 147–152.

WESSON, R. G. *The Russian Dilemma: A Political and Geopolitical View* (New Brunswick, N.J., 1974).

WIECZYNSKI, J. L. *The Russian Frontier: The Impact of the Borderlands upon the Course of Early Russian History* (Charlottesville, Va., 1976).

Peoples and Nationalities

ALLEN, W. E. D. *A History of the Georgian People* (New York, 1971).

ALLWORTH, EDWARD. *The Modern Uzbeks . . . : A Cultural History* (Stanford, Calif., 1990).

BARTOLD, V. V. "Slavs," in *Encyclopedia of Islam*, vol. 4, (Leiden, Holland, 1978).

BLUM, DIETER. *Russia, the Land and People of the Soviet Union* (New York, 1980).

DVORNIK, FRANCIS. *The Slavs in European History and Civilization* (New Brunswick, N.J., 1962).

GOLDHAGEN, ERICH. *Ethnic Minorities in the Soviet Union* (New York, 1968).

GREENBERG, L. S. *The Jews in Russia*, 2 vols. (New Haven, Conn., 1944, 1951).

GROUSSET, R. *The Empire of the Steppes: A History of Central Asia*, trans. N. Walford (New Brunswick, N.J., 1970).

HOOSON, DAVID. *The Soviet Union: People and Regions* (London, 1966).

HORAK, S., ed. *Guide to the Study of the Soviet Nationalities* (Littleton, Colo., 1982).

HRUSHEVSKYI, M. *A History of the Ukraine* (New Haven, Conn., 1941).

KOLARZ, WALTER. *The People of the Soviet Far East* (Camden, Conn., 1969).

LAND, DAVID M. *The Armenians: A People in Exile.* (Winchester, Mass., 1989).

LANG, D. M. *A Modern History of Georgia* (London, 1962).

OLCOTT, MARTHA. *The Kazakhs* (Stanford, Calif., 1987).

PIERCE, R. A. *Russian Central Asia, 1867–1917: A Study in Colonial Rule* (Berkeley, Calif., 1960).

RAUN, TOIVO. *Estonia and the Estonians* (Stanford, Calif., 1987).

SENN, A. R. *The Emergence of Modern Lithuania* (New York, 1959).

SUNY, ROBERT G. *The Making of the Georgian Nation* (Stanford, Calif., 1988).

VAKAR, N. *Belorussia: The Making of a Nation* (Cambridge, Mass., 1956).

WHEELER, G. *The Modern History of Soviet Central Asia* (London, 1964).

History to 1855

BILLINGTON, JAMES. *The Icon and the Axe: Interpretive History of Russian Culture* (New York, 1970).

BLACK, C. E. *Understanding Soviet Politics: The Perspective of Russian History* (Boulder, Colo., 1986).

BLUM, JEROME. *Lord and Peasant in Russia* (Princeton, N.J., 1961).

CRUMMEY, ROBERT O. *The Formation of Muscovy, 1304–1613* (London and New York, 1987).

CUSTINE, A. L. L. *Journey for Our Times* (New York, 1951).

EGAN, DAVID, AND M. EGAN. *Russian Autocrats from Ivan the Great to the Fall of the Romanov Dynasty: An Annotated Bibliography of English Language Sources* (Metuchen, N.J., 1987).

FENNELL, J. L. *Ivan the Great of Moscow* (London, 1961).

GREY, IAN. *Ivan the Terrible* (London, 1964).

HELLIE, R. *Enserfment and Military Change in Muscovy* (Chicago, 1971).

KEEP, JOHN H. *Soldiers of the Tsar: Army and Society in Russia, 1462–1874* (Oxford, Eng., 1985).

KLYUCHEVSKII, V. O. *Peter the Great* (New York, 1961).

LEDONNE, JOHN. *Ruling Russia: Politics and Administration in the Age of Absolutism* (Princeton, N.J., 1985).

LIKHACHEV, D. S. *The Great Heritage* (Moscow, 1982).

LINCOLN, W. B. *Nicholas I* (Bloomington, Ind., 1978).

MACKENZIE, D. AND M. CURRAN. *A History of Russia and the Soviet Union*, 3rd Edition (Homewood, Il., 1987).

MADARIAGA, ISABEL. *Russia in the Age of Catherine the Great* (New Haven, Conn., 1981).

MASSIE, ROBERT. *Peter the Great: His Life and World* (New York, 1980).

MILIUKOV, PAVEL N. *Outlines of Russian Culture*, 3 vols. (Philadelphia, Pa., 1942).

PASKIEWICZ, H. *The Making of the Russian Nation* (London, 1963).

PIPES, RICHARD. *Russia Under the Old Regime* (London, 1974).

PLATONOV, S. *The Time of Troubles* (Lawrence, Kans., 1970).

PRESNIAKOV, A. E. *The Formation of the Great Russian State* (Chicago, 1970).

PUSHKAREV, SERGEI. *The Emergence of Modern Russia, 1801–1917* (New York, 1963).

RIASANOVSKY, NICHOLAS V. *A History of Russia*, 4th ed. (New York, 1984).

———. *A Parting of the Ways: Government and the Educated Public in Russia, 1801–1855* (Oxford, Eng., 1976).

ROBINSON, GEROID T. *Rural Russia Under the Old Regime* (New York, 1949).

RYBAKOV, BORIS. *Early Centuries of Russian History* (Moscow, 1965).

SAWYER, P. H. *The Age of Vikings* (London, 1962).

SETON-WATSON, HUGH. *The Russian Empire, 1801–1917* (Oxford, Eng., 1967).

SPULER, BERTOLD. *The Mongols in History* (New York, 1971).

SUMNER, B. H. *A Short History of Russia* (New York, 1949).

TREADGOLD, DONALD. *The Great Siberian Migration* (Princeton, N.J., 1957).

VERNADSKY, G., AND M. KARPOVICH. *A History of Russia*, 5 vols. (New Haven, Conn., 1943–1969). (The most complete survey in English to 1689.)

VOYCE, ARTHUR. *Moscow and the Roots of Russian Culture* (Norman, Okla., 1964).

WARE, T. *The Orthodox Church* (Baltimore, Md., 1963).

WITTFOGEL, KARL. *Oriental Despotism* (New Haven, Conn., 1957).

WREN, MELVIN. *The Western Impact upon Russia* (Chicago, 1971).

CHAPTER TWO

REFORM AND REACTION, 1855–1904

THE GREAT REFORMS

Following defeats in major wars Russia has generally undergone significant reform or revolution. The Crimean defeat revealed that traditional serf Russia could not compete militarily or economically with more advanced west European nations. The death of the "Iron Tsar" in 1855 marked the end of a conservative old regime based upon serfdom, unlimited autocracy, and repressive censorship. Although his successor, Alexander II, was conservative by nature and training, his new regime undertook major changes in many aspects of Russian life. Of these the emancipation of the serfs was the greatest and most difficult. Emancipation was accompanied by basic reforms in Russia's economy, army, and society. Alexander II's Great Reforms, although incomplete, especially in the political sphere (see Figure 2.1), began to transform Russia into a more modern country. In many respects the Great Reforms are comparable with the manifold changes instituted by Mikhail S. Gorbachev in the USSR after 1985. (See Chapter 20.)

Alexander II *(Library of Congress)*

Serfdom, established legally in 1649, had bound some 85 percent of Russia's population to the land as private serfs or state peasants, condemning them to eke out a precarious and dependent existence focused on agriculture. As an economic system, serfdom had been declining for half a century as the realization grew among intellectuals and enlightened bureaucrats and landowners that it had outlived all usefulness. In 1860, some 60 percent of private serfs were mortgaged to state banks by an ever more indebted nobility. Alexander II, otherwise often indecisive and uncertain, played a vital role in preparing and carrying through the Emancipation, which represented the most far-reaching reform undertaken by any European government in the 19th century. Soon he realized that Russia could not remain a great European power or generate needed military and economic strength unless serfs and state peasants were liberated. Dmitrii A. Miliutin, subsequently his Minister of War, viewed serfdom as the chief obstacle to a modern army: "Serfdom does not allow us either to reduce the term of service or increase the number of unlimited leaves so as to diminish the present number of troops." Increasing numbers of bureaucrats tended to place interests of state and reform ahead of their personal concerns as landowners. Saddled with heavy debts and dependent upon state aid, most serf owners could not effectively resist governmental action. Roughly 70 years of criticism and

Figure 2.1 *Russian Imperial Government (1855–1905)*

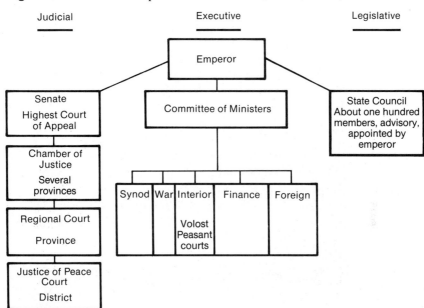

condemnation of serfdom by the Russian intelligentsia had helped prepare the way for its abolition. Finally, there had been rising peasant discontent and rural violence during the first half of the century, which Soviet scholars stress as the chief cause of emancipation. However, there is inadequate evidence to prove that Alexander II freed the serfs mainly out of fear of peasant revolution.

To guard his autocratic powers, Alexander had the Emancipation prepared secretly and bureaucratically, but pushed the nobility and his officials along and warned he would not tolerate delay. The Emancipation Act of 1861 granted private serfs personal freedom, but the servile economy persisted for many years because the process of providing them with land proved lengthy and complex. The state advanced about three fourths of the redemption cost directly to the landowners in interest-bearing bonds, deducting the landowners' debts. The peasants had to pay the remaining fourth as well as repaying the state over 49 years. This compromise settlement, still incomplete in 1905, satisfied neither party completely and left the Russian peasantry, hampered by ignorance and low yields per acre, with inadequate land. In the rich Black Soil region of the south, peasants lost about one quarter of the land they had worked before the Emancipation. Peasant land allotments varied in size by region—Black Soil, non-Black Soil, and steppe. Maximum and minimum norms were set for each province, but the landowner was, in any case, guaranteed at least one third of his estate. Extensive police powers hitherto wielded by the landowner, were mostly transferred to the peasant community (mir), which was thus retained for fiscal and administrative reasons and to maintain rural order and stability. Initially elated at their emancipation, many former serfs soon wondered whether their economic status had really been improved because they now had to pay for services they had formerly received from their lords. State and imperial peasants were freed in 1866 and 1863 respectively, receiving lands they had worked before the Emancipation in return for higher rents. Strip farming with traditional techniques and primitive plows and periodic redistribution of the land persisted in Russia proper, while between 1860 and 1914 the rural population roughly doubled. Despite universal conscription, some schooling, and the abolition of the poll tax (1886), peasants tended to remain at the bottom of the Russian social pyramid until 1917.

Other highly significant changes accompanied the Emancipation. Alexander II's government promptly relaxed censorship and travel restrictions, which promoted freer contacts with Europe and spurred a great growth in the towns of newspapers and periodicals expressing a variety of viewpoints. However, a capricious and limiting censorship of the press persisted. Universities were freed from most of the severe restrictions imposed under Nicholas I and were opened along with secondary schools to all social groups. The important zemstvo reform, necessitated by the gentry's loss of direct control over the peasantry, introduced limited provincial and district self-government in European Russian provinces that possessed an organized nobility. Zemstvo assemblies were to be elected by landowners, peasants, and townspeople according to land and real property they held, allowing the nobility to dominate them, especially at the provincial level. With money raised from property taxes, but with severely limited budgets, zemstva were to establish and operate primary schools, build roads and bridges, erect prisons, and found clinics. However, zemstva were denied permission to operate in volosti (townships) or above the provincial level. Decisions of their executive boards could be vetoed by the regular provincial bureaucracy, and accounts of their proceedings could be censored. Serving initially as schools of self-government, the zemstva, despite many shortcomings, gradually undermined the autocratic principle and agitated for liberal reform and national representation. Similarly, the municipal law of 1870 established a measure of urban self-rule and greatly improved city services.

A women's movement for emancipation and access to education arose in Russia in the 1860s, simultaneously with those in western Europe. In both areas, the rise of feminism was stimulated by the heritage of the Enlightenment, French Revolution, and Utopian Socialism. As emancipation of the serfs neared, the liberalized Russian press of the late 1850s voiced ideas of liberating women from their traditional bondage to men. The legal basis for women's subservience in 19th-century Russia was the declaration in the Code of Russian Laws (1836): "The woman must obey her husband, reside with him in love, respect, and unlimited obedience, and offer him every pleasantness and affection as the ruler of the household."[1] The few women educated in Russia before 1860 were prepared for motherhood and domesticity in a few secondary schools open mostly to daughters of the gentry. Even before the Emancipation gentry women began to petition and agitate for access to higher education. In 1859, women were admitted to university lectures, only to be barred once again from attending lectures in 1861. Access to education and employment were to be the initial focuses of the Russian feminist movement, led by gentry women.

The court system, harsh and inequitable under Nicholas I, was greatly altered by the law of November 1864, which set up independent regular courts of a western European type, initially free from administrative controls, with irremovable, trained judges and jury trials for major cases. Justice of the peace courts, established in district centers for lesser cases, proved efficient, popular, and fair. However, cases concerning peasants alone were still tried by separate peasant courts under police supervision; ecclesiastical courts handled all divorces and cases affecting the clergy. Later, political cases as well were removed from the purview of the new regular courts.

Finally, able and liberal War Minister Dmitrii A. Miliutin (1861–1881) transformed the Russian army over powerful aristocratic opposition. First, Miliutin reduced the term of service from 25 to 15 years and abolished most corporal punishments. Regional military districts largely replaced Nicholas's overcentralized and overstaffed army administration. Military gymnasia with a broad curriculum and open to all classes superseded exclusive cadet corps; primary schools were set up in the army to make many recruits literate. The principles of the judicial reform were extended to army courts. Finally, the law of 1874 introduced universal military training, with a maximum term of six years, decreasing according to educational attainment. "The defense of the fatherland," declared the law, "forms the sacred duty of *every* Russian [male] citizen."

---

[1] Richard Stites, *The Women's Liberation Movement in Russia* (Princeton, N.J., 1978), pp. 6–7.

Universal service allowed Russia to establish trained reserves, reduced social barriers, and raised army morale.

Despite limitations and bureaucratic opposition, the Great Reforms changed Russia fundamentally. The all-class principle, at the heart of most of them, reduced noble privilege and increased rights of other groups. The masses could now be educated and gradually integrated into society. Concepts of equality before the law, universal military service, local self-government, and greater press freedom weakened autocracy. The reforms, note Soviet historians, marked Russia's transition from feudalism to capitalism, though there were many feudal survivals and persisting inequalities. However, legally, Alexander II remained an autocrat and blocked any move toward a constitution or national parliament. He controlled the executive branch, where no cabinet was permitted to develop, by appointing and dismissing all ministers. An appointed State Council of some 100 officials debated prospective laws, but its decisions lacked binding force because the emperor and his ministers initiated all legislation. Failure to achieve real political change at the top would prove fateful for tsarism.

Trends toward liberal change were strongest from 1856 to 1861 when most of the Great Reforms were conceived. A subsequent conservative countertrend was reinforced by D. V. Karakozov's attempt on the life of Alexander II in 1866. Count P. A. Shuvalov, chief of gendarmes and former large serf owner, dominated Alexander II for the next seven years and helped block completion of the reforms.

FOREIGN AFFAIRS, 1815–1881

Shifting Policies Toward Europe

Imperial Russia from 1815 to 1914 adopted a generally defensive posture toward other European powers. Abandoning for the most part the aggressive expansionism of previous centuries that had brought Russian power deep into central Europe, Russian leaders in the 19th century sought to preserve and defend the generous European boundaries accorded them in 1815 by the Congress of Vienna. After absorbing Finland, most of Poland, and Bessarabia during the Napoleonic era, Russia, without further legitimate or pressing territorial claims in Europe, became essentially a satiated power in that region. Backward economically and socially relative to western Europe, Russia aimed to consolidate its gains and, except for the Crimean debacle, managed to avoid armed conflicts with other great powers. Until 1890, Russia often cooperated with Austria, Prussia, and later Germany, states with similar political and social systems. Russia was linked with Europe by dynastic marriages, common use of French as the diplomatic language, and manifold ties between Russian and European aristocracies. Thus, in general, imperial Russia, during its final century, unlike Soviet Russia later, sought to work within and uphold the European order created at the Vienna Congress, which benefited and protected it. Russia sought to guard its preeminence in eastern Europe by perpetuating the partitions of Poland (in which the German powers had shared) and uphold conservative, legitimate monarchy throughout Europe against challenges posed increasingly by nationalism, liberalism, and socialism. Russia sought to achieve its limited aims by cautious diplomacy, adjustment, and compromise.

From the Congress of Vienna until the Crimean War, Russia espoused a defensive conservatism. For those 40 years it remained the dominant land power in Europe, cooperating with equally conservative Austrian and Prussian monarchies. Threats to the Vienna settlement and European peace were resolved by periodic meetings of leaders of the great powers, which produced compromise solutions. Alexander and Nicholas I departed only occasionally from support of legitimate monarchy to provide sporadic backing to Serb and Greek national movements in the Balkans.

The Crimean defeat caused significant changes in Russian policies toward Europe. No self-respecting power could be expected to acquiesce indefinitely in the defenseless Black Sea coast and absence of naval bases imposed by the Treaty of Paris. Nor could the Romanov dynasty feel secure, until its prestige and European role, shaken in the Crimea, had been reaffirmed. For centuries Russian foreign policy had been essentially that of tsar or emperor who could determine it at will: making war or peace, signing treaties, and hiring and firing his ministers without having to accept advice from anyone. However, Alexander II had less grasp of foreign affairs and less self-confidence than his immediate predecessors and left everyday policy to subordinates. Frequently indecisive and susceptible to various influences, Alexander displayed a strong and growing personal tie with his uncle, King William I of Prussia. Alexander promptly selected A. M. Gorchakov, a native Russian who had been ambassador to Vienna during the Crimean War, as foreign minister (1856–1882). Advocating revival of Russia's leading diplomatic role in Europe, Gorchakov with his fluent French and close ties with European aristocrats, favored negotiation and peace. These were essential for a Russia with a depleted treasury and absorbed in domestic reform.

During the first years after the Crimean War, Russia cooperated with France, especially in Italy and the Balkans, until the Polish Revolt of 1863 induced Russia to seek Prussia's support instead. Russia's benevolent neutrality in 1866 and 1870 aided the outstanding Prussian statesman,

Otto von Bismarck, to unify Germany under Prussian leadership. During the Franco-Prussian War (1870–1871), Gorchakov, with German support, scored his greatest personal triumph: By denouncing the Black Sea clauses of the Paris Treaty, he regained for Russia the right to fortify its Black Sea coast. The exorbitant price Russia had to pay for this was the formation on its western frontier of a powerful, dynamic German Empire, which would invade Russia during two world wars. In 1873, at Bismarck's initiative, the rulers of Russia, Germany, and Austria-Hungary formed the Three Emperor's League, an entente designed to preserve the status quo in eastern Europe.

Balkan Policies

Meanwhile in the Balkan Peninsula, Gorchakov had been seeking to rebuild Russia's influence and safeguard its traditional interests. These were to protect and head its Christian, especially Orthodox, peoples; ensure free passage through the Turkish Straits for Russian commerce, and eventually to dominate or control those waterways; and to establish one or more Balkan client states. However, this opened the way for a group of bellicose Panslavs and Russia-firsters to exert increasing influence on Russia's Balkan policies. Panslavism, a movement to unite the Slav peoples resembling efforts to unite Italians and Germans, had developed initially among Austrian Slavs as a cultural movement to resist Germanization. Russian Panslavism of the 1860–1870s, the obstreperous offspring of Slavophilism and militant nationalism, advocated a forceful national imperialism. Regarding Russia as a superior "big brother" for smaller and weaker Slav peoples of the west and south, some Russian noblemen, courtiers, journalists, and army officers expounded doctrines laced with Social Darwinism and racism. Thus N. Ia. Danilevskii's *Russia and Europe* (1872), sometimes dubbed "the Bible of Panslavism," predicted victory for Russia and its Slav allies in an "inevitable conflict" with the German world and formation of an all-Slav federation centering in Constantinople. R. A. Fadeev, a retired major general, proclaimed that Russia must "extend her preeminence to the Adriatic" in leading Orthodox Slavs in a war against the Germans, until "the Russian reigning house covers the liberated soil of Eastern Europe with its branches under the supremacy of the tsar of Russia...."[2] In western Europe, Fadeev's provocative pamphlet raised the spectre of Russian imperial rule over a series of east European satellite states. Such nationalistic views were shared widely in the Asiatic Department of the Foreign Ministry, whose

---

[2]R. A. Fadeev, *Opinion on the Eastern Question* (London, 1876).

Map 2.1 *Russia and the Balkans, 1876–1885*

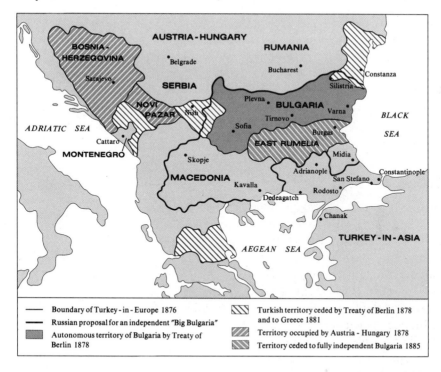

talented director, N. P. Ignatiev, became Russian ambassador in Constantinople (1864–1877). Favoring a unilateral Russian solution of the "Eastern Question" involving the future of the Ottoman Empire, Turkish Straits, and Balkan Christians, Ignatiev coordinated the activities of Russian diplomats in the Balkans and Near East and opposed Gorchakov's pro-European, frenchified Diplomatic Chancellery.

These divergent policies—one pro-European, the other unilateralist—were tested in the Balkan Crisis (1875–1878). In July 1875, Orthodox Serbs in the Turkish provinces of Bosnia and Herzegovina revolted and received support, at first unofficially, from Serbia, Montenegro, and Russian Slav Committees. (See Map 2.1.) Officially, Russia proclaimed nonintervention, but Count N. P. Ignatiev, its ambassador in Constantinople, encouraged Balkan Slavs to aid the insurgents, while Panslavs in Russia organized medical and financial aid for them. Early in 1876, the Slav Committees sent retired General M. G. Cherniaev to Serbia and recruited several thousand Russian volunteers to serve under his command in the ensuing Serbo-Turkish War. When the Turks

Map 2.2 *Central Asia, 1850–1914*

defeated Cherniaev's motley Serbo-Russian army, official Russia was soon drawn reluctantly into a Russo-Turkish War (1877–1878), which ended in a Russian victory. Upon defeated Turkey, Count Ignatiev imposed the Treaty of San Stefano (March 1878), which reflected his Panslav aims, and envisioned a Big Bulgaria under Russian military occupation. When Great Britain and Austria-Hungary threatened war unless Russia submitted this treaty to all the powers, Alexander II, to prevent another disastrous conflict with a European coalition, agreed to the Congress of Berlin (June-July 1878). Directed by Germany's Bismarck as "honest broker," it reduced Russian gains and alienated the frustrated Panslavs. Austria-Hungary occupied Bosnia and Herzegovina and dominated the western Balkans; Russian influence was confined to a shrunken, autonomous Bulgaria.

Asia and America

Russia's policies in the Asiatic sphere were more dynamic and successful as it played the role of an imperialist European power toward more backward, weaker neighbors. (See Map 2.2.) By 1863, the guerrilla resistance of Muslim mountaineers in the Caucasus had been broken, and the region pacified by Field Marshal Bariatinskii and D. A. Miliutin. The Caucasus provided Russia with secure natural boundaries in the south and firm bases for expansion in Central Asia. That vast area, lying east of the Caspian Sea and south of Siberia, had mostly been annexed to the Russian Empire by 1895. Between 1730 and 1850, the broad Kazakh steppe (now the Kazakh SSR) was occupied. Then, beginning in the 1860s, for reasons resembling those of European overseas neoimperialism, Russia moved southward deep into the Muslim oasis region. The War Ministry favored filling a major power vacuum, while frontier generals and governors, seeking promotion and glory, spurred the process along. The imperial family, tempted by the prestige of easy victories, sanctioned most conquests and rewarded those responsible, while the Foreign Ministry sought to justify military advances on the grounds of inexorable necessity. Beginning in 1864, small Russian forces seized northern Turkestan from weak, feuding Muslim khanates, culminating in the assault on Tashkent by General Cherniaev (June 1865). In 1867, Alexander II appointed General K. P. Kaufman as the first governor-general of Turkestan; he built an administration, won native respect, and began developing its silk and cotton resources. Kaufman greatly expanded Russian Turkestan, a process completed in 1895, giving Russia natural frontiers in the Pamir Mountains with Afghanistan and India. By 1905, railroad lines had linked this vast Central Asian colony firmly with the Russian motherland.

Simultaneously, Russia was liquidating its Alaskan holdings and establishing a firmer foothold on the shores of the Pacific. In Alaska, the fur trade was dwindling, the inefficient Russian-America Company continued to pile up debts, and the region had become indefensible. Thus the Russian government in 1867 sold Alaska to a reluctant United States for a paltry $7.2 million. Meanwhile in the Far East, exploiting the weakness and disintegration of Manchu China in the face of Western imperialism, Governor-General M. N. Muraviev (Amurskii) of eastern Siberia seized the Amur and Ussuri river valleys and founded the city of Vladivostok ("Ruler of the East") in July 1860. That December, Count Ignatiev negotiated the Treaty of Peking with helpless China, superseding the Treaty of Nerchinsk (1689), which left the Amur region to China, and confirming Russia's possession of what became the Maritime Province. A century later Communist China would claim that these territories had been seized illegally at gunpoint.

DOMESTIC AFFAIRS, 1881–1904

Counterreform Under the Last Two Tsars

Alexander II's assassination in March 1881 by terrorists of the People's Will inaugurated two decades of reaction and political stagnation. To combat such terrorism the government, in February 1880, had set up a Supreme Executive Commission under Count M. T. Loris-Melikov, a former war hero, who was given full police powers. Loris-Melikov's so-called dictatorship of the heart dissolved the infamous Third Section, establishing a new department of police under the Interior Ministry. That August, with terrorism apparently checked, Loris-Melikov urged creation of a legislative commission with representatives appointed by zemstva, and cities to advise the State Council on legislative bills. Called by some the Loris-Melikov constitution, this innocuous proposal was approved by Alexander II on March 1, 1881, the day of his assassination. However, the poorly educated and unimaginative new ruler, Alexander III (1881–1894), at the demand of his tutor and chief adviser, Constantine Pobedonostsev, shelved Loris-Melikov's scheme, and liberal ministers resigned. Alexander III, rabidly religious, conservative, and nationalistic, relied chiefly upon Pobedonostsev, who as procurator of the Holy Synod and tutor to his son, Nicholas II, largely determined the outlooks and policies of the last two tsars.

Pobedonostsev elaborated a complete and consistent theory of autocracy, gentry rule, and status quo conservatism derived from Uvarov's triad of autocracy, orthodoxy, and nationality. As the "gray eminence" of moribund tsarism, Pobedonostsev contributed heavily to a "dogma of autocracy," which blocked essential political change and provoked radical opposition. Pobedonostsev believed that by nature people were unequal, weak, and vicious. Russians, he argued, as shown by their history, required firm leadership and control. Western ways and institutions, warned this Slavophile, could not be grafted onto the Russian tree. Favoring concentrating political power in the autocrat and central administration, he opposed self-government as divisive and counted on traditional bonds between tsar and people. To him, constitutional government would poison the entire Russian organism. A distinguished jurist, Pobedonostsev nonetheless rejected the rule of law and civil liberties as restrictions on autocracy. Orthodoxy, he declared, was the only true faith, and only one religion was tolerable in an autocratic state. Rigid censorship by the Holy Synod must shield Russians from false Western liberal and radical doctrines; the Orthodox Church through its press and schools would imbue them with correct ideas. Unity was indispensable—one tsar, one faith, one language—thus national and religious minorities should be converted, assimilated, or expelled by ruthless Russification. Pobedonostsev's program was mainly negative: to preserve paternalistic noble, bureaucratic, and clerical authority and the status quo. To a remarkable extent, he persuaded his imperial pupils to accept and implement these outdated principles.

Thus Alexander III sought obediently to nullify the Great Reforms of his father with bureaucratic counterreforms. The land captain law of 1889 abolished most justice of the peace courts and transferred their functions to judges appointed by the Interior Ministry. Land captains, usually influential hereditary noblemen, were to supervise peasant affairs and could rescind decisions of village assemblies and peasant courts. In 1890, peasant representation in zemstva assemblies was reduced, and the Interior Ministry's authority over them was tightened. City electorates were drastically reduced. The central authorities sought to curtail local self-government and stifle local initiative. Nonetheless, zemstva and city assemblies continued to achieve much, and tension persisted between the bureaucracy and institutions of local government.

Alexander III's sudden death by stroke in 1894 brought his son Nicholas II to the throne amidst hopes of liberal change. Though more intelligent than his father and privately charming, Nicholas was irresolute and wholly ignorant of the forces shaping the modern world. Shortly before his accession, he married Alexandra of Hesse, "Alix," a deeply religious German woman who dominated him and reinforced his own pious conservatism. Sincerely devoted to wife and family, Nicholas became increasingly isolated from Russian reality. He never visited factories and blamed social unrest on Jews and revolutionaries. His chief interests, reflected in a carefully kept diary, were military reviews, hunting, tennis, and yachting. Early in 1895, he dashed hopes for change at a reception warning liberals to abandon "senseless dreams" about an increased role for zemstva: ". . . I, devoting all my strength to the welfare of the people, will uphold the principle of autocracy as firmly and unflinchingly as my late unforgettable father." Dominated by Pobedonostsev and the reactionary Prince V. P. Meshcherskii, Nicholas believed that constitutions and parliaments were evil. At first he displayed reasonable judgment in state affairs and retained capable men like Sergei Witte in office, but increasingly he listened to irresponsible adventurers and reactionaries. Although the first decade of Nicholas II's reign was outwardly calm and uneventful, beneath the surface opposition movements germinated.

Active discrimination against the Russian Empire's numerous national and religious minorities intensified from 1881 to 1905. Favoring Great Russians and the Orthodox church everywhere and fueled by Pobedonostsev's reactionary theories, the regime pressured non-Russians to renounce their languages and religions. Fostered by an intolerant

Alexandra and Nicholas II *(Library of Congress)*

central bureaucracy and police, Russification was supported by the Orthodox clergy and military. Among those who suffered severely were
Baltic Germans, Finns, and Armenians, who had displayed unswerving
loyalty toward the imperial regime. In Finland, which formerly had
enjoyed broad autonomy as a grand duchy, the independent postal
service was abolished in 1890; Russian was introduced forcibly into
certain Finnish institutions. Under a narrow-minded governor-general,
A. I. Bobrikov (1898–1904), the separate Finnish army was abolished,
and sessions of the Finnish Senate had to be conducted in Russian. In
1903 the Finnish Constitution was suspended. The governor-general's
assassination by a Finn in 1904 produced strong animosity between

Finland and Russia. In Russian Poland, all school subjects except Polish had to be taught in Russian. Alexander III and Nicholas II, both anti-Semitic and tutored by Pobedonostsev, enacted harsh laws against Jews. Pogroms—unofficial mob violence against Jews and their shops—intensified and were often condoned by the police. "Temporary Rules" of 1882, enforced until 1905, forbade Jews to live outside towns or large villages and forced them into business and certain professions. Strict Jewish quotas were established for secondary schools and universities. Jewish responses to such persecution were to emigrate, especially to the United States, or enter the revolutionary movement. Bigoted decrees undermined the loyalty of minorities, especially in the western borderlands, and helped stimulate revolutions in 1905 and 1917.

Economic and Social Development

The Crimean defeat ushered in a new chapter in Russian economic history marked by development of a capitalist economy. Soviet historians, regarding the entire period of 1861 to 1917 as a capitalist phase, assert that Russia was transformed swiftly into a capitalist country. Most Western scholars regard 1861–1890 as preparatory years of slow growth for more rapid development after 1890. First, numerous obstacles blocking the path of industrialization had to be overcome: shortage of investment capital, a totally inadequate transportation system, lack of a skilled labor force, and a weak internal market. The role of the state would prove crucial in removing the first two of these barriers. Learning the sad lessons of the Crimean defeat to which lack of railways south of Moscow had contributed, Alexander II's government promptly recognized their military value and later their economic benefits. Finance Minister Michael Reutern wrote Alexander: "Without railways and mechanical industries Russia cannot be considered secure in her boundaries. Her influence in Europe will fall to a level inconsistent with her international power and her historic significance."[3] Because the impoverished treasury could not then finance railroad construction, foreign loans were sought, and private companies encouraged. After 1865, the government provided subsidies and guarantees for construction of lines deemed essential by the state. There ensued an orgy of construction and speculation, but many such small concerns went bankrupt in the depression of 1873–1876, and others became heavily indebted to the state. In the 1880s, the government constructed major lines itself, bought up many private railways, and created an expanding state-owned system. By 1890, major economic

---

[3]T. von Laue, *Sergei Witte and the Industrialization of Russia* (New York, 1963), p. 9.

At the Portsmouth Peace Conference in August 1905. Left to right: Count Sergei Iu. Witte, Russia's chief delegate; Baron Roman Rosen, second delegate; U.S. President Theodore Roosevelt; Foreign Minister Baron J. Komura and K. Takahira (SOVFOTO)

regions had been interconnected and linked with major ports as the railway network grew from only 600 miles in 1857, to 11,730 in 1876, and over 22,000 miles in 1890.

The Finance Ministry became the key agency promoting Russian economic development. Under Reutern (1861–1878), it faced complex and interrelated problems of stabilizing the currency, balancing the budget, achieving an active trade balance, and attracting foreign investment. One step forward was to create a new State Bank with branches throughout Russia. Another was to establish (1862) a unified state budget enabling the Finance Ministry to coordinate economic activities and develop some state planning. An extraordinary budget, financed by foreign loans, was set up to pay for industrial equipment, arms, and railway construction. Lowered tariffs encouraged an influx of foreign products and capital and sharply increased Russian grain exports paid for foreign loans. However, neither Reutern nor his immediate successors could find the formula to overcome Russia's persisting poverty, and their progress was slowed by heavy expenditures in the Russo-Turkish War.

Until 1890, industrial growth proceeded at a modest pace. At first, the emancipation settlement did little to assist it, contributing instead to an industrial slump in the early 1860s, especially in Ural metallurgy, which had employed mostly serf labor. Meanwhile, the mir (peasant commune) blocked permanent migration of peasant labor to the cities. However, relaxation of restrictions on importing foreign capital and goods and judicial and administrative reforms of the 1860s created a better climate for business activity. The government, gradually losing its fear of industrialization, began to consider it necessary in order to strengthen Russia's role in world affairs. Among domestic manufacturers, textiles alone had an assured and expanding home market as per capita consumption of cotton goods roughly doubled between 1860 and 1880. Sugar refining expanded markedly. During the 1880s, the Donets Basin became an important iron and steel producing region with factories owned mostly by foreign capitalists. Large factories, like that built at Iuzovka by John Hughes, an English capitalist, were more modern and productive than Ural enterprises. Private capitalism flourished as joint-stock companies were formed with government encouragement.

These achievements during the preparatory era brought significant financial gains and fostered the industrial boom of the 1890s, both attributable largely to Finance Minister Sergei Iu. Witte (1893–1903). Self-confident and dynamic, Witte had forged a brilliant career in private business before entering state service as a railway expert. He soon reformed the Finance Ministry into an efficient general staff for economic development. In his first budget report, Witte affirmed government responsibility for the whole economy and warned: "International competition does not wait." Unless Russian industry developed swiftly, foreign concerns would predominate, and Russia would become an economic colony of the West: "Our economic backwardness may lead to political and cultural backwardness as well." His work, therefore, was filled with a sense of urgency: Russia's industrialization was viewed as a race against time. The "Witte System" called for stimulating private enterprise and exploiting domestic resources through a vast state-sponsored program of railway construction, which would trigger expansion of heavy industry, notably metallurgy and fuels. Their development would spark light industry, and eventually agriculture would prosper as growing industrial cities demanded more foodstuffs. General prosperity would raise tax yields and recompense the government for heavy initial capital outlays.

Witte's program, concentrating on heavy industry and substituting the role of the state for inadequate private capital, foreshadowed Stalin's more ruthless Five Year Plans. (See Chapter Eleven.) An experiment in state capitalism, it might enable a backward country to overtake the industrial leaders. To fuel Russia's first industrial boom, Witte channeled about two thirds of government revenues into economic development. His most ambitious project was building the Trans-Siberian Railroad. Besides constructing this vital transcontinental line, he promoted peasant colonization of Siberia and envisioned the railroad as a means to penetrate and dominate Asian markets. Russia's European railroads were doubletracked and lines built to more seaports. From 1898 through 1900, almost 2,000 miles of railroads were constructed annually, fueling a boom in the Donets Basin's iron and steel industry. The Witte upsurge produced an average industrial growth rate for the 1890s of some 8 percent annually, the highest of any major European country. During that decade, pig iron output trebled, oil production rose two and one half times, and coal output doubled.

Witte financed his program chiefly with a state liquor monopoly and other indirect taxes, which fell largely on peasants and townspeople. The high tariff of 1891 also brought large sums into the treasury. For railway construction he relied mainly on foreign loans. Witte was favored by abundant foreign private funds seeking investment and the Franco-Russian Alliance of 1893, which induced the French government to foster private investment in Russia. Witte had to borrow heavily abroad to balance the budget overall, but his prompt payment of dividends in gold maintained a high Russian credit rating. To preserve a favorable trade balance, he pushed grain exports and curtailed imports. In 1897, after stabilizing the paper ruble and building state gold reserves, he finally put Russia on the gold standard, enhancing her international prestige and encouraging further foreign investment. However, Witte's vast authority and advocacy of further reforms such as abolition of the mir aroused opposition from conservatives, notably Pobedonostsev, who accused him of causing growing foreign economic influence and supposed agricultural decline. They and Nicholas II, opposing Witte's efforts to adapt Russian autocracy to 20th-century needs, blamed him for the economic slump of 1900–1903. Nonetheless, his system laid a sound basis for subsequent Russian industrial development and proved that rapid economic growth was possible in a backward country by state mobilization of its resources.

Under the impact of the Great Reforms and industrialization, Russia's social structure underwent profound change after 1860. Officialdom continued for census purposes to use the old categories of the class (soslovie) system, but new elements emerged that rejected the old patterns: a professional middle class of lawyers, doctors, and journalists, a better-off peasant element, and an industrial working class. Industrialization, urbanization, and reform legislation promoted social mobility. The new courts largely disregarded estate, title, and wealth while universal military service, abolition of the poll tax (1886), schools, and participation in zemstva lessened peasant isolation. Increasing sales of noble lands to merchants and peasants reduced the nobility's economic power and social prestige. However, after 1881, the rise of new social groupings was hampered by a conservative regime anxious to preserve the traditional order and by the failure of new groups to form economic organizations to promote their interests.

Among the peasantry, still the overwhelming bulk of the Russian population, differentiation was proceeding, spurred by the developing money economy, causing much controversy. Between 1877 and 1905, the average land allotment per peasant household in European Russia declined by about one third. Whereas Populists (see p. 60) affirmed that the mir remained unshaken and that Russian peasants were still fundamentally equal in land and wealth, V. I. Ulianov (Lenin) asserted in his *The Development of Capitalism in Russia* (1899) that about one sixth had become kulaks ("rural bourgeoisie"), and over one tenth "rural proletarians" without arable land or livestock. Communal agriculture, he concluded, was disintegrating and doomed. Western scholars concur that the Emancipation, by leaving some 4 million peasants landless or with dwarf allotments had fostered differentiation.[4] Nevertheless, the collective traditions of the mir remained predominant because even in 1905 almost three fourths of peasant allotments in European Russia were subject to periodic repartition. However, kulaks, a small minority of thrifty, hardworking peasants, were acquiring livestock, renting and buying more land, and hiring impoverished peasants to work for them.

Industrial workers, still listed as peasants in the 1897 census, were slow to become genuine proletarians in the Marxist sense. But Soviet accounts claim that the working class was far larger than tsarist statistics suggested. Workers employed in manufacturing, mining, and transportation in European Russia, affirms Lenin, grew from 706,000 (1865) to 2,208,000 (1900–1903). Recent Western studies, on the other hand, portray tsarist Russian industrial workers as still half peasant in 1905. Migrating to new industrial centers nearby, peasants were slow to master industrial skills or become integrated into urban life. As late as 1905, 90 percent of Russian urban workers still belonged to communes, sent money to families or relatives in villages, and returned there periodically themselves. Low industrial wages and miserable living conditions delayed formation of a hereditary proletariat. Some 60 percent of workers, noted the 1897 census, lived alone, many in filthy barracks owned by their employers. Johnson states: "The typical worker had one foot in the village

---

[4]Lenin emphasized differentiation to discredit the populists and justify Marxist predictions.

and one in the factory, but showed little inclination to commit himself irrevocably to either alternative."[5] The state acted belatedly to protect industrial workers and regulate factory conditions. The law of 1897 set an $11\frac{1}{2}$ hour maximum for all workers and 10 hours for night work, but many manufacturers evaded the law. Before 1905, few Russian workers were unionized, they lacked rights to strike or bargain collectively, and their wages were far lower than those of workers in western Europe.

Russian women also were struggling to escape their traditional inferior status. Developing after 1860 were parallel movements of feminism, nihilism, and political radicalism. Seeking solutions within the bounds of existing tsarist society, liberal feminism aimed at gradual, peaceful reforms to improve women's status, especially in education and employment. Reformist feminists, mostly well-educated gentry women led by Maria Trubnikova, Nadezhda Stasova, and Anna Filosofova, attacked patriarchal social mores and by petitions and through the press campaigned for women's education. During the 1860s, some 150 women's secondary schools with some 10,000 students were opened. In the 1870s, feminist victories in higher education, despite opposition from conservatives and the Education Ministry, were aided by a favorable public and official fears that if denied education in Russia, women would study abroad. In 1872, university courses for women were created in Moscow and soon after at other Russian universities. A Russian medical school for women opened in St. Petersburg in 1872. By 1880, in quality and range of women's university education, Russia was unequalled in Europe (though behind the United States) and had the most practicing women doctors on the continent.

Alexander III's accession in 1881 undermined this promising movement as Pobedonostsev conservatives equated feminism with revolution. Medical facilities and women's university courses (except in St. Petersburg) were closed, and the institutional weakness of Russian feminism was revealed. An impassioned appeal by Maria Tsebrikova to Alexander III denouncing "bureaucratic anarchism" and urging him to eliminate poverty, hunger, and disease in the villages brought her banishment to a remote province. About 1895 began a halting revival, but Russian feminism, lacking suffrage societies, remained largely apolitical, disorganized, and ineffectual until 1905.

---

[5]Robert Johnson, *Peasant and Proletarian* . . . (New Brunswick, N.J., 1979), p. 50.

FOREIGN AFFAIRS, 1881–1904

From 1878 to 1904 Russia's internal economic development was fostered by a rare generation of peace. With Alexander III rarely interfering directly in foreign affairs, policy was directed ably by Foreign Minister N. K. Girs, a prudent professional diplomat, who restrained nationalists and militarists and kept Russia firmly aligned with the German powers until 1890. Alexander's lone foray into foreign policy-making during the Bulgarian Crisis (1885–1887) proved a fiasco. After Bulgaria's unification in 1885, which he had not authorized, Alexander removed its prince and Russian officers assumed control of Bulgaria. Eventually, Bismarck and Girs surmounted the resulting crisis, which threatened to embroil Russia with Austria-Hungary, by negotiating the Reinsurance Treaty of 1887. However, three years later when Emperor William II of Germany refused to renew it and fired Bismarck, Russo-German relations deteriorated rapidly, fostering rapprochement between France and Russia, despite profound differences in their regimes, policies, and ideologies. This produced the extraordinarily important Franco-Russian Alliance of 1893, in which longstanding rivals buried the hatchet in the face of German military power. At one stroke this reversed Russia's traditional alignment with the German powers. If either France or Russia were attacked by Germany, the other pledged to assist its partner with all its forces. Their defensive alliance opposed the Triple Alliance (1882) of Germany, Austria-Hungary, and Italy, splitting Europe dangerously between two formidable power blocs. Meanwhile, after 1887, Russia pursued a pacific, low-profile policy in the Balkans culminating in Austro-Russian agreements in 1897 and 1903 to preserve the status quo there. Only if the moribund Ottoman Empire collapsed would they divide its European lands. Absorbed elsewhere, the major Balkan imperial rivals agreed to keep that region quiet and the Turkish Straits closed to foreign warships.

Anglo-Russian rivalry in the Middle East persisted until the settlement of 1907. Tension between them had almost resulted in war during the Afghan Crisis of 1885, then gradually subsided. Britain and Russia competed for influence in corrupt and prostrate Persia (now Iran), where military and civilian agents steadily extended Russian influence, and a Cossack Brigade (founded in 1879) served as an anti-British spearhead. While London considered Persia an outpost in the defense of British India, Russia viewed it as ripe for the plucking. "The entire northern part of Persia," declared Count Witte, "was intended, as if by nature, to turn in the future . . . into a country under our complete protectorate." In Persia, the British, whose chief interests lay in the south and west, were losing ground to Russia in competition for trade, influence, and railway building. Their contest can be compared with recent U.S.-Soviet tensions in the same region.

Russia had emerged as a Pacific power, after acquiring the Amur region and Vladivostok by 1860. Until the late 1890s, Russian interests in the Far East were growing, but limited. The Treaty of St. Petersburg (1875) with emerging Japan provided Russia with the large offshore island of Sakhalin, but Siberia's settlement lagged, and Russian naval facilities and overland communications remained inadequate. A group of Russian scholars, journalists, and military men known as Vostochniki (Easterners), like the Panslavs for the Balkans, advocated imperial expansion in Asia. Russia, with its essentially non-European culture, they asserted, was destined to develop or incorporate much of Asia and protect Europe against the "yellow peril." Mongolia and Sinkiang longed to join Russia, affirmed the explorer, M. N. Przhevalskii. Prince E. E. Ukhtomskii, a journalist who influenced Nicholas II, believed that once opened by modern communications, Siberia would become Russia's Eldorado. Count Witte translated such vague imperial dreams into a degree of reality by inducing the government, in 1891, to begin constructing the Trans-Siberian Railroad; he envisioned it as the spearhead of Russian economic expansion in the Far East.

By revealing China's helplessness, the Sino-Japanese War of 1894 stimulated European imperial powers, including Russia, to press forward. In 1895, Witte, with Franco-German diplomatic support, compelled a reluctant Japan to return the Liaotung Peninsula with its warm-water ports to China. In 1896, the Li- Lobanov Agreement authorized a Russian-controlled corporation to build and operate a Chinese Eastern Railroad across northern Manchuria. (See Map 2.3.) In 1898, Nicholas II, urged on by military and naval leaders, and over Witte's strong objections, ordered seizure of strategic Port Arthur, the naval base on the Liaotung Peninsula, and forced China to lease to Russia the very region she had compelled Japan to renounce! Construction of a South Manchurian Railroad, northward from Port Arthur to a junction with the Chinese Eastern, allowed Russia to dominate all of Manchuria. After the Boxers, a nationalist Chinese society, attacked Russian railway properties in 1900, War Minister A. N. Kuropatkin dispatched troops to occupy Manchuria; he told Witte that it would become a Russian protectorate.

Its government gravely divided over Far Eastern policy, Russia embarked on a reckless, aggressive course in the Orient. While Witte and the Foreign Ministry favored continued peaceful economic penetration of China and an alliance with her, adventurers led by former Guards officer, A. M. Bezobrazov, obtained the Yalu River timber concession on the Manchurian-Korean border, a move toward eventual Russian annexation of Korea. Japan sought a compromise settlement with Russia,

Map 2.3 *Russia in the Far East to 1914*

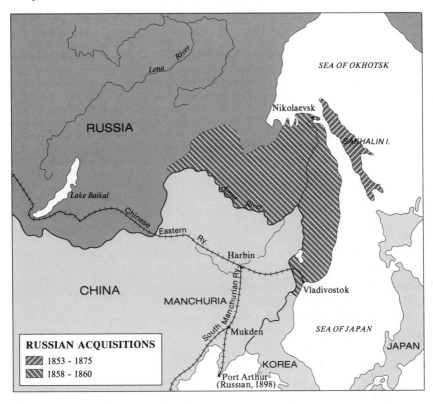

which Witte repeatedly urged Nicholas II to accept, but Interior Minister V. K. Pleve declared that bayonets had made Russia, not diplomats: "In order to restrain revolution [at home], we need a little victorious war." Nicholas II, blissfully confident, wrote William II, emperor of Germany: "There will be no war [with Japan] because I do not wish it." Thus Russia rejected reasonable Japanese peace offers and blundered ill prepared into a needless and disastrous war.

The Russo-Japanese War (1904–1905) began in January 1904 with sudden Japanese attacks on the scattered Russian fleet. Invading Manchuria from Korea, the Japanese besieged Port Arthur, the chief Russian naval base in the Far East. In Manchuria, Japanese armies repeatedly defeated General Kuropatkin and drove him north; Port Arthur surrendered ignominiously to them. Seeking to redress the military balance, Russia's Baltic Fleet sailed around Africa, only to suffer virtual annihilation by Admiral Togo's main fleet in Tsushima Strait. With Japan nearing the end of its limited resources and Russia engulfed by revolution, both sides willingly allowed President Theodore Roosevelt of the United States to mediate their conflict. The Treaty of Portsmouth, New Hampshire, ending the war, transferred southern Manchuria to Japan and confirmed its preeminence in Korea; Russia retained northern Manchuria and the Chinese Eastern Railroad. The Russo-Japanese War, halting Russia's imperial drive in the Far East and weakening the Franco-Russian Alliance, ended British fears of Russian imperialism and naval power. Japan's victory, its first over a great European power and the initial defeat for white imperialism in Asia, discredited the tsarist regime at home and helped induce it to grant important concessions to the Russian people.

Suggested Additional Reading

BALMUTH, DANIEL. *Censorship in Russia, 1865–1905* (Washington, D.C., 1979).

BLACK, E. E., ed. *The Transformation of Russian Society . . . since 1861* (Cambridge, Mass., 1960).

BLACKWELL, WILLIAM. *The Industrialization of Russia*, 2d ed. (Arlington Heights, Ill., 1982).

BRADLEY, JOSEPH. *Muzhik and Muscovite: Urbanization in Late Imperial Russia* (Berkeley, Calif., 1985).

CRANKSHAW, EDWARD. *The Shadow of the Winter Palace . . . 1825–1917* (New York, 1976).

CRISP, OLGA. *Studies in the Russian Economy Before 1914* (New York, 1976).

EMMONS, TERENCE. *The Emancipation of the Russian Serfs* (New York, 1970).

FIELD, DANIEL. *The End of Serfdom* (Cambridge, Mass., 1976).

FISCHER, G. *Russian Liberalism . . .* (Cambridge, Mass., 1958).

FITZPATRICK, ANNE L. *The Great Russian Fair: Nizhnii-Novgorod, 1840–90* (New York, 1989).

GADDIS, JOHN. *Russia, the Soviet Union, and the United States* (New York, 1978).

GATRELL, PETER. *The Tsarist Economy, 1850–1917* (New York, 1986).

GEYER, DIETRICH. *Russian Imperialism . . . 1860–1914* (New Haven, Conn., 1987).

GREENBURG, LOUIS. *The Jews in Russia*, 2 vols. (New Haven, Conn., 1951).

KAZEMZADEH, FIRUZ. *Russia and Britain in Persia, 1864–1914* (New Haven, Conn., 1968).

KEEP, J. L. H. *The Rise of Social Democracy in Russia* (Oxford, Eng., 1963).

KOLCHIN, PETER. *Unfree Labor: American Slavery and Russian Serfdom* (Cambridge, Mass., 1987).

LENIN, V. I. *The Development of Capitalism in Russia* (Moscow, 1956).

MACKENZIE, DAVID. *The Lion of Tashkent . . .* (Athens, Ga., 1974).

MALOZEMOFF, A. *Russian Far Eastern Policy, 1881–1904* (Berkeley, Calif., 1958).

McNeal, Robert. *Tsar and Cossack, 1855–1914* (New York, 1987).

Mosse, W. E. *Alexander II and the Modernization of Russia* (New York, 1962).

Owen, T. C. *Capitalism and Politics in Russia . . . 1855–1905* (Cambridge, England, 1981).

Pearson, Thomas S. *Russian Officialdom in Crisis: Autocracy and Local Self-Government, 1861–1900* (Cambridge, England and New York, 1989).

Pintner, W. M., and D. K. Rowney, eds. *Russian Officialdom* (Chapel Hill, N.C., 1980).

Rieber, Alfred, ed. *The Politics of Autocracy . . .* (Paris, 1966).

Robinson, G. T. *Rural Russia Under the Old Regime* (New York, 1949).

Rogger, Hans. *Russia in the Age of Modernisation and Revolution, 1881–1917.* (London and New York, 1983).

Romanov, B. A. *Russia in Manchuria, 1892–1906,* trans. S. Jones (Ann Arbor, Mich., 1952).

Simms, J. Y. "The Crisis in Russian Agriculture at the End of the 19th Century: A Different View," *Slavic Review, 36* (September 1977), pp. 377–398.

Stites, Richard. *The Women's Liberation Movement in Russia . . .* (Princeton, N.J., 1978).

Sumner, B. H. *Russia and the Balkans, 1870–1880* (Oxford, Eng., 1937).

Thaden, E. C. *Conservative Nationalism in 19th Century Russia* (Seattle, 1964).

Tugan-Baranovsky, M. I. *The Russian Factory in the 19th Century,* trans. A. Levin et al. (Homewood, Ill., 1970).

von Laue, T. H. *Sergei Witte and the Industrialization of Russia* (New York, 1963).

Vucinich, W. S., ed. *The Peasant in Nineteenth Century Russia* (Stanford, Calif., 1968).

Westwood, J. N. *A History of Russian Railways* (London, 1964).

Witte, S. Iu. *The Memoirs of Count Witte* (New York, 1921).

Zaionchkovskii, P. A. *The Russian Autocracy Under Alexander III,* trans. D. D. Jones (Gulf Breeze, Fla., 1976).

CHAPTER THREE

OPPOSITION TO TSARISM

Never assume that the Russian people have always remained docile and obedient under a repressive regime. While modern Russian history has involved the growth of political autocracy, serfdom, and repression, it has also witnessed several massive peasant revolts and two great revolutions in 1905 and 1917. Whenever autocratic government weakened or controls were relaxed, popular upheavals erupted, virtually unmatched in violence and destructiveness. To suggest Russia's ideologies and forces of dissent, we will now trace liberal and radical movements against tsarism, notably from 1855 to the eve of the Revolution of 1905.

During the 17th and 18th centuries occurred four major and a number of minor popular revolts. Provoked by the development of serfdom and a centralized autocratic state, these peasant and Cossack revolts, lacking cohesion and disciplined armies, were all doomed to eventual suppression by the Muscovite tsardom. During the first "time of troubles" an ex-galley slave and Cossack, Ivan Bolotnikov, led peasants and have-nots from towns in southern Muscovy against the "boyars' tsar,"

Vasili IV, only to meet defeat in 1607. From 1667 to 1671, a great revolt raged in the Don frontier region against Moscow, led by Stepan ("Stenka") Razin, a fearless, hard-drinking Cossack warrior. After winning wide support in "the wild field" (frontier), Razin's movement was eventually crushed by the army of Tsar Alexis, bequeathing a legacy of glorious defiance and popular legend. Under another Cossack leader, Kondraty Bulavin, the Don frontier rose again, 1707–1709, against Peter I, a westernizing autocrat, and against reforms the rebels believed were subverting their traditional faith and freedoms. Finally, in 1773–1774 the Pugachev Revolt, called "the Peasant War" by Soviet scholars, was the greatest rural upheaval of Russian and European history down to 1905. Led by a Don Cossack, Emelian Pugachev, who claimed to be the legitimate tsar, Peter III, it spread like wildfire through the Ural and Volga regions until defeated by Catherine II's army. "The entire populace was for Pugachev," wrote the great poet Alexander Pushkin. "Only the nobility openly supported the government." All these uprisings were suppressed brutally by a tsarist regime, which instead of remedying popular grievances, fastened even tighter controls over an enslaved people. There would be no recurrence of large-scale peasant revolts until after 1900.

Plainly, leadership by the educated would be required before successful warfare could be waged against the bastions of tsarism and serfdom. Such leadership arose with the emergence under Catherine II in the 1780s of a Russian intelligentsia. This was defined aptly by a Populist historian, Ivanov-Razumnik, as an hereditary group outside estate or class, seeking the physical, mental, social, and personal emancipation of the individual from oppression. Under Catherine, it comprised only a handful of enlightened noblemen led by Novikov and Radishchev, but its ideas circulated among the elite of Moscow and St. Petersburg. They were passed on to the Decembrists, who elaborated them further, drew up extensive programs of reform and revolution, and attempted, albeit unsuccessfully, to overturn autocracy and serfdom in 1825. The intelligentsia movement broadened during the Slavophile-Westernizer debate of 1838–1848 to include offspring of the middle class, such as the radical literary critic Vissarion Belinskii, who in 1847 from Austrian exile excoriated the autocratic system of the "Iron Tsar":

> Russia sees her salvation not in mysticism, not in asceticism, not in pietism, but in the achievement of civilization, enlightenment and humanitarianism . . . , an awakening in her people of the sense of human dignity.

And Belinskii pointed the way forward with other Westernizers toward the goal of a new, free Russia:

The most topical, the most vital national questions in Russia today are the abolition of serfdom, the repeal of corporal punishment, and the introduction as far as possible, of the strictest application of at least those laws which are already on the books.[1]

Alexander Herzen (1812–1870), the founder of Populism and the first important Russian socialist, combined elements of Slavophilism and Westernism into a radical ideology. From the Slavophiles, Herzen derived his passion for Russian institutions and values. Rejecting the modern industrialism and urban life of western Europe, he viewed the Russian peasant commune (mir) as the basis for a decentralized peasant Russian socialism. Going into exile in 1847, Herzen published in London the biweekly *Bell (Kolokol)* from 1857 to 1867. This most influential Russian émigré newspaper of all time attacked the evils of the old regime and called for freedom and emancipation. Meanwhile a vibrant new intellectual climate marked the first decade of Alexander II's reign as numerous liberal and radical newspapers and periodicals appeared. "Everyone is talking, everyone is studying, including people who never before read anything in their lives," wrote the historian K. D. Kavelin. Contacts with Europe, severed by Nicholas I, were renewed; hopes for drastic change soared.

In the post-Crimean epoch, a diversified liberal and radical opposition developed against the autocracy. Liberals, aiming to reform and improve the system peacefully, competed with revolutionaries who sought to overthrow it. Liberals found it difficult to pursue their work in the face of governmental repression and without a parliament. Determined radicals, often using despotic methods and organizations, answered police repression with terrorism, secrecy, and ruthlessness. Before 1890 they looked mostly to the peasantry as their army of revolution; afterward, Marxism grew rapidly, and its adherents wooed a rising urban working class. Soviet historians devote most attention to Marxist Social Democrats and claim that only a workers' party could have taken Russia to socialism. Recent Western scholars, often rejecting this thesis, have turned more to agrarian socialists and liberals. Why did Russian liberalism remain relatively weak? Why did radical movements develop so many splits? Was a Marxist triumph in Russia inevitable as Soviet accounts suggest? Did the autocracy help determine the opposition's aims and means?

The relaxation of censorship increased contacts with Europe, and government overtures stimulated liberal gentry to advocate reform. In

---

[1]"Letter to N. V. Gogol," in M. Raeff, *Russian Intellectual History: An Anthology* (New York, 1966), p. 254.

Tver province, liberal gentry leaders A. M. Unkovskii and A. A. Golovachev composed a memorandum that criticized the bureaucracy and official reform proposals and advocated full and immediate emancipation, as well as an equal role for gentry committees in working it out. The Tver gentry committee's majority project (1858) urged landowners to favor emancipation with land, abolition of *barshchina* (labor service) and patrimonial rights, and an all-class, elected local administration. Other liberals urged reform of army recruitment and the courts, accountability of bureaucrats to the courts, and public primary schooling. Strongly influenced by liberal European thought and Russian university lectures, such liberal views won considerable support among the provincial gentry.

Liberal gentry ideology evolved further in their provincial assemblies of 1859–1860. The Tver assembly protested government violations of noble rights and affirmed a major public role for the gentry. When the authorities exiled Unkovskii for this, he wrote Alexander II:

> I never thought that the problem of peasant emancipation could be decided by the gentry or its representatives, but I have always been convinced that for the success of this transformation the conscious sincere cooperation of the gentry is necessary.[2]

These gentry assemblies were unprecedented in Russia. Summoned to discuss national issues in elected bodies for the first time, the provincial gentry discussed economic, political, and legal reform. As official reform plans matured, however, the regime gradually restricted public initiative and, in November 1859, forbade gentry assemblies to debate the peasant question. Nonetheless, they continued to voice strong opposition to extension of bureaucratic control and demanded full local self-government in return for the imminent loss of seignorial rights. The most vocal assemblies advocated immediate obligatory redemption of land by the peasantry, drastic judicial reform, and all-class elective local self-government.

After the Emancipation, gentry assemblies pressed for political and administrative change and criticized the emancipation statutes. The Tver provincial gentry assembly resolved (February 1862):

> Gentry are deeply convinced that the government is not capable of realizing [further reforms]. The free institutions to which these reforms lead can come only from the people. . . . The gentry . . . indicate that the path onto which [the government] must venture for the salvation of itself and of

---

[2]Quoted in T. Emmons, *The Russian Landed Gentry* (Cambridge, Eng., 1968), p. 281.

society . . . is the gathering of representatives from the entire people without distinction as to class.

To dramatize gentry demands for local self-government, the Tver Assembly went on to renounce its class privileges:

> The gentry, by virtue of class advantages, have so far escaped fulfillment of the most important public obligations. Sovereign, we consider it a grievous fault to live and enjoy the benefits of the public order at the expense of other classes. . . . We most loyally request Your Majesty to be allowed to take upon ourselves a part of state taxes and obligations. . . .[3]

Instead of meeting with the Tver leaders or heeding their recommendations, Alexander II ordered their arrest.

During 1861–1862, Russian publicists abroad, such as A. I. Koshelev and Herzen, fostered a semiconstitutional gentry movement for a consultative assembly, or *zemskii sobor*. Underground leaflets advocated a constitution, responsible ministers, jury trials, and freedom of religion and the press. The regime blocked gentry constitutionalism and punished its leaders while conceding to gentry wishes by facilitating redemption of land and outlining liberal zemstvo and judicial reforms. This took the steam out of gentry opposition, and a Moscow petition (1865) for a national consultative assembly was gentry constitutionalism's last gasp.

After 1865, gentry liberalism centered in the new zemstva. Leaders such as I. I. Petrunkevich of Chernigov aimed to convert them into "a school of self-government, and by this means prepare the way for a constitutional state order." They aimed to expand zemstva activities to the maximum and take from the autocracy most control over rural affairs. In Chernigov, Petrunkevich's program to aid the peasantry included free primary education, improving material conditions, and justice under law.[4] Such liberals sought a society where the individual would be central and self-governing, private property would be guaranteed, and law would be supreme. Zemstva liberals strove to persuade the regime to accept their "small deeds" in raising popular cultural and material well-being, hoping that eventually it would grant a national zemstva or even a constitution.

Meanwhile young intellectuals, led by N. G. Chernyshevskii and N. A. Dobroliubov, determined to remake the world through reason, turned enthusiastically to radicalism. Some were priests' sons estranged from existing values and institutions and convinced that partial reforms were

---

[3]Emmons, *The Russian Landed Gentry*, pp. 341–343.
[4]Charles Timberlake, "Ivan Il'ich Petrunkevich . . . ," *Essays on Russian Liberalism* (Columbia, Mo., 1972), p. 18 ff.

Nikolai G. Chernyshevskii, 1828–1889, leading
radical of the 1860s and author of *What Is To
Be Done?* *(SOVFOTO)* (See pg 70

useless. Radicals gathered around a journal, *The Contemporary*. Soviet
scholars regard Chernyshevskii, a leading contributor, as the chief pre-
cursor of Bolshevism and praise his materialism and scorn for liberalism.
Chernyshevskii dreamed of changing history's course by building a
perpetual motion machine to abolish poverty. He and Dobroliubov
stressed the intellectual's duty to awaken, educate, and lead the toiling
masses. Viewing the mir (peasant commune) as the basis for decentralized agrarian socialism, Chernyshevskii affirmed that Russia,
unlike Europe, could avoid capitalism and move directly to socialism. In
What Is To Be Done?, (Chto delat?), composed in prison (1863), he described
a socialist utopia achieved by relentless, practical revolutionaries who
would "impose their character on the pattern of events, and hurry their
course." Now few, they would multiply rapidly, and "in a few years . . .
people will call unto them for rescue, and what they say will be performed
by all." Chernyshevskii's "toiler's theory" asserted that labor was entitled
to all that it produced, but he derived his socialism more from Fourier

than from Marx. Twenty years in Siberian exile made him a revolutionary martyr.

Dmitri Pisarev (1840–1868) reflected the uncompromising radicalism of intelligentsia "sons" of the 1860s who attacked the values and beliefs of the "fathers" of the 1840s. "Here is the ultimatum of our camp: what can be smashed should be smashed; what will stand the blow is good; . . . at any rate hit out left and right." This thrilled rebellious adolescents fighting the establishment. The writer Ivan Turgenev dubbed their ideology nihilism, and Bazarov, the hero of his novel *Fathers and Sons* (1862), was Pisarev thinly disguised. A convinced Westernizer, Pisarev believed that an educated elite with modern science and European technology would uplift the masses and destroy autocracy.

During the early 1860s, small groups of intelligentsia discussed ways to spread propaganda and achieve revolution. N. Shelgunov's dramatic leaflet, *To the Younger Generation* (1861), urged the educated youth to reject Western parliamentary models and rely upon the mir. "We trust in our own fresh forces. We believe that we are called upon . . . to utter our [own] words and not follow in the wake of Europe." Another leaflet, *Young Russia* (1862), by Peter Zaichnevskii, a Moscow University student, proposed a republic and local assemblies based on the peasant commune: "Russia is entering the revolutionary period of its existence. The interests of the masses are irreconcilable with those of the Imperial party, landowners, officials, and Tsar. Their plundering of the people can only be stopped by a bloody, implacable revolution." The police speedily dissolved such groups.

In the mid-1860s, a small group of Moscow intelligentsia led by Nicholas Ishutin, a follower of Chernyshevskii, plotted direct, violent action. A secret band of terrorists known as Hell was to destroy autocracy. In April 1866, a student, Dmitri Karakozov, Ishutin's cousin, shot at the tsar. He missed (and apologized to Alexander II before being executed!), and the Ishutin circle was broken up.

In the ensuing reaction, Russian exiles developed conspiratorial ideas. In 1869, Sergei Nechaev, a Moscow University student in Geneva, Switzerland, and the romantic revolutionary Mikhail Bakunin composed *Catechism of a Revolutionary,* which stressed that revolutionaries must be professional, dedicated, and disciplined:

> The revolutionary is a doomed man. He has no interests, no affairs, no feelings, no attachments of his own. . . . Everything in him is wholly absorbed by one sole, exclusive interest . . . revolution. He must train himself to stand torture and be ready to die. . . . The laws, the conventions, the moral code of civilized society have no meaning for him. . . . To him whatever

promotes the triumph of the revolution is moral, whatever hinders it is criminal.[5]

Later Lenin, praising the *Catechism* highly, patterned his Bolshevik Party upon it. Nechaev returned briefly to Russia in 1870 and set up a small organization, the People's Reckoning *(Narodnaia Rasprava)*, which murdered a member who planned to betray it to the authorities.[6]

REVOLUTIONARY POPULISM

In the 1870s, a broader movement of revolutionary intelligentsia heeded Herzen's appeal: "Go to the people." Populism *(Narodnichestvo)* combined idealistic faith in the peasantry with determination to overthrow the old social and political order by force. Lacking central organization or a cohesive ideology, Populism advocated a peasant socialism derived largely from Herzen. The Populists regarded European large-scale factory industry as degrading and dehumanizing, denied that an industrial revolution must precede socioeconomic progress, and believed that only agriculturists led the good, natural life. Using intelligence and free will, Russians could avoid European errors. Like Rousseau, Populists believed that bad institutions had corrupted people and that the state had fostered inequality, injustice, and oppression. Popular revolution, not parliaments, would produce a decentralized socialist order. Populists idealized the people *(narod)*, especially the peasantry, as a mystical, irresistible, and virtuous force whose traditional institutions—the mir and the primitive producers' cooperative *(artel)* with their collective landholding and quasi self-government—would become socialist once the old order was destroyed. Convinced that peasants in the mir were practicing rudimentary socialism, Populists disregarded clear signs of its disintegration before an advancing money economy. They emphasized ethical and humanitarian values and faith in collective institutions, but they disagreed about revolutionary organization, the intelligentsia's relationship to the people, and how and when to achieve revolution. In the early 1870s, the émigrés Bakunin and Lavrov had small followings of socialist youth; later P. N. Tkachev's conspiratorial views tended to prevail.

Mikhail Bakunin, a founder of anarchism with long experience in tsarist prisons, urged an immediate, spontaneous mass uprising *(bunt)* by

---

[5]A. Yarmolinsky, *Road to Revolution* (London, 1957, reprint Princeton, N.J., 1986), pp. 156–157.

[6]Fyodor Dostoyevsky based his novel *The Possessed* on this incident and the character Peter Verkhovenskii on Nechaev.

the peasantry. Regarding much of the intelligentsia as a privileged elite that despised the people, Bakunin appealed not to reason or science, but to emotion, feeling, and mass instincts: "The Russian peasantry are socialists by instinct and revolutionaries by nature. . . . We must not act as schoolmasters for the people; we must lead them to revolt." The existing state must be totally destroyed, and a free federation of peasant communes should replace it. A romantic apostle of freedom, Bakunin opposed "the authoritarian communism of Marx and the entire German school." He helped inspire the "going to the people" movement of 1874, and his influence grew during the 1870s, but no true Bakuninist organization was ever established in Russia. When the anticipated popular uprisings failed to break out, Bakunin's following dwindled.[7]

P. L. Lavrov's more moderate, cautious approach grew popular. Lavrov, a mathematics professor, achieved prominence with his legally published *Historical Letters* (1870). For their education, intellectuals owed a debt to the people and should repay it by preparing them for revolution: a "critically thinking" elite should propagandize and agitate among the people. Abroad, in his journal, *Forward!*, Lavrov developed a complete Populist program. He borrowed Marx's tenets of the increasing misery of the masses and the worldwide socialist revolution, but was uncertain whether revolution in Russia would precede or follow full capitalist development. He emphasized careful preparation of a peasant revolution by the intelligentsia. (Bakuninists derisively dubbed his followers "the preparationists.") Dedicated intellectual revolutionaries were to explain socialism to the masses and recruit members from their ranks. (Lavrov worked it all out mathematically!) Local uprisings, directed by a revolutionary organization, would fuse in a nationwide revolution. Afterward, a strong central government would be needed temporarily, but Lavrov repudiated dictatorship.

P. N. Tkachev, the heir of Nihilism and Ishutin, led a small Jacobinist faction that rejected Lavrov's patient approach. Tkachev's views in the émigré newspaper *The Tocsin* combined Populism, Marxism, and Blanquism.[8] Like Bakunin he urged immediate action, but believed that a centralized, elite organization of revolutionaries must lead the masses, a disciplined party able to impose its will. Tkachev's writing was filled with urgency: Unless revolution came soon, capitalism would destroy the mir. "This is why we cannot wait. This is why we insist that a revolution in Russia is indispensable . . . at the present time." A temporary dictatorship

---

[7]Franco Venturi, *Roots of Revolution* (New York, 1960), pp. 429–436.
[8]Named after Auguste Blanqui, a French revolutionary who advocated armed insurrection and dictatorship by a revolutionary minority.

would follow armed overthrow of the old order, but it would wither away once the people had been educated in socialism. Tkachev appealed desperately for immediate revolution until finally he went insane. Later, Lenin described his plan for seizing power as majestic.

Populism's practical achievements were few. Its main early organization, the Chaikovskii Circle (Lavrovist) was broken up by arrests. In 1873–1874, after a famine in the Volga region, more than 3,000 young urban intellectuals "went to the people" to spread socialist ideas and prepare revolution, but the peasants responded to this unorganized, naive "children's crusade" by turning over many of the ragged agitators to the police; the rest returned home disillusioned. The failure of the "going to the people" episode discredited Lavrovism and dissipated some of the naive idealism of Russian Populists. In 1876, a broader Populist organization, the second Land and Liberty (the first was founded in 1861), demanded all land for the peasants and conducted the first mass revolutionary demonstration in Russia at Kazan Cathedral in St. Petersburg. The police arrested its leaders, and two big trials were held. In 1879, Land and Liberty split mainly over the issue of terrorism; moderates founded their own organization and newspaper, *Black Repartition,* which repudiated terrorism and violence, but soon its leaders (Plekhanov, Deutsch, and Zasulich) fled abroad. An extremist, proterrorist element created *Narodnaia Volia,* the People's Will, based on ideas of Nechaev and Tkachev. Its secret Executive Committee plotted to assassinate the tsar and other high officials in order to disorganize the regime and trigger popular revolution. In March 1881, the People's Will murdered Alexander II, but within two years the police had destroyed it and broken the revolutionary movement.

Before the 1860s, few women played a role in revolutionary activity. Under Alexander II, female radicalism at first involved only acts of individual defiance and participation in radical circles. Revolutionary proclamations of the 1860s, often distributed by women, mostly failed to mention women's rights except for Zaichnevskii's pamphlet, *Young Russia* (1862), which demanded complete women's emancipation, civil and political equality, and abolition of marriage and the family. Becoming the Bible for Russian feminists and revolutionaries, Chernyshevskii's novel *What Is To Be Done?* described the development of Vera Pavlovna, the new socialist woman, who frees herself from family control and escapes an arranged marriage. Love and sexual fulfillment, she concludes, are less important for women than economic independence. Only about 65 of some 2,000 Russian revolutionaries in the 1860s were women, but they were involved in radical circles such as Ishutin's and workshops such as the Dressmaking Shop of the Ivanova sisters in Chernyshevskii's novel, where educated women and lower-class seamstresses lived, worked, and read radical authors together.

That women composed about one eighth of revolutionary Populists of the 1870s, most of them well educated, reflected the growing women's movement. As revolutionaries, women could aspire to equality and rise to top leadership posts, proving themselves capable of things undreamed of by traditional society. About one third of the Executive Committee of the People's Will were female, and they were subsequently incarcerated in the worst prisons alongside male terrorists. A prominent leader of the People's Will was Vera Figner (1852–1942), an aristocratic woman who studied medicine and worked among the peasantry as a Populist follower of Bakunin. In 1876, she joined Mark Natanson and others in Land and Liberty to organize a massive peasant uprising. Concluding that only violent revolution could overturn tsarism, she joined the Executive Committee and held the People's Will together for two years after Alexander II's assassination. Betrayed to the police, she served 22 years solitary confinement in a fortress, then was exiled, finally returning to Soviet Russia after 1917. Another prominent woman revolutionary was Sofia Perovskaia (1853–1881), daughter of the St. Petersburg governor-general. Revolutionaries admired her for her simplicity, love of common people, stoicism, coolness, and courage. During the "going to the people" movement, she agitated among St. Petersburg workers and was prominent in the Chaikovskii Circle. As a leader of the Executive Committee, Perovskaia prepared Alexander II's assassination, placed the bomb throwers, and gave the signal. Apprehended with her lover, terrorist Andrei Zheliabov, she confessed freely, and was the first Russian woman political prisoner to be hanged (1881).

Women played a vital and growing role in the Russian revolutionary movement, both in its Populist phase and later in the Marxist movement. Setting an example of dedication to violent struggle, they created precedents for numerous women participants in the revolutions of 1905 and 1917. Wrote V. I. Lenin in 1918: "From the experience of all liberation movements, it can be noted that the success of revolution can be measured by the extent of the involvement of women in it."[9]

THE DEVELOPMENT OF MARXISM

By 1881, the more naive, idealistic elements of the intelligentsia had been eliminated or discredited. The Populist movement, after the failure of "going to the people" and faced with police persecution following the

---

[9]Lenin, *Polnoe Sobranie Sochinenii*, 5th ed. (Moscow, 1960), vol. 36, p. 186.

tsar's assassination, was in disarray. Urban-bred revolutionaries,. still idealizing the peasantry, had not bridged the gulf in education, attitudes, and life-styles with the rural masses. Economic conditions were changing rapidly, and an industrial working class with more revolutionary potential was emerging. Alexander III's stifling autocracy, allied with rising business, heightened the revolutionaries' despair and isolation. Radical youths of the 1880s, dismayed by Populist defeats and illusions, searched for a new, comprehensive theory to explain disturbing new economic facts. Some found their answer in Marxism, which began to attract intellectuals, and link them with the industrial working class.

Fundamentals of Marx's Theory

Karl Marx (1818–1883), whose forebears had been Jewish rabbis, and Friedrich Engels (1820–1895), son of a wealthy German manufacturer, derived their cohesive theory of "scientific socialism" from many sources, weaving others' ideas ingeniously into a system to explain the "laws of history." Their complex and sometimes contradictory theory reflected European ideas of progress and human perfectibility. Marx, the philosopher, and Engels, the publicist, combined in a unique intellectual partnership. Marx owed much to the system of dialectical idealism of the outstanding German philosopher G. F. Hegel, accepting his method of reasoning (dialectic) and his belief that conflict of opposites and the resulting synthesis produces progress, unfolding in stages and culminating in perfection. However, Marx rejected Hegel's conservative political and social views and his belief that ideas create reality. Marx adopted Ludwig Feuerbach's atheism and materialism: How man earns his daily bread determines his actions and outlook ("Man is what he eats"). Antagonistic social classes (for example, bourgeoisie versus proletariat), affirmed Marx, contend over the means of production (land, factories, and tools). Economic elements (means of production and worker-owner relationships), he argued, make up the substructure of society and determine basically its superstructure (government, law, religion, ideas). A person's economic and social status largely determine what he or she does, writes, and thinks. Nonetheless, Marx retained a strong belief in human dignity and the goal of freedom.

Applying their philosophy to history (historical materialism), Marx and Engels shared Hegel's view of human evolution by inexorable laws through a series of stages toward freedom. Each successive historical stage—primitive communism, slavery, feudalism, capitalism, and socialism—reflects a more mature form of production. Passage from one stage to the next results inevitably from conflict between a class (for example, the bourgeoisie) controlling the means of production and the one it

Karl Marx, 1818–1883, founder of "scientific socialism." *(EASTFOTO)*

exploits (proletariat). As one mode of production yields to a more advanced one, and the exploited class achieves greater freedom, a new stage develops, usually by revolution.

Capitalism, explained Marx, is that historical stage in western Europe during which the bourgeoisie (especially factory owners) exploits the proletariat. At first, with its numerous small, competing firms, capitalism is revolutionary and dynamic, the most productive system yet devised. However, the worker, the creator of value, receives back in wages only a fraction of the value his labor creates; the capitalist pockets the rest ("surplus value") as profit. As weaker firms succumb, competitive capitalism will evolve into its opposite—monopoly. The industrial work force will absorb much of the peasantry and lesser bourgeoisie until the proletariat becomes the vast majority of the population. As overproduction and unemployment grow, so will worker dissatisfaction and class consciousness. Fully developed capitalism will produce mountains of goods, which miserably paid workers cannot afford to buy.

Revolutions, Marx predicted, would occur first in advanced capitalist countries. They would be led by communists—class-conscious workers and intellectuals—defined as "the most advanced and resolute section of the working-class parties of every country . . . which pushes forward all others." In 1848, Marx believed that revolutions would mostly be violent because ruling capitalists and feudal lords would not yield wealth and power voluntarily, but they would be democratic since the vast oppressed majority would dispossess a tiny minority of exploiters. In 1872, Marx declared that there were countries such as America, England, and perhaps Holland, where the workers might achieve their goal peacefully. These differing views on the necessity of revolution would be reflected later in a split between European democratic socialists and Russian Bolsheviks.

Following the demise of capitalism, a transitional era of unspecified length—the dictatorship of the proletariat (which Marx never defined clearly) would prevail. Workers the world over would unite to cast off their chains and establish socialism everywhere. A workers' state would run the government and economy, distribute goods fairly to the people, and educate them in socialist values. Coercing only former exploiters, it would be more democratic than "bourgeois democracy" because it would represent the workers, the vast majority. Once it had achieved its purposes, the workers' state, or at least its coercive aspects, would wither away. Private property, class struggle, and exploitation would disappear, yielding to a perfect socialist order of abundance and freedom called *communism*. Marx described this system in 1875:

> . . . After the subordination of the individual to the division of labor, and therewith also the antithesis between mental and physical labor has vanished . . . ; after the productive forces have also increased with the all-round development of the individual, and all the springs of cooperative wealth flow more abundantly—only then can the narrow horizon of bourgeois right be crossed in its entirety and society inscribe on its banner: From each according to his ability, to each according to his needs![10]

Did Marxian theory, conceived for western Europe with its more liberal, humanitarian traditions, apply to backward, autocratic Russia? Marx learned Russian, read Chernyshevskii, and corresponded with Russian socialists, but his and Engels's views on Russia were uncertain and inconsistent. Thus Marx suggested in 1877 that Russia could escape capitalism and move directly from feudalism to socialism *if* capitalist elements within the mir were eliminated and *if* proletarian revolutions occurred soon in western Europe. In 1881, anxious to see tsarism overthrown, Marx replied to Vera Zasulich, a leading Russian Populist, that his research on the mir had "convinced him that this community is

---

[10]Quoted in Robert Tucker, *The Marx-Engels Reader*, 2d ed. (New York, 1978), p. 531. For more on Marxism see R. N. Carew-Hunt, *The Theory and Practice of Communism* (New York, 1958) and *Marxism: Past and Present* (New York, 1954).

the mainspring of Russia's social regeneration," provided it could "eliminate the deleterious influences which assail it from every quarter. . . ."[11] However, after Marx's death Engels wrote sadly that these conditions had not been fulfilled, so that Russia was doomed to undergo capitalism after all. On Russia, Marx and Engels proved to be hesitant Marxists.

From *Das Kapital* to *What Is To Be Done?*

In the 1870s Marxist ideas began to circulate in Russia. The abstruse and technical *Das Kapital* (1867) was published openly, as were other nonpolitical Marxist works. In 1875 the first significant worker organization in Russia, the South Russian Workers Alliance, opened in Odessa, but soon its leaders were arrested. Three years later, the Northern Alliance of Russian Workers, with more than 200 active members, arose in St. Petersburg, but until the mid-1880s Russia had few Marxists and no Marxist movement.

George Plekhanov (1856–1918), though of noble origin, "reared a whole generation of Russian Marxists," Lenin said. Earlier, Plekhanov had sought to create a scientific Populism, but even then he had stressed the industrial workers' revolutionary potential. In 1879, he became editor of *Black Repartition,* the moderate Populist newspaper, but discouraged by its failure and the poor results of agitation among the peasantry, in 1880, he fled into Swiss exile. Realizing that in Russia the commune was disintegrating and industry was developing, Plekhanov in Geneva converted to Marxism. He was attracted by its orderliness and by Marx's claim to have discovered the laws of historical development. In Switzerland he, Paul Akselrod, and Vera Zasulich set up an independent Marxist group, the Liberation of Labor (1883), which for the next two decades acted as an embryo Russian social democratic party. Its members translated Marxist works and sent pamphlets into Russia, but at first Russians remained apathetic. In *Our Differences* (1885), Plekhanov denounced the People's Will for urging terrorism and minority insurrection. Industry was growing in Russia: "We must recognize that in this sphere the present as much as the [near] future belongs to capitalism in our country." Plekhanov affirmed that Russia, like western Europe, must pass through capitalism to reach socialism; only the proletariat, sparked by the intelligentsia, could organize a true socialist revolution. He balanced between voluntarist and determinist aspects of Marxism: the proletariat needed knowledge and organization, but the laws of history

---

[11]Tucker, *Marx-Engels Reader,* p. 675.

would surely bring defeat to the bourgeoisie. "The Social Democrats," he exulted, "are swimming along the current of history."

The Russian intelligentsia viewed Marxism and Populism as separate, competing movements. In 1885, a Bulgarian student, D. Blagoev, established the first Marxist study group in Russia; soon these became popular among university students and workers. The famine of 1891, revealing peasant helplessness, stimulated Marxism's growth as younger intellectuals such as V. I. Ulianov, later known as Lenin, rejected Populism and turned to the workers. In St. Petersburg, a Central Workers Circle linked worker groups and Marxist intellectuals, and in 1893 Ulianov joined one of them, beginning an illustrious revolutionary career. Marxist literature then mostly stressed determinism: Capitalist development was undermining the mir and proving Populism wrong. Arkadi Kremer's pamphlet, *On Agitation* (1894), however, warned that Marxists must not just study and theorize but also learn workers' grievances and exploit them. His associate, Julius Martov, met Ulianov and merged his Vilna group with ones in Petersburg. In 1895, major strikes in the textile industry revealed the workers' revolutionary energy and dispelled naive faith in Marxist study circles, but many Marxist leaders, including Ulianov and Martov, were arrested and exiled to Siberia.

Some Russian Marxists, influenced by European currents, turned away from revolution. Eduard Bernstein, a German Social Democrat, was attacking some of Marx's main premises, claiming that socialism could be reached by gradual, nonviolent, democratic means. In Russia, Peter Struve and S. Bulgakov argued that capitalism would evolve gradually into socialism. The movement of Economism developed, stressing "spontaneous" development and peaceful agitation to encourage workers to demand economic benefits from employers. Many Russian workers seemed more interested in shorter hours and higher pay than in revolution. Meanwhile, an attempt by Russian Marxist "politicals," who advocated active struggle against the regime, to form a national social democratic party, failed when the leaders of the initial secret congress of the Social Democrats (SDs) of 1898 in Minsk were arrested.

The youthful Lenin (Ulianov), by insisting on the necessity for violent revolution to achieve socialism, helped reinvigorate Russian Marxism. Vladimir Ilich Ulianov had been raised in the conservative, disciplined, and religious household of Ilia N. Ulianov, a dedicated teacher and provincial school inspector, in Simbirsk (now Ulianovsk) on the mid-Volga River. At age three, Vladimir Ilich became a nobleman when his father, because of his promotion to superintendent of schools, acquired hereditary nobility (his Soviet biographers fail to mention this). He and his older brother, Alexander, whom Vladimir greatly admired, were both excellent students and avid readers. In 1887, Alexander was executed for

Vladimir Ilich Lenin (1870–1924) *(Library of Congress)*

conspiring with remnants of the People's Will to assassinate Alexander III. His brother's death and Alexander's favorite author, Chernyshevskii, influenced Vladimir Ilich profoundly. Chernyshevskii's *What Is To Be Done?* convinced him that "strong personalities" impose their patterns on history. Admitted in 1887 to the law faculty of Kazan University up river from Simbirsk, Ulianov was expelled only months later after a student demonstration. Following private study, he passed the bar examination in St. Petersburg and practiced law briefly in Samara. Though admiring the dedication of the members of the People's Will, his disciplined mind was attracted to Marxism, and by 1892 he had become a convert. In one of his first writings, a pamphlet, *Who Are the Friends of the People?* (1894), Ulianov attacked the Populists, insisting that Russia was irrevocably committed to capitalist development. He developed this thesis fully in his major work written in Siberian exile, *The Development of Capitalism in Russia* (1899), arguing that differentiation of the peasantry into a rural proletariat and rural bourgeoisie (kulaks) proved that a disintegrating peasant commune was doomed to disappear.

After his exile, Lenin with Plekhanov became orthodox Marxism's chief spokesmen against revisionism. Restating Plekhanov, Lenin affirmed that revolution was absolutely essential in Russia and urged Social Democrats to lead an organized, class-conscious working class. Attacking the view of the Economists, a faction of Russian Marxism, that workers could develop cohesion spontaneously while improving their economic status, he argued that by itself the working class could develop only trade unionism. Marxists must provide conscious leadership, not trail behind the masses. In 1900, Lenin and Martov joined older émigrés of the Liberation of Labor (Plekhanov, Akselrod, and Zasulich) to found the newspaper, *Iskra (The Spark)* in Stuttgart, Germany, to combat revisionism and consolidate Marxist ideology and organization. In its first issue, using his pseudonym for the first time, Lenin stressed the need for active political work.

> The task of Social Democracy is to instill social democratic ideas and political consciousness into the mass of the proletariat and to organize a revolutionary party unbreakably tied to the spontaneous labor movement. . . . We must train people who will dedicate to the revolution not a free evening but the whole of their lives. . . .

What Is To Be Done? (1902), a lengthy pamphlet derived from his lead articles for *Iskra,* contained Lenin's main ideas on the nature and organization of the party. Stressing the need for discipline and cohesive organization to combat the Russian autocracy, he wrote:

> We are marching in a compact group along a precipitous and difficult path, firmly holding each other by the hand. We are surrounded on all sides by enemies, and we have to advance almost constantly under their fire.

Frequent use of military metaphors would characterize the writings of Lenin and other Bolsheviks. Lenin argued that it was essential to create a small, centralized body of professional revolutionaries from the intelligentsia to serve as the vanguard of the working class in its struggle to achieve socialism. "Class political consciousness can be brought to the workers *only from without.* . . ." Lenin further defined the party:

> The organization of the revolutionaries must consist first and foremost of people who make revolutionary activity their profession. . . . Such an organization must perforce not be very extensive and must be as secret as possible.

With such a party, success would be assured: "Give us an organization of revolutionists and we will overturn the whole of Russia."[12]

Iskra's leaders moved to reorganize Russian social democracy. In July 1903, a Second Congress (the abortive Minsk meeting of 1898 was designated the first) convened in Brussels, Belgium. Because *Iskra* controlled 33 of the 43 delegates, some of whom had more than one vote, its program was mostly approved. After the Belgian authorities compelled the congress to move to London, a struggle developed within the *Iskra* group between Lenin and Martov over party membership and organization. Arguing for an elite party, Lenin insisted that membership be limited to active participants in a party organization. Martov advocated a broad, mass party: "The more widely the title of party member is extended the better." That, Lenin objected, would inundate the party with opportunists. Plekhanov, the party's elder statesman, sided with Lenin, but at first Martov's more democratic formula prevailed 28 to 22. After the congress had rejected the Jewish Bund's demand for autonomy, however, the Bundists walked out; they were soon joined by the defeated Economists. These walkouts, engineered by Lenin, who worked frantically to secure victory, gave his "hard" faction a majority of two over Martov's "softs." Lenin promptly dubbed his group Bolsheviks (majority men) and obtained a psychological edge over Martov's faction, which meekly accepted the name Mensheviks (minority men). Lenin sought to exploit his slim majority to impose his views on membership and organization and make the party a centralized organization of professional revolutionaries. Instead, the Second Congress split the Social Democrats irreconcilably. Soon after the congress, the Mensheviks took over *Iskra* and won a majority on the central committee as well. Less disciplined and united than the Bolsheviks, the Mensheviks believed that the first revolution in Russia must be bourgeois and establish a democratic republic. Menshevik differences with the Bolsheviks, at first over seemingly minor matters of party organization, widened steadily. Mensheviks favored a broad, democratic, and genuine workers' party, not a narrow conspiratorial elite mainly of intellectuals. In 1905, Paul Akselrod, a leading Menshevik, urged Russian workers to form their own trade unions and party under worker leadership, to draft their own program rather than accept dictation from professional intellectual revolutionaries like Lenin. As Bolsheviks and Mensheviks feuded and his former *Iskra* colleagues accused Lenin of dictatorial methods and of creating a state of siege in the

---

[12]V. I. Lenin, *What Is To Be Done?* (New York, 1969), pp. 11, 78–79, 109.

SD party, young Leon Trotskii (Lev Bronstein), a brilliant polemicist and orator, stood between the factions and sought to mediate their differences.

FROM POPULISM TO THE SOCIALIST REVOLUTIONARIES

Populism recovered slowly from the destruction of the People's Will. Populist ideologists of the 1880s and early 1890s denounced capitalism and argued desperately that it must never come to Russia. Younger Populists, however, calling themselves Socialist Revolutionaries (SRs), agitated among new factory workers of peasant origin. In the capitals, the Marxists outdid them, but in provincial centers the SRs won much support. Some Populist exiles returned, such as Catherine Breshko-Breshkovskaia, who won converts around the country and became known as "the grandmother of the revolution."

In the late 1890s, three centers of SR activity emerged. In 1896, the Union of Socialist Revolutionaries was founded in Saratov and won followers in the Moscow and Volga regions. *Our Tasks* (1898) proclaimed: "Propaganda, agitation, and organization . . . , such are the tasks of preparatory work at present." It emphasized winning political freedom and deferred revolution to an indefinite future. A southern element from Voronezh and the Ukraine advocated a constitution, agitation among the peasantry, strikes by agricultural workers, and boycotts against landlords. A third group formed in Minsk by Breshko-Breshkovskaia and A. Gershuni, a young Jewish scientist, featured terror as its chief weapon against autocracy. In 1898, the police frustrated an attempt to establish an SR party in Russia, but in 1900, an underground organization and newspaper, *Revolutionary Russia*, were set up in Kharkov. Two years later, elements from the various SR groups met in Berlin to establish the Socialist Revolutionary Party.

Its chief ideologist was Victor Chernov (1876–1952), an SR organizer in Tambov province, who accepted some Marxist doctrines and recognized capitalist development in Russia. Urging SRs to agitate in factories and include workers in "the people," Chernov admitted that the proletariat would lead the revolution against capitalism, but affirmed that the peasantry would be "the fundamental army." In the new society, socialized enterprise in the towns would complement reorganized socialist communes. Like the Populists but unlike the Marxists, Chernov stressed free will, passion, and creativity, but he stood ready to collaborate with Marxists and urban workers to overturn capitalism.

Contrary to the Social Democrats, the dynamic, rapidly growing SR party never had a large or well-disciplined formal membership. Forming many local groups around various leaders, they propagandized vigorously among peasants and factory workers. Unlike their Populist forebears, SRs enjoyed considerable support from workers and white-collar people in provincial towns, though they remained peasant oriented. The SRs never produced a truly outstanding leader and lacked the organizational cohesion to link their massive peasant following with a town-bred intellectual leadership. Within the party, but actually independent, was the small, highly disciplined Combat Detachment, led by terrorists A. Gershuni and Evno Azev. Between 1902 and 1905, it assassinated two interior ministers, the Moscow governor-general, and other officials. Thus the tsarist police considered the SRs more dangerous than the more academic, theoretical SDs.

LIBERALISM ORGANIZES

Nineteenth-century Russian liberalism, despite considerable achievements in education and public health through the zemstva, never attained cohesion, but on the eve of the 1905 Revolution, reinforced with former revolutionaries, it broadened into a vigorous, effective national movement seeking a national zemstva union, constitutional reform, and civil liberties.

Until 1898, zemstva remained the main liberal arena and gradualism the chief approach. Zemstvo leaders, anxious to promote public welfare, felt keenly the lack of a national organization, but their activities continued to expand despite official restrictions. By 1900, zemstva employed more than 70,000 agronomists, doctors, and teachers. This professional personnel, known as the "Third Element," helped democratize the zemstva until both their gentry and professional members supported constitutional reform and civil rights. The Slavophile liberals' chief spokesman, the conscientious D. N. Shipov (1851–1920), chairman of the Moscow provincial zemstvo board, favored joint administration of Russia by tsar and people through a national consultative assembly and hoped the tsar would heed his appeals. Petrunkevich, active in the Chernigov and Tver provincial zemstva since 1868, led zemstvo constitutionalists. Slavophile liberals still awaited governmental concessions, and Shipov, despite official rebuffs, sought to extend zemstva to additional provinces and create a national zemstvo union. The regime's refusal to permit that, its repressive actions of 1899–1900, and the Slavophile liberals' submissiveness strengthened the constitutionalists.

Defectors from revolutionary socialism reinforced liberalism among the professional intelligentsia. During the 1890s, the Legal Populists, led by N. K. Mikhailovskii, stressing ethical principles and the individual, abandoned revolutionary views to cooperate with the liberals. Legal

Marxists, headed by N. Berdiaev and P. Struve, likewise rejected revolution. Struve, author of the Marxist manifesto of 1898 at Minsk, broke with the SDs to advocate liberal gradualism. The Economists, S. Prokopovich and his wife, Kuskova, like the English Webbs, advocated "pure trade unionism" to satisfy the workers' economic needs. Kuskova's *Credo* (1899), depicting orthodox Marxists as narrow sectarians, urged Economists to support the liberals.

At the turn of the century, Russian liberals acquired a press and a more cohesive political program. The liberal gentry set up *Beseda*, a private discussion group, including Slavophiles and constitutionalists. After 1896, zemstvo liberals of all shadings met irregularly to agitate for a national zemstvo union, and in May 1902, the first congress of zemstvo officials, 52 leaders from 25 provinces, met without official authorization at Shipov's home. This semilegal action set a pattern for liberals in 1905. The founding in Stuttgart, in 1902, of the periodical, *Osvobozhdenie (Liberation),* edited by Struve, with money from a Moscow landowner, established a militant liberal press organ. Adopting a radical constitutionalist line, it became almost as influential as Herzen's *Bell.* In 1903, a Union of Liberation, designed to unite the entire non-Marxist intelligentsia, was formed in Switzerland with many outstanding theorists and activists. In January 1904, its leaders met in private apartments in St. Petersburg and pledged to work to abolish autocracy, establish constitutional monarchy, and achieve universal, secret, and direct suffrage in equal constituencies—the "four-tailed" suffrage—for a national parliament. The Union's national council met regularly until the 1905 Revolution.

Before 1905, the opposition movements were developing greater cohesion and clearer programs. The liberals, led by such pro-Western intellectuals as Paul Miliukov, were supported by much of the growing professional middle class and some provincial zemstvo gentry. Socialists generally agreed on the need to overthrow the tsarist autocracy and establish a less rigidly centralized popular government. They differed sharply, however, over timing and means, over how their movement or party should be organized, and over which elements should constitute and lead it. The SRs with an urban intellectual leadership, and mainly peasant rank and file, opposed a Marxist workers' party, the SDs, itself split among Bolsheviks, Mensheviks, and smaller factions. Both liberal and radical opposition to the tsarist regime was rising on the eve of the 1905 Revolution.

Suggested Additional Reading

ANDERSON, T. *Russian Political Thought* (Ithaca, N.Y., 1967).

ASCHER, A. *Pavel Axelrod and the Development of Menshevism* (Cambridge, Mass., 1972).

BALABANOFF, ANGELICA. *My Life as a Rebel* (New York, 1938).

BARON, S. H. *Plekanov: The Father of Russian Marxism* (Stanford, Calif., 1963).

BILLINGTON, JAMES. *Mikhailovsky and Russian Populism* (New York, 1958).

BYRNES, R. F. *Pobedonostsev: His Life and Thought* (Bloomington, Ind., 1969).

CARR, E. H. *Mikhail Bakunin* (New York, 1961).

CHERNYSHEVSKY, N. G. *What Is To Be Done?* (New York, 1961). (Novel.)

DAN, FEDOR. *The Origins of Bolshevism*, translated and edited by Joel Carmichael (New York, 1970).

EMMONS, T. *The Russian Landed Gentry* (Cambridge, Eng., 1968).

ENGEL, B. A. *Mothers and Daughters: Women of the Intelligentsia of 19th Century Russia* (Cambridge, Eng., 1983).

FIGNER, VERA. *Memoirs of a Revolutionist* (New York, 1927).

FISCHER, GEORGE. *Russian Liberalism* (Cambridge, Mass., 1958).

FRÖHLICH, K. *The Emergence of Russian Constitutionalism, 1900–1904* (The Hague, 1982).

GETZLER, J. *Martov* (New York, 1967).

GLEASON, ABBOTT. *Young Russia: The Genesis of Russian Radicalism in the 1860s* (New York, 1980).

HAIMSON, LEOPOLD. *The Russian Marxists . . .* (Cambridge, Mass., 1955).

HARE, RICHARD. *Pioneers of Russian Social Thought* (New York, 1964).

HERZEN, A. I. *My Past and Thoughts*, 6 vols. (New York, 1924–1928 and reprints).

KEEP, J. L. *The Rise of Social Democracy in Russia* (Oxford, Eng., 1963).

KROPOTKIN, PETER. *Memoirs of a Revolutionist* (New York, 1927 and reprints).

LAMPERT, E. *Sons Against Fathers . . .* (London, 1965).

————. *Studies in Rebellion* (London, 1957).

LANE, DAVID. *The Roots of Russian Communism* (University Park, Pa., 1968).

LAVROV, P. L. *Historical Letters*, ed. J. Scanlan (Berkeley, Calif., 1967).

MILLER, MARTIN. *The Russian Revolutionary Emigres, 1825–1870* (Baltimore, 1986).

OFFORD, DEREK. *The Russian Revolutionary Movement in the 1880s* (London and New York, 1986).

PIPES, RICHARD, ed. *The Russian Intelligentsia* (New York, 1961).

POMPER, PHILIP. *The Russian Revolutionary Intelligentsia* (New York, 1970).

————. *Sergei Nechaev* (New Brunswick, N.J., 1979).

RANDALL, F. N. *N. G. Chernyshevskii* (New York, 1967).

SCHAPIRO, LEONARD. *Rationalism and Nationalism in Nineteenth Century Russian Thought* (New Haven, Conn., 1967).

SEDDON, J. H. *The Petrashevtsy . . .* (Manchester, Eng., 1985).

SETON-WATSON, HUGH. *The Russian Empire 1801–1917* (Oxford, Eng., 1967).

THADEN, E. C. *Conservative Nationalism in Nineteenth Century Russia* (Seattle, 1964).

TIMBERLAKE, CHARLES, ed. *Essays on Russian Liberalism* (Columbia, Mo., 1972).

TREADGOLD, DONALD. *Lenin and His Rivals, 1898–1906* (New York, 1955).

TURGENEV, IVAN. *Fathers and Sons,* trans. Constance Garnett (New York, Modern Library, 1950). (Novel.)

VENTURI, FRANCO. *Roots of Revolution . . . (New York, 1960).*

WILDMAN, A. K. *The Making of a Workers' Revolution* (Chicago, 1967).

WOLFE, BERTRAM. *Three Who Made a Revolution* (New York, 1964).

WORTMAN, RICHARD. *The Crisis of Russian Populism* (London, 1967).

YARMOLINSKY, A. *Road to Revolution* (London, 1957).

ZAIONCHKOVSKY, P. A. *The Russian Autocracy in Crisis, 1878–1882,* trans. and ed. G. M. Hamburg (Gulf Breeze, Fla., 1979).

CHAPTER FOUR

REVOLUTION, REACTION, AND REFORM, 1905–1914

The decade of 1905–1914 witnessed a crucial race in Russia between reform and revolution and alternating periods of radicalism and reaction. The major revolution, which erupted in 1905, brought masses of workers and peasants, under intelligentsia leadership, for the first time into a broad, popular movement against the autocracy. Although the revolution failed and was succeeded by iron-handed political reaction, the tsarist system was altered significantly. A semiconstitutional monarchy with a national parliament sought, albeit hesitantly, to grapple with Russia's perplexing problems. Important agrarian reform was undertaken, and industrialization resumed. While the armed forces were being reorganized and modernized, a weakened Russia sought simultaneously to recover prestige abroad and avoid conflict. By 1914, a measure of success seemed to have crowned these efforts. Partially industrialized Russia, though plagued by social turmoil, was moving ahead economically and maturing politically. Why did the Revolution of 1905 break out? Why did it fail to overthrow tsarism? How genuine was the constitutional monarchy that succeeded unlimited autocracy? Was Russia in 1914 truly moving toward parliamentary government, prosperity, and social harmony or toward imminent, massive social revolution?

THE REVOLUTION OF 1905

Historians differ widely over the meaning of the Revolution of 1905. Most Western scholars regard it, like the European revolutions of 1848, as a liberal-democratic movement in which workers and peasants acted largely spontaneously. Early Soviet accounts, such as Pokrovskii's, agreed, but Stalinist historians dramatized and glorified Bolshevik leadership of the proletariat in a "bourgeois-democratic revolution." Most scholars affirm that 1905 was the dress rehearsal for the greater 1917 revolutions because similar parties and mass elements participated, though with less cohesion and militancy in the first case.

Revolution occurred in 1905 because industrial workers, intellectuals, peasants, and ethnic minorities found their repressive, unresponsive government unbearable. Supporting the government, on the other hand, were a large and cohesive bureaucracy, a vast police network, the nobility, the church, and the army, but until Witte was returned to office (October 1905), the regime used these still powerful elements ineptly. The depression of 1900–1903 and bad harvests had brought hard times to Russia, and an increasingly articulate opposition sought political freedom, civil liberties, and social reform. Spurring the revolution were Japanese victories in the Far East, which discredited the government, eroded its prestige, inflated prices, and caused rising disaffection in the armed forces. Each setback in Asia reinforced dissatisfaction and opposition in European Russia.

The assassination (July 1904) of Interior Minister V. K. Pleve had removed the only dynamic government figure. Replacing him with the mild Prince Peter Sviatopolk-Mirskii, Nicholas II made minor concessions to the public. In Paris in October 1904, the Liberation movement and socialists agreed to agitate for the replacement of autocracy with a democratic regime based on universal suffrage, and by December most educated Russians were criticizing the regime. In many cities, political banquets were held similar to those before the Paris revolution of 1848.

The revolution began on "Bloody Sunday" (January 9, 1905). With police cooperation, the priest Father George Gapon had organized St. Petersburg factory workers to deflect them from revolutionary ideas. When news came of Port Arthur's fall, a strike of locomotive workers spread through the giant Putilov plant and several other St. Petersburg factories. Gapon urged the workers to petition the tsar to end the war, convene a constituent assembly, grant civil rights, and establish an eight-

Bloody Sunday (January 9, 1905). The demonstrators are fired upon by tsarist troops in front of Narva Gate in St. Petersburg.

hour workday, all also goals of the Liberationists. On January 9, a snowy Sunday morning, Gapon led one of several columns of workers from various parts of the city toward the Winter Palace. The marchers—men, women, and children—bore icons, sang hymns, and clearly intended no violence. When they disregarded orders to halt, the tsar's uncle, Grand Duke Vladimir Aleksandrovich, ordered troops to fire on the crowd, and hundreds of the unarmed workers were slaughtered.

Bloody Sunday united the Russian people against the autocracy and undermined its faith in the tsar. During January, half a million workers struck, and assemblies of nobles and zemstva issued sharp protests. As students and professional people joined the workers, St. Petersburg became the center of nationwide agitation. Except for Socialist Revolutionary terrorists, however, there was relatively little violence. At their congress in March, the Liberationists demanded a constituent assembly, universal suffrage (including women), separation of church and state, autonomy for national minorities, transfer of state and crown lands to the peasants, an eight-hour workday, and the right to strike. Revolutionary socialists, mostly in exile, squabbling over tactics, played little part in this movement.

Bloody Sunday. The demonstrators led by Father Gapon are attacked by the tsar's cavalry in St. Petersburg.

Bloody Sunday. Taking refuge behind a hastily assembled barricade, the demonstrators fire on the tsar's troops.

The battleship, *Potemkin,* named after Catherine II's influential favorite and launched in 1900, was the last Russian predreadnought ship to be built. Constructed in Nikolaev shipyard, it combined French and German designs. The *Potemkin* weighed 13,000 tons and was 378 feet long. The mutineers who took over the ship in June 1905 later surrendered to the Romanian authorities. *(Heller model 1:400 constructed by Bruce MacKenzie)*

In May and June, the opposition organized, the strike movement expanded, and a naval mutiny erupted. Fourteen unions of professional people established the Union of Unions to coordinate their campaign for a constituent assembly. Paul Miliukov, head of the Union of Liberation, was elected its president, giving liberals in 1905 a unity that socialists and conservatives lacked. Although Bolsheviks and many Socialist Revolutionaries favored armed insurrection, other socialists cooperated with the Union. At the textile center of Ivanovo-Voznesensk, virtually the entire work force struck, some 70,000 workers. Their strike committee, calling itself a soviet (council), took on governmental functions such as price regulation. On June 14, the crew of the new battleship *Potemkin* mutinied under a red flag and forced the government to deactivate the Black Sea Fleet.

Some minority nationalities of the Empire, notably in Russian Poland, the Baltic provinces, Finland, and the Caucasus, took uncoordinated but sometimes violent action during 1905 aiming chiefly to win autonomy within the Russian Empire. At the same time Ukrainian nationalism emerged for the first time as a considerable force, combining intelligentsia and peasantry. In August 1905 Muslims organized politically at Nizhnyi-Novgorod, demanding elimination of all legal discrimination against their faith.

Nicholas II's response to all this was to announce the Bulygin Duma (named after the new Minister of Interior, A. G. Bulygin), a consultative assembly to be elected by a limited suffrage favoring rural elements. It would be able to speak but not act, and autocracy would be preserved. This temporarily split the opposition three ways: zemstvo moderates favored participating in such elections, the Union of Unions urged a boycott and agitation for a constituent assembly, and revolutionaries advocated an armed uprising.

The spreading mass unrest forced greater governmental concessions. Peasant disorders grew in many regions. Radical demands by the Peasant Union, formed in July, revealed that contrary to official expectations, the peasantry had joined the opposition. The workers forced the government's hand: History's first general strike began spontaneously September 19 with a walkout by Moscow printers, which then was joined by bakers and factory workers. Spreading to St. Petersburg, it halted railroad, telegraph, and telephone service completely. In all Russia, only one newspaper, a conservative Kiev daily, was published, and in mid-October mobs controlled the streets of leading cities. The workers' strike committee in St. Petersburg became a soviet and selected a 22-man executive committee under Leon Trotskii and a Menshevik, G. Khrustalev-Nosar.

Powerless to halt the strike, the regime fell into panic and virtual paralysis. Count Witte advised either a military dictatorship or a constitution. Unable to find a dictator, and faced with general revolt in town and countryside, the tsar yielded. His October Manifesto (October 17 old style) promised a constitution, civil liberties, and a national parliament (Duma) elected by a broad suffrage without whose consent no bill was to become law. It also legalized most strikes and ended peasant redemption payments. Two days later, Nicholas revived the Council of Ministers, creating a unified executive branch, and named Witte premier. Nicholas was in despair because he had broken his pledge to maintain autocracy unaltered.

The tsar replaced reactionary ministers, but liberal leaders refused to join the government, and socialists and left liberals spurned the Manifesto. The two months after it was issued were the most disorderly of 1905. In those "days of freedom," the St. Petersburg Soviet, coordinating a growing soviet movement, decreed the end of censorship, newspapers ignored censorship restrictions, and the public began exercising rights that the Manifesto had promised. In October and November, rural violence reached its peak, and national minorities agitated for autonomy or independence. Naval mutinies broke out at Kronstadt, Vladivostok, and Sevastopol, and in November postal and telegraph workers struck, touching off new railroad strikes. Government troops suppressed peasant revolts and arrested the St. Petersburg Soviet's leaders, but the Soviet, supported by the Peasant Union and the socialists, proclaimed economic war against the regime and called for another general strike. In December, the Moscow Soviet led a week-long armed workers' rebellion, but it was suppressed after bitter street fighting reminiscent of the Paris "June Days" of 1848; thousands of Moscow workers were shot or deported. The regime had now recovered its nerve, and after the Moscow Soviet called off its faltering general strike, the Revolution gradually subsided. Opposition newspapers were closed, and the "days of freedom" ended.

Tsarism survived 1905 for reasons not present in the fatal crisis of 1917. Quick and honorable conclusion of the Russo-Japanese war in August localized disaffection in the armed forces, and mutinies were suppressed; most peasant soldiers remained loyal. The timely political and economic concessions of the October Manifesto satisfied most moderates, isolated radical elements, and divided advocates of social change from advocates of political change. Many top revolutionaries were in exile. Mass groups were uncoordinated and lacked good leadership, and their protest movements peaked at different times. On the other hand, the bureaucracy and police backed the regime solidly. Finally, at a crucial time Witte secured a large loan from France, which was anxious to prop up its ally, Russia, so it would not have to face Germany alone. Nonetheless, the Revolution of 1905 aroused the Russian people politically and gave them a taste of freedom. The government restored order but not the awe it had formerly inspired in the masses. Tsarism had a last chance but under altered conditions.

CREATION OF THE DUMA MONARCHY, 1905–1906

The most dangerous time for a bad government, noted the 19th-century French writer Alexis de Tocqueville is when it begins to change for the better. Bloody Sunday had shattered the myth of the tsar as a benevolent, omniscient father. A new principle of political authority was needed, but as the revolution ebbed, Nicholas II salvaged most of his autocratic powers, fired Witte, and blocked creation of a true parliamentary regime. Further trouble portended between "society" and the government as the Manifesto's promises were hedged with restrictions, infuriating the left liberals and making them into defiant obstructionists.

Decrees and acts of the next six months laid foundations for a regime satisfying neither side. To the liberals' dismay, an imperial manifesto of

Figure 4.1 *Russian Imperial Government (1906–1917)*

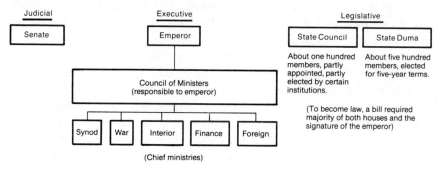

February 1906 created a bicameral legislature. (See Figure 4.1.) The hitherto wholly appointive State Council was reorganized as a conservative upper chamber, half of it appointed by the emperor, half of it elected by various social bodies (zemstva, municipal dumas, the nobility, and universities, for example). Though most males over the age of 25 could vote for deputies to the lower house, the State Duma, the electorate was divided into the traditional classes: landowners, peasants, and townspeople. A weighted, indirect franchise favored landowners and peasants and excluded many workers. It represented the belated realization of Speranskii's scheme of 1809,[1] not the "four-tailed" suffrage of liberal demands. The government expected the Duma to be a conservative assembly.

The Duma's powers were very limited. Russia's constitution, the Fundamental Laws of April 1906, described the emperor now as "autocrat" instead of "unlimited autocrat." He retained power to declare war and appoint and dismiss ministers of state, who were responsible to him alone. Duma members could question ministers, but the latter did not have to give satisfactory replies, and the crown retained all powers not specifically given to the legislature. To become law, a measure had to pass both houses, and the emperor retained absolute veto power. Article 87 of the Fundamental Laws further restricted Duma authority by authorizing ministers to govern by decree during Duma recesses, provided the Duma approved such decrees subsequently. The Duma's ability to obstruct the executive was slight because the emperor determined the duration of its sessions and could prorogue it at will if he set a date for new elections. The Duma could not overturn the ministry nor revise the Fundamental Laws,

---

[1]As chief adviser to Alexander I, M. Speranskii proposed comprehensive political reforms to give Russia representative bodies and the rule of law.

Table 4.1 *Russian Political Parties and Programs, 1905–1917*

Party	Program
RSDLP (Social Democrats), 1898 (splits 1903 into: 1. Bolsheviks 2. Mensheviks)	Marxist (overthrow of tsarism, establishment of a workers' state) 1. Stress violent revolution 2. Orthodox Marxists; move toward nonviolent, parliamentary socialism
SRs (Socialist Revolutionaries), 1900	Peasant socialism (violent overthrow of tsarism; establishment of federal state; confiscation of estates without compensation)
KD (Constitutional Democrats), 1905	Liberal-democratic (constitutional monarchy or a republic, all civil rights, ministerial responsibility, land reform)
Trudoviks (Labor faction), 1906	Radical groups favor drastic land reform, national autonomy for minority peoples, civil liberties
Octobrists, 1905	Conservatives (program of "October Manifesto"; limited monarchy, mild reform, rule of law)
United Nobility, 1906	Faction or pressure group to promote noble interests; mainly conservative
Union of the Russian People, 1905	Extreme conservatives (advocate "orthodoxy, autocracy, and nationalism"; racist)

and its control of the purse was severely restricted. (It had no control over court expenses and little over the army or state debt.) Could any legislature operate effectively under such limitations?

Amidst continuing revolutionary disturbances, the electoral campaign for the First Duma began in December 1905. Excitement and expectancy gripped Russia as for the first time political parties, though still not legal, contended in national elections. The SRs, deciding at their first open congress in Finland to boycott the elections and promote violent revolution, demanded socialization of the land, its issuance to peasants on the basis of need, and a federal system with full national self-determination for non-Russians. At their Fourth Congress in Stockholm (spring 1906), the SDs restored surface unity, but serious Bolshevik-Menshevik differences persisted. Initially, most SDs favored boycotting the elections, and then the Mensheviks decided to participate. Arguing that Bolsheviks could use the Duma to denounce tsarism, Lenin shocked his colleagues by voting with the Mensheviks. As revolutionary parties scarcely competed in the elections, peasants voted mostly for the Trudovik (Labor) group, largely SR in ideology but peaceful in tactics. Among the nonrevolutionary parties, the most radical was the Constitutional Democrats (Kadets, KD), led ably by Miliukov and Struve from the Union of Liberation and Petrunkevich from the zemstva. Abandoning temporarily their call for a constituent assembly, the Kadets campaigned for full parliamentary rights for the Duma, alienation of large estates with compensation, and more rights for labor. The Octobrist Party, led by A. I. Guchkov, representing moderate zemstvo leaders, business, and liberal bureaucrats, accepted the October Manifesto. Aiming to strengthen constitutional monarchy and civil liberties, it opposed real land reform and national self-determination. The extreme Right, especially the ultranationalist Union of the Russian People, denounced the Duma and the Jews and demanded restoration of unlimited autocracy.

The election revealed Russia's radical mood and dismayed the government. The Kadets (180 seats) with their allies organized and dominated the First Duma, and the peasant Trudoviks had about 100 deputies. There were 18 Menshevik Social Democrats, 17 Octobrists, 15 extreme Rightists, and about 100 deputies from national and religious minorities.

In the Winter Palace's elegant St. George's room, the tsar opened the First Duma on May 10, 1906. He, his court, and ministers, magnificent and bejeweled, occupied one side of the hall. Opposite sat the staid State Council, and behind them crowded the 500 Duma delegates: bearded peasants, Mensheviks in worker blouses, and minority groups in national costume. The contrast between the elite and popular representatives resembled that at the French Estates-General of 1789. In a brief, colorless "Address from the Throne," Nicholas II, like Louis XVI, gave the legislature no directives.

Organizing the Duma, the Kadets elected one of their own, Sergei Muromtsev, as speaker. Their reply to the tsar's "Address" demanded fully democratic suffrage, abolition of the State Council as an upper house, ministerial responsibility to the Duma, and amnesty for all political prisoners, but Nicholas and his ministers refused such exorbitant demands. Obsessed by European precedents and blind to Russian realities, Miliukov spurned compromise. I. L. Goremykin, the faded and servile bureaucrat who had replaced Witte as premier, responded for the tsar that the Duma's requests were all "inadmissible." The Duma promptly declared no confidence in the government, which simply ignored it. Because the Kadets failed to use existing Duma powers, vital issues such as land reform, minority rights, and education were neglected. Secret Duma discussions with the tsar on a Kadet or coalition ministry proved fruitless. The Kadets' doctrinaire approach and Nicholas's suspicion doomed the First Duma and ultimately the constitutional experiment. When the Duma appealed directly to the public on the land question, Nicholas dissolved it without ordering new elections.

The Kadets responded with illegal defiance. When troops closed the Duma, some 180 delegates, mostly Kadets and Trudoviks, went to Vyborg, Finland, where Muromtsev proclaimed it reconvened. Miliukov drew up the Vyborg Manifesto, which urged Russians not to pay taxes or supply army recruits until the Duma met again, but there was little public response and the Manifesto's signers were tried, jailed briefly, and disfranchised. Losing many talented leaders, the Kadets never fully recovered their political leadership.

Originally dedicated to promoting the broad, liberal development of Russia into a parliamentary democracy, the Kadets gradually became a narrower party of the professional middle class confined largely to towns and increasingly suspicious of the masses. After 1906, the Kadets began to hedge on their democratic aims, tending to prefer constitutional monarchy. To many workers and peasants the Kadets were "bourgeois," a party favoring gradual change while preserving upper-class privilege and social order.

After the Duma's dissolution, P. A. Stolypin, since July 1906 premier and minister of interior, made frequent use of Article 87, which allowed the executive to rule by decree. This last statesman of imperial Russia dominated the political scene for the next five years. Stolypin, a well-to-do landowner, had been a provincial marshal of nobility who in 1905, as governor of Saratov province, had ruthlessly repressed peasant disorders. He was an impressive orator, thoroughly convinced of his rectitude, who favored bold measures and strong-arm tactics. A Russian nationalist, Stolypin viewed repression as the prelude to reform by an enlightened autocracy. Proclaiming a state of emergency, he instituted field courts-martial against SR terrorists, who were killing hundreds of police, priests, and officials. By the spring of 1907, the trials had effectively broken the revolutionary movement.

To the government's chagrin, the short-lived Second Duma (February–June 1907) was more extreme and less constructive than the first. Both SDs and SRs participated in the elections, but Stolypin declared leftist parties illegal and forbade their campaign literature. Almost half those elected were socialists, but they failed to form a bloc and disdained collaboration with the Kadets, who had lost ground. The Duma debated Stolypin's agrarian reforms (see pp. 90–91) heatedly, then refused to approve them. Violent SD attacks on the army infuriated the tsar who, urged on by the Union of the Russian People, dissolved the Duma. The first constitutional phase ended in complete deadlock between the Duma and the executive.

POLITICAL DEVELOPMENT, 1907–1914

Stolypin's decree of June 1907, dubbed a coup d'état, altered the original electoral laws arbitrarily to produce a Duma "Russian in spirit." Declared Stolypin: "We don't want professors, but men with roots in the country, local gentry, and the like." Blatantly violating the Fundamental Laws, his measure ensured that subsequent elections would be far from democratic. The government reduced peasant representation drastically, guaranteeing that noblemen would choose almost half the electors: Non-Russians lost most of their seats. Only about 2.5 percent of the population voted for the Third Duma, in which the Octobrists emerged as the largest party, the Right was greatly strengthened, and the Kadets were further weakened. On the Left, Trudoviks and Social Democrats each had 14 deputies. This "Masters' Duma" proved so satisfactory to the government that it was allowed to serve out its full five-year term. Though the State Council blocked many progressive laws, the Duma nonetheless approved Stolypin's agrarian reforms, promoted universal education, extended local self-government and religious freedom, and expanded its control of the budget. Even the Third Duma marked an advance over the Pobedonostsev era: All political points of view were represented, political parties operated openly, and newspapers debated public issues. Whenever possible, the Duma protected and broadened civil liberties by drawing public attention to government abuses.

Outwardly, the Fourth Duma (1912–1917), more than half noblemen, seemed still more conservative. The strengthening of Right and Left at the expense of the political center revealed dangerous political polarization, but even many conservative deputies defended the Duma and observed parliamentary forms. The Duma's tragedy, notes Thomas Riha, was that "too few were learning too slowly" in a political oasis far from the masses. The government often treated it as a mere department, and the emperor, until dissuaded by his ministers, considered making the Duma merely advisory.

Non-Russian elements were strongly represented in the First Duma of 1906. There were 51 Polish deputies united in a Polish Circle, about 40 Ukrainian nationalists, and 30 Muslims, most of whom cooperated with the Kadets. Under this pressure the imperial government restored the Finnish Diet as a single chamber of 200 members elected for a three-year term by a system of proportional representation and virtual universal suffrage of both sexes. Finland thus became the first country in eastern Europe to grant the vote to women.

From this atmosphere of reluctant concessions to the nationalities by a beleaguered imperial regime in 1905, their situation deteriorated sharply during the years 1907–1914. They faced a conservative imperial government and hostility by most of the Russian people. Polish schools reverted to their russified condition prior to 1905, and the Ukrainian nationalist movement was subjected to vigorous repression. Baltic Germans were favored by the Russian regime, whereas other Baltic peoples (Estonians, Latvians, and Lithuanians) were suppressed. A law of the Russian Duma in 1910 reduced the Finnish Diet to the status of a provincial assembly before dissolving it altogether; Finland was then governed dictatorially by decree as an occupied and hostile country. Simultaneously, persecution of the Jews was intensified. The policies of the Russian imperial government generally alienated most national minorities completely, preparing the way for their common revolt against Russian rule in 1917–1918.

Until late in 1911, Stolypin ran the executive branch capably, if high-handedly. He used Article 87 to bypass the legislature whenever it obstructed his measures. At first he enjoyed Nicholas II's confidence and support; later he offended the imperial family. In September 1911, Stolypin was assassinated in the Kiev opera house by a double agent who received a ticket from the chief of police! Succeeding him as premier was Finance Minister V. N. Kokovtsov, who was able and moderate, but lacked his predecessor's independence and dynamism. In late 1913, the emperor removed him under pressure from the empress and Grigori Rasputin, whose influence Kokovtsov had opposed consistently. The aged and incompetent Goremykin replaced him.

The revolutionary movement, though plagued by police infiltration, recovered somewhat after 1912 from its eclipse under Stolypin. The SRs were appalled by the exposure of Evno Azev, head of their Combat Detachment, as a police agent. Arrests and double agents also weakened the SDs. According to Trotskii, Bolshevik membership had shrunk, in 1910, to 10,000. Early in 1914, Roman Malinovskii, Bolshevik leader in the Duma, was exposed as a police spy. Abroad, Lenin maintained his own organization and blocked efforts to reunite the party. In 1912, he convened a conference in Prague, and set up a separate Bolshevik party. Later that year the so-called August Bloc under Martov and Trotskii held a separate Menshevik conference, and in 1913 separate Menshevik and Bolshevik factions were formed in the Duma. The Bolsheviks retained their revolutionary fervor while the Mensheviks tried to create a legal, trade-union-oriented labor movement run by the workers themselves.

How were the Bolsheviks faring in 1914? Some Western accounts, emphasizing their demoralization, cite declining circulation of *Pravda* (their party newspaper), Lenin's isolation in SD ranks, a small, weak party in Russia, and loss of popularity among Russian workers. Only the outbreak of World War I, claims British scholar Leonard Schapiro, prevented the Bolsheviks' demise. A Soviet source, however, asserts that by July 1914 the Bolsheviks had the support of four fifths of Russian workers and were leading a militant strike movement in St. Petersburg. Leopold Haimson, an American historian, agrees that Bolsheviks were outdoing Mensheviks in the capitals because their revolutionary program and tactics appealed to many new workers. Bolshevik success, if success it was, reflected worker militancy more than skillful, perceptive leadership.

ECONOMIC AND SOCIAL DEVELOPMENT

Important economic and social change occurred between 1906 and 1914. Industrial growth was lifting Russia out of backwardness, and the Stolypin agrarian reforms were creating a basis for a new class of independent farmers. Social inequality was lessening as workers and peasants obtained higher incomes, greater mobility, and more rights.

Stolypin agreed with the socialists that a communal peasantry was potentially revolutionary. His government's aim, therefore, was to abolish the mir (peasant commune), free the peasant from it, and foster individual farming. Stolypin explained to the Duma in 1908: "The government has put its wager not on the drunken and the weak but on the sober and the strong—on the sturdy individual proprietor." In November 1906, he decreed after the First Duma that in communes without a general repartition since 1882, a householder could claim ownership of all plow land worked in 1906. In case of a repartition, he could demand land held before 1882, plus land received in a repartition provided he paid the commune the original redemption price. This policy encouraged peasants to shift from repartitional to hereditary tenure. The law of June 1910 dissolved all communes with no general repartition since 1861. After one peasant in such a commune applied for an ownership deed, all land in it became private. In repartitional and hereditary communes, the head of the household received ownership of the land, a policy that encouraged or even forced younger males to go to the city. Stolypin's ultimate objective was consolidation of scattered strips into Western-style farms.

How successful were these land reforms? Stolypin stressed the need for 20 years of peace to implement them, but they were halted in 1915. Though the government appointed many surveyors and exerted great pressure, results were inconclusive. By 1915, over half of Russian peasant households had hereditary ownership of their allotments, but less than 10 percent were fully consolidated individual farms.[2] Agricultural techniques and output improved considerably on such farms, but village collectivism, though weakened, remained prevalent. Many communes, supposed to be dissolved by the law of 1910, never were. After a big initial push, state enforcement lagged. Thus, in 1917, most Russian peasant households still lived in the traditional mir.

Who benefited from the reforms? According to Soviet accounts, only a minority of wealthy peasants. Stolypin sought to end strip farming and carry through an agricultural revolution, reply recent Western accounts. Viewing the process as a race against time, Lenin feared that Stolypin's reforms would transform the dissatisfied peasantry, upon which he counted in the future, into a class of loyal, conservative peasant proprietors.

The government encouraged colonization of Siberia to absorb dispossessed younger peasants and to increase farm output. About half of Siberian wheat was exported abroad or to other parts of Russia. Siberia, however, lacking a local nobility, promoted rugged individualism and a bourgeois ethos that distressed conservatives. After a visit in 1910, Stolypin called Siberia "an enormous, rudely democratic country which will soon throttle European Russia." The government also promoted peasant land purchases through the Peasant Bank. In 1914, European Russian peasantry owned over four times as much land as the nobility (460 to 108 million acres). The vast state and imperial holdings (390 million acres) were mostly unsuited to agriculture. By 1917, most Russian crop land was already in peasant hands.

After 1905, significant industrial progress occurred, though the government did not promote it with Witte's single-minded determination. The economy now was more mature, and the official role less marked. The Finance Ministry, despite creation of a separate Ministry of Trade and Industry, still controlled the keys to industrial development but used them more cautiously. Finance Minister Kokovtsov (1906–1913), stressing balanced growth, sought to maintain the gold standard and a high tariff to uphold Russia's foreign credit and to balance the budget. Thanks to a spurt in new railroad building, the growth rate almost equalled that of the Witte period. Excellent harvests, large exports, and wider prosperity enhanced Russia's overall economic perfor-

---

[2]In 1915 of the some 14 million peasant allotments, some 5 million remained under repartitional tenure. About 1.3 million were subject to automatic dissolution, but had not actually been dissolved, and 1.7 million had been affected to some degree. About 4.3 million holdings had fully hereditary title in scattered strips, and more than 1.3 million had been partially or completely consolidated into farms. Gerold T. Robinson, *Rural Russia* (New York, 1949), pp. 215–216.

mance, although in 1914 it still had the lowest per capita wealth of the major powers, and its industry trailed those of England, Germany, the United States, and France.[3] Industrial progress now, instead of impoverishing the population, was combined with agricultural growth and modest prosperity. Russia had overcome its backwardness, claimed Kokovtsov, and only the Bolshevik Revolution interrupted its "swift and powerful development."

Geographical distribution of Russian industry changed little, but consolidation and foreign ownership increased. In 1912, the central industrial region produced more than one third of all manufactures, followed by the Ukraine, the northwest, and the Urals. In manufacturing, the largest labor force was in metalworking, cottons, and other textiles. Soviet accounts stress that foreign interests initiated most industrial combinations in this "era of imperialism." In 1902, French capitalists fostered creation in southern Russia of Prodameta, a metallurgical cartel; by 1910, its member firms produced about three fourths of the empire's iron products and almost half its rails. The Duma, however, prevented it from becoming a full-fledged trust, a circumstance that revealed big industry's limited influence in imperial Russia. Other combinations formed in sugar (1887) and oil (1904). Foreign influence and investment in Russian industry were considerable, but Soviet claims that Russia had become a semicolonial appendage of Western capitalism seem exaggerated. A tsarist source estimated foreign investment in Russia, in 1916, at 2,243 million rubles, over half in mining, metallurgy, and metalworking with the French holding almost one third of this total, followed by the British, Germans, and Belgians.

Railroad construction remained the key to Russian industrial booms. The 6,600 miles of line built between 1902 and 1911 triggered an annual industrial growth rate of almost 9 percent between 1909 and 1913 and overall economic growth of about 6 percent annually between 1906 and 1914. Private railroad lines were more efficient, but the state owned about two thirds of the network, and rising revenues from its lines enabled the government to pay interest on railroad loans and still have a surplus. Nonetheless, in 1914, Russia's external debt (5.4 billion rubles) was one of the world's largest.

Russia's foreign trade increased considerably in volume, but its direction and structure changed little. In 1913, exports were worth more than 1.5 billion rubles and imports 1,374 million. Russia still exported

---

[3] In total volume of industrial production in 1913, France exceeded Russia 2.5 times, England 4.6, Germany 6, and the United States 14.3. P. Liashchenko, *History of the Russian National Economy* (New York, 1949), p. 674.

mostly agricultural goods (grain 44 percent, and livestock and forest products 22 percent). Industrial exports (10 percent) went mostly to backward Asian lands. Germany bought about 30 percent of Russian exports and supplied 47 percent of its imports; Britain stood second with 17.5 percent and 13 percent, respectively.

The empire's population rose by almost one third between 1897 and 1913, to more than 165 million (excluding Finland). Mainly responsible were a birthrate much higher than in western Europe and a declining deathrate. The east had the highest growth rates, but three fourths of the population resided in European Russia. Despite industrialization and urban growth, cities in 1913 contained only 16 percent of the population.

Russian society in 1914, undergoing transition and with numerous inequities and frictions, remained dominated by a nobility that guarded its privileges jealously against the bourgeoisie. Impoverished lesser gentry were selling their lands rapidly, but large landowners retained much wealth and strengthened their influence at court. After 1906, a pressure group, the Council of the United Nobility, protected their interests. Within the Church, the elite black (monastic) clergy remained in control and blocked needed reform. In an expanding bourgeoisie, Moscow entrepreneurs led the commercial and industrial elements; St. Petersburg remained the financial center. Outside the capitals, the bourgeoisie was often cautious and stodgy and engaged mainly in local trade and industry. Within the Russian middle class, liberal professions exceeded industrial and commercial elements in numbers and influence.

Among the peasantry, slow differentiation was speeded somewhat by the Stolypin reforms, but the mass of middle peasantry was still growing numerically. There were tensions in the village between an upper crust of kulaks and proletarian and semiproletarian elements, but the basic rural rivalry pitted peasant against noble. Peasant isolation was diminishing, and with freedom of movement gained after 1906, many younger peasants migrated to the cities. Peasant inferiority and poverty were lessening, but remained potential dangers to the regime.

Far from suffering increasing misery, as Marx had predicted, Russian industrial workers after 1905 found their status and economic position improving. Sharply reduced summertime departures for the village revealed growth of a largely hereditary proletariat. By 1914, over 3 million workers labored in mines and factories, about one half in enterprises with over 1,000 employees. Such large factories enhanced worker consciousness and solidarity and facilitated agitation by socialists and union organizers. Real wages rose considerably, but still lagged far behind those in Europe because of a plentiful labor supply and low labor productivity. Increasingly unionized skilled and semiskilled workers were now usually paid enough to maintain a normal family life. Working conditions were also improving. After 1912, the 10-hour day prevailed, accident and sickness compensation, partly paid by employers, was instituted, and factory inspection increased. Theoretically legalized in 1905, strikes remained virtually prohibited, and unions were barred from organizing public meetings. Strikes were few in 1907–1910, but an industrial revival and a massacre of workers in the British-owned Lena goldfields (April 1912) sparked a resurgence: some 700,000 workers struck in 1912, 900,000 in 1913, and about 1.5 million in the first half of 1914. St. Petersburg metalworkers, the most literate, highest paid workers, were also the most militant.

Wage levels and living conditions, bad enough for working men, remained far worse for women, who generally received only about two thirds the pay of males. Many working women remained below a normal subsistence level as conditions in small sweatshops were appalling and unregulated. Nonetheless, the poorly educated working women in tsarist Russia were mostly docile and obedient and proved difficult to organize in unions or politically. Women's education and literacy lagged far behind that of men. (In 1903–1905 only 13.7 percent of Russian women were literate compared with 32.6 percent of men.)

No genuine Russian women's movement emerged until the 1905 Revolution, which brought women consciousness and organization but few tangible benefits. Two separate movements developed: a feminist women's suffrage organization and a socialist movement sharply opposed to it in methods and goals. Early in 1905, the feminist All-Russian Union for Women's Equality was formed, seeking "freedom and equality before the law without regard to sex." Centering in St. Petersburg, it developed branches all across Russia. In April in the capital, the first political meeting convened for women in Russian history, drawing about 1,000 people and laying a basis for the Union's first congress in Moscow in May. The Union demanded an immediate constituent assembly elected without distinctions of sex, nationality, or religion; equality of the sexes under law; protection of women workers; and equal educational opportunity for women at every level—in July it joined the Union of Unions. During and after 1905, the feminist movement focused on the issue of women's suffrage, which was denied by the October Manifesto but supported increasingly by liberal and radical political parties. However, in 1908, under pressure of political reaction the Women's Union collapsed as antagonism escalated between feminists and socialists. In 1910, feminist activity revived around the weekly *Women's Cause*. The largest feminist organization in Russia had under 1,000 members by 1917, minuscule compared to the West. Most feminists came from the middle class and were led chiefly by nongentry university graduates. Confronting powerful foes on left and right, Russian feminism failed to persuade the Duma to give the vote to women.

Also emerging from the 1905 Revolution was a small women's socialist movement, which encountered hostility or indifference from male workers and most Social Democratic leaders. Its outstanding leader was Alexandra Kollontai, born in 1872, an energetic nonconformist, who began as a Populist before becoming a Marxist follower of Plekhanov. The Revolution of 1905 turned Kollontai into a dedicated revolutionary, who wrote and distributed socialist literature, raised money, and marched with workers. "Women and their fate have occupied my whole life," she recalled later. Finding support in the Union of Textile Workers, mostly women, she gave Marxist lectures and organized public meetings that emphasized the themes of exploitation and social liberation. After spending the years of reaction abroad, Kollontai returned to lead a revival of the women's socialist movement (1912–1914), remaining its chief link with the European International Socialist Women's Movement. In March 1913, Kollontai promoted the first celebration of International Women's Day in Russia.

FOREIGN AFFAIRS, 1906–1914

Defeat in the war with Japan, the 1905 Revolution, and indebtedness restricted Russia's freedom of action abroad, and dreams of an expanded Asian empire lay shattered. Settling outstanding disputes in the Far and Near East, Russia concentrated again on Europe and the Balkans in an effort to regain lost prestige. The Foreign Ministry's task was to prevent exploitation of Russia' military weakness by other powers. Until 1914, it averted disaster by repeated diplomatic retreats under German pressure.

In the Far East, relations between Russia and Japan were transformed as Russian leaders learned from their defeat. Both powers were anxious to protect their mainland interests and moved toward partnership. The United States' Open Door policy, an apparent screen for economic penetration of Manchuria, fostered a series of Russo-Japanese agreements. In 1910, Russia recognized Japan's special interests in Korea and south Manchuria in return for Japan's pledge to respect Russian domination of northern Manchuria and Outer Mongolia. Russia encouraged Mongolia to escape Chinese control; in 1912 it proclaimed its "independence" and became de facto a Russian protectorate. On the eve of World War I, Russia's position in the Far East was secure.

Powerful imperial Germany absorbed much of Russia's attention. In 1904–1905, William II, to undermine the Franco-Russian Alliance, had offered the tsar the defensive Björkö Treaty. Although the naive tsar signed it, Foreign Minister Lamsdorf and Count Witte persuaded him to ignore it and stick to Russia's alliance with France. When Germany sought to humiliate France in Morocco (1905–1906), Russia backed France loyally at the Algeciras Conference in return for a large French loan. The French alliance remained the cornerstone of Russian foreign policy until the end of the empire, and growing German military and naval strength fostered rapprochement between Russia and England. German leaders believed that Anglo-Russian imperial rivalries were insoluble, but Japan's defeat of Russia caused London to abandon fears of Russian expansionism. The friendship of Russia and England with France encouraged the British Liberal cabinet, realizing that it could not defend Persia, to seek agreement with Russia. Foreign Secretary Lord Grey wrote: "An entente between Russia, France, and ourselves would be absolutely secure. If it is necessary to check Germany, it could then be done."

Serious obstacles had to be overcome on the Russian side. Foreign Minister Alexander Izvolskii (1906–1910), who reasserted his ministry's role (sometimes rashly), had to neutralize pro-German feeling at court and overcome the old Turkestan military men who coveted all of Persia. The Anglo-Russian Convention of August 1907 left Afghanistan and Tibet in the British sphere, while unfortunate Persia was partitioned into a British sphere in the southeast and a huge Russian zone in the north, separated by a neutral area. Anglo-Russian rivalry in Persia continued, but became tolerable and peaceful. By 1914, Russia dominated most of it, but England accepted this as the price of containing Germany.

Izvolskii hoped that Britain would now assist him to revise the Straits Convention to let Russian warships pass through the Bosphorus, but he was disappointed. His interest in the Straits coincided with Austria's more dynamic Balkan policies. Conrad von Hötzendorf, Austrian chief of staff, wished to crush Serbia by preventive war, while Alois von Aehrenthal, the Foreign Minister, aimed to annex Bosnia and Herzegovina, which Austria had occupied since 1878. (See Map 4.1.) At Buchlau (September 1908), Aehrenthal and Izvolskii agreed that Russia would support their annexation by Austria in return for Austrian backing to revise the Straits Convention. Austria annexed Bosnia and Herzegovina, but Izvolskii could not win the other power's consent on the Straits question. Angered by Austria's absorption of two Serbian-speaking provinces, Serbia demanded territorial compensation, but because Germany backed Austria, Russia dared not support Serbia's claims. Russia and Serbia had to back down before the German powers. The Bosnian crisis discredited Izvolskii and gave warning of a general war over the Balkans.

Succeeding Izvolskii as foreign minister was S. D. Sazonov (1910–1916), a conscientious diplomat who lacked firm control over his subordinates. As Panslav tendencies revived, Russian consuls N. G. Hartvig in Belgrade and A. Nekliudov in Sofia advocated a forward policy. In 1912,

Map 4.1 *Russia and the Balkans, 1912–1914*

Countries with Austrian and German influence against Russia
Russia's Balkan allies

with their warm encouragement, a Balkan League of Serbia, Bulgaria, Montenegro, and Greece was formed. In October, disregarding official Russian and Austrian warnings, the League attacked Turkey and conquered Macedonia. Austria, however, blocked Serbia's aspiration to Adriatic ports, and Russia yielded again to German threats. In a second Balkan war of 1913, Bulgaria, seeking control of Macedonia, attacked the Serbs and Greeks, but they, aided by Romania and Turkey, defeated Bulgaria, and seized Bulgarian Macedonia. This victory smashed the Balkan League, turned embittered Bulgaria toward the Central Powers (Germany, Austria-Hungary, and Italy), and damaged Russian prestige. Serbian nationalism intensified further as the Austrian military awaited an opportunity to crush Serbia completely.

In the Balkans before 1914, Russian and Austrian imperialism clashed and Russo-German tension was sometimes severe, but war between Russia and the Central Powers was far from inevitable. Russo-German friction over the Berlin to Bagdad Railway and over German attempts to dominate the Straits was settled peacefully. The Romanovs remained pro-German, supported by the Duma Right, which sought to buttress autocracy against Western liberal parliamentarism.

Suggested Additional Reading

BOCK, MARIA. *Reminiscences of My Father, Peter A. Stolypin* (Metuchen, N.J., 1970).

CHARQUES, RICHARD. *The Twilight of Imperial Russia* (London, 1958, 1974).

EDELMAN, R. *Gentry Politics on the Eve of the Russian Revolution: The Nationalist Party, 1907–1917* (New Brunswick, N.J., 1980).

———. *Proletarian Peasants: The Revolution of 1905 in Russia's Southwest* (Ithaca, N.Y., 1987).

EDMONDSON, L. H. *Feminism in Russia, 1900–17* (Stanford, Calif., 1984).

FLORINSKY, MICHAEL. *The End of the Russian Empire* (New York, 1931, 1961).

GAPON, GEORGE. *The Story of My Life* (London, 1905).

GURKO, V. I. *Features and Figures of the Past . . .* (Stanford, Calif., 1939).

HAIMSON, LEOPOLD. "The Problem of Social Stability in Urban Russia, 1905–1917," *Slavic Review, 23,* pp. 619–642; and *24,* pp. 1–22. Comments by Mendel and von Laue in *24,* pp. 23–46.

HARCAVE, SIDNEY. *The Russian Revolution of 1905* (London, 1970).

HEALY, A. E. *The Russian Autocracy in Crisis: 1905–1907* (Hamden, Conn., 1976).

HENNESSY, R. *The Agrarian Question in Russia, 1905–1917. The Inception of the Stolypin Reform* (Giessen, W. Germany, 1977).

HOSKING, GEOFFREY. *The Russian Constitutional Experiment . . . 1907–1914* (New York, 1973).

IZVOLSKY, A. P. *Recollections of a Foreign Minister* (New York, 1921).

KOKOVTSOV, V. N. *Out of My Past* (Stanford, Calif., 1935).

LINCOLN, W. BRUCE. *In War's Dark Shadow: The Russians Before the Great War* (New York, 1983).

MAKLAKOV, V. A. *The First State Duma* (Bloomington, Ind., 1964).

MANNING, R. T. *The Crisis of the Old Order in Russia* (Princeton, N.J., 1983).

MCCAULEY, M., & P. WALDRON, eds. *Octobrists to Bolsheviks . . . Documents . . .* (Baltimore, 1984).

MCNEAL, ROBERT, ed. *Russia in Transition, 1905–1914* (New York, 1970).

MEHLINGER, H. D., and J. M. THOMPSON. *Count Witte and the Tsarist Government in the 1905 Revolution* (Bloomington, Ind., 1972).

MILIUKOV, PAUL. *Political Memoirs, 1905–1917,* ed. A. Mendel (Ann Arbor, Mich., 1967).

———. *Russia and Its Crisis* (Chicago, 1905, 1962).

MILLER, M. S. *Economic Development of Russia, 1905–1914,* 2d ed. (London, 1967).

OBERLANDER, E., et al. *Russia Enters the Twentieth Century . . .* (New York, 1971).

OWEN, L. A. *The Russian Peasant Movement, 1906–1917* (London, 1937; reprint New York, 1963).

PARES, BERNARD. *Russia Between Reform and Revolution* (New York, 1962).

POSPIELOVSKY, D. *Russian Police Socialism: Experiment or Provocation?* (London, 1971).

REICHMAN, HENRY. *Railwaymen and Revolution: Russia, 1905* (Berkeley, Calif., 1987).

RICE, CHRISTOPHER. *Russian Workers and the Socialist-Revolutionary Party Through the Revolution of 1905–07* (New York, 1988).

RIHA, THOMAS. *A Russian European: Paul Miliukov . . .* (Notre Dame, Ind., 1968).

"The Russian Revolution of 1905–07. 80th Anniversary," *Russian History, 12,* no. 1 (Spring 1985).

SABLINSKY, WALTER. *The Road to Bloody Sunday* (Princeton, N.J., 1976).

SCHLEIFMAN, NURIT. *Undercover Agents in the Russian Revolutionary Movement: The SR Party, 1902–14* (New York, 1988).

SCHWARZ, S. M. *The Russian Revolution of 1905 . . . ,* trans. G. Vakar (Chicago, 1967).

STAVROU, T. G., ed. *Russia Under the Last Tsar* (Minneapolis, 1969).

SZEFTEL, MARC. *The Russian Constitution of April 23, 1906* (Brussels, 1976).

THADEN, EDWARD. *Russia and the Balkan Alliance of 1912* (University Park, Pa., 1965).

TROTSKY, L. D. *1905,* trans. A. Bostock (New York, 1972).

VERNER, ANDREW M. *The Crisis of Russian Autocracy: Nicholas II and the 1905 Revolution* (Princeton, N.J., 1990).

WILLIAMS, ROBERT C. *The Other Bolsheviks: Lenin and His Critics, 1904–1914* (Bloomington, Ind., 1986).

ZENKOVSKY, A. V. *Stolypin: Russia's Last Great Reformer,* trans. M. Patoski (Princeton, N.J., 1986).

CHAPTER FIVE

CULTURAL DEVELOPMENTS, 1855-1917

The late 19th century witnessed a spectacular flowering of Russian culture. Nicholas I's death removed an oppressive weight from Russian life and ushered in a relatively liberal era that, combined with a powerful national upsurge, produced remarkable cultural creativity. Individuals in literature, art, music, and architecture began to experiment with new modes of expression. Frank discussion of the plight of the peasantry and emancipation focused attention on this long neglected segment of society. The daily lives of commoners and the drama and pathos of peasant life captured the imagination of Russian artists.

LITERATURE

Russian literature entered a Golden Age associated primarily with Turgenev, Dostoevsky, and Tolstoy, all among the world's greatest novelists. This triumvirate, building upon the legacy of Pushkin, Lermontov, and Gogol, became the most consummate practitioners of literary realism. Under their tutelage, Russian literature achieved great international acclaim.

Turgenev (1818–1883)

Ivan Turgenev, a nobleman, was well educated by private tutors, studied at Moscow and St. Petersburg universities, then studied philosophy at Berlin University and became an ardent Westerner. Through his works this most Western of Russia's major writers taught Europeans to appreciate Russian literature. After his return to Russia his short stories about peasant life, based on personal observation, appeared in *The Contemporary*, the leading "thick journal" of literature and of literary and social criticism, and later were published as *A Sportsman's Sketches (1852)*, winning him wide recognition as a leading author. The stories constituted a powerful indictment of serfdom, while portraying the serf as compassionate and dignified. Despite sharp official criticism, the book affected public opinion deeply. Publication that same year of his laudatory obituary of Nicholas Gogol, author of biting satires on government corruption and social injustice, brought brief imprisonment and banishment to his provincial estate. In 1853, pardoned and allowed to return to the capital with his reputation enhanced, Turgenev was regarded as literary Russia's chief spokesman.

Turgenev embodied the new spirit pervading Russian life. In his first novels, *Rudin* (1856) and *Nest of Gentlefolk* (1859), he depicted the misguided idealism of the older generation, well intentioned but unrealistic. In the novel *On the Eve* (1860), he described the aspirations of the new generation. These works, hailed as models of literary realism, tried to show life as it really was and faced the toughest issues of the day. In them the critics found neither sentimentality nor fantasy, only beauty and truth, simplicity and sensitivity. Both conservative and radical critics hailed his descriptive powers, portrayal of character, and insight.

In 1862 appeared Turgenev's most famous novel, *Fathers and Sons*, which dealt with generational conflict between men of the 1860s—Arkadi and the novel's hero, the Nihilist Bazarov—and the 1840s—Arkadi's father and uncle. Right-wing critics condemned Turgenev for unduly publicizing and apparently approving radicalism by depicting Bazarov too positively. The left criticized Bazarov as a caricature of the younger generation's aspirations. Except for Dmitri Pisarev (the model for Bazarov), who praised the novel, most radical critics claimed Turgenev had exhausted his talent. After many triumphs, the general rejection of *Fathers and Sons* crushed Turgenev's ego. Settling in western Europe, he made only a few brief visits home. His novel *Smoke* (1867) expressed his disillusionment with Russia and stressed the arrogance,

Ivan Turgenev (1818–1883) *(Library of Congress)*

narrowmindedness, and deceitfulness of Russian aristocrats and émigrés.

Turgenev's last novel, *Virgin Soil,* analyzed the "going to the people" movement of the early 1870s, (see Chapter 3, p. 62), but revealed that he had lost touch with Russian life in exile even as his fame grew in Europe. The first Russian author with an international reputation, Turgenev felt more at ease among Europe's literary elite than among Russians, whom he treated disdainfully. Unreconciled with his beloved homeland, Turgenev died in a village near Paris.

Dostoevsky (1821–1881)

If Turgenev was the stylistic master of realism, Feodor Dostoevsky strove to be a "realist in a higher sense," plumbing the depths of mankind's soul

Feodor Dostoevsky (1821–1881)
(*Library of Congress*)

and laying bare conflicts within human nature. His metaphysical realism dealt with the meaning and purpose of life. For him ideas had a tangible, palpable quality. Seeking to overcome divisions in Russian life, he discovered that only by surmounting the division between mankind and God could Russian life be restored to wholeness. Dostoevsky wrote:

> I am a child of the age, a child of unbelief and skepticism. I have been so far, and shall be I know to the grave. . . . If anyone proved to me that Christ was not the truth, and it really was a fact that the truth was not in Christ, I would rather be with Christ than the truth.[1]

Throughout his life he sought to know and understand Christ. Believing deeply in Russia and its people, he tried similarly to believe in God. A character in *The Possessed* blurts out: "I believe in Russia. I believe in Orthodoxy. . . . I believe that Christ will come again in Russia." This was Dostoevsky's own conviction, proclaimed in his writings.

The son of a well-to-do but miserly doctor, Dostoevsky was an engineering student in St. Petersburg when he learned of his father's murder

---

[1]Cited in E. H. Carr, *Dostoevsky* (New York, 1931), pp. 281–282.

by peasants. With his inheritance he soon resigned his army commission to devote himself to literature.

"We have all sprung from Gogol's 'Overcoat,' "[2] Dostoevsky once remarked. Indeed, his first novel, *Poor Folk* (1845), is related to "The Overcoat." An exchange of letters between a young girl and an aging government clerk exposes the pathos and constant struggle of the downtrodden for human dignity. The novel revealed Dostoevsky's intense concern with psychological torment, self-sacrifice, and alienation— key themes of his later great novels. At 23, hailed as a new Gogol, he was recognized overnight as a leading Russian author. But when his second novel, *The Double* (1846), was greeted coolly, his vanity was deeply wounded. Abandoning his literary friends, he attended the radical Petrashevskii Circle partly out of boredom and curiosity. But Nicholas I's regime equated nonconformity with treason. The Petrashevtsy and Dostoevsky were arrested in April 1849. Confined in Peter and Paul Fortress, he was convicted of crimes against the state. At the execution site, Dostoevsky's death sentence was commuted to eight years' exile in Siberia. Being snatched from the jaws of death affected him profoundly, stimulating his deep interest in human psychology and torments of the mind. For almost a decade Dostoevsky languished in prison and exile.

Dostoevsky recorded his prison sojourn vividly in letters to his brother Mikhail then in *Notes from the House of the Dead* (1861), resembling Alexander Solzhenitsyn's *Gulag Archipelago* (see Chapter 17). He wrote Mikhail:

> For five years I have lived under the control of warders in a crowd of human beings, and have never been alone for a single hour. To be alone is a necessity of normal existence, like drinking and eating; otherwise, in this forced communal life you become a hater of mankind. The society of people acts like a poison or an infection, and from this insufferable torment I have suffered more than anything these four years.[3]

Imprisonment, a turning point in Dostoevsky's life, caused an intellectual reorientation profoundly affecting his entire outlook. He discovered two vital sources of inspiration basic for his later views: the New Testament and "the people" of Russia.

Allowed to return to St. Petersburg in 1859, Dostoevsky and his brother entered journalism as partners. After initial success, disaster struck involving suppression by the authorities and financial failure. In 1864 the deaths of his wife and beloved brother plunged him into grief;

---

[2]A famous short story written by Gogol in 1842.
[3]In Helen Muchnic, *An Introduction to Russian Literature* (New York, 1947), pp. 129–130.

his debts brought him close to bankruptcy. In that disastrous year Dostoevsky ventured into philosophy in *Notes from Underground*. Releasing his despair, he sought to answer Chernyshevskii's utopian novel, *What Is to Be Done?* (see Chapter 3). Chernyshevskii believed people were inherently good and rational; Dostoevsky argued that people could use their free will to choose between good and evil; he presented people as irrational and contradictory. A man's ability to choose, claimed Dostoevsky, was the root of his freedom. He developed these ideas further in his major novels.

The great novels *Crime and Punishment* (1866), *The Idiot* (1869), *The Possessed*, (1871–1872), and the profound final work, *The Brothers Karamazov* (1879–1880), constitute a related cycle dealing with contemporary Russian issues, reflecting stages in Dostoevsky's elaboration of Christianity, and portraying the "underground man." *Crime and Punishment* reveals the tragic failure of Raskolnikov, a poor student, to assert his individuality "without God" by senselessly murdering a pawnbroker and her sister. Raskolnikov succeeds only in denying his humanity and Christian spirit. In *The Idiot* Dostoevsky portrays saintly idiocy—a long revered Russian trait, in Christlike Prince Myshkin, an impotent epileptic, long confined in mental institutions. Returning to society, he becomes enmeshed in the lives of "ordinary" people who find him amusing and wholly gullible. Exploiting his kind generosity, they turn him into a real madman. By his actions Myshkin fosters Christian compassion and, like Christ, is ridiculed and abused.

The Possessed deals with socialism's alleged destructive qualities. A ruthless Nihilist, Peter Verkhovenskii, persuades his followers to murder a fellow conspirator suspected of wishing to squeal to the police (see Chapter 3). Reacting to the "Nechaev Affair," an actual event of his day, Dostoevsky was convinced of socialism's moral bankruptcy. *The Possessed,* based on the "Nechaev Affair," dramatized the alienation resulting, he felt, from rejecting Christianity. In this novel the theater of the struggle between good and evil is all of Russia. Dostoevsky feared that socialism, destroying individuals like Raskolnikov and Verkhovenskii, threatened Russia with destruction. A powerful indictment of the revolutionary movement, the novel provoked criticism in the press. The left vilified Dostoevsky as a writer without talent and a traitor to his principles. The right denounced him for the prominence his novel gave to the revolutionary movement. Undaunted, he continued his quest for personal spiritual peace and salvation for Russia.

In his greatest novel, *The Brothers Karamazov,* Dostoevsky tried to resolve issues that long had tormented him. Old Feodor Karamazov is murdered by one of his four sons, provoking a great theological debate between Ivan Karamazov and his younger brother Alyosha over the existence of God. The debate culminates in the famous "Legend of the Grand Inquisitor," portraying in parable form the human conflict between material well-being and belief in God. Christ reappears in Spain during the Inquisition and is recognized by the Grand Inquisitor, who threatens to burn him at the stake because Christ asks people to grant Him allegiance freely without coercion. Freedom of choice, warns the Grand Inquisitor, threatens the happiness of people who beg for authoritarianism in order to be free of the responsibility of freedom. Like the Grand Inquisitor, socialist revolutionaries offered people material well-being at the cost of their freedom, contended Dostoevsky. Society was doomed unless it embodied Christ's ideal; the Russian people possessed a Christlike harmony that could redeem mankind. Russia's and mankind's salvation were to be found in spiritual rebirth by voluntary acceptance of Christ's spirit.

Tolstoy (1828–1910)

Leo Tolstoy came from a prosperous noble family with estates south of Moscow. Tutored at home, he attended Kazan University, but abandoned his studies to open a school for peasant children on his estate. Joining the army in 1851, he served in the Caucasus, beginning his literary career there with a semiautobiographical trilogy, *Childhood, Boyhood and Youth* (1852–1857), which won him wide acclaim. At the siege of Sevastopol during the Crimean War, he recorded his impressions in *Sevastopol Stories*. After the war Tolstoy resigned from the army, traveled in Europe, and supported the reforms launched by Alexander II following the Crimean War. Marrying in 1862, he settled down on his estate, devoting himself to writing and his family.

His great novels, *War and Peace* and *Anna Karenina,* stem from this tranquil period. *War and Peace* (1869), a vast literary canvas of the momentous Napoleonic period, probes the lives of people from all social groups. Vast panoramas, great battles, agonizing retreats, and the historic encounter of Napoleon and Kutuzov serve as backdrop for Tolstoy's historical and moral philosophy. The novel's heroine and Tolstoy's ideal woman is Natasha Rostov, an ordinary woman with extraordinary qualities, who mirrors mighty historical forces. Ordinary people move history, not vaunted heroes like Napoleon, he believed. Tolstoy viewed Napoleon as a mere puppet, manipulated by forces beyond his control. To Tolstoy history had its own inner logic working itself out through people as agents, not as its creators.

> History, that is, the unconscious, general hive life of mankind, uses every moment of the life of kings as a tool for its own purposes.

Count Leo Tolstoy (1828–1910) in his study *(Library of Congress)*

Though Napoleon at that time, in 1812, was more convinced than ever that it (war) depended on him . . . he had never been so much in the grip of inevitable laws, which compelled him, while thinking that he was acting on his own volition, to perform for the hive life—that is to say, for history— whatever had to be performed. Leo Tolstoy, *War and Peace*, translated by Louise and Aylmer Maude, New York, 1942, p. 67.

Despite a huge cast of characters and a bewildering variety of human experience, *War and Peace* is a remarkably unified masterpiece in which Tolstoy's philosophy integrates perfectly with his artistry.

In *Anna Karenina*, an outstanding social novel of smaller dimensions, written between 1873 and 1877 and published serially in 1876–1877, Tolstoy expounded on family issues, judicial reform, emancipation, the role of women, and the nobility's economic decline. The focus is the triangle of Anna, her husband, Alexis, and her lover, Count Vronskii. Contrasting with Anna's and Vronskii's tempestuous affair is Kitty's marriage to the idealistic landowner, Levin. Anna and Vronskii struggle against social conventions that deny them happiness together. Bitterness and guilt corrupt their relationship until Anna, to achieve peace, commits suicide and Vronskii's life is ruined.

Tolstoy's later works lack the scope, intensity, and depth of these two masterworks. In the late 1870s Tolstoy underwent a religious conversion dramatically recounted in *A Confession* (1882). Rejecting conventional

Orthodoxy for a rationalistic Christianity based on nonresistance to evil, he urged rejection of all coercive institutions: church, state, and private property. His critique of contemporary society brought his public excommunication in 1901. Tolstoy's denunciation of the nobles' greed and his repudiation of private property caused conflict with them while the state viewed him as a dangerous revolutionary. His unconventional views on marriage and the family expressed in *The Kreutzer Sonata* (1889) and *The Devil*, published posthumously, provoked bitter family dissension. At 82, signing over his property to his estranged wife, Tolstoy set out on a pilgrimage and died a few days later at a house in Riazan province. Justifiably, he is known as the last "true giant of the reformist aristocratic intelligentsia." He searched restlessly for answers to the meaning of life and history.

Chekhov (1860–1904)

Anton Chekhov was the last great figure of 19th-century Russian literature. Born in Taganrog on the Sea of Azov as son of a greengrocer and grandson of a serf, he grew up in poor health amidst provincial boredom, middle-class piety, and straitened finances. When his family moved to Moscow, Anton remained in Taganrog, supporting himself by tutoring and running errands. He was a carefree youth with an extraordinary sense of humor, evident in his later stories. His literary career began in 1880 with stories hastily written for pulp magazines under a pseudonym. Besides paying for medical school, his writings gave him the reputation of a prolific but mediocre writer. When one story was noticed by the literary elite upon its publication in 1885, Chekhov was invited to St. Petersburg and met Alexis Suvorin, editor of *New Times*, a prominent daily. Impressed with Chekhov's ability, Suvorin urged him to make writing his career. Much flattered, Chekhov continued writing short stories whose quality improved as their quantity decreased. In 1888 the Academy of Sciences gave him the prestigious Pushkin Prize. Amidst this growing success came warnings of tuberculosis, which would end his life prematurely. Foreseeing death, Chekhov between 1889 and 1897 wrote many fine stories reflecting personal restlessness and a belief that Russia required sweeping changes. Recurrent themes are human vanity, weaknesses, and melancholia. His characters often yearn for a richer, more beautiful future.

Always fascinated by the theater, Chekhov in 1895 composed a serious play, *The Sea Gull*, but its first performance flopped because the director and actors misunderstood it. Two years later it was presented by a new theatrical company formed by K. S. Stanislavskii and V. I. Nemirovich-Danchenko, the famous Moscow Art Theater. Its directors

Anton Chekhov (1860–1904)
(Library of Congress)

(Stanislavskii and Nemirovich-Danchenko) and actors understood its subtleties, and *The Sea Gull* became a sensation. In close association with Stanislavskii's theater, Chekhov from 1899 to 1903 wrote the immortal plays, *Uncle Vania, The Three Sisters,* and *The Cherry Orchard.* Lacking clear plots or dramatic climaxes, they are studies in human psychology. Understatement, lack of suspense, little action—Chekhov's literary characteristics—succeed brilliantly on stage. Chekhov wrote with great enthusiasm for life and unfaltering optimism about the future. He lived in a Russia entering a century of momentous change. A character in his last story, "A Marriageable Girl," reflects the apprehension he and his generation felt about the future:

> The whole town was so outmoded and antiquated, she felt. Was it awaiting its own end? Or expecting something fresh and original to begin? It was never quite clear which. Oh, if it would only hurry up and begin . . . that brave new world where you can face your own destiny boldly, where you can be cheerful and free, knowing you're in the right! Now, such a life *will* come about sooner or later.[4]

Chekhov died in the summer of 1904, during a health cure in Germany, leaving a rich legacy of plays, stories, letters, and essays that deeply influenced writers in Russia and abroad. He brought the Golden Age to a close, though Russian literature continued to be creative and

---

[4]*The Oxford Chekhov,* trans. and ed. R. Hingley (London, 1975), vol. 9, p. 222.

Maxim Gorkii (1869–1936) *(Library of Congress)*
[Alice Boughton]

original. The last tsarist decades witnessed another outburst of creative energy, called the Silver Age. The transitional figure was Maxim Gorkii (1869–1936), whose literary credo evolved from classical realism, through neoromanticism, to socialist realism.

Gorkii (1868–1936)

From a lower middle-class family, Maxim Gorkii (born A. M. Peshkov), saw his modest social status deteriorate rapidly after his father's premature death. On the streets at a tender age, he obtained his education by surviving in hostile Nizhnii-Novgorod. Gorkii wandered ceaselessly through southern Russia, learning much from those he met and gaining insight into life's vicissitudes. (The pseudonym Gorkii means "bitter" or "miserable" and was for him a constant reminder of the miserable and bitter childhood he had as a street urchin in Nizhnii-Novgorod.) He acquired understanding of and sympathy for the downtrodden. Acquaintances from these early years later appeared in his writings. Gorkii's first published work was *Makar Chudra* (1892), a tale of love, passion, and violence among gypsies. Written realistically, his early works reflect preference for broad social themes and his humanitarianism. His stories were well received because they portrayed vividly to readers a little-known world. His collected stories, issued in two popular volumes in

1898, made his reputation as a talented, forceful writer. In 1902 he was elected an honorary member of the Imperial Russian Academy of Sciences. When the government annulled the election on political grounds, he became all the more popular. On close terms with revolutionaries and arrested in 1900, he supported the Social Democrats and after 1903 often the Bolsheviks.

Encouraged by his friend Chekhov, Gorkii began writing plays. In 1902 Stanislavskii's Moscow Art Theater staged with limited success his drama, *The Lower Depths,* an unconventional play set in a decaying boardinghouse filled with social dregs—drunks, prostitutes, and thieves. In translation it soon became a hit in western Europe. In this play, a call for freedom, Gorkii defended the dignity of people ground down by tsarism. The authorities banned it in the provinces and branded Gorkii a dangerous radical.

Gorkii's massive and tendentious novels were less successful artistically. He wrote one, *Mother* (1907), on an ill-fated visit to the United States. Participating in the 1905 Revolution, Gorkii had been arrested again, then released on the provision that he leave Russia. Disillusioned with the United States, he criticized American society bitterly in a collection of stories about New York, *The City of the Yellow Devil* (1907). He finally settled in Italy, where his villa on the Isle of Capri became a haven for political exiles and an artists' and writers' colony. In his absence his reputation in Russia dwindled, but his great autobiographical work, *Childhood* (1913), and *Among Strangers* (1915) restored his renown. During a political amnesty honoring the Romanovs' tercentenary, he returned to Russia in 1913, wrote for the Bolshevik press, and edited a Marxist journal, *Annals.* Gorkii rejoiced at tsarism's collapse in March 1917, but was unenthusiastic about the Bolshevik coup in November. Although he quarreled frequently with Lenin, Gorkii eventually made peace with him and continued writing in the Soviet era.

Decadence and Symbolism

Other writers criticized Gorkii for his continued commitment to a literary realism they considered outmoded. Many became preoccupied with form and beauty. A general European romantic revival influenced these new trends in Russia, where it was called the Decadent movement and later Symbolism. Such writers and poets emphasized aesthetics and "art for art's sake." Mysticism, individualism, sensualism, and demonism were its hallmarks. Language became vague and obscure to create symbolic images and sounds; poetry revived. Younger Symbolists included the great Alexander Blok, Andrei Beli, and Nicholas Gumilev. These poets formed a closely knit group that met frequently, contributed to the same journals, and created poetry of technical perfection, pure tonal harmony, and sheer beauty. These writers were little affected at first by World War I and Russia's growing social crisis. Most welcomed the March but not the November Revolution. Afterward some sought exile abroad; others remained in Russia hoping to influence revolutionary developments. War and revolution took their toll on Russian culture but pointed in new and uncharted directions.

In music, painting, and architecture, developments paralleled, though belatedly, those in literature. Painting and music, following literature's lead, responded favorably to the upsurge of national consciousness among Russians following the Crimean War and were influenced by the new realistic aesthetics. Architecture was less affected until the turn of the century.

MUSIC

The Russian Music Society, founded in 1859, helped foster musical activity in Russia, promoted conservatory training, and encouraged music appreciation among the public. Anton Rubinstein, a distinguished pianist and composer, was the moving force behind it. With his younger brother, Nicholas, he established branches of the Music Society in Moscow and some 30 provincial centers. Conservatories were founded in St. Petersburg, Moscow, Kiev, Kharkov, Saratov, Tbilisi, and Odessa to provide musical education. The Society organized several symphony orchestras and smaller performing ensembles and sponsored concerts by Russian and foreign artists all over Russia to bring music to wider audiences. Conservative in musical taste and theory, the Society followed the lead of the Rubinsteins, who viewed the German classical and romantic schools of composition as the models to emulate.

The Five

Despite the Society's remarkable popular success and an upsurge of interest in music, its conservative credo did not go unchallenged. A small group of musicians formed to initiate a revolution in Russian music and direct it along new paths—the famous "Five," or the so-called Mighty Handful. One could scarcely imagine a more unlikely group to revolutionize the field of music. Its leader and organizer was Mily Balakirev (1837–1910), its only trained musician, an excellent pianist and conductor, but mediocre as a composer. Cesar Cui (1835–1918) was trained as an engineer and eventually became a general of army engineers. Modest Musorgskii (1839–1881) was a Guards officer and later an official in the Transport Ministry. Alexander Borodin (1834–1878), trained as a doctor of medicine, eventually became chemistry professor at the St. Petersburg Medical-Surgical Academy. Nicholas Rimskii-Korsakov (1844–1908) became a naval officer and later a professor of music at the St. Petersburg Conservatory. These men, from diverse backgrounds and differing professional interests, did not always agree, but they shared common musical ideals and attitudes.

The Five, considering themselves the legitimate successors of Glinka and Dargomyzhskii (earlier successful composers), aimed to create a Russian national school of music based on native folk and church music. Rejecting strict Western rules of technical form, they preferred a freer, more flexible style associated with folk music. They abhorred imitation of foreign models and scorned the canons of Italian opera as shallow devices to glorify the voice. Italian opera, they believed, was devoid of content and dramatic effect. Not surprisingly, bitter polemics erupted between Rubinstein's conservatives and Balakirev's musical nationalists, which failed to resolve their fundamental differences but publicized and popularized music. In 1862, to counter the influence of Rubinstein's Music Society, the Five organized the Free School of Music to promote their musical theories in teaching and through performances of their works. The great champion of the Five, the Free School of Music, and the nationalist musical trend was the distinguished art and music critic V. V. Stasov (1824–1906), whose caustic polemics and enthusiastic reviews won for the Five a large and loyal following.

Balakirev and Borodin were the creators of the Russian symphonic school, and both contributed significantly to symphonic theory. Musorgskii, Rimskii-Korsakov, and Borodin were the geniuses of Russian opera, whose works have survived fluctuating tastes and remain in the repertoire throughout the world. Borodin worked 18 years on his great opera, *Prince Igor,* first performed in 1890 with great success. Based on the disputed 12th-century epic, *The Tale of the Host of Igor,* it is a heroic national saga. Modest Musorgskii is renowned for his monumental music drama, the opera *Boris Godunov,* one of the greatest works of art produced in Russia. The composer first studied the history and language of the 16th century carefully and was influenced by old Russian church music. The opera's hero was to be not Tsar Boris but the suffering Russian people, epitomized by a simpleton. Thus Musorgskii, adapting Pushkin's play, wrote much of the libretto himself and declared: "My music must reproduce the people's language even in the most insignificant nuances."[5] *Boris Godunov,* in its original stark, terse version, without any female lead, was rejected as insufficiently operatic by the Marynskii Theater of St.

[5]V. Seroff, *Modeste Moussorgsky* (New York, 1968), p. 90.

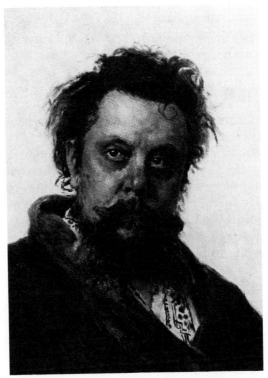

Modest Musorgskii (1839–1881) *(Library of Congress)*

Petersburg. Musorgskii then completely revised the opera, adding a "Polish" third act with Marina as prima donna and a revolutionary scene. His revised version was performed successfully from 1874 until 1882, then it was withdrawn under pressure from Alexander III's regime, which disliked its revolutionary implications. Rimskii-Korsakov, Musorgskii's friend, completely reorchestrated *Boris,* and his polished version scored triumphs throughout Europe and America. Musorgskii also composed most of *Khovanshchina,* a second folk opera based on the Moscow *streltsy* (musketeers') revolt of 1682. Completed and revised by Rimskii-Korsakov, it has remained a perennial favorite. Musorgskii also composed *A Night on Bald Mountain,* one of the first Russian tone poems, and a piano suite, *Pictures at an Exhibition,* best known in the orchestral version by Maurice Ravel.[6] Rimskii-Korsakov's operas, somewhat less

---

[6]See David MacKenzie, "Modest Petrovich Musorgskii," in *Modern Encyclopedia of Russian and Soviet History* (Gulf Breeze, Fla., 1982), vol. 24, pp. 17–23.

well-known outside of Russia, include *The Snow Maiden,* a fantastic Russian fairy tale; *Sadko,* an old folktale of Novgorod; and *The Golden Cockerel (Le Coq d'Or),* also based on a fairy tale.

Tchaikovsky (1840–1893)

Among the first students at the St. Petersburg Conservatory, opened in 1862, was Peter Tchaikovsky, destined to become the best known and most beloved Russian composer. His name became synonymous with Russian music, and his works remain favorites throughout the world. Like so many of his contemporaries, Tchaikovsky was trained not for a musical career but for the civil service and briefly served as a minor official in the Ministry of Justice. Music was his passion, and he studied privately until enrolling in the Conservatory. He soon resigned his civil service post to devote himself to full-time study. He was such a distinguished music student that he was invited to join the faculty of the new Moscow Conservatory in 1866; for the next dozen years he worked and taught there. His association with the Rubinsteins, and with Moscow, fostered antagonism between him and the Five in St. Petersburg, which unfortunately often obscured how much they shared and how close they were in musical tastes and attitudes. Their antagonism frequently was more personal than professional. Some critics have characterized Tchaikovsky's music as cosmopolitan and Western, while calling that of the Five nationalist and Russian. This superficial distinction ignores their common origins and national feelings.

In Moscow, Tchaikovsky composed some of his finest and most enduring music. Despite recurring mental crises, he completed four symphonies, many operas, including *Eugene Onegin* (adapted from Pushkin), concertos, much incidental music, and his greatest ballet, *Swan Lake.* Then followed a period of acute depression and nervous tension, which prevented him from composing with the same intensity and creative power. Another burst of sustained creative energy began in 1889 with his second great ballet, *The Sleeping Beauty,* followed in 1892 by a third, *The Nutcracker,* one of his most popular compositions. Traveling in western Europe in 1892, Tchaikovsky rediscovered his old facility in composition, which had eluded him for years, and realized that his Sixth Symphony ("Pathetique") would be his masterpiece. First performed in St. Petersburg in October 1893, under the composer's direction, it has been acclaimed universally not only as Tchaikovsky's greatest work but also one of the greatest of all Russian musical works.

More than any other 19th-century Russian composer, Tchaikovsky acquired even in his lifetime an international reputation. In his last years, he traveled extensively, conducting his music all over the world, and was specially honored at ceremonies opening Carnegie Hall in New York City in 1891. Despite or perhaps because of his international reputation, nationalists criticized his music as too Western and imitative of foreign models. This criticism was justified in the sense that Tchaikovsky was influenced by European musical traditions, but it did not mean that his music was not Russian. Igor Stravinsky, his worthy successor, emphasized repeatedly its uniquely Russian quality:

> Tchaikovsky's music, which does not appear specifically Russian to everybody, is often more profoundly Russian than music which has long since been awarded the facile label of Muscovite picturesqueness. This music is quite as Russian as Pushkin's verse or Glinka's song. While not especially cultivating in his art the "soul of the Russian peasant," Tchaikovsky drew unconsciously from the true popular sources of our race.[7]

By the turn of the century, Russian music had achieved unprecedented maturity, international recognition, and respect. A whole group of brilliant teachers took up the cause in Russian conservatories and helped mold a new generation of composers, which carried on the traditions of the Five and Tchaikovsky. Among the most talented were Sergei Rachmaninov (1873–1943), A. E. Glazunov (1865–1936), A. Liadov (1855–1914), M. M. Ippolitov-Ivanov (1859–1936), and Sergei Taneev (1850–1918). None achieved the status or reputation of the Five or Tchaikovsky, nor did they possess quite the same creative spark, but they contributed nonetheless many original and creative compositions to Russian music.

Meanwhile, a pair of young, innovative Russian composers opened up entirely new vistas, much as the Symbolists had introduced new forms of poetic expression. Alexander Scriabin (1871–1915) came from a musical family and revealed a precocious talent, which was nurtured by excellent teachers. Enrolled at the Moscow Conservatory at the age of 16, he revealed prodigious ability as a pianist and as a composer. He dabbled in mysticism, devoured Decadent poetry, and wrote poetry himself. Scriabin went on a successful concert tour of Russia and Europe, but he suffered from nervous disorders that cut short his career. Influenced by the Symbolists, Scriabin rejected the musical realism of the Five and Tchaikovsky's academic conventions and charted a new musical course. Inspired by mysticism, romanticism, the occult, and the Decadents, Scriabin concluded that art must transform life. Pain, ugliness, and evil would be transformed into beauty and joy by art; life would be transformed into the Kingdom of God on earth. He viewed the artist as a new

---

[7]Cited in R. A. Leonard, *A History of Russian Music* (London, 1956), p. 197.

messiah, capable of redeeming humankind and infusing life with new creative energy, lifting a human to the level of a god. He composed music, such as *The Poem of Ecstasy,* of eerie, haunting qualities, music which he characterized as mystico-religious, the basis for a new harmonic system. His influence remained limited outside Russia, but his compositions, especially his piano music, affected Stravinsky, Sergei Prokoviev, and Dmitri Shostakovich. Today his music is experiencing a revival in the West.

Stravinsky (1882–1971)

Stravinsky marks a watershed in the history of Russian music because he represents the first tide of musical influence flowing *from* Russia *into* Europe. Unlike most of his contemporaries, Stravinsky was self-taught, until tutored by Rimskii-Korsakov. His early career was closely associated with the famous Russian impresario, Serge Diagilev (1872–1929), who heard two of his works at a private concert in 1908 and was deeply impressed. At the time, Diagilev was preparing the program for the first season of the revolutionary Ballet Russe de Monte Carlo in Paris, and he asked Stravinsky to orchestrate two Chopin pieces for the ballet. Thus began one of the most revolutionary and productive associations in musical history—Diagilev, the organizer and man of ideas; Stravinsky, the musical innovator whose scores would revolutionize music; Michael Fokine, the choreographer whose ballets would become modern classics against which all other dance was measured; Leon Bakst, the brilliant set and costume designer, who with Alexandre Benois revolutionized set design; and finally, Vaslav Nijinsky, perhaps the greatest of all ballet dancers. Together, in 1910, they created a stunning and opulent production of *The Firebird,* based on an old Russian folktale, with music by Stravinsky, choreography by Fokine, and sets by Bakst. The result was an international triumph of extraordinary importance. In 1911, the company staged *Petrushka,* a ballet teeming with new ideas and musical forms. Stravinsky introduced a radical orchestral style and boldly innovative music, which shocked many listeners. In 1913 Diagilev staged Stravinsky's even more radical ballet, *The Rite of Spring,* which created a public scandal because of its brutal realism, violence, and extraordinary vitality, which to many was sheer lunacy and cacophony, insulting to a generation still steeped in sentimental romanticism. Stravinsky was the musical descendant of Musorgskii's realism and a musical nationalist in these early works, using the rich tradition of Russian folk music. After these amazing early successes, Stravinsky sought still newer musical forms, which led him away from Russian traditions. Before World War I, he settled in Switzerland, and after the war he lived in France. At the

Igor Stravinsky (1882–1971) *(Library of Congress)*

outbreak of World War II, he moved to the United States. War and revolution cut him off from Russia, which he revisited triumphantly only in his final years. The creativity of Russian music in the last decades of the monarchy, epitomized by Stravinsky, parallels in many ways the flowering of Russian literature during its Golden Age.

PAINTING

Russian painting developed rapidly during the late 19th century, though less dramatically than music. Painting was finally emancipated from the neoclassical style, long imposed by the Academy of Arts. As in literature and music, young artists challenged older artistic conventions, and strove to develop realism and nationalism in painting. In 1863, the entire graduating class of the Academy openly challenged the rigid policies of the artistic establishment. Opposition to Academy policies and to its monopoly over art surfaced after "The Festival of the Gods in Valhalla" was decreed as compulsory subject matter for the annual competition to determine those who would be selected to continue their studies in Italy.

Refusing to participate in such a competition, the students demanded the right to select their own subjects freely so as best to display their artistic talents. When the authorites demurred, 14 students resigned from the Academy in protest and formed their own artistic cooperative *(artel),* which soon evolved into the Society of Traveling Art Exhibitions; it dominated Russian art from 1870 into the 1890s. The Society was organized by young nationalist artists who rejected the Academy's cosmopolitan and neoclassical approach. Annual exhibitions were organized in St. Petersburg, which then went on tour throughout Russia. The exhibitions of the so-called Itinerants, as artist members of the Society were called, acquainted wide audiences with recent works by Russia's best artists. Most talented artists were affiliated formally or informally with the Society. The critic Vladimir Stasov, who had served as public spokesman for the Five, was a staunch defender of the Itinerants.

These Itinerants, declaring war on the Academy's conventions, promoted artistic realism based on a portrayal and interpretation of Russian life as it existed around them. They emphasized content more than form and composition, but they were by no means indifferent to composition, color, and design. They stressed social comment, often protesting against injustice, inequality, and exploitation, but they recognized that for their art to make serious social statements, it had to display sound form, too. They regarded themselves as artists first, not as mere propagandists.

The moving force behind the Society of Traveling Art Exhibitions was Ivan Kramskoi and, to a lesser extent, Vasili Perov. They were organizers and enterpreneurs as well as skillful artists. Kramskoi was a fine painter whose portraits of prominent leaders reveal great psychological insight and understanding. Perov, of humble origin, portrayed most powerfully lower-class life and problems. His scathing criticisms of the hypocrisy and moral turpitude of the Orthodox clergy brought him into conflict with the authorities.

The most famous and successful 19th-century Russian artist was Ilia Repin (1844–1930), whose canvases still evoke a powerful response. Though of lower-class origin, he studied at the Academy of Arts and won a prestigious traveling scholarship to study in Italy. *The Volga Boatmen,* painted between 1870 and 1873, and designed as a group portrait of the human beasts of burden who hauled heavy barges up river, against the Volga's current, won him a European reputation. This painting portrayed the brutal exploitation so widespread in Russia. Repin knew each of the characters depicted in the painting and recorded their tragic lives in his memoirs. Equally devastating as a critique of social evils was his *Religious Procession in Kursk Province* (1880–1883), which suggested the clergy's arrogance and aloofness, the brutality of the police, the quiet suffering of the peasantry, and the haughty superiority of the nobility.

Ilia Repin (1844–1930) self-portrait *(Library of Congress)*

Repin became known as the most talented Russian painter and an outspoken critic of contemporary society. In the 1880s, he turned to history, choosing subjects such as *Tsar Ivan and the Body of His Son* (1881–1885), a painting that showed Ivan IV moments after he had clubbed his eldest son to death. It criticized implicitly the corrupting influence of unlimited autocratic power. Repin helped win greater European recognition for Russian art, but after the Bolshevik Revolution he retired to his country house in Finland and refused to return to Soviet Russia.

Such artists as V. V. Vereshchagin (1842–1904) likewise enhanced the growing reputation of Russian painting. A military painter, he sought to promote pacifism and international peace by portraying realistically the horrors of war he had observed firsthand as artist-correspondent in the Russo-Turkish War of 1877–1878. Exhibited extensively in Europe and the United States, Vereshchagin enjoyed a wider reputation than almost any other Russian artist of the period. Thus Russian artists tried to create a truly national art form, just as the writers sought to guard against foreign influences, yet their work paralleled the genre and historical painting prevalent in many European countries.

Beginning in the 1890s, the Russian art world, like literature and music, experienced a revolt against the canons of realism and nationalism by younger artists, notably Mikhail Nesterov (1862–1942) and Mikhail Vrubel (1856–1911). Both broke with the realism of the Itinerants. Nesterov was a deeply religious man whose paintings on religious themes revealed a strength and simplicity, formal structure, and symbolic design reminiscent of iconography. His paintings were studies in mystical idealism, designed to capture the essence of an otherworldly reality revealed in lives of saints, hermits, and monks.

Vrubel's abbreviated and tragic career was perhaps more important in turning Russian art away from realism. He studied philosophy before enrolling in the Academy of Arts and was interested in aesthetic theory and art history, especially classical art and Russian iconography. He became a successful designer and mural painter, skilled at church decoration. In an artwork, every element was important to him: form, line, color, design, and subject matter, not for their total effect but in themselves. Vrubel became an advocate of "art for art's sake," art created for aesthetic purposes, which the realists considered outrageous. Suffering from serious mental stress, Vrubel was obsessed with demons, particularly after illustrating a commemorative edition of Lermontov's story "The Demon." Vrubel produced a powerful, brooding devil, but still unsatisfied, he continued painting devils and finally produced a huge figure with contorted features and an expression of terrifying bitterness and despair, which mirrored his own accelerating breakdown. This figure was placed against a background of dark swirling colors reminiscent of the Art Nouveau movement and Impressionism in Europe. After completing this tour de force, he went insane and was confined in an asylum until his death. In his short career Vrubel did much to shake Russian art loose from crystallized forms of realism and influenced the poets and composers of his age.

The foundations of a new direction in Russian art were firmly established in 1898, with formation of a group known as *Mir Iskusstva* (The World of Art), named after the journal the group published between 1898 and 1904. This group of young, cosmopolitan aristocrats was led by Serge Diagilev, Alexander Benois, Leon Bakst, and Dmitri Filosofov. Diagilev, the moving force and impresario, began his activities with successful exhibitions of advanced Russian and European art. The journal attracted the most talented and avant-garde artists, essayists, and poets who wrote daring, controversial articles on a variety of topics. The journal openly advocated "art for art's sake" and tried to popularize new artistic trends. The success of *Mir Iskusstva* encouraged such similar publications as *Byloe* (Past Years), *The Golden Fleece,* and *Apollon,* which informed their readers of the latest European trends and attempted to

A. V. Shchusev (1873–1949) *(Library of Congress)*

reintegrate Russian and European art. The resulting excitement and enthusiasm carried over into every facet of Russian culture. Symbolism, Futurism, Cubo-Futurism, Cubism, and Abstract Impressionism all found supporters and practitioners in Russia. The best known Russian artists of this period included the young Marc Chagall, M. Larionov, N. Goncharova, V. Borisov-Musatov, V. Kandinskii, and K. Malevich, all artists who helped to shape the development of modern art.

ARCHITECTURE

Russian architecture did not reveal the same originality and striving for national forms of expression as did literature, music, and painting, and it continued to be dominated largely by foreign architects and styles. Only toward 1900 did some Russian architects seek consciously to create a new national architectural style based upon Russian structures and styles of the medieval period. The Slavic Revival, a rebirth of interest in Russia's past, affected all aspects of Russian culture. Iconography was rediscovered as a developed art form, and the carefully prescribed iconographic principles influenced many architects who found inspiration in the stylized forms of architecture portrayed in iconography. The Slavic Revival encouraged architects to turn to traditional Russian wooden structures as a source of inspiration and to translate these traditional styles into stone and brick structures. Slavic Revival architecture, found all over Russia, was particularly prevalent in Moscow, the traditional center. The Historical Museum there, completed in 1883, is an excellent example of this revival of traditional national forms. A leader in this revival was A. V. Shchusev (1873–1949), who designed a number of Orthodox churches in traditional Novgorod and Pskov style, built Moscow's Kazan Railroad Station, and designed the Russian pavilion at the Venice International exhibition, all in the style of 17th-century Muscovy.

The history of Russian culture, between the Crimean War and World War I is one of tremendous vitality and originality in most fields of cultural endeavor. During this period the world discovered the richness of the Russian accomplishments in the arts. For the first time Russian culture began to influence international culture rather than merely responding to or imitating Western trends. On the eve of World War I, Russian culture was extraordinarily dynamic and diverse, exciting and energetic. War and revolution dampened spirits, but did not destroy the creative impulses of the Russian intelligentsia.

Suggested Additional Reading

ASAFIEV, BORIS. *Russian Music from the Beginning of the Nineteenth Century,* trans. A. Swan (Ann Arbor, Mich., 1953).

BENOIS, A. *The Russian School of Painting* (London, 1919).

BERLIN, I. *The Hedgehog and the Fox: An Essay on Tolstoy's View of History* (New York, 1953).

BOUSOVA, E. and G. STERNIN. *Russian Art Nouveau* (New York, 1988).

CALVOCORESSI, M. D. *A Survey of Russian Music* (London, 1944).

EIKHENBAUM, B. M. *The Young Tolstoy,* trans. G. Kern (Ann Arbor, Mich., 1972).

EMERSON, CARYL. *Boris Godunov: Transpositions of a Russian Theme* (Bloomington, Ind., 1987).

FANGER, D. L. *Dostoevsky and Romantic Realism* (Cambridge, Mass., 1965).

FAUCHEREAU, SERGE. *Moscow, 1900–1930* (New York, 1988).

GRAY, C. *The Great Experiment: Russian Art 1863–1922* (London, 1962).

GROSSMAN, L. *Dostoevsky: A Biography,* trans. M. Mackler (New York, 1975).

GUSTAFSON, RICHARD F. *Leo Tolstoy: Resident and Stranger* (Princeton, N.J., 1986).

HELDT, BARBARA. *Terrible Perfection: Women and Russian Literature* (Bloomington, Ind., 1987).

HINGLEY, R. *Chekhov: A New Biography* (New York, 1976).

LEONARD, R. *A History of Russian Music* (New York, 1968).

MAUDE, AYLMER. *The Life of Tolstoy,* 2 vols. (Oxford, Eng., 1987).

OBOLENSKY, CHLOE. *The Russian Empire: A Portrait in Photographs* (New York, 1979).

RABINOWITZ, STANLEY, ed. *The Noise of Change: Russian Literature and the Critics (1891–1917)* (Ann Arbor, Mich., 1986).

SIMMONS, E. J. *Chekhov: A Biography* (Boston, 1962).

TROYAT, H. *Tolstoy* (Garden City, N.Y., 1967).

VALKENIER, E. *Russian Realist Art: The State and Society: The Peredvizniki and Their Tradition* (Ann Arbor, Mich., 1977).

———. *Ilyia Repin* (New York, 1990).

YARMOLINSKY, A. *Turgenev. The Man, His Art and His Age* (New York, 1959).

CHAPTER SIX

WAR AND REVOLUTION, 1914–1917

In August 1914, imperial Russia, its armed forces still being reorganized, refused to yield to Austro-German pressure and entered World War I. Initially, the war produced unity, patriotic resolve, and predictions of quick victory. As it dragged on, it revealed Russia's bureaucratic ineptitude, disunity in the army and government, and financial disarray. Military defeats and the regime's incompetence undermined morale among soldiers and civilians alike. In March 1917, in the midst of this great conflict, the tsarist regime was overthrown by a popular revolution. What caused the sudden collapse of the Romanov regime, which had ruled Russia for over 300 years? Was it economic backwardness, bureaucratic bungling, or incompetent military leadership—or a combination of these—that encompassed Russia's defeat in World War I? This chapter probes the complex relationship between the war and the coming of revolution in March 1917.

RUSSIA ENTERS WORLD WAR I

On June 28, 1914, a Bosnian student linked with the Serbian national movement assassinated Archduke Francis Ferdinand, heir to the Austrian throne, in Sarajevo, Bosnia, sparking war among the European powers, Japan, and later the United States. The assassination alone did not cause the war. World War I resulted from increasingly rigid alliance systems, which divided Europe between the Triple Alliance (Germany, Austria-Hungary, and Italy) and the Triple Entente (Great Britain, France, and Russia) and involved the prestige of all powers; from a precipitous growth of armaments and militarism; from intense nationalism, especially in Serbia and France, expressed in hatred of their national enemies, Austria and Germany; and from imperial rivalries. In this tense, intolerant atmosphere, diplomats could not reach reasonable compromises.

Russian leaders, at first not unduly alarmed by the Sarajevo murder, went on vacation. The Russian public and press, while mostly anti-Austrian and pro-Serbian, were not violently so. In mid-July, the Russian government even sent the quartermaster-general on a routine mission to the Caucasus. By July 20, Russian leaders had returned to St. Petersburg to greet President Poincaré of France, who spent three days there on a previously arranged state visit. French and Russian chiefs reaffirmed their solemn obligation under the Franco-Russian Alliance.

No sooner had Poincaré departed than Austria-Hungary issued an ultimatum to Serbia that was so framed as to be unacceptable. Russian Foreign Minister S. D. Sazonov exclaimed: "That means European war," but he urged Serbia to make a conciliatory reply, appeal to the powers, and not resist Austria militarily. He requested Austria to give the Serbs more time to answer, but Russia, assured of French support, resolved not to back down.

The mobilization of Russia's army became a vital factor in the last days before war broke out. On July 24, the Council of Ministers empowered the War Minister to mobilize only districts facing Austria. Sazonov saw this as mainly a diplomatic move to back Serbia. War Minister Sukhomlinov and Chief of Staff Ianushkevich agreed to this partial mobilization, though subordinates objected that there were no plans for it and that to improvise them might disrupt full mobilization later. On July 25, the tsar and his ministers, learning that Serbia's reply had not satisfied Austria, agreed to support Serbia at any cost. Austria mobilized and, on July 28, declared war on Serbia, and Sazonov announced that Russia would carry out partial mobilization.

Meanwhile, Russian staff officers had convinced their chiefs, and finally Nicholas II and Sazonov, that partial mobilization was impractical.

On July 29, with the Austrians bombarding Belgrade, the Russian chief of staff gave General Dobrovolskii the decree of Nicholas II, authorizing full mobilization. Nicholas, receiving the Kaiser's telegram warning of the consequences, rescinded this order, but on July 30, Sazonov and the military chiefs persuaded him to authorize general mobilization. Germany demanded that Russia demobilize; when it refused, Germany declared war on Russia, then on France. After Germany violated Belgian neutrality, England joined France and Russia on August 4. The Central Powers (Germany and Austria-Hungary) faced a coalition of Serbia, Russia, France, and England.

Russia's responsibility for World War I remains debatable. German and Western revisionist historians argue that its general mobilization doomed German and British efforts to head off conflict. But the tsar and Sazonov, who opposed war, concluded that partial mobilization would disorganize the Russian army. Another retreat in the Balkans, they believed, might destroy Russia's credibility as a great power. Also, Austria was the first to mobilize, declare war, and begin hostilities against Serbia, an ally of Russia. Like all great European powers in 1914, Russia bore some responsibility, but its leaders went to war reluctantly after failing to find a peaceful solution. Soviet historians, following Lenin, have considered World War I a clash of rival imperialist powers with Germany and Austria-Hungary bearing primary responsibility.

WAR AIMS AND WARTIME DIPLOMACY

Russia entered the war without clear aims except to protect itself and Serbia. At first no specific territorial claims were made against Germany, and Sazonov merely denounced German militarism and pledged to restore a "free" Poland. In September 1914, he told the French and British ambassadors that Russia advocated reorganizing Austria-Hungary into a triple monarchy, ceding Bosnia, Herzegovina, and Dalmatia to Serbia and restoring Alsace-Lorraine to France. As an afterthought he requested free passage for Russian warships through the Turkish Straits. Grand Duke Nicholas, Russia's commander in chief, urged the peoples of Austria-Hungary to overthrow Hapsburg rule and achieve independence, but other Russian leaders did not pursue this nationalist tack. Like other members of the Entente, Russian leaders expected victory to provide them with a program of war aims.

Early defeats and Turkish entry into the war ended official Russian reticence. After Germany persuaded the Ottoman Empire to join the Central Powers (November 1, 1914), the tsar favored expelling it from Europe and solving "the historic task bequeathed to us by our forefathers on the shores of the Black Sea." Nationalists and liberals in the Duma and press took up the refrain. Only securing Constantinople, Professor Trubetskoi of Moscow University declared, would guarantee Russia's independence. Paul Miliukov, leader of the Kadets and the liberal opposition in the Duma, echoing the general nationalist euphoria, demanded that Russia seize the Straits and Constantinople, and to do so became the principal Russian war aim.

The Entente powers pledged, in September 1914, not to conclude a separate peace and to consult on peace terms, but they disagreed over war plans and aims. As a basis for a future peace they concluded secret treaties and agreements. In December 1914, Grand Duke Nicholas, lacking forces to capture or garrison the Straits, urged Sazonov to obtain them by diplomacy. London, to keep Russia fighting, responded warmly. "As to Constantinople, it is clear that it must be yours," the English king told the Russian ambassador. In 1915, the British undertook a Dardanelles campaign to force open the Straits and develop a supply line to Russia; its failure helped doom Russia instead to eventual defeat. In March 1915, Sazonov insisted that if the Entente won, the Straits and environs go to Russia; England, then France, agreed. The tsar told the French ambassador, Maurice Paléologue: "Take the left bank of the Rhine, take Mainz; go further if you like." Later, secret inter-Allied agreements arranged a partition of the Ottoman Empire. Russia would obtain the Straits, eastern Anatolia, and part of the southern coast of the Black Sea. The former Crimean powers promised this, knowing that without Russia they would lose the war. Thus the Russian government and liberals were committed to an imperialistic peace, which aroused no popular enthusiasm at home.

THE ARMY AND THE FRONTS

Russia began World War I with unity, optimism, and loyalty to the Crown, a situation unlike the public apathy prevalent at the beginning of the Japanese war. Domestic quarrels and differences seemed forgotten, and the strike movement, so threatening in July, ended abruptly. Virtually the entire Duma pledged to support the war effort, except for a few socialists who refused to vote war appropriations. The enthusiasm was largely defensive; the Russian people believed that the war was being fought to defend Russia and Serbia. In the cities this spontaneous patriotism became anti-German: the name of St. Petersburg was changed to Petrograd and there were anti-German riots. The villages, however, remained ominously silent.

At first the generals and nationalist press proclaimed that the Russian "steamroller" would move to Berlin and end the war in a few weeks. In the West, this myth of Russian invincibility was widely believed. Actually, the army, its leadership split between "patricians" and "praetorians" (aristocratic and professional elements), reflected the deep rifts in Russian government and society. Though contemporaries claimed that the army had been unprepared, the military *was* prepared for a replay of the Russo-Japanese War. As the German General Staff realized, the Russian army had recovered completely from that defeat and possessed more infantry and mobile guns in the east than the Germans did. What hampered the Russian army in 1914 was divided command, incompetent leadership, and failure to mobilize industry. Grand Duke Nicholas, the impressive-looking six-foot-six commander in chief, appointed at the last moment, lacked real authority and knew neither his subordinates nor military plans. In General Polivanov's words, he "appeared entirely unequipped for the task and . . . spent much time crying because he did not know how to approach his new duties." His military bearing made him popular with the men, who mistook his severity for competence. In August 1915, Nicholas II, who knew even less, replaced him, continuing a disastrous Romanov tradition of placing members of the imperial family in top military posts. War Minister V. A. Sukhomlinov, who had put through needed reforms before the war, succumbed to intrigues by his political and military foes.[1] High army commands, despite Sukhomlinov, were filled largely by seniority, not proven ability. Abler company-grade officers, killed in large numbers in the first months, could not be replaced, producing a grievous officer shortage.

General conscription swelled a peacetime force of 1.35 million men to almost 6.5 million, with no comparable increase in trained officers. During the war, over 15 million men were called up—some 37 percent of all Allied soldiers—but only a fraction could be equipped; they were poorly led and early in the war were inadequately supplied. The rank and file were mostly illiterate peasants ignorant of why they fought. Red tape and lack of a unified command or agreed war plan produced much confusion. Shortages of shells and rifles soon developed mainly from lack of planning and failure to mobilize industry.

Within the army command, prewar controversies between those favoring an offensive against weaker Austria-Hungary and others advocating an invasion of Germany remained unresolved. The army was split between competing fronts, strategies, and generals jealous of one another; men and resources were wasted. Appeals for help from the hard-

---

[1]Sukhomlinov, notes Norman Stone in his revisionist treatment of Russia in World War I, was hated by Duma liberals for his autocratic methods and by old guard, aristocratic military elements for his reforms. Accused of corruption, he was imprisoned by the tsarist and Provisional governments, though the charges were never proven. *The Eastern Front* (New York, 1975), pp. 24–32.

pressed French and British in the west persuaded the Russian high command to dispatch two armies under Generals Rennenkampf and Samsonov (personal enemies) into East Prussia. Inadequate maps, inaccurate intelligence, and poor coordination between the armies and their commanders produced defeat. The Germans rushed in reinforcements from France, and General von Hindenburg trapped Samsonov's army at Tannenberg. Some 300,000 men were lost, Samsonov apparently shot himself, and Russian morale was seriously damaged. Revealing German tactical superiority and ending Russian dreams of a march to Berlin, Tannenberg proved "that armies will lose battles if they are led badly enough."[2] However, a Russian offensive against the smaller, poorly armed, and unreliable Austro-Hungarian army led to occupation of Galicia and heavy Austrian losses and ended hopes by the Central Powers for quick victory in the east.

Unlike the positional trench warfare in France, a war of maneuver persisted on the eastern front. In April 1915, the Germans, reinforcing their armies, scored a breakthrough in Russian Poland. A devastating four-hour artillery bombardment smashed Russian trenches and scared their ill-trained defenders from their posts. Galicia was reconquered, and the Russians retreated hastily, abandoning Poland and part of the Baltic provinces. An unwise Russian scorched-earth policy produced swarms of refugees who poured into Russian cities and demoralized the population. Severe shortages of war matériel and even food plagued the Russian forces: Their artillery had few shells, while German guns fired ceaselessly; many Russian soldiers even lacked rifles. Losses and desertions soared, officers lost faith in their men, and morale plummeted. Rumors spread: "Britain will fight to the last drop of Russian blood." Commented one Russian solider: "We throw away our rifles and give up because things are dreadful in our army, and so are the officers."[3] Only swampy terrain, overextended German supply lines, and the heroism of the Russian soldier prevented utter collapse. During 1915, while the western front had a long breathing spell, Russia bore the main pressure of the Central Powers.

In the winter of 1915–1916 began a surprising recovery. Though few of the promised war supplies came from Russia's allies, Russian industry in a great effort produced over 11 million shells during 1915, proving its capacity to support a modern war. Unofficial efforts, by zemstva, Duma deputies, and other public-spirited groups, left the army far better equipped and supplied. By mid-1916, the Russian army enjoyed a

---

[2]Stone, *Eastern Front,* p. 59.
[3]Stone, *Eastern Front,* p. 170.

Map 6.1 *Russia in World War I, 1914–1918*

Major battle sites   Major Russian railways   Farthest Russian advance 1916

Russian border 1914   Farthest Russian advance in Germany and Austria, 1914

considerable superiority in both men and matériel over the Central Powers. The new War Minister, A. A. Polivanov, and Chief of Staff M. Alekseev were abler than their predecessors. General A. A. Brusilov's sudden but carefully prepared attack in Galicia, May 1916, shattered Austrian lines and forced the Germans to send reinforcements. This action revealed Russia's renewed ability to fight and induced Romania to join the Allies. In the Caucasus, Russian forces prevailed against poorly organized Turkish armies, capturing Erzurum and Trebizond in 1916 and penetrating deep into Anatolia.

Thus the Russian army, despite poor command and organization, played a vital part in World War I. It tied down much of the Central Powers' strength and repeatedly saved the western front from disaster. However, the cost to Russia was staggering: over 3 million soldiers killed and wounded and 2.7 million captured and missing. Though coping well with Austrians and Turks, Russian forces were usually defeated by the Germans. These defeats, speeding deterioration of relations between Russian officers and their men, demoralized the army and contributed greatly to the downfall of the tsar's regime.

THE HOME FRONT

Modern war, the supreme test of a nation's soundness, reveals strengths and hidden weaknesses. On the one hand, World War I triggered rapid growth of Russian machinery and chemical industries as well as of the industrial proletariat. On the other hand, it exposed Russia's inadequate transport, fumbling government, and chaotic finances. It revealed the tsar's incompetence and isolation, heightening contradictions between a disintegrating regime and a disgruntled public. The terrible weakness of the home front, more than military shortcomings, produced defeat and revolution.

The Economy

Agriculture suffered less than industry from the ill-considered mobilization of Russian manpower. Because of rural overpopulation and prewar wastage of labor, peasant farms were able to operate almost normally despite the loss of most male laborers. In some unoccupied provinces, acreage under cereal crops actually increased as women, children, and old men took up the slack. Large estates, which had produced most of the surplus for home and foreign markets, were harder hit because they could not obtain hired laborers, machinery, or spare parts. Despite increased demand, the total Russian grain and potato harvest and meat production fell by about one third during the war. At first, peasant soldiers ate better in the army than they had at home, but by 1917 the front was receiving less than half the grain it required. As commanders searched for food, their soldiers grew hungry and dissatisfied.

Even in 1917 Russia possessed enough food for both civilians and soldiers. The virtual cessation of food exports and diminished use of grain to manufacture vodka roughly balanced production declines. Government policy contributed to shortages; artificially low state prices for grain deprived farmers of production incentives; meanwhile, prices of manufactured goods they desired rose rapidly. Peasants, therefore, consumed more grain and brewed their own alcohol, while speculators hoarded grain and awaited higher prices. Because shipping foodstuffs to the cities was complicated by a worsening transport crisis, by 1917 the cities in the northern consuming provinces were hungry, while in the Ukraine and Siberia food was relatively abundant.

Transportation, the economy's weakest link, was nearing breakdown by 1917. The railroad system, which had barely met ordinary peacetime needs, had a low carrying capacity and inferior connections with seaports. (Only a narrow gauge line went to Archangel, and not until 1916 was a railroad built to the new port of Murmansk.) Wartime needs virtually monopolized a railway system further overburdened by the retreat in Poland and massive evacuation of civilians. Railroad cars and spare parts, formerly obtained largely in western Europe, became critically short. The government spent 1.5 billion rubles to improve the network and build additional lines; it ordered American railway equipment, but this arrived only late in 1917. On the eve of the March Revolution, a crisis in railroad transport worsened the problems of industry and food supply.

Because at first the government had no deferment system, industry was crippled by mobilization of irreplaceable skilled labor. Much of the labor force came to be composed of women, children, and war prisoners. Initially, many factory owners pursued "business as usual," and some curtailed production because of mobilization, disruption of foreign business connections, and expected decrease in domestic demand. Unprecedented need for munitions and war supplies placed an intolerable burden on industry, which could not get essential raw materials and fuel. (More shells were used in a month than in a year of the Russo-Japanese War.) The loss in 1915 of Russian Poland, the Empire's most industrialized region, reduced production by about one fifth. To be sure, certain branches of industry, spurred by war demand, grew rapidly: metalworking trebled in 1916 and chemicals expanded 250 percent. Rifle production in August 1916 was eleven times that of 1914 but was still insufficient.

Red tape and lack of government planning further complicated industry's problems. The official hands-off policy lasted until appalling

Hungry Petrograd in World War I *(Library of Congress)*

munitions shortages spurred public action. During 1915, industrialists, Duma members, zemstva, and municipalities formed military-industrial committees, which improved the supply picture greatly. But government action was too little and too late. By 1917, industrial production was falling sharply in a growing economic crisis. Yet Soviet accounts exaggerate the wartime growth of monopolies and trusts to support their claims that in Russia finance capitalism was maturing, thus preparing the way for socialism.

The war badly disrupted Russian foreign trade. In the first year, exports fell to about 15 percent of the prewar level and recovered later to only 30 percent. Imports, dropping sharply at first in 1916, were double the prewar value, mainly war supplies and equipment sent by the Allies through Siberian ports. Instead of the 47 million ruble export surplus of 1913, the wartime Russian trade deficit totalled some 2.5 billion rubles.

Incompetent government wartime financing damaged the Russian economy. At the outset, Russia seemed in better financial shape than in the Russo-Japanese War, but the Treasury expended as much in a month of World War I as in a year against Japan. A drastic fall in customs and railway receipts cut Treasury revenues, and an incredible blunder robbed it of the liquor tax. The Finance Minister ordered state liquor stores closed during mobilization and introduced legislation to raise liquor prices to combat drunkenness. A decree of August 1914 kept liquor stores closed throughout the war. Such pioneering in prohibition cost the Treasury about 700 million rubles annually, about 25 percent of its total revenue. Peasants brewed their own liquor, and illicit vodka sales brought huge profits to dealers but nothing to the Treasury. New wartime taxes barely covered this loss, and state revenues fell far short of war expenditures. Income and war profits taxes were low and introduced too late. Huge domestic and foreign loans and massive use of the printing press financed the war. Foreign nations, chiefly Britain, loaned Russia some 8 billion rubles, accelerating a sharp decline in the ruble's exchange value, which produced rampant inflation, loss of confidence in the currency, and a rapid rise in living costs. Russia grew ever more dependent financially upon its allies.

The serious economic strain of the war helped bring on revolution and made it more profound. The basic economic framework, especially of peasant agriculture, remained sound, but food supplies in the swollen cities of Petrograd and Moscow became increasingly inadequate as the overstrained railway system deteriorated. With paper rubles losing their value, there was little incentive for peasants to ship their grain to the cities. Although the masses' purchasing power rose, people found little to buy. Russian resources were wasted and misused by incompetent officials.

The Government

During the war, the tsarist regime revealed its inability to govern the country and disintegrated rapidly. Nicholas II, retaining faith in autocracy, orthodoxy, and nationality, failed to supply leadership; he believed that constitutional government was evil and that the public could not be allowed to help run Russia. Though interfering little with the Duma, he largely ignored it, and absorbed himself in family affairs and problems. Ever more dominated by Empress Alexandra, he and his family were estranged from the public and the bureaucracy. "The characteristic feature of the imperial family," noted a trusted minister, "is their inaccessibility to the outside world, and their atmosphere of mysticism." Empress Alexandra, who hated the Duma and liberal ministers with a passion, was largely responsible for this isolation, and as Rasputin's hold over her grew, she interfered more and more in state affairs. The most influential of several "men of God" to influence the superstitious empress, Rasputin had been introduced at court in November 1905. She found this semiliterate, debauched (his motto was: "Redemption through sin"!), but dynamic Siberian peasant indispensable to preserve her hemophiliac son, Alexis (born 1904), and the dynasty. Rasputin managed through hypnotism to stop the tsarevich's bleeding, and to the imperial couple he embodied the Russian people.

When Nicholas II took command of the army in September 1915, control over the government passed to the empress and Rasputin. Believing that she could save Russia from revolution, Alexandra relied completely on Rasputin, who lacked clear political aims; she was surrounded with unscrupulous, greedy adventurers. When the more competent, liberal ministers, appointed under public pressure early in 1915, protested Nicholas's decision to become army chief, the empress, to preserve autocracy, removed them from office. A nonentity, Boris Stürmer, was named premier. "A country cannot be lost whose sovereign is guided by a man of God," Alexandra wrote Nicholas. "Won't you come to the assistance of your hubby now that he is absent . . . ?" Nicholas queried. "You ought to be my eyes and ears there in the capital. . . . It rests with you to keep peace and harmony among the ministers."[4] The final disgraceful year of Romanov rule was marked by "ministerial leapfrog" as the empress and Rasputin shifted ministers with bewildering speed. The last premier, Prince N. D. Golitsyn, begged to be relieved of his tasks, which he did not know how to perform. Late in 1916, Rasputin's behavior became intolerable even to loyal monarchists. An ultraconservative Duma delegate, V. M. Purishkevich, and two grand dukes invited Rasputin to a banquet, fed him cake laced with cyanide, shot him, and finally drowned him in a canal. This was a terrible blow to the empress, but she and A. D. Protopopov continued to rule and hold seances to recall Rasputin from the dead. On the eve of the March Revolution, the government was inactive, divided, and in an advanced state of decay.

Meanwhile, the Duma had risen to unprecedented national leadership. After the war began, the Duma set up a provisional committee to aid the wounded and war sufferers and to coordinate its war work. At first, the Duma supported the government unconditionally, but early in 1915 it agitated with zemstvo and municipal representatives for a responsible ministry. That summer, about two thirds of the Duma, excluding the extreme Left and Right, formed a Progressive Bloc led by Kadets and

---

[4]*The Letters of the Tsar to the Tsaritsa, 1914–1917* (London, 1929), and *Letters of the Tsaritsa to the Tsar, 1914–1916* (London, 1923).

Octobrists, which advocated a government capable of winning public confidence, political amnesty, religious freedom, and freedom for trade unions. Though most of the ministers accepted this program, Premier Goremykin stubbornly rejected it as an illegal attempt to limit the autocrat's power. During 1916, the Duma's relations with the executive branch deteriorated sharply when deputies led by Miliukov accused the government and the tsarina of conspiring with the Germans. Censorship deleted the sharpest Duma attacks, but its debates were widely publicized, and it was winning a public following. The fatal weakness that prevented the Duma from representing and leading the Russian people in 1917 was an electoral process of indirect and weighted voting that favored the landed nobility. Thus, the majority of Russians were still not politically represented.

The Revolutionary Movement

The government's ineffectiveness and inability to win liberal support provided revolutionaries with a rare opportunity. In 1915, after the defeat in Galicia, strikes grew more numerous and continued to mount until the March Revolution, but the socialist parties in Russia remained too disorganized and fragmented to prepare a revolution. Their leaders mostly remained in exile in Siberia or Europe, out of touch with Russia. Initially, the SDs in the Duma denounced the war as the product of aggressive capitalism and urged the proletariat to oppose it. The Bolshevik deputies, more aggressively antiwar than the Mensheviks, were soon arrested, tried, and exiled to Siberia. Social Democrats abroad were divided by the war. Plekhanov, splitting with Lenin and the majority, urged Russian workers to fight against Prussian imperialism and with the Western democracies to final victory. Lenin, in his *Theses on War* (1914), written in Switzerland, denounced World War I as imperialist and exhorted Russian workers to help defeat tsarism and to turn the conflict into a civil war and prepare revolution. Lenin accused the Second International and its leader, Karl Kautsky, of betraying the proletariat by voting for a fratricidal war. At international socialist conferences at Zimmerwald (1915) and Kienthal (1916), the minority Leninist left urged a civil war of workers against all capitalist governments, but most European socialists supported their governments in World War I.

The Bolsheviks' Russian rivals were likewise divided. The Menshevik organizational committee in Switzerland, including Martov, Akselrod, and Martynov, denounced the war and advocated eventual revolution, but sought to restore unity to international socialism. Rather than favor Russia's defeat, they exhorted workers to exert pressure on all governments to conclude a democratic peace without annexations and indemnities. In Russia, an important Menshevik group around the publication *Our Dawn (Nasha Zaria)* advocated noncooperation with the regime without hampering the war effort; later it favored defense of Russia against invasion. The SRs, still dispirited, were split between a right actively supporting the war effort, Chernov's pacifist center, and a sizable left internationalist wing favoring defeat of tsarism. In Russia and abroad, socialists divided into three main groupings: patriots, centrists (defensists and pacifists), and defeatists advocating revolution.

Bolshevik organizations in Russia were tougher and more resilient than their rivals. The British scholar Leonard Schapiro claims that Bolshevik wartime activity was intermittent and ineffective, but Soviet accounts assert that the Bolsheviks led the workers' struggle against the war from the start, steadily expanded their organization, and followed Lenin's instructions. Although the police "liquidated" the Petrograd Committee 30 times and arrested more than 600 Bolsheviks, the party nonetheless expanded its membership and activities. By late 1916, the Bolsheviks, numbering perhaps 10,000, were led by A. G. Shliapnikov (Lenin's man), V. M. Molotov, and P. A. Zalutskii. Though Soviet historians exaggerate Bolshevik strength and leadership of the workers, the party did represent a considerable force ready, unlike Mensheviks and SRs, to exploit a revolutionary situation.

THE MARCH REVOLUTION

In five days—March 8–12, 1917 (February 23–27 Old Style),[5] a mass movement in Petrograd overturned the tsarist government. The eyewitness accounts of N. N. Sukhanov, a moderate socialist, and French ambassador Maurice Paléologue stress that it was spontaneous and not led by a party or organization. Western historians and early Soviet accounts, such as Trotskii's *History of the Russian Revolution*, accept this view, whereas Stalinist historians overstate Bolshevik leadership of the masses.

In previous months, the Petrograd strike movement had steadily gathered momentum. A strike by some workers at the Putilov factory, Russia's largest, became general, and on March 7 the management locked out the workers. Though the government and tsar had received numerous warnings of impending revolution (from foreign ambassadors and Duma president M. V. Rodzianko), they made no concessions. Nicholas II, confident that nothing unusual was afoot, left his palace at Tsarskoe Selo near Petrograd on March 7 for military headquarters at Mogilev.

---

[5]New Style dates, like those in western Europe, will be used from this point onward.

The authorities had a detailed plan to suppress an uprising: first the 3,500 police were to be used, then Cossacks with whips, and finally troops from the 150,000 man garrison. The plan, though later implemented, proved ineffective.

Revolution began in Petrograd on March 8, international women's day. In the large factories of Vyborg district, women in bread lines and strikers began spontaneous demonstrations, which spread to the Petersburg side. (See Map 7.1.) Women textile workers, the most downtrodden segment of the Petrograd proletariat, supplied the impetus. In the streets appeared placards with slogans: "Down with the war!" "Give us bread!" and "Down with autocracy!" That day, notes Sukhanov, "the movement in the streets became clearly defined going beyond the limits of the usual factory meetings. . . . The city was filled with rumors and a feeling of 'disorders.'" Fearing conflict with the authorities while the party was weak, the Bolsheviks, who controlled Vyborg Borough Committee, relegated revolution to the indefinite future, not realizing that one was in progress. In March, noted Trotskii, the higher the revolutionary leaders, the further they lagged behind the masses. Next day (March 9), continued Sukhanov, "the movement swept over Petersburg like a great flood. Nevskii Prospect [the main shopping street] and many squares in the center were crowded with workers." Mounted police were sent to disperse the demonstrations, then Cossacks were ordered out. They charged the crowds halfheartedly and often chatted amicably with the workers.

By March 10, "the entire civil population felt itself to be in one camp united against the enemy—the police and the military." Proclamations of the garrison commander, General Khabalov, threatening stern punishment for demonstrators, were torn down, police were disarmed or vanished from their posts, and factories and streetcars halted operation. Khabalov sent in troops, but the crowds, avoiding clashes with them, sought to win them over.

Early on Sunday, March 11, workers advanced from outlying districts toward Petrograd's center. Stopped at the bridges, they poured across the solidly frozen Neva River, dodging bullets. At the tsar's orders, Khabalov sent thousands of infantry into the streets. On Nevskii Prospect, soldiers fired on crowds, killing many and terrorizing the rest; that afternoon the Vyborg Committee considered calling off the strike. The critical moment of the revolution had come. In the evening, after police fired on a crowd, soldiers of the passing Pavlovskii Regiment mutinied, fired on the police, then returned to barracks, resolved not to fire again at strikers, and appealed to their comrades to join them. This was the military's first revolutionary act of 1917.

Tsar Nicholas and family, the tsar seated second from left *(Library of Congress)*

On the fifth day (March 12) workers streamed into the factories and in open meetings resolved to continue the struggle. Armed insurrection grew irresistibly from events, while the Bolshevik headquarters staff looked on despondently, leaving the districts and barracks to their own devices. Soldiers mutinied in growing numbers and joined crowds of workers.

New centers of authority sprang up before old ones had disappeared. The government had ordered the Duma prorogued, but on March 12 some members elected a Provisional Committee under the Duma president, Rodzianko, representing all groups except the Right, "to restore order in the capital and establish contact with public organizations and institutions." Reflecting views of the Progressive Bloc, the Committee sought to save the dynasty with a responsible ministry. Simultaneously, the Petrograd Soviet was reborn while mutinous troops freed worker and socialist leaders from the city's prisons. Proceeding with the troops to the Tauride Palace and aided by the trade union leaders, they created the Provisional Executive Committee of the Soviet of Workers' Deputies. At the Petrograd Soviet's first meeting that evening some 250 delegates were present, but new ones kept entering the noisy, chaotic session. No political party proposed a definite plan or took decisive leadership. When soldier deputies asked to join, the organization became the Soviet of Workers' and Soldiers' Deputies. Henceforth, this spontaneous fusion of popular elements led the revolution.

The tsarist government and dynasty came to a swift, unlamented end. By March 14, the entire garrison of Petrograd had defected, and the tsarist ministers were arrested. The Duma's Provisional Committee selected a Provisional Government from liberal members of the Progressive Bloc, the "government having public confidence," which the bourgeoisie had long sought. Learning of the deteriorating situation in Petrograd, Nicholas II decided to rejoin his family at Tsarskoe Selo, but railroad workers halted his train and forced him to return to Pskov, headquarters of the northern front. Behind events as usual, he agreed now to a responsible ministry, but his commanders unanimously advised abdication. On March 15, delegates Guchkov and Shulgin, sent to Pskov by the Provisional Committee, secured Nicholas's abdication in favor of his brother, Grand Duke Michael. Rumors of Michael's impending rule caused such indignation among the workers that he wisely renounced his claims and, on March 15, 1917, Romanov rule ended in Russia.

PROBLEM 1
Did World War I Cause the Collapse of Tsarism?

What is the relationship between the defeat of a regime in war and its overthrow? What is the connection between war and revolution? Did Germany's defeat of the Russian imperial army cause or trigger the collapse of tsarism in March 1917? Without war, was it likely that the regime could have survived in liberalized form, turning perhaps into something resembling the British constitutional monarchy? Or, conversely, did the war delay tsarist collapse by generating a final outburst of Russian patriotism? Was the regime's disintegration so far advanced in 1914 that it would soon have collapsed in any case? Were social and political tensions rising or declining in Russia in 1914? Finally, could either the tsarist regime, without war or a liberal successor, have confronted 20th-century problems successfully?

THE SOVIET POSITION

History of the Communist Party of the Soviet Union (Moscow, 1960). This official Soviet account, written during the rule of N. S. Khrushchev, emphasizes the approaching collapse of tsarist Russia and the revolutionary upsurge just before World War I, as well as the growing strength and cohesion of the Bolsheviks in leading the discontented masses:

The cost of living was rising, and the position of the worker was deteriorating. An official industrial survey revealed that while annual wages averaged 246 rubles, annual profit per worker averaged 252 rubles. . . . Incredible poverty reigned in the countryside. Stolypin's agrarian policy had, as its direct result, the mass impoverishment of the peasants and enrichment of the kulak [better-off peasants] bloodsuckers. . . . The Russian countryside presented a picture of omnipotent feudal landlords, bigger and richer kulak farms, the impoverishment of a vast mass of middle peasants, and a substantially increased mass of landless peasants. . . . The situation left no doubt whatever that the Stolypin policy had collapsed.

Its collapse brought out more saliently than ever the profound contradictions throughout Russia's social and political system. It demonstrated anew that the tsarist government was incapable of solving the country's basic social and economic problems. . . . Poverty, oppression, lack of human rights, humiliating indignities imposed on the people—all this, Lenin emphasized, was in crying contradiction to the state of the country's productive forces and to the degree of political understanding and demands of the masses. . . . Only a new revolution could save Russia. . . .

The Bolsheviks' prediction that a new revolutionary upsurge was inevitable proved to be true. Everywhere there was growing discontent and indignation among the people. The workers saw in the Bolshevik revolutionary slogans a clear-cut expression of their own aspirations. . . . Of all the political parties then active in Russia, only the Bolsheviks had a platform that fully accorded with the interests of the working class and the people generally. . . .

The workers' movement continued to grow in scope and strength. There were over one million strikers in 1912, and 1,272,000 in 1913. Economic struggles were intertwined with political ones and culminated in mass revolutionary strikes. The working class went over to the offensive against the capitalists and the tsarist monarchy. . . . In 1910–1914, according to patently minimized figures, there were over 13,000 peasant outbreaks, in which many manor houses and kulak farmsteads were destroyed. . . . The unrest spread to the tsarist army. . . . Mutiny was brewing in the Baltic and Black Sea fleets. A new revolution was maturing in Russia.

Together with the rise of the working-class movement, the party of the working class, the Bolshevik Party, grew and gained in strength. . . . Amidst the difficulties created by their illegal status, the Bolsheviks *reestablished a mass party*, firmly led and guided by its Central Committee. . . . Everywhere—in mass strikes, street demonstrations, factory gate meetings—the Bolsheviks emphasized that revolution was the only way out, and put forward slogans expressing the people's longings: a democratic republic, an eight-hour working day, confiscation of the landed estates in favor of the peasants.

Meanwhile the waves of the working-class movement rose higher and higher. In the first half of 1914 about 1,500,000 workers were involved in strikes. . . . On July 3 the police opened fire on a workers' meeting at the Putilov Works in St. Petersburg. A wave of indignation swept over the country. The St. Petersburg Bolshevik Committee called for immediate strike action. . . . Demonstrations began in protest against the actions of the tsarist authorities and the war, which everyone felt was about to break out. The strike wave spread to Moscow; barricades were thrown up in St. Petersburg, Baku, and Lodz.

Russia was faced with a revolutionary crisis. The landlords and capitalists were accusing each other of inability to put out the flames of revolution. . . . The tsarist government adopted "emergency" measures, the capital was turned into a veritable military camp. . . . The advance of the revolution was interrupted by the outbreak of the world war (pp. 163–164, 167, 169–170, 173, 175–176, 182–183).

THE PESSIMISTS' VIEW

Leopold Haimson in "The Problem of Social Stability in Urban Russia, 1905–1917, II," *Slavic Review, 24,* no. 1 (March 1965), presents an interesting analysis of conditions in Russia on the eve of World War I in some ways refuting and in others supporting the preceding Soviet assertions:

The four-day interval between the last gasps of the Petersburg strike and the outbreak of war may not altogether dispose of the thesis of Soviet historians that only the war prevented the strike movement of July, 1914, from turning into a decisive attack against the autocracy. . . . Yet surely much of the conviction of this argument pales in the light of the two glaring sources of political weakness that the strike revealed from its very inception . . . the failure of the clashes in St. Petersburg to set off anything like the all-national political strike, which even the Bolshevik leaders had considered . . . a necessary condition for the armed assault against the autocracy . . . [and] the inability of the Petersburg workers to mobilize, in time, active support among other groups in society. . . . No demonstrations, no public meetings, no collective petitions—no expressions of solidarity even barely comparable to those that Bloody Sunday had evoked were now aroused. . . . Thus, . . . the most important source of the political impotence revealed by the Petersburg strike was precisely the one that made for its "monstrous" revolutionary explosiveness: the sense of isolation, of psychological distance, that separated the Petersburg workers from educated, privileged society. . . . The crude representations to be found in recent Soviet writings of the "revolutionary situation" already at hand in July, 1914, can hardly be sustained. Yet when one views the political and social tensions evident in Russian society in 1914 in a wider framework and in broader perspective, any flat-footed statement of the case for stabilization appears at least equally shaky. . . .

By July, 1914, along with a polarization between workers and educated, privileged society . . . , a second process of polarization—this one between the vast bulk of privileged society and the tsarist regime—appeared almost equally advanced. Unfolding largely detached from the rising wave of the labor movement, this second process could not affect its character and temper but was calculated to add a probably decisive weight to the pressure against the dikes of existing authority. By 1914, this second polarization had progressed to the point where even the most moderate spokesmen of liberal opinion were stating publicly, in the Duma and in the press, that an impasse had been reached between the state power and public opinion, which some argued could be resolved only by a revolution of the left or of the right. . . .

Indeed, by the beginning of 1914 any hope of avoiding a revolutionary crisis appeared to be evaporating even among the more moderate representatives of liberal opinion. Under the impact of the blind suicidal course pursued by the government and its handful of supporters, the Octobrist Party had split at the seams. . . .

Indeed, many signs of economic and social progress could be found in the Russian provinces of the year 1914—the introduction of new crops, new techniques and forms of organization in agriculture, and the industrialization of the countryside; growing literacy among the lower strata and invigorated cultural life among the upper strata of provincial society. But no more than in the major cities were these signs of progress and changes in the localities to be viewed as evidence of the achievement or indeed the promise of greater social stability. . . . "Official" and "unofficial" Russia had now turned into two worlds completely sealed off one from the other . . . (pp. 1, 2, 3, 8, 9, 10).

THE OPTIMISTS' VIEW

Leonard Schapiro, a British historian, in *The Communist Party of the Soviet Union* (New York, Random House, 1959) stresses the weakness and disorganization of the Bolsheviks on the eve of World War I, providing a sharp contrast to Soviet accounts:

The Bolsheviks, or those of them who supported Lenin, could now [1914] no longer persist in their policy of maintaining the split [with the Mensheviks] at all costs. . . . There was also more unity now on the non-Bolshevik side than ever before. . . . If Lenin were isolated in his intransigence, there was every chance that many of his "conciliator" followers, who had rejoined him in 1912, would break away again. The Bolshevik organization was, moreover, in a poor state in 1914, as compared with 1912. The underground committees were disrupted. There were no funds, and the circulation of *Pravda* had fallen drastically under the impact of the split in the Duma "fraction."

Intensive propaganda for unity now began inside Russia. The Mensheviks and organizations supporting them drew up an appeal to the Russian workers, blaming the Bolsheviks for the split, and urging support for the efforts of the International to reunite the whole party. But it was too late. War broke out . . . and before long, the Russian social democrats were rent asunder by new and even less reconcilable dissensions [pp. 139–140].

Alexander Gerschenkron, an American economic historian, argues that Russia was following the path that western Europe had taken earlier and suggests that without war, it would have avoided revolution:

Russia before the First World War was still a relatively backward country by any quantitative criterion. . . . Nevertheless . . . Russia seemed to duplicate what had happened in Germany in the last decades of the 19th century [in industrial development]. One might surmise that in the absence of the war Russia would have continued on the road of progressive westernization. . . . The likelihood that the transformation in agriculture would have gone on at an accelerated speed is very great. . . .

. . . As one compares the situation in the years before 1914 with that of the 90s, striking differences are obvious. In the earlier period, the very process of industrialization with its powerful confiscatory pressures upon the peasantry kept adding . . . to the feeling of resentment and discontent until the outbreak of large-scale disorders became almost inevitable. The industrial prosperity of the following period [1906–1914] had no comparable effects, however. Modest as the improvements in the situation of peasants were, they were undeniable and widely diffused. Those improvements followed rather than preceded a revolution, and accordingly tended to contribute to a relaxation of tension. . . .

Similarly, the economic position of labor was clearly improving. . . . There is little doubt that the Russian labor movement of those years was slowly turning toward revision and trade-unionist lines. As was true in the West, the struggles for general and equal franchise to the Duma and for a cabinet responsible to the Duma, which probably would have occurred sooner or later, may well have further accentuated this development. . . .

. . . It seems plausible to say that Russia on the eve of the war was well on the way toward a westernization or, perhaps more precisely, a Germanization of its industrial growth ("Patterns of Economic Development," in C. Black, *The Transformation of Russian Society* [Cambridge, Mass., 1960], in excerpts, pp. 57–61).

CONCLUSION

Neither "optimists" nor "pessimists" have proved their case fully, yet both present valid arguments. Unquestionably, there was serious social tension and a major worker upsurge early in 1914, yet to call this a

Alexander II reforms

"revolutionary situation" appears as misleading as to claim that one existed in 1861. The workers remained largely isolated from the rest of Russian society; their movement was confined mainly to the larger cities. To be sure, the alienation of educated society from a narrow-minded regime was evident and growing, as was fragmentation of the political parties (notably Kadets and Octobrists). On the other hand, Russia for the first time was experiencing self-sustaining industrial and agricultural growth, as well as an unparalleled degree of prosperity.

Suggested Additional Reading

BERNSTEIN, H. *The Willy-Nicky Correspondence, 1914–17* (New York, 1918).

BRUSSILOV, A. A. *A Soldier's Notebook, 1914–18* (Westport, Conn., 1971).

BUCHANAN, G. W. *My Mission to Russia,* 2 vols. (New York and London, 1923).

CHERNIAVSKY, M. *Prologue to Revolution . . . 1915* (Englewood Cliffs, N.J., 1967).

DE JONG, ALEX. *The Life and Times of Grigorii Rasputin* (New York, 1982).

EDELMAN, R. *Gentry Politics on the Eve of the Russian Revolution* (Brunswick, N.J., 1980).

FLORINSKY, M. T. *The End of the Russian Empire* (New Haven, Conn., 1931).

FRANCIS, S. R. *Russia from the American Embassy* (New York, 1971).

GOLDER, F. *Documents of Russian History, 1914–17* (New York, 1927).

GOLOVIN, N. N. *The Russian Army in the World War* (New Haven, Conn., 1931).

GRAYSON, B. L. *Russian-American Relations in World War I* (New York, 1979).

GRONSKY, P. P., and N. I. ASTROV. *The War and the Russian Government* (New Haven, Conn., 1929).

GURKO, V. I. *War and Revolution in Russia, 1914–1917* (New York, 1919).

HASEGAWA, T. *The February Revolution: Petrograd 1917* (Seattle, 1981).

KATKOV, GEORGE. *Russia 1917: The February Revolution* (New York, 1967).

KNOX, A. *With the Russian Army: 1914–1917* (New York, 1921).

KOHN, S. *The Cost of the War to Russia . . .* (New Haven, Conn., 1932).

MANDEL, DAVID. *The Petrograd Workers and the Fall of the Old Regime* (New York, 1984).

MASSIE, R. *Nicholas and Alexandra* (New York, 1967).

MICHELSON, A. M., et al. *Russian Finance During the War* (New Haven, Conn., 1928).

NOLDE, B. E. *Russia in the Economic War* (New Haven, Conn., 1928).

ODINETS, D. M., and P. J. NOVGORODTSEV. *Russian Schools and Universities in the World War* (New Haven, Conn., 1929).

PALEOLOGUE, M. *An Ambassador's Memoirs,* 3 vols. (New York, 1972).

PARES, BERNARD. *The Fall of the Russian Monarchy . . .* (New York, 1939; reprint, New York, 1961).

———., ed. *The Letters of the Tsar to the Tsaritsa, 1914–1917* (London, 1929).

———. *The Letters of the Tsaritsa to the Tsar . . .* (London, 1923).

PAVLOVSKY, G. *Agricultural Russia on the Eve of Revolution* (London, 1930).

PEARSON, R. *The Russian Moderates and the Crisis of Tsarism, 1914–1917* (New York, 1977).

POLNER, T. I., et al. *Russian Local Government During the War and the Union of Zemstvos* (New Haven, Conn., 1930).

PURISHKEVICH, V. M. *The Murder of Rasputin*, ed. M. Shaw (Ann Arbor, Mich., 1985).

RODZIANKO, M. V. *The Reign of Rasputin* (London, 1927).

RUTHERFORD, W. *The Russian Army in World War I* (London, 1975).

SENN, A. E. *The Russian Revolution in Switzerland* (Madison, Wisc., 1971).

SIEGELBAUM, L. H. *The Politics of Industrial Mobilization in Russia, 1914–1917* (New York, 1983).

SMITH, C. J. *The Russian Struggle for Power, 1914–17* (New York, 1956).

SOLZHENITSYN, A. *August 1914* (New York, 1972). (Historical novel.)

STONE, N. *The Eastern Front* (New York, 1975).

STRUVE, P. B., et al. *Food Supply in Russia During the War* (New Haven, Conn., 1930).

WILDMAN, A. K. *The End of the Russian Imperial Army . . .* (Princeton, N.J., 1979).

ZAGORSKY, S. O. *State Control of Industry in Russia During the War* (New Haven, Conn., 1928).

CHAPTER SEVEN

FROM MARCH TO NOVEMBER 1917

The politically freest, most exciting year in Russian history was 1917, and it has generated more controversy than any other. Bolshevik victory in November brought to power an intransigent, antiliberal element. Ever since 1917, Soviet and Western historians have debated why the Bolsheviks won and what it signified for humankind. The Soviet view, now more flexible and sophisticated, presents Bolshevik victory as the inevitable result of historical development. The Bolsheviks, it notes, assumed power for the proletariat under Lenin, their revered leader. A few Western historians, such as E. H. Carr, agree that the Bolsheviks were bound to triumph because of their clear purpose and determination. Some Western accounts, especially Robert Daniels's *Red October,* stress spontaneity and the role of chance in 1917. Others cite conspiracy as the decisive factor, but most Western histories reject an explanation of the outcome on the basis of a single factor.

How do the Revolutions of March and November 1917 compare with one another? Were the events and outcome in 1917 predetermined? Did the Provisional Government's liberal democratic experiment founder because of Russia's weak constitutional tradition, because it failed to keep its promises, or because it kept Russia in World War I? What produced Bolshevik victory: Lenin's and Trotskii's leadership, superior organization, an attractive program, mass action, or a combination of these elements? Did the Bolsheviks win because of their strengths or their opponents' weaknesses and blunders?

THE "DUAL POWER"

In March 1917, a "Dual Power," to use Trotskii's phrase, succeeded tsarism. Dual power, he notes, does not necessarily imply equal division of authority or a formal equilibrium, and it arises from class conflict in a revolutionary period when hostile classes rely upon incompatible ruling institutions—one outlived, the other developing. The Provisional Government, argued Trotskii, represented a Russian bourgeoisie too weak to govern long; the Petrograd Soviet was a proletarian organ, which surrendered power initially to the bourgeoisie. Both convened, at first, in the Tauride Palace, where they competed for loyalty and popular support.

The Provisional Government represented landed and industrial wealth, privilege, and educated society. Its Premier and Interior Minister, Prince G. E. Lvov, a distinguished aristocrat and wealthy landowner, had been a prominent zemstvo leader and member of the right wing of the Kadet party. "I believe in the great heart of the Russian people filled with love for their fellow men. I believe in this fountain of truth, verity, and freedom," declared this idealistic Slavophile liberal. "An illustrious but notoriously empty spot," commented Trotskii. Lvov's government, despite good intentions, was poorly equipped to maintain order or to govern Russia. Its dominant figure and real brains was Foreign Minister Paul Miliukov, the erudite but unrealistic history professor who had led the Kadet Party since 1905. War Minister Alexander I. Guchkov, a big Moscow industrialist, strove to preserve army discipline and create reliable military support for the regime. Finance Minister M. I. Tereshchenko owned property worth some 80 million rubles, spoke excellent French, and was a ballet connoisseur. Only A. F. Kerenskii, Minister of Justice and leader of the leftist Labor Group, represented even vaguely those who had unseated the tsar. A young lawyer of rare oratorical power and febrile energy, he believed fully in the revolution and his own destiny, but Kerenskii, noted Trotskii, "merely hung around the revolution." The Petrograd Soviet had barred its members from the Government, but Kerenskii, a vice-chairman of the Soviet, after a dramatic speech, secured permission to enter the cabinet.

A. F. Kerenskii (1881–1970) *(Library of Congress)*

This liberal Provisional Government was to exercise authority only until a democratically elected constituent assembly could establish a permanent regime. "Its orders," noted War Minister Guchkov, are "executed only insofar as this is permitted by the Soviet . . . which holds in its hand the most important elements of actual power such as troops, railroads, the postal and telegraph service." The Provisional Government pledged to prepare national elections with all possible speed, and the constituent assembly became an article of faith—the holy grail of Russian democracy—for moderates and revolutionaries, including Bolsheviks. Meanwhile the Government took what steps it could toward democracy by granting full freedom of speech, press, assembly, and religion and equality to all citizens. An amnesty released political prisoners and allowed exiles to return. Provincial governors were abolished, and local governmental officials were to be elected. Unprecedented freedom and euphoria prevailed in Russia. All restrictive legislation imposed on national and religious minorities under tsarism was abolished, and the administration of the borderlands was placed mostly in local hands.

The Petrograd Soviet, hastily formed and ill-defined in membership, powers, and procedure, promptly took charge in the capital and coordinated other soviets that sprang up throughout Russia. On March 15, it had 1,300 members; a week later soldier delegates swelled the number to more than 3,000. Even when reduced to its former size, it was too large and noisy to do much real business. A small Executive Committee, chaired by the Menshevik N. S. Chkheidze, was chosen to reach and implement important decisions. Moderate socialists dominated it and the Soviet, with Bolsheviks in opposition. At first, party affiliations were unimportant in the Soviet.

The drama of Russia in 1917 was captured wonderfully by this eyewitness, the radical American journalist John Reed:

> Lectures, debates, speeches—in theatres, circuses, schoolhouses, clubs, Soviet meeting-rooms, Union headquarters, barracks. . . . Meetings in the trenches at the front, in village squares, factories. . . . What a marvellous sight to see the Putilov factory pour out its 40,000 to listen to Social Democrats, Socialist Revolutionaries, Anarchists, anybody, whatever they had to say, as long as they would talk! For months in Petrograd, and all over Russia, every street-corner was a public tribune.[1]

The Soviet approved the Government's initial program and measures, but their relations soon grew strained over control of the army and foreign policy. On March 14, the Soviet's army section issued Order No. 1, which authorized all army units to elect soldier committees and send representatives to the Soviet. Enlisted men were to obey their officers and the Government only if their orders did not conflict with the Soviet. This Order, confirmed most reluctantly by War Minister Guchkov, prevented the Government from controlling the army and further undermined army discipline. Meanwhile, Foreign Minister Miliukov insisted that the March Revolution had not changed Russian foreign policy: Russia would fulfill its commitments to the Allies and fight for "lasting peace through victory." Allied governments and the United States, which had entered the war in April, quickly recognized the Provisional Government and supplied it generously with war credits. Russia, insisted Miliukov, must obtain Constantinople and the Straits and "merge the Ukrainian provinces of Austria-Hungary with Russia." This expansionist program based on secret inter-Allied treaties provoked a Soviet appeal, on March 27, to

---

[1]John Reed, *Ten Days That Shook the World* (New York, 1987), p. 11.

Map 7.1 *Petrograd, 1917*

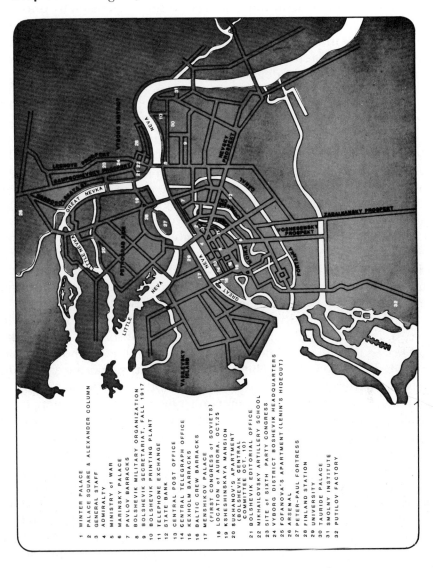

1 WINTER PALACE
2 PALACE SQUARE & ALEXANDER COLUMN
3 GENERAL STAFF
4 ADMIRALTY
5 MINISTRY of WAR
6 MARINSKY PALACE
7 PAVLOV BARRACKS
8 BOLSHEVIK MILITARY ORGANIZATION
9 BOLSHEVIK SECRETARIAT, FALL 1917
10 BOLSHEVIK PRINTING PLANT
11 TELEPHONE EXCHANGE
12 STATE BANK
13 CENTRAL POST OFFICE
14 CENTRAL TELEGRAPH OFFICE
15 KEXHOLM BARRACKS
16 BALTIC CREW BARRACKS
17 MENSHIKOV PALACE
    (FIRST CONGRESS of SOVIETS)
18 LOCATION of AURORA, OCT.25
19 KSHESHINSKAYA MANSION
20 SUKHANOV'S APARTMENT
    (BOLSHEVIK CENTRAL
    COMMITTEE OCT.10)
21 BOLSHEVIK EDITORIAL OFFICE
22 MIKHAILOVSKY ARTILLERY SCHOOL
23 SITE of SIXTH PARTY CONGRESS
24 VYBORG DISTRICT BOSHEVIK HEADQUARTERS
25 FOFANOVA'S APARTMENT (LENIN'S HIDEOUT)
26 ARSENAL
27 PETER-PAUL FORTRESS
28 FINLAND STATION
29 UNIVERSITY
30 TAURIDE PALACE
31 SMOLNY INSTITUTE
32 PUTILOV FACTORY

European peoples to overthrow their imperialist governments and achieve a just and democratic peace "without annexations and indemnities." Meanwhile, until peace came, the Russian Revolution must defend itself. Within the Government, Miliukov and Guchkov contended with ministers who repudiated an imperialist peace, though for the time being an atmosphere of democratic unity muted these differences.

THE BOLSHEVIKS GAIN LEADERS AND A PROGRAM

Moderates controlled the Government and Soviet, but the Bolsheviks grew into a formidable opposition. Late in March, L. B. Kamenev and Joseph Stalin (I. V. Djugashvili) returned to Petrograd from Siberian exile. Briefly turning the Bolsheviks to the right, they pledged to support the Provisional Government in a defensive struggle against Germany. (Later Stalin blamed Kamenev for this rightist orientation, claiming that he had always opposed the Provisional Government and the war.) Though described by N. N. Sukhanov in 1917 as "a grey blur," Stalin was an able organizer and contributed from behind the scenes to Bolshevik victory, but neither he nor Kamenev supplied dynamic leadership.

Lenin's return to Russia in mid-April proved vital to Bolshevik success. In Switzerland, directing a small group of socialist émigrés, he had feared that he would not live to see the revolution. Though taken unaware by the March Revolution, he grasped its significance immediately and telegraphed his party comrades: "Our tactic: absolute lack of confidence, no support to the new Government. . . ." His "Letters from Afar" to *Pravda*, the Bolshevik newspaper, envisioned an armed seizure of power by the proletariat fused with an armed populace. To arrange his return home, Lenin negotiated through Swiss socialists with the German government, which readily consented to send home socialists dedicated to overthrowing a pro-Allied government and ending Russia's participation in the war. Temporary identity of interests and even Lenin's receipt of "German gold," though, does not prove his opponent's assertion that he was a German agent. Lenin was prepared to accept help from whatever source (only the Germans provided it) without compromising his principles or altering his goals. He and other Russian socialist exiles passed through Germany on a sealed train.

At Petrograd's Finland Station on April 16, the Bolsheviks gave Lenin a triumphal welcome, although he had been in neither the Soviet nor the Duma. The Soviet's chairman, Chkheidze, greeted him: "We think that the principal task of the revolutionary democracy is now the defense of the revolution from any encroachment, either from within or without . . . , the closing of democratic ranks. We hope that you will pursue these goals together with us." Lenin, disregarding Chkheidze, turned to the entire Soviet delegation:

> Dear Comrades, Soldiers, Sailors and Workers! I am happy to greet in your persons the victorious Russian revolution, and greet you as the vanguard of the worldwide proletarian army. . . . The piratical imperialist war is the beginning of civil war throughout Europe. . . . The worldwide socialist revolution has already dawned. . . . Germany is seething. . . . Any day now the whole of European capitalism may crash. The Russian revolution accomplished by you has prepared the way and opened a new epoch. Long live the worldwide socialist revolution.[2]

Lenin's exhortation caused dismay and incredulity among most Bolshevik leaders who were moving toward accommodation with the Provisional Government.

The following day—April 17—Lenin presented a series of proposals, known as his "April Theses," to the Petrograd Bolshevik Committee. "The basic question," explained Lenin, "is our attitude toward the war." Because the new Provisional Government favored continuing in World War I, he condemned it as "imperialistic through and through." There must be "no support for the Provisional Government; exposure of the utter falsity of all its promises." He added, "Not the slightest concession must be made to 'revolutionary defensism'! . . . since the war on Russia's part remains a predatory imperialist war. . . . Russians must transform this 'imperialist war' into a civil war against capitalism." According to Lenin, Russia was moving from the first, bourgeois, stage of the revolution to its second stage, "which is to place power in the hands of the proletariat and the poorest strata of the peasantry. . . ." The Bolsheviks must tell the masses that the Soviet of Workers' Deputies was "the only possible form of revolutionary government." Spurning western parliamentary democracy, Lenin advocated a republic of soviets of workers and peasant deputies. The police, army, and bureaucracy were to be abolished. Private lands must be confiscated and all land in Russia nationalized. All banks should be merged into one general national bank under the soviet. Bolsheviks should seize the initiative to form a revolutionary international. However, the Petrograd Committee rejected Lenin's "April Theses" 13 to 2, *Pravda* dubbed them "unacceptable," and Plekhanov, the father of Russian Marxism, declared: "A man who talks such nonsense is not dangerous." Lenin argued, cajoled, and persuaded until three weeks later an all-Russian Bolshevik conference approved his

---

[2]N. Sukhanov, *The Russian Revolution* (New York, 1962), vol. 1, pp. 272–273.

program by a wide margin. The Bolsheviks took over the initial soviet program: bread, land, and peace.

In May, Leon Trotskii returned from exile in New York and, in July, joined the Bolsheviks with his followers. Lenin had adopted (or stolen) Trotskii's idea of permanent revolution: Instead of awaiting full development of capitalism, Russia could move directly to socialism by revolution. When Trotskii, the most effective orator of the Revolution, joined Lenin, its ablest strategist and organizer, the Bolsheviks gained a great advantage in leadership.

THE REVOLUTION MOVES LEFT (MAY–JULY)

As Lenin won control of the Bolsheviks, a severe crisis shook the Provisional Government. It was touched off by Foreign Minister Miliukov's May 1st Note, which rejected a separate peace, and pledged Russia would fight to the end to secure "sanctions and guarantees." The profoundly patriotic Kadet Party, led by Miliukov, wished almost unanimously to fight to final victory. This stance alienated the Kadets from war-weary soldiers and workers. The Soviet viewed Miliukov's Note as a thin disguise for an imperialist peace, notably seizure of the Turkish Straits, which he had advocated repeatedly. Massive, spontaneous demonstrations of workers and soldiers erupted in Petrograd and Moscow with slogans: "Down with Miliukov!" "Down with the Provisional Government!" The demonstrators could have overturned the Government, but when the latter disavowed the Note, the Soviet prohibited further demonstrations. Nonetheless, Miliukov, disliked for his cool arrogance, and Guchkov, the conservative war minister, were forced to resign.

Since the Soviet's Executive Committee now permitted member parties to join the Provisional Government, the cabinet was reorganized as a coalition of nine nonsocialist (mainly Kadet) and six socialist ministers. Its dominant figure was Alexander Kerenskii, a right-wing SR, as war and navy minister. Victor Chernov, the SRs chief ideologist, became minister of agriculture. Supported by most peasants and many soldiers, the SRs retained, by far, the largest popular following, but they were starting to disintegrate. During 1917, they achieved none of their social program, especially drastic land reform. Their mass support became dissatisfied with the leadership. By entering the Government, moderate socialists became vulnerable to Bolshevik criticism of their inaction, mistakes, and continuation of the war. The extremist Bolsheviks, like the Jacobins (radicals in the French Revolution), profited from the moderates' passivity and incompetence as rulers and war leaders.

The coalition ministry's policies differed little from its predecessor's. Caught between Allied insistence upon a total military effort and Soviet pressure for a democratic peace, the Government issued vague statements to mask internal divisions. War Minister Kerenskii, Foreign Minister Tereshchenko, and Premier Lvov advocated an active war role. Responding to French pleas to tie down German troops in the east, Kerenskii prepared a great offensive in Galicia, hoping thereby to revive army morale, provide the regime with reliable troops, and secure Allied financial and political support. A patriot and a democrat, he believed that a free Russia was linked indissolubly with the Allied cause. Conservatives of the Kadet Party expected an offensive to restore order in Russia and perhaps bring military victory. Kerenskii toured the front to whip up patriotic enthusiasm. Special volunteer "shock battalions" were recruited to lead the way. Kerenskii's oratory was applauded warmly, but it had few lasting effects on the war-weary Russian troops.

In June 1917, moderate socialists seemed securely in control of the Government and the Soviet. When the first all-Russian Congress of Soviets opened on June 16, the Bolsheviks and their allies had only 137 out of 1,000 delegates. The Menshevik Tseretelli told the delegates that the Government was safe; no party in Russia would say: "Give us power!" To his surprise Lenin shouted: "Yes, there is one!" and attacked the bourgeoisie, demanding that the war be ended and capitalist aid repudiated. The moderate majority disregarded Lenin, but in the factories Bolshevik strength and worker radicalism were rising. On June 23, the Bolsheviks, pressed by workers and soldiers, agreed to lead a demonstration against the Government, but the next day the Congress of Soviets called it off. A week later, however, a demonstration organized by the Congress to display revolutionary unity was dominated by such Bolshevik slogans as "End the war!" The Bolsheviks, not the Soviet, now clearly led the Petrograd workers.

On July 1, Kerenskii's much heralded offensive began in Galicia with a great artillery barrage. After initial gains against the Austrians, it was halted after 12 days, and on July 19 German and Austrian forces counterattacked and easily broke through Russian lines. Demoralized Russian troops threw down their weapons and fled. Their panicky retreat ended only after all Galicia had been lost and enemy attacks ceased. On July 25, the Government restored the death penalty for desertion, but this action failed to revive the army's will to fight.

As the Russian offensive faltered, disorders broke out in Petrograd (July 16–18), following the resignation from the Provisional Government of four Kadet ministers, who opposed the cabinet's decision to grant demands for autonomy by the Ukrainian *Rada* (assembly). Troops of the garrison, sailors from the Kronstadt naval base, and factory workers clashed with Government supporters. The Bolshevik-dominated First Machine Gun Regiment, after refusing to leave for the front, began the demonstrations. Some 500,000 soldiers and workers marched on the Tauride Palace to force the Soviet to assume power. Radical Bolsheviks from the Military Organization and Petersburg Committee supported this movement, but more cautious Central Committee leaders considered it premature. The Bolshevik Party finally decided, reluctantly, to lead the demonstration. The Soviet's Executive Committee, though frightened, refused to take power or implement Bolshevik demands. Without clear purpose, the demonstrators, after roughing up some ministers, gradually dispersed and the July Days petered out. Later, Stalin explained the curious Bolshevik tactics: "We could have seized power [in Petrograd] . . . , but against us would have risen the fronts, the provinces, the soviets. Without support in the provinces, our government would have been without hands and feet." Lenin, too, believed that national support for the Bolsheviks was still inadequate. Their unwillingness to lead damaged the Bolsheviks temporarily among militant soldiers and workers.

KORNILOV AND THE RIGHTWARD SHIFT (JULY–SEPTEMBER)

As the July Days ended, the Provisional Government and Petrograd Soviet regained control. Guards regiments in Petrograd, hearing that Lenin was a German agent, rallied to the Government, and a reaction set in against the Bolsheviks as newspapers published documents accusing their leaders of treason. The Government disarmed the First Machine Gun Regiment and occupied Bolshevik headquarters. The next day, troops searched *Pravda*'s editorial office, wrecked its press, and closed down Bolshevik newspapers. The Bolshevik Military Organization wished to resist, but the workers were cowed. Realizing that the party had suffered a severe setback, Lenin convinced the Central Committee of the need to retreat. He considered standing trial to refute the Government charges, but fearing that he might be murdered in prison, Lenin took refuge in Finland. Trotskii and some other Bolshevik leaders were arrested.

Kerenskii, reshuffling the coalition cabinet on July 25, replaced Prince Lvov as premier. Mensheviks and SRs held most ministerial posts, but the moderate Government failed to implement the measures that the impatient masses demanded. Kerenskii, the democrat, began his rule with halfhearted repression. Insurgent troops and civilians mostly retained their arms, and though the central Bolshevik apparatus was shaken, Bolshevik support in Petrograd's factories continued to grow. By mid-August, the Bolshevik Party numbered about 200,000 members, compared with 80,000 in April, and had outstripped the Mensheviks, whose support declined partly because of the inactivity of the Provisional Government.

Early in August, Kerenskii again reshuffled his cabinet and moved into the Winter Palace, seat of the tsars. To build support for his shaky regime before the elections to the Constituent Assembly, he convened the Moscow State Conference drawn from Russia's elite: members of the four Dumas, the soviets, the professions, and army leaders. The Bolsheviks boycotted the Conference (August 26–28) and sought to embarrass it with a general strike in Moscow. Instead of strengthening Kerenskii's government, the Conference exposed the chasm between conservatives and moderate socialists.

As the Moscow State Conference met, General Lavr Kornilov emerged as leader of the conservatives. The son of a Siberian Cossack with a reputation for bravery and rigid discipline, he had been appointed commander in chief of the army by Kerenskii on July 31. Though Kornilov lacked political acumen (General Alekseev described him as "a man with the heart of a lion and the brains of a sheep"), he headed a movement of bourgeoisie, landowners, and the military organized by Rodzianko and Miliukov. About August 20, he ordered his Cossacks and Caucasian Wild Division to take up positions within striking distance of Moscow and Petrograd. After talking with Kerenskii, Kornilov told his chief of staff: "It is time to hang the German supporters and spies with Lenin at their head and to disperse the Soviet . . . once and for all." When Kornilov entered the chamber of the Moscow State Conference, the Right cheered wildly; the Left applauded Kerenskii with equal warmth. The Conference convinced Kornilov that Kerenskii was too weak to restore order in Russia. Supported by conservative Duma leaders, financiers, and the Allied powers, Kornilov pushed plans to march on Petrograd and crush the revolution. Learning of the conspiracy, Kerenskii secured authorization from socialist members of his cabinet to take emergency measures, but the Kadet ministers resigned. Kerenskii's dismissal of Kornilov as commander in chief, on September 9, forced the general's hand.

The threat of a military coup united Petrograd socialists, who mobilized workers and soldiers to defend the revolution. While Kerenskii postured equivocally, hoping that Kornilov would crush the Bolsheviks and leave him in command, the Soviet's Executive Committee set up a "Committee for Struggle Against Counterrevolution" to coordinate resistance. Bolshevik leaders were released and directed the Committee's work, and arms were gathered everywhere to equip the Red Guard, a workers' militia. Kronstadt sailors, pouring in to defend Petrograd, swiftly rounded up Kornilovites. The Executive Committee instructed army committees and railroad and telegraph workers to obstruct Kornilov's advance; his small forces were enveloped and never reached Petrograd. His troop trains were delayed or derailed while Bolshevik agitators turned his soldiers against their officers. The Wild Division, won over by a Moslem delegation, elected a committee that apologized to the Petrograd Soviet for participating in a counterrevolutionary plot. Kornilov and his supporters were arrested, and the only serious rightist attempt in 1917 to seize power fizzled out ingloriously.

THE RISING TIDE (SEPTEMBER–NOVEMBER)

After Kornilov's defeat, the Bolsheviks rode a wave of mass discontent that finally overwhelmed the weak Provisional Government. In the Kornilov affair, the party had displayed leadership and control of the workers, who were becoming increasingly radical. On September 13, the Petrograd Soviet approved a Bolshevik resolution for the first time; five days later this action was repeated in Moscow. On September 22, when the Petrograd Soviet again voted Bolshevik, the moderate Executive Committee, interpreting this as a vote of no confidence, resigned, and soon thereafter Trotskii was elected chairman. Control of the principal soviets gave the Bolshevik Party a strategic base as important as radical Paris was for the French Jacobins in 1792.

Kerenskii's moderate regime might still have survived had it acted swiftly to begin land reform, end the war, and convene the Constituent Assembly, but it did none of these. Alexander Verkhovskii, the new war minister, urged Russia and the Allies to conclude a just peace and carry out immediate social reforms, but the Provisional Government, ignoring his suggestions, soon removed him. Instead, Kerenskii made more cabinet changes and proclaimed Russia a republic. On September 27, he convened a 1,200-man Democratic Conference in Petrograd, drawn from soviets, trade unions, zemstva, and cooperatives. Representing mostly the Russian educated classes whose influence and popular support were dwindling, this Conference voted to establish the Council of the Republic, or Preparliament, dominated by moderate socialists but including nonsocialists and some Bolsheviks. At the Council's first meeting, on October 20, Trotskii denounced it and the Bolsheviks walked out; the other deputies took no action.

Extreme elements were growing at the expense of the moderates. Between July and October, while the Bolshevik vote in Moscow city elections rose from 11 to 51 percent, and the Kadets (now the conservatives) from 17 to 26 percent, the moderate SRs dropped from 58 to 14 percent. Chernov, the only SR leader of real stature, was a theoretician, not a practical politician. Its other leaders (Kerenskii and Savinkov) grew more conservative, whereas the militant rank and file drew closer to the Bolsheviks. As the SRs neared an open split, the Mensheviks were losing worker support to the Bolsheviks. The radical masses were rejecting moderate leaders and parties and moving the revolution to the left.

The breakdown of the army, which had been developing since March, contributed greatly to extremism. Kornilov's fiasco hastened the collapse of discipline among the exhausted troops; the men regarded officers as enemies of the revolution. For months thousands of peasant soldiers had been deserting their units and filtering back to their villages, ragged, hungry, and disgruntled. Soldier soviets in most army units swung toward the Bolsheviks, who accelerated the trend with leaflets and agitation. National groups demanding independence also helped dissolve the army until by November few reliable units remained.

The peasantry moved spontaneously during 1917 to seize and divide up landowners' estates, though at first they had waited and listened to Government promises. In May, the first National Peasant Congress in Petrograd, wholly SR-dominated, outlined a program: All property in land was to be abolished, even for smallholders, and land was to belong to the entire people. Anyone might use land if he tilled it himself; hired labor was to be prohibited. Final solution of the land question was to be left to the Constituent Assembly. By midsummer, angered by official grain requisitioning, shortages of manufactured goods, and post-ponement of land reform, the peasants began to act. Violent land seizures and murders of landowners grew in number week by week, reaching a peak in October and November. The Bolsheviks did not lead the peasants, but exploited their discontent. The Government, helpless to protect landlord property, reluctantly recognized local peasant committees and soviets, which controlled much of the countryside. By November, most peasants backed leftist SRs who were cooperating with the Bolsheviks.

The workers grew more discontented as they were squeezed by galloping inflation, dwindling food supplies, and shrinking real wages. Food riots and long lines of hungry workers became common in the cities. Disorder mounted in factories as strikes intensified and industrial sabotage and murders of hated foremen by workers increased. The owners, lacking essential raw materials and fuel, shut down many factories, but the workers believed that such closures were meant to prevent strikes for higher wages. The Government could neither mediate between workers and employers nor coerce the workers. By November, the rapidly growing trade union movement had more than 2 million members. Moderate socialists retained influence in central trade union conferences, but by June more radical local factory committees were endorsing Bolshevik proposals for worker control of the factories; by November, factory committees and district soviets in Petrograd were firmly Bolshevik. The largely spontaneous and militant worker movement converged with the Bolshevik drive for political power and supplied the mass base for the

Bolshevik Revolution. By November, peasants were seizing the land, workers the factories; soldiers were deserting and making peace, and soviets were taking power. All this coincided with the Bolshevik short-term program.

With increasing urgency national minorities—almost half the population of the Russian Empire—demanded autonomy or independence. In March 1917, the Provisional Government, while promising the Poles independence and making concessions to the Finns, refused to recognize Ukraine as a separate administrative entity. Ukrainian moderates established a Central Council (Rada) in Kiev that favored autonomy, but Ukrainian radicals soon dominated the Rada and pushed it toward independence. In June, the Rada demanded that Petrograd recognize Ukrainian territorial and administrative autonomy and permit separate Ukrainian army units. Though sympathetic, the Provisional Government avoided specific promises and admonished: "Wait until the Constituent Assembly." By July, the Rada was virtually an independent government, but the Ukrainian national movement remained fragmented. Ukrainian quarrels with Petrograd over the extent of autonomy merely weakened liberal and moderate socialist elements in Russia. Native nationalist movements also developed rapidly in the Baltic provinces, soon to become independent as Latvia, Lithuania, and Estonia. In Central Asia, the Russians had crushed a Kazakh revolt in 1916, but during 1917 Kazakh congresses in Orenburg demanded a "Greater Kirghizia." Almost everywhere, the Provisional Government's control over the borderlands was slight, moderate socialists leading the Petrograd government temporized, and the Bolsheviks exploited the resulting confusion.

Kornilov's defeat signaled a sharp upturn in Bolshevik popularity. To Lenin, still hiding in Finland, the achievement of Bolshevik majorities in leading soviets proved that it was time to strike. The soviets could become the foundation for a revolutionary regime. "They represent a new *type* of state apparatus which is incomparably higher, incomparably more democratic," he wrote. Crucial for Lenin were majorities in the chief soviets, not victories in parliamentary elections. The Bolsheviks now were strong in the capitals, Volga cities, the Urals, Donets Basin, and Ukrainian industrial centers, while their allies, the Left SRs, had widespread support among peasants and soldiers. No longer could an isolated Red Petrograd be crushed by the rest of Russia.

Lenin and Trotskii, certain that it was time to seize power, had to convince the Central Committee in Petrograd. Lenin's slogan was "Insurrection now!" With majorities in the Petrograd and Moscow soviets, he wrote the Central Committee in late September, "The Bolsheviks can and must take power into their own hands." To await the Constituent Assembly, warned Lenin, would merely enable Kerenskii to surrender

Red Guards on a street in Petrograd (© *Mary Evans Picture Library/Photo Researchers, Inc.*)

Petrograd to the Germans. "The main thing is to place on the order of the day *the armed uprising in Petrograd and Moscow. . . . We will win absolutely and unquestionably.*" Insurrectionary detachments should be formed and placed in position immediately. Shocked by Lenin's urgent messages, the Central Committee burned one of his letters and disregarded the other.

Early in October, Lenin moved to Vyborg, closer to the capital. Bolshevik leaders in Petrograd were calling for the Second Congress of Soviets, set for early November, to assume power peacefully. In the pamphlet *Will the Bolsheviks Retain State Power?* Lenin insisted that the masses would support a purely Bolshevik government. Nothing except indecision could prevent the Bolsheviks from seizing and keeping power until the world socialist revolution triumphed. As the central Committee stalled, Lenin wrote in *The Crisis Has Matured* (October 12): "We are on the threshold of a world proletarian revolution" that the Bolsheviks must lead. If the Central Committee showed misguided faith in the Congress of Soviets or Constituent Assembly, its members would be "miserable traitors to the proletarian cause." When this, too, was disregarded, Lenin threatened to resign and campaign in the lower ranks of the party.

On October 20, Lenin came to Petrograd in disguise to convert the Central Committee to armed insurrection. He and 11 Committee members argued through the night of October 23–24 in the apartment of the unsuspecting Sukhanov. They approved a Political Bureau (subsequently Politburo) of seven: Lenin, Zinoviev, Kamenev, Trotskii, Stalin, Sokolnikov, and Bubnov. After long debate, the idea of armed uprising was approved in principle, though Zinoviev and Kamenev, arguing that armed insurrection would be contrary to Marx's teachings, remained opposed and kept the party leadership in turmoil until the November Revolution. Trotskii urged that the insurrection be coordinated with the imminent Second Congress of Soviets, thus giving it a measure of legitimacy, and he stuck to this position despite Lenin's demand for immediate action. Without Lenin's and Trotskii's leadership, it seems unlikely that the Bolsheviks would have taken power.

THE NOVEMBER REVOLUTION

Unlike the spontaneous overthrow of tsarism, the November Revolution was an armed seizure of power by one party under cover of the Second Congress of Soviets. Had the Bolsheviks not acted in November, Trotskii concludes, their opportunity would have passed.

Preparations for an armed showdown were haphazard on both sides. Trotskii, chairman of the Petrograd Soviet and its Military Revolutionary Committee (MRC), directed the insurrection and was the most active Bolshevik leader at large in Petrograd. The MRC and the Bolshevik Military Organization won over or neutralized the 150,000-man Petrograd garrison. Composed mostly of overage, sick, or green troops, the garrison leaned politically toward the SRs, but was loyal to the Soviet and to whoever kept it away from the front. The MRC sent revolutionary commissars to all its regiments, ousted government commissars, and won control. When the garrison recognized MRC and Soviet authority on November 5, the government was virtually powerless, but the uprising was "postponed" until the meeting of the Second Congress of Soviets on November 7.

The government remained outwardly confident. Colonel G. P. Polkovnikov, commander of the Petrograd Military District, announced he was ready for trouble. Premier Kerenskii hoped the Bolsheviks would act so that the government could crush them. The government had a thorough defense plan that anticipated most Bolshevik moves and concentrated on holding the city center and Neva bridges. Kerenskii had some 1,000 military cadets, officers, and Cossacks—sufficient, he believed, to paralyze Bolshevik centers if used boldly.

As both sides waited, government strength ebbed. On November 5, Trotskii and Lashevich literally harangued the garrison at Peter and Paul Fortress into surrendering and procured weapons there for 20,000 Red Guards. Next morning, the government sent military cadets to close

Leon Trotskii (1879–1940) *(United Press International)*

down Bolshevik newspapers and moved to the Winter Palace the Women's Battalion of Death, recruited by Kerenskii in June to shame Russian males into fighting. Accusing Lenin of treason and ordering MRC leaders arrested, Kerenskii sought plenary powers from the Pre-parliament to crush the Bolsheviks.

Government moves and Lenin's exhortations prodded the MRC into counteraction. "The situation is impossibly critical. . . . A delay in the uprising is equivalent to death," Lenin told the Central Committee. Early on November 7, Red Guards and sailors occupied railroad stations, the State Bank, and the central telephone exchange without resistance. Kerenskii lacked troops that would defend his regime and left Petrograd to locate loyal units outside. The capture of the Winter Palace that evening was anticlimactic and virtually bloodless. About 10 P.M., when the Women's Battalion tried a sortie, the besiegers rounded it up, raped a few, and dispersed the rest. The ministers surrendered meekly to invading Red Guards and were placed under house arrest. In this "assault," unduly glorified in Soviet accounts, only six attackers and no defenders were killed. The Provisional Government had fallen almost without resistance.

Bolshevik Petrograd withstood Kerenskii's counterattack combined with an internal revolt. At Pskov, Kerenskii had persuaded General N. N. Krasnov to move on Petrograd with about 700 Cossacks, and on November 12 they occupied Tsarskoe Selo, just to the south. The previous day, however, an uprising in Petrograd by military cadets organized by moderate socialists had been crushed. Red Guards and sailors repelled Krasnov's feeble attack on Petrograd, and his force, neutralized by Red propaganda, melted away. Kerenskii escaped in disguise and eventually reached England.

In most of Russia, the Bolsheviks established control in a few weeks. In Moscow, there were several days of severe fighting before the Red Guards[3] overcame military cadets and stormed the Kremlin November 15, but there was no active defense of the Provisional Government elsewhere. Georgian Mensheviks set up a nationalist regime, and in Kiev the Ukrainian Rada took over, but these actions did not then threaten Bolshevik rule. The Bolsheviks generally favored nationalist movements against the old Russian Empire.

Screened by the Second Congress of Soviets, the Bolsheviks created a new regime even before the Government yielded. Lenin emerged from hiding the afternoon of November 7 to tell the Petrograd Soviet: "The oppressed masses themselves will form a government. The old state apparatus will be destroyed root and branch. Now begins a new era in the history of Russia." That evening the Second Congress of Soviets convened with Bolsheviks predominating (390 out of 650 delegates). After verbal fireworks, the moderate socialists denounced the Bolshevik coup as illegal, walked out, and went into opposition. The remainder (Bolsheviks and Left SRs) set up an all-Bolshevik regime: Lenin became president of the Council of People's Commissars, Trotskii foreign commissar, and Stalin commissar of nationalities. Lenin read his Decree on Peace, which urged immediate peace without annexations and indemnities, the end of secret diplomacy, and publication of all secret treaties. To win peasant support, he issued the Decree on Land, which

---

[3]The Red Guards numbered about 20,000 in Petrograd and between 70,000 and 100,000 in all Russia. D. N. Collins, "A Note on the Numerical Strength of the Russian Red Guard in October 1917," *Soviet Studies*, 24, no. 2 (October, 1972), pp. 270–280.

confiscated state and church lands without compensation. Lenin was acting swiftly to implement his promises.

PROBLEM 2
Why Did the Bolsheviks Win?

The seizure of power by the Bolshevik Party of Lenin and Trotskii in November 1917 (October by the "old style" calendar), was a crucial turning point in Russia's political history, and one of the most momentous events in modern world history. This and the subsequent bitter civil war placed Russia squarely on a path leading toward Stalin's totalitarianism and the epic transformations of agriculture and industry in the 1930s. The Russian Revolutions of 1917, unlike the French, American, or Chinese conquest of power, occurred in wartime amidst military defeat, economic collapse, and governmental disintegration. How did a Bolshevik Party, with scarcely 250,000 members and apparently weaker than its socialist rivals, the Mensheviks and SRs, achieve power in a vast peasant country whose people had just discarded the 300-year authoritarian regime of the Romanovs and made Russia briefly into "the freest country in the world"? Was this Bolshevik takeover, condemned by many contemporary Russian socialists as Blanquism, or insurrection for its own sake, consistent with Marxism? In the 1840s, Marx had predicted that socialism would inevitably replace capitalism through a violent revolution, but initially in fully developed capitalist countries. Was Bolshevik victory the inevitable outcome of Russia's historical and economic development, or an accidental by-product of Russia's defeat and breakdown in 1917?

Soviet and many Western scholars would ascribe Bolshevik success primarily to the Bolsheviks' strengths. Official Soviet accounts, holding to the orthodox Marxist view, emphasized that the November Revolution was the inevitable outcome of Russian historical development, ascribing also great importance to the decisive role of the Bolshevik Party as a whole and Lenin's individual qualities of leadership. Declared *The History of the USSR* in 1967:

> The October armed insurrection in Petrograd was the first victorious proletarian uprising. The insurrection triumphed because the Bolshevik Party was armed with the Leninist theory of socialist revolution and utilized the experience of past uprisings of the workers. The Party, guided by the teachings of Marxism, treated insurrection as an art, insured its organization and decisiveness. The Central Committee of the party correctly utilized revolutionary forces. . . . V. I. Lenin worked out the plan of insurrection and conscientiously executed it. . . .

The success of the October insurrection was the result of the vast organizational activity of the Bolshevik Party and its Central Committee. The Bolsheviks were at the head of the insurgents. By their bravery and courage, their unexampled devotion to the revolution, they raised the masses to this heroic feat. The soul and brain of the insurrection was the great Lenin. Wherever he was in the hours of insurrection . . . , he was in the center of events. . . . The October armed uprising in Petrograd . . . showed what heroic deeds the people can accomplish when led by the Marxist-Leninist party.[4]

The 27th Party Congress in 1986 adopted a revised "Program of the Communist Party of the Soviet Union," which reiterated these themes, attributing Bolshevik victory to the well-organized, revolutionary Russian working class led by the Bolsheviks under Lenin. The March Revolution, argued that document, had failed to deliver the Russian masses "from social and political yokes" or from the burden of the "imperialist war," and it had not resolved social contradictions. "Thus a socialist revolution became an undeniable demand."

The working class of Russia was distinguished by great revolutionary qualities and organization. At its head stood the Bolshevik Party, hardened in political struggles and possessing an advanced revolutionary theory. V. I. Lenin armed it with a clear plan of struggle after formulating theses on the possibility of the victory of a proletarian revolution under conditions of imperialism originally in one of a few separate countries.

At the summons of the Bolshevik Party and under its leadership the working class undertook a decisive struggle against the power of capital. The Party united in one powerful stream the proletarian struggle for socialism, peasant struggle for the land, the national-liberation struggle of the oppressed peoples of Russia, into a general [obshchenarodnoe] movement against the imperialist war and for peace, and directed it with the overthrow of the bourgeois order.[5]

Many Western accounts also consider the Bolshevik victory as the inevitable outcome of the momentum of an invincible party, or the product of clever, even diabolical, plotting by Lenin. On the surface in November 1917, the Bolsheviks possessed many strengths: a highly centralized, disciplined organization; leadership; and mass support. Although indecisive, unsure, and weak back in March, the party allegedly had become a potent instrument under Lenin and Trotskii, who combined organizational skill, intellectual and oratorical power, and ruthless purpose to exploit opportunities that arose late in 1917. The Bolsheviks'

---

[4]*Istoriia SSSR s drevneishikh vremen do nashikh dnei* (Moscow, 1967), vol. 7, pp. 145–146.
[5]*Programma Kommunisticheskoi Partii Sovetskogo Soiuza* (Moscow, 1989), pp. 6–7.

mass following—the industrial workers of Petrograd and Moscow—were militant, impatient, and readily mobilized, living mostly in well-defined workers' quarters. Lenin's short-term program—outlined in his "April Theses," of bread, land, peace, and all power to the soviets—coincided largely with the workers' aspirations at that moment.

However, one can also view the reasons for Bolshevik success in more negative terms: the product of fortunate accidents, circumstances, and divisions, weaknesses, and mistakes of their opponents. The Bolsheviks' chief socialist rivals—the SRs and Mensheviks—were badly split internally; indeed, the SRs by November were becoming two parties, a right wing favoring peaceful methods and moving toward democratic socialism, and a radical, terrorist left that would ally with the Bolsheviks. Both of these rivals lacked cohesion and discipline, failed to put forward practical programs, and proved unable to mobilize mass support. The thesis of Professor Crane Brinton about the weaknesses of moderates in periods of revolution seems pertinent: "The moderates in control of the formal machinery of government are confronted by . . . radical and determined opponents. . . . This stage [dual sovereignty] ends with the triumph of the extremists." Continues Brinton:

> Little by little the moderates find themselves losing the credit they had gained as opponents of the old regime, and taking on more and more of the discredit [as] . . . heir to the old regime. Forced on the defensive, they make mistake after mistake.[6]

Thus the Right SRs, Mensheviks, and Kadets were all moderate parties caught between an intransigent leftist opposition (Bolsheviks) and a weak and incompetent Provisional Government, which they had joined and whose blunders and foot-dragging exacerbated their internal weaknesses. The Provisional Government's ineffectiveness provided the Bolsheviks with the opportunity to take power. Establishing in March 1917 broad personal and political freedom in Russia, that government failed to implement promptly its most important pledge: to prepare elections to the Constituent Assembly. Had that Assembly been convened in late summer or early fall 1917, as was wholly feasible, Bolshevik opportunities might have disappeared with the creation of a legitimate and permanent Russian government. Instead, Premier Kerenskii resorted to legalistic devices, harangues, and exhortations and kept Russia locked in a disastrous and unpopular war. Given the deepening mood of popular extrem-

---

[6]Crane Brinton, *The Anatomy of Revolution*, rev. ed. (New York, 1965), p. 137. In his classic study, Brinton compares the English, American, French, and Russian revolutions.

ism in the fall of 1917, his democratic regime was virtually foredoomed to failure.

In sharp contrast to the Soviet thesis that the Bolsheviks succeeded because of their correct theory, careful plans, and decisive action with mass support, the American scholar Robert Daniels affirms that Moscow has fostered a myth with little basis in reality and that the Bolshevik Revolution succeeded because of an incredible series of accidents and miscalculations by their opponents:

> One thing that both victors and vanquished were agreed on . . . was the myth that the insurrection was timed and executed according to a deliberate Bolshevik plan. . . . The stark truth about the Bolshevik Revolution is that it succeeded against incredible odds in defiance of any rational calculation that could have been made in the fall of 1917. . . . While the Bolsheviks were an undeniable force in Petrograd and Moscow, they had against them the overwhelming majority of the peasants, the army in the field, and the trained personnel without which no government could function. . . . Lenin's revolution . . . was a wild gamble with little chance that the Bolsheviks' ill-prepared followers could prevail against all the military force that the government seemed to have, and even less chance that they could keep power even if they managed to seize it temporarily. To Lenin, however, it was a gamble that entailed little risk, because he sensed that in no other way and at no other time would he have any chance at all of coming to power. . . .

Nor was the subsequent exaltation of Lenin's leadership really accurate:

> . . . There is some truth in the contentions, both Soviet and non-Soviet, that Lenin's leadership was decisive. By psychological pressure on his Bolshevik lieutenants and his manipulation of the fear of counterrevolution, he set the stage for the one-party seizure of power. But . . . in the crucial days before October 24, [November 6] Lenin was not making his leadership effective. The party, unable to face up directly to his brow-beating, was tacitly violating his instructions and waiting for a multi-party and semi-constitutional revolution by the Congress of Soviets. Lenin had failed to seize the moment, failed to nail down the base for his personal dictatorship—until the government struck on the morning of the 24th of October. Kerenskii's ill-conceived countermove was the decisive accident.[7]

Despite such revisionist Western views, in the USSR the concept of a carefully conceived, Marxist revolution with wide popular support has been cultivated assiduously and on the whole successfully. This is accompanied by the rather incongruous assertion that the success of this revolution depended heavily on the individual leadership and driving

---

[7]Robert Daniels, excerpted from *Red October: The Bolshevik Revolution of 1917.* Copyright © 1967 Robert V. Daniels. Reprinted with the permission of Charles Scribner's bons.

energy of the genius, Lenin. This evident contradiction reflects the persistent dichotomy in Marxism between determinism (inexorable laws) and voluntarism (dynamic leadership).

Suggested Additional Reading

ABRAHAM, RICHARD. *Alexander Kerensky* (New York, 1987).

ADAMS, A., ed. *The Russian Revolution and Bolshevik Victory* (Boston, 1972).

AVRICH, PAUL. *The Russian Anarchists* (Princeton, N.J., 1967).

BOLL, N. M. *The Petrograd Armed Workers Movement in the February Revolution (February–July 1917)* (Washington, D.C., 1979).

BRINTON, CRANE. *The Anatomy of Revolution* (New York, 1965).

BROWDER, R., and A. KERENSKY, eds. *The Russian Provisional Government, 1917*, 3 vols. (Stanford, Calif., 1961).

BROWER, DANIEL R., ed. *The Russian Revolution: Disorder or New Order?* (Arlington Heights, Ill., 1986).

BUNYAN, J., and H. H. FISHER, eds. *The Bolshevik Revolution, 1917–1918. Documents and Materials* (Stanford, Calif., 1934).

CARR, E. H. *The October Revolution: Before and After* (New York, 1971).

CHAMBERLIN, W. H. *The Russian Revolution, 1917–1921*, 2 vols. (New York, 1935).

CHERNOV, VICTOR. *The Great Russian Revolution* (New Haven, Conn., 1936).

CURTISS, J. S. *The Russian Revolution of 1917* (Princeton, N.J., 1957).

DANIELS, ROBERT. *Red October: The Bolshevik Revolution of 1917* (New York, 1967).

———. *The Russian Revolution* (Englewood Cliffs, N.J., 1972).

ELWOOD, R. C., ed. *Reconsiderations on the Russian Revolution* (Cambridge, Mass., 1976).

FERRO, M. *October 1917. A Social History of the Russian Revolution*, trans. N. Stone (Boston, 1980).

———. *The Russian Revolution of February 1917 . . .* , trans. J. Richards (Englewood Cliffs, N.J., 1972).

GALILI, ZIVA. *The Menshevik Leaders in the Russian Revolution* (Princeton, N.J., 1989).

GILL, G. J. *Peasants and Government in the Russian Revolution* (New York, 1979).

HARTLEY, L. *The Russian Revolution* (New York, 1980).

HEALD, EDWARD. *Witness to Revolution: Letters from Russia, 1916–1919*, ed. James Gidney (Kent, Ohio, 1972).

HILL, C. *Lenin and the Russian Revolution* (New York, 1978).

KAISER, DANIEL H., ed. *The Workers' Revolution in Russia, 1917: The View from Below* (Cambridge, Eng., 1987).

KATKOV, G. *The Kornilov Affair . . .* (London, 1980).

KERENSKII, A. F. *The Catastrophe* . . . (New York, 1927).

———. *The Crucifixion of Liberty* (New York, 1934).

———. *Russia and History's Turning Point* (London, 1965).

KOENKER, D. *Moscow Workers and the 1917 Revolution* (Princeton, N.J., 1981).

KOENKER, DIANE, and W. G. ROSENBERG. *Strikes and Revolution in Russia, 1917* (Princeton, N.J., 1990).

LOCKHART, R. H. B. *The Two Revolutions: An Eyewitness Study of Russia, 1917* (London, 1957).

LUXEMBURG, R. *The Russian Revolution* (New York, 1981).

MAWDSLEY, E. *The Russian Revolution and the Baltic Fleet* (London, 1978).

MELGUNOV, S. P. *The Bolshevik Seizure of Power* (Santa Barbara, Calif., 1972).

MILIUKOV, P. N. *The Russian Revolution. Vol. I: The Revolution Divided: Spring 1917*, trans. T. & R. Stites (Gulf Breeze, Fla., 1978).

MOHRENSCHILDT, D. VON, ed. *The Russian Revolution of 1917: Contemporary Accounts* (New York, 1971).

PALEOLOGUE, M. *An Ambassador's Memoirs*, 3 vols. (New York, 1972).

PETHYBRIDGE, R. *The Spread of the Russian Revolution: Essays on 1917* (London, 1972).

———, ed. *Witnesses to the Russian Revolution* (London, 1964).

PIPES, RICHARD, ed. *Revolutionary Russia: A Symposium* (New York, 1969).

RABINOWITCH, A. *Prelude to Revolution: . . . the July Uprising* (Bloomington, Ind., 1969).

———. *The Bolsheviks Come to Power* (New York, 1976).

RADKEY, O. H. *The Agrarian Foes of Bolshevism: . . . Russian Socialist Revolutionaries* . . . (New York, 1958).

REED, JOHN. *Ten Days That Shook the World* (New York, 1919, and reprints).

ROSENBERG, WILLIAM. *Liberals in the Russian Revolution: The Constitutional Democratic Party, 1917–1921* (Princeton, N.J., 1974).

SAUL, N. E. *Sailors in Revolt: The Russian Baltic Fleet in 1917* (Lawrence, Kans., 1978).

SCHAPIRO, LEONARD. *The Russian Revolution of 1917: The Origins of Modern Communism* (New York, 1984).

SERGE, VICTOR. *Year One of the Russian Revolution* (New York, 1972).

SLUSSER, ROBERT. *Stalin in October: The Man Who Missed the Revolution* (Baltimore, Md., 1987).

SOBOLEV, P. N., ed. *The Great October Socialist Revolution*, trans. D. Skvirskii (Moscow, 1977).

SUKHANOV, N. N. *The Russian Revolution of 1917*, 2 vols., ed. J. Carmichael (New York, 1962).

SUNY, R. G. *The Baku Commune 1917–1918* . . . (Princeton, N.J., 1972).

SUNY, RONALD, and ARTHUR ADAMS, eds. *The Russian Revolution and Bolshevik Victory. Problems in European Civilization*, 3d ed. (Lexington, Mass., 1990). (Includes and discusses various viewpoints.)

THOMPSON, J. M. *Revolutionary Russia, 1917* (New York, 1981).

TROTSKY, LEON. *The History of the Russian Revolution,* 3 vols. (New York, 1932).

WADE, REX. *The Russian Search for Peace: February–October 1917* (Stanford, Calif., 1969).

WILDMAN, ALLAN. *The End of the Russian Imperial Army* . . . (Princeton, N.J., 1980).

WILLIAMS, A. R. *Through the Russian Revolution* (New York, 1978).

CHAPTER EIGHT

WAR COMMUNISM, 1917–1921

After the November Revolution it took the Bolsheviks, governing a divided, war-torn country, a decade to achieve full military and political control and begin to build a new autocracy. After making peace with the Central Powers with the Treaty of Brest-Litovsk, they defeated their domestic counterrevolutionary opponents in a bitter civil war (1918–1921) complicated by foreign intervention.[1] They moved simultaneously to destroy the old state, political parties, society, and economic order and erect new socialist ones. By 1927, they had succeeded in their destructive mission, but had taken only initial and tentative steps in socialist construction. One can divide this first decade of Bolshevism in power into the hectic initial months, a period of extremism and revolutionary fervor (1918–1921), and one of recovery, compromise, and power struggle (1921–1927). In 1918–1919, it seemed dubious that the Soviet regime

---

[1] The Bolsheviks were known as the Reds whereas their disunited opponents, spanning the political spectrum from SRs (Socialist Revolutionaries) to monarchists, were known as the Whites.

could retain power in semibackward Russia without revolutions abroad. Provided they succeeded, could the Bolsheviks build socialism in isolated Soviet Russia? Why and how did they win the Civil War? Why did the Allies intervene, and how did this affect the outcome? Was "War Communism" an unplanned response to the war crisis or a conscious effort to build socialism?

FIRST STEPS, 1917–1918

After the Bolshevik coup in Petrograd, many Russian and foreign leaders believed that their rule would be but a brief interlude and that Lenin could not implement his program of bread, land, and peace. Predicting that 240,000 Bolsheviks, running Russia for the poor, could "draw the working people . . . into the daily work of state administration," Lenin counted on imminent European revolutions to preserve his infant regime; otherwise, its prospects appeared dim. Bolshevik leaders recalled the Paris Commune of 1871, in which radical Paris was crushed by conservative France, and their initial measures seemed designed to make a good case for posterity in case world capitalism overwhelmed them.

Bolshevik power spread swiftly from Petrograd over central Russia, but it met strong opposition in borderlands and villages, from other socialist parties, and even from some Bolsheviks. (See p. 181.) Lenin, however, acted decisively to crush other socialist parties, dissident Bolsheviks, and workers' groups in Russia proper. Mensheviks and Right SRs were demanding a regime of all socialist parties without Lenin and Trotskii, who had led the "un-Marxian" November coup. Right Bolsheviks under Gregory Zinoviev and Lev Kamenev temporarily left the Central Committee and proclaimed: "Long live the government of Soviet parties!" Retorting that the Congress of Soviets had approved his all-Bolshevik regime, Lenin called the rightists deserters and until they submitted, threatened to expel them from the party. Bringing a few Left SRs into his government, Lenin hailed it as the dictatorship of the proletariat (Bolsheviks) and poor peasantry (Left SRs). This action completed the split of the SRs.

The Constituent Assembly represented a severe political challenge because during 1917 the Bolsheviks had pledged to convene it. Even after November *Pravda* proclaimed: "Comrades, by shedding your blood, you have assured the convocation of the Constituent Assembly." Lenin knew his Bolshevik party could not win a majority, but he found it too risky to cancel the scheduled and promised elections. Held only three weeks after the Bolshevik coup, the elections to the Constituent Assembly were the only fundamentally free elections contested by organized and divergent political parties under universal suffrage ever held in Russia. Despite

Bolshevik Headquarters, Smolny Institute in Leningrad, where the Revolution was first declared won *(Michael Curran)*

continuing political turmoil, over 40 million votes were cast using secret, direct, and equal suffrage. Despite some intimidation and restrictions imposed on the Kadets and the Right, the elections were remarkably fair and orderly. The SRs obtained about 58 percent of the vote, the Bolsheviks 25, other socialists 4, and the Kadets and the Right 13 percent. Soviet accounts stress that major cities returned Bolshevik majorities and that many SR votes were cast for pro-Bolshevik Left SRs. Nonetheless, non-Bolshevik parties had won the elections.

Lenin swiftly neutralized, then dissolved the Assembly. In December, the Kadets were banned as counterrevolutionary, and their leaders and many right-wing socialists were arrested. The Constituent Assembly, warned Lenin, must accept the Soviet regime and its measures or be dissolved. When the Assembly convened in Petrograd January 18, 1918, it was surrounded with sharpshooters, and armed Red soldiers and sailors packed its galleries. After Bolshevik resolutions were defeated and Chernov, a moderate SR, was elected president, the Bolsheviks walked out. Early next day on Bolshevik orders, a sailor told Chernov to suspend the session because "the guards are tired." Red troops then closed down the Assembly and dispersed street demonstrations in its behalf. Moderate socialists during the Civil War tried to use the Assembly as a rallying point only to find that most peasants knew nothing about it. The Constituent Assembly's dissolution marked the demise of parliamentary democracy in Russia.

Old political agencies, principles, and parties were crushed ruthlessly. Decrees abolished the Senate, zemstva, and other organs of local self-government. Even before counterrevolutionary threats materialized, the sinister Cheka (Extraordinary Commission), an incipient Soviet secret police, began Red terror under the dedicated Polish revolutionary Felix Dzerzhinsky. The imperial family, transported to Ekaterinburg (Sverdlovsk) in the Urals, was murdered at Lenin's orders in a cellar in July 1918.[2] The Left SRs, who left the cabinet after Brest-Litovsk and sought to overthrow the regime, were expelled from the soviets and proscribed. At the December 1920 Congress of Soviets, individual Mensheviks and SRs appeared legally for the last time.

At first Lenin sought to achieve his short-term economic program without antagonizing mass elements. The peasantry were allowed to seize landowners' estates and divide them up into small holdings. Worker committees were authorized to take over factories. "Workers' control" undermined private capitalism, dislocated production, and fed economic chaos. All banks, railroads, foreign trade, and a few factories were nationalized, but a mixed economy functioned for the time being. The Supreme Council of National Economy (*Vesenkha*) was created to coordinate economic affairs and supervise regional economic councils (*sovnarkhozy*), which ran local activities. These initial efforts at economic planning proved rather ineffective.

The Bolsheviks acted promptly to destroy the traditional patriarchal family, army, and church associated with the tsarist regime and clear the way for a new socialist society. Early in 1918 they adopted the Western calendar. Marriage and divorce were removed from church control, and only civil marriage was recognized. One spouse could cancel a marriage before a civil board without citing reasons, then notify the absent partner of the "divorce" by postcard. Incest, bigamy, and adultery were no longer considered crimes. In the army, ranks and saluting were abolished, and officers were to be elected. A major campaign against the Orthodox Church began because Lenin considered religion as part of the Marxist superstructure that must reflect economic conditions. Declared Lenin: "God is before all a complex of ideas produced by the stupefying oppression of man"; he predicted a struggle between religion and the

---

[2]Unsubstantiated reports abound that the tsar's daughter Anastasia—or even the entire family—escaped execution and went abroad.

socialist state, until the former disappeared. Orthodoxy's link with tsarism, the Bolsheviks believed, made it counterrevolutionary and an obstacle to building socialism. Lenin warned, however, that attacking religious "superstitions" directly might alienate the masses from the Soviet state. Instead, a multifaceted campaign began to pen the church in a corner until it withered and died. A decree of February 1918 separated church and state and deprived churches of property and rights of ownership. The church hierarchy was destroyed and its lands, buildings, utensils, and vestments nationalized. Believers had to apply to a local soviet to secure a place of worship and religious articles, and parish churches could operate only with irregular donations of believers. Twenty years of intensive Soviet persecution of all religions had begun.

Lenin had promised peace, and the Russian army had disintegrated to the point where it could no longer fight. When the Allies failed to respond to his Decree on Peace, Lenin urged a separate peace, but only German advances on Petrograd, in February 1918, overcame Central Committee opposition to such a peace. Lenin considered the Treaty of Brest-Litovsk (Soviet Russia's separate peace with the Central Powers), despite its severity, essential for his regime's survival. The Baltic provinces and the entire Ukraine were surrendered to German occupation. As he predicted, it provided a breathing space, allowed demobilization of the army, and perhaps saved the Soviet regime.

CIVIL WAR, 1918–1920

The Russian Civil War between the Bolsheviks (Reds) and their political opponents (Whites) did as much to create the USSR as the Revolutions of 1917, affirms an American work.[3] Bolshevik objectives in November 1917 were unclear, but the merciless civil strife between Reds and Whites laid the foundations of the autocratic Soviet system. The Bolshevik Party was hardened and militarized, systematic terror began, extreme economic policies were adopted, and implacable hostility developed toward the West. The Civil War, though not wholly responsible for these, made Bolshevik policies much more draconian.

After moving to Moscow early in 1918, Lenin's regime came under intense military and political pressure. As White forces approached, Lenin set up a ruthless emergency government, which sought to mobilize central Russia's total resources. "The republic is an armed camp,"

---

[3] Peter Kenez, *Civil War in South Russia: The First Year of the Volunteer Army* (Berkeley, Calif., 1971).

Nicholas Bukharin declared. "One must rule with iron when one cannot rule with law." Relatively democratic norms of party life in 1917 yielded to dictatorship, and local popular bodies were suppressed. Lenin made major political and economic decisions and reconciled jealous subordinates. Wisely, he let Trotskii handle military affairs, confirmed his decisions, and defended the able war commissar against intrigues by Stalin and others. Jakob Sverdlov ran the party organization until his death in 1919; Stalin then assumed that role. The Eighth Party Congress in 1919 created the first operating Politburo with five full members (Lenin, Trotskii, Stalin, Kamenev, and N. M. Krestinskii) and three candidates (Bukharin, Zinoviev, and M. Kalinin) constituting Bolshevism's general staff.

In January 1918, Lenin, proclaiming the Third Congress of Soviets the supreme power in Russia, had it draft a constitution. At the Congress some delegates advocated genuine separation of powers and autonomy for local soviets, but the successful Stalin-Sverdlov draft outlined, instead, a highly centralized political system, which concentrated all power in top government and party bodies. The Constitution of 1918, disfranchising former "exploiters" (capitalists, priests, and nobles) and depriving them of civil rights, supposedly guaranteed all democratic freedoms to the working class. Urban workers received weighted votes to counteract the peasantry's huge numerical superiority. Between congresses of soviets, a 200-member Central Executive Committee was to exercise supreme power and appoint the executive, the Council of People's Commissars. A hierarchy of national, regional, provincial, district, and local soviets was to govern Soviet Russia. The Constitution, however, omitted mention of the Bolshevik Party, possessor of all real political power!

As the Soviet regime consolidated political control over central Russia, long repressed national aspirations for independence disintegrated the former tsarist empire until Russia was reduced virtually to the boundaries of 1600. The Civil War, like the Time of Troubles (see Chapter 1), brought political conflict, social turmoil, foreign intervention, and ultimate national Russian resurgence and reunification. Soviet accounts stress heroic Russian resistance in both instances to foreign aggression. The southern frontier—the "Wild Field"—again became a refuge for rebels against a shaky regime in Moscow, and western borderlands broke away to secure independence. Anti-Communist Finns defeated Bolshevik-supported Red Finns to create an independent Finland, and the Baltic states of Latvia, Lithuania, and Estonia, assisted by German occupiers, declared independence and retained it until 1940. In the Ukraine a moderate General Secretariat signed a treaty with the Germans who occupied that region and set up a puppet regime under "Hetman" Skoropadski, opposed by Bolsheviks and many Ukrainian nationalists. In Byelorussia an anti-Communist group, the Hromada, declared independence, but the national movement there was less developed and lacked a broad popular following. In the Caucasus a Transcaucasian Federative Republic existed briefly in 1918 before yielding to separate regimes in Georgia, Armenia, and Azerbaijan under British protection. In Central Asia Tashkent was an isolated Bolshevik fortress in a sea of disunited Moslems. The SRs created regimes in western Siberia and at Samara on the Volga, while Cossack areas of the Urals and the North Caucasus formed a Southeastern Union. Russia had almost dissolved.

To undermine the tsarist empire and Provisional Government, the Bolsheviks had used the slogan of national self-determination. However, as early as 1903, most Russian Social Democrats, preferring, like Marx, large, centralized states, had rejected federalism. Viewing nationalism as a capitalist by-product that would disappear under socialism, the Bolsheviks underestimated its power and attractiveness, though Lenin exploited national movements to bring his party into power. He advocated political self-determination in 1917 for every nation in the Russian Empire, but aimed to reunite them subsequently with a Russian socialist state. Grigorii Piatakov, a Bolshevik leader in the Ukraine, expressed the party's view bluntly:

> On the whole we must not support the Ukrainians, because their movement is not convenient for the proletariat. Russia cannot exist without the Ukrainian sugar industry, and the same can be said in regard to coal (Donbass), cereals (the black earth belt), etc. . . .[4]

Realizing that without the resources of the western borderlands Soviet Russia would not be a major power, Lenin strove to reconcile advocacy of national self-determination with Soviet Russian unity. At his instruction Joseph Stalin formulated a Bolshevik doctrine of "proletarian self-determination" limited to "toilers," denying it to the bourgeoisie and intelligentsia. National independence would be recognized only "upon the demand of the working population . . . ," meaning in fact local Bolsheviks subject to control by Moscow.

Civil War and Allied Intervention, 1918–1920

Opposition to Lenin's government began in November 1917 but at first was disorganized and ineffective. Many Russians believed that the Soviet regime would soon collapse, and an ideological gulf divided conservative

---

[4]Cited in R. Pipes, *The Formation of the Soviet Union* (Cambridge, Mass., 1954), p. 68.

V. I. Lenin and sister in Moscow, 1920 (*Library of Congress*)

military elements from moderates and socialists. In August 1918, Fania Kaplan, a terrorist, attempted to kill Lenin and wounded him severely. In the Don region, General M. V. Alekseev, former imperial chief of staff, began organizing anti-Bolshevik elements soon after November into the Volunteer Army, which became the finest White fighting force. Before the Bolsheviks seized Russian military headquarters at Mogilev, some leading tsarist generals (Kornilov, A. I. Denikin, and others) escaped and joined Alekseev. The anti-Bolshevik White movement included socially and ideologically disparate elements lacking in unity and coordination. Former tsarist officers exercised military and often political leadership and played a disproportionate role. Though some were of humble origin, their education and status separated them from a largely illiterate peasantry. White soldiers were mostly Cossacks, set apart from ordinary peasants by independent landholdings and proud traditions. Officers and Cossacks had little in common ideologically with Kadet and SR intellectuals except antipathy for Bolshevism.

Facing this motley opposition was a Red Army, created in January 1918. At first an undisciplined volunteer force, by late 1918—after Trotskii had become war commissar—it became a regular army with conscription and severe discipline imposed by former imperial officers. Trotskii defended this risky and controversial policy as "building socialism with the bricks of capitalism." To get Red soldiers to obey their officers, officers' families were often held hostage to ensure the officers' loyalty. Trotskii raised uncertain Red Army morale by appearing in his famous armored train at critical points. In August 1918 at Sviiazhsk near Kazan he rallied dispirited Red troops and helped turn the tide against the SRs. Soviet historians still give him little credit for this brilliant feat of inspiration and organization, which saved the regime.

Full-scale civil war and Allied intervention followed an uprising in May 1918 of the Czechoslovak Brigade in Russia. The Czechs had joined the imperial Russian army during World War I and, surviving its collapse, remained perhaps the best organized military force in Russia. Wishing to go to the western front to fight for an independent Czechoslovakia, the Czechs quarreled with Soviet authorities. Then they seized the Trans-Siberian Railroad, cleared the Reds from most of Siberia, and aided their White opponents. The Allies, claim Soviet accounts, employed the Czechs to activate all enemies of Red power and intervened militarily to over-throw the Soviet regime. Western accounts affirm that Allied interven-tion was designed to restore a Russian front against Germany. President Wilson allowed United States participation in the Allied expeditions to north Russian ports in the summer of 1918 only after the Allied com-mand insisted it was the sole way to win World War I.[5] Such individual Allied leaders as Winston Churchill and Marshal Foch, however, did aim to destroy Bolshevism through intervention. The Soviet-Western contro-versy over its nature and purpose still rages.

The Civil War, fought initially with small Russian forces of uncertain morale, grew in scope and bitterness. Villages and entire regions changed hands repeatedly in a fratricidal conflict in which both sides committed numerous atrocities. At first the main threat to the Soviet regime came from the east. In August 1918, SR troops, encouraged by the Czechs' revolt, captured Kazan and the tsarist gold reserve and formed SR regimes in Samara and in Omsk in western Siberia. After the Red Army regained Kazan, the SRs in Omsk were ousted by Admiral A. Kolchak, who won Czech and later Allied support, for his conservative Siberian regime. Early in 1919, pledging to reconvene the Constituent Assembly, Kolchak moved westward toward Archangel and Murmansk, controlled by the Allies and the White Russian army of General Evgenii Miller. By late summer, however, the Red Army had forced him back across the Urals. (See Map 8.1.) White and Allied armies hemmed in the Bolsheviks on every side. In the west, General Iudenich, commanding a British-equipped White army in Estonia, advanced close to Petrograd in October

---

[5]George Kennan, *Russia and the West Under Lenin and Stalin* (Boston, 1960), p. 64.

Map 8.1 *The Civil War, 1919*

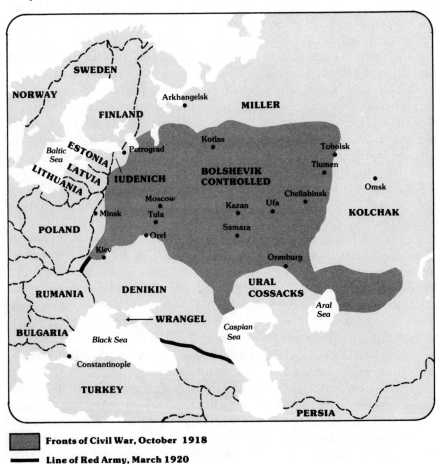

Fronts of Civil War, October 1918

Line of Red Army, March 1920

Source: Treadgold, Donald W., *Twentieth Century Russia*, Fourth Edition, © 1976, 1972, 1959, by Rand McNally College Publishing Company, Chicago. Map, page 114.

1919, but Trotskii rallied its defenders and Iudenich's army dissolved. The chief military threat came from the south. Early in the fall of 1919, General Denikin, commanding Don Cossacks and the elite Volunteer Army equipped with British tanks, reached Orel, 250 miles south of Moscow. Then numerically superior Red forces counterattacked and drove him back, and in March 1920 the British evacuated the remnants of his army from Novorossiisk.

The Bolsheviks gradually reasserted military and political control over the tsarist borderlands, except for Poland, Finland, and the Baltic

The monument to the Legendary Machine Gun Cart at Kakhovka, site of an important battle of the Civil War fought in the Ukraine. Horse-drawn machine gun carts of this type were instrumental in the Bolsheviks' victory in the Civil War. *(Michael Curran)*

states. In the west, they dissolved the Byelorussian Rada and incorporated Byelorussia. After the Central Powers withdrew from the Ukraine at the end of 1918, the Ukrainian nationalist Directory ousted their puppet, Hetman Skoropadski. Conservative and liberal nationalist elements competed with the Red Army for control of a Ukraine, which experienced anarchy and turmoil. Early in 1919, the Red Army removed the Directory, but much of the Ukraine was conquered by Denikin's Whites. In 1920, Red forces restored the rule of Ukrainian communists now wholly subservient to Moscow, virtually ending the abortive Ukrainian struggle for independence. Though the Allied powers recognized de facto independence of the three Caucasian republics early in 1920, Moscow's rapprochement with Turkish nationalists paved the way for Soviet incorporation of the Transcaucasus. That spring, the Red Army occupied Azerbaijan; in December unfortunate Armenia succumbed; and in March 1921 Red forces conquered Menshevik-controlled Georgia against strong resistance. In Central Asia, the Bolsheviks conquered the khanates of Khiva and Bukhara and set up several artificial client national states. Bands of mounted Basmachi guerrillas resisted Red rule in Turkestan until the mid-1920s. With most of the former Russian Empire reunited forcibly with its Great Russian core, the way was prepared for creation of the Soviet Union.

By then the Allies, except for the Japanese in Vladivostok, had departed and White resistance had weakened, but a Soviet-Polish war prolonged Russia's agony. To reconstitute a Greater Poland, the forces of Marshal Joseph Pilsudski invaded the western Ukraine and captured Kiev in May 1920. A Soviet counteroffensive carried General M. N. Tukhachevskii's Red Army to Warsaw's outskirts, and Lenin sought to communize Poland. The Poles, however, with some French support, rallied, drove out the Red Army, and forced Soviet Russia to accept an armistice and later the unfavorable Treaty of Riga (March 1921). Soviet preoccupation with Poland enabled Baron Peter Wrangel, Denikin's successor and the ablest White general, to consolidate control of the Crimea. Wrangel employed capable Kadet leaders to carry through land reform, won peasant support, and occupied considerable areas to the north. After the Soviet-Polish armistice in October 1920, the Red Army smashed Wrangel's resistance and forced the evacuation of some 150,000 Whites to Constantinople.

The Whites had lacked coordination and were plagued by personal rivalries among their leaders. They denounced Bolshevism, but affirmed nothing. Denikin and Kolchak were moderates, who lacked effective political or economic programs. Their slogan: "A united and indivisible Russia" alienated national minorities and played into Bolshevik hands. White generals made military blunders, but their political mistakes and disunity proved decisive. Allied intervention was of dubious value: Foreign arms and supplies aided the Whites, but were insufficient to ensure victory and let the Reds pose as defenders of Mother Russia. Bolshevik propaganda portrayed White generals (wrongly) as reactionary tools of Western imperialism and (more correctly) as aiming to restore the landlords. Conversely, the Reds possessed able leadership, a disciplined party, clever propaganda, and a flexible policy of national self-determination. The Red Army had central positions, better discipline, and numerical superiority. Retaining worker support in the central industrial region and controlling its railways, the Bolsheviks won the Civil War as they had won power in 1917 with superior leadership, unity, and purpose.

Russian women, theoretically granted full civil, legal, and electoral equality in January 1918, by the new Bolshevik regime, played significant roles, some quite novel, during the Civil War. Their participation in medical services and combat was far broader than in World War I. In the Civil War, Russian women fought on every front and with every weapon; the female machine-gunner made frequent appearances in early Soviet literature. From October 1919, women's activities were coordinated by Zhenotdel (Women's Department) of the Party's Central Committee, and by 1920 women were being conscripted for noncombatant service and held important positions in the Red Army's political departments. Inessa

Nedezhada K. Krupskaia (1869–1939), Lenin's
wife, women's activist, who unsuccessfuly
opposed Stalin's drive for power *(SOVFOTO)*

Armand, a close friend of Lenin, was Zhenotdel's first director. She, along
with Alexandra Kollontai and Nadezhda Krupskaia, Lenin's wife, were
leaders of women's rights in early Soviet Russia. An estimated 74,000
women participated in the Russian Civil War, suffering casualties of
about 1,800.

"War Communism": An Economic Disaster

During the Civil War, the government adopted War Communism, an
emergency program of nationalization, grain requisitioning, and labor
mobilization. With the Whites holding the richest food-producing regions, in Lenin's words: ". . . Hunger and unemployment are knocking at
the doors of an ever greater number of workers . . . , there is no bread."
In May 1918, he launched a "crusade for bread," and in June all large-
scale industry was nationalized and labor conscripted. This development
marked the true beginning of War Communism. State administration of
industry by the Supreme Council of National Economy *(Vesenkha)* and its
numerous boards proved to be inefficient. Almost one fourth of
Petrograd's adult population became officials, perhaps outnumbering
actual factory workers. According to Maurice Dobb, an English economist, representatives of some 50 boards surrounded a dead mare in the

streets of Petrograd and disputed responsibility for disposing of its carcass! In a speech made in Moscow in 1922, Lenin admitted:

> Carried away by a wave of enthusiasm . . . , we thought that by direct orders of the proletarian state, we could organize state production and distribution of products communistically in a land of petty peasants. Life showed us our mistake.

By 1920, industrial production—a victim of inefficiency and civil war— had fallen to one fifth of the 1913 level.

In the countryside, as the Bolsheviks denounced "rich" peasants (kulaks), Sverdlov warned that the Soviet regime would survive "only if we can split the village into two irreconcilably hostile camps, if we succeed in rousing the village poor against the village bourgeoisie." Red Army detachments aided "committees of the poor" (*kombedy*) to seize "surplus" grain—everything above a bare minimum for subsistence—from kulaks and middle peasants. Compulsory grain deliveries, though later regularized, amounted to virtual confiscation because peasants were paid in almost worthless paper currency. When farmers hid their grain, sold it on the black market, or brewed vodka, the government responded with forcible seizures. Lacking incentives, the peasantry reduced sowings, and agricultural output under War Communism fell to about one half of what it had been. Government attempts to organize collective farms and cooperatives failed because few peasants would enter them voluntarily, and only fear that the Whites would restore landlordism kept some peasants loyal to the Bolshevik regime.

With most state expenditures financed by the printing of money as needed, the ruble was undermined and paper currency became almost worthless. Worker rations were free, and wages were paid mostly in kind. As doctrinaire Bolsheviks rejoiced at an increasingly moneyless economy, production plummeted. With the government unable to obtain enough food for the cities, illegal bagmen brought foodstuffs to city dwellers in return for consumer goods. A black market thrived.

Once the Civil War ended, the population found War Communism unbearable. In the winter of 1920–1921, in the Don and Volga regions, Ukraine and north Caucasus peasant uprisings broke out. Soviet sources blame SR-led kulaks, but most middle peasants joined the revolts as the worker-peasant alliance, the cornerstone of Soviet power, tottered. Grain requisition detachments were attacked everywhere, and the Cheka, in February 1921, reported 118 separate peasant uprisings. In Tambov province, Alexander Antonov, a former SR, led almost 50,000 insurgent peasants demanding "Down with Communists and Jews!" and "Down with requisitioning!" From all over Russia, peasant petitions demanded a fixed tax on agricultural produce instead of grain seizures. In the towns, the situation was equally dismal: Industry and transport lay idle, workers starved, and city life was falling apart. Despite the Reds' military victory, Soviet Russia seemed about to collapse.

The Kronstadt Revolt of 1921

In March 1921 a major revolt by sailors of the Kronstadt naval base on Kotlin Island near Petrograd confirmed Lenin's decision to yield to peasant demands to scrap War Communism. Ironically, Red sailors, the most revolutionary, pro-Bolshevik element during 1917, led an insurrection against the Bolshevik regime only four years later. As in March 1917, hunger was again a factor. A one third reduction in the bread ration triggered worker strikes and demonstrations in Petrograd in February. These encouraged the crews of two warships of the disaffected Baltic Fleet to draw up a list of demands. Their Petropavlovsk Resolution condemned War Communism, demanded elections to the soviets by secret ballot, the abolition of grain requisitioning and state farms, and full freedom for peasants on their land. Advocating anarcho-syndicalism, the sailors sought land, liberty, and a federation of autonomous communes. The Resolution appealed to the Soviet regime to live up to its Constitution of 1918 and grant rights and freedoms that Lenin had proposed during 1917. A Provisional Revolutionary Committee led by S. M. Petrichenko, a sailor of Ukrainian peasant background, seized control of Kronstadt, whose Communist Party virtually dissolved. During their two-week regime the Kronstadt rebels recaptured briefly the enthusiastic idealism and freedom of the March Revolution.

Fearing for their power, the Bolshevik authorities, realizing the Kronstadt uprising might ignite a massive rebellion in Russia, sought from the start to discredit it as a White-émigré plot manipulated from abroad. They depicted Kronstadt sailors of 1921, whom Trotskii in 1917 had called "the pride and glory of the Russian Revolution," as demoralized, drunken roughnecks. Actually, the revolt was native and spontaneous. Declared Petrichenko: "Our revolt was an elemental movement to get rid of Bolshevik oppression . . . [so] the will of the people will manifest itself." Spurning conciliation or concessions that might have averted bloodshed, Bolshevik leaders headed by Trotskii demanded that the "counterrevolutionary mutineers" immediately lay down their arms. When the rebels rejected his ultimatum, the Red Army launched an infantry assault across the ice from Petrograd, only to be repulsed. In the final attack of March 16 some 50,000 Red troops finally conquered defiant Kronstadt. The bloody suppression of the revolt revealed the Bolshevik regime as a repressive tyranny relying on naked force. Kronstadt, admitted Lenin, "lit up reality better than anything else." Revealing the need for new economic policies and a relaxation of state pressure, the revolt marked the end of the Russian revolutionary movement.[6]

Suggested Additional Reading

ADAMS, ARTHUR. *The Second Ukrainian Campaign of the Bolsheviks* (New Haven, Conn., 1963).

AVRICH, PAUL. *Kronstadt 1921* (Princeton, N.J., 1970).

BASIL, J. D. *The Mensheviks in the Revolution of 1917* (Columbus, Ohio, 1984).

BRADLEY, JOHN F. *Civil War in Russia, 1917–1920* (New York, 1975).

BRINKLEY, GEORGE. *The Volunteer Army and the Allied Intervention in South Russia, 1917–1921* (Notre Dame, Ind., 1966).

BROVKIN, VLADIMIR. *The Mensheviks After October . . .* (Ithaca, N.Y., 1988).

BUNYAN, J., and H. H. FISHER, eds. *Intervention, Civil War and Communism in Russia, April–December 1918: Documents and Materials* (Baltimore, Md., 1936).

BURBANK, JANE. *Intelligentsia and Revolution: Russian Views of Bolshevism, 1917–1922* (Oxford, Eng., 1989).

DENIKIN, ANTON. *The Russian Turmoil* (London, 1922).

FISCHER, LOUIS. *The Life of Lenin* (New York, 1964).

FOOTMAN, DAVID. *Civil War in Russia* (New York, 1962).

GETZLER, ISRAEL. *Kronstadt, 1917–1921: The Fate of a Soviet Democracy* (Cambridge, Eng., 1983).

KAZEMZADEH, FIRUZ. *The Struggle for Transcaucasia, 1917–1921* (New York, 1951).

KENEZ, PETER. *Civil War in South Russia: The First Year of the Volunteer Army* (Berkeley, Calif., 1971).

KENNAN, GEORGE F. *Soviet-American Relations, 1917–1920*, 2 vols. (New York, 1967).

KINGSTON-MANN E. *Lenin and the Problem of Marxist Peasant Revolution* (Oxford, Eng., 1983).

LEHOVICH, DMITRY. *White Against Red: The Life of General Denikin* (New York, 1974).

LINCOLN, W. BRUCE. *Red Victory: A History of the Russian Civil War* (New York, 1989).

LOCKHART, R. H. BRUCE. *British Agent* (New York, 1933).

LUCKETT, RICHARD. *The White Generals . . .* (London, 1987).

MORLEY, JAMES W. *The Japanese Thrust into Siberia, 1918–1920* (New York, 1957).

RADKEY, OLIVER. *The Election to the Russian Constituent Assembly of 1917* (Cambridge, Mass., 1950).

———. *The Unknown Civil War in Russia* (Stanford, Calif., 1976).

---

[6]Paul Avrich, *Kronstadt 1921* (Princeton, N.J., 1970).

RESHETAR, JOHN S., JR. *The Ukrainian Revolution, 1917–1920* (Princeton, N.J., 1952).

SHOLOKHOV, MIKHAIL. *And Quiet Flows the Don* (New York, 1966). (Historical novel of the Civil War.)

STRAKHOVSKY, LEONID. *The Origins of American Intervention in North Russia* (Princeton, N.J., 1937).

ULLMAN, R. H. *Intervention and the War: Anglo-Soviet Relations, 1917–1920,* 2 vols. (Princeton, N.J., 1961, 1968).

UNTERBERGER, BETTY. *America's Siberian Expedition, 1918–1920* (Durham, N.C., 1956).

VERNECK, ELENA. *The Testimony of Kolchak and Other Siberian Material* (Stanford, Calif., 1935).

WHITE, JOHN A. *The Siberian Intervention* (Princeton, N.J., 1950).

WRANGEL, PETER N. *The Memoirs of General Wrangel* (London, 1929).

CHAPTER NINE

THE NEW ECONOMIC POLICY AND POWER STRUGGLE, 1921–1927

In March 1921 in the face of a rising tide of peasant uprisings and the Kronstadt Revolt, the 10th Congress of the Soviet Communist Party under Lenin's leadership scrapped the disastrous economic policies of War Communism. In their place were instituted the basic elements of a New Economic Policy (NEP), described by Lenin as a step backward toward capitalism in order to prepare the way for a subsequent surge forward toward the promised land of socialism. NEP promoted the recovery of the Soviet economy devastated by seven years of war and doctrinaire Bolshevik economic experimentation. NEP also relaxed somewhat the economic and political pressures exerted by the state and allowed more scope to individual enterprise and creativity. Did NEP represent a genuine retreat toward capitalism or the initial stage of socialist construction? Did it signify Lenin's abandonment of the more extreme features of the Bolshevik dictatorship in favor of moderate policies and the slower advance toward socialism advocated by N. I. Bukharin?

Lenin suffered his first cerebral stroke in May 1922, which triggered a major struggle over the succession among the principal Soviet leaders. Stalin and Trotskii soon became the chief contenders for power, but neither was given Lenin's full blessing. How did Stalin, a "grey blur" in 1917, eventually defeat his rivals and achieve absolute power in the Soviet Union? Did Stalin's triumph signify a logical continuation of Leninist rule and principles or a dastardly betrayal of the ideology of Marxism-Leninism?

ECONOMIC AND POLITICAL CONTROLS OF NEP

Lenin had written that tactical retreats would sometimes be necessary. To save the regime, the peasantry had to be wooed and the worker-peasant alliance restored. To achieve this, Lenin, overcoming objections to "compromise with capitalism," persuaded the 10th Party Congress to end grain requisitioning and approve a fixed tax in kind per acre. Initially, the New Economic Policy was a limited move to stimulate peasant production for the urban market, but by late 1921 private buying and selling had swept the country. Private ownership was restored in consumer sectors, while the state retained control over the "commanding heights"—large industry, transport, and foreign trade.

Postponing socialist agriculture indefinitely, NEP stimulated small private farming. Class war in the village was abandoned, and richer peasants were allowed to prosper. Once they had paid their tax in kind, farmers were free to dispose of their surplus and were guaranteed secure tenure. Within limits, they could lease additional land and hire labor. With these stimuli, agriculture recovered rapidly until threatened by the "scissors crisis" of 1922–1923. Marketing their grain in order to buy consumer goods, farmers found that industrial prices, kept up by inefficient state trusts, were three times higher relative to agricultural prices than before World War I. Farmers again curtailed marketings and purchases of manufactures. When this threatened economic recovery by reducing urban food supplies and piling up consumer goods, the government forced state industry to lower prices and to prune excess staff. These measures overcame the worst effects of the scissors.

Scrapping War Communism also fostered industrial recovery. Denationalization began in May 1921, and soon about 4,000 small firms controlled three fourths of retail and 20 percent of wholesale trade. Inefficient state enterprises were forced to close, and free contracts among remaining state firms gradually replaced centralized allocation of raw materials and equipment. State-owned big industry employed more than 80 percent of all workers, but handicrafts and small firms with up to 20 employees were private. Real wages recovered roughly to prewar

Red Army passing in review before Trotskii (first from left, marked with a cross) in Red Square, c. 1918 *(Library of Congress)*

levels, but unemployment became an increasing problem. By 1923, the USSR possessed the first modern mixed economy with state and private sectors. A degree of economic planning was achieved by Gosplan (State Planning Commission).

In 1924–1925, the mixed NEP economy, overcoming currency difficulties and the price scissors, reached its peak. As state-controlled big industry coexisted with individual and family enterprises, production in industry and agriculture neared prewar levels. In 1927, about 25 million individual farms composed 98.3 percent of all agricultural units, while state and collective farms included only a tiny minority of peasants and land. Some 350,000 peasant communes, with their village assemblies, not local soviets, dominated rural life. More than 90 percent of the peasantry belonged to mirs and had reverted to traditional strip farming and periodic land redistribution. Millions of households still used wooden plows, and half the 1928 grain harvest was reaped by scythe or sickle! Whereas Soviet sources divide the peasantry neatly into kulaks, middle peasants, and poor peasants, actually each group shaded into the next. Middle peasants, poor by European standards, often lacked horses. Redefined to suit political convenience, kulaks were estimated at 5 to 7 percent of the total, yet only 1 percent of households employed more than one laborer. Nonetheless, the resurgence of the kulaks suggested peasant differentiation and capitalist revival. Individual farmers sought to consolidate their land and increase production for the market, but success meant being labeled "kulak exploiters." In 1925, the sown area was about that of 1913, but the grain harvest was some 10 percent smaller. Whereas Stalin claimed that only half as much grain was marketed in 1927 as in 1913, recent studies affirm that marketings in 1927 almost equaled the 1909–1913 average. Urban demand for grain was rising while peasants, discouraged by low prices, ate better and sold less. Grain exports, which reached 12 million tons in 1913, were only 300,000 tons in 1927–1928.

Party moderates, led by Bukharin, advocated continuing NEP indefinitely in order to reach socialism. Peasant prosperity, they argued, would stimulate rural demand for industrial goods and increase marketable agricultural surpluses. In 1925, Bukharin declared: "Peasants, enrich yourselves!" but soon had to repudiate that slogan. The party's goal, he stated, was "pulling the lower strata up to a high level," because "poor peasant socialism is wretched socialism." Lower industrial prices would spur peasant demand and achieve socialism without coercion "at a snail's pace."

Serious economic problems still faced Russia in 1927. A primitive peasant agriculture barely surpassed prewar levels of productivity. An overpopulated countryside inundated towns with unskilled workers, threatening Bolshevik industrial goals and urban-rural market relationships. As industrial growth leveled off, the economy, unable to draw from capital accumulated under tsarism, faced hard decisions on how to generate more investment and savings. Grain marketings were insufficient to support industrial progress, yet short of coercion, the only ways to increase them were to provide cheaper consumer goods or to raise farm prices significantly.

The experience and results of NEP were debated and reassessed in the USSR under Gorbachev after 1985. At the 27th Party Congress of February 1986, Gorbachev himself advocated "something like a Leninist food tax (*prodnalog*) in the new conditions of today" to stimulate lagging agricultural production. The numerous Soviet articles in 1987–1989 that referred to NEP were overwhelmingly favorable and often exaggerated its beneficial economic results. Soviet specialists attributed NEP's successes primarily to the economic freedom it gave the peasant. Some stressed the efficiency of individual peasants producing for the marketplace whereas others, apparently with official approval, argued for the need of voluntary peasant cooperatives for any long-term solution of agrarian problems. Many Soviet intellectuals praised the NEP years as an era of political, legal, and cultural freedom.[1]

But how much did Soviet women benefit from this increased freedom? Proclaiming a women's emancipation and equality that they failed to implement fully in practice, the Bolsheviks had created Zhenotdel, directed after Inessa Armand's death by Alexandra Kollontai (1920–1921). She emphasized the liberation of "women of the East," notably Muslim women of Central Asia, from their traditional subservience. Opposing the increasing centralism and bureaucracy overtaking the Bolshevik Party, Kollontai advocated creative efforts by the workers themselves; in 1921, she drafted and distributed the program for the Workers' Opposition faction, advocating syndicalism. Lenin and his colleagues, denouncing the Workers' Opposition as a threat to Party unity and discipline, removed Kollontai from Zhenotdel and packed her off to Norway on a minor diplomatic mission. Her political career was over, but later she became the first Soviet ambassador to Sweden. Lenin's regime, while providing educational and economic equality for women, granted them little political power. Before November 1917, only three women had served in the party leadership; few thereafter even reached the Central Committee, and no woman served on the Politburo until Ekaterina Furtseva achieved full membership, 1957–1961. Observed Kollontai correctly in 1922: "The Soviet state is run by men." Soviet women enjoyed broad civil rights but little political power.

Under NEP, though a degree of freedom persisted, political controls were tightened. Remaining Menshevik and SR leaders were exiled, and late in 1921, a party purge excluded about one fourth the Bolshevik membership. Within the party, factions were banned and political dissent became more dangerous. Punitive powers of the expanding central party apparatus over the members increased, and decision making by top leaders grew more arbitrary. Party decrees, however, failed to end debate

---

[1] R. W. Davies, ed., *Soviet History in the Gorbachev Revolution* (Bloomington, Ind., 1989), pp. 28 ff.

or factions during NEP, even though the defeated might be expelled or lose their posts.

The Constitution of 1918 had proclaimed federalism, but relations among Soviet republics remained undefined until in December 1922 a unified, centralized Union of Soviet Socialist Republics replaced the several independent republics. Within the huge Russian Republic (RSFSR) were 17 autonomous republics and regions for national minorities, all ruled from Moscow. Other republics, such as Ukraine and Byelorussia, had to accept the RSFSR's constitution verbatim. Because the soviets were subordinate to party direction and other Communist parties were Russian led, the Russian Party's Central Committee exercised full de facto power everywhere. The RSFSR government became the highest state authority in all areas occupied by the Red Army. Recent Soviet histories, minimizing national resistance to integration in Soviet Russia, attribute the USSR's formation partly to "imperialist" pressure and foreign plots to overthrow Soviet power. Actually, it resulted mainly from the Red Army's subjugation of tsarist borderlands, such as Transcaucasia. When Red troops entered Vladivostok in 1922, following Japanese withdrawal, the Far Eastern Republic dissolved instantly and merged with the RSFSR. The nominally independent republics of Khiva and Bukhara in Central Asia were abolished in 1924 and their territory distributed arbitrarily among five new Soviet republics: Uzbek, Turkmen, Tajik, Kazakh, and Kirghiz.

The new USSR was an apparent compromise between Bolshevik desires for centralization and autonomist aims of nationalists and federalists in the borderlands. The Bolsheviks viewed the USSR as a stage in the advance toward an ultimate worldwide Soviet state. Within it, national minorities often enjoyed less autonomy than under tsarism. Gone were their political parties, separate religious and cultural institutions, though they received linguistic autonomy, distinct national territories, and political representation—a fake federalism concealing complete Russian and Bolshevik predominance; it failed to win the support of the nationalities.

Once Lenin achieved power, his doctrines changed considerably. Before the November coup he had declared in *State and Revolution:*

> To destroy officialdom immediately, everywhere, completely—this cannot be thought of. . . . But to *break up* at once the old bureaucratic machine and to start immediately the construction of a new one which will enable us gradually to reduce all officialdom to naught, this is *no* Utopia, it is the experience of the [Paris] Commune, the . . . direct and urgent task of the revolutionary proletariat.[2]

---

[2]Lenin, *Polnoe Sobranie Sochineniia,* 5th ed. (Moscow, 1962), vol. 33, pp. 48–49.

Capitalism had so simplified governmental functions, Lenin believed, that ordinary workers could perform such "registration, filing and checking." He had conceived of a "state apparatus of about 10, if not 20 million" class-conscious workers as part-time civil servants. (How poorly he understood the problems of running an industrial society!) Once in power, the flexible Lenin discarded former views that proved inapplicable. The transition to socialism, he admitted in 1918, would require bourgeois experts, and in 1920 he conceded sadly: "We have to administer [the proletarian state] with the help of people belonging to the class we have overthrown" and pay them well. In his final years, Lenin, in his writings, grew cautious and reformist. Criticizing War Communism's "furious assaults," he described "exaggerated revolutionism" as dangerous in domestic policy and advocated "conquering peacefully" by careful economic construction. The contrast between his militant views in 1917–1920 and the reformist, evolutionary emphasis of 1921–1923 makes one wonder which was the "real" Lenin.

Nonetheless, Lenin bequeathed an elitist doctrine and party as one foundation of a new autocracy (others were provided by tsarism, the Civil War, and War Communism). His central doctrine—the dictatorship of the proletariat—he had defined as "power won and maintained by the proletariat against the bourgeoisie, power unrestricted by any laws." Having designed a theoretically centralized party able to strike ruthlessly and outlawing factions within it (which failed to end factionalism), he hoped that "democratic centralism" would encourage free intraparty debate, then unanimous action. Discussion was to be free until a decision was reached, then all party members were expected to execute it loyally. Although Lenin prevailed within the party not by force, not because of any position he held, but by persuasion, charisma, and moral stature, nevertheless he left to Stalin certain tools which Stalin used to build his brutal dictatorship: a centralized party, predominant central organs, subservient soviets, and police terror. It was Lenin who authorized creation of a secret police and who banned factionalism within the party. By applying these elements ruthlessly and vindictively, Stalin altered the Soviet system fundamentally. (See Chapter 10, pp. 219 ff.)

THE STRUGGLE OVER SUCCESSION

In May 1922, Lenin suffered his first stroke. By his writings, pragmatic leadership, and ability to handle people, he had dominated Bolshevism since its inception, and his semiretirement sparked a struggle for succession within the party. Lenin named no successor, and his "Testament," or "Letter to the Congress" of December 1922, found fault with all the leading contenders. Increasingly dismayed by Stalin's Great Russian chauvinism and brutal domination of the party apparatus, Lenin wrote: "Comrade Stalin, having become *gensek* [General Secretary] has concentrated boundless power in his hands, and I am not sure that he will always manage to use this power with sufficient caution." He had a second stroke in December 1922. In January 1923, he added: "Stalin is too rude. . . . I propose to the comrades that they devise a way of shifting Stalin from this position. . . ." Apparently, only a third stroke in March 1923 prevented Lenin from removing Stalin. Concern for the party and their own positions induced other contenders at first to form a collective leadership and present a united front. Behind the scenes the struggle for succession went through several phases until Stalin triumphed. These issues were debated fiercely: Where was the Revolution heading? Would NEP lead to capitalism or socialism? How should Russia be industrialized? Factions, though illegal, were too ingrained in party traditions to be easily eradicated, though politics grew ever more dangerous and secretive. At Lenin's death in 1924, four major groups had formed: a Stalin faction, the Trotskii Left, Bukharin's moderates, and a Zinoviev-Kamenev group based in Leningrad.

Joseph Stalin, the eventual winner, was born in 1879 as Iosif Vissarionovich Djugashvili of semiliterate Georgian parents descended from serfs. As a boy, Soso was devoted to his mother and rebelled against a drunken father and all authority. An excellent student who expected to excel in everything, he idealized Koba, a fearless 19th-century Caucasian mountain chieftain, and adopted his view of vindictive triumph as a worthy goal in life. He resented the strict discipline at the Tiflis Orthodox seminary and was expelled as a socialist in 1899. Between 1902 and 1917, he was arrested and exiled repeatedly for underground revolutionary activity. He became a Bolshevik soon after the faction's formation; as Lenin's admiring disciple, he modeled himself after his hero and adopted the name, Stalin, partly because it resembled Lenin. Stalin adopted a Great Russian outlook and dedicated his life to revolution. His *Marxism and the National Question* (1913) established him as a major leader and a mature Marxist. In 1917, as party organizer and close colleague of Lenin, he belonged to the Bolshevik general staff. The SR memoirist, N. Sukhanov, however, recalled Stalin then as "a grey blur, looming up now and then dimly, and not leaving any trace." During the Civil War, he gained military experience and political influence but was intensely jealous of Trotskii, who overshadowed him. The traditional Western view of Stalin as a nonintellectual "organization man," building the party state, however, fitted Sverdlov better. Stalin handled crises well, but he was too impatient, hot tempered, and uncooperative to be a gifted organizer or administrator. In 1923, he confided to Kamenev: "The

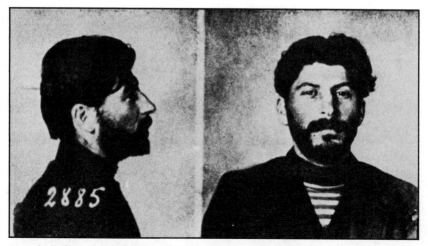

Joseph Stalin: Tsarist police photograph (*John Massey Stewart*)

greatest delight is to mark one's enemy, prepare everything, avenge oneself thoroughly, and then go to sleep."

Aiming to control the Bolshevik movement, Stalin achieved his commanding position by the politics of power and influence and by cultivating a political following built up over the years. In exile, using Machiavelli's *The Prince* as a primer, he studied the strategy and tactics of politics. He had an intuitive eye for men's strengths and weaknesses and how to exploit them. After Sverdlov's death in 1919, Stalin acquired key posts in the Orgburo (concerned with organizational matters), Politburo, and Secretariat, and election as General Secretary consolidated his organizational position. Stalin dominated the party apparatus that Sverdlov had built, forged his personal machine, and obtained a controlling voice on party bodies that selected and placed personnel.

Stalin exploited cleverly the cult of Lenin, which developed during the leader's final illness. Lenin had prohibited public adulation of himself and detested ceremony, but after his death his teachings—Leninism—became sacred doctrine. Official decrees ordered monuments to Lenin erected all over the USSR, renamed Petrograd as Leningrad, and authorized a huge edition of his writings. Stalin urged that Lenin's body be embalmed and placed on public display in a tomb on Red Square, although his widow, Trotskii, and Bukharin protested that this was un-Marxian. As Lenin's devoted disciple, Stalin gathered the reins of power and won public acclaim.

Before achieving full power, Stalin survived some tense moments. In May 1924, a Central Committee plenum heard Lenin's "Testament,"

Stalin's birthplace, surrounded by the Stalin museum, in Gori, Georgia *(Michael Curran)*

which urged Stalin's removal as General Secretary. But Zinoviev and Kamenev, who had formed a triumvirate with Stalin in 1922, supported him from fear of Trotskii. Stalin used the triumvirate to undermine Trotskii, whose inept tactics and arrogance antagonized many party members; Trotskii also spurned overtures from Kamenev and Zinoviev when Stalin's rise might still have been prevented. Only after his rivals had voted him into all positions of power did Stalin begin an open struggle with them. His repetitious, catechistic style won support from younger, semieducated Bolsheviks, who sought a single authoritative chief to lead their party forward.

In 1925, the triumvirate broke up: Zinoviev and Kamenev drifted belatedly toward Trotskii, while Stalin joined Bukharin's moderates. At the 14th Congress, Kamenev, too late, challenged Stalin's credentials as the new party chief, but Stalin's machine defeated him and broke up Zinoviev's Leningrad organization. Because Stalin still lacked enough prestige to seize sole power, his alliance with Bukharin proved most advantageous. As chief theorist and spokesman for NEP, Bukharin shielded Stalin from accusations that he was usurping Lenin's place and compensated for his lack of ideological clout. Through 1927, Stalin supported NEP, Bukharin's gradualist economics, and his ideological warfare against Trotskii.

During the growing debate over socialist construction, Stalin developed his major theory: socialism in one country. (See p. 233.) He had declared at a Bolshevik conference, in April 1917: "The possibility is not excluded that Russia will . . . blaze the trail to socialism." In 1925, Bukharin affirmed that the USSR could build its own socialism gradually but added, "Final practical victory of socialism in our country is not possible without the help of other countries and of world revolution." Posing as a moderate and Lenin's true interpreter, Stalin restated the Leninist view in *Foundations of Leninism* (1924):

> To overthrow the bourgeoisie the efforts of one country are sufficient; for the final victory of socialism, for the organization of socialist production the efforts of one country, particularly of a peasant country like Russia, are insufficient; for that the efforts of the proletariats of several advanced countries are required.[3]

To prove that Trotskii and his theory of world revolution were anti-Leninist, however, Stalin later that year suddenly asserted that Russia alone could organize a completely socialist economy with advanced industry and high living standards. He developed the nationalistic view that Russia alone might blaze the trail of socialist construction. Soviet Russia, the pioneer of proletarian revolution, could construct a fully socialist society by its own exertions with or without revolutions abroad. To ensure that the old order would not be restored, however, the proletariat must win power in "at least several other countries." Carefully selecting his quotations, Stalin insisted that this was Lenin's theory, too. Stalin's program of Russian self-sufficiency in building socialism proved highly effective, especially among new, young party members, and a burgeoning Soviet officialdom, composed largely of semieducated worker and peasant elements. These greedy and often incompetent officials welcomed Stalin's nationalism and growing "personality cult." The new bureaucracy, manipulated by Stalin, replaced the proletariat as the bearer of socialism.[4] The doctrine of socialism in one country made Stalin an authoritative ideological leader, who could shrug off his opponent's belated criticisms.

---

[3]Quoted in R. Tucker, *Stalin as Revolutionary, 1879–1929* (New York, 1973), p. 371.
[4]See Moshe Lewin, "The Social Background of Stalinism," in R. Tucker, ed. *Stalinism* (New York, 1977), pp. 111 ff.

Table 9.1 *Participants in the Soviet Power Struggle, 1922–1929*

1922–1925	Triumvirate: Stalin-Zinoviev-Kamenev
1925–1928	Stalin-Bukharin versus Trotskii-Kamenev-Zinoviev
1929–1953	Stalin in power

In 1926–1927, Stalin defeated and silenced the Left with support from the Bukharinists. Trotskii and Zinoviev were removed from the Politburo, and the latter was ousted as Comintern chief. Trotskii's denunciations of the Stalin-dominated Politburo as "Thermidorean," his critique of its blunders in foreign policy, and his street demonstration of November 1927 hastened his expulsion from the party and exile. As Zinoviev and Kamenev recanted their views to save their party membership, only the Bukharinists stood between Stalin and complete power.

Soviet Russia, under NEP, was a one-party dictatorship modified by social pluralism, an economic compromise between socialism and capitalism. Though the state sector predominated in industry and was growing, the private sector remained vital and dominant in agriculture. Most Soviet citizens, especially peasants, worked and lived far from party or state control, which did not extend far outside the urban centers. NEP was an era of rival theories, contention, and exciting experiments. Tolerance of political, economic, and social diversity marked it as a period of liberal Communism, recovery, and civil peace. As Stalin built his party autocracy, however, these compromises could not long endure.

PROBLEM 3
From Lenin to Stalin—Continuity or Betrayal?

Who, if anyone, was responsible for putting Soviet Russia on a course leading to renewed autocracy, repression, and massive purges? Was this the work of Lenin or Stalin, or was it inherent in Bolshevism, or the previous development of Russian history? Were there fundamental differences in approach, policy, and personality between Lenin and Stalin? Was Stalin's regime the logical culmination of Leninism, or did his one-man rule and personality cult represent a breach with and repudiation of Bolshevik ideals and practice? Did Stalin's dictatorship constitute an aberration, a temporary interruption of a Bolshevik tradition of "collective leadership," as N. S. Khrushchev would later intimate?

Until 1960, most Western scholars stressed elements of continuity between early Bolshevism and the Stalin era. This theory of the "straight line" was reinforced more recently by Alexander Solzhenitsyn's *The Gulag Archipelago,* which traced the roots of mass terror and the system of forced labor camps to the first days of Lenin's regime. (See the "Soviet Émigrés" section.) Western scholars tended to view Stalin's "great transformation" of 1929–1933 as perfecting an inherent, inevitable totalitarianism. Recently, some Western historians, using newly accessible Soviet materials, have challenged this continuity thesis. These revisionists argue that Stalinism differed fundamentally from earlier Bolshevism, that Stalin's policies were so violent and extreme that they changed the very nature of the Soviet state and Bolshevik Party. By emphasizing statism, Great Russian nationalism, and anti-Semitism and by encouraging his own deification, Stalin repudiated the beliefs of Lenin and his "Old Bolshevik" colleagues, such as Trotskii, Zinoviev, and Bukharin. To view Stalinism as merely the outgrowth of the militant Lenin of *What Is to Be Done?* (1902), argues Stephen Cohen, is a grievous oversimplification. Instead, Bolshevism evolved over the years from an unruly, loosely organized group of independent-minded revolutionaries into the centralized, bureaucratic organization of the 1920s; under Stalin the Communist Party was terrorized and its influence sharply reduced. In actuality, the Bolshevik Party had never been quite the disciplined vanguard of professionals advocated in *What Is to Be Done?* Even official party historians complained repeatedly that its history was one of "factional struggle." Despite the ban on factions engineered by Lenin in 1921, the party remained oligarchical or, as Bukharin put it, "a negotiated federation between groups, groupings, factions, and tendencies." Thus, Cohen concludes, the party's "organizational principles" did not produce Stalinist dictatorship and conformity.[5]

Indicative of the widely disparate views on the relationship between the regimes of Lenin (1917–1923) and Stalin (1928–1953) are the following excerpts from official Soviet publications, a work by a Soviet dissident scholar, excerpts from a very recent Soviet biography of Stalin, two statements by émigrés from the Soviet Union, and two Western accounts.

---

[5]S. Cohen, "Bolshevism and Stalinism," in R. Tucker, *Stalinism,* pp. 19–29. See also Tucker, *The Soviet Political Mind* (New York, 1963).

OFFICIAL SOVIET INTERPRETATIONS

1. *History of the Communist Party of the Soviet Union (Bolsheviks). Short Course* (New York, 1939). This is the official party history prepared ostensibly by the Central Committee following the Great Purge. It was edited and perhaps partly written by Joseph Stalin and reflects the "classical" Stalinist interpretation of the purges: The "dregs of humanity" referred to in the text included the leading "Old Bolsheviks," the closest colleagues of Lenin—the original leaders of Soviet Russia, the Bolshevik Party, and the Third International (Comintern)! (See Chapter 10 for a discussion of Stalin's Great Purge.)

In 1937, new facts came to light regarding the fiendish crimes of the Bukharin-Trotsky gang. The trial[s] . . . all showed that the Bukharinites and Trotskyists had long ago joined to form a common band of enemies of the people, operating as the "Bloc of Rights and Trotskyites." The trials showed that these dregs of humanity, in conjunction with the enemies of the people, Trotsky, Zinoviev, and Kamenev, had been in conspiracy against Lenin, the Party, and the Soviet state ever since the early days of the October Socialist Revolution. The insidious attempts to thwart the Peace of Brest-Litovsk at the beginning of 1918, . . . the deliberate aggravation of differences in the party in 1921. . ., the attempts to overthrow the Party leadership during Lenin's illness and after his death, . . . the vile assassination of Kirov . . .—all these and similar villainies over a period of 20 years were committed, it transpired, with the participation or under the direction of Trotsky, Zinoviev, Kamenev, Bukharin, Rykov and their henchmen, at the behest of espionage services of bourgeois states.

The trials brought to light the fact that the Trotsky-Bukharin fiends, in obedience to the wishes of their masters—the espionage services of foreign states—had set out to destroy the Party and the Soviet state, to undermine the defensive power of the country, to assist foreign military intervention, to prepare the way for the defeat of the Red Army, to bring about the dismemberment of the U.S.S.R., to destroy the gains of the workers and collective farmers, and to restore capitalist slavery in the U.S.S.R. These Whiteguard pygmies, whose strength was no more than that of a gnat, apparently flattered themselves that they were the masters of the country, and imagined that it was really in their power to sell or give away the Ukraine, Byelorussia, and the Maritime Region. . . . These contemptible lackeys of the fascists forgot that the Soviet people had only to move a finger, and not a trace of them would be left. The Soviet court sentenced the Bukharin-Trotsky fiends to be shot. . . . The Soviet people approved the annihilation of the Bukharin-Trotsky gang and passed on to the next business [pp. 346–348].

2. *History of the Communist Party of the Soviet Union* (Moscow, 1960). Issued during the modified one-man rule of N. S. Khrushchev, this

party history reflects denunciation of Stalin's crimes after 1934, balanced by praise for his economic achievements, as expressed by the 20th Party Congress of 1956. Note that no attempt is made here to rehabilitate "Old Bolshevik" leaders like Trotskii, Zinoviev, and Bukharin.

The victory of socialism created favorable conditions for the extension of Party and Soviet democracy. But in spite of that, there were direct violations of Party and Soviet democracy resulting from what was later defined by the Party as the cult of Stalin's personality. Stalin began to develop into a law certain restrictions in inner-Party and Soviet democracy that were unavoidable in conditions of bitter struggle against the class enemy and his agents. He began to violate the standards of Party life worked out by Lenin, the principle of collective leadership, deciding many important questions on his own. In Stalin's actions a discrepancy arose between word and deed, between theory and practice. . . . Starting from correct Marxist premises, he warned against impermissible exaggerations of the role of the individual in history, but in practice he encouraged the cult of his own personality.

Stalin rightly stressed the necessity of strengthening the Soviet State in every possible way, of keeping a watchful eye . . . on the machinations of the hostile capitalist encirclement; . . . to be on guard against . . . the routed opposition groups of the Trotskyists, Zinovievites . . . On the other hand, in 1937, when Socialism was already victorious in the U.S.S.R., Stalin advanced the erroneous thesis that the class struggle in the country would intensify as the Soviet State grew stronger. . . . In practice it served as a justification for mass repressions against the Party's ideological enemies who had already been routed politically. Many honest Communists and non-Party people, not guilty of any offense, also became victims of these repressions. During this period the political adventurer and scoundrel, Beria,[6] who did not stop short at any atrocity to achieve his criminal aims, worked his way into responsible positions in the State, and, taking advantage of Stalin's personal shortcomings, slandered and exterminated many honest people, devoted to the Party and the people. In the same period a despicable role was played by Yezhov . . . Many workers, both Communists and non-Party people, who were utterly devoted to the cause of the Party, were slandered with his assistance and perished. Yezhov and Beria were duly punished for their crimes.[7] . . . Although the mistakes resulting from the cult of Stalin's personality retarded the development of Soviet society, they could not check it, and still less could they change the Socialist nature of the Soviet system (pp. 512–513).

---

[6]After the Great Purge had reached its climax in 1937 under N. I. Ezhov, Stalin had him executed and made Lavrenti Beria head of the security police (NKVD).
[7]Yezhov was executed, apparently at Stalin's orders, in 1938. Beria was purged in June 1953 after apparently attempting to overthrow the government and was executed either before or after his "trial."

DISSIDENT HISTORIAN

..dvedev is a Soviet Marxist scholar, who became absorbed in study
..e Stalin era after Khrushchev's revelations at the 20th and 22nd
..rty Congresses. However, by the time he had completed his book, *Let
History Judge: The Origins and Consequences of Stalinism* in 1968, the
Brezhnev regime was moving toward a partial rehabilitation of Stalin,
and it had to be published in the United States. Medvedev subsequently
was expelled from the party, but remains a Marxist living in the Soviet
Union. This book represented an "insider's" view of the Stalin phenomenon. Medvedev accepted Khrushchev's view that Stalinist terror and the
personality cult were temporary departures from an essentially sound
Soviet system, but he was much more vigorous in denouncing that terror.

To many people in the Soviet Union the mass repression of 1937–38 was
an incomprehensible calamity that suddenly broke upon the country and
seemed to have no end. Explanations abounded, some of them representing
a search for the truth, but more attempting to escape the cruel truth, to find
some formula that would preserve faith in the Party and Stalin. . . . One
widespread story was that Stalin did not know about the terror, that all those
crimes were committed behind his back. Of course it was ridiculous to
suppose that Stalin, master of everyone and everything, did not know about
the arrest and shooting of members of the Politburo and the Central
Committee, . . . about the arrest of the military high command and the
Comintern leaders. . . . But that is a peculiarity of the mind blinded by faith
in a higher being. This naive conviction of Stalin's ignorance was reflected in
the word, *ezhovshchina,* "the Ezhov thing," the popular name for the tragedy
of the thirties. . . , a new version of the common people's faith in a good tsar
surrounded by lying and wicked ministers. But it must be acknowledged that
this story had some basis in Stalin's behavior. Secretive and self-contained,
Stalin avoided the public eye; . . . he acted through unseen channels. He
tried to direct events from behind the scenes, making basic decisions by
himself or with a few aides . . . preferring to put the spotlight on other
perpetrators of these crimes, thereby retaining his own freedom of movement.

Some confusion about the nature of Stalin's power must be cleared away.
By the end of the twenties and the early thirties he was already called a
dictator, a one-man ruler. . . , but the unlimited dictatorship that he established after 1936–38 was without historical precedent. For the last fifteen
years of his bloody career Stalin wielded such power as no Russian tsar ever
possessed. . . . In the years of the cult, Stalin held not only all political power;
he was master of the economy, the military, foreign policy; even in literature,
the arts, and science he was the supreme arbiter. . . .

It was an historical accident that Stalin, the embodiment of all the worst
elements in the Russian revolutionary movement, came to power after
Lenin, the embodiment of all that was best. . . . The Party must not only

condemn Stalin's crimes; it must also eliminate the conditions that facilitated them. . . . Stalin never relied on force alone. Throughout the period of his one-man rule he was popular. The longer this tyrant ruled the USSR, coldbloodedly destroying millions of people, the greater seems to have been the dedication to him, even the love, of the majority of people. . . .

One condition that made it easy for Stalin to bend the Party to his will was the hugely inflated cult of his personality. . . . The deification of Stalin justified in advance everything he did. . . . All the achievements and virtues of socialism were embodied in him. . . . Not conscious faith, but blind faith in Stalin was required. Like every cult, this one tended to transform the Communist Party into an ecclesiastical organization with a sharp distinction between ordinary people and leader-priests headed by their infallible pope. The gulf between the people and Stalin was not only deepened but idealized. The business of state in the Kremlin became as remote and incomprehensible for the unconsecrated as the affairs of the gods on Olympus. . . . Just as believers attribute everything good to God and everything bad to the devil, so everything good was attributed to Stalin and everything bad to evil forces that Stalin himself was fighting. "Long live Stalin!" some officials shouted as they were taken to be shot (pp. 289–290, 355, 362–363).[8]

A CONTEMPORARY SOVIET HISTORIAN

D. A. Volkogonov, a prominent military historian, has written *Triumph and Tragedy*, the first complete biography of Stalin published in the USSR. Volkogonov explained: "I want to show that the triumph of one person can turn into a tragedy for the whole people." As Director of the Institute of Military History, Volkogonov used many reminiscences and documents from the hitherto secret archives of the Defense Ministry, stressing how Stalin's psychotic personality resulted in tragedies for the Soviet people. "I am profoundly convinced that the socialist development of society could have avoided those dark stains . . . if a deficit of popular authority had not developed after the death of Lenin." But none of the other available leaders, Volkogonov concluded, would have been preferable to Stalin:

> If Trotskii had been in charge of the Party, even more burdensome experiences would have awaited it, involving loss of our socialist achievements—all the more because Trotskii did not have a scientific and clear programme for the construction of socialism in the USSR. Bukharin had

[8]Roy A. Medvedev, *Let History Judge: The Origins and Consequences of Stalinism* (New York, 1968).

such a programme . . . , but in spite of his great attractiveness as a person . . . and his humanity Bukharin for a long time did not understand the necessity of a sharp leap by the country in the growth of its economic power.[9]

SOVIET ÉMIGRÉS

1. VICTOR SERGE (VIKTOR L. KIBALCHICH): *From Lenin to Stalin* (New York, 1973).   Born in Brussels, Belgium, in 1890 of Russian émigré parents, Serge became a radical socialist and after the Russian Revolution returned to Soviet Russia. He joined the Bolshevik Party and became prominent in the Comintern barely escaping to the West before the Great Purge. Like his "Old Bolshevik" contemporaries, Serge greatly admired and idealized Lenin, but was profoundly disillusioned by Stalinist tyranny.

> Everything has changed. The aims: from international social revolution to socialism in one country. The political system: from the workers' democracy of the soviets, the goal of the revolution, to the dictatorship of the general secretariat, the functionaries, and the GPU [secret police]. The party: from the organization, free in its life and thought and freely submitting to discipline, of revolutionary Marxists to the hierarchy of bureaus, to the passive obedience of careerists. The Third International: from a mighty organization of propaganda and struggle to the opportunist servility of Central Committees appointed for the purpose of approving everything, without shame or nausea. . . . The leaders: the greatest militants of October are in exile or prison. . . . The condition of the workers: the equalitarianism of Soviet society is transformed to permit the formation of a privileged minority, more and more privileged in comparison with the disinherited masses who are deprived of all rights. Morality: from the austere, sometimes implacable honesty of heroic Bolshevism, we gradually advance to unspeakable deviousness and deceit. Everything has changed, everything is changing, but it will require the perspective of time before we can precisely understand the realities . . . (pp. 57–58).

2. ALEXANDER SOLZHENITSYN: *The Gulag Archipelago, 1918–1956*, 3 vols., (New York, 1973).   This massive work by a great contemporary Russian writer forcibly exiled from the USSR in 1974, describes the labor camp system in the USSR and its history, based on personal experience and 227 witnesses. Begun in 1958, it was first published

---

[9]D. A. Volkogonov, "Fenomen Stalina," *Literaturnaia gazeta*, December 9, 1987; *Trud*, June 19, 1988; and *Pravda*, June 20, 1988. These are excerpts from Volkogonov's book, *Triumf i Tragediia: Politicheskii portret I. V. Stalina* (Moscow, 1989).

abroad in 1973. Arbitrary arrest and detention, argues Solzhenitsyn, originated with Lenin in 1918 and was merely extended and intensified under Stalin. He sees repression as an inalienable part of an evil Soviet totalitarianism. Note how Solzhenitsyn's interpretation of Lenin differs from that of Roy Medvedev, who considers him a true Marxist, invariably adhering to norms of socialist legality.

When people today decry the *abuses of the cult* [of Stalin's personality], they keep getting hung up on those years which are stuck in our throats, '37 and '38. And memory begins to make it seem as though arrests were never made *before* or *after,* but only in those two years. . . . The *wave* of 1937 and 1938 was neither the only one nor even the main one, but only one, perhaps, of the three biggest waves which strained the murky, stinking pipes of our prison sewers to bursting. *Before* it came the wave of 1929 and 1930 . . . which drove a mere 15 million peasants, maybe even more, out into the taiga and the tundra. . . . And *after* it was the wave of 1944 to 1946 . . . when they dumped whole *nations* down the sewer pipes, not to mention millions and millions of others who . . . had been prisoners of war, or carried off to Germany and subsequently repatriated. . . .

It is well known that any *organ* withers away if it is not used. Therefore, if we know that the Soviet Security organs or *Organs* (and they christened themselves with this vile word), praised and exalted above all living things, have not died off even to the extent of one single tentacle, but instead, have grown new ones and strengthened their muscles—it is easy to deduce that they have had *constant* exercise. . . .

But even before there was any Civil War, it could be seen that Russia . . . was obviously not suited for any sort of socialism whatsoever. . . . One of the first blows of the dictatorship was directed against the Kadets—the members of the *Constitutional Democratic Party*. At the end of November 1917 . . . the Cadet Party was outlawed and arrests of its members began. . . . One of the first circulars of the NKVD [initially the Cheka, renamed NKVD in 1934], in December 1917, stated: "In view of sabotage by officials . . . use maximum initiative in localities, *not excluding* confiscations, compulsion, and arrests." . . . V. I. Lenin proclaimed the common, united purpose [in January 1918] of "purging the Russian land of all kinds of harmful insects." And under the term *insects* he included not only all class enemies but also "workers malingering at their work. . . ." It would have been impossible to carry out this hygienic purging . . . if they had had to follow outdated legal processes and normal judicial procedures. And so an entirely new form was adopted: *extrajudicial reprisal,* and this thankless job was self-sacrificingly assumed by the Cheka . . . , the only punitive organ in human history which combined in one set of hands investigation, arrest, interrogation, prosecution, trial and execution of the *verdict* (vol. 1, pp. 24–28, excerpts).

WESTERN VIEWS

1. GEORGE F. KENNAN: *Russia and the West Under Lenin and Stalin* (Boston, 1960). An American specialist in Russian affairs, Kennan served in the American Foreign Service, 1926–1953, including a stint as ambassador in Moscow. Following retirement, he became professor at the Institute for Advanced Studies in Princeton, New Jersey, where he wrote *Soviet-American Relations, 1917–1920,* 2 vols. (New York, 1956–1958). *Russia and the West* is derived from lectures delivered at Oxford and Harvard universities, 1957–1960. After World War II Kennan won renown as the author of the "containment theory" that advocated preventing Soviet expansion with non-Communist alliances and bases.

It remains only to mention the contrast between Stalin, as a statesman and [Lenin]. . . . The differences are not easy ones to identify, for in many instances they were only ones of degree and of motive. Lenin, too, was a master of internal Party intrigue. He, too, was capable of ruthless cruelty. He, too, could be unpitying in the elimination of people who seriously disagreed with him. . . . No less than Stalin, Lenin adopted an attitude of implacable hostility toward the Western world.

But behind all this there were very significant differences. Lenin was a man with no sense of inferiority. Well-born, well-educated, endowed with a mind of formidable power and brilliance, he was devoid of the angularities of the social parvenu, and he felt himself a match for any man intellectually. He was spared that whole great burden of personal insecurity which rested so heavily on Stalin. He never had to doubt his hold on the respect and admiration of his colleagues. He could rule them through the love they bore him, whereas Stalin was obliged to rule them through their fears. This enabled Lenin to run the movement squarely on the basis of what he conceived to be its needs, without bothering about his own. And since the intellectual inventory of the Party was largely of his own creation, he was relieved of that ignominious need which Stalin constantly experienced for buttressing his political views by references to someone else's gospel. Having fashioned Leninism to his own heart's desire out of the raw materials of Marx's legacy, Lenin had no fear of adapting it and adjusting it as the situation required. For this reason his mind remained open throughout his life—open, at least, to argument and suggestions from those who shared his belief in the basic justification of the second Russian Revolution of 1917. These people could come to him and talk to him, and could find their thoughts not only accepted in the spirit they were offered but responded to by a critical intelligence second to none in the history of the socialist movement. They did not have to feel, as they later did under Stalin, that deep, dangerous, ulterior meanings might be read into anything they said, and that an innocent suggestion might prove their personal undoing.

This had, of course, a profound effect on the human climate that prevailed throughout the Soviet regime in Lenin's time. Endowed with this temperament, Lenin was able to communicate to his associates an atmosphere of militant optimism, of good cheer and steadfastness and comradely loyalty, which made him the object of their deepest admiration and affection and permitted them to apply their entire energy to the work at hand. . . . While Lenin's ultimate authority remained unquestioned, it was possible to spread initiative and responsibility much further than was ever the case in the heyday of Stalin's power. This explains why Soviet diplomacy was so much more variegated and colorful in Lenin's time than in the subsequent Stalin era. In the change from Lenin to Stalin, the foreign policy of a movement became the foreign policy of a single man.

2. STEPHEN COHEN, *Bukharin and the Bolshevik Revolution* . . . (New York, 1971). Stephen Cohen, professor of politics at Princeton University, has specialized in the Soviet period and written an outstanding biography of Nikolai Bukharin, a leading theoretician and close colleague of Lenin:

While the internal party battles of 1923–9 constituted prolonged attempts to reconstruct the power and authority previously exercised by Lenin, the idea that there could be a successor—a "Lenin of today"—was impermissible. Lenin's authority within the leadership and in the party generally had been unique. Among other things, it had derived from the fact that he was the party's creator and moving spirit, from his political judgment which had been proved correct so often and against so much opposition, and from the force of his personality, which united and persuaded his fractious colleagues. In no way did it derive from an official post. As Sokolnikov pointed out: "Lenin was neither chairman of the Politburo nor general secretary; but nonetheless, Comrade Lenin . . . had the decisive political word in the party." It was . . . a kind of charismatic authority, inseparable from Lenin as a person and independent of constitutional or institutional procedures.

Some of his heirs intuitively understood this and commented on it in different ways. "Lenin was a dictator in the best sense of the word," said Bukharin in 1924. Five years later, describing Lenin as the singular "leader, organizer, captain, and stern iron authority," and contrasting his preeminence with Stalin's brute machine power, Bukharin tried to explain further.

"But he was for us all *Ilich,* a close, beloved, person, a wonderful comrade and friend, the bond with whom was indissoluble. He was not only 'Comrade Lenin,' but something immeasurably more . . ." (pp. 223–224).[10]

CONCLUSION

A wide divergence of views persists among scholars about the relationship between Lenin's rule and that of Stalin. Among Soviet scholars, Lenin remains a generally respected, even revered figure, but viewpoints about Stalin range from hero worship by Russian and Georgian neo-Stalinists, to the relatively balanced verdicts of the Khrushchev years, to bitter denunciation by Roy Medvedev and most writers and historians under Gorbachev. Many Soviet citizens, notably workers, still appear to believe that Stalin's positive contributions to the USSR outweighed his monstrous crimes. Those crimes were downplayed under Brezhnev when the emphasis once again was placed on Stalin's achievements as collectivizer, industrializer, and war leader. Even under Gorbachev many military memoirs continue to praise Stalin's leadership during World War II. Solzhenitsyn's view, on the other hand, repudiates Soviet totalitarianism in toto, Lenin included, in favor of Russian nationalism and neo-Orthodoxy. Whether Stalin's regime represented a continuation of Lenin's principles and rules or their antithesis remains debated.

Suggested Additional Reading

CARR, E. H. *A History of Soviet Russia*, 10 vols. (New York, 1951–1972).

CHASE, WILLIAM. *Workers, Society, and the Soviet State: Labor and Life in Moscow, 1918–1929* (Champaign, Ill., 1990).

COHEN, STEPHEN. *Bukharin: A Political Biography* (New York, 1974).

D'AGOSTINO, ANTHONY. *Soviet Succession Struggles . . . from Lenin to Gorbachev* (Winchester, Mass., 1987).

DANIELS, ROBERT. *The Conscience of the Revolution: Communist Opposition in Soviet Russia* (Cambridge, Mass., 1960).

DESAI, MEGHNAD, ed. *Lenin's Economic Writings* (Atlantic Highlands, N.J., 1989).

DEUTSCHER, ISAAC. *The Prophet Unarmed: Trotsky, 1921–1929* (Oxford, Eng., 1951).

FISHER, HAROLD. *The Famine in Soviet Russia, 1919–1923 . . .* (Stanford, Calif., 1927).

KOLLONTAI, ALEXANDRA. *The Workers' Opposition in Russia* (Chicago, 1921).

KRUPSKAIA, NADEZHDA. *Memories of Lenin* (London, 1942).

LEWIN, MOSHE. *Lenin's Last Struggle* (New York, 1968).

MEYER, ALFRED. *Leninism* (Cambridge, Mass., 1957).

PAGE, STANLEY. *Lenin and World Revolution* (New York, 1959).

PIPES, RICHARD. *The Formation of the Soviet Union* (Cambridge, Mass., 1954).

READ, CHRISTOPHER. *Culture and Power in Revolutionary Russia . . .* (New York, 1990).

REIMAN, MICHAL. *The Birth of Stalinism: The USSR on the Eve of the "Second Revolution,"* trans. George Saunders (Bloomington, Ind., 1987).

SCHAPIRO, LEONARD. *The Origin of the Communist Autocracy, 1917–1922* (Cambridge, Mass., 1955).

SERGE, VICTOR. *From Lenin to Stalin* (New York, 1973).

TARBUCK, KEN. *Bukharin's Theory of Equilibrium* (Winchester, Mass., 1989).

TROTSKY, LEON. *The Revolution Betrayed* (Garden City, N.Y., 1937).

TUCKER, ROBERT. *Political Culture and Leadership in Soviet Russia from Lenin to Gorbachev* (New York, 1987).

———. *Stalin as Revolutionary, 1879–1929* (New York, 1973).

———, ed. *Stalinism: Essays in Historical Interpretation* (New York, 1977).

ULAM, ADAM. *The Bolsheviks* (New York, 1965).

VON LAUE, THEODORE. *Why Lenin? Why Stalin?*, 2d ed. (Philadelphia, 1971).

ZALESKI, EUGENE. *Planning for Economic Growth in the Soviet Union, 1918–1932* (Chapel Hill, N.C., 1971).

CHAPTER TEN

THE POLITICS OF STALINISM, 1928–1941

Stalin had ousted Trotskii and the "Left Opposition" by 1928 and taken major steps away from Lenin's collective leadership and freer intraparty debate and toward personal rule in a totalitarian system. After 1928, Stalin moved to secure total power over party and state by crushing the "Right Opposition" and purging other colleagues of Lenin who retained influential positions. He manipulated the Lenin cult and created the monstrous myth of his own omniscience. To win autocratic power, the Stalin regime crushed passive opposition from the peasantry and secured control over the countryside by forcibly collectivizing agriculture. With the rapid industrialization of the Five Year Plans, it won support from an increasing working class. (For collectivization and industrialization see pp. 237 ff.) The state swallowed society as most Soviet citizens became state employees, subject to increasing party supervision and controls. After all significant opposition seemingly had been overcome, Stalin launched the Great Purge of 1936–1938, which eliminated the Old Bolsheviks and left his minions triumphant over a purged party, army, and state, and over a supine and frightened populace. In the Stalinist political system, theory and practice were often totally at odds. The federal system and Constitution of 1936 gave national minorities and the Soviet people the appearance of self-government and civil rights; actually all power resided in a self-perpetuating party leadership in Moscow. Did Stalin's aims and methods derive from Ivan the Terrible? Was he a loyal Marxist and true heir of Lenin, or an Oriental despot paying mere lip service to Marxism-Leninism? How did Stalin's political system function? Why did he undertake the Great Purge?

INTRAPARTY STRUGGLES AND CRISES, 1929–1934

A growing personality cult aided Stalin's drive to dominate the party, and rule the USSR. Launched cautiously at the 14th Congress in 1925, it developed notably after Stalin's 50th birthday (December 21, 1929), celebrated as a great historic event. In contrast with Lenin's modest, unassuming pose, the Stalin cult by the mid-1930s took on grandiose, even ludicrous forms. At a rally during the Purges in 1937, N. S. Khrushchev, Stalin's eventual successor, declared:

> These miserable nonentities wanted to destroy the unity of the party and the Soviet state. They raised their treacherous hands against Comrade Stalin. . . , our hope; Stalin, our desire; Stalin, the light of advanced and progressive humanity; Stalin, our will; Stalin, our victory.[1]

Within the party, the area of dissent narrowed, then disappeared. As Stalin crushed the "Left" in 1926–1927, it became clear that he would exclude factions or individuals who opposed his personal authority. But though Trotskii and the rest were stripped of influential positions, they still underestimated Stalin. Trotskii's expulsion from the USSR in 1929 brought predictions that power would pass to a triumvirate of Bukharin, Alexis Rykov, and M. P. Tomskii, who appeared (mistakenly) to dominate the Politburo selected after the 15th Congress.

Once the "Left" had been broken, Stalin adopted a moderate stance, and split with the "Right" led by Bukharin. The Stalin-Bukharin struggle developed behind the scenes during a growing economic crisis: Better-off peasants (kulaks), taxed heavily by the regime, withheld their grain from the market. Whereas Bukharin favored further concessions to the peasantry, including raising state grain prices, Stalin began urging strong action against the kulaks and officials who sympathized with them. Denouncing the still unnamed opposition for blocking industrialization,

---

[1]Quoted in E. Crankshaw, *Khrushchev's Russia* (Harmondsworth, Eng., 1959), p. 53.

Joseph Stalin (1879–1953) *(United Press International)*

Stalin used his control of the Secretariat and Orgburo to remove Bukharin's supporters from key party and government posts. Belatedly contacting Kamenev from the broken "Left," Bukharin warned: *"He* [Stalin] will strangle us." He added:

> Stalin . . . is an unprincipled intriguer who subordinates everything to the preservation of his power. He changes his theories according to whom he needs to get rid of at any given moment. . . . He maneuvers in such a way as to make us stand as the schismatics.[2]

By early 1929, Stalin attacked the "Right" openly and told a Politburo meeting: "Comrades, sad though it may be, we must face facts: a factional group has been established within our party composed of Bukharin, Tomskii, and Rykov" that was blocking industrialization and collectivization. Though the "Right" controlled the Moscow party organization, Stalin won majority support in the Politburo, bypassed the Moscow leaders, and broke their resistance. In April 1929, the Central Committee

---

[2]Quoted in I. Deutscher, *Stalin* (London, 1949), p. 314.

Figure 10.1 *Politics of Stalinism*

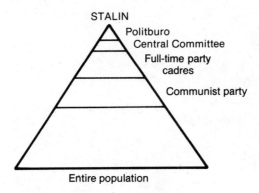

STALIN
Politburo
Central Committee
Full-time party
cadres

Communist party

Entire population

condemned the "Right" and removed its leaders from their posts; in November they surrendered, recanted their views, and bought themselves a few years of grace. (See Figure 10.1.)

Open political opposition in the party ended, but during 1932–1933 Stalin faced a grave economic and political crisis. Forced collectivization had brought on famine and hunger in the cities and provoked widespread nationalist opposition, especially among Ukrainian peasants. As Stalin's popularity fell to its nadir, Trotskii's *Bulletin of the Opposition* declared abroad: "In view of the incapacity of the present leadership to get out of the economic and political deadlock, the conviction about the need to change the leadership of the party is growing." Trotskii reminded his readers of Lenin's "Testament," which had urged Stalin's removal as General Secretary. In November 1932, after Nadezhda Allilueva, Stalin's second wife, spoke out about famine and discontent, the overwrought Stalin silenced her roughly, and she apparently committed suicide. Victor Serge notes that Stalin submitted his resignation, but none of the Politburo's obedient Stalinist members dared accept it. Finally, V. M. Molotov said: "Stop it, stop it. You have got the party's confidence," and the matter was dropped.

Stalin surmounted this personal danger and the economic and political crisis in the country. Opposition remained unfocused, confused, and leaderless. In 1932, Stalin had Kamenev and Zinoviev expelled from the party and exiled to Siberia, but after more abject recantations, they were allowed to return. After similar admissions of guilt, other Old Bolsheviks received responsible posts. They might have tried to kill Stalin, but who would rule in his place? Even Trotskii declared: "We are concerned not with the expulsion of individuals but the change of the system." Stalin temporarily adopted a moderate, conciliatory course. His speech of January 1934 called for consolidating earlier gains and inaugurated a brief period of relative liberalism. Within the Politburo the youthful and popular Leningrad party chief, S. M. Kirov, backed by Voroshilov and Kalinin, supported concessions to the peasantry and an end to terror; hard-liners such as Molotov and Kaganovich opposed this. During 1934, Stalin apparently wavered between these groups.

THE GREAT PURGE

This interlude ended with Kirov's murder in December 1934. The supposed assassin, Nikolaev, and his accomplices were promptly apprehended, tried secretly, and shot. They were described officially as Trotskyites working for the clandestine, foreign-directed "United Center," which had allegedly plotted to kill Stalin and other top leaders. Zinoviev and Kamenev, supposedly implicated in the plot, were sentenced to penal servitude.

Ominous changes proceeded in the political police. Early in 1934, the secret police (GPU), which had gained a sinister reputation, was dissolved. Its tasks were assumed by the People's Commissariat of Internal Affairs (NKVD), which combined control over political, regular, and criminal police. Henrikh Iagoda, its first chief, perhaps fearing that Kirov's liberal line threatened his power, may have engineered the assassination at Stalin's order. NKVD employees were highly paid and obtained the best apartments and other privileges. This "state within a state" maintained a huge network of informers, kept dossiers on millions of persons, and spied on all party agencies. Special sections watched the NKVD's own regular personnel, whose members were expected to show primary loyalty to the NKVD and only secondarily to the party. Special NKVD courts, exempt from control by government or judicial agencies, were set up to conduct secret trials.

While surface calm prevailed, Andrei Zhdanov, Kirov's successor as Leningrad party chief, conducted a ruthless purge there, deporting tens of thousands of persons to Siberia, and the NKVD prepared the greatest mass purge in history. In May 1935 a Special Security Commission was created to investigate all party members, "liquidate enemies of the people," and encourage citizens to denounce suspected counterrevolutionaries and slackers. Its members included Stalin, N. I. Ezhov (later head of the NKVD), Zhdanov, and Andrei Vyshinskii, subsequently chief prosecutor at the public trials. That spring, 40 members of Stalin's personal bodyguard were tried secretly for conspiracy, and "terrorists" were hunted in every party and Komsomol (Young Communist League) agency. As the rapidly growing NKVD justified its existence by uncovering conspiracies everywhere, Stalin ordered careful surveillance even of Politburo members.

A reign of terror was unleashed, dwarfing that of the French Revolution. Perhaps that precedent had previously deterred Stalin, who once remarked: "You chop off one head today, another one tomorrow. . . . What in the end will be left of the party?" Unlike the French case, terror in Russia reached its murderous peak two decades after the Revolution. The French terror claimed about 40,000 victims; Stalin's from 1935 to 1938 killed hundreds of thousands and sent millions into exile.[3] Stalin, not the NKVD, initiated the Great Purge and approved executions of prominent figures. A Stalinist account explained:

> The Trotsky-Bukharin fiends, in obedience to the wishes of their masters—the espionage services of foreign states—had set out to destroy the party and the Soviet state, to undermine the defensive power of the country, to assist foreign military intervention . . . [and] to bring about the dismemberment of the USSR . . . , to destroy the gains of the workers and collective farmers, and to restore capitalist slavery in the USSR.[4]

The party had to become an impregnable fortress to safeguard the country and the gains of socialism from foreign and domestic enemies. Stalin added: ". . . As long as capitalist encirclement exists, there will be wreckers, spies, diversionists, and murderers in our country, sent behind our lines by the agents of foreign states." The Soviet public found this distorted view credible.

Three great public trials of party leaders accused of treason were held in Moscow. At the "Trial of the Sixteen" (August 1936), Prosecutor Vyshinskii accused Kamenev, Zinoviev, and others of conspiring to overthrow the regime and to remove Stalin and other Politburo leaders. After confessing and incriminating the "Right" Opposition, the defendants were convicted and shot. When this severe treatment of Lenin's old colleagues provoked opposition in the Central Committee, Stalin removed Iagoda and appointed as NKVD chief Ezhov, under whom the purge reached its bloody climax. Each group of defendants incriminated the next in a chain reaction of denunciations. At the "Trial of the Seventeen" (January 1937), featuring Piatakov, Muralov, and Radek (all "Old Bolshevik" leaders), the accused confessed to treasonable dealings with Germany and Japan. The greatest public spectacle of them all, the "Trial of the Twenty-One" (March 1938) included Bukharin, Rykov, and Iagoda. Foreign espionage agencies, claimed the prosecutor, had set up a

---

[3] In 1989 Paul Robeson, Jr., estimated that the USSR during the Stalin era had about 29.3 million "excess deaths" from terror and famine.

[4] *Short History of the Communist Party* (New York, 1939), p. 347.

"bloc of Rightists and Trotskyists" on Soviet soil to bring a bourgeois-capitalist regime to power and detach non-Russian regions from the USSR. Allegedly Bukharin had been a traitor since 1918. Vyshinskii concluded his prosecution with the invariable appeal: "Shoot the mad dogs!" and the leading defendants would be executed.

Why did the accused, many of them prominent, courageous revolutionaries, publicly admit crimes they could not have committed, when their confessions constituted the only legal basis for conviction? Most had recanted several times already, each time admitting greater guilt, and hoped to save their lives, positions, and families. Some believed that the party, to which they had dedicated their lives, must be right. The defendants, mostly middle aged, were broken down by lengthy NKVD interrogations and sleeplessness, or were hypnotized by the terror. Doubtless, they hoped to save something from blasted careers by bowing to Stalin's tyranny.

Those who were tried and executed, or died by other means, included all surviving members of Lenin's Politburo, except Stalin and Trotskii, the defendant in chief tried in absentia. A former premier, two former chiefs of the Comintern, the trade union head, and two chiefs of the political police were executed. Survivors must have wondered how the great Lenin could have surrounded himself with so many traitors and scoundrels. In 1914, to be sure, Roman Malinovskii, Lenin's close colleague, had been exposed as a police agent. The legacy of police infiltration of revolutionary organizations under tsarism provided some basis for believing the revelations of the 1930s.

The Great Purge decimated the leadership corps of the Soviet armed forces. The military chiefs, especially Marshal Tukhachevskii, who had made the Red Army an effective fighting force, apparently had been highly critical of the early trials. In May 1937, he and other prominent generals were arrested, accused of treasonable collaboration with Germany and Japan, and shot. None of them resisted or attempted a military coup. Purged later were most members of the Supreme War Council, 3 of 5 marshals, 14 of 16 army generals, and all full admirals. About half the entire officer corps was shot or imprisoned, a terrible insult to Red Army patriotism and a grave weakening of the armed forces. (After Stalin's death, all leading military figures who were purged were rehabilitated, many posthumously, and declared innocent of all charges brought against them. See Problem 6 in Chapter 14.)

In addition to Old Bolsheviks, many Stalinist party leaders were eliminated. Purged were 70 percent of the Central Committee members and candidates chosen in 1934. At the 18th Party Congress in 1939, only 35 of 1,827 rank and file delegates from the previous congress were present! From the party and army the purge reached downward into the general populace as friends and relatives of those purged were arrested. Thousands of ordinary citizens were denounced orally or by poison-pen letters, often out of jealousy and meanness, of crimes they had not and could not have committed. For two years (1937–1938), most of a helpless population lived in abject terror of sudden arrest and deportation. Special targets for arbitrary arrest included former members of other political parties and former White soldiers, priests, intellectuals (especially writers), Jews and other national minorities in Russian towns, and professionals who had been abroad. Many ordinary workers and peasants were also denounced and forced to confess to imaginary crimes against the state. Stalin even issued orders to arrest a percentage of the population. His bloodthirstiness grew as members of all social groups were rounded up.

Why this terrible bloodbath? wondered the survivors. Some victims were scapegoats for economic failures of the early 1930s. Stalin's chief motive, suggests the British scholar Isaac Deutscher, was to destroy those who might lead an alternate regime or criticize his policies. This strategy required killing or exiling party and military men trained by purged leaders, then rebuilding the chief levers of Soviet power: the party, the army, and the security forces. The general public may have been involved deliberately to create the climate of fear essential to Stalin's total control. The need for millions of forced laborers in the Arctic and Siberia supplied a reason for mass deportation of workers and peasants. Perhaps Stalin became utterly mad, making pointless the search for rational explanations. Certainly casualties were too great to be justified by ordinary political or social aims. Robert Conquest's estimate of about 8 million purge victims in camps by 1938, plus another million in prisons, seems reasonable. During the 1930s, a huge NKVD empire of forced labor camps and prisons, begun in the White Sea area under Lenin and described graphically in Alexander Solzhenitsyn's *The Gulag Archipelago*, mushroomed in European Russia and Siberia. Major projects included constructing the White Sea and Moscow-Volga canals, double-tracking the Trans-Siberian Railway, and gold mining in the frigid Kolyma region. Usually fed below the subsistence level and working under extremely arduous conditions, the inmates died off rapidly only to be replaced by new millions.

In December 1938, with the arrest of master purger Ezhov, blamed for excesses ordered by Stalin, the purge's intensive phase ended. By then, half the urban population of the USSR was on police lists, and 5 percent had actually been arrested.[5] Large-scale terror remained

---

[5]See R. Conquest, *The Great Terror* (New York, 1968).

endemic to the Soviet system, until Stalin's death. The epilogue to the Great Purge was the brutal murder of Trotskii in Mexico (August 1940) by an NKVD agent, the son of a Spanish Communist. Besides terrorizing the USSR, the purge opened up numerous vacancies in civil and military posts, filled by obedient but often inexperienced men who ensured Stalin's omnipotence. The Politburo lost most of its power and became Stalin's rubber stamp, while his private Secretariat became a modern Oprichnina. Otherwise the purge altered the Soviet political system remarkably little.

The Great Purge necessitated the rewriting of Communist Party history. Directed by Zhdanov and Stalin's secretaries, historians prepared the *History of the All-Union Communist Party (Bolshevik), Short Course* (1938). Apparently, Stalin corrected the manuscript and wrote the section on philosophy. Portraying Stalin as Lenin's only true disciple, the *History* claimed that other Old Bolsheviks had conspired against Lenin and the party since 1917. Thus the all-powerful dictator had altered history to serve his present purposes. After 1938, Stalin worked intensively to foster patriotism, restore unity, and rebuild the army leadership and the armed forces as the Nazi threat to the USSR grew.

GOVERNMENT AND PARTY ORGANIZATION

The Stalin regime combined systematic terror and massive use of force with a democratically phrased constitution, apparent federalism, and representative institutions. Operating ostensibly through a hierarchy of soviets, the political system was run actually by the party leadership and NKVD. Often theory and practice were wholly at odds, and in many ways Stalinism marked a return to tsarist autocracy. Stalin himself, no longer the apparently patient, humble, and accessible party functionary of the early 1920s, retreated into the Kremlin's recesses or to his country villa at nearby Kuntsevo. Rarely appearing in public, he clothed himself in mystery, and many in the younger generation regarded him and his oracular pronouncements with awe and reverence. Once his rivals had been eliminated, he grew more dictatorial and, after 1938, became an all-powerful father figure. His Politburo contained bureaucrats and party officials, not active revolutionaries or creative ideologists, as in Lenin's time. Men such as Molotov, Kaganovich, and Kuibyshev, though able administrators, were narrow and ignorant of foreign lands. In the Politburo, Stalin listened impatiently to their arguments, then often decided an issue with a sarcasm or vulgar joke. All important matters were decided there, under the dictator's jealous eye.

The legal basis of this Soviet political system was the Constitution of 1936. Constitutions under Marxism were supposed to reflect existing socioeconomic conditions and had to be altered as this situation changed. Earlier Soviet constitutions (1918 and 1924), with a franchise heavily weighted to favor urban elements and excluding "exploiters," represented the proletarian dictatorship's first phase. In November 1936, Stalin explained to the Eighth Congress of Soviets that because rapid industrialization and collectivization had eliminated landlords, capitalists, and kulaks, "There are no longer any antagonistic classes in [Soviet] society . . . [which] consists of two friendly classes, workers and peasants." Restrictions and inequalities in voting could be abolished, and a democratic suffrage instituted. The Stalin Constitution, he claimed, would be "the only thoroughly democratic constitution in the world." It was designed to win approval abroad.

The promises of the Stalin Constitution (finally superseded by a new one in 1977) often meant little in practice. "The USSR," it proclaimed, "is a federal state formed on the basis of a voluntary union of equal Soviet socialist republics." Most republics, however, had been conquered or incorporated forcibly, and the predominance of the Russian Republic, with about half the population and three fourths the area of the Union, negated equality. Theoretically, a republic, as formerly, could secede, but to advocate secession was a crime, and a "bourgeois nationalist deviation." Only the working class, through its vanguard, the Soviet Communist Party, could approve secession or create and abolish republics. In 1936, Transcaucasia split into Azerbaijan, Armenia, and Georgia, which were admitted as separate republics; then the Kazakh and Kirghiz republics in Central Asia were added. A Karelo-Finnish Republic was created partly out of territory taken from Finland in 1940, but it was abolished equally arbitrarily in 1956. Also in 1940, the Moldavian Republic was established, mostly from territory acquired by treaty with Hitler, and the formerly independent Baltic countries of Estonia, Latvia, and Lithuania were occupied and became Soviet republics. An amendment of 1944 permitted republics to establish relations with foreign countries (none has ever done so), and the Ukraine and Byelorussia obtained separate United Nations representation in 1945. Smaller national groups (more than 100 in the Russian Republic alone) obtained autonomous republics and national areas, plus legislative representation.

Soviet federalism provided an illusion of autonomy and self-government, but the central government, retaining full power, repressed any group or individuals who advocated genuine autonomy or independence, especially in the Ukraine, populous and agriculturally valuable. Each nationality received its own territory, language, press, and schools, but the Russian-dominated all-Union Communist Party supervised and controlled them. This federal system, in Stalin's words "national in form, socialist in content," though preferable to tsarism's open Russification and assimilation, perpetuated Russian rule over most areas of the old empire. National feeling persisted nonetheless among many minority peoples of the USSR.

Under the Stalin Constitution a bicameral Supreme Soviet became the national legislature, and supposedly the highest organ of state authority. The Council of the Union was directly elected from equal election districts, one deputy per 300,000 population. The Council of Nationalities represented the various administrative units: 25 deputies from each union republic, 11 from autonomous republics, and so on. Delegates elected for four-year terms by universal suffrage received good pay during brief sessions, but unlike United State Congressional Representatives, retained their regular jobs and had no offices or staffs. A Presidium, elected by both houses, could issue decrees when the Soviet was not meeting, and its chairman was titular president of the USSR. Bills became law when passed by both houses, but the Supreme Soviet under Stalin never recorded a negative vote. It was a decorative, rubber-stamp body without real discussion or power of decision. Below it lay a network of soviets on republic, regional, provincial, district, and village or city levels—over 60,000 soviets in all—with some 1,500,000 deputies elected for two-year terms. Sovereign in theory, soviets were controlled in fact at every level by their party members and parallel party organizations. Elections were uncontested with only one candidate in each election district, selected by the party.

The Constitution entrusted executive and administrative authority to the Council of People's Commissars (called the Council of Ministers since 1946). Some ministries operated only on the all-union level, others there and in the republics, and still others in the republics only. Theoretically, but not in practice, these ministries were responsible to the soviets. Coordinating the administrative and economic system, the Council of People's Commissars possessed more power than the Constitution suggested. The Supreme Court of the USSR headed a judicial system including supreme courts in the republic, regional, and people's courts. Lower courts were elected and higher ones chosen by the corresponding soviet. Judges, supposedly independent, were subject to party policies, and many important cases were tried in secret by the NKVD.

Article 125 of the Constitution promised Soviet citizens freedoms of speech, conscience, press, assembly, and demonstrations "in conformity with the interests of the working people and in order to strengthen the socialist system." Citizens were guaranteed the right to work, education, rest, and maintenance in sickness and old age. Article 127 pledged freedom from arrest except by court decision. In fact, the Soviet people never enjoyed most of these rights. As the new constitution was printed, the NKVD was conducting mass arrests and deportations without trial.

The state assigned workers to jobs arbitrarily and prohibited strikes and independent trade unions. Constitutional rights could be used only to support the regime, not to criticize it.

The Stalin Constitution, unlike its predecessors, at least suggested in Article 126 the true role of the Communist Party:

> . . . The most active and politically conscious citizens in the ranks of the working class, working peasants, and working intelligentsia voluntarily unite in the Communist Party of the Soviet Union, which is the vanguard of the working people in their struggle to build communist society and is *the leading core of all organizations of the working people, both public and state.* [Italics added for emphasis.][6]

Still organized on Leninist principles, the party remained the elite force of about 4 percent of the population in which intellectuals and bureaucrats outnumbered ordinary workers. Operating supposedly by democratic centralism, it exercised decisive authority over domestic and foreign affairs. Under Stalin all power passed to higher party organs coopted by the leaders, not elected democratically as the party rules stipulated. The rank and file could merely criticize minor shortcomings and lost all influence over the self-perpetuating leadership. The party became Stalin's monolithic, disciplined, and increasingly bureaucratic instrument. Intraparty debate avoided major issues and was limited to *how* to implement decisions, not to discuss alternative policies or leaders.

The all-union congress, a periodic gathering of leaders from the entire USSR, theoretically exercised supreme authority within the party. Once factions were banned (1921) and the "Right" was defeated (1929), however, congresses lost power to initiate policies. Important decisions were made in advance by the Politburo and approved unanimously by the congress, which merely ratified policies of the leadership pro forma. In Lenin's time, the Central Committee, supposedly elected by the congress to direct party work between congresses, was an important decision-making body; under Stalin it grew in size (to 125 full members and 125 candidates in 1952), but declined in power. It comprised mostly regional party secretaries and ministers from the all-union and republic governments.

The Central Committee, stated the party rules, elected three subcommittees: the Politburo, Orgburo, and Secretariat; in fact, they determined the Committee's membership and policies. With about a dozen full members and a few candidates, the Politburo ostensibly "directs the work

---

[6]*Constitution (Fundamental Law) of the Union of Soviet Socialist Republics* (Moscow, 1957), p. 103.

of the Central Committee between plenary sessions." It has always included the most powerful party and state officials and decided the chief domestic and foreign policy issues; since 1920 it has been the main power center in the USSR. Its meetings have been secret and its debates presumably free. Stalin purged the Politburo, refilled it with his own men, and made it an instrument of his personal power. During the 1930s, it experienced great insecurity and high turnover; since then its members have enjoyed much stability of tenure. The Orgburo, Stalin's original power base, directed the party's organizational work until its merger with the Politburo in 1952. The Secretariat directed the party's permanent apparatus. Stalin, as General Secretary with four assistants, managed its professional staff and controlled all party personnel and appointments.

With five levels the party, like the soviets, was directed centrally by its all-union organs. (See Figure 10.2.) Thus the Ukrainian Party, run generally by Great Russians, was controlled from Moscow, which decided its policies and personnel. Lower party officials were often sacrificed as scapegoats for unpopular or mistaken national policies. Some regional party secretaries became miniature Stalins, who dictated to frightened subordinates. At the bottom of the party hierarchy stood some 350,000 primary organizations, or cells, composed of at least three members, in villages, collective farms, factories, offices, and military units. Acting like nerves of the human body, they permeated and controlled all organizations and agencies.

Party membership was open, in theory, to all persons over 21 years of age (over 18 for Komsomol members). Applicants filled out a detailed questionnaire, submitted recommendations from three members in good standing to a primary party organization, and served at least a year's candidacy. Applications had to be approved by the primary organizations and ratified by the district party unit. Rank and file members performed party work besides their regular jobs. They had to pay dues, work actively in agitation and propaganda among their fellows, explain Marxian theory and the party line, and set examples of leadership and clean living. Their rewards included power and influence because the party was the only road to political success, plus material benefits. Disobedient or undisciplined members were reprimanded, censured, or in graver cases, expelled. Periodic purges were designed to cleanse the party of opportunists, slackers, and the disloyal. Under Stalin, Communists occupied the key positions in most walks of life; factory managers, collective farm chairmen, school superintendents, and army officers were generally party members. Within the party, urban elements predominated over rural ones and Great Russians over national minorities.

The highly centralized Stalinist political system was based on interlocking presidia of the party and the state. The main decisions, made

Figure 10.2 *Soviet Power Centers Under Stalin*

Both the Communist Party of the Soviet Union and the Soviet government were organized on five levels from the all-union hierarchy at the top and the local bodies at the bottom. At each level the party organization controlled the corresponding governmental (soviet) bodies. Of the 15 Soviet socialist republics, the Russian Republic was by far the largest. Among the others were Ukraine, Byelorussia, Georgia, and Armenia. Each republic possessed its own Supreme Soviet and ministries. Autonomous republics (for smaller nationalities) also had their own supreme soviets and councils of ministers. The Communist Party of each republic was subordinated to the All-Union Party organs.

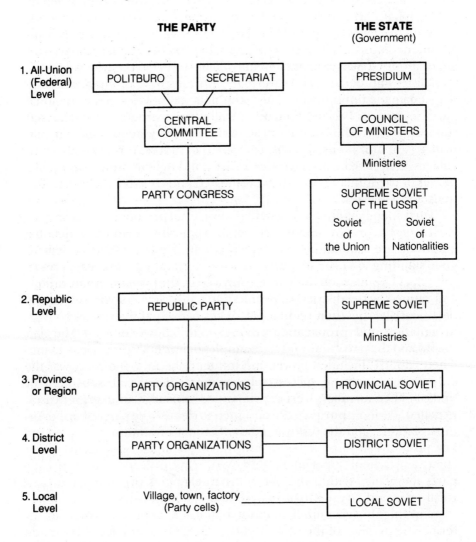

by Stalin personally and approved by the Politburo, were transmitted by lower party organs, soviets, trade unions, and media of mass communication to the people. The party manipulated the soviets skillfully to maintain links with the population and provide a semblance of legitimate rule. The main weaknesses were lack of local initiative and the absence of any legal means to transmit power from one leader or group of leaders to another. This intensified intrigue, suspicion, and power struggles behind the scenes at the top.

STALINISM

Stalin had risen in the party as an organizer and administrator, not an ideologist. Marx had been a theorist, not an active revolutionary; in Lenin, the two aspects were in rare balance. At first, Stalin marched carefully in Lenin's footsteps (his chief theoretical work was *Problems of Leninism*), but once in power he altered and gravely distorted the doctrines of Marx and Lenin. Stalin's major doctrinal innovation—socialism in one country—had developed accidentally and pragmatically during his struggle with Trotskii. (See Chapter 9.) Trotskii's apparently contrasting theory of "permanent revolution" stressed using the Comintern (Communist International, organization of Communist parties) to foment revolutions abroad; Stalin emphasized building socialism in Russia first. They differed somewhat over means and tactics, but shared the goal of an eventual global triumph of Communism. But could socialism be *completely* built in a single country? Stalin claimed in 1936 that it had already been *essentially* constructed in Russia, although final victory must await worldwide revolution. Stalin's national emphasis won him continuing support from industrial workers, the intelligentsia, and military men, as well as from a party anxious to believe that Russians could build socialism themselves. Socialism in one country provided the ideological basis and social support for forced collectivization and the five-year plans.

Because Stalin affirmed that socialism had triumphed in the USSR and that class enemies had been broken, why was proletarian dictatorship not withering away, as Marx had predicted? Stalin had already answered this question in rather cynical fashion at the 16th Party Congress in 1930:

> We are in favor of the state dying out, and at the same time we stand for the strengthening of the dictatorship of the proletariat, which represents the most powerful and mighty authority of all forms of state which have existed up to the present day. The highest possible development of the power of the state with the object of preparing the conditions of the dying out of the state?

Is this contradictory? Yes, it is contradictory. But this contradiction is a living thing and completely reflects Marxist dialectics.[7]

the art of examining the validity of a theory

Apparently, Stalin derived this view from Lenin's statement that state machinery must be perfected in the lower phase of socialism before withering. To justify strengthening the proletarian state, Stalin argued that hostile capitalist powers, surrounding the USSR, threatened armed intervention. Until "capitalist encirclement" was replaced by socialist encirclement of capitalism, the proletarian state must remain strong and alert, eliminate "bourgeois survivals," and hasten the transition to the final goal—Communism.

Stalin was reacting instinctively against a Marxian internationalism that had already been undermined by the apparent failure of world revolution. For Stalin, the interests of the Soviet fatherhood clearly preceded those of the international proletariat and foreign Communist parties. Thus in the years before World War II, Soviet nationalism and patriotism were developed partly as an affirmation of what the working class had built in the USSR and partly to counter separatism in the borderlands. Pride in Soviet industrial and technological achievements was fostered by the regime, with considerable success among workers and the younger generation. The shift away from internationalism was reflected in the repudiation by the Stalin regime of the works of the Marxist historian M. N. Pokrovskii, who had condemned Russian tsars and imperialism unreservedly. From the mid-1930s occurred a selective rehabilitation, and even praise of such rulers as Peter the Great and Ivan the Terrible for unifying and strengthening Russia. Tsarist generals such as Suvorov and Kutuzov, and certain admirals in the Crimean War, were glorified for defending their country heroically. New Soviet patriotism contained elements of traditional Great Russian nationalism, which Stalin had adopted. Through Soviet nationalism—one positive aspect of socialism in one country—Stalin sought to overcome and replace narrower national loyalties within the USSR.

The Stalinist political system established patterns of authority, many of which—unlike Stalin's cult of personality—have persisted to the present. With maximum use of force and terror, Stalin crushed all political opposition, as Ivan the Terrible had sought but failed to do. Stalin created perhaps the most powerful, centralized state in history with a developed industry and a vast bureaucracy. In so doing, he, though a believing Marxist, perverted Marxist ideology almost beyond recognition by accumulating personal power analogous to that of Oriental despotism.

---

[7]*Problems of Leninism* (Moscow, 1933), vol. 2, p. 402.

The Communist Party, though supreme over obedient soviets, was itself transformed into a bureaucracy of frightened automatons by the Great Purge. Stalin's successors would repudiate mass terror and the cult of individual dictatorship but not centralized autocracy.

Suggested Additional Reading

ADAMS, ARTHUR. *Stalin and His Times* (New York, 1972).

ARMSTRONG, JOHN. *The Politics of Totalitarianism: The Communist Party of the Soviet Union from 1934 to the Present* (New York, 1962).

AVTORKHANOV, A. *Stalin and the Soviet Communist Party* (New York, 1959).

BAUER, R., A. INKELES, and C. KLUCKHOHN. *How the Soviet System Works* (Cambridge, Mass., 1956).

BERMAN, HAROLD J. *Justice in the USSR* (New York, 1963).

CARMICHAEL, JOEL. *Stalin's Masterpiece: The Show Trials and Purges of the Thirties* . . . (New York, 1976).

CARR, E. H. *The Bolshevik Revolution: Socialism in One Country, 1924–1926*, 3 vols. in 4 parts (London, 1958–1964).

CONQUEST, ROBERT. *The Great Terror* (New York, 1968).

———. *Inside Stalin's Secret Police: NKVD Politics, 1936–1939* (Stanford, Calif., 1985).

———. *Stalin and the Kirov Murder* (Oxford, Eng. and NY, 1990).

DALLIN, D., and B. NICOLAEVSKY. *Forced Labor in Soviet Russia* (New Haven, Conn., 1947).

DANIELS, ROBERT, ed. *The Stalin Revolution* (Lexington, Mass., 1990).

DAY, RICHARD B. *Leon Trotsky and the Politics of Economic Isolation* (New York, 1973).

DE JONG, ALEX. *Stalin and the Shaping of the Soviet Union* (New York, 1986).

DEUTSCHER, ISAAC. *Stalin: A Political Biography*, 2d ed. (New York, 1967).

DJILAS, MILOVAN. *The New Class* (New York, 1957).

ERICKSON, JOHN. *The Soviet High Command* . . . *1918–1941* (New York, 1962).

FAINSOD, MERLE. *How Russia Is Ruled*, 2d ed. (Cambridge, Mass., 1963).

———. *Smolensk Under Soviet Rule* (Cambridge, Mass., 1958).

FRIEDRICH, CARL J., and Z. K. BRZEZINSKI. *Totalitarian Dictatorship and Autocracy*, 2d ed. (New York, 1966).

GETTY, J. A. *Origins of the Great Purges* . . . *1933–1938* (Cambridge, Eng., 1985).

HAZARD, J. N. *The Soviet System of Government*, 5th ed. (Chicago, 1980).

HYDE, A. M. *Stalin, the History of a Dictator* (New York, 1982).

KATKOV, GEORGE. *The Trial of Bukharin* (New York, 1969).

KOESTLER, ARTHUR. *Darkness at Noon* (New York, 1951). (Novel relating to the Great Purge.)

LEVYTSKY, BORYS, comp. *The Stalinist Terror in the Thirties: Documentation from the Soviet Press* (Stanford, Calif., 1974).

MEDVEDEV, ROY A. *Let History Judge: The Origins and Consequences of Stalinism* (New York, 1971, 1973).

MOORE, BARRINGTON, JR. *Soviet Politics: The Dilemma of Power* (Cambridge, Mass., 1957).

NOVE, ALEC. *Stalinism and After*, 3d ed. (London, 1989).

ORWELL, GEORGE. *1984* (New York, 1949). (Novel on totalitarianism.)

SCHAPIRO, LEONARD. *The Communist Party of the Soviet Union*, rev. ed. (New York, 1970).

SERGE, VICTOR. *Memoirs of a Revolutionary, 1901–1941* (New York, 1963).

SOLZHENITSYN, A. *The Gulag Archipelago, 1918–1956*, 3 vols. (New York, 1974–1975).

———. *One Day in the Life of Ivan Denisovich* (New York, 1963). (Novel about labor camps under Stalin.)

SOUVARINE, BORIS. *Stalin: A Critical Survey of Bolshevism* (New York, 1939).

THORNILEY, DANIEL. *The Rise and Fall of the Rural Communist Party, 1927–39* (New York, 1988).

TROTSKY, L. D. *Stalin: An Appraisal of the Man and His Influence.* (New York, 1941).

TROTSKY, LEON. *The Revolution Betrayed* (Garden City, N.Y., 1937).

———. *Trotsky's Notebooks, 1933–1935*, trans. and ed. Philip Pomper (New York, 1986).

TUCKER, R., ed. *Stalinism: Essays in Historical Interpretation* (New York, 1977).

TUMARKIN, NINA. *Lenin Lives! The Lenin Cult in Soviet Russia.* (Cambridge, Mass., 1983).

ULAM, ADAM. *Stalin: The Man and His Era* (New York, 1973).

URBAN, G. R., ed. *Stalinism: Its Impact on Russia and the World* (New York, 1982).

VON LAUE, THEODORE. *Why Lenin, Why Stalin?*, 2d ed. (Philadelphia, 1971).

VYSHINSKY, ANDREI. *The Law of the Soviet State* (New York, 1948).

WEISSBERG, ALEX. *The Accused* (New York, 1951).

CHAPTER ELEVEN

THE GREAT
TRANSFORMATION

Once the economy recovered to prewar levels and Stalin had consolidated his power, he launched the "Second Socialist Offensive" of rapid industrialization and forced collectivization of agriculture. This policy followed a bitter debate within the party over how to modernize the Soviet economy. In the decade after 1928, the USSR became a major industrial country, collectivized its agriculture, and acquired the basic economic and social forms that characterize it today. The price paid for these advances by the Soviet people, however, was very high. Did Stalin's "revolution from above" reflect Marxist-Leninist principles or betray the ideals of 1917? Were rapid industrialization and forced collectivization necessary and worth their terrible cost, or was Bukharin's alternative of gradual evolution toward socialism preferable? Should Stalin be called "the great" for overcoming Russia's backwardness and weakness? If so, then 1929 marks a greater turning point in Russian history than 1917. After continuing to smash or remodel traditional social pillars, the family, school, and church, why did Stalin retreat toward tsarist patterns in the later 1930s and make concessions to the church?

THE GREAT INDUSTRIALIZATION DEBATE, 1924–1928

During the mid-1920s, leading Soviet politicians and economists debated Russia's economic future. They agreed on goals of socialism and industrialization, but disagreed on how they could best be achieved. The success of the New Economic Policy (NEP) meant that survival was not at issue, but in a largely hostile world, the USSR, unlike tsarist Russia, had to rely on its own resources to industrialize.

The party "Left," led by Trotskii but with Evgeni Preobrazhenskii as chief economic spokesman, advocated rapid industrial growth at home while promoting revolutions abroad. The key to industrialization and socialism, Preobrazhenskii argued, was "primitive socialist accumulation": Lacking colonies to exploit, the USSR must obtain necessary investment capital by keeping farm prices low and taxing private farmers heavily. NEP, he believed, could restore the economy, but it could not produce the vast capital required for industrialization and the development of transportation and housing. Central state-planning would permit immediate major investment in heavy industry. The "Left" accused the Stalin-Bukharin leadership of favoring kulaks, "surrendering" to NEP-men, and isolating the USSR. It stressed the intimate connection between developing Soviet socialism and ending "our socialist isolation." Opposing forcible expropriation of kulaks, Trotskii believed that revolutions in advanced countries would promote Soviet industrialization.

Bukharin, chief official spokesman and later leader of the "Right," urged the continuation of NEP until the USSR gradually "grew into" socialism. Leftist "superindustrializers and adventurers" would alienate better-off peasants, undermine the worker-peasant alliance, and threaten the regime. Taxing peasants heavily would price industrial goods beyond their reach and induce them to market less grain. Instead, industrial prices should be cut and peasants encouraged to produce and save freely. Agricultural surplus would provide investment capital, expand the internal market, and stimulate industrial production. Citing Lenin's last writings, Bukharin advocated gradual "agrarian cooperative socialism." He overestimated peasant economic power and considered the peasant-worker alliance inviolable. Unless Soviet industrialization were more humane than under capitalism, he warned, it might not produce socialism. "We do not want to drive the middle peasant into communism with an iron broom." Bukharin spoke of "moving ahead slowly . . . dragging behind us the cumbersome peasant cart," and of creeping "at a snail's pace. . . ."

All leading Bolsheviks viewed industrialization as a vital goal and realized that it must rely mainly on internal resources. Agreeing that investment capital must be shifted from agriculture into industry, they differed over how much to take and how to take it. Bukharin emphasized the development of the internal market, imposition of progressive income taxes, and voluntary savings. Such methods, retorted the "Left," would produce too little capital because peasants would consume most of the surplus. Bolsheviks agreed that central planning was needed, but what did this involve? The "Left" advocated a single state-imposed plan, stressing rapid growth of heavy industry. Bukharin called that "a remnant of War Communist illusions," which disregarded market forces of supply and demand; instead he would stress consumer industry.

The factions also argued about capitalist elements in the countryside. Official figures of 1925 stated that poor peasants composed 45, middle peasants 51, and kulaks 4 percent of the peasantry. Asserting that more than 7 percent were kulaks, who were exploiting and dominating the village, the "Left" argued that continuing NEP would restore capitalism. Peasant differentiation had increased, replied Bukharin, but kulaks were still less than 4 percent, and state control of large-scale industry prevented any serious capitalist danger. Class conflict in the countryside, he predicted, would subside as the economy approached socialism.

As the debate continued, these differences lessened. Bukharin began to admit the need for rapid growth; Preobrazhenskii warned of its considerable risks. The chief beneficiary of this apparent synthesis was Stalin. Supporting Bukharin during the debate, he expelled the "Left" and stole its plank of rapid industrialization. To break peasant resistance, he combined it later with forced collectivization and demanded industrial goals far higher than those of the "Left."

Bukharin's gradualist solution was doomed as the private sector lost its ability to compete with the state sector. Taxing heavily the profits of private producers, imposing surcharges for transportation and exorbitant levies on kulaks, the state squeezed private producers severely. By cutting industrial prices despite severe shortages of industrial goods, the state undermined the basis of NEP, which was based upon a free market and incentives. To the party the stagnation of the restored Russian economy by 1926 was intolerable because without rapid growth the party's élan and morale would deteriorate.

Some recent Soviet accounts claim that the demise of the NEP was natural and inevitable. Unlike capitalist countries, the USSR could not exploit colonies, conduct aggressive wars, or obtain foreign credits. To achieve socialism the state had to industrialize quickly by concentrating resources in its hands and tapping all sources of internal capital, especially agriculture. Accepting most of Preobrazhenskii's theory of primitive socialist accumulation, some Soviet historians conclude that the populace, especially the peasantry, had to make major sacrifices in order to achieve industrialization. Recent Western studies, however, conclude that NEP agriculture could have satisfied immediate urban needs; they question the necessity and value of collectivization, either to solve the grain problem or to increase capital formation.[1]

COLLECTIVIZATION

Stalin's adoption in 1929 of a policy of forced collectivization of agriculture provoked a grim struggle between the regime and the peasantry. One factor in his decision was an apparent grain crisis in 1927–1928. Farm output had reached prewar levels, but grain marketings remained somewhat lower (though higher than Stalin claimed), largely because of government price policies. Better-off peasants, awaiting higher prices, withheld their grain, and the state could not obtain enough to feed the cities or finance new industrial projects. Peasants, roughly 80 percent of the Soviet population, operated about 25 million small private farms; collective and state farms were few and unimportant.[2] Most peasants still carried on traditional strip farming and remained suspicious of the Soviet regime. Kulaks tended to be literate, enterprising, and hard working, envied by other peasants for their relative prosperity, but respected for their industry. Employing a hired worker or two and perhaps renting out small machines to poorer neighbors, kulaks performed most of their own labor, and scarcely qualified as capitalists or semicapitalists, as Soviet historians describe them.

Marx and Lenin—and even Stalin before 1928—had never suggested *forced* collectivization. Marx intimated that large industrial farms would evolve gradually. Lenin considered collective, mechanized agriculture essential to socialism but warned that amalgamating millions of small farmers "in any rapid way" would be "absolutely absurd." Collective farming must develop "with extreme caution and only very gradually, by the force of example without any coercion of the middle peasant."[3] Following this advice closely, Stalin told the 15th Party Congress in 1927:

> What is the way out? The way out is to turn the small and scattered peasant farms into large united farms based on cultivation of the land in common, go over to collective cultivation of the land on the basis of a new higher technique. The way out is to unite the small and dwarf peasant farms *gradually but surely, not by pressure but by example and persuasion*, into large farms

---

[1] J. Karcz, "From Stalin to Brezhnev...," in J. Millar, *The Soviet Rural Community* (Urbana, Ill., 1971), p. 36 ff. See also R. W. Davies, *Soviet History in the Gorbachev Revolution* (Bloomington, Ind., 1989), especially pp. 40–46.
[2] In 1928, individual farmers tilled 97.3 percent of the sown area, collectives 1.2 (of which 0.7 percent were of the loose *toz* type), and state farms 1.5 percent.
[3] Lenin, *Collected Works* (New York, 1927–1942), vol. 30, p. 196.

based on common, cooperative collective cultivation of the land. . . . There is no other way out.[4] [Italics added for emphasis.]

Perhaps from ignorance or misinformation, Stalin disregarded Lenin's warnings and his own statements. Touring the Urals and Siberia in January 1928, he arbitrarily closed free markets, denounced hesitant officials, and had grain seized from the peasants. His "Urals-Siberian method" marked a return to War Communism's forced requisitioning. Faced with strong "Rightist" protests, Stalin retreated temporarily, but during 1928–1929 this brutal method was used repeatedly in scattered areas. Bukharin objected to it as "military-feudal exploitation" of the peasantry and referred to Stalin as Chingis-khan. Until he had destroyed the "Right," Stalin refrained from a general assault on private agriculture, and the First Five Year Plan approved in 1929 proposed that state and collective farms provide only 15 percent of agricultural output. The predominance of private farming seemed assured indefinitely.

Late in 1929, after crushing the "Right," Stalin moved abruptly to break peasant resistance and secure resources required for industrialization. Voluntary collectivization had clearly failed, and most Soviet economists doubted that the First Plan could be implemented. Recalled N. Valentinov, a Menshevik: "The financial base of the First Five Year Plan was extremely precarious *until Stalin solidified it by levying tribute on the peasants in primitive accumulation by the methods of Tamerlane.*"[5] Stalin may have viewed collectivization also as a means to win support from younger party leaders opposed to kulaks, NEP-men, and the free market. Privately, he advocated "industrializing the country with the help of *internal* accumulation," à la Preobrazhenskii. Once the peasantry had been split and rural opposition smashed, Stalin believed that rural proletarians would spearhead collectivization under state direction. The grain shortage induced the Politburo to support Stalin's sudden decision for immediate, massive collectivization.

A great turn was underway, Stalin asserted in November. The Central Committee affirmed obediently that poor and middle peasants were moving "spontaneously" into collectives. In secret, Stalin and his colleagues had ordered local officials to try out massive collectivization in selected areas. When results seemed positive (the number of collective farmers had allegedly doubled between June and October), Stalin ordered general collectivization, led by some 25,000 urban party activists. Entire villages had to deliver their grain to the state at low prices. Kulaks were deliberately overassessed for grain deliveries, then expropriated for

---

[4]Stalin, *Works* (Moscow, 1953–1955), vol. 10., p. 196.
[5]Ruthless Central Asian conqueror of the early 15th century.

failure to obey. The party had not discussed how to implement collectivization, and so initial measures were sudden, confused, and ill prepared. Many officials interpreted them to mean incorporating all peasants in kolkhozy (collective farms). Stalin and Molotov pressed for speed, overruled all objections, and rejected proposals for private peasant plots and ownership of small tools and livestock. Local officials took Stalin at his word.

The initial collectivization drive provoked massive peasant resistance and terrible suffering. Isaac Deutscher notes that rebellious villages, surrounded by Red Army detachments, were bombarded and forced to surrender. So much for voluntary, spontaneous collectivization! Within seven weeks about half the peasantry had been herded into collectives, but bringing in as little as possible, the peasants slaughtered over half the horses, about 45 percent of the large cattle, and almost two thirds of the sheep and goats in Russia. In December 1929, Stalin authorized liquidation of the kulaks:

> Now we are able to carry on a determined offensive against the kulaks, eliminate them as a class. . . . Now dekulakization is being carried out by the masses of poor and middle peasants themselves. . . . Should kulaks be permitted to join collective farms? Of course not, for they are sworn enemies of the collective farm movement.[6]

Poor neighbors often stole kulaks' clothing and drank up their vodka, but Stalin prohibited their dividing kulak land because he thought if they did so they would be reluctant to enter collectives. By a decree of February 1930, "actively hostile" kulaks were to be sent to forced labor camps; "economically potent" ones were to be relocated and their property confiscated. The "least noxious" kulaks were admitted to collectives. A recent party history claims that only 240,757 kulak families were deported, but eventually deportation overtook nearly all so-called kulaks, up to 5 million persons counting family members. Few ever returned, thousands of families were broken up, and millions of peasants were embittered. Soviet sources claim that such excesses reflected peasant hatred of kulaks, but there is little evidence of this. In March 1930, with the spring sowing threatened by lack of seed grain, Stalin in an article, "Dizzy with Success," called a temporary halt and blamed overly zealous local officials for excesses he had authorized. Interpreting this as repudiation of compulsory collectivization, the majority of peasants hastily left the kolkhozy.

---

[6]Cited in *Istoriia KPSS* (Moscow, 1959), p. 441.

Table 11.1 *Agricultural Output During Collectivization*

Category	1928	1929	1930	1931	1933	1935
Grain (million tons)	73.7	71.7	83.5	69.5	68.4	75.0
Cattle (million)	70.5	67.1	52.5	47.9	38.4	49.3
Pigs (million)	26.0	20.4	13.6	14.4	12.1	22.6
Sheep and goats (million)	146.7	147.0	108.0	77.7	50.2	61.1

After a brief pause, peasants were lured into collectives by persuasion and discriminatory taxation. By 1937, nearly all land and peasants were in kolkhozy, and remaining individual peasants worked inferior land and paid exorbitant taxes. But kolkhoz peasants were demoralized: Crops lay unharvested, tractors were few, and farm animals died of neglect. Large grain exports to western Europe in 1930–1931 exhausted reserves, and city requirements increased. In 1932, amidst widespread stealing and concealment of grain, collectivization hung by a thread and was maintained by force. In the Ukraine and north Caucasus, the state seized nearly all the grain, causing a terrible famine, which the Soviet press failed to report. Table 11.1 reveals the impact of collectivization.[7] Between 1928 and 1933, forced collectivization cost the Soviet Union roughly 27 percent of its livestock and contributed to the death of some 5 million persons, mostly peasants, in the famine of 1932–1934, notes J. Karcz. Damage to agriculture during this period was so severe that it could contribute little to the initial five-year plans. Collectivization was supposed to ensure more agricultural products for towns and industry, but though state grain procurements increased dramatically from 1928 to 1931, procurement of other products, notably meat and industrial products, declined sharply.

At first, collective farm organization and management were confused. The city activists sent to supervise collectivization and manage the farms misunderstood the peasantry and made many blunders. Peasant rights in kolkhozy were few and vague, and pay was low. The regime initially favored state farms (*sovkhozy*) as being fully socialist, but their inefficiency and costliness provoked second thoughts, and after 1935 they received less emphasis.

The "Model Statute" of 1935 described the kolkhoz as supposedly a voluntary cooperative whose members pooled their means of produc-

---

[7]Adapted from A. Nove, *The Soviet Economy*, 2d ed. (New York, 1967), p. 186.

tion, ran their own affairs, and elected their officials in a general meeting. Actually, local party organizations nominated farm chairmen and issued orders to farms, while state procurement agencies and Machine Tractor Stations (MTS) assured party control. The state-controlled MTS received all available machines and tractors and rented them to kolkhozy. Only after fixed requirements were met (taxes, insurance, capital fund, administration, and production costs) were kolkhoz members paid from what remained according to their work. Wages varied sharply according to skill and the farm's success, but as late as 1937, 15,000 kolkhozy paid their members nothing at all. The Statute recognized the peasant's right to a private plot of up to one acre per household and some livestock. This grant created the chief private sector in the economy. After 1937, kolkhozy produced mainly grain and industrial crops (cotton, sugar beets, flax); private peasant plots provided most meat, milk, eggs, potatoes, fruits, and many vegetables. Peasants sold these products after paying taxes. Low state prices, however, discouraged agricultural output. Industrial prices in 1937 were far higher than in 1928–1929, a recurrence of the price "scissors" against the peasant. On kolkhozy there was much coercion and unhappiness, but as the output of private plots increased, living conditions gradually improved.

During the last prewar years, arbitrary state decisions, ignoring local conditions, caused agriculture to stagnate or decline. In 1939, the party reduced the allowable size of private plots and transferred millions of acres to collective control. Stricter discipline and compulsory minimums of labor days were instituted for collective farmers, and fodder shortages brought a decline in already low kolkhoz livestock production. Crop yields and private livestock ownership declined substantially, but state procurements for urban consumption and for exports rose. Providing few incentives, collective farming remained very unpopular with Soviet peasants. Even by Soviet official figures, agricultural output increased very little during the 1930s. To achieve rapid industrialization and socialism, Stalin had uselessly sacrificed Russia's best, most enterprising farmers. This suggests that less compulsory methods, such as those of NEP, might well have proved less costly and more effective.

INDUSTRY: THE FIVE YEAR PLANS

One rationale for collectivization was to ensure food supplies adequate to support the rapid industrialization of the First Five Year Plan, which aimed immediately to provide a powerful heavy industry and only later an abundant life. The plan's psychological purpose was to induce workers and young people to make sacrifices, by holding before them a vision of the promised land of socialism in their own lifetimes. The state would benefit because the economy would become fully socialist, production and labor would be wholly state controlled, and security against capitalist powers would be strengthened. Stalin stated in February 1931: "We are 50 to 100 years behind the advanced countries. We must cover this distance in 10 years. Either we do this or they will crush us." Ten years and four months later Hitler invaded the USSR!

The First Five Year Plan did not inaugurate Soviet economic planning. Under NEP, Gosplan (State Planning Commission) had operated and there had been annual control figures. (See Chapter 9.) As private market forces declined, central economic control increased. The goods famine of 1926–1927 promoted state distribution of key commodities, especially metals, and regulation of production. Soviet economists had long discussed a five-year plan, but serious work on one began only in 1927.

Realistic early drafts of the First Plan in 1928 yielded to optimistic (and fantastic) variants in 1929. In 1927, Gosplan's mostly nonparty professional staff outlined a plan for relatively balanced growth, with industry to expand 80 percent in five years; it recognized probable obstacles. Party pressure, however, soon forced estimates upward, and resulting variants represented overly optimistic predictions made largely for psychological purposes. The version of S. G. Strumilin, a leading party planner, allowed for possible crop failures, little foreign trade or credits, and potentially heavier defense spending, but it set goals far exceeding those of the "Left," which Stalin had denounced as superindustrialist. Stalin boasted in 1929:

> We are going full steam ahead toward socialism through industrialization, leaving behind the age-long "Russian" backwardness. We are becoming a land of metals. . . , automobiles . . . , tractors, and when we have put the USSR on an automobile and the muzhik on a tractor, let the noble capitalists . . . attempt to catch up. We shall see then which countries can be labeled backward and which advanced.[8]

Because 1928 was a successful year, goals were boosted higher. In April 1929, the 16th Congress approved an optimal draft of the Plan, which assumed that no misfortunes would occur. Gross industrial output was to increase 235.9 percent, labor productivity 110 percent; production costs were to fall 35 percent and prices 24 percent. To fulfill such goals would require a miracle (in which Stalin presumably did not believe!). In

---

[8]Quoted in Maurice Dobb, *Soviet Economic Development Since 1917* (New York, 1948), p. 245.

December 1929, a congress of "shock brigades" urged the Plan's fulfillment in four years; soon this became official policy. Constantly sounding notes of urgency, Stalin forced the tempo and brought former party oppositionists into line. Riding a wave of overoptimism, party leaders chanted: "There is no fortress that the Bolsheviks cannot storm." Perhaps Stalin knowingly adopted impossible targets largely for political reasons. Those urging caution were denounced as "bourgeois" wreckers working for foreign powers.

During the First Plan some wholly unanticipated obstacles appeared. The Great Depression in the United States and Europe made Soviet growth look more impressive, but it dislocated world trade and made imported foreign machinery more expensive relative to Soviet grain exports. Defense expenditures, instead of declining, were increased due to Japanese expansion in east Asia. Ignorance and inexperience of workers and managers caused destruction or poor use of expensive foreign equipment, blamed on deliberate wrecking and sabotage. Resources were used inefficiently: Industrial plants often lacked equipment or skilled workers. The inexorable drive for quantity brought a deplorable decline in quality as strains and shortages multiplied.

The First Plan had mixed results. Vast projects were undertaken, but many remained unfinished. Some, such as the Volga-White Sea Canal, were built by forced labor; others reflected genuine enthusiasm and self-sacrifice. At Magnitogorsk in the Urals, previously only a village, a great metallurgical center arose as workers and technicians labored under primitive conditions to build a bright socialist future. As industrial output rose sharply, the regime announced late in 1932 that the Plan had been basically fulfilled in four years and three months, but goals were surpassed only in machinery and metalworking, then partly by statistical manipulation.[9] Nonetheless, the new powerful engineering industry reduced Soviet dependence on foreign machinery. Fuel output rose considerably, but iron and steel fell far short because necessary plants took longer to complete than anticipated. Supposed increases in consumer production concealed sharp declines in handicrafts. To the party, the First Plan was a success (though goals for steel were fulfilled only in 1940, for electric power in 1951, and for oil in 1955) because industrial expansion and defense output could now be sustained from domestic resources. Lifting itself by its own bootstraps, the USSR was vindicating

---

[9]Overfulfillment in machinery resulted chiefly from assigning high prices in 1926–1927 rubles to many new machines, thus increasing the "value" of total output. See A. Nove, *The Soviet Economy* (New York, 1967), p. 192.

Map 11.1 *Industry and Agriculture to 1939*

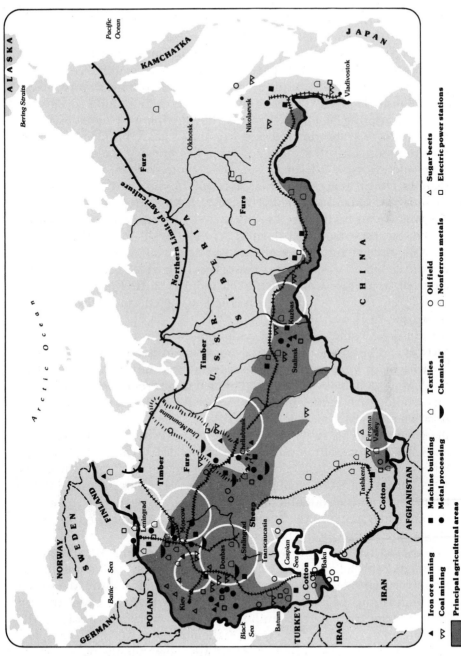

Source: Adapted from *A History of Russia, Second Edition* by Nicholas V. Riasanovsky. Copyright © 1969 by Oxford University Press, Inc. Used by permission.

Stalin's idea of socialism in one country. Consumer production, agriculture, and temporarily military strength, however, were sacrificed to a rapid growth of heavy industry (See Map 11.1.)

Labor was mobilized and lost much freedom. Once the state controlled all industry, Stalin declared trade union opposition anti-Marxist: How could the proletariat strike against its own dictatorship? Early in 1929, Tomskii and other trade union leaders were removed and replaced by Stalinists. Henceforth, trade unions were to help build socialist industry by raising labor productivity and discipline. Unions exhorted workers to raise production and organize "shock brigades." Factory directors took control of wages, food supplies, housing, and other worker necessities. Russian workers, losing the right to strike or protest against their employer, reverted to their status of 75 years earlier, and Stalin's attitude toward labor resembled that of early Russian capitalists. By 1932, unemployment disappeared in towns and a seven-hour day was introduced, but real wages fell sharply. As millions of untrained peasants, escaping collectivization, sought industrial jobs, labor discipline deteriorated. Machinery was ruined, and workers hunted for better conditions. (In 1930 the average worker in the coal industry shifted jobs three times!) Cities grew rapidly, housing construction lagged, and urban services were grievously overtaxed.

Raising incomes without a comparable rise in consumer goods or services and burgeoning industrial employment spurred inflation. Seeking to achieve impossible goals, managers hired more and more labor, sending wage bills skyrocketing. Rationed goods remained cheap, leaving people much money but little to buy. By 1929, a wide gap opened between official and private prices. To absorb excess purchasing power, the government in 1930 instituted the turnover tax in place of many excise levies. Generally imposed at the wholesale level, it amounted to the difference between the cost of production and the retail selling price. In 1934, for instance, the retail price of rye was 84 rubles per centner (100 kilograms), of which 66 rubles was turnover tax. Its burden fell mainly on the peasantry because the state paid them so little for their grain; so agriculture indirectly financed the Five Year Plan.

A Soviet account in the Brezhnev period, claiming that the situation at home and abroad required rapid industrialization, barely mentioned Stalin's crucial role in launching it. The First Plan, it continued, erected the foundations of a socialist economy and turned the USSR into an industrial-agrarian state as enthusiastic shock workers completed the plan ahead of schedule. The workers themselves, resolving to complete the plan in four years, were supported by the party and the plan's success represented a great victory for socialism. While admitting serious shortcomings, these Soviet historians asserted that the party quickly remedied the difficulties.[10]

By 1932, the Soviet economy was badly overstrained; 1933 brought shortages and privation. The Second Five Year Plan, redrafted during its first year, was adopted in February 1934 by the 17th Congress. More realistic than the First Plan, its execution was aided by more experienced planners and managers. Unlike its predecessor, final goals were lower than preliminary ones. Heavy industrial targets were mostly met, and machinery and electric power output rose dramatically. Labor productivity surpassed expectations, and technical sophistication improved as the First Plan's investments bore fruit. The Second Plan stressed consolidation, mastering techniques, and improving living standards. Initially, a greater increase was planned for consumer goods than for heavy industry, but then came a shift toward heavy industry and defense. Consumer goals were underfulfilled and per capita consumption fell below the 1928 level. Completed metallurgical works in Magnitogorsk, Kuznetsk, and Zaporozhye further reduced Soviet dependence on foreign capital goods, relieved the strain on the balance of payments, and permitted repayment of earlier debts. By 1937, the basic tools of industry and defense were being made in the USSR. Growth followed an uneven pattern: After a bad year, 1933, came three very good ones in industry and construction, and then relative stagnation began in 1937 (between 1937 and 1939 steel production actually declined). Table 11.2 shows some results of the two plans.[11]

During the Second Plan, labor productivity rose substantially and industrial employment fell below estimates as training programs gradually created a more skilled labor force. Pay differentials widened, rationing was gradually abolished, and more consumer goods were made available. After 1934, high prices of necessities stimulated harder work under the prevailing piecework system. Labor productivity was improved by Stakhanovism, a by-product of "socialist competition." In September 1935, Alexis Stakhanov, a Donets coal miner, by hard work and intelligent use of unskilled helpers, produced 14 times his norm. Fostered by the party, Stakhanovism spread to other industries and low labor norms were raised. Harsh penalties for absenteeism and labor turnover reduced these and improved labor discipline. However, the Great Purge, Soviet historians later admitted, swept away managers, technicians, statisticians, and even foremen. The shaken survivors often

---

[10]*Istoriia SSSR* (Moscow, 1967), vol. 8, pp. 475–483.
[11]Adapted from Nove, *Soviet Economy*, pp. 191, 225.

Table 11.2 *First and Second Plan Results*

Category	1927–1928	1932 (target)	1932–1933 (actual)	1937 (target)	1937 (actual)
National income in 1926–1927 rubles (billions)	24.5	49.7	45.5	100.2	96.3
Gross industrial output (billions of rubles)	18.3	43.2	43.3	92.7	95.5
Producers' goods	6.0	18.1	23.1	45.5	55.2
Consumers' goods	12.3	25.1	20.2	47.1	40.3
Gross agricultural production (billions of 1926–1927 rubles)	13.1	25.8	16.6	—	—
Electricity (100 million Kwhs.)	5.05	22.0	13.4	38.0	36.2
Hard coal (million tons)	35.4	75.0	64.3	152.5	128.0
Oil (millions tons)	11.7	22.0	21.4	46.8	28.5
Steel (million tons)	5.9	19.0	12.1	17.0	17.7
Machinery (millions of 1926–1927 rubles)	1,822.0	4,688.0	7,362.0	—	—

rejected responsibility. This reaction, and the growing shift of resources into arms production, created an industrial slowdown after 1937.

The diversion of resources into defense plagued the Third Five Year Plan (1938–1941), which the Nazi invasion interrupted. Industrial output increased an average of less than 2 percent annually, compared with 10 percent under the first two plans. Progress remained uneven, with much growth in production of machinery, but little in steel and oil. New western frontier territories such as the Baltic states considerably increased productive capacity. Labor was severely restricted in mobility and choice of occupation, the work week rose to 48 hours, and workers required permission from their enterprise to change jobs. A million high school students were conscripted for combined vocational training and industrial work.

In summary, rapid industrialization (1928–1941) brought increases in heavy industrial production unprecedented in history for a period of that length as shown in Table 11.3.[12]

The USSR became a leading industrial power, but living standards, real wages, and housing conditions declined. Dire predictions made during the industrialization debate came true: Bukharin foresaw the

---

[12]Stanley H. Cohn, *Economic Development in the Soviet Union* (Lexington, Mass., 1970), p. 39.

Table 11.3 *Selected Statistical Indicators, 1928–1940 (1928 = 100)*

Category	1940 output (in percent of 1928)
Industrial production	263
Industrial materials	343
Ferrous metals	433
Electric power	964
Chemicals	819
Machinery	486
Consumer goods	181
Agricultural production	105
Crops	123
Animal products	88
Individual consumption (per capita)	93
Real wages	54
Capital stock	286
Urban housing space (per capita)	78

human sacrifices and inflation, and Preobrazhenskii's concept of primitive socialist accumulation was implemented by methods that appalled him. (He was executed for protesting the excesses of collectivization.)

SHIFTS IN SOCIAL POLICIES

A continued assault on social institutions associated with the old regime accompanied the Second Socialist Offensive. After 1933 or 1934, policy shifted to consolidation of Soviet institutions that often resembled their tsarist models, and emphasis on discipline and social stability was renewed to overcome unfavorable effects of the preceding offensive. Social policies of 1934–1941 represented "a great retreat,"[13] or Soviet Thermidor, except that they coincided with the bloody terror of the purges.

Efforts to undermine the traditional family in order to strengthen the socialist state continued during the First Five Year Plan. Husbands and wives were often assigned to different cities, yet any available job had to be accepted. When a teacher complained of being separated from her

---

[13]See Nicholas Timasheff, *The Great Retreat* (New York, 1946).

husband, the Labor Board advised her to find a husband at her new job. In Stalingrad, "socialist suburbs" featuring single rooms were built, but only bachelors would live in them. Such policies did weaken family ties, but the by-products were grim. Free divorce and abortion caused a serious decline in birthrates, which threatened the supply of labor and army recruits. In Moscow medical institutions in 1934 there were only 57,000 live births and 154,000 abortions. Early in 1935, divorces numbered more than 38 per 100 marriages. Communities were confronted with spiraling juvenile delinquency and hooliganism. Children were beating up their schoolteachers!

In 1934–1935, the regime—largely for economic reasons—shifted course abruptly. "The family," it was now stated officially, "is an especially important phase of social relations in socialist society" and must be strengthened. Marriage is "the most serious affair in life" and should be regarded as a lifelong union; men who changed their wives like shirts were threatened with prosecution for rape. In 1939, the journal of the Commissariat of Justice proclaimed:

> The State cannot exist without the family. Marriage is a positive value for the Socialist State only if the partners see in it a lifelong union. So-called free love is a bourgeois invention and has nothing in common with the principles of conduct of a Soviet citizen.[14]

Marriage was now dignified with well-staged ceremonies in comfortable registration centers. Soon wedding rings were being sold again, and non-Communists frequently reinforced the civil ceremony with a church wedding. Strict regulations, replacing the quickie divorce of earlier days, greatly curtailed divorces and raised fees sharply. Divorce became more difficult and expensive to obtain in the USSR than in many of the United States, and unregistered marriage, instituted in 1926, was abolished. After June 1936, abortion was permitted only if the mother's life were endangered or to prevent transmission of serious illness. Parental authority was reinforced, and young people were urged to respect and obey parents and elders. Motherhood was glorified (Stalin made a pilgrimage to Tiflis to show how much he loved his old mother), and mothers of large families were compensated. After destroying the old extensive patriarchal family, the authorities reinforced the new Soviet nuclear family.

Joseph Stalin, the self-styled "man of steel," emphasized women's economic and personal dependence, reflecting the attitude of male superiority prevalent in the Caucasus and Central Asia. To Stalin, women epitomized ignorance and conservatism, threatening social progress:

---

[14]Quoted in Timasheff, *The Great Retreat*, p. 198.

"The woman worker . . . can help the common cause if she is politically conscious and politically educated. But she can ruin the common cause if she is downtrodden and backward. . . ." Under Stalin's rule there was strong emphasis on women's duties and responsibilities at home and at work, while less and less was heard of their former oppression. In the Stalin era, the role of women was transformed primarily by industrialization, collectivization, and urbanization. Their massive influx into the Soviet work force after 1929 coincided with greatly expanded educational opportunities, growth of child-care institutions, and protective legislation for all workers, but not equal pay. However, unlike early Bolshevik libertarian concern with female emancipation, the Soviet aim was no longer to enhance women's independence, but to improvise a response to urgent needs created by rapid urbanization and burgeoning female employment. Development of social services, such as child-care centers, because of the low priority assigned to them by the Stalin regime, failed conspicuously to keep pace with demands.

Experimentalism in education yielded, during the First Plan, to a structured, disciplined school program. Not Leninist theory, but industry's insistent demands for trained specialists triggered the shift. Applicants to higher educational institutions were found to be woefully deficient in reading skills and parroted vague generalizations. In 1929, A. Lunacharskii, chief exponent of experimentalism, was removed, and a shift to serious study began under the slogan "Mastery of knowledge." In 1931–1932 came partial curricular reforms: Teaching of Marxism was reduced, history revived, and "progressive education" was largely abandoned. Book learning, academic degrees, systematic textbooks, and traditional grading practices were reemphasized. Examinations were reinstituted after a 15-year lapse. Noisy, undisciplined classrooms disrupted by hooligans yielded to quiet, disciplined ones as the authority of teachers and professors was restored. Decrees from above specified every detail of instruction and school administration as a new Soviet school emerged, patterned after the conservative tsarist school of the 1880s. Curricula resembled tsarist and European ones, and pupils were dressed in uniforms like those of the 1880s. For pragmatic reasons, a retreat to traditional models began earlier in education than in other fields. The authoritarian school reflected the Stalinist autocracy.

Soviet religious policies fluctuated. During the First Plan, there was a widespread campaign to close churches. In 1930, the Soviet press reported the burning of icons and religious books by the carload, and restrictions, disfranchisement, and discriminatory taxation plagued the clergy. The atheist League of Militant Godless, featuring the young and growing to almost 6 million members, induced many collective farms to declare themselves "godless." Then between 1933 and 1936, partly to allay peasant discontent, came some relaxation of persecution. The Stalin Constitution of 1936 restored the franchise to clergymen and gave them full civil rights. The Purge of 1937–1938 brought another wave of persecution, but few priests were executed. After 1938, a more tolerant religious policy developed to win popular support and counter the rising threat of Nazi Germany. Christianity was now declared to have played a progressive, patriotic role in Russian history. Violence against churches and believers was forbidden, and the closing of churches and political trials of clergymen were halted. The regime adopted a subtler approach of emphasizing that scientific advances had made religion outmoded. Soviet leaders, recognizing the persistence of religious belief, sought to use it to consolidate their power. The Soviet census of 1937 had revealed that more than half the adult population still classified themselves as believers. (The census takers were sent to Siberia!) Meanwhile, the Orthodox Church recognized the regime and wished to cooperate with it to achieve greater social discipline, a strong family, and restriction of sexual activity. Twenty years of official persecution greatly weakened the church as an organization and reduced markedly the numbers of the faithful, but strengthened their faith. Marxism-Leninism proved an inadequate substitute for religion.

During the 1930s, the Stalin regime, abandoning experimentalism and radical policies, retreated toward tradition and national and authoritarian tsarist patterns. There emerged an increasingly disciplined, status-conscious society headed by a new elite of party bureaucrats, economic managers, engineers, and army officers, which differed sharply in attitudes and habits from the revolutionary generation.

PROBLEM 4
Collectivization: Why and How?

The transformation of Russian agriculture under Stalin from 25 million individual farms into several hundred thousand collective and state farms was one of the 20th century's most dramatic and important events. It involved a massive conflict between the Soviet regime and the peasantry, the destruction of many of the best Soviet farmers and much of the livestock, and produced a terrible famine in 1933. Soviet collectivized agriculture, plagued by low productivity, lack of incentives for farmers, and incompetent organization, has sought ever since without conspicuous success to satisfy domestic needs. Was forced collectivization necessary or wise? Why was it undertaken? Who was responsible for the accompanying mass suffering? Here these issues are explored from various viewpoints, including Stalin's contemporary speeches, a Soviet account from 1967, and the work of a Soviet historian published in the West.

STALIN'S VIEW

Stalin and his Politburo colleagues claimed in 1929 that it was necessary to collectivize agriculture to achieve economic progress and socialism. They affirmed that the decision to collectivize was imposed upon them by kulak treachery and the insistent demands of an expanding industry. Poor and middle peasants, Stalin claimed, were entering collective farms voluntarily and en masse. Declared Stalin as forced collectivization began:

> The characteristic feature of the present collective farm movement is that not only are the collective farms being joined by individual groups of poor peasants . . . but . . . by the mass of middle peasants as well. This means that the collective farm movement has been transformed from a movement of individual groups and sections of the laboring peasants into a movement of millions and millions of the main mass of the peasantry. . . . The collective farm movement . . . has assumed the character of a mighty and growing *anti-kulak* avalanche . . . paving the way for extensive socialist construction in the countryside [speech of December 27, 1929].

At the beginning of forced collectivization, Stalin, summarizing the party's problems and achievements in agriculture, stressed the rapid development of a new socialist agriculture against desperate resistance from "retrogade" elements:

> The party's third achievement during the past year . . . [is] the *radical change* in the development of our agriculture from small, backward *individual* farming to large-scale advanced *collective* agriculture, to joint cultivation of the land . . . , based on modern techniques and finally to giant state farms, equipped with hundreds of tractors and harvester combines.
> . . . In a whole number of areas we have succeeded in *turning* the main mass of the peasantry away from the old, *capitalist* path . . . to the new *socialist* path of development, which ousts the rich and the capitalists and reequips the middle and poor peasants . . . with modern implements . . . so as to enable them to climb out of poverty and enslavement to the kulaks onto the high road of cooperative, collective cultivation of the land. . . . We have succeeded in bringing about this *radical change* deep down in the peasantry itself and in securing the following of the broad masses of the poor and middle peasants in spite of incredible difficulties, in spite of the desperate resistance of retrograde forces of every kind, from kulaks and priests to philistines and Right Opportunists.
> . . . Such an impetuous speed of development is *unequalled* even by our socialized large-scale industry. . . . All the objections raised by "science"

against the possibility and expediency of organizing large grain factories of 40,000 to 50,000 hectares each have collapsed. . . .

What is the new feature of the present collective-farm movement? . . . The peasants are joining the collective farms not in separate groups, as formerly, but as whole villages, *volosts,* districts, and even *okrugs.* And what does that mean? It means that *the middle peasant is joining the collective farm* [November 1929].

Only a month later, however, Stalin hinted that forcible means were having to be employed after all:

It is necessary . . . *to implant* in the village large socialist farms, collective and state farms, as bases of socialism which, with the socialist city in the vanguard, can drag along the masses of peasants. . . .

In March 1930, at his colleagues' insistence, Stalin temporarily halted forced collectivization. His article, "Dizzy with Success," blamed local party workers and extremists for errors and perversions of official policy:

. . . People not infrequently become intoxicated by such successes, . . . overrate their own strength. The successes of our collective-farm policy are due . . . to the fact that it rests on the *voluntary character* of the collective-farm movement and *on taking into account the diversity of conditions* in various regions of the USSR. Collective farms must not be established by force. That would be foolish and reactionary. The collective-farm movement must rest on the active support of the main mass of the peasantry. . . . In a number of the northern regions of the consuming zone . . . , attempts are not infrequently made to *replace* preparatory work for the organization of collective farms by bureaucratic decreeing . . . , the organization of collective farms on paper.

. . . Who benefits from these distortions, . . . these unworthy threats against the peasants? Nobody, except our enemies! In a number of areas of the USSR . . . attempts are being made . . . to leap straight away into the agricultural commune. . . . They are already "socializing" dwelling houses, small livestock, and poultry. . . .

How could there have arisen in our midst such blockhead excesses in "socialization," such ludicrous attempts to overleap oneself? . . . They could have arisen only in the atmosphere of our "easy" and "unexpected" successes on the front of collective farm development . . . as a result of the blockheaded belief of a section of our Party: "We can achieve anything!" [March 2, 1930].

In his report to the 17th Congress in January 1934, Stalin hailed the results of rapid collectivization in the USSR:

. . . From a country of small individual agriculture it has become a country of collective, large-scale mechanized agriculture. . . . Progress in the main branches of agriculture proceeded many times more slowly than in industry, but nevertheless more rapidly than in the period when individual farming predominated. . . . Our Soviet peasantry has completely and irrevocably taken its stand under the Red banner of socialism. . . . Our Soviet peasantry has quit the shores of capitalism for good and is going forward in alliance with the working class to socialism.[15]

THE OFFICIAL POSITION: 1967

The *History of the USSR* (Moscow 1967), issued early in the Brezhnev era, while defending the necessity and correctness of collectivization and stressing the voluntary entry of many peasants into kolkhozy, admitted the widespread use of force and "administrative methods" (secret police). It credited the party (not Stalin) with successfully implementing collectivization, but criticized the extremism of some party leaders. Stalin was reprimanded mildly, and his role in deciding upon and implementing collectivization was deemphasized.

Under conditions of worsening international relations, increasing economic difficulties, and the growth of class struggle within the USSR, the Communist Party had to achieve simultaneously industrialization and the socialist reconstruction of agriculture. Life demanded a colossal application of energy by party and Soviet people and sacrifices. . . .

In the course of fulfilling the First Five Year Plan, the Communist party came out decisively for speeding the tempo of constructing socialism. Collectivization was part of that construction. The decision that it was necessary to reduce the period of implementing it ripened gradually. . . . In the spring of 1929 were heard the words "full collectivization" for the first time as a practical task. . . . In the second half of 1929 the village seethed as in the days of the revolution [of 1917]. At meetings of the poor peasants, at general village assemblies only one question was raised: organizing kolkhozy. From July through September 1929 were attracted into *kolkhozy* as many peasants as during the whole 12 years of Soviet power. And during the last three months of 1929 the numerical growth of *kolkhozy* was twice as fast again. This was, as the party emphasized, "an unprecedented tempo of collectivization, *exceeding the most optimistic projections.*". . .

The choice of the moment for a transition to massive collectivization was determined by various reasons. Among them the most important was the spurt in the country's economy. Socialist construction was advancing at an accelerating pace. The industrial population was growing considerably faster than had been assumed. The demand for commercial grain and raw materials rose sharply. The inability of small peasant production to supply a growing industry with food . . . became unbearable. It became clear that the

---

[15]J. Stalin, *Works* (Moscow, 1955), vol. 12, pp. 131–138, 147, 155, 198–206; vol. 13, pp. 243–261.

economy of the country could not be based on two different social foundations: big socialist industry and small individual peasant farming. . . .

One of the new methods of struggle of the kulaks against the policy of the Soviet state in 1928–29 was so-called kulak self-liquidation. The kulaks themselves reduced their sowings, sold their stock and tools. "Kulak self-liquidation" thus began before the state shifted to a policy of consistent liquidations of the kulaks as a class. . . .

Along with the achievements in socialist reconstruction of the village, inadequacies were revealed. . . . Such a leap was to a significant degree caused by serious extremes, by the broad use of administrative measures. . . . In a majority of cases local leaders themselves forced by every means the process of collectivization. . . . Leaders of one region issued at the beginning of 1930 the following slogans: "Collectivize the entire population at any cost! Dekulakize no less than seven percent of all peasant farms! Achieve all this by February 15 [1930] without delaying a moment!" . . . Administrative methods, violation of the voluntary principal in *kolkhoz* construction, contradicting the Leninist cooperative plan caused sharp dissatisfaction among the peasantry. . . . All that represented a serious danger for the country, for the alliance of the working class with the peasantry. In the struggle against these extremes rose all the healthy forces of the party. The Central Committee was inundated by letters of local Communists, workers, and peasants. . . . Numerous signals of the dissatisfaction of the peasantry with administrative methods of *kolkhoz* construction caused serious concern in the Central Committee. Thus the party and government in February and March 1930 took a series of emergency measures to correct the situation in the countryside. . . . On March 2, 1930, was published the article of I. V. Stalin, "Dizzy with Success" . . . against leftist extremes. . . . Many people noted, to be sure, that it had come too late when extremes had taken on a massive character. . . . One must note that in describing the causes of the extremes, I. V. Stalin was one-sided and not self-critical. He placed the entire blame for mistakes and extremes on local cadres, accused them of dizziness and demanded harsh measures against them. This caused a certain confusion among party workers, which hampered the task of eliminating excesses.[16]

A DISSIDENT SOVIET HISTORIAN

Roy Medvedev, a Soviet historian, in *Let History Judge* (New York, 1973), recently published in the USSR, castigates forced collectivization and Stalin's role in it. Unlike the previous selection, which ascribed "mistakes" mainly to a few "leftists," Medvedev points directly at Stalin and the Politburo and suggests that forced collectivization was unwise and unnecessary. He ascribed Stalin's decision for forced collectivization and elimi-

---

[16]*Istoriia SSSR* (Moscow, 1967), vol. 8, pp. 443, 541–543, 553–557.

nation of the kulaks mainly to economic conditions, for which Stalin and his colleagues were responsible:

> The economic miscalculations of Stalin, Bukharin, and Rykov and the kulaks' sabotage of grain procurement brought the USSR at the end of 1927 to the verge of a grain crisis. . . . Mistakes . . . in the previous years did not leave much room for political and economic maneuvering, [but] there were still some possibilities for the use of economic rather than administrative measures, that is for the methods of NEP rather than War Communism.

Medvedev attributed the traumatic implementation of collectivization to Stalin's incompetent and disastrous leadership:

> . . . His inclination toward administrative fiat, toward coercion, instead of convincing, his oversimplified and mechanistic approach to complex political problems, his crude pragmatism and inability to forsee the consequences of alternative actions, his vicious nature and unparalleled ambition—all these qualities of Stalin seriously complicated the solution of problems that were overwhelming to begin with.
>
> . . . Stalin could not appraise correctly the situation taking shape in the countryside. At the first signs of progress [of collectivization] he embarked on a characteristically adventurous course. Apparently, he wanted to compensate for years of failures and miscalculations in agricultural policy and to astonish the world with a picture of great success in the socialist transformation of agriculture. So at the end of 1929, he sharply turned the bulky ship of agriculture without checking for reefs and shoals. Stalin, Molotov, Kaganovich, and several other leaders pushed for excessively high rates of collectivization, driving the local organizations in every possisble way, ignoring . . . difficulties. . . .
>
> Although at the beginning of the 30s, grain production decreased, bread was in short supply, and millions of peasants were starving, Stalin insisted on exporting great quantities of grain. . . . Moreover, Soviet grain was sold for next to nothing. . . . The most galling aspect of the sacrifices that the people suffered—the peasants most of all—is that they were unnecessary. . . . The scale of capital investment in industry, which Stalin forced in the early 1930s, was too much for the economy to bear. . . .

Stalin was likewise responsible, claims Medvedev, for the extreme tempo and excessive socialization of the initial collectivization drive. The Central Committee's draft decree had suggested a slower pace:

> At his [Stalin's] insistence the draft was stripped of rules indicating what portion of livestock and farm implements should be collectivized. In the final version the period of collectivization was reduced in the North Caucasus and Mid-Volga to one to two years and rules were omitted concerning socialization of the instruments of production. . . . The peasants' right to keep small livestock, implements, and poultry was omitted. Also deleted were guidelines for liquidating the kulaks. . . . Material and financial resources needed

to organize hundreds of collective farms had not been set aside. . . . Most of the local party, soviet, and economic organs . . . were not prepared for total collectivization in such a short time. In order to carry out the orders that came from above . . . , almost all party and Soviet organs were forced to put administrative pressure on the peasants and also on the lower officials. . . . Such methods absolutely contradicted the basic principles of Marxism-Leninism.[17]

SOVIET VIEWS UNDER GORBACHEV

Under the Gorbachev regime, Soviet writings about Stalin's policy of forced collectivization have much continuity with critiques from the Khrushchev period. However, there has been far more outright condemnation of forced collectivization as a whole as well as of Khrushchev's agricultural policies. Thus academician V. A. Tikhonov claimed that the kulaks had virtually disappeared during the Civil War period (1918–1920), so that those "dekulakized" by Stalin from 1929 to 1933 were peasants who produced somewhat more than the average—that is, the ablest and thriftiest Soviet farmers; Tikhonov described forced collectivization as an unmitigated disaster. Sociologist V. Shumkin stated bluntly:

> Stalin decided to eliminate NEP prematurely, using purely administrative measures and direct compulsion; this led, speaking mildly, to pitiable results. Agricultural production was disrupted; in a number of districts of the country famine began. In towns measures against artisans and small producers in practice destroyed a whole sphere of services. The lives of tens of millions of people . . . were filled with incredible deprivations and difficulties, often at the limit of purely biological existence.

And the economist V. Seliunin castigated Stalin's "Year of the Great Break" (1929) instituting forced collectivization as the "year of the breaking of the backbone of the people."[18]

A WESTERN VIEW

The most recent Soviet critiques of forced collectivization tend to confirm the findings of an outstanding recent Western study by Moshe Lewin,[19] who generally endorsed Medvedev's conclusions. Lewin affirms that

---

[17]Roy Medvedev, *Let History Judge* (New York, 1973), pp. 69 ff.

[18]R. W. Davies, *Soviet History in the Gorbachev Revolution* (Bloomington, Ind., 1989), pp. 49–50. The three Soviet articles cited by Davies were all published in 1987 or 1988.

[19]Lewin, *Russian Peasants and Soviet Power: A Study of Collectivization* (New York, 1975).

Stalin, in asserting that the middle peasant was entering the kolkhoz voluntarily, was arguing from false premises:

> There were no grounds for suggesting that there had been a change of attitude among the mass of the peasantry with regard to the *kolkhozes*. The supposed change was a product of Stalin's peculiar form of reasoning which consisted of taking the wish for the deed. It followed that the peasants were being won over because this spring *there would be* 60,000 tractors in the fields, and in a year's time there would be over a hundred thousand.

As to the results of forced collectivization, Lewin concludes:

> The rash undertaking of the winter 1929–30 costs the country very dearly. . . . Indeed, it is true to say that to this day Soviet agriculture has still not fully recovered from the damaging effects of that winter.

The cost of collectivization was enormous: "Seldom was any government to wreak such havoc in its own country."[20] Economically, forced collectivization was counterproductive even in the short run, concludes James Millar; in the long run it had no economic rationale at all.[21] It is revealing that forced collectivization à la Stalin was not tried elsewhere in eastern Europe. Instead, wealthier farmers were squeezed out, as Lenin had suggested, by economic measures and their managerial talents used in the collective farms.

Suggested Additional Reading

BELOV, FEDOR. *A History of a Soviet Collective Farm* (New York, 1955).

BERGSON, ABRAM. *The Real National Income of Soviet Russia Since 1928* (Cambridge, Mass., 1961).

BERLINER, JOSEPH S. *Factory and Manager in the USSR* (Cambridge, Mass., 1957).

BLACKWELL, WILLIAM. *The Industrialization of Russia . . .* (New York, 1982).

BROWN, EMILY. *The Soviet Trade Unions and Labor Relations* (Cambridge, Mass., 1966).

CARR, E. H. *Foundations of a Planned Economy, 1926–1929* (New York, 1972).

CONQUEST, ROBERT. *The Harvest of Sorrow: Soviet Collectivization and the Terror-Famine* (New York, 1986).

CURTISS, JOHN S. *The Russian Church and the Soviet State* (Boston, 1953).

DANIELS, R. V., ed. *The Stalin Revolution* (Lexington, Mass., 1972).

DAVIES, R. W. *The Soviet Collective Farm, 1929–1930* (Cambridge, Mass., 1980).

---

[20]Lewin, *Russian Peasants. . .* , pp. 457, 515.
[21]Millar, "Mass Collectivization. . . ," *Slavic Review,* Dec. 1974, p. 766.

———. *The Industrialization of Soviet Russia*, vol. 3: *The Soviet Economy in Turmoil 1929–1930* (Cambridge, Mass., 1989).

DEUTSCHER, ISAAC. *The Prophet Outcast: Trotsky, 1929–1940* (Oxford, Eng., 1963).

DUNMORE, T. *The Stalinist Command Economy* (New York, 1980).

ERLICH, A. *The Soviet Industrialization Debate* . . . (Cambridge, Mass., 1960).

FITZPATRICK, SHEILA, ed. "Sources on the Social History of the Prewar Stalin Period," *Russian History, 12,* nos. 2–4.

GERSCHENKRON, A. *Economic Backwardness in Historical Perspective* (Cambridge, Mass., 1962).

HODGEMAN, DONALD R. *Soviet Industrial Production, 1928–1951* (Cambridge, Mass., 1954).

HOLZMAN, FRANKLYN D. *Soviet Taxation* (Cambridge, Mass., 1955).

INKELES, ALEX, and R. A. BAUER. *The Soviet Citizen* . . . (Cambridge, Mass., 1959).

JASNY, NAUM. *Soviet Industrialization, 1928–1952* (Chicago, 1961).

KRAVCHENKO, VICTOR. *I Chose Freedom* (New York, 1946).

LAIRD, ROY D., ed. *Soviet Agriculture and Peasant Affairs* (Lawrence, Kans., 1963).

LEWIN, MOSHE. *Russian Peasants and Soviet Power* . . . (New York, 1975).

MALE, D. J. *Russian Peasant Organization Before Collectivization* . . . (Cambridge, Eng., 1971).

NOVE, ALEC. *Was Stalin Really Necessary?* (London, 1964).

PREOBRAZHENSKY, E. A. *The Crisis of Soviet Industrialization*, ed. D. Filtzer (White Plains, N.Y., 1979).

SCOTT, JOHN. *Behind the Urals* (Boston, 1943).

SHOLOKHOV, MIKHAIL. *Virgin Soil Upturned* (New York, 1959). (Novel.)

SMITH, KEITH, ed. *Soviet Industrialization and Soviet Maturity: Economy and Society* (London, 1986).

STALIN, JOSEPH. *Problems of Leninism* (Moscow, 1940).

SWIANIEWICZ, S. *Forced Labor and Economic Development* . . . (London, 1965).

TIMASHEFF, NICHOLAS. *The Great Retreat* (New York, 1946).

VIOLA, LYNNE. *The Best Sons of the Fatherland: Workers in the Vanguard of Soviet Collectivization* (New York, 1989).

WHEATCROFT, S. G., and R. W. DAVIES, eds. *Materials for a Balance of the Soviet National Economy, 1928–1930* (Cambridge, Eng., 1985).

ZALESKI, E. *Stalinist Planning for Economic Growth*, trans. and ed. M. C. MacAndrew and J. Moore (Chapel Hill, N.C., 1979).

CHAPTER TWELVE

CULTURE IN THE SOVIET ERA, 1917-1929

From the very outset of the Soviet state, culture became the handmaiden of politics and could not be viewed or understood in isolation from politics. From 1917 to 1929 Soviet culture passed through two clearly defined stages of development. During the so-called era of War Communism (1917–1921) there was no real official policy on cultural affairs because Bolshevik leaders were too preoccupied with the survival of their new regime, beset on all sides by enemies, both foreign and domestic. In those turbulent years many of Russia's outstanding writers, artists, and musicians sought refuge abroad, and some remained in foreign exile. From 1921 to 1928, the period of the New Economic Policy, a generally liberal approach prevailed toward the arts: Experimentation and debate were largely accepted as essential to a healthy cultural life. Some of those intellectuals who had emigrated during the Civil War now returned to Soviet Russia.

The November Revolution that catapulted the Bolsheviks into power did not precipitate an immediate and abrupt break with established cultural patterns and traditions. Indeed, during the first years of the Soviet regime and particularly after the Civil War and the period of liberalization represented by the New Economic Policy introduced in 1921, the Russian cultural scene appeared little changed from what it had been before the Revolution. This static condition was due in part to the fact that the Bolsheviks, once they had seized power, were intent on retaining it and were thus concerned with critical questions of political consolidation, economic reconstruction, and military preparedness, all of which left little time or energy to devote to the arts. Even if inclined to introduce wide-ranging control of all aspects of social and cultural activity, the Bolsheviks realized that they could not do so with the limited cadres of trained and experienced personnel at their disposal. On the other hand, the disruptions of war, revolution, and civil war meant that for a time not much of enduring cultural value was produced. Relatively little was published as scarce reserves of paper were quickly consumed to print militant propaganda leaflets and revolutionary tracts designed to persuade the populace of the advantages of Bolshevism. Painters and sculptors who managed to continue work found little demand for or even interest in their output. Basic materials—paints, clay, canvas, paper— were all in short supply and what was available was usually of poor quality. Composers and musicians faced similar problems. Concert halls, instead of ringing with symphonic melodies and rousing choruses, were more often filled with raucous political debates and revolutionary agitation. Moreover, the intelligentsia had been reduced by deaths from hunger, disease, war, and execution. Emigration was one avenue of escape from what must have appeared to many as the beginnings of the apocalypse. Many prominent artists chose to live abroad as transients or permanent exiles rather than face the uncertainties of life in the Soviet Union. The list of émigrés was impressive, including such prominent names as Maxim Gorkii, Ivan Bunin, Ilia Ehrenburg, Alexis Tolstoy, Dmitri Merezhkovskii, Zinaida Hippius, Igor Stravinsky, Serge Prokofiev, Serge Rachmaninov, Serge Diagilev, Marc Chagall, and Vasili Kandinskii. Some returned to the Soviet Union later, while others became permanent residents abroad.

The chaos and the uncertainty of the early years of Soviet rule constituted only part of the larger obstacle to elaborating a coherent cultural policy. From an ideological or theoretical vantage point there was equal confusion and uncertainty. In the Marxist scheme culture and the arts constitute part of the superstructure rather than the material base. Only changes in the substructure—in the mode or method of production—would bring about corresponding changes in culture and the arts. A new socialist culture would emerge only gradually after a new economic order had been established and a genuinely proletarian society achieved.

Nevertheless, it would be an error to think that Russian culture was unaffected by the Revolution or that the Bolsheviks were uninterested in culture and formulation of policy for the arts.

Lenin outlined his none too radical view of the arts as follows:

> Art belongs to the people. It must have its deepest roots in the broad masses of the workers. It must be understood and loved by them. It must be rooted in, and grow with their feelings, thoughts, and desires. It must arouse and develop the artist in them. Are we to give cake and sugar to a minority while the mass of workers and peasants still eat black bread? So that art may come to the people, and people to art, we must first of all raise the general level of education and culture.[1]

There was really nothing very new, nor even particularly Marxist, about this view. In many ways, it echoed what had been espoused by Vladimir Stasov in his defense of the art of the Itinerants and the music of the Five during the 19th century. Art had to be rooted in the life of the people, it had to be clear and understandable, and it had to serve a useful purpose: to educate the people. Such was to become the essence of the Soviet concept of art.

LUNACHARSKII: THE POLITICS OF CULTURE

The man responsible for translating Lenin's views on culture and art into reality was Anatol Lunacharskii (1875–1933), son of a successful tsarist civil servant, who spared no sacrifice or expense to provide him with the best education available in Russia and western Europe. Lunacharskii studied philosophy and literature and became refined, sophisticated and urbane, his tastes cosmopolitan and progressive. He joined the Bolshevik Party in 1904 and often described himself as "an intellectual among Bolsheviks, and a Bolshevik among the intelligentsia." As the Bolshevik Party's leading cultural authority, Lunacharskii was the natural choice to be the first People's Commissar of Education. From 1917 to 1929, Lunacharskii guided the Soviet regime's efforts to improve education and develop a socialist culture in conformity with Lenin's views. Lunacharskii proved to be a skillful and imaginative administrator, who exercised his considerable authority with flexibility and tolerance. The tasks facing him were formidable: First to initiate and oversee a program of basic education designed to teach the illiterate masses, variously estimated at 60 to 70 percent of the population, to read and write. He also needed to begin winning the allegiance of the artistic intelligentsia and

---

[1]Cited in Sheila Fitzpatrick, *The Commissariat of Enlightenment* (New York, 1971), p. 24.

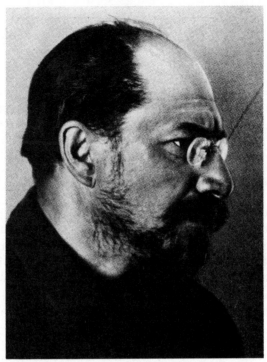

Anatol Lunacharskii (1875–1933) *(Library of Congress)*

persuade intellectual workers of their social responsibilities, obligations to the state, and need for a common purpose. Finally, he had to convince the hard-pressed party leadership of the paramount importance of the arts in order to secure financial backing to carry on an effective cultural program. He recognized the need to maintain a delicate balance between traditional values of more conservative elements of society and fanatical enthusiasm for entirely new directions and demands for a complete break with the past by more radical supporters of the regime. He had to work frantically at times to prevent wanton destruction of cultural monuments, especially churches and other buildings and sculptures associated with the old regime, by those who wished to obliterate old "bourgeois culture." Although determined to preserve the best of the old heritage, Lunacharskii refused to be limited by it.

His immediate efforts among the intelligentsia were not confined to attempts to restrain enthusiasm by proletarian supporters of the regime. At the same time he had to persuade opponents of the Bolsheviks to forsake open hostility in favor of neutrality or support. Persuasion and patience, he believed, were superior to pressure and coercion. His was a voice of calm and reasonableness in an era of impatience and often frenzied intolerance. Lunacharskii's actions were generally sensible and humane in an inhumane and often irrational age. While he was Commissar of Education, he encouraged a give-and-take, which would contrast sharply with later rigid Stalinist authoritarianism. The 1920s were in many ways the "Golden Era" of the Soviet culture. It was an age of experimentation and innovation in many spheres, and Lunacharskii was able to chart a reasonable course through turbulent waters.

Social life and schools were soon affected by the "ideological reorientation" implied by the revolution. Some radical social reformers predicted the "withering away" of the traditional family and encouraged a breach with bourgeois patterns of social behavior. In education, the curriculum was drastically revised to give learning practical value by promoting economic specialization and material production and to develop socially responsible individuals. Schools were to be socially nondiscriminatory, free, secular, and compulsory to the age of 17. Schooling and work experience were to be integrated, and ideological loyalty and Soviet patriotism became integral parts of the curriculum. Schools were designed to be political and economic instruments to overcome Russia's backwardness. Lunacharskii's Commissariat made significant progress in education in a very short time, despite shortages of buildings, teachers, and books. By 1926, an estimated 51 percent of those over age nine were literate.

PROLETKULT AND OTHER VANGUARD GROUPS

In order to implement a wide-ranging program in education and culture, Lunacharskii saw the need to recruit "bourgeois specialists" of the prerevolutionary era. A comprehensive educational system could not be organized without experienced personnel. "Bourgeois specialists" were needed to train "socialist specialists" of the future. Wishing to alienate no one, Lunacharskii authorized and helped finance numerous literary, artistic, and educational groups that retained much freedom and autonomy. Cultural groups proliferated. Among the leading groups sponsored by Lunacharskii's Commissariat was the Association of Proletarian Cultural and Educational Organizations (Proletkult). Proletkult had been founded in 1917, before the November Revolution, by A. A. Bogdanov to provide an outlet for working-class cultural activity and leadership and to give direction to a broad educational program. Proletkult promoted establishment of workers' clubs (to foster literature, art, drama, and music) and workers' universities and palaces of culture to introduce proletarians to culture and education. In August 1918, Proletkult sponsored a conference of proletarian writers that called for setting up an All-Russian Union of Writers of "working class origin and viewpoint," the first effort to organize proletarian cultural workers into a unified group. This resolution was not acted upon then, but the idea was not forgotten. The aggressive stance of Proletkult caused friction with Lunacharskii's Commissariat, and the two institutions often worked at cross-purposes. Their overlap and competition finally persuaded Lenin to intervene in 1920. He ordered Proletkult merged with the Commissariat, ending the former's autonomy. Proletkult was always far more radical and ideological than the Commissariat. Lenin would not allow Proletkult to undermine Lunacharskii's more traditional program.

In contrast to Proletkult's aim of drastic reorientation of culture, a group of writers emerged dubbed the "Fellow Travelers" by Trotskii. These were the "bourgeois specialists" in literature, mostly established prerevolutionary writers who remained in Soviet Russia. They sought in their works to analyze the acutely felt problems of adjustment in a new and alien world. They wrote of the Revolution, the Civil War, and their effects on individual human beings. They were less interested in cosmic historical forces than the more ideologically oriented proletarian writers. The Fellow Travelers wrote about romantic love, violence, and passion. In 1921, a group of Fellow Travelers formed a fraternity known as the Serapion Brotherhood (borrowing the name from a hermitlike character created by the early 19th-century German Romantic writer E. T. A. Hoffmann). This rather loosely organized group had no clearly articulated esthetic doctrine to which all members subscribed, but it sought to preserve artistic freedom. "Most of all," wrote one of the founders, "we were afraid of losing our independence, of suddenly finding ourselves a 'Society attached to the People's Commissariat of Public Enlightenment' or to some other institution." They wished to write according to their own principles and convictions. Interest in literature and the belief that it could be produced only in a totally free atmosphere bound the members together. But the Serapion Brotherhood's unity began to crumble as early as 1924.

Another literary group of this period was *Pereval* (The Mountain Pass), more closely aligned with the party than the Serapion Brotherhood. Founded in 1924 with the active cooperation of the Old Bolshevik Alexander Voronskii, editor of *Red Virgin Soil*, *Pereval* was the first important Soviet "thick" journal (a "thick" journal was one with serious, intellectual content) with essays on politics, economics, literature, and the arts. The *Pereval* group's emergence reveals the confusion and uncertainty of the early 1920s. The group consisted largely of young writers dedicated to the Revolution and over half were party members. They looked upon emerging Soviet society as transitional between old and new. Their writing probed Soviet society, criticizing as well as praising. Favoring artistic freedom, they advocated literary "sincerity" and artistic "realism" and stressed each writer's unique personality and psychological insight as critical in developing literary talent. Theirs was a humanistic outlook uncomplicated by doctrinaire ideology. The *Pereval* writers' individualism and humanism brought them into conflict with the militant proletarian writers, who accused them of "defeatism" and lack of revolutionary enthusiasm. Lunacharskii had to monitor such disputes and prevent them from becoming disruptive.

Opposed to the Serapion Brotherhood and *Pereval* were larger, more influential organizations of proletarian writers that grew from the Proletkult movement. The Moscow Association of Proletarian Writers (MAPP) was founded in 1923, the Russian Association of Proletarian Writers (RAPP) in 1925, and the All-Union Combined Association of Proletarian Writers (VOAPP) in 1928. These groups claimed to be the only true spokespersons for the working class in literature. From the beginning they were aggressive, attacking the Fellow Travelers and *Pereval* writers in their journal, *On Literary Guard*. Early in 1925, the proletarian groups organized the first all-Union Conference of Proletarian writers as a forum to attack nonproletarian writers. Fellow Travelers were accused of writing works against the revolution and of espousing bourgeois values of nationalism, mysticism, and individualism. Many of their accusations against the Fellow Travelers were groundless. Still there was open debate, not intimidation: The Fellow Travelers responded with a ringing defense of their literary freedom and intellectual integrity.

These debates became so intense that the party intervened, and issued "The Policy of the Party in the Field of Artistic Literature," the first formal party statement on cultural affairs. It revealed that many Bolsheviks in positions of authority were sophisticated culturally and understood that development in the arts could not be dictated. The party acknowledged that a variety of literary trends existed, reflecting the diversity of the NEP period, and it refused to endorse a single literary trend as "correct." The party announced it would remain aloof from partisan debate and advocated fair competition between the groups. This guaranteed that cultural ferment would persist and that the proletarian writers would not devour the Fellow Travelers.

Painting and music revealed similar patterns. The 1920s witnessed a struggle between "left" and "right" factions in art and music. The Soviet musical world was split by the intense, often vitriolic debates between two warring factions: the modern-oriented Association for Contemporary Music (ASM) and the Russian Association of Proletarian Musicians (RAPM). The members of the former were dubbed proponents of the *asmovskii* position, signifying decadent-modernist formalism. Members of RAPM were known as adherents of the *rapmovskii* position, that signified simplistic musical primitivism. These adjectives concealed deep practical and ideological ifferences. ASM maintained close ties with the musical life of western Europe and thus assured Soviet composers contact with the most advanced and progressive Western ideas. At the same time, ASM sought to acquaint the West with the best music of Soviet composers. These Western contacts were especially stimulating to young composers such as Dmitri Shostakovich (1906–1975). Furthermore, the members of ASM completely rejected the idea that music was a political tool. One member declared, "Of course I am not a 'proletarian' composer in the sense that I do not write commonplace music 'for the masses.' " He went on to argue that "music is music, not ideology."

The opponents of the ASM were the proletarian musicians, many of whom had participated in the ill-fated Proletkult movement, which had collapsed in 1920. The Russian Association of Proletarian Musicians was founded in 1923 to organize proletarian ideology in music. The members of RAPM rejected most past composers and displayed a thoroughly negative attitude toward the classical heritage. They declared war on the more traditional composers of ASM and announced a life and death struggle between their "revolutionary realism" and "decadent formalism" of the "bourgeois" composers. Lunacharskii tried to mediate and cautioned the proletarian musicians not to press too hard in efforts to "revolutionize" Russian music. Uneasy coexistence prevailed in music until the end of the 1920s.

LITERATURE

Two Poets of the Revolution

A mood of uncertainty and ambiguity pervaded Russian literature during the early Soviet period. This ambiguity was clearly expressed in the last works of the brilliant Symbolist poet Alexander Blok (1880–1921), considered by many the greatest Russian poet of the 20th century. Well-established and respected in 1917, Blok welcomed the Revolution as the painful birth of a new world order. Yet the violence that accompanied it sickened and frightened him. He stood precariously over a widening gulf between old and new, uncertain where to leap. He wrote two famous poems in 1918, amidst revolution and civil war, which reflected his—and the intelligentsia's—ambiguous reaction to the Revolution. Blok's *The Scythians* celebrated the Revolution as an elemental expression of the Russian national spirit. "Yea, we are Scythians,/ Yea, Asians, a slant-eyed, greedy brood." Russia, he proclaimed, had long shielded a haughty and

Alexander Blok (1880–1921) *(Library of Congress)*

ungrateful Europe from the ravages of the Mongol hordes. Now it would collect on that debt and beckoned to Europe to join and promote peace and cooperation and the welfare of humanity. "Come unto us from the black ways of war,/ Come to our peaceful arms and rest./ Comrades, before it is too late,/ Sheathe the old sword; may brotherhood be blest." Should Europe refuse to heed this call to peace, he warned, a Scythian and Asiatic horde would descend upon it to destroy corrupt and dying Western civilization. Warned *The Scythians:* Join us in the pursuit of social justice, peace, and harmony or face annihilation.

Even more sombre and controversial was Blok's foreboding poem *The Twelve,* which elicited enormous interest and impassioned debate. *The Twelve* is ambiguous—we are not certain whether Blok intended it to affirm the Revolution or predict destruction of a refined and ancient culture. Was it a hymn of praise or a deceitful blasphemy? The "twelve" are Red Army soldiers tramping through Petrograd in a blizzard, intent on murder and pillage against the hated bourgeois enemy. The poem begins forebodingly: "Black night,/ White snow./ The wind, the wind!/ It

all but lays you low./ The wind, the wind,/ Across God's world it blows!"
The Revolution, like the wind, sweeps all before it. Having recorded the
soldiers' bloody acts, the poem ends cryptically: "Forward as a haughty
host they tread./ A starved mongrel shambles in the rear./ Bearing high
the banner, bloody red,/ That He holds in hands no bullets sear—/
Hidden as the flying snow veils veer,/ Lightly walking on the wind, as
though/ He Himself were diamonded snow,/ With mist-white roses
garlanded!/ Jesus Christ is marching at their head."[2] Thus 12 terrorists
are transformed into the 12 apostles, vanguard of a new era, following
Christ and leading mankind forward to a new millennium, justifying a
destructive revolution. Is this what Blok had in mind?

These were Blok's last two poems. He died in 1921, a victim of chaotic
times. His final diary entries confirm his despair and personal incom-
patibility with the Soviet era. "At this moment, I have neither soul nor
body; I am ill as I have never been before. Vile, rotten Mother Russia has
devoured me, . . . as a sow gobbles one of its suckling pigs."[3] Having tried
to leap to the new, he had slid into the abyss.

Another major poet destined to be devoured by Mother Russia and
the Revolution was Vladimir Mayakovskii (1893–1930). No other writer
was so closely identified with the Revolution, none was the object of such
adulation. A prominent and respected Futurist poet before 1917,
Mayakovskii hailed the November Revolution, joined the Bolshevik
Party, and confidently set out to create a new "proletarian art" appropriate and appealing to the masses. He was one of the "cultural radicals" who
rejected all bourgeois art as obsolete. He insisted: "The White Guard is
turned over to a firing squad: Why not Pushkin?" A new age required a
new art, an art to celebrate the Revolution, the proletariat, the machine,
the city, all modern life. The Futurists viewed themselves as the vanguard
of proletarian culture, and Mayakovskii was in the forefront. To accomplish these grandiose aims, Mayakovskii and his friends organized LEF
(Left Front in Art). Its members shared no uniform theoretical doctrine,
but LEF proclaimed a functional, utilitarian art, useful to the state. "I
don't want to be a wayside flower," Mayakovskii intoned, "plucked after
morning in an idle hour." "Art for the sake of art" repelled him: To
engage in idle dilettantism during historic change was to betray art.
Instead, he commented on current issues, practiced poetic journalism,
and even put his poetry to work selling goods and products. His poetry
was enlisted in the service of the people and the Revolution.

---

[2]A. Yarmolinsky, ed., *An Anthology of Russian Verse, 1812–1960,* trans. Babette Deutsch
(New York, 1962), pp. 109, 120.
[3]Cited in Marc Slonim, *Modern Russian Literature* (New York, 1953), p. 206.

Typical of his approach was the poem *150,000,000*, published in 1920. "150,000,000 [the 1919 population of the USSR] is the name of the creator of this poem./ Its rhythms—bullets,/ its rhymes—fires from building to building./ 150,000,000 speak with my lips. . . ./ Who can tell the name/ of the earth's creator—surely a genius?/ And so/ of this/ my/ poem/ no one is the author."[4] The poem portrays the struggle between good and evil, socialism and capitalism, Ivan and Woodrow Wilson, Moscow and Chicago, 150,000,000 Russians and the rest of the world. These blatantly propagandist works were failures. Lenin chastised Lunacharskii for issuing *150,000,000* in 5,000 copies—1,500 for "libraries and cranks" would have been enough, Lenin thought.

Among Mayakovskii's most popular works are two plays, *The Bedbug* and *The Bathhouse*, performed in 1929 and 1930 respectively. Both reveal Mayakovskii's growing disillusionment with the Soviet regime, which seemed to him increasingly remote from the heroic dreams of the Revolution. In *The Bedbug* a worker, Prisypkin, becomes a self-important bureaucrat who indulges his bourgeois tastes and values. A fire set by his drunken guests disrupts his wedding day. Everyone except Prisypkin and a lone bedbug are incinerated. Fifty years later, Prisypkin and the bedbug are found perfectly preserved in a block of ice. Prisypkin makes a full recovery after being thawed out, but his miraculous resurrection is a mixed blessing for the purified and refined Communist society of the future into which he is now introduced. His bourgeois attitudes and habits—drinking, smoking, and swearing, for example—and especially the "ancient disease" of love are all dangerously contagious and potentially disruptive. As a result of these fears, the authorities incarcerate him and the bedbug in a cage, and they are displayed as curiosities. Prisypkin symbolized everything Mayakovskii hated in himself and in the Soviet citizen of the late 1920s. Already the revolutionary fervor and willingness to make sacrifices was beginning to fade, to be replaced by what he considered to be bourgeois values—self-satisfaction and complacency and the pursuit of material happiness. Soviet society, he feared, was fostering a whole generation of Prisypkins.

The Bathhouse was an even more direct indictment of Soviet life and particularly the emerging Stalinist bureaucracy, which already was radiating the pettiness and vulgarity characteristic of the Stalinist dictatorship at its worst, with all its anti-intellectualism, crudeness, and sterility. Mayakovskii was continuing a well-established literary tradition, dating back at least to Gogol, in which literature was a vehicle used to expose bureaucratic inefficiency, abuse of power, and corruption. The

---

[4] Cited in Edward J. Brown, *Russian Literature Since the Revolution* (New York, 1969), p. 54.

inspiring dreams given substance by the Revolution were beginning to dissipate, in Mayakovskii's view, like so many bubbles in the air. The enthusiasm and spontaneity of the NEP period were rapidly giving way to a soulless bureaucratic state, supported by a vast police apparatus reminiscent of tsarist times. Mayakovskii's sincere efforts to publicize and expose to public ridicule what he felt to be the dangers and shortcomings of Soviet society were viciously attacked, as could be expected, by the petty and narrow-minded bureaucrats, who had themselves felt the sting of his sharp criticism. Their attacks on him only served to convince him of the accuracy of his assessment.

Harassed by enemies and opponents, adrift in a society that no longer met his high standards and expectations, beset with personal problems, and suffering from boredom and isolation, Mayakovskii shot himself in April 1930. His suicide note was entirely rational and devoid of despair and self-pity. "Don't blame anyone for my death, and please don't gossip about it. The deceased hated gossip." His tragic death sent shock waves through the entire intelligentsia. He had always been *the* poet of the Revolution, the poetic spokesman of the working class, the leading proponent of socially useful literature, and yet his suicide seemed to many to be a slap in the face to the Revolution. Whether it was or not we shall never know, for even in death Mayakovskii served the Revolution. His legacy as a poet and a symbol has been enormous, and despite all the vicissitudes of the Soviet cultural policy since 1930, his image remains untarnished, his poetic genius unchallenged.

Two Novelists of Dissent

The prose counterpart of Mayakovskii was Eugene Zamiatin (1884–1937), author of the brilliant and influential antiutopian novel *We*. As a young man Zamiatin joined the Bolshevik Party but quickly found the atmosphere sectarian, petty, and doctrinaire, and so he left the party before the 1917 Revolution. He was never an enthusiastic supporter of the Bolsheviks or the November Revolution. He was trained as a naval engineer and shipbuilder, although his first love and real interest was literature. Zamiatin began publishing stories in 1911 and was a well-known author at the outbreak of World War I. During the war he spent a great deal of time in England, supervising the construction of ships for the Russian navy. After the Revolution, he found it difficult to fit into the new Soviet society and only with the help of his friend and fellow writer, Maxim Gorkii, was Zamiatin finally able to secure employment as a lecturer on literature at the Petrograd House of the Arts. Zamiatin continued to publish and eventually became the spiritual godfather of the

Serapion Brotherhood, although not a formal member of the group. *We,* completed in 1920 and circulated but never published in the USSR until 1989, was published in English translation in 1924, the first of a series of Soviet writings that have enjoyed great success in the West.

Zamiatin revealed in *We* a frightening vision of the society he saw emerging in the Soviet Union. He foresaw a degeneration of Communism and feared the destruction of human freedom and individuality by the monolithic state. *We* is a satirical portrait of a future utopian city in which science and technology have provided every convenience (including an Astrodome-like glass cover to protect the city from the elements), but the inhabitants have been reduced to ciphers rather than individuals (men are known by consonants and numbers, women by vowels and numbers). Every facet of human activity—work, thought, leisure activity, sexual love—is carefully controlled by the "wise authorities." Transparent living quarters and constantly monitored activity make privacy, or any concept of privacy, a thing of the past. Every thought, action, and utterance is recorded; every deviation from the norm is ruthlessly suppressed. The main character of the novel is D-503, who has rebelled against the sterile conformity and has dared to engage in free thought, to entertain feelings of genuine love, and to develop a passionate interest in nature and the world about him—he is a more sophisticated Prisypkin. D-503 is eventually destroyed or, more accurately, reprogrammed, and his "irrationality" is destroyed by the "wise authorities."

Zamiatin's novel may be interpreted as a warning, an alarm about future potential dangers, stemming from the regime's unethical manipulation of science and technology to deprive people of their freedom and individuality. Such a document was, of course, unacceptable for publication in the Soviet Union. (*We* was the forerunner of Aldous Huxley's *Brave New World* and George Orwell's *1984*.) Many of Zamiatin's other writings annoyed the Soviet authorities, and a vicious campaign of vilification and denunciation (practices later all too familiar) was mounted against him in 1929. *We* was singled out as the worst example of Zamiatin's malicious attacks on Soviet society. He was prevented from publishing, forced to resign his teaching position, and ostracized by friend and foe alike. His old friend Gorkii finally came to his assistance in 1931 and delivered Zamiatin's letter of appeal to Stalin himself. Zamiatin began with dignity:

> The writer of this letter, a man condemned to the supreme penalty, appeals to you . . . to commute that penalty. You probably know my name. For me as a writer to be deprived of the opportunity to write is a sentence of death. Matters have reached a point where I am unable to exercise my

profession because creative writing is unthinkable if one is obliged to work in an atmosphere of systematic persecution that grows worse every year.[5]

(Boris Pasternak or Alexander Solzhenitsyn could have written similar lines later.) Owing to Gorkii's personal intercession with Stalin, Zamiatin and his wife were finally allowed to leave the Soviet Union in 1932. He died in Paris in 1937, conscious that his impact on Russian literature had been slight and that his major contribution had been training a generation of young writers. He proudly claimed that he taught them to write with "90-proof ink."

Zamiatin's contemporary, Boris Pilniak (the pen name of Boris Vogau, 1894–1937), was one of the most popular and influential of the Fellow Travelers. His influence on Soviet literature in the 1920s was probably greater than that of any other writer. A productive and popular author, his works were widely read and discussed. His first, and in many ways his greatest achievement, was his novel *The Naked Year* (1922), woven out of a series of vignettes of the revolutionary era. These sketches, rather loosely tied together, recount the intense cruelty and impassioned hatreds unleashed by the Revolution and portray the suffering, heroism, and optimism of the age with compelling pathos and energy. Pilniak's sympathies were not with the Bolsheviks (though he wrote about them positively) but with those seeking to free humankind from all compulsion and restraints, whether they were anarchists, Socialist Revolutionaries, or disillusioned Bolsheviks. He shared Zamiatin's concern about the dangers to human freedom and individuality engendered by efforts to organize all life according to some preconceived plan. Pilniak's clearest statement of his concerns was "The Tale of the Unextinguished Moon" (1926), which closely resembles the actual death of the Red Army's commander in chief, Michael Frunze. A Red Army hero of the Civil War falls ill and is ordered by the party to undergo surgery even though he knows instinctively such surgery will kill him. The party leader, known as Number One, insists that the hero, as a useful worker, ought to be repaired to continue being useful, just like a piece of machinery. Pilniak castigates this callous, dehumanizing attitude, and in the story the Red Army commander dies on the operating table as if he had been cut down on the field of battle. This provoked a storm of criticism; the journal in which the story appeared was recalled, and Pilniak and the journal's editors were forced to denounce the story publicly as "a gross error."

Pilniak was thus already suspect when his short novel *Mahogany* appeared in Germany in 1929. Pilniak had, like many Soviet writers, sent

---

[5]Cited by Michael Glenny in "The Introduction" to E. Zamiatin's *We* (New York, 1972), p. 12.

his manuscript to Germany to be published simultaneously with the Soviet edition in order to gain international copyright protection. (The Soviet Union did not then subscribe to the International Copyright Convention.) Unacceptable as written in the Soviet Union, the novel was only published in 1930 after complete rewriting, under the title *The Volga Falls to the Caspian Sea*. It deals with the construction of a dam and a hydroelectric plant that will destroy an ancient, historic town. The theme is the struggle between the "old" and the "new," between "history" and "technological progress." Pilniak's sympathies were clearly with "history," and his heroes were not the construction workers but the mahogany collectors who cherish true craftsmanship and traditions and preserve what they can of the "old" in face of the advance of the "new."

THE CINEMA

Lenin was among the first to recognize the value of the cinema: "The cinema is for us the most important of all the arts." As a means of communication in an era of mass culture, the cinema is unsurpassed. Highly sophisticated messages can be recorded on film, duplicated in countless copies, distributed throughout a country, and projected on screens for millions of people with a minimum of technical equipment and trained personnel. Thus the atmosphere was right for the development of Soviet cinema. There had been a well-established Russian movie industry before the Revolution, but almost all film directors, actors, and technical personnel gathered up their equipment and left Russia after the Revolution. The Soviet cinema had no "bourgeois specialists" to depend on or worry about as was the case in literature, music, and painting. The Soviet cinema was free to develop without opposition or tradition. Young enthusiasts were the first Soviet directors, and their spontaneity, ingenuity, and artistic sense left a deep impression on Soviet filmmaking.

Two of the earliest Soviet directors of importance were Lev Kuleshov, who directed his first film at the age of 17, and Dziga Vertov, placed in charge of film coverage of the Civil War when he was 20. Vertov's documentary accounts of the Civil War helped to shape future Soviet films. Vertov developed the concept of the "camera-eye" (*kinoglaz*), which records what is occurring. Beyond that, the director's task is to give meaning to the raw experience recorded by the camera, through the process of cutting and arranging—editing—the film. In this manner, the film becomes a powerful instrument of interpretation and education. Vertov carried his techniques further after the Civil War, recording scenes from Soviet life all over the country, editing them, and arranging them into the equivalent of filmed newspapers. He called these documentaries "film truth" (*kino-pravda*), after the newspaper *Pravda*.

The director Lev Kuleshov sought to apply Vertov's techniques to the feature film. He attempted to use Vertov's documentary realism to stimulate imagination and anticipation in the viewer, to make film an intellectual as well as a visul experience. The technical sophistication of his equipment may not have been very high, but he used it very creatively and intelligently. He combined documentary footage with pure fiction to create an artistic montage, which paved the way for the greatest of all Soviet film directors, Serge Eisenstein (1898–1948).

Eisenstein was trained as an architect, worked as a poster artist during the Civil War, and joined the Proletkult theater as a set designer, where he came under the influence of the director V. E. Meierhold. Eventually, he staged his own theatrical productions and moved to cinema only in 1924. He combined Meierhold's theatrical techniques, including a stress on the purely visual, caricature, contrast, and contradiction, and combined them with Kuleshov's imaginative documentary montage to develop an original and imaginative style of his own. Eisenstein's first film, *Strike* (1924), began as a documentary but evolved into a powerful and imaginative portrait of the inequities of capitalist Russia. Eisenstein's use of visual symbolism enhanced the psychological impact of the film. He wanted to jolt his audiences with powerful scenes, shock them with startling visual effects, to create a "film-fist" (*kino-kulak*) to pummel the viewer with imaginative and thought-provoking images. *The Battleship Potemkin* (1926) was Eisenstein's greatest cinematic triumph. The film portrayed the brief revolt of the crew of the battleship *Potemkin* in Odessa during the Revolution of 1905. The hero of the film is the battleship itself, which sparks and sustains the revolutionary enthusiasm of the crew. The film was a powerful indictment of the callousness and inhumanity of the tsarist regime represented by such powerful images as the mechanical march down the famous steps of Odessa harbor by a phalanx of tsarist troops and the unforgettably repulsive image of maggot-infested meat being given to the battleship crew by inhumane officers. *Potemkin* demonstrated just how powerful a political instrument the cinema could be. Still, Eisenstein's films, including *Potemkin*, were not great popular successes during the 1920s. Audiences seemed to prefer the lighter touch of foreign imports, and party censors and critics were always suspicious of Eisenstein's unorthodox methods. By the late 1920s he was beginning to have difficulties with the authorities.

Another great Soviet director of the 1920s was Vsevolod Pudovkin, whose works were less original than Eisenstein's but more accessible to audiences and thus more popular. He attempted to transfer the theater to film. He relied on professional actors and a clear story line, assets that gave his works a smoothness and continuity lacking in Eisenstein's more experimental films. Pudovkin drew his subject matter from works of fiction and attempted in his films to involve the viewer in the psychological development of individual characters rather than in great historic events. His films were often sentimental and unsophisticated, but were extremely influential in the development of Soviet cinema. Pudovkin's most critically acclaimed film is *Mother* (1926).

By the late 1920s, party authorities began to take a greater interest in the cinema and attempted to control it as they did other aspects of culture. The party supported Vertov and his followers, advocates of the "film-eye" documentary techniques, now to be harnessed to the industrialization drive of the 1930s. Eisenstein and other more imaginative directors, along with a number of prominent film actors, emigrated in protest.

EDUCATION

From the inception of the Bolshevik regime, the party placed high priority on eliminating illiteracy, which was especially widespread in rural areas but also affected many urban workers. As early as 1919, a campaign was inaugurated to eradicate illiteracy, the *likbez* (liquidation of illiteracy). It aimed at expanding the educational system, emphasizing practical education and hands-on experience. In 1921, so-called *rabfaki* (workers' schools) were established in factories to offer instruction in basic reading, writing, and arithmetic. Evening classes were held in factories; their success may be measured by the millions who learned the rudiments of literacy in their crash courses.

An effort to create a "workers' culture" resulted from the desire to develop a new cultural and educational level worthy of the new era. However, this often caused a lowering of the overall cultural level as many intellectuals, officials, and white-collar workers sought to identify completely with the new "leading class" and began to dress and speak like workers, carefully disguising their more refined tastes and attitudes.

Despite the assault on illiteracy and creation of a new workers' culture, the party did not neglect higher education. Intent on training a new generation of scientists with the proper political and intellectual outlook, the party established a Communist Academy rivaling the old Imperial Academy of Sciences and staffed largely by members of the old guard. A number of Communist universities were also established. A limited coexistence between these institutions prevailed until the late 1920s. In general, Bolshevik attitudes prevailed in the social sciences (economics, history, politics), whereas prerevolutionary views predominated in the natural sciences and humanities.

Education at all levels had two fundamental purposes: (1) to train a new generation in socialist thinking and counteract lingering bourgeois influences and (2) to establish a solid foundation for a new socialist culture expressed in all the arts and sciences. A correct socialist world outlook among the students was emphasized. If that could be established early, then continuously reinforced, the subjects studied would assume an appropriate "socialist character" no matter what they were—literature, chemistry, economics, or astronomy. Intensive efforts were made to open up educational opportunities for the former lower classes, notably workers.

SCIENCE

As the 1920s progressed, a period of relative freedom and peaceful coexistence between the Marxist and non-Marxist camps, tensions grew and a showdown was clearly inevitable, the outcome of which was never really in doubt. Scientists experienced a growing intolerance at the hands of the party on issues of central scientific and philosophical importance such as Freudian psychology, Einstein's theory of relativity, quantum mechanics, and modern genetic theory. Intellectual debates over inter-pretation of these theories, crucial to the development of 20th-century science, acquired political overtones. Serious scientists found it increas-ingly difficult to reconcile dialectical materialism, as interpreted by the party, with basic principles of quantum mechanics or Einstein's relativity theory. Many scientists chose to retreat from public debate about sci-entific theory and pursue their own research unobtrusively. Thus many gifted scientists shunned controversial theoretical work, which was viewed as politically dangerous if one ended up on the losing side of a theoretical debate.

Nowhere were these dangers more apparent than in genetics. The controversies that plagued Soviet genetics for more than a generation were typical of those affecting many aspects of Soviet intellectual life. Traditional geneticists agreed that a gene reproduces itself essentially unchanged from generation to generation, with very infrequent in-stances of mutation. Soviet scientists tended to reject that view as not squaring with Marxism's dialectical materialism. Some Soviet geneticists now suggested that evolution involved a series of adaptations to environ-mental conditions capable of transmission to subsequent generations, that is, the inheritance of acquired characteristics. Such a view was consistent with the Soviet view that the USSR had created an entirely new and superior social environment from which triumphant Soviet men and women would emerge. The debate between traditionalists and Soviet Lamarckians moved back and forth during the 1920s. (Lamarck, a pre-Darwinian philosopher, had formulated the idea that acquired charac-teristics could be transmitted to successive generations.) Only with the emergence under Stalin of a young pseudoagronomist, Trofim Lysenko, would the genetics debate take on real and dire political dimensions. During the New Economic Policy, politics did not impinge seriously on scientific work, but the spectre of dialectical materialism hung malevolently over an infant Soviet science like the sword of Damocles. The agony of Soviet genetics would begin with the emergent Stalinist dictatorship of the 1930s.

Toward the end of the 1920s, tension and unease developed in scientific circles and in all realms of Soviet culture, as the party manifested impatience at the slow pace of development. In 1928, a mere 6 percent of all scientific workers were members of the Communist Union of Scientific Workers (*Varnitso*). Among scientists the party was winning few adherents, and the Academy of Sciences remained impervious to party influence. The frightening possibility arose that the party might be excluded from the country's intellectual life. Advocacy of peaceful coexistence between party and nonparty scientists was deleted abruptly from official pronouncements as the party began with increasing regularity to assert its authority in scientific matters. With the consolidation of Stalin's position and the rise of the cult of personality, Stalin began to intervene in scientific debates. Soon his arbitrary view became official and exclusive in all branches of learning.

Suggested Additional Reading

ABRAHAM, GERALD. *Eight Soviet Composers* (London, 1943).

ALEXANDROVNA, VERA (pseud.). *A History of Soviet Literature*, trans. M. Ginsburg (Garden City, N.Y., 1963).

BAROOSHIAN, V. D. *Russian Cubo-Futurism, 1910–1930* (The Hague, 1974).

BEREDAY, G. F., et al., eds. *The Changing Soviet School* (Boston, 1960).

BROWN, E. J. *Major Soviet Writers: Essays in Criticism* (London, 1973).

———. *Russian Literature Since the Revolution* (Cambridge, Mass., 1982).

CHAPPLE, R. L. *Soviet Satire of the Twenties* (Gainesville, Fla., 1980).

EASTMAN, MAX. *Artists in Uniform: A Study of Literature and Bureaucratism* (New York, 1934).

ENTEEN, G. M. *The Soviet Scholar-Bureaucrat: M. N. Pokrovskii and the Society of Marxist Historians* (University Park, Pa., 1978).

ERMOLAEV, HERMAN. *Soviet Literary Theories, 1917–1934* (New York, 1963, 1977).

FAUCHEREAU, SERGE. *Moscow, 1900–1930* (New York, 1988).

FITZPATRICK, SHEILA. *The Commissariat of Enlightenment . . . 1917–1921* (Cambridge, Eng., 1970).

GASINOWSKA, XENIA. *Women in Soviet Fiction, 1917–1964* (Madison, Wis., 1968).

GORKII, MAKSIM. *On Literature* (Seattle, 1973).

GOVEHAKOV, NIKOLAI. *The Theater in Soviet Russia* (New York, 1957).

GUERMAN, M. *Art of the October Revolution* (New York, 1979).

HINGLEY, RONALD. *Nightingale Fever: Russian Poets in Revolution* (New York, 1981).

JANECEK, GERALD. *The Look of Russian Literary Avant-Garde Visual Experiments, 1900–1930* (Princeton, N.J., 1984).

KOPP, ARISTOTLE. *Soviet Architecture and City Planning, 1917–1953* (New York, 1970).

LUCKYI, G. N. *Literary Politics in the Soviet Union, 1917–1934* (New York, 1956).

MAGUIRE, ROBERT A. *Red Virgin Soil: Soviet Literature in the 1920's* (Princeton, N.J., 1968).

OLKHOVSKY, ANDREI. *Music Under the Soviets: The Agony of an Art* (New York, 1955).

POGGOLI, R. *The Poets of Russia, 1890–1930* (Cambridge, Mass., 1930).

Soviet Art: 1920s–1930s (Russian Museum, Leningrad, 1988).

STANISLAVSKY, C. *My Life in Art,* trans. J. J. Robbins (London, 1967).

STRUVE, GLEB. *Russian Literature Under Lenin and Stalin.* (Norman, Okla., 1971).

TROTSKY, LEON. *Literature and Revolution* (Ann Arbor, Mich., 1960).

CHAPTER THIRTEEN

SOVIET CULTURE UNDER STALIN, 1929–1953

Stalin referred to 1929 as "the year of the great break," and in reality it was a far more revolutionary and devastating period than any preceding era. The First Five Year Plan and forced collectivization, beginning in 1928–1929, determined the entire future development of the Stalin regime and the Soviet Union. Stalin's "revolution from above" would alter irrevocably the nature of Soviet society and restructure the very face of the country. Cultural and scientific life could not escape these momentous transformations. As Stalin's role loomed ever larger in all spheres of life, the relatively freewheeling culture of the NEP era, with its lively debates and numerous controversies, came abruptly to an end. Ominously, things became simplified into either party or antiparty positions. No longer could one afford to remain neutral or aloof; independent views were no longer tolerated. Party-mindedness *(partiinost)* became the measure of all things.

Tightened controls on Soviet intellectual life began with an attack on the Academy of Sciences, which had struggled valiantly to remain aloof from political involvements. Using a method by which he had often advanced his own political fortunes, Stalin insisted that membership in the Academy be expanded and proceeded to nominate carefully selected candidates. By 1929, old guard academicians had been relegated to obscurity, replaced by aggressive party-minded members who transformed the Academy into a tool of Stalinist cultural policy. After a pliable majority had been seated, some distinguished older members were arrested, beginning late in 1930. The latter included Sergei Platonov and Evgenii Tarle, two highly respected nonparty historians. The purpose of this campaign was to bring the prestigious Academy into line and harness its talents in support of the Five Year Plan. Many resisted or evaded the party's demands, only to pay dearly for this lack of cooperation during the Great Purge of 1935–1938.

For the first time the party now intervened in fields such as linguistics. Nicholas Marr, a distinguished linguist, had tried to apply Marxist theory to the study of linguistics. Language, Marr argued, was an aspect of social life, which reflected productive relations. In other words, language as part of the superstructure, would reflect fundamental changes in the socioeconomic base. Thus, suggested Marr, a new socialist language would emerge with the development of socialist productive relations. From his study of linguistic usage by Soviet writers, Marr discerned the beginnings of such a new socialist language, in both Russian and the non-Russian languages of the USSR. After Marr's death in 1934, Stalin distorted his views on linguistics to claim that Russian was socialism's international language, and that non-Russian languages must yield to Russian. This served as the theoretical basis for a new wave of Russification imposed on national minorities.

The most flagrant example of the party's interference in Soviet intellectual life was in genetics. (See Chapter 12, "Science.") Agricultural collectivization opened the way for unscrupulous individuals to win party support for the most preposterous theories. T. D. Lysenko, an agronomist, argued that classical genetics had disregarded dialectical change and thus had misinterpreted the genetic process. Lysenko claimed that hereditary characteristics resulted from the dialectical interaction of an organism with its environment. He argued that natural properties of organisms could be changed by altering the environment, and these changes could then be communicated to succeeding generations. This rather astounding theory was supplemented by the belief that organisms could somehow select which acquired characteristics could be transmitted to future generations. This belief coincided with, and reinforced, the conviction that the Great October Socialist Revolution had inaugurated an entirely new era in which a new and superior Soviet individual would emerge. Change the environment and you can change humankind! With conditions ripe for a different approach to genetics, Lysenko became the intellectual man of the hour.

Stalin, discerning in the young agronomist's views the promise of a new era of agricultural productivity, readily backed Lysenko. Lysenko asserted that he could turn winter wheat into spring wheat merely by treating the seeds. Eventually, he claimed that he could transform one species into another, for example, wheat into rye. Officially, his experiments were hailed as the very epitome of socialist science, although they were never duplicated outside his own laboratories. That Lysenko could persuade very few scientists with his unverified experiments was immaterial because the all-powerful Stalin accepted his scientific claims fully. Thus Lysenko soon acquired enormous power, destroyed his enemies, and gave his views the force of "scientific law." Even Nikolai Vavilov, hitherto the most distinguished Soviet geneticist with an established international reputation (elected president of the International Congress of Genetics in 1939), fell victim to the Stalin-backed Lysenko, eventually perishing in prison after valiant efforts to maintain his scholarly integrity. Lysenko's impact on Soviet agriculture and biology was disastrous. His harebrained schemes inflicted untold damage on crops and livestock. But so formidable was this "dictator of biology" that many agronomists falsified results of the application of his theories for fear they themselves might be "planted" for failure to cooperate. Spreading on the heels of Stalinist-induced fear, Lysenkoism destroyed most research in Soviet genetics for more than a generation.

Scientists, like artists, were expected to serve unequivocally the interests of the party and Stalin. Thus the spirit of inquiry, which had long characterized Russian and Soviet science, ended abruptly and many branches of science suffered irreparable harm. Science, art, and literature all became the humble servants of the party. Many talented people retreated into abstract and theoretical study, hoping thereby to avoid the risks and dangers of applied science that when not yielding the expected results could compromise them and endanger their positions and their lives. Writers composed for their desk drawers; scientists retreated from the laboratory to their private offices where risks were reduced. Zhores Medvedev, himself, a distinguished scientist and chronicler of the Lysenko affair, portrayed the general atmosphere eloquently:

> An unprecedented number of discussions took place in 1935–37 in all fields of science, the arts and literature. As a rule, because of the historical conditions, they were all harsh. Differences of opinion, approach, method, and evaluation of goals are completely natural occurrences in science. Truth is born from argument. But in the environment of the massive repressions of the thirties, the spy hunts and centralized inflaming of passions, and under the conditions of a feverish search after the "enemies of the people" in all

spheres of human activity, any scientific discussion tended to become a struggle with political undertones. Nearly every discussion ended tragically for the side represented by the more noble, intellectual, honest, and calm men, who based their arguments on scientific facts.[1]

Only the strength and courage of many men and women dedicated to the pursuit of truth allowed Soviet science and culture to survive at all in this hostile environment.

The political ambiguity of many works of the Fellow Travelers in literature and the lack of conformity in other cultural fields could no longer be tolerated in Stalinist Russia. By 1929, Stalin's personal dictatorship started to impinge directly on the lives of Soviet citizens as industrialization and collectivization began in earnest. Stalinist controls were now extended over every aspect of culture. One sign of the shift away from the tolerance of NEP days was Lunacharskii's removal as Commissar of Education early in 1929. Shortly after came the first signs of tightening party control over literature.

LITERATURE

The technique by which party control was extended to literature became the classic Stalinist pattern, repeatedly used and continually refined: to settle on scapegoats who could be used to intimidate and terrorize an entire group into acquiescence. The scapegoats on this occasion were Pilniak, Chairman of the All-Russian Union of Writers, and Zamiatin, Chief of the Leningrad Union of Writers. The attack on them and, by implication, on all Fellow Travelers, signaled a sharp change in literary policy. The charges against Pilniak and Zamiatin, that they had arranged for publication of their works abroad to avoid Soviet censorship, were totally bungled by the prosecution (a mistake not so readily made in the future). Both writers presented solid evidence that works of theirs published abroad were totally unauthorized by them. The embarrassed accusers shifted their attack to the alleged anti-Soviet nature of these works. Attention was drawn to the supposedly anti-Soviet nature of Fellow Travelers' works. "Anti-Soviet" was defined as any hostile or neutral position. One was either for socialist construction in the USSR or was considered an "enemy of the people." The message was clear: The Fellow Travelers must cease to write unless they changed their ways and wrote "correct," politically acceptable literature.

---

[1] Zhores A. Medvedev, *The Rise and Fall of T. D. Lysenko*, trans. I. M. Lerner (New York, 1971), pp. 5–6.

Zamiatin and Pilniak, along with their supporters, were removed from leadership of the Union of Writers, over half its membership was purged, and its name was changed to All-Russian Union of Soviet Writers with the emphasis on "Soviet." The freedom and tolerance of NEP ended abruptly; the era of "party-oriented" literature began. The Fellow Travelers were henceforth expected to participate fully in the mighty industrialization effort, to prove their "solidarity" with the proletariat; their literary efforts were to serve the party and help in the construction of socialism. The Russian Association of Proletarian Writers (RAPP) won virtual control over the literary scene. Pilniak recanted, but Zamiatin stood his ground and eventually wrote his courageous and successful appeal to Stalin. (See Chapter 12, "Literature.") RAPP, led by Leopold Averbakh, Alexander Fadeev, and Iuri Libedinskii, exerted heavy pressure on the Fellow Travelers and attacked "neobourgeois elements" in literature.

RAPP proved a disappointing weapon of literary control because its members did not accept the party view that literature could be produced on demand or by directive, nor the simplistic approach of a 1930 *Pravda* editorial: "Literature, the cinema, and the arts are levers in the hands of the proletariat which must be used to show the masses positive models of initiative and heroic labor." The emphasis was on the "positive," too simple and one-sided a view even for sincere proletarian writers like Averbakh and Fadeev. To them literature had to present honest, full-scale portraits of life—the bad and the good, the corrupt and the virtuous, the negative and the positive. Despite their enthusiastic support of the regime and willingness to serve as literary watchdogs, Averbakh and the proletarian writers of RAPP were out of step with party authorities who wanted literature and art to portray the heroic struggles to industrialize and collectivize the country only in positive and optimistic fashion. Culture was conceived as a weapon in the hands of party leaders to propagandize, inspire, and mobilize the masses. Despite their proletarian biases and sympathies, RAPP writers were still too wedded to "objective art" and individualism. The next step in bringing literature to heel was to dissolve RAPP in 1932. Diverse literary groupings were abolished; henceforth all writers were to be members of a single national Union of Soviet Writers completely dominated by the party. To some Fellow Travelers these developments came as a welcome respite from arrogant goading by RAPP. Others, more perceptive and attuned to what was happening, saw this situation as the beginning of direct interference by Stalin and the party in the creative process.

A New Aesthetic: Socialist Realism

More than two years passed before the full impact of the 1932 decisions was felt. Clearly, a great deal of opposition to party control of literature had to be overcome before the authorities could venture to convene an open congress of writers to formalize the situation. The First All-Union Congress of Soviet Writers met in August 1934. Of the 590 Soviet delegates attending, more than 60 percent were party members. There were many prestigious foreign guests. At this First Writers' Congress Andrei Zhdanov (1896–1948) first emerged as the party's new authority on cultural affairs. He presented the main address, which clearly outlined the current status of the literary scene and outlined the future form and content of Soviet literature: *having deliberate bias*

> Our Soviet literature is not afraid of being called tendentious, because it *is* tendentious. In the age of the class struggle a non-class, non-tendentious, apolitical literature does not and cannot exist. In our country the outstanding heroes of literary works are the active builders of a new life. . . . Our literature is permeated with enthusiasm and heroism. It is optimistic, but not from any biological instinct. It is optimistic because it is the literature of the class which is rising, the proletariat, the most advanced and most prospering class.[2]

This was the genesis of "socialist realism," the aesthetic that until very recently dominated every facet of Soviet culture. Zhdanov defined "socialist realism" as the portrayal of "real" life in all its revolutionary development, the aim of which was to promote the ideological re-education of the masses in the spirit of socialism. The new doctrine was given respectability by the endorsement of Gorkii, who presided over the Congress and lent his enormous prestige to the new policy. Delegate after delegate rose almost mechanically to reiterate Zhdanov's remarks and endorse the new party-oriented literary principle. So carefully orchestrated was the Congress that even the most prominent and respected writers dared not protest openly against a conception of literature so closely and completely identified with the party's political and economic goals. It was not known just how far Stalin was prepared to go to ensure conformity to his "literary" and "cultural" views. In 1934, it was evident that if one expected to be a practicing writer, one had to be a member of the Writers' Union; to be a member one had to accept its statutes, which embodied Zhdanov's concept of literature as a weapon in the party's hands. How sharply this contrasted with the tolerant attitude of the 1925 party resolution on literature!

---

[2]A. Zhdanov et al., *Problems of Soviet Literature* (New York, n.d.), p. 21.

The enormous significance of the First Congress of Soviet Writers was not immediately recognized, nor was the full impact of socialist realism immediately felt. For one thing, literary contacts with Western writers increased, and a flurry of flattering literary criticism and many translations of progressive Western authors appeared in the Soviet Union. (More than a hundred works by American authors alone were translated into Russian, including works by Hemingway, Dreiser, and Dos Passos.) Moreover, despite the imposition of the narrowly defined socialist realism and the paralyzing atmosphere of the Great Purges in the mid 1930s, some tolerably good literature was produced during this period, a testimony to the indomitable spirit and vitality of literary traditions and to the skill of some authors in skirting around socialist realism as defined by Zhdanov. One example is Iuri Krymov's *Tanker Derbent* (1938), which superficially applied socialist realism in recounting the personal problems and uncertainties of men engaged in intense competition in the oil shipping business on the Caspian Sea. Many themes and concerns of the presocialist realism period continued to find a place in the literature of the 1930s. One genre in which socialist realism tended to be less obtrusive was historical fiction, which enjoyed a real renaissance in the 1930s.

Russian nationalism was powerfully stimulated by the rise of Nazism in Germany and gathering war clouds in the 1930s. In the year of the ideological reorientation of literature a new orientation in the writing of history was also decreed. M. N. Pokrovskii (1868–1932), friend and collaborator of Lunacharskii, had almost single-handedly created a Marxist orientation among professional historians in the Soviet Union and had been responsible for virtually eliminating national history from school curricula. History was thus reduced to vague sociological categories involving the class struggle. National heroes ceased to play any meaningful role in history texts, and a whole generation of Soviet schoolchildren grew up with little knowledge of their past. Beginning in 1934, Pokrovskii and his historical school were denounced as anti-Marxists, who failed to appreciate the progressive character of Russian historical development. The upshot was a reintroduction of national history and a cult of national heroes, which was reflected in the arts. Patriotic themes were developed by many authors who chose historical settings for their plays and novels. Many of these works dealt with the great military struggles of the Russian people against foreigners. Sergei Borodin wrote about the struggles against the Tatars in his novel *Dmitri Donskoi* (1937); Sergei Sergeyev-Tsenskii's portrayal of the Crimean War, *The Ordeal of Sevastopol* (1937–1938), was well received, and Alexis Novikov-Priboi used the site of the famous naval battle of the Russo-Japanese War as the setting for his novel *Tsushima* (1932–1935). Perhaps the most successful historical novel of the period was Alexis Tolstoy's unfinished three-volume *Peter I* (1929–1944), which became one of the great popular successes of Soviet literature, often considered a worthy companion of another great historical novel by a distant relative, Leo Tolstoy's *War and Peace*. Based on extensive historical research, *Peter I* presented a very positive portrait of the "Great Transformer of Russia," one which Stalin greatly admired.

Other themes emphasized were World War I, the Revolution, and the Civil War. Comparable to Tolstoy's novel, *Peter I*, was the simultaneous appearance of Mikhail Sholokhov's four-volume *Quiet Don* (1928–1940), which portrayed masterfully the lives of peasants and Cossacks during war, revolution, and civil war. He was less concerned with the nation's heroic struggle than with the moral and psychological problems of individuals struggling to grasp the significance of events that were engulfing them. Soviet critics have always claimed that *The Quiet Don* is the classic example of socialist realism, but in fact it bears little resemblance to the socialist realism of Zhdanov and the hack writers of the 1930s. Conceived on a scale comparable to *War and Peace*, *The Quiet Don* begins in 1912 and traces life in a quiet Cossack village before World War I. The outbreak of war disrupts the village and Sholokhov tries to measure the war's impact on individuals and families. The second volume deals with the difficulties of war, growing discontent, and the Revolution and its impact on the village and individual lives. The last two volumes record the bitter fighting of the Civil War. The novel touched a responsive chord in the Soviet reading public, who discovered in Sholokhov's writing more substance, originality, and power than in all the five-year-plan novels of the proletarian writers put together. Indeed, so powerful and moving was the impression left, especially in the first parts of the novel by an unknown writer, that skepticism about the work's authorship was widespread. Wondering at the enormous ability of the author, some claimed that Sholokhov had obtained a manuscript written by a White army officer killed during the Civil War and had passed it off as his own work. Such charges have been investigated and officially denied, but still rumors persist (hinted at most recently by Solzhenitsyn) that Sholokhov is not the author of *The Quiet Don*. In the absence of concrete evidence to the contrary, it must be assumed that Sholokhov wrote the novel and that he is a major writer whose study of human resiliency and fortitude represents one of the few bright spots of Soviet literature in the Stalin era.

Literary Victims of Stalinism

The period of the Great Purges (1935–1938) was one of the most frightening, debased, and sterile periods in Soviet history when virtually no one felt safe. The purge eventually cut deeply into the ranks of the Soviet intelligentsia. (Solzhenitsyn claimed in the 1970s that more than 600 writers disappeared during the purges.) Many established writers were publicly branded Trotskyite, "enemies of the people," and diasppeared without trace until hastily rehabilitated in the post-Stalin period. Many others simply disappeared. The literary intelligentsia was encouraged, indeed ordered, to devour itself as the Soviet cultural world was terrorized. The history of those terrible years was a picture of awesome contrasts—enormous heroism, abject cowardice, hypocrisy, and shrewd maneuvering. Some stumbled over themselves in their haste to denounce friend and foe alike as traitors, spies, saboteurs, and Trotskyites. Others tried to remain unnoticed and uncontaminated. Still others merely waited with patient resignation. The result was disastrous for Soviet literature and culture in general as the untalented and un- scrupulous came to the fore as spokespersons for Soviet culture. The list of great talents lost during the purge reads like a Who's Who of Soviet literature.

Prominent among these distinguished literary victims of Stalinism was Osip Mandelshtam (1892–1938), a highly educated poet of Jewish birth and one of the most talented writers of the 20th century. His elaborate poetry was replete with magnificent archaisms, which revealed strong Greek Orthodox influence. In 1933–1934, his work was criticized for not reflecting Soviet life and "distorting reality." Unusual outspokenness doomed Mandelshtam. Recalled the writer, V. Kataev: "He was a real opponent of Stalin. . . . [In 1936 or 1937] he was shouting against Stalin; what a terrible man Stalin was." For an acid poem about the dictator, he was arrested during the Great Purges and died in a labor camp in 1938.[3]

The Nazi invasion of June 1941 offered some respite from the terror of the purges and the concerns of socialist realism. The struggle for national survival against the Nazi onslaught required unity, cooperation, and common purpose only possible in a more tolerant and flexible atmosphere. Literature and the arts were enlisted in the war effort, party controls, including censorship, were relaxed, and writers and artists found themselves freer to develop their talents. Many writers became war correspondents, went to the front, and sincerely appealed to the national spirit of the people, reporting countless stories of personal heroism, great battles, and partisan activities. Some of this was sheer propaganda to bolster morale, while some was first-rate eyewitness reporting. On occasion, pieces would appear that qualified as literature. Ilia Ehrenburg

---

[3]Under *glasnost*, Mandelshtam has been rehabilitated and his poetry is again in fashion.

(1891–1967) wrote a memorable two-volume collection of pieces entitled simply *War* (1941–1942), an extraordinarily moving portrait of a nation struggling to survive the Nazi *Blitzkrieg*. There was no lack of motivation for writers as the Soviet people rallied to defend Mother Russia. The sieges of Leningrad and Stalingrad (especially K. Simonov's *Days and Nights* on the siege of Stalingrad), the transfer of industry, countless cases of personal sacrifice and heroism provided raw materials for hundreds of war novels, narrative poems, plays, and short stories, which inspired and informed the masses. This literary outpouring reflected the party's greater tolerance and flexibility early in the war, reminiscent of some of the diversity of the 1920s. As long as the writers and artists contributed to the war effort, they were allowed greater latitude than they had enjoyed since the 1920s.

As the war drew to a victorious end, the war-weary Soviet people anticipated a more relaxed and humane era in which to pursue their interests without interference. Terrible sacrifices had brought victory and unprecedented prestige to the Soviet Union. Most people believed it was time to reap the benefits, a loosening of the heavy-handed Communist dictatorship and a better way of life for all. There were hints of change to be found everywhere during the war. Strident party ideology was toned down during wartime cooperation with the Western democracies. The Soviet people anticipated a continuation of these trends, only to be disillusioned by a rapid return to prewar harshness. The siege mentality of the war years was to be continued into the postwar era.

Shrewd observers were aware how transitory was wartime liberalism as early as 1943, when the immediate threat to the survival of the Soviet Union had been removed and the Red Army went on a sustained offensive. As the tide of battle turned, the party began to express concern over erosion of ideological orthodoxy, which might undercut the political reliability of the Soviet intelligentsia. The first indication of renewed party vigilance on the ideological front was an attack, at the end of 1943, on the popular satirist and short-story writer Mikhail Zoshchenko (1895–1958), whose short, humorous autobiographical sketches, *Before Sunrise*, were being successfully serialized in a Soviet journal. Abruptly, they were attacked in party publications as insipid, unpatriotic, and examples of "vulgar philistinism" (a favorite term of opprobrium in the postwar period). Publication of further installments was immediately halted. Several other prominent writers also came under fire for not following party guidelines with sufficient enthusiasm. This was a chilling reminder that there were limits to the party's tolerance. Even though it was preoccupied with the war, there was still time to watch the writers. The policies of cultural control remained. Still, many hoped that liberal changes in party policies toward culture could be encouraged in the postwar period. Some delegates to the first postwar conference of Soviet writers (May 1945) even went on record against any resumption of party interference in literature and culture in general. The party, it was argued, should not try to create a "miracle" in literature, a polite way of saying that great works of art could not be produced on command.

Such harmful attitudes had to be quickly corrected before they got out of hand. The party lost no time in making it clear that any temporary lapses of discipline during the war would no longer be tolerated. On August 14, 1946, the party's Central Committee issued a resolution condemning two prominent Leningrad journals, *The Star* and *Leningrad,* for publishing ideologically harmful, apolitical works, adopting a servile attitude toward contemporary bourgeois culture, and disparaging Soviet life and the Soviet people. This party resolution contained the essential ingredients of the so-called *Zhdanovshchina,* the era of Andrei Zhdanov's ideological dominance. After the Central Committee attack, *Leningrad* was closed down, and *The Star* was saddled with a party bureaucrat as editor, who was admonished to clean house and banish from the pages of the journal the "debased" works of authors like Zoshchenko, the poet Anna Akhmatova (1888–1966), and others who shared their "antiparty" views. Once again, the party singled out "scapegoats" to initiate a new policy of strict control. The choice of scapegoats was not arbitrary. The focus was on Leningrad, its journals and authors, revealing the fear of party authorities, more accurately of Stalin, of the traditional Western orientation of Leningrad and its peculiar sense of independence, stemming from heroic survival of a three-year siege during the war. The choice of Zoshchenko and Akhmatova was no accident either. Both were influenced by prerevolutionary models, both had won recognition in prerevolutionary times, neither had been enthusiastic about the Soviet regime. Furthermore, Zoshchenko had come under fire earlier as a literary maverick.

Zhdanov elaborated on the Central Committee resolution at a meeting of Leningrad writers. His language was more virulent and vulgar than that of the original resolution. He bitterly denounced Zoshchenko's story "The Adventures of a Monkey," which had appeared in *The Star* in 1945. The story was a harmless satire about a monkey who escapes from a zoo. Zhdanov saw something sinister in the story.

> If you will read that story carefully and think it over, you will see that Zoshchenko casts the monkey in the role of supreme judge of our social order, and has him read a kind of moral lesson to the Soviet people. The monkey is presented as a kind of rational principle having the right to evaluate the conduct of human beings. The picture of Soviet life is deliber-

Anna Akhmatova (1888–1966) *(Library of Congress)*

ately and vilely distorted, and caricatured so that Zoshchenko can put into the mouth of his monkey the vile, poisonous anti-Soviet sentiment to the effect that life is better in the zoo than at liberty, and that one breathes more easily in a cage than among Soviet people. Is it possible to sink to a lower political and moral level? And how could the Leningraders endure to publish in their journals such filth and nonsense?[4]

Zhdanov concluded that Zoshchenko's work was "a vile obscenity." Unless he changed his ways there would be no place for him in Soviet literature.

Zhdanov turned with even greater vituperation to Akhmatova, a most distinguished Russian poet. The main themes of her poetry were love and religion, which required her to remain silent during most of the 1930s. She began publishing again during and after the war in Leningrad journals. Zhdanov said about her poetry:

---

[4]Cited in Edward J. Brown, *Russian Literature Since the Revolution*, pp. 226–227.

[Her] subject matter is throughout individualist. The range of her poetry is pathetically limited. It is the poetry of a half-crazy gentlelady, who tosses back and forth between the bedroom and the chapel. . . . Half-nun and half-harlot, or rather both nun and harlot, her harlotry is mingled with prayer.[5]

This was no idle criticism, but a lethal vendetta.

These official denunciations were quickly translated into action. Both writers were expelled from the Writers' Union. Zoshchenko was a broken man who lived in poverty and loneliness until he died in 1958. Akhmatova, too, was forced to remain silent, living in isolation and poverty, sustained only by her great moral courage, until she could publish again in the post-Stalin period.

ANTICOSMOPOLITANISM AND THE ARTS

The campaign against noncomformity was not limited to the literary sphere; it engulfed also cinema and the arts. Numerous films and other artistic works were pilloried as insufficiently ideological, or too Western-oriented. To make sure there was no doubt about the party's new ideological policies, the Central Committee began publishing a weekly newspaper *Culture and Life*, which announced in its very first issue that "all the forms and means of ideological and cultural activity of the party and the state—whether the press, propaganda and agitation, science, literature, and art, the cinema, radio, museums, or any cultural and educational establishment—must be placed in the service of the communist education of the masses." *Culture and Life* spearheaded the attack on the "degenerate bourgeois culture of the West," which, party authorities felt, had too strong a following in the Soviet Union. One of the most serious accusations against nonconformists was "cosmopolitanism," defined as servility before Western bourgeois culture. As part of the campaign against "cosmopolitanism" came demands to glorify everything Soviet and stress Stalin's genius. The creation of *Culture and Life*, Zhdanov's speeches, and the growing "cult of personality" were all part of a program designed to spell out within narrow limits what cultural workers must do. The results were disastrous. Soviet culture was reduced to a parody of itself. Everything in Soviet life was idealized, and the Soviet people were touted as the world's most advanced and progressive people, enjoying the most creative and original culture. The harsh facts of life in the postwar Soviet Union were ignored. Any attempt to provide a realistic picture of Soviet life was branded a "slander."

---

[5]Brown, *Russian Literature* . . . , p. 227.

The "anticosmopolitan campaign" did not get underway fully until after the mysterious premature death of Zhdanov in 1948. Anticosmopolitanism had its roots in the immediate postwar period, and received its first elaboration in Zhdanov's 1946 speeches. "Cosmopolitan" became synonymous with "unpatriotic," with "anti-Soviet." Everything in the West was decried, and imitation of Western models was considered "toadyism" or servility before Western bourgeois culture. Any deviation from approved party policies could be labeled "cosmopolitanism," the equivalent of treason. Writers ceased to write, or wrote for "the desk drawer" (not for publication), or produced party-approved drivel, then tried to make peace with themselves.

MUSIC

The only branch of cultural activity to survive the deadening party directives was music, perhaps because the USSR boasted some of the most talented and famous composers in the world: Prokofiev, Shostakovich, Khachaturian, and Miaskovskii. They were idolized by party and public as the finest examples of Soviet creativity and were awarded every honor and prize the Soviet Union could bestow year after year. There was, likewise, a group of remarkable performers, such as the violinist, Oistrakh, the pianist Rikhter, and the cellist Rostropovich.

Direct and oppressive political intervention by the party began in 1936 against Shostakovich's opera *Lady Macbeth of Mtsensk,* based on Nikolai Leskov's novella of the same title written in 1865. His most innovative and controversial work, Shostakovich's opera had enjoyed a triumphant premiere in Leningrad in January 1934. During the next two years, *Lady Macbeth* had achieved unparalleled success for a new Soviet work with over 170 performances in Moscow and Leningrad. Soviet critics, while critical of the opera's more lurid aspects, hailed it as reflecting "the general success of socialist construction, of the correct policy of the party." Such an opera, they gushed, "could have been written only by a Soviet composer brought up in the best traditions of Soviet culture." The youthful Shostakovich had "torn off the masks and exposed the false and lying methods of the composers of bourgeois society." So poorly were the implications of socialist realism then understood, noted a Western critic, that *Lady Macbeth* was then accepted as its epitome.

All went well for *The Lady* and its composer until Stalin saw the opera. Having just heard and praised a patriotic piece by Dzerzhinskii for its realism and positive hero, Stalin, whose musical tastes were very conservative, found *Lady Macbeth* repulsive, raucous, and obscene. An unsigned and therefore authoritative article in *Pravda* on January 28, 1936, entitled "Confusion Instead of Music," denounced the work as formalist and vulgar, a repudiation of operatic form:

> The listener is flabbergasted from the first moment of the opera by an intentionally ungainly, muddled flood of sounds. Snatches of melody, embryos of musical phrases, drown, escape and drown once more in crashing, gnashing, and screeching. Following this "music" is difficult, remembering it is impossible.

A week later, another *Pravda* article denounced Shostakovich's ballet on Soviet themes, *A Limpid Stream*, destroying his career as a ballet composer.[6] With the Great Purge underway, the composer's friends climbed swiftly aboard the bandwagon of criticism. This was a clear warning to composers and other creative artists to conform to the dictates of socialist realism as interpreted by the party and by Stalin personally.

Then the storm subsided allowing the chastened Shostakovich and other composers to resume writing, but they were more careful to avoid experimental forms of musical expression. During World War II, Shostakovich and Prokofiev in particular were once more in vogue, rewarded generously for compositions such as the former's Symphony no. 7 (1942), the *Leningrad* Symphony, and the latter's opera, *War and Peace*, based on patriotic themes. Until the beginning of 1948, the Soviet musical world enjoyed a degree of artistic freedom and creative independence, out of reach of the literary and artistic intelligentsia. Suddenly, in January 1948, Zhdanov announced that this adulation had been a terrible mistake, that these "great" composers were anti-Soviet hacks, unworthy to use the title "Soviet composer." How did this abrupt about-face occur?

A curious silence descended over the Soviet musical world, beginning in December 1947 when some long-awaited premiere performances went practically unnoticed in the press and a number of secondary musical figures simply disappeared without mention. Then in January 1948, Zhdanov presided over a turbulent meeting of composers and musicians. On February 10th, the party Central Committee issued a resolution on music comparable to that on literature of 1946. This resolution on music viciously attacked long-honored and respected artists. The resolution announced:

> The state of affairs is particularly bad in the case of symphonic and operatic music. The Central Committee has here in mind those composers who persistently adhere to the formalist and anti-people school—a school which has found its fullest expression in the works of composers like

---

[6]D. MacKenzie, "D. D. Shostakovich," in *MERSH, 32* (1983), pp. 33–34; Boris Schwarz, *Music and Musical Life in Soviet Russia* (Bloomington, Ind., 1983), pp. 119 ff.

Comrades Shostakovich, Prokofiev, Khachaturian, Shebalin, Popov, Miaskovskii, and others. Their works are marked by formalist perversions, anti-democratic tendencies which are alien to the Soviet people and their artistic tastes.

The composers were further accused of creating music incomprehensible to the masses. "Disregarding the great social role of music, [these composers] are content to cater to the degenerate tastes of a handful of estheticizing individualists." The intent of the resolution was to drag serious music down to the level of "pop music."

> The divorce between some Soviet composers and the people is so serious that these composers have been indulging in the rotten "theory" that the people are not sufficiently "grown up" to appreciate their music. They think it is no use worrying if people won't listen to their complicated orchestral works, for in a few hundred years they will. This is a thoroughly individualist and anti-people theory, and it has encouraged some of our composers to retire into their own shells.[7]

Thus music was not serving as a vehicle to reeducate the masses in the spirit of socialism! Give the people what they want, Zhdanov told the composers—simple ditties they could sing and hum while they merrily filled, or overfilled, their production quotas.

The impact of the decree on Soviet music was as disastrous as that of the 1946 decree on literature. Khachaturian and Prokofiev adapted themselves as best they could to the new party demands. Shostakovich publicly repented for past "errors" then went right on composing as he always had, making an occasional obeisance to the party authorities. Miaskovskii, already an elderly man whose career stretched back into prerevolutionary times, was destroyed by the resolution, and died embittered and defeated in 1951. Prokofiev's work deteriorated in his last years, a change for which the resolution on music of 1948 was at least in part responsible. Furthermore, these decrees on music and literature must be viewed as part of a general anti-intellectual policy, designed to drag culture down to the level of the masses rather than lift the masses up to the level of a sophisticated, creative culture. The *Zhdanovshchina* represented the triumph of the Stalinist bureaucratic mentality, which enjoyed kicking around those with genuine talent and ability. Zhdanov died in August 1948, but unfortunately his policies did not die with him. One of the supreme ironies of the postwar era was the renaming of the famous University of Leningrad to honor this man who had done

---

[7]Cited in A. Werth, *Russia: The Postwar Years* (New York, 1971), pp. 356, 358.

so much to poison the intellectual climate of the Soviet Union. It took the death of Stalin to unleash winds of change and usher in a more tolerant and creative atmosphere.

PROBLEM 5

Socialist Realism

Why did the Communist Party, during the 1930s, feel compelled to establish precise guidelines for art and literature and, to some extent, also for music? Did socialist realism emerge full blown immediately, or did it develop gradually over time? What were its main characteristics? By what means was it imposed on Soviet writers, artists, and composers? Was there a degree of flexibility in official interpretations of socialist realism? Did Soviet officials remain consistent in enforcing its principles and criteria?

By the late 1920s, the party was reluctant to permit independent or autonomous groups within society, which might offer alternatives to the official Marxist-Leninist line, particularly in the cultural arena where, during NEP, various aesthetic views competed for the allegiance of writers, artists, and composers. Just as the Soviet regime could not permit a private landowning peasantry, neither could it tolerate independent artists who might challenge or ignore the momentous changes produced by the First Five Year Plan. Artists, like peasants, had to be controlled and coerced by the Soviet regime.

Unlike the forced collectivization of Russian agriculture, cultural controls were not established abruptly. The first definite indication that the party intended to intervene more directly in cultural affairs was the Central Committee Resolution of December 28, 1928, "On Serving the Mass Reader with Literature," which stated in part:

> Recognizing that the subject matter of the mass book is not satisfactory . . . , it is necessary: (a) to give special attention to the publication of books popularizing the Marxist-Leninist history of the Communist Party and the revolutionary movement; (b) to strengthen the publication of mass literature on production, raising the level of workers' and peasants' technical knowledge; (c) to develop the publication of popular scientific books, linking them up with the socialist reconstruction, and adapting them to the demands of self-education; (d) to broaden the publication of belles-lettres, especially those works which develop present-day political themes, and which are directed against bourgeois influences, philistinism, decadence, etc.; (e) to

guarantee the greatest possible accessibility of the mass book (in its form and its expression) to a wide reading audience.[8]

Directed at the publishing industry, this resolution revealed that the authorities, deeply concerned with what Soviet citizens were reading, were prepared to set up fairly precise guidelines as to what should be published. The tone of this resolution departed sharply from the more tolerant attitudes of the early 1920s. Several essential priorities were established by this resolution, which emphasized the construction of socialism. It stressed political education and indoctrination by easily comprehended works on the history of the party and revolutionary movement. To appreciate sacrifices demanded of them, the people needed to understand the role of the party and the significance of the Revolution of 1917. The great Stalinist era of construction, launched in 1929, would be doomed to failure without greater technical knowledge among workers and peasants. Literature must have a strong political content featuring contemporary issues, such as building socialism and maintaining vigilance against the insidious and decadent influence of bourgeois philistinism. Finally, literature must be "accessible" to a wide audience whose educational level was only beginning to rise. Thus literary works had to be comprehensible to the broad, poorly educated masses.

The full impact of the party's official intervention in cultural life became evident in 1930, when another step was taken toward creation of a party-controlled literature. Consolidation began of the numerous independent literary groups that had flourished under NEP; organizational and ideological conformity replaced the open debates and discussions characteristic of the lively 20s. The Russian Association of Proletarian Writers (RAPP) absorbed many smaller groups, which were pressured to surrender their independence. Occasionally, Stalin intervened personally, but there was yet no blunt coercion by the authorities. Two prestigious nonparty writers, Zamiatin and Pilniak (see Chapter 12), were accused of publishing novels abroad without permission, novels which were insulting to Soviet dignity. They were harassed, forced to resign as heads respectively of the Leningrad and Moscow sections of the Soviet Writers' Union in 1930, and then vilified as "traitors" who were "trafficking with the enemy." The portent for the future was ominous.

Beginning to intervene personally in literary affairs, Stalin issued pronouncements that became instantly *official* policy. Speaking through the Central Committee and occasionally directly to individual writers,

---

[8]Cited in Edward J. Brown, *The Proletarian Episode in Russian Literature* (New York, 1953), pp. 199–200.

Stalin set guidelines for both style and content of literature. All human endeavor had now to be harnessed in behalf of economic advance, including art, fiction, music, drama, poetry, and the cinema.

A Central Committee Resolution of April 23, 1932, finally and formally established party-oriented conformity as the only allowable standard. The freedom and experimentation of the 20s had ended irrevocably.

> The Central Committee ascertains that as a result of the considerable successes of socialist construction, literature and art in the past few years have exhibited enormous growth in quality and quantity. A few years ago, when literature was still under the strong influence of alien elements, which flourished particularly in the early years of NEP when the ranks of proletarian literature were still relatively weak, the Party aided by every means at its disposal, to create special proletarian [writers'] organizations in the spheres of art and literature, in order to strengthen the position of proletarian writers and art workers.
>
> Now that the cadres of proletarian literature have had time to grow and new writers have come forward from factories, mills and collective farms, the framework of the existing literary organizations (VOAPP, RAPP, etc.) has become too narrow and restrains the serious development of literary creativity. This situation creates the danger that these organizations may be transformed from a means for the greater mobilization of Soviet writers and artists around tasks of socialist construction into a means to cultivate group insulation and isolation from the political tasks of the day and from those significant groups of writers and artists who sympathize with the aims of socialist construction. Hence, the necessity for an appropriate reorganization of the literary-artistic associations and for the extension of the basis of their work.
>
> Therefore, the Central Committee resolves:
>
> 1. To liquidate the Association of Proletarian Writers (RAPP);
>
> 2. To unite all writers upholding the platform of Soviet power and striving to participate in socialist construction into a single Union of Soviet Writers with a Communist [Party] fraction therein;
>
> 3. To promote a similar change in the spheres of other forms of art;
>
> 4. To entrust to the Orgburo the elaboration of practical measures for the application of this resolution.[9]

Thus all other literary organizations were abolished. Created in their stead was a single union under firm party control. Henceforth, the form and content of literature could readily be compelled to conform with party directives.

---

[9]"O perestroike literaturno-khudozhestvennykh organizatsii," *Pravda*, April 24, 1932, p. 2.

The First Congress of Soviet Writers was held in Moscow on August 17, 1934. Andrei A. Zhdanov, a rising star in the Soviet ideological firmament, presented the party's authoritative view on literature:

> The key to the success of Soviet literature is to be sought for in the success of socialist construction. Its growth is an expression of the successes and achievements of our socialist system. At the same time it is the richest in ideas, the most advanced and the most revolutionary literature. Never before has there been a literature which has organized the toilers and oppressed for the struggle to abolish once and for all every kind of exploitation and the yoke of wage slavery. Never before has there been a literature which has based the subject matter of its works on the life of the working class and peasantry and their fight for socialism. . . . There is not, there cannot be in bourgeois countries a literature which consistently smashes every kind of obscurantism, every kind of mysticism, bigotry, and superstition, as does our literature.[10]

Zhdanov continued:

> Comrade Stalin has called our writers engineers of human souls. What does this mean? What duties does the title confer upon you? In the first place, it means knowing life so as to be able to depict it truthfully in works of art, to depict it not in a dead, scholastic way, not simply as "objective reality," but to depict reality in its revolutionary development. In addition to this, the truthfulness and historical concreteness of the artistic portrayal should be combined with the ideological remolding and education of the working people in the spirit of socialism. This method in literature and literary criticism is what we call the method of socialist realism.
>
> I think that every one of our Soviet writers can say to any dull-witted bourgeois, to any philistine, to any bourgeois writer who may talk about our literature as tendentious: "yes, our Soviet literature is tendentious, and we are proud of this fact, because the aim of our tendency is to liberate the toilers, to free all mankind from the yoke of capitalist slavery."[11]

This view, enunciated in 1934, changed little during the ensuing half century. A leading Soviet critic, A. Ovcharenko, stated in 1978:

> Socialist realism at its present stage of development is based upon a definite view of the world, life and man, a definite view of art and its mission. The philosophical aspect of this view of the world and man is freedom from all mythology; perception of reality in its continuous revolutionary formation and an active attitude on the part of the artist, art, and the positive hero towards the world as material to be remolded on the basis of "freedom, beauty, and—respect for people." The aesthetic corollaries of this view of the world are: the expression of life's truth in artistic images as broadly and as

---

[10]Andrei A. Zhdanov, *Essays on Literature, Philosophy, and Music* (New York, 1950), p. 9.
[11]Zhdanov, *Essays on Literature* . . . , pp. 12–13.

profoundly as possible, the historical method of perceiving and depicting reality, clarity in the author's position, and a harmonic unity in art of the elements of reflection, representation, and re-creation.[12]

The Union of Writers, in the more than 50 years of its existence as the only officially recognized authors' organization, has grown from 1,500 members in 1930 to well over 8,000 members, some of whom were unwilling to accept without question party dictates. One of the most celebrated challenges to socialist realism came when Andrei Siniavskii, writing under the pseudonym Abram Tertz, published abroad without party approval a work entitled *On Socialist Realism,* which began as follows:

> What is socialist realism? What is the meaning of this strange and jarring phrase? Can there be a socialist, capitalist, Christian, or Mohammedan realism? Does this irrational concept have a natural existence? Perhaps it does not exist at all; perhaps it is only the nightmare of a terrified intellectual during the dark and magical night of Stalin's dictatorship? Perhaps a crude propaganda trick of Zhdanov's or a senile fancy of Gorki's? Is it fiction, myth, or propaganda?[13]
>
> . . . The most exact definition of socialist realism is given in a statute of the Union of Soviet Writers: "Socialist realism is the basic method of Soviet literature and literary criticism. It demands of the artist the truthful, historically concrete representation of reality in its revolutionary development. Moreover, the truthfulness and historical concreteness of the artistic representation of reality must be linked with the task of ideological transformation and education of workers in the spirit of socialism."
>
> The Purpose (with a capital P) is Communism, known in its early stage as socialism. A poet not only writes poems but helps, in his own way, to build Communism; so, too, do sculptors, musicians, agronomists, engineers, laborers, policemen, and lawyers, as well as theaters, machines, newspapers, and guns.[14]

Tertz, quoting Nikita Khrushchev, stated:

> ". . . for the artist who truly wants to serve his people, the question does not arise of whether he is free or not in his creative work. For him, the question of which approach to the phenomena of reality is clear. He need not conform for himself; the true representation of life from the point of view of Communist *partiinost* is a necessity of his soul. He holds firmly to these positions, and affirms and defends them in his work."[15]

---

[12]A. Ovcharenko, *Socialist Realism and the Modern Literary Process,* Moscow, 1978, p. 115.
[13]Tertz, *On Socialist Realism* (New York, 1960), p. 23.
[14]Tertz, *On Socialist Realism,* p. 26.
[15]Tertz, pp. 41–42.

Rising to a note of strident sarcasm and irony, Tertz claimed that Soviet artists who were willing advocates of socialist realism were prepared to accept any "official" pronouncement as their guide and source of inspiration in the creative process.

> It is with the same joyous facility that this artist accepts the directives of the Party and the government, from the Control Committee and its First Secretary. For who, if not the Party and its leader, knows best what kind of art we need? It is, after all, the Party that leads us to the purpose (of Communism) in accordance with all the rules of Marxism-Leninism, the Party that lives and works in constant contact with God. And so we have in it and in its leaders the wisest and most experienced guide, who is competent in all questions of industry, linguistics, music, philosophy, painting, biology, etc. He is our Commander, our Ruler, our High Priest. To doubt his word is as sinful as to doubt the will of God.[16]

Finally, Tertz suggests that socialist realism will ultimately lead to a dead end.

> It seems that the very term "socialist realism" contains an insoluble contradiction. A socialist, i.e., a purposeful, a religious, art cannot be produced with the literary method of the nineteenth century called "realism." And a really faithful representation of life cannot be achieved in a language based on theological concepts. If socialist realism really wants to rise to the level of the great world cultures and produce its *communiad*, there is only one way to do it. It must give up the "realism," renounce the sorry and fruitless attempts to write a socialist *Anna Karenina* or a socialist *Cherry Orchard*. When it abandons its effort to achieve verisimilitude, it will be able to express the grand and implausible sense of our era.[17]

As we will see in Chapter 17, socialist realism continued to be imposed on cultural workers until *glasnost* emerged as official policy in 1986 under Gorbachev. Since then efforts to control the form and content of artistic expression have been abandoned. Freedom of choice and pluralism have been officially recognized as the only way to ensure artistic freedom. Thus socialist realism is dead as an imposed aesthetic doctrine. Individual artists may continue to adhere to its principles out of habit or genuine commitment, but there is no attempt to compel this. The perceived sense of intellectual and cultural separation felt by Soviet artists and writers because of compulsory acceptance of socialist realism now has been largely overcome. Soviet intellectuals and artists seek integration once again into the international artistic community. Cultural workers now

---

[16]Tertz, p. 42.
[17]Tertz, p. 91.

must compete for public recognition and are free to choose how to do so. Subjects and approaches formerly considered "decadent," "immoral," "unacceptable," or "anti-Soviet" are recognized today as legitimate. Many view this as restoring Soviet culture to the mainstream of world culture as Soviet writers, artists, composers, and other culturally creative individuals seek recognition abroad for their cultural achievements.

Suggested Additional Reading

BOWLT, J. E., ed., and trans. *Russian Art of the Avant-Garde . . . , 1902–1934* (New York, 1976).

BOWRA, C. M. *Poetry and Politics, 1900–1960* (Cambridge, Eng., 1966).

BROWN, E. J. *The Proletarian Episode in Russian Literature, 1928–1932* (New York, 1953, 1971).

DUNHAM, V. *In Stalin's Time: Middle-Class Values in Soviet Fiction* (New York, 1976).

ERMOLAEV, HERMAN. *Mikhail Sholokhov and His Art* (Princeton, 1982).

FITZPATRICK, S. *Education and Social Mobility in the Soviet Union, 1921–1934* (New York, 1979).

GLEASON, A., et al., eds. *Bolshevik Culture: Experiment and Order in the Russian Revolution* (Bloomington, Ind., 1985).

GRAHAM, LOREN. *Science and Philosophy in the Soviet Union* (New York, 1970).

GUNTHER, HANS. *The Culture of the Stalin Period* (New York, 1990).

HAYWARD, M., and L. LABEDZ, eds. *Literature and Revolution in Soviet Russia, 1917–1962* (New York, 1963).

HAYWARD, MAX. *Writers in Russia: 1917–1978*, ed. Patricia Blake (San Diego, 1983).

JORAVSKY, DAVID. *The Lysenko Affair* (Cambridge, Mass., 1970).

KREBS, S. D. *Soviet Composers and the Development of Soviet Music* (New York, 1970).

MATHEWSON, R. W. *The Positive Hero in Russian Literature* (Stanford, Calif., 1978).

MEDVEDEV, ZHORES A. *The Rise and Fall of T. D. Lysenko*, trans. I. M. Lerner (Garden City, N.Y., 1971).

NESTYEV, ISRAEL. *Prokofiev*, trans. F. Jonas (Stanford, Calif., 1960).

RÜHLE, J. *Literature and Revolution . . .* (New York, 1969).

SCHWARZ, BORIS. *Music and Musical Life in Soviet Russia, 1917–1981* (Bloomington, Ind., 1983).

SLONIM, M. *Soviet Russian Literature . . . , 1917–1967* (New York, 1967).

STEWART, B. H. *Mikhail Sholokhov: A Critical Introduction* (Ann Arbor, Mich., 1967).

STRUVE, GLEB. *Russian Literature Under Lenin and Stalin, 1917–1953* (Norman, Okla., 1971).

VARSHAVSKY, S., and BORIS REST. *The Ordeal of the Hermitage: The Siege of Leningrad, 1941–1944* (Leningrad and New York, 1985).

YARMOLINSKY, A., ed. *A Treasury of Russian Verse* (New York, 1949).

CHAPTER FOURTEEN

SOVIET FOREIGN RELATIONS TO 1941

Since the Bolshevik Revolution, Soviet foreign policy has comprised an intricate combination of national and ideological elements. Some Western historians, stressing the elements of continuity between tsarist Russian and Soviet policies, have argued that geography and historical experience determine a country's basic interests, regardless of political regime. Emphasizing such persistent aims as the desire for security, urge for access to the sea, manifest destiny in Asia, and the leadership of the Slav peoples, they contend that Soviet policy was pragmatic and power oriented. Other foreign scholars (notably Western ex-Communists), at least until the 1960s, considered Marxism-Leninism paramount and a blueprint for world domination. Soviet leaders, they argued, sought by every means to create a world Communist system run from Moscow and regarded relations with the capitalist world as a protracted conflict that would last until one side triumphed. Believing that all Soviet moves aimed to promote world revolution, this group concluded it was fruitless, even harmful for the West to make agreements with the USSR. A middle view interpreted Soviet foreign policy as combining traditional and ideological elements: Revolutionary beliefs and ideology predominated at first, then pragmatic nationalism increased as Soviet leaders gradually reverted to more conservative policies based on power, geography, and history.

An important ideological foundation for Soviet foreign policy was provided by Lenin's pamphlet *Imperialism, the Highest Stage of Capitalism* (1916), which long remained established doctrine in Soviet Russia. Written in Swiss exile in the midst of World War I, it updated and globalized Marxism despite being singularly unoriginal. (It was based chiefly on works of two European socialists, J. A. Hobson and Rudolf Hilferding.) The pamphlet revealed Lenin's thinking about the capitalist world, positing an inevitable and protracted conflict between it and Soviet socialism. Lenin defined imperialism as finance or monopoly capitalism, controlled by bankers, which had developed from the earlier industrial capitalism of Marx's time:

> Imperialism is capitalism in that stage of development in which the domination of monopoly and finance capital has taken shape; in which the export of capital has acquired pronounced importance; in which the division of the world by international trusts has begun, and in which the partition of all the territory of the earth by the greatest capitalist countries has been completed.

A relentless search for raw materials, markets, and investment opportunities had provoked quarrels among leading capitalist countries, ending in World War I. That war, Lenin predicted, would bring capitalism crashing down, breaking first like a chain at its weakest link, perhaps in Russia. Eventually, imperialism would succumb to its internal contradictions: among imperialist powers and power blocs, and between individual imperialist countries and their rebellious overseas colonies. The final outcome, gloated Lenin, could only be worldwide socialist revolution and the demise of capitalism.

What were the major aims of Soviet foreign policy down to 1941? At first Lenin and Trotskii strove to foment revolution abroad because they believed that otherwise world capitalism would crush Soviet Russia. War-weary Europe, especially Germany, seemed ripe for revolution, and Comintern leaders long remained confident that one would occur. A second, apparently conflicting aim soon emerged and became paramount: to preserve the Soviet regime and power base, if need be at the expense of foreign Communists. Moscow, therefore, sought to divide capitalist powers, prevent anti-Soviet coalitions, and woo colonial peoples. As long as their military weakness persisted, Soviet leaders aimed to avoid war with major capitalist powers.

To achieve these goals Soviet leaders forged a variety of instruments. The Comintern and Soviet party coordinated the Communist parties that developed in most foreign countries. Because until 1945 the USSR was the only Communist power, most foreign Communists looked to Moscow for inspiration and direction. Especially under Stalin, Communist parties abroad became subservient to Soviet policy. Each had a legal organization, which propagated Soviet views in democratic countries, was represented in legislatures, led labor unions, and criticized anti-Soviet cabinets. Illegal underground bodies, operating if the open ones were suppressed, conducted subversion and sabotage. Soviet commercial missions and skillful radio and newspaper propaganda supplemented the work of these parties.

The Soviet regime instituted a new diplomacy. As commissar of foreign affairs, Trotskii believed initially that diplomacy would soon disappear because world revolution was supposedly imminent. He declared confidently: "We'll issue a few decrees, then shut up shop." At Brest-Litovsk he had repudiated the norms and even the dress of old secret European diplomacy, but once the revolutionary wave subsided, Soviet diplomacy became important and its diplomats donned traditional formal dress. Moscow, however, scorned permanent accommodation with other nations, and Soviet diplomacy prepared the way for future expansion by lulling capitalist countries into false security, winning temporary concessions, and splitting the capitalist camp. Whereas under Lenin diplomacy remained innovative and flexible, Stalin bound his diplomats with rigid, detailed instructions.

The Soviets before 1941 made little use of force—the ultimate sanction in foreign policy—because of military weakness. During the Polish-Soviet War of 1919–1920, they attempted unsuccessfully to spread revolution on Red Army bayonets, but only in 1939–1940 was force used effectively against weaker Finland and the Baltic states.

In matters of foreign policy, Lenin's voice proved decisive. In the first months of the regime, policies were debated freely in the Central Committee and Politburo, and sometimes he was outvoted. Then the Politburo, under Lenin's direction, became the chief policy-making body in foreign affairs, and its decisions were transmitted to *Narkomindel* (People's Commissariat of Foreign Affairs) for implementation. Lenin formulated foreign policy and built up the Soviet diplomatic service; the foreign commissar had no more independence than a tsarist foreign minister. Noted Foreign Commissar Georgi Chicherin:

> In the first years of the existence of our republic, I spoke with him by telephone several times a day, often at length, and had frequent, personal interviews with him. Often I discussed with him all the details of current

diplomatic affairs of any importance. Instantly grasping the substance of each issue . . . , Vladimir Ilich [Lenin] always provided in his conversations the most brilliant analysis of our diplomatic situation and his counsels . . . were models of diplomatic art and flexibility.[1]

The autocratic tsarist tradition in foreign affairs was restored fully by Stalin. Let us now examine Soviet policies chronologically. Each of the five periods between 1917 and 1941 reflected a different approach toward the antagonist, the capitalist world.

FIRST REVOLUTIONARY ERA, 1917–1921

For the new Soviet government, a first priority was to redeem Bolshevik pledges to take Russia out of World War I. That war, which Lenin had long proclaimed to be an imperialist struggle, had undermined both the tsarist regime and its successor, the Provisional Government. Lenin's "Decree on Peace," approved on November 7, 1917, by the Second All-Russian Congress of Soviets had been foreshadowed by his fourth "Letter from Afar" in March where he had stated that the Petrograd Soviet should repudiate treaties concluded by previous Russian governments. The "Decree on Peace" proposed to all warring peoples and their governments "to begin immediately negotiations for a just and lasting peace . . . without annexations . . . and indemnities." It continued: "The [Soviet] government abolishes secret diplomacy and . . . expresses the firm intention to carry on all negotiations absolutely openly before all the people and immediately begins to publish in full the secret treaties concluded or confirmed by [previous Russian governments]."[2] Following this declaration was President Wilson's "Fourteen Points" (January 1918), which resembled it closely in phraseology. Lenin urged all belligerents to conclude an immediate armistice, during which their representatives could negotiate a permanent and nonimperialistic peace settlement. One purpose of his "Decree" was to provoke general peace negotiations so that a weak Soviet Russia need not face the Central Powers alone. Bolshevik leaders may have believed also that the appeal would touch off revolutions throughout Europe.

The Allied powers ignored Lenin's appeal and his Soviet regime, but the German imperial government responded eagerly to his call for an armistice. Disregarding Lenin's demagogic appeal to German workers, the Berlin government and high command saw great potential strategic

---

[1]*Izvestiia*, January 30, 1924, p. 2.
[2]A. Rubinstein, *The Foreign Policy of the Soviet Union* (New York, 1972), pp. 51–52.

and psychological advantages from conclusion of a separate peace with Soviet Russia. By liquidating the eastern front, Germany could shift millions of troops westward and perhaps deliver a knockout blow in France to Allied armies before American troops could arrive in great force.

Leon Trotskii, after firing diplomats of the Provisional Government, had taken charge of the new People's Commissariat of Foreign Affairs (Narkomindel). Believing world revolution to be imminent, Trotskii considered traditional European secret diplomacy to be outmoded. Therefore, he directed the new agency haphazardly with inexperienced personnel until replaced in March 1918 by Georgi Chicherin, who restored order and improved efficiency.

Peace negotiations between Soviet Russia and the Central Powers dragged on with interruptions from late December 1917 until March 1918 at Brest-Litovsk, German headquarters for the eastern front. The Soviet delegation, soon headed by Trotskii himself, proposed a peace without annexations and delivered inflammatory revolutionary appeals over the heads of the German delegates to the war-weary peoples of Europe. General Max von Hoffman of Germany, however, aiming to erect satellite states in western Russia, insisted that all German-occupied areas be separated from Russia. To obtain Ukrainian resources, the Germans reached agreement with the anti-Bolshevik Rada (February 9th) and detached the entire Ukraine from Russia. These stiff German territorial demands caused Trotskii in January to suspend negotiations and return to Petrograd. The Bolshevik Central Committee now held its first great debate over foreign policy. Left Bolsheviks and left SRs urged a revolutionary war to promote the triumph of world revolution. On the other hand, Lenin argued that preservation of revolution in Russia must take precedence over the uncertain prospects of world revolution and over the interests of the international proletariat. He demanded an immediate end to the war: "For the success of socialism in Russia, . . . not less than several months will be necessary . . . to vanquish the bourgeoisie in our own country." However, the Central Committee approved Trotskii's compromise formula of "no war, no peace": that is, Russia would neither fight nor sign a treaty with Imperial Germany. The Germans responded with a swift offensive toward Petrograd. As they advanced, the alarmed Bolshevik leaders, including Lenin, favored seeking aid from the Allies. Despite efforts in this direction by unofficial Allied agents in Russia, Allied governments ignored these overtures. With the Germans approaching Petrograd, Lenin finally convinced the majority of the Central Committee to accept new, harsher German peace terms.

In the summer of 1918 the Allies intervened militarily in Russia's civil war. (See Chapter 8.) According to Soviet historians, they sought to overthrow Bolshevism, set up spheres of interest, and exploit Russia's resources. Claimed *Pravda* in September 1957:

> The organizer and inspirer of armed struggle against the Soviet Republic was international imperialism . . . [which] saw in the victory of the socialist revolution a threat to its own parasitical existence, to its profits and capital. To throttle the young Soviet republic, the imperialists, led by the leading circles of England, the USA, and France, organized military campaigns against our country.

But George Kennan, a leading American diplomat, asserted that the Allies had aimed to restore an eastern front, win the war, and keep their supplies out of German hands. British and French military leaders pushed for intervention, but President Wilson sent token U.S. forces most reluctantly. Allied troops did little fighting in Russia, but the Allies equipped and supplied Russian White forces long after World War I ended. Proponents (Churchill) argued that Allied intervention prolonged White resistance and stalled world revolution; recent opponents (Kennan) claim that it helped alienate Soviet Russia from the West. Allied intervention produced international stalemate because neither Soviet Russia nor the West could destroy the other; this situation suggested that outside powers cannot decide a civil war in a major country.

Allied hostility fed the extreme Soviet policies of those years. As German revolutionary socialists (Spartacists) fought for power in Berlin, Lenin, in January 1919, invited leftist European socialists to the First Comintern Congress. Of 35 delegates who attended, only 5 came from abroad, and even they did not truly represent their parties. Russian-dominated from the start, the Comintern, or Third International, gave Lenin a nucleus for a world Communist movement, though it was too feeble then to organize revolutions abroad. During the Second Comintern Congress of August 1920, as the Red Army advanced in Poland, delegates from 41 countries waxed optimistic over prospects for world revolution until Soviet defeat before Warsaw dashed their hopes. Twenty-one conditions for admission, which sought to impose the Russian party's tight discipline, were approved, but for some years the Comintern remained a loose collection of parties with factions and heated debates. By 1924, when it became a disciplined tool of Soviet policy, revolutionary opportunities abroad had dwindled.

The Allies excluded war-torn Soviet Russia from the Paris Peace Conference of 1919. Soviet-Western ideological and military antagonisms were at their peak, and in the West people were searching for Communists under every bed. Before the Conference, Prime Minister Lloyd-George of Britain wrote:

Map 14.1 *Soviet Russia and Europe, 1919–1938*

SOVIET RUSSIA AND EUROPE,
1919 – 1938

BARENTS SEA

PETSAMO

MURMANSK

WHITE SEA

ARKHANGELSK

N. DVINA

SWEDEN

FINLAND

BALTIC SEA

L. LADOGA

VIIPURI

TURKU

HELSINKI LENINGRAD

VOLODGA

UFA

TALINN NARVA

ESTONIA NOVGOROD

VOLGA

TARTU

PSKOV

RIGA

LATVIA

LITH. DVINSK

KALININ

MOSCOW

ULYANOVSK

KUIBYSHEV

MEMEL

E.

PRUSSIA

KOVNO

VILNA

W. DVINA

SMOLENSK

SARATOV

MINSK

WARSAW BREST

DON

STALINGRAD

ASTRAKHAN

KIEV

DNIEPER

KHARKOV

CZECH.

LVOV

DNIESTER

DNEPROPETROVSK

ROSTOV-ON-DON

CASPIAN

SEA

HUNGARY

KISHINEV ODESSA

RUMANIA

NOVOROSSISK

ORDZHONIKIDZE

BLACK SEA

0   MILES   500

FINLAND INDEPENDENT
1917 (1918)

LATVIA,LITHUANIA AND
ESTONIA, INDEPENDENT 1918

POLAND, INDEPENDENT 1918

VILNA REGION,CEDED TO
LITHUANIA BY RUSSIA AND
SEIZED BY POLAND,1920

BESSARABIA SEIZED BY
RUMANIA 1918

RUSSIAN BORDERS IN POLAND,
LITHUANIA AND S. W. RUSSIA (N. E
GALICIAN FRONTIER) 1914

CURZON LINE

RUSSIAN BOUNDARY
1921-1938

OTHER INTERNATIONAL
BOUNDARIES AFTER THE
VERSAILLES SETTLEMENTS

Personally, I would have dealt with the Soviets as the de facto government of Russia. So would President Wilson. But we both agreed that we could not carry to that extent our colleagues at the Congress nor the public opinion of our countries which was frightened by Bolshevik violence and feared its spread. . . .[3]

Preoccupied with Germany, the Allies neglected Soviet Russia and its relationship with Europe. (See Map 14.1.) This rebuff fed Bolshevik hostility to the peace settlement and the League of Nations, which the Soviets regarded as a potential capitalist coalition against them, and drew the two outcasts—Weimar Germany and Soviet Russia—together.

In 1919, halfhearted private Allied overtures to Soviet Russia failed, but during 1920 relations began to improve. Once the Allies withdrew from Russia and the White armies were defeated, the Bolsheviks sought Western aid to restore Russia's wrecked economy. Lloyd-George, favoring recognition of Soviet Russia and restoration of normal economic ties, helped end the Allied blockade. "We have failed to restore Russia to sanity by force. I believe we can save her by trade," he told Parliament. The Polish-Soviet War delayed normal relations, but by early 1921 Red Army defeats in Poland and Western desires to win Russian markets laid a basis for accommodation.

ACCOMMODATION, 1921–1927

Lenin warned Moscow leftists late in 1920 that an era of coexistence with capitalism was dawning. European capitalist economies were reviving, and even the intransigent Trotskii admitted: "History has given the bourgeoisie a fairly long breathing spell. . . . The revolution is not so obedient, so tame that it can be led on a leash as we imagined." The Polish conflict, ended by the Treaty of Riga (March 1921), left Soviet Russia weakened. The Ukraine proper became a Soviet republic, but Poland acquired parts of Byelorussia and the western Ukraine. After seven years of strife, Russia' economy faced collapse. Lenin, confronting peasant uprisings and the Kronstadt revolt, launched the New Economic Policy at home and a conciliatory policy toward the West.

To strengthen itself for subsequent conflict, Soviet Russia now sought diplomatic recognition, trade, and credits from the West. Recognition would provide some security against attack and aid Soviet efforts to divide capitalist countries and win trade concessions. The West reacted favorably because European industries needed export markets and their gov-

---

[3]Quoted in George Kennan, *Russia and the West Under Lenin and Stalin* (Boston, 1960), p. 124.

ernments, never truly committed to overthrow the Soviet regime, longed for normal relations. Obstacles to settlement included Comintern propaganda in the West and its colonies and, in particular, Russian debts. Western claims, totalling about 14 billion rubles (roughly 7 billion dollars), included pre–World War I tsarist debts, wartime borrowing, and compensation for nationalized European property; the Soviets made huge counterclaims for damage done by Allied intervention. The West agreed that wartime debts and Allied damage to Russia nearly cancelled each other out, but the French especially sought repayment of the prewar debt, most of which they held, and reimbursement for confiscated property. When Russia demurred, debt negotiations broke down; but the Soviets, making token concessions on propaganda, obtained some short-term credits, trade agreements, and diplomatic recognition from all major powers except the United States. Even this refusal of recognition did not prevent extensive U.S. technological assistance and some Soviet-American trade during the 1920s.

The shift to accommodation enhanced the role of Soviet diplomacy directed by an able professional, Georgi Chicherin (Foreign Commissar, 1918–1930). An ex-Menshevik of noble birth who had once worked for the tsarist foreign ministry, Chicherin was an idealistic socialist, dedicated, scholarly, and hard working. However, with his dubious past (from a Bolshevik standpoint), he never achieved high rank or influence in the Soviet Communist Party. Abroad, he had to contend with the Comintern, Profintern (international trade union organization), secret police, and foreign trade and tourist agencies. Furthermore, the Narkomindel lacked even the degree of authority enjoyed by the tsarist foreign office. After 1919, formulation and decision making in foreign and domestic affairs were concentrated in the Politburo of the Russian Communist Party, rather than the Party Congress or Central Committee. During Lenin's illnesses of 1922–1923, the Politburo decided foreign policy issues collectively, then transmitted its decisions to Chicherin for implementation. However, when healthy, Lenin formulated basic theoretical and practical concepts of foreign policy himself and devoted much attention to organizing the new Soviet diplomatic service. His fertile political imagination and tactical skill made him preeminent in determining the general outlines of early Soviet foreign policy. With Lenin acting basically as his own foreign minister, Chicherin's position resembled that of Foreign Minister Gorchakov in the 1860s—executing policies already determined by the head of state. The Politburo frequently bypassed the Narkomindel, the rival Comintern did not keep it informed, and the government, affirming that the Comintern was an independent agency, disclaimed responsibility for its moves. Nonetheless, Chicherin achieved real gains by persistent diplomacy.

The Genoa Conference (April 1922) marked his, and Soviet Russia's, diplomatic debut. In western Europe, Genoa was conceived as an international effort to restore Europe's depressed economy by drawing in both of its pariahs—Weimar Germany and Soviet Russia. At the opening session of the Conference, Chicherin declared:

> While maintaining ... their communist principles ..., the Russian delegation recognize that in the present period of history, which permits the parallel existence of the old social order and of the new [socialist] order now being born, economic collaboration between the states representing these two systems of property is imperatively necessary for the general economic reconstruction.[4]

To the West, Chicherin held out alluring prospects of extensive trade with Soviet Russia and lucrative investment in nascent Siberian industries, coupling this with a proposal for general disarmament. However, his main objective remained to separate Weimar Germany from the victor powers and reach a diplomatic accord with it.

Chicherin achieved this brilliantly at Rapallo, Italy. Exploiting Western coolness and snubs toward the Germans at Genoa, he induced Weimar delegates to meet with him at nearby Rapallo. To the consternation of the British and French, Germany and Soviet Russia promptly concluded the Treaty of Rapallo involving mutual diplomatic recognition, cancellation of debts and claims, and agreements to expand and normalize trade. While western liberals viewed Rapallo as a sinister Soviet-German conspiracy, the Germans regarded it as inaugurating for them an independent foreign policy and escape from the consequences of defeat in World War I. The Soviets considered Rapallo a model agreement with a bourgeois state, leaving them full freedom of action. They interpreted it as splitting European capitalism and enabling them to reach useful accords with the weaker segment. Rapallo, Moscow concluded, scotched dangers of European economic action against Soviet Russia and brought it out of diplomatic and economic isolation. Simultaneously, clandestine military cooperation was taking shape: The Germans were constructing arms factories in Soviet Russia and trying out new weapons, including tanks, prohibited to them by the Treaty of Versailles. (The Soviets had a share of the weapon production.) During the severe crisis that confronted Weimar Germany during 1923, policy differences surfaced between Narkomindel and the Comintern. While Chicherin supported the Weimar government and Soviet Russia shipped

---

[4]Jane Degras, ed., *Soviet Documents on Foreign Policy* (New York, 1951–1953, 1983), vol. 1, p. 298.

grain to Germany, the Comintern backed efforts by the German Communist Party to overthrow it. The Comintern suffered a grave reverse as evidence mounted that prospects for a Communist revolution in Germany were all but dead. Continuing rivalry between Narkomindel and Comintern, however, reflected merely differing tactics, not a conflict of basic aims.

Chicherin's policy of normalizing relations with the rest of Europe, while generally successful, also suffered setbacks. During Anglo-Soviet negotiations for trade and credits, erupted the "Zinoviev Letter" (October 1924), whose authenticity remains disputed. Containing supposed instructions from the Comintern president to British Communists to subvert the armed forces, the letter caused a furor. The "Letter" provoked a "Red scare" in Britain, contributed to the downfall of the Labor government, and strained Anglo-Soviet relations severely. Another diplomatic reverse followed: The Locarno Agreements of 1925 between Germany and the former Allied powers excluded the USSR completely and achieved a brief era of apparent European unity and harmony. Despite such reverses, Chicherin's diplomacy, by ending Soviet isolation and reaching accord with Weimar Germany, enhanced Soviet security and contributed to its economic recovery. Only a year after Locarno the Soviet-German Treaty of Berlin (April 1926), reaffirming the provisions of Rapallo, stipulated neutrality if either country were attacked by a third power.

However, Soviet hostility toward the League of Nations persisted. From its inception the League had been viewed in Moscow as a concealed capitalist coalition against Soviet Russia. This resulted partly from the latter's exclusion from the Paris Peace Conference of 1919 and partly because the League was dominated in the interwar period by leading capitalist powers, Britain and France. Furthermore, international stability and prosperity, fostered by the League, would reduce Communist prospects for world revolution. A Soviet press statement on the League of Nations declared in November 1925:

> We regard the League of Nations . . . not as a friendly association of peoples working for the general good, but as a masked league of the so-called Great Powers, who have appropriated to themselves the right of disposing of the fate of weaker nations. . . . Certain Powers are counting on using Germany to assist in carrying out . . . their hostile designs against the USSR. . . . The League is a cover for the preparation of military action for the suppression of small and weak nationalities.[5]

---

[5]Degras, *Soviet Documents . . .* , vol. 2, pp. 65–66.

Not until 1934 would the Soviets alter their hostility toward the League.

Asia had remained secondary in Soviet policy. Lenin recognized the revolutionary potential of colonial peoples in undermining Western imperialism, but Soviet Russia was too weak to exploit it. Soviet Russia promptly repudiated tsarist imperial privileges and spheres of interest, most of which it could not retain anyway. To weaken Franco-British influence in the Near East and enhance Soviet security, Lenin supported such nationalists as Kemal Pasha of Turkey. The Soviets appealed to colonial peoples, notably at the Comintern-sponsored Baku Congress of September 1920. Zinoviev told delegates from 37 nationalities: "The Communist International turns today to the peoples of the East and says to them: 'Brothers, we summon you to a Holy War first of all against British Imperialism.'" This was purely a propaganda campaign, but later many Asian revolutionaries were trained in the USSR with profound consequences for the West.

Justifiably, Soviet leaders regarded China as the key to Asia. They promptly condemned European imperialism there and renounced most special Russian privileges, though in 1921 the Red Army entered Outer Mongolia, ostensibly pursuing White generals, and established a Communist puppet government. Mongolia has served ever since as a buffer and Russian base on China's frontier. During the early 1920s, Moscow maintained formal relations with the weak Beijing government while Soviet agents, led by Michael Borodin, penetrated the Canton regime. Its leader, Sun Yat-sen, who had led the Chinese Revolution of 1912, aimed to expel foreign imperialism and to achieve national unity and social reform. With Borodin's aid, he built the Kuomintang (Nationalist Party) on the model of the Soviet Communist Party. Sun's death in 1925 left a vacuum in Canton soon filled by Chiang Kai-shek, a young Moscow-trained nationalist officer. The Stalin-Trotskii struggle affected Soviet policy: Convinced that China was entering her bourgeois-democratic revolution, Stalin favored proletarian participation in a national bloc including peasants and bourgeoisie and urged the Communists to enter the Kuomintang. Trotskii, however, advocated an armed Communist uprising and a direct transition to socialism in China. Stalin's policy prevailed, but during his northward expedition in 1926, Chiang slaughtered Communists in Shanghai, expelled Soviet advisers, and soon ruled much of China. Soviet policies there, based on inadequate knowledge of the situation, had plainly failed.

NEOISOLATIONISM, 1928–1933

Stalin's ascendancy brought a return to autocracy in Soviet domestic and foreign policies and produced a docile and subservient Comintern. Removing potential and actual rivals from positions of power and influence at home and launching forced collectivization and massive industrialization, Stalin abroad raised as a smokescreen the danger of imminent attacks on the USSR by powerful capitalist states. Envious and distrustful of cosmopolitan, intellectual Old Bolsheviks such as Zinoviev and Bukharin, he acted to undermine their influence and sever ties with European socialism. In these years occurred a marked growth of deliberate isolation from European affairs.

In his report to the 15th Party Congress (December 1927), Stalin intimated that a major shift in Soviet foreign policy was imminent and raised the spectre of renewed capitalist assaults against the USSR:

> Whereas a year or two ago it was possible and necessary to speak of . . . "peaceful coexistence" between the USSR and the capitalist countries, today . . . *the period of "peaceful coexistence" is receding into the past,* giving place to a period of imperialist assaults and preparation for intervention against the USSR.[6]

Soon afterward Stalin accused France, which he considered the dominant European power, of making preparations to attack the Soviet Union, which he surely did not believe and for which there was not a shred of evidence. The Sixth Comintern Congress of September 1928, an obedient Stalinist body, proclaimed the USSR to be the sole bastion of world revolution and stressed that all Communist parties owed exclusive allegiance to Moscow; their local interests must be subordinated to preserving the USSR.

While accusing Western capitalist nations of plotting war, Stalin emphasized that Soviet foreign policy sought consistently to preserve peace. At the 16th Congress of June 1930 he affirmed:

> As a result of this policy of negotiating trade and non-aggression pacts . . . we have succeeded in maintaining peace . . . in spite of a number of provocative acts . . . of the warmongers. We will continue to pursue this policy of peace with all our might. . . . We do not want a single foot of foreign territory, but we will not surrender a single inch of our territory to anyone.

---

[6]Stalin, *Works* (Moscow, 1955), vol. 10, pp. 282 ff.

Indeed, despite Stalin's intransigent and frequently alarmist tone, Soviet foreign policy in these years remained cautious and pacific, avoiding confrontations with capitalist powers. Stalin appears to have counted on the preservation of world peace during the First Five Year Plan and continued to sound this theme down to 1939.

The Great Depression (1929–1933) convinced Moscow of the correctness of its policy line against western democratic socialists. Predicting the imminent demise of world capitalism, Soviet leaders concluded that this would leave social democrats as the only important remaining barrier throughout the world to the conquest of power by the working class led by the Communists. Declared Politburo member V. M. Molotov: "Social fascism with its 'left' wing is the last resource of the bourgeoisie among the workers."

Stalin's theory of "social fascism," which claimed that Western socialists had adopted Fascist policies, helped undermine democracy in Weimar Germany and bring Adolf Hitler to power. Stalin detested the democratic, pro-Western policies of the German Social Democrats (SPD), but he also distrusted the large and volatile German Communist Party (KPD) and doubted he could control it if it achieved power. Thus, Stalin, playing Communists against Social Democrats, ordered the KPD to collaborate with the Nazis against a Weimar Republic undermined by the Depression. Believing that the capitalists were already in power in Germany and that the Nazis were likewise bourgeois, Stalin concluded that Hitler in power, rather than launch a revolution against capitalism, would crush moderate socialism and cause Germany's defection from the western camp and its dependence on the USSR. To desperate pleas by German Social Democrats for Communist aid against the Nazis, the reply of the Soviet embassy was: The road to a Soviet Germany lies through Hitler. Thus Stalin bears considerable responsibility for the triumph of Nazism in Germany, which later would prove so costly to the USSR. Even after Hitler assumed power (January 1933), Stalin persisted in regarding France as the chief Soviet foe, apparently out of ignorance about German conditions and excessive faith in Leninism.

In the Far East, Stalin pursued a cautious, defensive course. In 1928, he severed relations with Chiang's nationalist regime, and the next year, after local authorities seized the Chinese Eastern Railway, the Red Army restored it to Soviet control. Once Japan seized Manchuria in 1931 and turned it into the puppet state of Manchukuo, Stalin became gravely concerned about Japanese militarism. Reinforcing the Red Army in the Far East, he sought agreement with Japan, even offering to sell it the Chinese Eastern Railway. He restored relations with Chiang, tried to prevent Sino-Japanese cooperation against the USSR, and sought rapprochement with the United States.

Meanwhile, the USSR was advocating peace and disarmament for Europe. Maxim Litvinov, Chicherin's longtime assistant who succeeded him as foreign commissar in 1930, proposed total disarmament at the Geneva Disarmament Conference of 1932 but found little response. In January 1933, Hitler assumed power in Germany and influenced Stalin to alter his foreign policy. Deep in the Depression, the West no longer threatened the USSR, but the chief beneficiaries were not Communism but aggressive German Nazism and Japanese militarism.

COLLECTIVE SECURITY, 1934–1937

Worried by the rising Nazi threat, Stalin gradually abandoned isolationism and opposition to the Versailles system to seek reconciliation with the West. During 1932, the Soviets had normalized relations with such neighbors as Finland, Estonia, Poland, then with France. In 1934, Soviet diplomacy tried to erect an east European alliance to protect its western borders, but Poland demurred. Meanwhile, diplomatic relations were established with the United States. Soviet leaders, admiring American enterprise and efficiency, had long desired recognition from the United States, but conservative Republican presidents, Communist propaganda, and unpaid Russian debts had blocked it. Invited to Washington by President Franklin Roosevelt, Litvinov provided assurances on propaganda and legal protection for Americans in the USSR. In November 1933, the United States recognized the USSR, and William Bullitt, who had led an unofficial mission to Russia in 1919, became the first American ambassador there. Receiving him warmly and ignoring strong American isolationism, Stalin mistakenly expected the United States to block Japanese penetration of China.

By 1934, after the Polish-German pact, Stalin realized that Nazism represented a real danger to the USSR. Though holding out an olive branch to Hitler, he noted that "revanchist and imperialist sentiments in Germany" were growing. Hitler's nonaggression pact with Poland roused Soviet fears that he might encourage the Poles to seize the Ukraine. Growing concern over Germany accelerated a Soviet shift toward the Western democracies.

In September 1934, the USSR finally joined the League of Nations, and abandoned its hostility to the Paris peace settlement. Maxim Litvinov, a Jew, an anti-Nazi, and a pro-Westerner, became a convincing spokesman for Soviet cooperation with the West. He used the League of Nations to proclaim a Soviet policy of peace, disarmament, and collective security against aggression. Contrary to assumptions in the West, Litvinov never made policy but merely executed Stalin's orders. His sincere belief in the new line won the confidence of Western liberals and socialists, but the

Maxim M. Litvinov (1876–1951) as Soviet
Ambassador to the U.S. (1941–1943) in his
Washington, D.C., office with Lenin looking
over his shoulder. Litvinov as Commissar of
Foreign Affairs, 1930–1939, was associated
with a policy of collective security against Hitler
(SOVFOTO)

League's failure to halt Italy in Ethiopia in 1935 revealed once again its
weakness as a peacekeeping instrument.

Stalin also sought security through mutual defense pacts. In May
1935, France and the USSR, driven together again by fear of Germany,
concluded a mutual assistance pact, but it lacked the military teeth of the
old Franco-Russian Alliance; politically divided France took almost a year
to ratify even a watered-down version. The USSR pledged to aid Czechoslovakia militarily against a German attack if the French did so first, as
Stalin insured cautiously against being drawn into war with Germany
while the West watched.

The Comintern obediently adopted a new Popular Front policy. Its
Seventh (and last) Congress of July–August 1935, announced that all
"progressive forces" (workers, peasants, petty bourgeoisie, and intelligentsia) should cooperate against Fascism, the most dangerous form of
capitalist imperialism. Communists were instructed to work with so-

cialists and liberals while retaining their identity within the Popular Front.

Failures of collective security in 1936 caused growing Soviet disillusionment. In March, Nazi troops marched into the Rhineland in clear violation of the Versailles and Locarno treaties, using French ratification of the pact with the USSR as justification. Disregarding feeble French and British protests, the Germans refortified the Rhineland. This action shattered the collective security approach, and by weakening the French position, undermined the Franco-Soviet pact, shifting the balance of power to Germany. Stalin realized that he could not count upon the West to resist Nazi aggression, which was now likely to turn eastward. Soon Stalin began the Great Purge, eliminating rivals in case he later had to deal with Hitler. The West's apathy toward the Spanish Civil War, beginning in July, reinforced Stalin's suspicions. While Germany and Italy supported General Franco's Fascist revolt against the Spanish Republic, the West proclaimed nonintervention. The USSR, explaining that it was aiding the Popular Front against Fascism, provided important military aid to the Republic, saved Madrid from early capture, and greatly prolonged the conflict. Stalin may have hoped to draw the West into the war or thought that lengthy Fascist involvement in Spain would delay a move against the USSR. However, during 1937 he withdrew most military aid from Spain and purged Russian Communists associated with it as Trotskyites. Soviet efforts to cooperate with the West against Hitler before World War II virtually ended.

THE NAZI-SOVIET PACT

The formation of the Axis (Germany and Italy) in October 1936 and its conclusion of the Anti-Comintern Pact with Japan in November apparently deepened antagonism between Communism and Fascism, but Stalin was already abandoning collective security. For him, 1937 was a year of watchful waiting abroad and relentless purge at home. Litvinov covered his retreat by continuing to advocate collective resistance to Fascism.

Nazi gains during 1938 demolished the remnants of collective security and alienated the USSR from the appeasement-minded West. Hitler's annexation of Austria drew only ineffectual Western protests, and Stalin doubtless concluded that the West would not fight Hitler to save eastern Europe. Litvinov warned repeatedly that time was running out if the West wanted Soviet cooperation against Fascism. Collective security's last gasp was the May Crisis between Germany and Czechoslovakia: The Czechs mobilized, the West and the USSR pledged aid if Czechoslovakia were attacked, and Hitler backed down. But at the Munich Conference in

Foreign Commissar Viacheslav M. Molotov (1890–1986) signing Nazi–Soviet Pact in August 1939. He served as foreign commissar and foreign minister 1939–1949 and 1953–1957. Standing left to right: German Foreign Minister von Ribbentrop, Stalin, and V. Pavlov (*UPI/ Bettmann*)

October, with the USSR excluded, France and Britain surrendered the Czech Sudetenland to Hitler and made Czechoslovakia indefensible. Western appeasement and Stalin's purge of the Red Army, which weakened the USSR, had destroyed collective security.

Tension with Japan stimulated Stalin's desire to settle with Hitler. He had tried to appease Japan by selling it the Chinese Eastern Railway in 1935. The outbreak of the Sino-Japanese War in 1937 temporarily relaxed pressure on the USSR. Stalin signed a friendship treaty with China, and supplied Chiang with arms and credits. When the Japanese army probed the Soviet border in major attacks at Changkufeng (July 1938) and Nomonhan (May 1939), it was repulsed with heavy losses, apparently convincing Tokyo that expansion into Siberia would be too costly.

By 1938, Stalin had eliminated all opposition and could dictate to the Politburo. "Stalin thought that now he could decide all things alone and that all he needed were statisticians," recalled N. S. Khrushchev. "He treated all others in such a way that they could only listen to and praise him." In May 1939, V. M. Molotov, Stalin's loyal secretary, replaced Litvinov as foreign commissar, suggesting that Stalin was preparing a major move in foreign policy. Molotov imposed rigid conformity upon the hitherto flexible and cosmopolitan Narkomindel.

During early 1939 the West and the Nazis vied for Soviet support. In March, Hitler's occupation of the rest of Czechoslovakia finally ended Western appeasement. France and Britain belatedly guaranteed the integrity of Poland and Romania but failed to convince Stalin that they would really fight Hitler. In a speech to the 18th Party Congress in March, Stalin, accusing the West of trying to provoke a Soviet-German conflict, warned that the USSR would not be drawn into a war "to pull somebody else's chestnuts out of the fire." In August, the West finally sent military missions to Russia, but it had moved too slowly and indecisively. Hitler, having decided to attack Poland, had already begun intensive negotiations with the USSR.

On August 23, 1939, the Nazi-Soviet Pact, concluded in Moscow between former ideological archenemies, shocked the world. (See p. 329.) That fateful agreement included a public nonaggression pact pledging absolute neutrality if either partner were attacked by a third power. Securing Hitler's eastern flank, the Pact encouraged him to invade Poland September 1. A secret territorial protocol partitioned Poland, with the USSR to receive roughly the eastern third. Latvia, Estonia, Finland, and Bessarabia were assigned to the Soviet sphere, and Lithuania was added to it later. (See Map 14.2.) Reflecting the worst traditions of the old secret diplomacy, the two dictators' cynical bargain resembled the alliance of 1807 between Napoleon and Alexander I. Once again Russia, bribed with temporary peace and east European territory, gave a Western tyrant a free hand to deal with Europe and England. Stalin then apparently interpreted the Pact as a diplomatic masterstroke, securing the USSR from invasion, giving it a buffer zone, splitting the capitalist world, and encouraging its parts to fight, all of which might enable Russia to become the arbiter of Europe.

If so, Stalin's hopes were soon shattered. He was appalled at the awesome Nazi *Blitzkrieg* that rolled over Poland, the Low Countries, and France; he watched helplessly as the Soviet Union, having agreed to supply Germany with raw materials, became economically dependent on Germany. At Hitler's insistence the Soviet-controlled Comintern abandoned its hostility to Nazism. Seeking compensation, Stalin occupied the Baltic states militarily, deported many of its citizens to Siberia, then engineered a sham plebiscite that, Moscow affirmed, overwhelmingly (over 99 percent) approved their annexation to the USSR. The Soviets

Map 14.2 *Territorial Changes, 1939–1941*

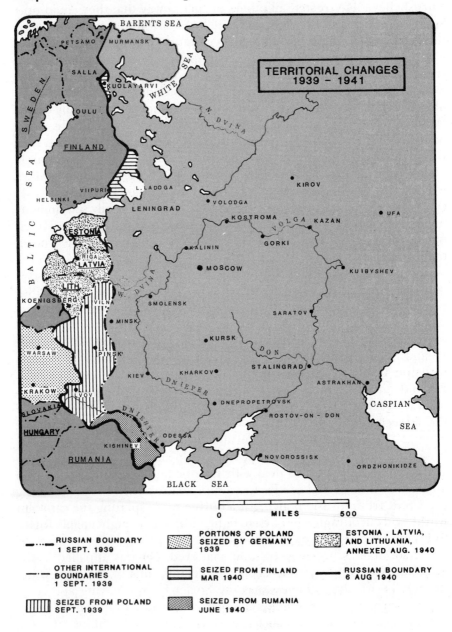

TERRITORIAL CHANGES
1939 – 1941

BARENTS SEA

PETSAMO MURMANSK

SALLA

KUOLAYARVI

WHITE SEA

OULU

N. DVINA

SWEDEN

FINLAND

KIROV

VIIPURI

L. LADOGA

HELSINKI

VOLODGA

LENINGRAD

UFA

KOSTROMA KAZAN

BALTIC SEA

ESTONIA

KALININ

VOLGA

GORKI

RIGA

LATVIA

MOSCOW

KUIBYSHEV

LITH.

W. DVINA

KOENIGSBERG

VILNA

SMOLENSK

SARATOV

MINSK

WARSAW

PINSK

KURSK

DON

KRAKOW

LVOV

KIEV

KHARKOV

STALINGRAD

DNIEPER

ASTRAKHAN

SLOVAKIA

DNIESTER

DNEPROPETROVSK

CASPIAN
SEA

HUNGARY

KISHINEV

ODESSA

ROSTOV-ON-DON

RUMANIA

NOVOROSSISK

ORDZHONIKIDZE

BLACK SEA

0 MILES 500

RUSSIAN BOUNDARY
1 SEPT. 1939

PORTIONS OF POLAND
SEIZED BY GERMANY
1939

ESTONIA , LATVIA,
AND LITHUANIA,
ANNEXED AUG. 1940

OTHER INTERNATIONAL
BOUNDARIES
1 SEPT. 1939

SEIZED FROM FINLAND
MAR 1940

RUSSIAN BOUNDARY
6 AUG 1940

SEIZED FROM POLAND
SEPT. 1939

SEIZED FROM RUMANIA
JUNE 1940

also demanded Finnish territory near Leningrad in exchange for part of Soviet Karelia. When the Finns refused, the Red Army attacked but met heroic resistance, suffered huge casualties, and displayed embarrassing weakness in the aftermath of the military purge. This unprovoked Soviet aggression, which the Soviets justified as an essential defensive measure, brought sharp Western condemnation, expulsion from the League of Nations, and almost provoked war with the West. Once Finnish defenses had been broken, Stalin hastily concluded peace, taking much of the Karelian Isthmus and many of the Finnish bases. Later in 1940 he seized Bessarabia and northern Bukovina from Romania to protect the vulnerable Ukraine.

Despite their large and mutually profitable trade, friction increased between Germany and the USSR. As early as July 1940, Hitler apparently decided to invade Russia, and Soviet stubbornness during the Molotov-Ribbentrop talks in November merely confirmed his decision. The German foreign minister tried in vain to turn Soviet aspirations southward to the Persian Gulf against Britain. Abandoning any pretense of Marxist internationalism, Molotov stated Soviet demands in pragmatic, power-political terms. The Soviet Union, he declared, would accept Ribbentrop's proposals on politicoeconomic cooperation:

1. Provided that the German troops are immediately withdrawn from Finland, which under the compact of 1939, belongs to the Soviet Union's sphere of influence. . . .

2. Provided that within the next few months the security of the Soviet Union in the [Turkish] Straits is assured by the conclusion of a mutual assistance pact between the Soviet Union and Bulgaria, which geographically is situated inside [its] security zone . . . and by the establishment of a base for land and naval forces of the USSR within range of the Bosphorus and Dardanelles by means of a long-term lease.

3. Provided that the area south of Batum and Baku in the general direction of the Persian Gulf is recognized as the center of the aspirations of the Soviet Union.

4. Provided that Japan [renounces] her rights to concessions for coal and oil in northern Sakhalin.[7]

Molotov's statement marked an evident return to traditional 19th-century tsarist objectives, secret diplomacy, and even language, that is, "spheres of influence," military bases, and long-term leases. Nazi-Soviet friction over Finland and the Turkish Straits resembled that between

---

[7]R. J. Sontag and J. Beddie, eds., *Nazi-Soviet Relations, 1939–1941* (Washington, D.C., 1948), pp. 258–259.

tsarist Russia and Napoleonic France preceding the French invasion of Russia in 1812.

PROBLEM 6
The Nazi-Soviet Pact: Then and Now

Prevalent historical opinion remains that the conclusion of the Nazi-Soviet Pact on August 23, 1939, gave Hitler the green light to invade Poland just eight days later, thus touching off World War II. Still disputed, however, is whether Stalin, the realistic statesman, had a genuine alternative in 1939 to an accord with Hitler. Could the Red Army, shattered by the terrible purge of its officer corps in 1937–1938, have resisted a Nazi invasion then? Would Hitler indeed have invaded the Soviet Union had Stalin aligned the USSR with the Western powers, Britain and France? Would Hitler have attacked Poland, already backed by the Western powers, without guaranteed neutrality from the Soviet Union? Was there a realistic chance for a military alliance between the xenophobic Stalin and the Western powers in 1939, given the abject surrender by France and Britain to the Axis powers at the Munich Conference in September 1938, which had excluded the USSR? How much responsibility for the outbreak of World War II therefore rests on the shoulders of Stalin's USSR?

Another series of questions relates to Stalin's motives and objectives, which recently have been scrutinized by Soviet historians and commentators. This debate centers around the secret additional protocol of August 23 on territorial divisions in eastern Europe and the subsequent protocol of September 28, 1939, under which the USSR secured Lithuania while surrendering Warsaw and portions of central Poland to Germany. Can Stalin's actions be defended on the grounds of security, that is, a defensive motive of creating a buffer zone to protect the USSR against a possible subsequent Nazi attack? Or was Stalin's objective primarily expansionist, that is, aggressive to secure control without risk of the Baltic states and eastern Poland and to agree with Hitler to destroy an independent Slav Poland? Probably it represented a combination of the two aims. Recent Soviet commentators have condemned the Pact and protocols as violations of Leninist principles in foreign affairs. Leaders in the Baltic republics have argued that their incorporation into the USSR in 1939–1940 took place forcibly against the background of secret agreements that were illegal both under international law and in the light of Leninist principles. If their incorporation was indeed involuntary, were the Baltic republics not therefore justified in demanding full independence and even secession from the USSR?

Some basis for answering these questions can be provided by examining the relevant documents from 1939: the Soviet-German Non-Aggression Pact, the secret territorial protocol of August 23, and the additional secret protocol of September 28th. Foreign Minister Molotov provided the official Soviet explanation of reasons for the Nazi-Soviet Pact. Half a century later, in 1989, the debate over the Pact intensified and excerpts from that Soviet debate, both Russian and Baltic, have been included.

EXCERPTS FROM THE TREATY OF AUGUST 23, 1939

1. Treaty of Non-Aggression Between Germany and the Union of Soviet Socialist Republics—August 23, 1939 [public portion].

Article 1: Both High Contracting Parties obligate themselves to desist from any act of violence, any aggressive action, and any attack on each other, either individually or jointly with other powers.

Article 2: Should one of the High Contracting Parties become the object of belligerent action by a third power, the other High Contracting Party shall in no manner lend its support to this third power. . . .

Article 4: Neither of the two High Contracting Parties shall participate in any grouping of powers whatsoever that is directly or indirectly aimed at the other party.

Disputes between the two nations were to be settled through "friendly exchange of opinion" or through arbitration (Article 5). The treaty was to run for 10 years; if neither party denounced it a year before its scheduled expiration, the treaty would be extended automatically for 5 more years.

Article 7: The present treaty shall be ratified within the shortest possible time. . . . The agreement shall enter into force as soon as it is signed.

For the government of	With the full power of
the German Reich	the Soviet government
J. von Ribbentrop	V. M. Molotov[8]

---

[8]R. J. Sontag and J. Beddie, eds., *Nazi-Soviet Relations, 1939–1941* (Washington, D.C., 1948), pp. 76–77.

EXCERPTS FROM THE SECRET ADDITIONAL PROTOCOL OF AUGUST 23, 1939

. . . The undersigned plenipotentiaries of each of the two parties discussed in strictly confidential conversation the question of the boundary of their respective spheres of influence in eastern Europe. These conversations led to the following conclusions:

1. In the event of a territorial and political rearrangement in the areas belonging to the Baltic States (Finland, Estonia, Latvia, Lithuania), the northern boundary of Lithuania shall represent the boundary of the spheres of Germany and the USSR. In this connection the interest of Lithuania in the Vilna area is recognized by each party.

2. In the event of a territorial and political arrangement of the areas belonging to the Polish state the spheres of influence of Germany and the USSR shall be bounded approximately by the line of the rivers Narew, Vistula and San. The question of whether the interests of both parties make desirable the maintenance of an independent Polish state and how such a state should be bounded can only be definitely determined in the course of further political developments. . . .

4. This protocol shall be treated by both parties as strictly secret.

v. Ribbentrop   V. Molotov[9]

THE SECRET SUPPLEMENTARY PROTOCOL OF SEPTEMBER 28, 1939

When German armies marched into Poland on September 1, 1939, the Soviet Union remained neutral according to the terms of the Non-Aggression Pact. On September 17 Soviet armies invaded eastern Poland and occupied the region assigned to it by the Secret Additional Protocol. At Soviet request, on September 28 in Moscow von Ribbentrop and Molotov signed a Secret Supplementary Protocol. This document amended the Secret Protocol of August 23 under Article 1 "to the effect that the territory of the Lithuanian state falls to the sphere of influence of the USSR, while, on the other hand, the province of Lublin and parts of the province of Warsaw fall to the sphere of influence of Germany. As soon as the Government of the USSR shall take special measures on Lithuanian territory to protect its interests, the present German-Lithuanian border . . . shall be rectified in such a way that the Lithuanian territory situated to the southwest of the line marked on the attached map

---

[9]Sontag and Beddie, *Nazi-Soviet Relations . . .* , p. 78.

should fall to Germany. . . ."[10] This Protocol confirmed that Nazi Germany had assigned all the Baltic states to the Soviet sphere.

THE OFFICIAL SOVIET EXPLANATION: 1939

On August 31, 1939, Foreign Minister Molotov provided this interpretation of the preceding Nazi-Soviet agreements in a speech to the Supreme Soviet of the USSR. Emphasizing the tense international situation that then prevailed in Europe and Asia, Molotov declared:

> In view of this state of affairs, the conclusion of a non-aggression pact between the USSR and Germany is of tremendous positive value, eliminating the danger of war between Germany and the Soviet Union. In order more fully to define the significance of this pact, I must first dwell on the negotiations which have taken place in recent months in Moscow with representatives of Great Britain and France . . . for conclusion of a pact of mutual assistance against aggression in Europe. . . . The initial proposals of the British Government were, as you know, entirely unacceptable . . . ; they ignored the principle of reciprocity and equality of obligations. . . . These negotiations encountered insuperable obstacles. . . . Poland, which was to be jointly guaranteed by Great Britain, France and the USSR, rejected military assistance on the part of the Soviet Union. . . . After this it became clear to us that the Anglo-French-Soviet negotiations were doomed to failure. . . . The British and French military missions came to Moscow without any definite powers and without the right to conclude any military convention. . . .
>
> The decision to conclude a nonaggression pact between the USSR and Germany was adopted after military negotiations with France and Britain had reached an impasse. . . . It is our duty to think of the interests of the Soviet people, the interests of the USSR. . . . In our foreign policy towards non-Soviet countries, we have always been guided by Lenin's well-known principle of the peaceful coexistence of the Soviet state and capitalist countries. . . . The Non-Aggression Pact . . . marks a turning point in the history of Europe, and not only of Europe. Only yesterday, the German fascists were pursuing a foreign policy hostile to us. . . . Today, however, the situation has changed and we are enemies no longer. The art of politics in the sphere of foreign relations . . . is to reduce the number of enemies and to make the enemies of yesterday good neighbors. . . . The two largest states of Europe have agreed to put an end to the enmity between them, to eliminate the menace of war and live in peace with the other. . . . Is it really difficult to understand that the USSR is pursuing and will continue to pursue its own

---

[10]Sontag and Beddie, p. 107.

independent policy, based on the interests of the peoples of the USSR and only their interests?[11]

Thus Molotov justified the agreements with Germany on the basis of Soviet national interests and the "insuperable obstacles" to an accord with the Western powers. He made no allusion whatsoever to the establishment of Soviet-German spheres of interest.

SOVIET VIEWS OF THE AGREEMENTS: 1989

A. N. Iakovlev, a member of the Soviet Politburo, in a *Pravda* interview published on August 18, 1989, declared that "serious researchers" agreed that when Stalin authorized Ribbentrop's visit to Moscow on August 22, 1939, the Soviet Union no longer had any choice of partners. Unable to prevent war by itself and having failed to enlist England and France as allies, "the only thing left for it to do was to think about how to avoid falling into the maelstrom of war for which the USSR was even less prepared in 1939 than in 1941. . . ." As to the Secret Additional Protocol of September 28, 1939, Iakovlev stated:

> From a political standpoint . . . , it represented a deviation from Leninist norms of Soviet foreign policy and from Lenin's break with secret diplomacy. . . . [The Protocol] conflicted with the sovereignty and independence of a whole series of countries [including the Baltic states] . . . and with the treaties which the USSR had previously concluded with those countries, with our commitments to respect their sovereignty, territorial integrity and inviolability. In my opinion, Stalin took an unjustified risk in giving his blessing to Molotov's signature to the "territorial-political rearrangement" of Poland. . . . The venture could have ended with the USSR's being drawn into the war rather than being given a breathing spell. . . . This way of acting by the Soviet leaders then in no way reflected the will of the Soviet people and was not in tune with their mood. I think we will be acting responsibly . . . by unequivocally condemning the prewar Soviet leadership's departure from Leninist principles of foreign policy. . . .

Asked to compare the Non-Aggression Pact of August 23, 1939, with the Secret Supplementary Protocol of September 28, Iakovlev found them to be qualitatively different:

> The first was a treaty made in peacetime; the second was concluded with a country [Nazi Germany] which had committed an overt act of aggression. The first was basically in keeping with the international practices of the time;

---

[11]V. M. Molotov, "The Meaning of the Soviet-German Non-Aggression Pact," Speech to the Supreme Soviet, August 31, 1939. In Alvin Rubinstein, *The Foreign Policy of the Soviet Union* (New York, 1960), pp. 145–151, excerpts.

the second essentially cast doubt on the USSR's status as a neutral—if it did not undermine that status—and pushed our country toward unprincipled cooperation with Nazi Germany. There was no direct need at all for the September 28 treaty. . . . For opportunistic motives, however, in late September Stalin made a move that entailed major political and moral costs in order, as he supposed, to fix Hitler firmly in a position of mutual understanding—not with the USSR, but with Stalin himself.[12]

On August 23, 1989—the fiftieth anniversary of the Non-Aggression Pact, an interview with F. N. Kovalev, director of the Foreign Ministry's Diplomatic Historical Administration, appeared in the Soviet newspaper *Izvestiia*. Discussing the forced incorporation of the Baltic republics of Latvia, Lithuania, and Estonia into the USSR, Kovalev said:

> When the agreements were signed in August 1939, what was primarily intended was to establish a definite boundary to German fascist expansion. And only that. It was certainly not intended, say, that the Baltic republics would eventually be incorporated into the USSR. The purport of Moscow's instructions to our representatives in the Baltic republics . . . was that Soviet garrisons stationed in the Baltic republics on the basis of treaties . . . concluded with them in late September and October 1939 should in no way interfere in those countries' internal affairs. There could be no question of any Sovietization of the three Baltic republics . . . but the presence of Soviet garrisons created an atmosphere in which leftist forces and democratic circles in the three republics began to step up efforts which ultimately led to the events that occurred in 1940 [incorporation]. From my viewpoint . . . , the Baltic republics then faced a very clear alternative; either side with Hitler or the USSR.[13]

On August 28, 1989, *Izvestiia* reported from the Lithuanian capital of Vilnius that the presidium of the Lithuanian Supreme Soviet had examined the conclusions reached by its commission studying the Soviet-German treaties of 1939. The assertion that Lithuania's incorporation into the Soviet Union in 1940 had been illegal, affirmed that Moscow newspaper, "is leading the republic of Lithuania into a political impasse and will be of little help during the transition to economic independence."[14]

---

[12]*Pravda*, August 18, 1989. Interview with A. N. Iakovlev.
[13]*Izvestiia*, August 23, 1989. Interview with F. N. Kovalev.
[14]"Search for the Road Together," *Izvestiia*, August 28, 1989.

CONCLUSION

Soviet views on the Nazi-Soviet agreements of 1939 have changed significantly in recent years. The Pact of August 23 has been disavowed as mistaken and "anti-Leninist," as have Soviet-German accords over spheres of influence. However, as of mid-1990, Moscow had not yet concluded that this required granting full independence to the Baltic republics.

Suggested Additional Reading

ADAMS, ARTHUR. *Readings in Soviet Foreign Policy* . . . (Boston, 1961).

ANGRESS, WERNER T. *Stillborn Revolution: The Communist Bid for Power in Germany, 1921–1923* (Princeton, N.J., 1963).

BELOFF, MAX. *The Foreign Policy of Soviet Russia, 1929–1941*, 2 vols. (London, 1947–1949).

BORKENAU, FRANZ. *World Communism: A History of the Communist International* (Ann Arbor, Mich., 1962).

BRANDT, C. *Stalin's Failure in China, 1924–1927* (Cambridge, Mass., 1958).

BROWDER, ROBERT P. *The Origins of Soviet-American Diplomacy* (Princeton, N.J., 1953).

BUDUROWYCZ, BOHDAN. *Polish-Soviet Relations, 1932–1933* (New York, 1963).

CARR, E. H. *German-Soviet Relations Between the Two World Wars, 1919–1929* (Baltimore, Md., 1951).

———. *The Soviet Impact on the Western World* (London, 1946).

———. *Twilight of the Comintern, 1930–1935* (New York, 1983).

CRAIG, GORDON, and FELIX GILBERT, eds. *The Diplomats, 1919–1939* (Princeton, N.J., 1953). (See chapters on Chicherin and Litvinov.)

DEGRAS, JANE. *Calendar of Soviet Documents on Foreign Policy, 1917–1941* (New York, 1948).

———, ed. *The Communist International, 1919–1943* (New York, 1956).

———, ed., *Soviet Documents on Foreign Policy, 1917–1941*, 3 vols. (New York, 1951–1953, 1983).

DMYTRYSHYN, BASIL, AND F. COX. *The Soviet Union and the Middle East: A Documentary Record of Afghanistan, Iran and Turkey, 1917–1985* (Princeton, N.J., 1985).

DRAPER, THEODORE. *American Communism and Soviet Russia* (New York, 1960).

EUDIN, X., and H. FISHER, eds. *Soviet Russia and the West, 1920–1927* (Stanford, Calif., 1957).

———, and R. NORTH, eds. *Soviet Russia and the East, 1920–27* (Stanford, Calif., 1957).

————, and R. SLUSSER, eds. *Soviet Foreign Policy, 1928–1934,* 2 vols. (University Park, Pa., 1966–1967).

FILENE, PETER G. *Americans and the Soviet Experiment, 1917–1933* (Cambridge, Mass., 1967).

FISCHER, LOUIS. *Russia's Road from War to Peace* . . . (New York, 1969).

————. *The Soviets in World Affairs* . . . *1917–1929,* 2d ed. (New York, 1960).

FISCHER, RUTH. *Stalin and German Communism* (Cambridge, Mass., 1948).

FREUND, GERALD. *Unholy Alliance: Russo-German Relations from the Treaty of Brest-Litovsk to the Treaty of Berlin* (New York, 1957).

GARRISON, MARK, and A. GLEASON, eds. *Shared Destiny: Fifty Years of Soviet-American Relations* (Boston, 1985).

GROMYKO, A. A., and B. N. PONOMAREV. *Soviet Foreign Policy, 1917–80,* 2 vols. (Moscow, 1981).

HASLAM, J. *Soviet Foreign Policy, 1930–33: The Impact of the Depression* (New York, 1983).

HILGER, GUSTAV, and ALFRED G. MEYER. *The Incompatible Allies: A Memoir History of German-Soviet Relations 1918–1941* (New York, 1953).

HULSE, JAMES W. *The Forming of the Communist International* (Stanford, Calif., 1964).

ISAACS, HAROLD R. *The Tragedy of the Chinese Revolution,* rev. ed. (Stanford, Calif., 1951).

KENNAN, G. F. *Russia and the West Under Lenin and Stalin* (Boston, 1960).

KOCHAN, L. *Russia and the Weimar Republic* (Cambridge, Eng., 1978).

McKENZIE, KERMIT E. *Comintern and the World Revolution, 1928–1943* . . . (New York, 1964).

McLANE, CHARLES B. *Soviet Policy and the Chinese Communists, 1931–1946* (New York, 1958).

MOSELY, P. E. *The Kremlin and World Politics* (New York, 1961).

PONOMARYOV, BORIS. *History of Soviet Foreign Policy, 1917–45* (Ontario, 1970).

RUBINSTEIN, A. Z., ed., *The Foreign Policy of the Soviet Union* (New York, 1972).

SONTAG, R. J., and J. BEDDIE, eds. *Nazi-Soviet Relations* (Washington, D.C., 1948).

TANG, PETER S. *Russia and the Soviet Policy in Manchuria, 1911–1931* (Durham, N.C., 1959).

TUCKER, R. C. "The Emergence of Stalin's Foreign Policy," *Slavic Review, 36* (December 1977), pp. 563–589.

ULAM, ADAM. *Expansion and Coexistence* . . . *1917–1973,* 2d ed. (New York, 1974).

ULDRICKS, T. J. *Diplomacy and Ideology: The Origins of Soviet Foreign Relations, 1917–1930* (London, 1980).

WEINBERG, G. *Germany and the Soviet Union, 1939–41* (New York, 1972).

WHITE, STEPHEN. *The Origins of Detente: The Genoa Conference and Soviet-Western Relations, 1921–1922* (London and New York, 1985).

ZENKOVSKY, SERGE A. *Pan-Turkism and Islam in Russia* (Cambridge, Mass., 1960).

CHAPTER FIFTEEN

WAR AND RECONSTRUCTION, 1941–1953

Between 1941 and 1945, the USSR fought the greatest war in Russian history. Despite poor military preparation and massive popular hostility to the Stalin regime, Soviet Russia eventually defeated the Nazi invasion, and the Red Army advanced triumphantly into central Europe. The USSR was joined by Britain and the United States, but Soviet relations with the West were complicated by suspicion and differences over strategy and war aims. The Soviet role in World War II and Stalin as wartime leader remain controversial (see Chapter 16, Problem 7): Was Soviet Russia caught by surprise in 1941 and, if so, why? Why did the Red Army suffer terrible early defeats, then recover and defeat Germany? How important was Allied aid in the Soviet victory, and how great were the respective Soviet and Western roles in defeating Germany and Japan?

When the war ended, Stalin reimposed tight controls over a Soviet people yearning for liberalization and relaxation. Reindoctrinating or imprisoning millions exposed to Western influences during the war, he again isolated the USSR and blamed the West for domestic hardships.

Heavy industry was stressed again at the consumer's expense, but reconstruction was rapid, and the USSR soon produced atomic and hydrogen weapons. Soviet Russia achieved dominance over eastern Europe, except for Yugoslavia, which escaped Stalin's grasp in 1948. Soviet expansion and Western resistance produced the Cold War between the two superpowers, and in Asia Communist China emerged as a huge Soviet ally. How did postwar Stalinism compare with the prewar regime? How and why did the Soviet Union win control of eastern Europe? Was Stalin mainly responsible for the Cold War?

INVASION

At dawn on June 22, 1941, more than 3 million German and auxiliary troops from Nazi-controlled Europe crossed the Soviet frontier on a 2,000-mile front. Their unprovoked attack inaugurated what the Soviets called "the great fatherland war," the greatest land conflict in world history, and a struggle that tested the Soviet regime and people to the limit. Despite accurate warnings from Soviet spies (such as Richard Sorge in Tokyo) and foreign intelligence of impending German attack, the Nazis achieved complete tactical surprise. At first, uncertain whether it was invasion or a provocation, Moscow ordered Soviet troops to remain passive. Apparently Stalin believed that Hitler would not attack if the USSR fulfilled its commitments under the Nazi-Soviet Pact. Finally, at noon on June 22, eight hours after the Nazis attacked, Deputy Premier Molotov informed the Soviet people of the German assault. Stalin, in a state of shock, remained in seclusion for several days at his dacha outside Moscow. When Ambassador Schulenburg delivered the German declaration of war, Foreign Minister Molotov queried: "Do you believe that we deserved this?"

Hitler's aim in Operation Barbarossa was to crush the "barbarian" USSR by crippling the Red Army in encirclements near the frontier, then to advance to the Archangel-Astrakhan line. Moscow, Leningrad, and most of European Russia would be occupied, and Russian remnants expelled into Asia. Nazi Germany would obtain sufficient oil, grain, and manpower to dominate Europe and defeat England. Hitler and his commanders were confident that this could be achieved before winter.

At first, Nazi victories exceeded even Hitler's expectations. Soviet frontier forces were overwhelmed and hundreds of planes destroyed on the ground as Soviet soldiers and civilians were stunned by the suddenness and power of the German onslaught. In four weeks General Heinz Guderian's tank forces pierced to Smolensk, only 225 miles from Moscow, while the northern armies sliced through the Baltic states toward Leningrad. Hundreds of thousands of demoralized Soviet troops surrendered; border populations in eastern Poland, the Baltic states, and the Ukraine welcomed the Germans with bread and salt as liberators from Stalinist tyranny.

Overconfidence and fanaticism caused Hitler and his associates to overlook or fumble golden military and political opportunities. On July 19, Hitler rejected Guderian's plea for an immediate strike against Moscow, ordering him instead against Kiev. That operation netted more than 600,000 Soviet prisoners, but produced fatal delay in assaulting Moscow, the key to Soviet power, which was very vulnerable in the fall of 1941. By October, the Germans had occupied most of the Ukraine and surrounded Leningrad, but Red Army resistance was stiffening. Guderian was now unleashed, and by early December reached Moscow's outskirts, but an early winter, lack of warm clothing and tracked vehicles, and major Siberian reinforcements stalled his advance. The year 1941 ended with a Soviet counteroffensive that drove the Nazis back from Moscow, opened a relief route into Leningrad, and recaptured Rostov in the south. (See Map 15.1.) Hitler's attempt to achieve quick victory in Russia had failed.

The Germans wasted unique chances to overturn Stalin's regime. Nazi agencies in Russia pursued conflicting policies. Many German army leaders and foreign officials sought Russian popular support, but Nazi party and SS elements treated the people as subhumans, exterminating or exploiting even those ready to cooperate with Germany. Alfred Rosenberg's Ministry for the East favored autonomous German-controlled satellite states in non-Russian borderlands, but Goering's economic agencies grabbed their resources for Germany. No single course was implemented consistently, but German eastern policy (*Ostpolitik*) was brutal and inefficient. The Nazis aimed to colonize choice areas with Germans and exploit Soviet resources, but they achieved remarkably little. Occupying some 400,000 square miles of Soviet territory with 65 million people and rich grain areas, the Germans obtained only a fraction of what they secured from France or from Nazi-Soviet trade agreements. Incompetent and corrupt German officials, who flooded the USSR like carpetbaggers, contributed to this economic failure as they disregarded popular aspirations for religious freedom, self-government, and decollectivization. Himmler's extermination detachments liquidated not just Bolsheviks but also thousands of innocent men, women, and children.

Why the initial Soviet collapse followed by recovery? Stalinists blamed setbacks on the Nazi surprise attack and credited recovery to a loyal populace that rallied to the motherland. Later, Khrushchev blamed early defeats mainly on Stalin's deafness to warnings of attack and inefficiency in using the breathing spell of the Nazi-Soviet Pact. In the West many

MAP 15.1 *USSR in World War II*

Axis and occupied areas
June 22, 1941

.... 1938 boundaries

▬▬▬ Russian boundary, 1941

Front lines in Russia

—·—· 1941 —··—· 1942

—···—· 1943 —····—· 1944

◀━━ **Russian and allied drives 1941–1945**

Source: Adapted from *A History of Russia, Second Edition* by Nicholas V. Riasanovsky.
Copyright © 1969 by Oxford University Press, Inc. Used by permission.

attributed Soviet collapse to a revolt of the borderlands and Soviet recovery mainly to Nazi brutality. The American political scientist George Fischer suggested that Stalin's initial paralysis of will had left an army and population used to dictation without instructions; once he reasserted leadership, the Soviet people again obeyed the regime.

By the end of 1941, the Soviet leadership had regained widespread public support. After two weeks of silence and seclusion (some reports claim he suffered a near nervous breakdown), Stalin appealed to the Soviet people by radio for national resistance to an invader seeking to turn them into "the slaves of German princes and barons" and restore the tsar and the landlords. A scorched earth policy must deny the Germans factories, food, and material. Stalin's call for guerrilla warfare behind German lines was reinforced by skillful patriotic propaganda. Soon forests in the German rear were infested with partisans who tied down many German troops and disrupted communications. A State Committee for Defense, headed by Stalin and including Molotov, Voroshilov, Beria, and Malenkov, became a war cabinet. As de facto commander in chief, Stalin concentrated military and political leadership in his own hands. In that capacity he made many arbitrary and harmful military decisions, often interfering in tactical matters, about which he knew little. Stalin's mistakes apparently contributed to major Red Army defeats, especially in the initial Nazi advance in 1941, yet his decision to remain in threatened Moscow in October 1941 halted panic provoked by the movement of diplomats and government offices to Kuibyshev on the Volga. If Stalin is partially to blame for early Soviet defeats, he deserves some credit for the Red Army's outstanding victories during 1944–1945.[1] His wartime leadership remains controversial.

The Grand Alliance—Britain, the USSR, the United States, and later France—formed against the Nazis and their allies in 1941 sent significant aid to the USSR. The day after the invasion Prime Minister Churchill of England offered the USSR friendship and military aid, while refusing to recant his earlier attacks on Bolshevism. After President Roosevelt's adviser Harry Hopkins went to Moscow in July, the United States began Lend-Lease assistance to Russia, which totaled some 15 million tons of supplies worth over $11 billion. Anglo-American aid contributed to the Soviet repulse of German attacks in 1942 and proved indispensable in subsequent Soviet counteroffensives. Japan's attack on Pearl Harbor in December 1941 brought the United States into the European war as well.

---

[1] A. Seaton, *Stalin as Military Commander* (New York, 1976), p. 271.

THE 1942 CAMPAIGN—THE TURNING POINT

In 1941, German losses had been so heavy that in 1942 Hitler's offensive had to be more limited. The Nazis still retained the potential to reach the Archangel-Astrakhan line and knock out the USSR, but Hitler removed most of his high command and interfered frequently in military decisions with disastrous results. Instead of trying to envelop and capture Moscow, he sought economic and psychological objectives: seizing the Caucasus oil fields and Stalingrad on the Volga.

In June, the Germans broke through the Don front, but Soviet resistance at Voronezh prevented an advance to the mid-Volga. Nazi armies rolled east, then southward into the Caucasus, but were halted short of the main oil fields. Stalingrad became the focus and symbol of the entire Soviet-German war. In bitter street fighting during August and September, Stalingrad was virtually reduced to rubble. Despite brave Soviet resistance, General von Paulus's Sixth Army captured most of the city, but his army was bled white in frontal assaults instead of crossing the Volga and encircling the city. Heroic Soviet defense, Siberian reinforcements, and U.S. equipment turned the tide. In November, a massive Soviet counteroffensive broke through Romanian and Italian lines on the exposed northern German flank and cut off the entire Sixth Army. After relief efforts failed, von Paulus and the hungry remnants of his army surrendered. Here was the psychological and perhaps military turning point of the Soviet-German war. After Stalingrad, the Nazis were mostly on the defensive and ultimate Allied victory in World War II became a matter of time and blood.

In 1942, the Nazis again neglected a major political weapon. In July, Lieutenant General Andrei Vlasov, an able Soviet commander, surrendered with his men and agreed to help Germany achieve a free, non-Bolshevik Russia. He denounced the Soviet regime, collective farms, and Stalin's mass murders. Some on the German General Staff wished to use him and several million Soviet war prisoners against Stalin. Named head of a Russian National Committee, Vlasov sought to form an army of liberation (ROA), but Hitler blocked its use until German defeat was inevitable. The Germans employed more than a million Soviet volunteers as cooks, drivers, and orderlies, but not in combat.

To counter an appalling desertion rate, Stalin appealed to Russian traditions and completed a reconciliation with the Orthodox Church. Soviet soldiers were told to serve the fatherland without socialist obligations. The army restored ranks, saluting, insignia, and officer privileges reminiscent of tsarist times, and the regime's tone became strongly nationalist. At the 25th anniversary of the Bolshevik Revolution (November 1942), Soviet leaders, instead of calling for world revolution, stressed

Slav solidarity. To convince the West that the USSR had abandoned world revolution, Stalin abolished the Comintern in 1943 and rewarded the loyal Orthodox hierarchy by restoring the patriarchate under state supervision. A church synod unanimously elected Metropolitan Sergei patriarch in September 1943; Sergei then proclaimed Stalin "the divinely anointed." These moves promoted unity and countered German efforts to foment disloyalty, but did not signify changes in Stalin's domestic or foreign aims.

Inter-Allied relations remained good in 1942 primarily because the USSR badly needed Lend-Lease supplies. Even then, friction developed over a second front and over Poland. Throughout 1942, Stalin pressed for a cross-Channel invasion; he was only partially mollified by the Allied invasion of North Africa in November. Stalin sought Western recognition of the USSR's June 1941 frontiers, but England and the United States, though making concessions, refused to sanction Soviet annexation of eastern Poland and the Baltic states.

SOVIET OFFENSIVES AND ALLIED VICTORY, 1943–1945

After Stalingrad, with brief exceptions, Soviet armies were on the offensive everywhere and bore the heaviest military burden until victory was achieved. After the defeat of a German offensive at Kursk in July 1943, producing the greatest tank battle in history, the Red Army attacked, jabbing ceaselessly at various points. U.S. tanks, trucks, and planes ensured the success of the Soviet drive westward by making the Red Army highly mobile. The Red Army's numerical superiority grew steadily. By the summer of 1944, the Germans were outnumbered about three to one, and the Soviets commanded the skies and used their artillery effectively. Named chief of the Soviet General Staff in 1941, Marshal Georgii Zhukov led the defense of Moscow later that year, and also directed the great Soviet counteroffensive of 1943–1945. His U.S. counterpart was General Dwight Eisenhower. The Germans could merely delay the Soviet advance and hope to exploit Allied divergences.

Once the Allies were advancing everywhere, their relations cooled. Both the Soviets and West feared that the other might make a separate peace, though there is little evidence that either planned to do so. As Soviet armies advanced, Stalin's attitude hardened as he sought to dominate eastern Europe and Germany. The Western allies, still sensitive in 1943 over the absence of a true second front, proved vulnerable to Stalin's diplomacy. Hitherto Soviet war aims had been defensive: to preserve Soviet frontiers, the Communist system, and Stalin's total control. Now Stalin sought also the Carpatho-Ukraine from Czechoslovakia to forestall Ukrainian disaffection. The USSR joined in the formation of the United Nations in 1942 and approved its high-sounding declarations, but Stalin never accepted Western democratic aims. He refused to alter his views or make major concessions to his partners. Stalin realized that the surest way to achieve his aims was to advance westward as far as possible, then secure what he wanted from the West. Stalin and Molotov, notes George Kennan, played their cards skillfully and carefully while the Western allies, holding a stronger hand, remained confused, divided, and unrealistic and let the Soviets score large gains.

Poland was the stickiest issue in inter-Allied relations. Early in 1943, the Germans discovered the corpses of thousands of Polish officers in the Katyn Forest near Smolensk. The Soviets accused the Nazis of the murders, but evidence is strong that Soviet security forces had killed the Poles in 1940.* Assertions of this by the Polish government in exile in London induced Stalin to sever relations with them. At Teheran in November 1943, Churchill proposed the Curzon Line of 1920 as Poland's eastern frontier, with Poland to be compensated in the west at German expense. Stalin promptly agreed and suggested the Oder-Neisse Line as the western boundary. Poland's drastic shift westward would make it dependent on Soviet favor. Churchill finally persuaded the London Poles to accept this bargain; but when their new leader, Stanislas Mikolajczyk, went to Moscow in July, the USSR had already recognized the Communist-dominated Lublin Committee political group in Poland and turned over to it liberated Polish territory. Because the Western allies took no firm stand, Mikolajczyk was powerless. In August 1944, with the Red Army in Praga, across the Vistula River from Warsaw, Poles aligned with the London exiles rose against the Nazis: General Bor's men fought heroically, but the Soviet army did not aid them. Once the Germans had destroyed this core of potential opposition to a Soviet-dominated Poland, the Red Army drove the Nazis from Warsaw.

The second front issue caused serious inter-Allied friction until the Normandy invasion of June 1944. At the Moscow foreign ministers' conference (October 1943), the Soviets sought a definite Western pledge to invade France by the next spring. At the Teheran Conference in November, Churchill's idea of invading the Balkans, partly to prevent Soviet control there, was blocked by Stalin, whose support of Overlord, the American plan to invade France, ensured its adoption. The Normandy invasion relieved Soviet fears of a Nazi-Western separate peace and speeded the end of the war. Later, Soviet historians claimed that Normandy was invaded to prevent a Soviet sweep to the Atlantic but had contributed little to Germany's defeat.

---

*In 1990, the Soviet Union admitted responsibility for the Katyn Forest Massacre.

Churchill, Roosevelt, and Stalin at Yalta, February 1945 *(United Press International)*

As Soviet forces advanced through Poland and the Balkans, Churchill sought to delimit postwar spheres of influence, a proposal Roosevelt repudiated as immoral. In October 1944, Churchill proposed a numerical formula for influence in eastern Europe: 90 percent Soviet influence in Romania and Bulgaria and similar British control in Greece; Yugoslavia and Hungary would be split 50–50. Such formulas, however, meant little: The USSR could gain total control in its sphere by military occupation.

In February 1945, with Allied armies at the border of or inside Germany, the Big Three met at Yalta in the Crimea to outline a postwar settlement. Because the Red Army controlled most of Poland, only united and determined Western action might have salvaged some Polish independence. The West (especially Roosevelt), however, wished to continue cooperation with the USSR after the war. In regard to Polish frontiers, Stalin insisted on the Curzon Line, overcoming halfhearted Western efforts to obtain Lvov and the Galician oil fields for Poland. In the west, Poland was to administer the region to the Oder-Neisse Line until the peace conference, and more than 7 million German residents were expelled. Stalin insisted that the West repudiate the London Poles and recognize the Soviet-controlled Lublin Committee as the core of a new Polish government; the West proposed a wholly new regime formed from all political parties. Finally, the Allies agreed to broaden the Soviet-dominated Polish provisional government and hold "free and unfettered elections" as soon as possible, but Stalin secured his basic aim: a Soviet-dominated Poland. Germany was to be de-Nazified, demilitarized, and occupied, and France was to receive an occupation zone from the Western share. The USSR would obtain half of a suggested total of $20 billion in German reparations. The Allies also agreed on voting in the United Nations and, by secret protocols, to Soviet entry into the Far Eastern war. Soviet gains at Yalta resulted from a strong military position, shrewd bargaining, and Western uncertainty.

After Yalta, Allied armies advanced swiftly. The Red Army overran Hungary, much of Austria, and crossed the Oder River. The Americans surged across the Rhine, and as Nazi resistance collapsed, the British urged them to occupy Berlin. General Eisenhower, however, halted at the Elbe River, then turned south to destroy the reputed German fortress in Bavaria. On April 17, Marshal Zhukov began his final offensive against Berlin, and on the 25th Soviet and American forces joined on the Elbe. While the Red Army was storming Berlin, Hitler committed suicide, and on May 8, 1945, his successors surrendered unconditionally.

THE USSR AND THE FAR EASTERN WAR

The United States had long sought Soviet participation in the war against Japan, but until victory in Europe was in sight, Stalin avoided the issue. Japanese neutrality in the German-Soviet war had permitted him to bring in Siberian troops to stop the Germans at Moscow and Stalingrad. Late in 1943, Stalin hinted to the United States that the USSR would enter the Pacific conflict soon after Germany's defeat. At Teheran, Roosevelt assured Stalin that Russia could recover territories lost in the Russo-Japanese War. U.S. military chiefs estimated before Yalta that without Soviet participation, it would take the United States 18 months and cost up to a million casualties to subdue Japan after Germany's surrender. Consequently, at Yalta to ensure Soviet entry into the war aganst Japan, Roosevelt accepted Stalin's demands for territory and spheres of interest in China and agreed to secure Chiang Kai-shek's consent to them.

On August 8, 1945, two days after the American atomic attack on Hiroshima, the USSR declared war on Japan. Justifying his action, Stalin cited somewhat lamely the "treacherous Japanese attack" in 1904 and the "blemish on the tradition of our country" left by Russia's defeat. "For 40 years we, the men of the older generation, have waited for this day." Stalin omitted to mention that in 1904 Russian Social Democrats had encouraged the Japanese to beat Russia quickly and later had celebrated Russia's defeat! Large Soviet forces overwhelmed the Japanese in Manchuria, continuing operations even after Japan's surrender on August 14. Soviet accounts claim that the Red Army's invasion of Manchuria, not the atomic bomb, caused Japan's surrender and brought the subsequent victory to the Chinese Communists. For one week's participation in the fighting, the USSR was rewarded generously: It recovered southern Sakhalin, Port Arthur, Dairen, and the Manchurian railways, secured all the Kurile Islands, and occupied North Korea. General MacArthur, however, rejected Soviet demands for an occupation zone in Japan.

The USSR's balance sheet in World War II revealed some gains in territory and population at enormous human and material cost. About 265,000 square miles of territory with some 23.5 million people were annexed forcibly to the Soviet Union of 1939: the Baltic states, eastern Poland, Bessarabia, northern Bukovina, eastern Karelia, the Carpatho-Ukraine, northern East Prussia, and the Kurile Islands. Estimates of Soviet war deaths range from 20 to 27 million, about half civilians.[2] By contrast, German casualties were about one third as great; U.S. losses of 295,000 were 72 times less! The Soviets suffered about 38 percent of all fatalities caused by World War II partly because the massive conflict was fought over their territory for three and one-half years, during which the invading Nazis sought deliberately to annihilate Jews and enslave other nationalities. The criminal negligence of its political and military leaders increased Soviet losses. At Stalin's orders Soviet commanders often sought to win battles at any cost, sending many soldiers to needless slaughter. Mass civilian starvation, notably in besieged Leningrad, and Stalin's deportation of over a million people from the Crimea and Caucasus led to additional deaths.[3] The Nazi invaders caused colossal material damage: They destroyed 1,710 towns and working settlements and over 70,000 villages, leaving 25 million Soviet citizens homeless; they wrecked some 32,000 industrial plants and tore up over 40,000 miles of railway.[4] At war's end western European Russia was devastated. The country emerged from the conflict depleted in manpower and its economy a shambles. Is it any wonder that the Soviet people long retained a pervasive fear of war?

---

[2]According to N. S. Khrushchev in 1961, Soviet deaths equalled 10 million soldiers and 10 million civilians. Soviet figures from 1973 (*Istoriia SSSR*, Moscow, 1973, vol. 10, p. 390) for the European republics listed as "killed and tortured to death" 6,844,551 civilians and 3,932,256 war prisoners. Western historians have come up with a total of 21.3 million— 13.6 million soldiers and 7.7 million civilians killed, or 11 percent of the Soviet population in 1941.

[3]Mikhail Heller and Alexander Nekrich, *Utopia in Power: The History of the Soviet Union from 1917 to the Present* (New York, 1982), pp. 443–444.

[4]*Istoriia SSSR* (Moscow, 1973), vol. 10, p. 390.

POSTWAR STALINISM

Domestic Affairs

As World War II ended, the exhausted Soviet people hoped for liberal change, freedom, and well-being. Instead Stalin restored total control, resumed rapid industrialization, and isolated the USSR from the West. After the brief euphoria of victory celebrations, Stalin reimposed terror and party dominance, concealing rather successfully from the West signs of mass discontent revealed early in the war.

At war's end some 5 million Soviet citizens were outside Soviet borders. At Yalta the Allies agreed to help one another bring home those of their citizens living abroad. About 3 million Soviet war prisoners, forced laborers, and defectors resided in areas under Western control, mostly Germany, and about 2 million in Soviet-occupied regions, who were nearly all recovered. Until 1947, Western authorities cooperated by urging or forcing (as with General Vlasov) Soviet citizens to return home. In displaced persons camps, U.S. troops forced many to leave with Soviet officials. Western leaders believed naively that with the war over, all but traitors and criminals would happily return home. About half a million "nonreturnables" stayed in the West by claiming they were Baltic or Polish nationals or by melting into the populace of disorganized Germany. The formerly pro-Soviet American journalist Louis Fischer noted that when Soviet Russians had a choice, they "voted against the Bolshevik dictatorship with their feet." Others committed suicide or redefected on the way to the USSR. Between 1945 and 1948, some 20,000 Soviet soldiers and officers defected from occupation forces, though until 1947 they were usually turned over to the Soviets for execution by their units. By 1948, Western cooperation ceased, but so did most opportunities to defect.

Returning Soviet soldiers and civilians, having seen Europe at first hand, confronted Stalin with a massive "debriefing" problem comparable with that of the tsarist regime after the Napoleonic Wars. Both governments solved it by repression and cutting ties with Europe, not with needed reforms. Isolation was essential for Stalin because Soviet living standards had fallen sharply while Russia's productive capacity had grown. His regime could not admit failure to produce abundance. Refusing economic dependence upon the West, Stalin found an alternative in quarantining his people. Thus, Stalin exiled many returning POWs to Siberia and other distant regions.

Even before the war ended, a campaign began against the supposedly decaying "bourgeois" West. Closed party meetings learned: "The war on Fascism ends, the war on capitalism begins" anew. Stalin's victory toast to the Russian people began the glorification of everything Russian while minimizing or ignoring debts to the West. In a February 1946 speech, Stalin reaffirmed that while capitalism survived, war was inevitable; he revived the bogey of capitalist encirclement to justify internal repression and economic sacrifice. In 1946, the _Zhdanovshchina_ began, an ideological campaign associated with Andrei Zhdanov, Leningrad party chief, who emerged during the war as heir apparent to Stalin. (See Chapter 10.) Zhdanov, who had proclaimed socialist realism _the_ acceptable art form in 1934, urged a struggle against foreign influences in Soviet life that amounted to ideological war with the West in order to demonstrate socialism's cultural superiority. "Our role . . . is to attack bourgeois culture, which is in a state of miasma and corruption." Soviet intellectuals were denounced for subservience to Western influence or using Western themes or sources. The economist Eugene Varga was castigated for doubting there would be a postwar depression in the United States. Zhdanov's campaign, demanding absolute conformity to party dictates, stifled Soviet intellectual development.

Stalin's assertions of Russian achievement reached absurd extremes. Russian or Soviet scientists were credited with almost every major scientific discovery of modern times. The desire to prove Russian self-reliance reflected a persistent Russian inferiority complex toward the West. In 1950, Stalin, attacking the late N. Marr's linguistic theories, suggested that in the socialist future a single superior language, presumably Russian, would prevail. As in the 1930s, T. D. Lysenko, an obscure plant breeder, was encouraged to denounce Western genetic theories and Soviet scientists who accepted them. (See p. 284.) Stalin combined xenophobic Russian nationalism and anti-Semitism: Jews were "homeless bourgeois cosmopolitans." Connected with Israel's emergence as a state and the desire of Soviet Jews to emigrate there, this campaign featured ugly anti-Semitic cartoons and severe persecution, though certain prominent Jews such as Lazar Kaganovich and the writer Ilia Ehrenburg were spared to "prove" that the regime was not anti-Semitic.

Soviet economic problems in 1945 were staggering. About one quarter of the nation's capital resources had been destroyed, including some two thirds in Nazi-occupied regions. Industrial and agricultural outputs were far below prewar levels; railroads were damaged or disrupted. United Nations relief and British and Swedish credits aided reconstruction, as did reparations from Germany and former Axis satellites such as Finland. Newly sovietized eastern Europe had to supply minerals, foodstuffs, and machinery, and German war prisoners helped rebuild devastated cities. Without major U.S. credits, which Stalin had hoped for, however, the reconstruction burden fell largely on the Soviet people. The Fourth Five Year Plan, stressing heavy industry and mineral production, aimed at complete rebuilding and at exceeding prewar levels in industry and agriculture. Prewar "storming" and rigid labor discipline were revived; slave labor controlled by the NKVD was used extensively. Heavy investment in construction sought to overcome a catastrophic urban housing shortage. In heavy industry the Plan was largely fulfilled, although spectacular industrial growth rates partly reflected restoration of existing capacity in western Russia. Over half the 2,500 industrial plants shifted eastward during the war remained there, heightening the importance of new Siberian industrial areas. Consumer production and agriculture, however, lagged seriously, and during Stalin's lifetime Soviet living standards remained among the lowest in Europe.

With drought and severe shortages of livestock plaguing agricultural recovery, food rationing continued until December 1947. Wartime peasant encroachments on collective farms were ended, and Khrushchev vigorously recollectivized the western Ukraine. By 1950, the 250,000 prewar collectives had been amalgamated into about 125,000, but Khrushchev's ambitious scheme to build agricultural cities (*agrogoroda*) with peasants living in massive housing projects foundered on peasant opposition and lack of funds. In 1948, in the eastern Ukraine, Stalin inaugurated a giant afforestation program, called modestly his "plan to transform nature," to stop drought and sandstorms, but it achieved little. Stalin continued to neglect agriculture as, ensconced in the Kremlin, he apparently believed stories of agricultural prosperity related by fearful subordinates. Meanwhile, collective farmers remained miserably poor and lacked incentives to produce.

Nonetheless, Stalin's draconian policies brought major heavy industrial growth and some agricultural recovery. By 1953, the USSR, the world's second greatest industrial power, was moving toward Stalin's seemingly fantastic 1960 goals of 60 million tons of steel, 500 million metric tons of coal, and 60 million metric tons of oil.

Foreign Affairs

In the first postwar years, the USSR greatly expanded its influence in Europe and Asia. Stalin, despite a U.S. atomic monopoly until 1949, built a bloc of satellite states in eastern Europe and promoted Communist victories in China, North Korea, and North Vietnam. His blustering tone and actions, however, then caused the West to rearm and ended opportunities for advances. Soviet expansion clashed with U.S. containment to produce the Cold War.

Between 1945 and 1948, the Soviet Union established complete control over eastern Europe. According to Soviet accounts, Communist states there emerged from native revolutions against exploitative landlords and capitalists. To construct a security shield against a German resurgence or possible Western action, Stalin ensured control in eastern European countries by "progressive elements," that is, pro-Soviet regimes. Stalin wished to use these countries' resources to rebuild the Soviet economy and their territory to influence events in central Europe.

Soviet methods of achieving control varied, but the general pattern was similar, except in Yugoslavia where Marshal Tito won power independently. Red Army occupation was the first step, except in Czechoslovakia and Yugoslavia. National Communist parties, decimated during the war, were rebuilt and staffed mainly with Soviet-trained leaders subservient to Moscow. Usually, the Soviets secured key levers of power for Communists—the army, police, and information media. Then coalition governments were formed from all "democratic, anti-Fascist" parties. With NKVD aid, political opposition was intimidated, disorganized, and fragmented. Conservative parties, accused (often falsely) of collaborating with the Nazis, were banned while socialist parties were split, then merged forcibly with the Communists. Resulting socialist unity parties allowed Communists to control the working class movement. Elections were often delayed until the Communists and their allies were assured of victory.

Poland, whose control was vital for Soviet domination of eastern Europe and influence in Germany, reflects these techniques clearly. Despite Yalta guarantees, Poland succumbed to Soviet domination after mild Western protests. During the war, the Nazis and Soviets had decimated its intelligentsia and officer class. Then the Red Army occupied Poland, and the Communist-dominated Lublin Committee formed the nucleus of a coalition government. Mikolajczyk and three other London Poles were included, but they were powerless against the Communists, who controlled the chief ministries and forced the socialists into a coalition. Mikolajczyk, very popular with peasants, democrats, and conservatives, probably would have won a free election, but the police intimidated members of his Peasant Party, and in the manipulated elections of 1947, the leftist bloc won and Mikolajczyk escaped into exile.

In Czechoslovakia the script was different but the results similar. It was the only eastern European country with an advanced industry and strong democratic traditions. A genuine democrat, Eduard Beneš, returned as president. At first, the Communists (and the USSR) were popular, won 38 percent of the vote in the 1946 elections, and took over several key ministries. Under Beneš, Czechoslovakia was friendly toward the USSR and sought to be a bridge between East and West, but Stalin could not tolerate a democracy on his borders. In February 1948, when democratic elements tried to force the Communist interior minister to resign, the Communists, supported by armed workers and a Red Army demonstration on the frontier, seized power and forced Beneš to resign.

Klement Gottwald established a Communist regime subservient to Moscow.

Soviet expansion in eastern Europe and tension over Germany helped produce the Cold War. In March 1945, Stalin and Roosevelt had exchanged heated notes over Poland; the Potsdam Conference in July revealed widening Soviet-Western differences. President Truman (who succeeded to the presidency after Roosevelt's death) and Foreign Minister Ernest Bevin of Britain (who replaced Churchill during the Conference) criticized Soviet policies in eastern Europe that violated the Yalta accords. Rapid deterioration of Soviet-Western relations stemmed partly from suspicion left after Western intervention in Russia in 1918–1919 and partly from deepened differences between Soviet and Western ideologies and political systems, after Stalin renewed autocracy in Russia. With the common enemy defeated, there was little to hold the USSR and the Western powers together. Stalin's xenophobia and paranoia were contributory: He considered the cessation of Lend-Lease in May 1945 and refusal of postwar American credits unfriendly acts, which they do not seem to have been. In his speech in February 1946, Stalin blamed the West for World War II and was pessimistic about prospects of future Soviet-Western friendship. Churchill's "Iron Curtain" speech at Fulton, Missouri, of March 5, 1946, cited by Western revisionist historians as having launched the Cold War, came a month later. Churchill described prophetically the Soviet domination of eastern Europe:

> From Stettin on the Baltic to Trieste on the Adriatic an iron curtain has descended across the Continent. All these famous cities and the populations around them lie in the Soviet sphere and are subject, in one form or another, not only to Soviet influence, but to a very high and increasing degree of control from Moscow.

The Iranian crisis was the first skirmish in the Cold War. During World War II, Allied troops had occupied Iran to guard supply routes to the USSR, but they were supposed to withdraw afterward. Soviet troops, however, remained in Iran ostensibly to protect the Baku oil fields while in the north the Soviets, barring Iranian troops, fostered a Communist-led movement for autonomy. Accusing the USSR of interfering in its domestic affairs, Iran appealed to the United Nations, where it received strong support from the United States and Britain. In April 1946, the Soviets, after signing an agreement with Iran for joint exploitation of its oil resources, reluctantly pledged to withdraw. Once the Red Army had left, Iran suppressed the northern separatists, and its parliament rejected the Soviet-Iranian treaty.

In the eastern Mediterranean, Soviet pressure and British weakness produced another crisis. Demanding "the return of Kars and Ardahan

(Russian from 1878 to 1918) and bases in the Turkish Straits, Stalin massed Soviet troops on Turkey's borders and conducted a war of nerves, but Turkey refused concessions. In neighboring Greece, the Soviets, Yugoslavia, and Bulgaria supported a Communist-led guerrilla movement against the conservative British-backed government. Because Roosevelt had hinted at Yalta that U.S. forces would withdraw from Europe within two years, Stalin hoped to dominate the region once Britain pulled out of Greece. To his surprise, President Truman in March 1947 pledged economic and military support to Greece and Turkey, describing the issue as a struggle between democracy and Communism. Reversing traditional U.S. isolationism, this "Truman Doctrine" began a permanent U.S. commitment to Europe. The USSR denounced it as subversive of the United Nations and a "smokescreen for expansion."

In June 1947, the U.S.-sponsored Marshall Plan for European recovery confronted Stalin with a difficult decision because all European states were invited to participate. Molotov attended preliminary meetings, and Poland and Czechoslovakia showed deep interest until Stalin abruptly recalled Molotov, forbade east European participation, and denounced the Marshall Plan as concealed American imperialism. Doing so was a serious blunder: Soviet acceptance probably would have doomed the Plan in the U.S. Congress, thus enhancing Soviet prospects of dominating western Europe. Instead, Stalin set up the Council of Mutual Economic Assistance (COMECON) as an east European equivalent. But until 1953, COMECON served largely as a device to extract resources from the satellites for the USSR.

George Kennan, a leading U.S. expert on the USSR, advocated in July long-term containment of the Soviet Union by strengthening neighboring countries until Soviet leaders abandoned designs of world domination. "For no mystical Messianic movement—and particularly not that of the Kremlin—can face frustration indefinitely, without eventually adjusting itself in one way or another to the logic of that state of affairs."[5] Kennan urged the West to adopt a patient policy of strength and await changes in Soviet conduct.

Creation of the Soviet-dominated Cominform (Communist Information Bureau) in Belgrade in September 1947, ostensibly to coordinate Communist parties of France, Italy, and eastern Europe, deepened ideological rifts with the West. At its founding congress, Zhdanov, confirming the end of Soviet-Western cooperation, described the division of international political forces into two major camps: imperialist (Western) and democratic (Soviet). Zhdanov, stating that coexistence between

---

[5]"The Sources of Soviet Conduct," *Foreign Affairs* (July 1947), pp. 575–582.

them was possible, warned that the United States had aggressive designs and was building military bases around the Soviet Union.

Soon the breach widened further. The Czech coup of February 1948 ended any Western illusions about Soviet policy in eastern Europe. Early that year the British and U.S. zones in Germany merged and a currency reform was implemented. Stalin responded in June by cutting off rail and road traffic to Berlin in order to expel the West from that city. (In 1945, the four victorious powers agreed to guarantee access to Berlin.) Some U.S. generals, such as Lucius Clay, favored forcing the blockade, but instead the United States flew in necessary supplies until Stalin lifted the siege in May 1949. Separate German regimes were soon formed: the Federal Republic in the west and the German Democratic Republic, a Soviet satellite, in the east. Alarmed and united by the Berlin crisis, the countries of western Europe and North America formed the North Atlantic Treaty Organization, a collective security system to counter huge Soviet conventional forces with European and American armies and atomic weapons.

In June 1948, Stalin's expulsion of the Yugoslav Communist Party from the Cominform opened a breach in east European communism. Previously, Tito had been a loyal Stalinist, but for Stalin his independent policies and tight control over his party and state proved intolerable. The Soviets accused the Yugoslavs of slandering the Red Army and the USSR and deviating from Marxism-Leninism. Behind the verbiage lay more fundamental conflicts: Tito, already dominant in Albania, aspired to lead a Balkan federation that would break Soviet domination. Stalin overrated Soviet power ("I will shake my little finger and there will be no more Tito. He will fall."), tried to remove Tito, and ordered his satellites to blockade Yugoslavia. But the Yugoslavs rallied behind Tito, who turned to the West for support, and danger of general war probably restrained Stalin from invading Yugoslavia. Tito developed a national communism that diverged markedly from that of the USSR in ideology, economy, and politics.

Stalin promptly purged other potential eastern European Titos. In Poland, Wladyslaw Gomulka was removed in 1949 as the party's general secretary; in other satellites there were show trials and forced confessions resembling the Soviet purges of 1937. Soviet control was ensured by an elaborate network that included Soviet troops, diplomats, secret police agents, and "joint companies" under Soviet control. Bilateral treaties enabled the USSR to exploit the satellites economically while Stalin's towering figure dominated a monolithic eastern European Bloc.

In October 1949, the Chinese Communist victory over the Nationalists created a huge Eurasian Communist Bloc of more than 1 billion people. Moscow, while aiding the Communists secretly, maintained formal ties with Chiang Kai-shek to the end. Mao Tse-tung, like Tito, had controlled a party and territory before achieving power, and China was too vast to become a satellite. In February 1950, after two months of tough bargaining in Moscow, Stalin and Mao concluded a mutual defense treaty against Japan and the United States. The USSR retained its privileges, treaty ports, and control of Outer Mongolia in return for modest amounts of economic aid, but a united Communist China would clearly be harder to control than a weak Nationalist China.

In his last years, Stalin continued a forward policy while carefully avoiding war. Soviet support for national liberation movements tied down large British and French forces in Malaya and Indochina. In June 1950, after Secretary of State Dean Acheson hinted that the United States would not defend South Korea, Stalin encouraged the Soviet-equipped North Koreans to invade it, but a prompt military response by the United States and other United Nations members prevented a Communist victory. Subsequent Chinese intervention in Korea, probably arranged by Stalin, produced a stalemate but enhanced China's independence of Moscow. The United States in 1951 concluded a separate peace with Japan, which emerged as its partner in the Pacific. Stalin's miscalculations in Asia revealed limitations of Soviet power and the fact that opportunities for expansion had vanished.

The 19th Party Congress and Stalin's Death

Stalin, in October 1952, convened the 19th Congress, the first party congress in 13 years. It approved the Fifth Five Year Plan, which featured the development of power resources, irrigation, and atomic weapons. The party now numbered more than 6 million members, but its top organs had become self-perpetuating and it had lost its proletarian character. Stalin instructed Khrushchev, former party boss of the Ukraine, to revise party statutes and carry through reform. Top party bodies were recast: A larger Presidium replaced the Politburo, and the Orgburo and Secretariat were merged. Georgi Malenkov had been Stalin's heir apparent since Zhdanov's sudden and mysterious death in 1948. Malenkov's 50th birthday in January 1952 had been celebrated with much fanfare, and he delivered the chief report at the Congress. But his position was under challenge, and before Stalin's death there was much jockeying for position within the party hierarchy.

Stalin had drawn the party line for the Congress in *Economic Problems of Socialism in the USSR*. Often considered his political testament, it discussed the transition from socialism to communism in the USSR without setting a timetable and emphasized the deepening crisis of capitalism. Stalin predicted that wars among capitalist states had become more likely than an anti-Soviet coalition. Stressing this theme at the Congress, Malenkov hinted that Soviet expansion would end temporarily while the USSR overtook the United States in military technology.

In January 1953, *Pravda* claimed that nine Kremlin doctors, six of them Jews, had hastened the deaths of high Soviet officials, including Zhdanov. This "Doctors' Plot," part of Stalin's crude anti-Semitic campaign, may have been engineered partly by Alexander Poskrebyshev, sinister head of Stalin's personal secretariat. Seemingly, it was one event in a power struggle between the nationalist former adherents of Zhdanov and the more internationally oriented faction of Malenkov and Beria, the secret police chief. The atmosphere of suspicion and fear in Moscow suggested strongly that Stalin was planning a new purge. On March 4, however, Stalin, who long had suffered from heart trouble and high blood pressure, had a massive stroke and died the next day. The Malenkov-Beria group, facing demotion or destruction at his hands, may have speeded his demise, ending a quarter century of personal dictatorship and bloody brutality unmatched in world history. But unlike Hitler, who left only ruins, Stalin bequeathed to his successors a powerful industrial state that owed much to his determination and satanic energy. Because Stalin failed to designate a successor, and the Soviet system provided no legal means to select one, a ruthless power struggle was inevitable.

Suggested Additional Reading

ANDERS, WLADYSLAW. *Hitler's Defeat in Russia* (Chicago, 1953).

ANDREYEV, CATHERINE. *Vlasov and the Russian Liberation Movement* . . . (Cambridge, Eng., 1987).

ARMSTRONG, J. A. *Soviet Partisans in World War II* (Madison, Wis., 1964).

ARONSEN, LAWRENCE, and M. KITCHEN. *The Origins of the Cold War in Comparative Perspective* . . . *1941–48* (New York, 1988).

BIALER, S. *Stalin and His Generals* . . . (New York, 1969).

BRZEZINSKI, ZBIGNIEW. *The Soviet Bloc: Unity and Conflict*, 2d ed. (Cambridge, Mass., 1961).

BUHITE, R. D. *Soviet-American Relations in Asia 1945–1954* (Norman, Okla., 1981).

CARRELL, P. *Scorched Earth: The Russian-German War, 1943–44* (Boston, 1970).

CHUIKOV, VASILI I. *The Battle for Stalingrad* (New York, 1964).

CLARK, ALAN. *Barbarossa: The Russian-German Conflict, 1941–1945* (New York, 1965).

CLEMENS, DIANE S. *Yalta* (New York, 1970).

CONQUEST, ROBERT. *The Nation Killers: Soviet Deportation of Nationalities* (New York, 1970).

COOPER, MATTHEW. *The Nazi War Against Soviet Partisans, 1941–1944* (New York, 1979).

COUNTS, GEORGE S. *The Country of the Blind: The Soviet System of Mind Control* (Westport, Conn., 1959).

CRAIG, W. *Enemy at the Gates: . . . Stalingrad* (New York, 1973).

DALLIN, A. *German Rule in Russia, 1941–45* (New York, 1957, 1980).

DALLIN, DAVID, J. *The Soviet Espionage* (New Haven, Conn., 1956).

DOUGLAS, R. *From War to Cold War 1942–48* (New York, 1981).

DMYTRYSHYN, BASIL. *Moscow and the Ukraine, 1918–1953* (New York, 1956).

DZIEWANOWSKI, M. K. *The Communist Party of Poland* (Cambridge, Mass., 1976).

ERICKSON, JOHN. *The Road to Berlin: Continuing the History of Stalin's War with Germany* (Boulder, Colo., 1983).

FEIS, H. *Churchill-Roosevelt-Stalin* (Princeton, N.J., 1957).

FISCHER, G. *Soviet Opposition to Stalin* (Cambridge, Mass., 1952).

FUGATE, B. *Operation Barbarossa* (Novato, Calif., 1984).

GALLAGHER, M. P. *The Soviet History of World War II . . .* (New York, 1963).

GOURÉ, LEON. *The Siege of Leningrad* (Stanford, Calif., 1962).

HAHN, W. G. *Postwar Soviet Politics . . . 1946–53* (Ithaca, N.Y., 1982).

HARBUTT, FRASER. *The Iron Curtain: Churchill, America, and the Origins of the Cold War* (New York and Oxford, 1986).

HERRING, G. *Aid to Russia, 1941–46 . . .* (New York, 1973).

KORIAKOV, MIKHAIL. *I'll Never Go Back; a Red Army Officer Talks,* trans. N. Wreden (New York, 1948).

KUZNETSOV, ANATOLI. *Babi Yar,* trans. D. Floyd (New York, 1970).

LIDDELL-HART, BASIL H. *The Red Army . . .* (Gloucester, Mass., 1956).

LUCAS, J. S. *War on the Eastern Front 1941–45* (New York, 1982).

LYONS, G., ed. *The Russian Version of the Second World War* (New York, 1983).

MASTNY, V. *Russia's Road to the Cold War . . .* (New York, 1979).

McCAGG, W. O. *Stalin Embattled, 1943–1948* (Detroit, 1978).

NEKRICH, A. M. *The Punished Peoples . . . ,* trans. G. Saunders (New York, 1978).

PAVLOV, DMITRI V. *Leningrad, 1941: The Blockade,* trans. J. Adams (Chicago, 1965).

PETROV, V., comp. *June 22, 1941* (Columbia, S.C., 1968).

SALISBURY, H. *The 900 Days: The Siege of Leningrad* (New York, 1969).

SEATON, A. *Stalin as Military Commander* (New York, 1976).

SHULMAN, MARSHAL. *Stalin's Foreign Policy Reappraised* (Cambridge, Mass., 1963).

SIMONOV, K. *Days and Nights* (New York, 1945). (Novel on Stalingrad.)

SNELL, J., ed. *The Meaning of Yalta* (Baton Rouge, La., 1956).

STEENBERG, S. *Vlasov* (New York, 1970).

VITUKHIN, I., ed. *Soviet Generals Recall World War II* (New York, 1981).

WERTH, A. *Russia at War, 1941–45* (New York, 1964, 1984).

ZAWODNY, J. K. *Death in the Forest: . . . the Katyn Forest Massacre* (Notre Dame, Ind., 1980).

————. *Nothing But Honour: The Story of the Warsaw Uprising, 1944* (Stanford, Calif., 1978).

ZHUKOV, G. E. *Marshal Zhukov's Greatest Battles* (New York, 1969).

ZINNER, PAUL. *Communist Strategy and Tactics in Czechoslovakia, 1918–1948* (New York, 1963).

CHAPTER SIXTEEN

THE KHRUSHCHEV ERA, 1953-1964

Stalin's death in March 1953 touched off a power struggle involving the major forces in the Soviet system: the party, the state, the army, and the police. As Stalin's successors tried new methods of rule and sought public support, controls over the USSR and eastern Europe were relaxed considerably. Nikita S. Khrushchev (1894–1971), the eventual winner, lacked Stalin's absolute authority and wooed the public by denouncing Stalin's crimes, improving living standards, and barnstorming around the country. Khrushchev retained the chief features of the Soviet system, but he instituted important changes. Abroad, revolts in Poland and Hungary loosened Soviet control over the satellites. Between the USSR and Communist China ideological and political conflict erupted, which produced a Communist world with several power centers and varying approaches. How and why did Khrushchev win the power struggle in the USSR? How great was his authority afterward? Why did he institute de-Stalinization, and what were its effects? How fundamental were differences between Khrushchev's Russia and Stalin's? How did the Soviet position in world affairs change under Khrushchev?

Stalin's coffin being carried out of the House of Trade Unions in March 1953. Right to left: L. Beria, G. Malenkov, Vassily Stalin (J. Stalin's son), V. Molotov, Marshal Bulganin, L. Kaganovich, and N. Shvernik. *(SOVFOTO)*

POLITICS: REPUDIATING STALINISM

After Stalin's death the principle of collective leadership revived, and individual dictatorship was repudiated. As Stalin was placed in the Lenin-Stalin Mausoleum, his chief pallbearers—Georgi Malenkov, Lavrenti Beria, and V. M. Molotov—appealed to the populace for unity and to avoid "confusion and panic." Briefly Malenkov held the two chief power positions of premier and first party secretary, but within two weeks he resigned as first secretary, and in September Khrushchev assumed that post. Marshal Zhukov, the World War II hero, became deputy defense minister as genuine collective rule and surface harmony prevailed.

In April 1953, *Pravda* announced that the "Doctors' Plot" had been a hoax. There was a shake-up in the secret police, and its chief, Beria, suddenly posed as a defender of "socialist legality" and urged liberal revisions of the criminal code. In June, his security forces apparently tried a coup, but party, state, and army leaders combined against him. Beria was arrested and may have been shot in the Kremlin by Marshal Zhukov. In December, his "execution" was announced, and he became an "unperson." Subscribers to the *Great Soviet Encyclopedia* were instructed to remove his biography, and paste in an enclosed article on the Bering Sea! The secret police came under closer party control.

For the rest of 1953, the Soviet press featured a jovial-looking Malenkov as the principal leader, who stressed consumer goods production and pledged that Soviet living standards would soon rise markedly. *Izvestiia*, the government newspaper, pushed this proconsumer line until December 1954, but *Pravda*, the party organ controlled by Khrushchev, denounced it as "a belching of the Right deviation . . . , views which Rykov, Bukharin, and their ilk once preached." (And they had been executed!) In February 1955, Malenkov resigned as premier, citing "inexperience" and accepting blame for agricultural failures. Marshal N. A. Bulganin, a political general and Khrushchev appointee, replaced him as premier.

Khrushchev, like Stalin, consolidated his power behind the scenes. A genuine man of the people, he epitomized the revolutionary principle: careers open to talent. Khrushchev was born in Kalinovka, a village in Kursk province near the Ukrainian border; his ancestors were serfs, his father a peasant, then a coal miner, and his own childhood full of hardships. His image while Soviet leader reflected his peasant heritage. Attending the parish school, Khrushchev was the first member of his family to become literate. He joined the Bolshevik Party in 1918, worked by day and attended school at night, fought in the Civil War, and revealed leadership and strong ambition. In 1929, still rough and uncouth, he was sent to the Moscow Industrial Academy to complete his education. By sheer ability and drive he came to lead its party organization. Three years later he became a member of the Central Committee and in 1935 headed the key Moscow party organization and guided it through the Great Purge. Invaluable to Stalin, he kept making speeches while others fell silent. In 1938, he was assigned to the Ukraine, completed ruthless purges there, and the next year entered the Politburo as a full member. During and after World War II he served as boss of the Ukraine. Throughout his career Khrushchev displayed toughness, resourcefulness, practicality, and a frank independence uncharacteristic of Stalin's henchmen. In 1950, surviving the failure of his untimely agricultural cities scheme, he stormed again into the inner circle of power.

After Malenkov's fall, Khrushchev was the most powerful member of the collective, sharing power with Premier Bulganin and Defense Minister Zhukov. During 1955–1956, he and Bulganin traveled to eastern Europe and Asia and undermined the power position of Foreign Minister Molotov. Meanwhile, Khrushchev was replacing his rivals' supporters in the Secretariat with his own men.

Khrushchev dominated the 20th Party Congress of February 1956. In a dramatic secret speech, he denounced the crimes of the Stalin era and began building up his own image as Lenin's loyal follower as steps toward full power. (See Problem 7 at the end of this chapter.) He overcame strong conservative opposition to the proposed speech by threatening to denounce Stalin publicly. In the speech, he accused Stalin of fostering a personality cult, claiming infallibility, and liquidating thousands of honest Communists and military leaders out of paranoidal suspicion. Stalin, he claimed, had gravely weakened the Red Army by executing its top leaders, and his inaction in June 1941 had brought the USSR to the brink of defeat. Khrushchev's speech established him as a reform leader campaigning for basic political changes and won him wide support from younger, provincial party leaders. He sought to break the hold that Stalin retained over the party even from the grave, absolve himself of responsibility for Stalin's crimes, and dissociate himself from the dictator's closest lieutenants, Molotov and Malenkov. Khrushchev depicted Stalinism as an aberration and urged a return to Leninism and collective leadership. Molotov's resignation as foreign minister in June 1956 confirmed the power of Khrushchev's forces.

Opposition to Khrushchev was weakened, not broken. The upheavals in Poland and Hungary in late 1956 (see p. 37) temporarily lowered his prestige. By creating regional economic councils (*sovnarkhozy*), Khrushchev aimed to break the technocrats' hold over the central economic ministries, but this action stimulated his opponents to desperate countermeasures. In June 1957, while Khrushchev and Bulganin visited Finland, his rivals united, secured a Presidium majority, and voted him out of office. Returning hastily, Khrushchev proved his mastery over the party apparatus. He weaned waverers (Voroshilov, Bulganin, Saburov, and Pervukhin) from his chief opponents (Malenkov, Molotov, Kaganovich, and Shepilov) and insisted that the Central Committee vote on his removal. With Marshal Zhukov's support, Khrushchev's provincial supporters were flown to Moscow. The Central Committee then reversed the Presidium's action and expelled his chief rivals, henceforth dubbed the "antiparty group." Through maneuver and compromise, Khrushchev had won a decisive though limited victory.

Khrushchev moved swiftly to consolidate his power. Marshal Zhukov, accused of building a personality cult in the Red Army, was removed from the Presidium and as defense minister and replaced by Marshal Rodion Malinovskii. In March 1958, Bulganin resigned and Khrushchev became premier, confirming his predominant role in party and state. He became an undisputed and very popular leader, with enthusiastic support from the Soviet people who enjoyed his informality, his appearances around the country, and his well-publicized trips abroad. However, even during his six years of personal rule, Khrushchev never possessed Stalin's authority. He could not dictate to the Presidium and he needed almost four years to remove his opponents from their posts. The "antiparty" leaders were exiled but not imprisoned, and even then Khrushchev's reform program was opposed strongly by a conservative group led by Mikhail Suslov.

Nikita Khrushchev represented something new and exciting for the Soviet public, an ordinary-looking Russian, open and garrulous, who had a real flair for public relations. Unlike Stalin, a suspicious paranoid ensconced within the Kremlin, Khrushchev plunged boldly into crowds and expressed his opinions flamboyantly. He was a risk taker and innovator who promised to improve living conditions for average people. He contrasted in character and approach from Stalin as dramatically as Gorbachev later would differ from his elderly predecessors. However, city intellectuals scorned Khrushchev for his ungrammatical Russian and boorish, often reckless behavior.

Once in power Khrushchev reduced the apparatus of terror and rebuilt the party as his chosen instrument of power. Malenkov had released some political prisoners, but Khrushchev released millions, especially in 1956. Victims of Stalin's terror were rehabilitated, often posthumously, notably Marshal Tukhachevskii and other Red Army leaders purged by Stalin. Police influence declined, and a more relaxed and hopeful political climate developed. Khrushchev sought popularity by mixing with the people, traveling around the USSR, and delivering homey speeches to workers and peasants. Unlike Stalin, the Kremlin recluse, Khrushchev remained informal, jovial and talkative, bringing new and able people from industry to revive the party, which Stalin had demoralized by terror. Promoting his youthful provincial supporters, he increased party authority over the technocrats. Like Lenin, Khrushchev stressed persuasion, not coercion, and party congresses, rare under Stalin, now met regularly.

In January 1959, Khrushchev convened a special 21st Congress to approve a Seven Year Plan to begin building communism (see pp. 367–368). Khrushchev launched a miniature personality cult, which described him as "Lenin's comrade-in-arms" and architect of the transition to communism. Urging preparation of a new party program, he stressed that the state's coercive aspects were "withering away" and that

Nikita Khrushchev *(United Press International)*

young communist league.

some administrative and police functions could be transferred to "public" organizations such as the *Komsomol*. Opponents, however, objected to any premature dissolution of the state, and after the Congress Khrushchev's erratic behavior and policy shifts revealed his continuing problems with the opposition.

The 22nd Congress of October 1961 convened mainly to adopt a new party program, which proclaimed: "The present generation of Soviet people shall live under communism." But at the Congress, Khrushchev renewed his anti-Stalin campaign and depicted Stalin's atrocities publicly in greater depth and detail. He accused Stalin of authorizing Kirov's assassination in 1934, which led to the Great Purge, and linked Molotov and Voroshilov with him in that affair. "Antiparty" elements, he claimed, had executed Stalin's repressive policies, whereas his own regime had broken cleanly with the past. In response to demands of some delegates, Stalin's body was removed from the mausoleum and reburied in the Kremlin wall. Moderates in the Presidium (Aleksei Kosygin, Mikhail Suslov, and Anastas Mikoian), however, blocked Khrushchev's efforts to expel "antiparty" leaders from the party. Then the Cuban missile crisis shattered his prestige (see p. 374), and only at the Central Committee's June 1963 plenum, which named Leonid Brezhnev and Nicholas Podgorny (his allies in the Presidium) as party secretaries, did Khrushchev seem to recover his authority. The "antiparty" leaders were expelled from the party but not tried. Khrushchev's 70th birthday in April 1964 was appropriately celebrated by the Soviet press, but he was not portrayed as absolute or indispensable. His struggle with the opposition remained inconclusive and his victory incomplete. Khrushchev's personal rule lasted only six years, 1958–1964.

After 1953, the relaxation of some totalitarian controls enhanced the Soviet regime's legitimacy for most of the population. With the overpowering authoritarian image of Stalin gone and with brutal police repression ended, a political reform movement developed among younger intellectuals and those released from Stalin's camps. This movement aimed at democratization, civil liberties, and preventing a reversion to Stalinism. Marxist-Leninist ideology became less effective and credible. The critical reaction of youthful dissidents ("sons") to the values of Stalinist "fathers" was reflected by reactions of Vladimir Osipov, later editor of the underground journal, *Veche,* to Khrushchev's secret speech:

> Overthrown was the man who had personified the existing system and ideology to such an extent that the very words "the Soviet power" and "Stalin" seemed to have been synonymous. We all, the future rebels, at the dawn of our youth, had been fanatical Stalinists [and] had believed with a truly religious fervor. . . . Khrushchev's speech and the 20th Congress destroyed our faith, having extracted from it its very core . . . , Joseph Stalin.[1]

The ensuing Hungarian Revolution profoundly affected Soviet university students. In Leningrad alone, some 2,000 were disciplined or expelled for condemning Soviet armed intervention in Hungary. They formed a number of political and literary groups that produced *samizdat* journals. (See Chapter 18, p. 432.)

Toward the non-Russian nationalities of the USSR Khrushchev pursued generally conciliatory policies while pushing efforts at linguistic and cultural Russification. Some of the peoples Stalin had deported during World War II were allowed to return home, but the Crimean

---

[1]Quoted in H. Morton and R. Tökes, *Soviet Politics and Society in the 1970s* (New York, 1974), p. 10.

Tatars and Volga Germans remained conspicuous exceptions. Finally, in 1964 Khrushchev rehabilitated the Volga Germans by decree, in an effort to improve relations with West Germany, but did not restore their autonomous republic. Crimean Tatar petitions to the government to permit their return to their ancestral homeland were pointedly ignored.

ECONOMY: A FOCUS ON AGRICULTURE

After 1953, despite some major policy changes, the Soviet economy retained the chief strengths and weaknesses of the Stalin period and was run by men trained under Stalin. It remained a centrally planned economy in which heavy industry and defense were emphasized, though the consumer sector now received more resources. Under Malenkov, the collective leadership, to win public support, pledged that for the first time since 1928 consumer industry would grow faster than heavy industry. In April 1953, food prices were considerably reduced, but since key items such as meat were in short supply, the result was long lines and shortages. Compulsory bond purchases were reduced, and the worker's take-home pay increased, but not the supply of available goods.

Khrushchev emphasized agriculture and began with a frank statement on its sad condition. Soviet collective farming in 1953 was unproductive and unworthy of a great power: Half the population barely fed the other half. Soviet livestock herds, noted Khrushchev, were smaller than in 1928 or even 1916. Heavy taxes on private peasant plots discouraged production of desperately needed meat, milk, and vegetables. These shortcomings must be overcome in two to three years, warned Khrushchev, always in a hurry. During the next five years, many steps were taken to foster agricultural growth. State prices for farmers' compulsory deliveries and over-quota shipments were raised sharply, especially for grains. In 1954, the average price paid for all agricultural products was more than double the 1952 level; in 1956 it was two and one half times higher. The state assumed most collective farm transportation costs, wrote off their old debts, and reduced taxes on private plots and limitations on private livestock holdings. Tractor and fertilizer production were expanded. Greater incentives to farmers and increased state investment in agriculture stimulated a 50 percent rise in output between 1953 and 1958.

Khrushchev's most controversial gamble was plowing up millions of acres of semiarid soil in the virgin lands of northern Kazakhstan. Reviving a plan of 1940 that had never been implemented, he sought to solve the grain shortage by greatly increasing the cultivated area of the

USSR. By the end of 1956, 88.6 million additional acres had been placed under cultivation, an area equal to the total cultivated land of Canada. Hundreds of new state farms were created, some 300,000 persons permanently relocated in Kazakhstan, and additional hundreds of thousands helped bring in the harvest. Leonid I. Brezhnev, then second party secretary of Kazakhstan, directed this campaign. In 1955, drought brought a poor crop and threatened Khrushchev's position, but an excellent harvest in 1956 apparently vindicated his risky experiment: Kazakhstan alone provided 16 million tons of grain.

The Sixth Five Year Plan, approved in 1956 by the 20th Congress, set ambitious goals for agriculture, including a grain output of 180 million tons. In 1957 began a hectic campaign to overtake the United States in per capita production of meat, milk, and butter, as Khrushchev toured the country, made many speeches, and dismissed numerous officials. He pushed the development of state farms at the expense of collectives (kolkhozy) and amalgamated the latter into larger units. (Kolkhozy decreased from 125,000 in 1950 to 69,100 in 1958.) In 1958, Machine Tractor Stations were abolished and kolkhozy were forced to purchase their machines.

Industrial growth in the 1950s continued to be rapid despite management problems. The Fifth Plan's goals were mostly fulfilled, and the Sixth Plan prescribed creation of a third major metallurgical base in Kazakhstan and western Siberia. Industrial management, however, became entangled with Khrushchev's drive for political supremacy. In February 1957, Khrushchev's scheme to scrap central industrial ministries in Moscow and replace them with regional economic councils (sovnarkhozy), eventually 107 in number, under Gosplan was approved. Causing a massive exodus of ministry personnel to the provinces, it made regional party secretaries virtual economic dictators. Khrushchev achieved his political aim of weakening the ministerial hierarchy but not the economic goal of greater industrial efficiency. The sovnarkhozy were supposed to overcome supply problems, avoid duplication, and improve regional planning, but they catered to selfish local interests, and individual enterprises often received no clear directives or got conflicting orders from various agencies. In the partial recentralization of 1963, sovnarkhozy were reduced in number and 17 larger economic planning regions were created. Khrushchev's insistence in 1962 on splitting party organizations into industrial and agricultural hierarchies caused much confusion and uncertainty especially because sovnarkhozy rarely corresponded with the new party units. By 1963, industrial and agricultural management were chaotic.

Meanwhile, in 1959, the Sixth Five Year Plan had been scrapped in mid-course in favor of Khrushchev's grandiose Seven Year Plan "to construct the bases of communism."[2] It featured heavy investment in the chemical industry, nonsolid fuels, and development of Asiatic Russia. In 1961, Khrushchev raised some of the Plan's goals, such as steel output. During its first years, industrial progress remained impressive, but thereafter declining growth rates in industry and agriculture made a mockery of Khrushchev's 1961 party program, which foresaw the attainment, by 1980, of industrial output and living standards far exceeding those of capitalist countries. In 1963, the Seven Year Plan was abandoned as impossible of achievement, a tacit admission that the party program likewise was unrealizable.

Agricultural stagnation and lagging labor productivity slowed overall Soviet economic growth after 1958. Agricultural output, supposed to rise 70 percent during the Seven Year Plan, increased only 14 percent (crops only 7 percent). Bad weather was a factor, especially in 1963, but other reasons were more important. The sudden dissolution of most Machine Tractor Stations and compelling the collective farms to purchase their machinery virtually bankrupted poorer farms. Dispersed among kolkhozy, the machines could not be properly maintained or repaired. Because kolkhozy lacked the capital to purchase new machinery, the agricultural equipment industry was brought to the verge of ruin. This poorly thought-out and irresponsibly executed reform had a depressing effect on collective farm production.

Equally harmful was Khrushchev's optimistic but ill-conceived campaign, announced in May 1957, to overtake the United States in production of meat, milk, and butter within three to four years. This provoked what the Medvedevs call "the Riazan fiasco." Responding to Khrushchev's appeal, A. N. Larionov, ambitious party secretary of Riazan province, pledged to more than double meat deliveries to the state in 1959. This was achieved by slaughtering beef and milk cows and buying animals and meat from other provinces; Larionov became a Hero of Socialist Labor. However, by 1960, Riazan's agriculture was ruined, its herds decimated, and its kolkhozy in debt. With Riazan unable to deliver even half its normal quota of meat and grain, the "heroic" Larionov shot himself; national production of meat fell sharply. Khrushchev's boast to overtake America in meat production became a bad joke.[3] Thus Khrushchev's personal campaigns, interference, and hasty reorganizations did consid-

---

[2]Khrushchev's Plan called for an increase of 62 to 65 percent in national income (58 percent was achieved); 80 percent in gross industrial output (84 percent achieved); grain, 164 to 180 million tons (121 million achieved); and meat, 6.13 million tons (5.25 million achieved).

[3]Roy Medvedev and Zhores Medvedev, *Khrushchev: The Years in Power*, trans. A. Durkin (New York, 1978), pp. 80–100.

erable harm. He did not create agricultural problems, but his policies often made them worse. In March 1962, he told the Central Committee:

> Communism cannot be conceived of as a table with empty places at which sit highly conscious and fully equal people. . . . It is necessary to double and triple the output of major farm products in a short period. . . . The development of agriculture is an integral part of the creation of the material and technical bases of communism.

Instead, Soviet grain production in 1963 fell 27 million tons below the high point reached in 1958, and millions of tons had to be imported from the United States and Canada. Poor economic performance after 1958 made Khrushchev increasingly vulnerable politically.

Beginning in 1958, the Soviet wage system was reformed with a trend away from the piece rates that had been prevalent under Stalin. New minimum wages in town and country gave the lowest paid workers substantial increases. To cut pay differentials, some higher salaries (for example, those of professors) were reduced. The work week was gradually shortened, maternity leaves were lengthened, and industrial pensions and disability benefits were much improved. The currency reform of 1961 exchanged 1 new ruble for 10 old ones; the rate of 4 rubles to the dollar was altered arbitrarily to 0.90 rubles per dollar. As direct taxes were further reduced, the turnover tax remained the chief source of state revenue.

In foreign trade important changes occurred under Khrushchev. The USSR abandoned Stalin's policy of exploiting the European satellites economically, scrapped the joint companies that had done so, and paid fairer prices for eastern European goods. In 1954, the multilateral Council for Mutual Economic Assistance (COMECON) had been revived, though most Soviet trade with eastern Europe remained bilateral. The USSR had moved into the foreign aid field and, in 1953 China received a long-term Soviet credit of 520 million rubles. (The Soviets had removed equipment worth more than three times that much from Manchuria in 1945!) After Khrushchev visited India in 1955, a major program of foreign economic aid to it began, partly to compete with the United States in the Third World. The Soviets supplied goods on credit, especially to India and Egypt, for later repayment in goods. Soviet imports and exports increased sharply. Using 1955 as the base year (100), imports in 1950 had been 54.6 and exports 56.7. By 1958, they were 148.4 and 130, respectively.[4]

---

[4]A. Nove, *An Economic History of the USSR* (London, 1969), p. 352.

Living standards of most Soviet citizens improved considerably under Khrushchev, but this rise whetted their appetites for more. Beginning in 1956, housing construction spurted and private home building received more state support. Even millions of new apartments, mostly in massive, ugly blocks, dubbed derisively "Khrushchev slums," however, could not satisfy demand. Between 1953 and 1964, the Soviet population rose from 188 to 228 million, mostly in cities. Just before his fall, Khrushchev declared that the chief task of the near future was "a further rise in the living standard of the people. . . . Now when we have a mighty [heavy] industry, the party is setting the task of the more rapid development of the branches that produce consumer goods. . . ." Performance did not match these promises.

FOREIGN AFFAIRS: CRISES IN THE COMMUNIST BLOC COUNTRIES

Soviet foreign policy quickly discarded its rigid Stalinist mold to adopt flexible, varied tactics. Malenkov began the shift, and Khrushchev, stressing peaceful coexistence with the West from February 1956, continued and extended this new approach. It had to overcome a conservative hardline opposition, led first by Molotov, and later apparently by Suslov, which favored a more aggressive, anti-Western course. Stalin's successors found it increasingly difficult to maintain leadership of the Communist Bloc and world Communist movement in the face of Chinese and Yugoslav challenges.

After Stalin's death, the collective leadership promoted détente with the West and China, as Premier Malenkov warned that nuclear war might destroy all humankind, not just capitalism. In July 1953, an armistice ended the Korean War, and at the Geneva Conference of 1954 the USSR supported settlement of the Indochina conflict, although no settlement was forthcoming. The tone and manners of Soviet diplomacy began to mellow. Unable to coerce China, Soviet leaders courted it, promising technical aid, loans, experts to assist Chinese industrialization, and agreed to end special privileges, abolish joint companies, and return Port Arthur to China.

Soviet leaders wished to prevent West Germany from rearming and entering NATO, but they refused to sacrifice their East German satellite. Early in 1954, a four-power conference called to reach a general German settlement ended in stalemate. After West Germany joined NATO, the Soviets set up the Warsaw Pact in May 1955, a defensive alliance of the satellites and the USSR, with the latter commanding all the military forces and legalizing the presence of Soviet troops in eastern Europe.

Foreign trips by top Soviet leaders, beginning in 1955, fostered a new image of Soviet foreign policy. Khrushchev made a pilgrimage to Belgrade, blamed the Soviet-Yugoslav breach of 1948 on Beria, and over Molotov's strong objections, achieved reconciliation with Marshal Tito. The expanding Soviet foreign aid program and the wooing of such neutral countries as India signified the replacement of Zhdanov's two-camp thesis (socialism versus capitalism) with a more flexible three-camp concept to include neutral countries. In May 1955, the USSR signed an Austrian peace treaty, which ended four-power occupation and made Austria a neutral country. (See Map 16.1.) Apparently, Moscow hoped that West Germany would leave NATO in order to achieve German reunification on a similar basis. This policy culminated in the Geneva Summit Conference (July 1955) between President Eisenhower and a smiling Khrushchev and Bulganin. The amiable "Geneva spirit" produced no substantive agreements, but reduced Cold War tensions and enhanced Khrushchev's prestige abroad.

A crisis confronted the USSR in eastern Europe in 1956. Without Stalin's awesome image, the unpopular satellite regimes proved vulnerable to public agitation for change. As Soviet controls relaxed and a degree of diversity appeared, a workers' uprising in East Germany (June 1953) had to be crushed by Soviet tanks. Khrushchev's secret speech further undermined the satellite regimes. In June 1956, riots in the Polish industrial city of Poznan swelled into a national movement of liberalization and brought the hasty restoration of Wladyslaw Gomulka, purged by Stalin, as first secretary of the Polish Communist Party. When top Soviet leaders stormed into Warsaw on October 19, the new Polish leadership presented a united front. In a compromise solution Poland won domestic autonomy while remaining in the Warsaw Pact and pledging loyalty to the USSR in foreign affairs. Such "domesticism" became a model for other eastern European countries. Preserving Soviet domination of the region, it freed the USSR from detailed supervision of domestic affairs in the satellites.

Meanwhile, in Hungary, a broad popular movement led by students and intellectuals demanded drastic political reforms. Premier Imre Nagy failed to halt Stalinist Hungary's rapid disintegration. After a revolt in Budapest (October 23), Nagy announced that Hungary would leave the Warsaw Pact, become a neutral country, and restore a multiparty system. Much of the Hungarian army joined the insurgents who appealed to the West for aid. Janos Kadar, hastily named the new first secretary of the Hungarian Party, "invited" in Soviet troops, which soon crushed the Hungarian rebels, as thousands of Hungarians fled into exile. The Soviet response showed in Hungary that the USSR would act militarily within its sphere of interest whenever Communist rule was threatened, a move that

Map 16.1 *USSR and Eastern Europe, 1945–1989*

FINLAND
• Viborg
• Leningrad

SWEDEN
• Reval

ESTONIA
Baltic Sea
• Pskov

Riga •
LATVIA

North Sea

Annexed by
Poland from
Germany

Memel LITHUANIA
Konigsberg • EAST
• Kovno
• Vilna

Bremen •
Stettin •
PRUSSIA
GERMANY
• Minsk

Berlin •
• Poznan
Warsaw •
• Bialystok

EASTERN GERMANY
• Pinsk

Bonn •
Erfurt • Dresden •
POLAND
• Breslau

SOVIET UNION

Nuremburg •
• Prague
Crakow •
Przemysl •
• Lvov

FRANCE
CZECHOSLOVAKIA
Galicia
• Chernovtsy

Munich •
AUSTRIA
Vienna •
• Uzhgorod

SWITZ.
• Budapest
Jassy •
• Kishinev
Bessarabia

HUNGARY

Trieste •
RUMANIA
*Semi-independent
since 1963*

Belgrade •
• Bucharest

ITALY
YUGOSLAVIA
*Independent
since 1948*
Black Sea

Adriatic Sea
BULGARIA
Sofia • *Strongly
pro-Soviet*

Tirana •
ALBANIA

GREECE
Aegean Sea
TURKEY

▨ **Russian occupied zones in Austria
(evacuated in 1955) and Germany**

▨ **Former German and Czechoslovak
territory annexed by Russia in 1945**

▨ **British, French, and American
occupied zones**

**Principal areas of anti-Soviet protest
and revolt 1953–1968 crushed by Soviet military
intervention (East Germany, Hungary, Czechoslovakia)
and by strong political pressure (Poland)**

〜〜 **The "Iron Curtain" in 1948**

Adapted with permission of Macmillan Publishing Co., Inc. from *Russian History Atlas*
by Martin Gilbert. Cartography by Martin Gilbert. Copyright © by Martin Gilbert.

demonstrated anew the existence of Communist control in eastern Europe based not on consent but on Soviet bayonets and the unreliability of satellite armies.

Toward the West, Khrushchev combined "peaceful coexistence" with bluster and threats. To him, coexistence meant avoiding war and preventing nuclear rearmament of West Germany. The USSR sponsored the Rapacki Plan (October 1957), named after the Polish foreign minister, for a nuclear free zone in central Europe. Khrushchev's caution in 1958 during crises over Taiwan and Lebanon involving the United States distressed hard-liners in Moscow and Beijing. The growing Chinese challenge helped provoke Khrushchev to deliver an ultimatum to the West over Berlin in November 1958, hoping to force Western powers out of that city. When his ultimatum instead stimulated Western unity and determination, Khrushchev backed down. His erratic policies toward the West reflected his weakness at home and vulnerability to conservative critics.

At a meeting in November 1957 to celebrate the 40th anniversary of the Bolshevik Revolution, the 12 ruling Communist parties issued the Moscow Declaration, which stressed the unity of the socialist camp headed by the USSR. The Yugoslavs, affirming that every country should determine its own road to socialism, refused to sign and accused the USSR of bureaucracy and departures from true Marxism-Leninism; Moscow retorted that Tito was a revisionist kowtowing to U.S. imperialism. Although the second Soviet-Yugoslav dispute (1958–1961) avoided an open breach, Yugoslav independence and the potential threat of national communism to Soviet leadership were reaffirmed.

After 1957, Soviet foreign policy was influenced strongly by the triangular Soviet–U.S.–Chinese relationship. Khrushchev was caught between his desire for détente with the West and the maintenance of Soviet leadership of the Bloc against more militant China. Seeking to score points against "American imperialism" in the Middle East, he backed Arab states against pro-Western Israel and Turkey and rattled his rockets. The growing Soviet commitment to the Arabs proved expensive, especially the construction for Egypt of the Aswan Dam, which the United States had refused to finance.

Renewed Soviet overtures to the United States ended in failure. After his Berlin ultimatum had failed to budge the West, Khrushchev at the 21st Congress (January 1959) made warm references to the United States, and in September he became the first Russian ruler to visit the United States. This trip was a personal triumph for Khrushchev and cemented his relationship with a flexible President Eisenhower; they agreed to hold a summit conference in Moscow in 1960. When a U.S. U-2 reconnaissance plane spying over Soviet territory was shot down and its pilot captured, Eisenhower took responsibility for the flight, but refused to apologize officially. An angry Khrushchev then sabotaged the summit and withdrew his invitation to Eisenhower to visit the USSR.

More serious was a growing rift between the USSR and China, which now became public and disrupted Bloc unity. Between 1957 and 1960, though their relations seemed harmonious, mounting Soviet criticism of China's industrial "Great Leap Forward" suggested that China might reach communism before the USSR. Khrushchev's party program of 1961 was in direct response to this Chinese challenge. The Chinese also condemned Soviet détente with the West. In 1960 began thinly concealed mutual vilification: the Chinese attacked Yugoslav "revisionism," the Soviets denounced the Stalinist Albanian regime, which sought Chinese support, as "dogmatic," but clearly they were striking at each other. Sino-Soviet tension was only partly ideological. Mao was now the senior leader of world communism, and in intra-Bloc disputes the Chinese adopted an orthodox, Stalinist line, which was supported by some of the Soviet "antiparty group." Militance in promoting revolution and national liberation won the Chinese widespread support in Asia and Africa. A unified Communist China challenged the Soviet position in Asia and posed a potential threat to underpopulated Siberia. Noting niggardly Soviet economic aid to them, the Chinese complained that Khrushchev was more generous to nonaligned India and Egypt. Asserting that tsarist Russia, in the 1850s, had acquired the Maritime Province unfairly, Chinese maps showed portions of the Soviet Far East as Chinese territory. Khrushchev withdrew some Soviet technicians from China and sought to dissuade the Chinese from developing nuclear weapons, but in 1959 Beijing decided to manufacture its own. In April 1960, *Red Flag*, a Beijing journal, denouncing Khrushchev's policy of coexistence with capitalism, affirmed that nuclear war would destroy imperialism but not the socialist camp. At the Romanian Party Congress in June, Khrushchev, quarreling violently with the Chinese delegates, castigated their leaders as nationalists, adventurists, and "madmen" seeking to unleash nuclear war.

Attempts to resolve the Sino-Soviet dispute failed. In the summer of 1960, a world Communist Congress in Moscow, representing 81 parties, sought to restore unity. Khrushchev, however, clashed with the Chinese over power-political issues. Soon afterward Albania, smallest and most backward of European Communist states, defied Khrushchev openly, praised Stalin, relied upon Chinese support, and boycotted the Soviet 22d Congress. Chou En-lai, after defending Albania at the Congress, left suddenly and was greeted vociferously in Beijing. Romania also began to assert independence of the USSR, especially in economic matters, and established good relations with China. In 1963, Romania proclaimed virtual neutrality in the Sino-Soviet dispute and even voted occasionally against the Soviet Union in the United Nations. The Sino-Soviet quarrel promoted polycentrism in the Communist world and disintegration of the Bloc.

After President John Kennedy's inauguration in 1961, Khrushchev sought concessions from the youthful American leader as compensation for his troubles in the Bloc. Cuba and Berlin were the key issues. In January 1959 Fidel Castro, heading a radical insurgent movement, took power in Cuba with Communist support and soon aligned himself with the Soviet Union. In April 1961 Cuban exiles supported by the United States sought unsuccessfully to overthrow the Castro regime in the inept Bay of Pigs invasion, whose failure revived Khrushchev's self-assurance. Meeting Kennedy in Vienna that June, Khrushchev threatened to sign a separate peace with East Germany unless an overall German settlement were reached soon. The ensuing Berlin crisis, however, revealed Kennedy's coolness and determination. To halt a westward surge of refugees, the East German regime built the Berlin Wall, which stood until late 1989. Finally, Khrushchev removed his time limit on a German settlement and advocated nuclear free zones in Europe and the Far East.

In the fall of 1962, the Cuban missile crisis threatened to provoke nuclear war between the USSR and the United States. Khrushchev had been seeking to conclude a German peace treaty and prevent China and West Germany from acquiring nuclear weapons. His decision to install medium-range missiles in Cuba was apparently a gamble to solve mounting domestic and foreign problems with one bold stroke: Once his missiles were installed, he might bargain with the West over Berlin and nuclear free zones. U.S. aircraft detected the Soviet installations, however, and President Kennedy ordered a sea blockade of Cuba (October 22). Khrushchev had the choice of withdrawing the missiles or fighting a United States far superior in long-range missiles and local naval power. Khrushchev prudently chose withdrawal only to be taunted by the Chinese for "adventurism" in placing the missiles in Cuba and cowardice in removing them!

Peaceful resolution of the missile crisis improved Soviet-American relations. In 1963, the United States, the USSR, and Britain agreed to ban the testing of nuclear weapons in the atmosphere. A "hot line" was set up between Washington and Moscow to reduce the danger of accidental nuclear war. Khrushchev's freedom of maneuver was sharply restricted by the Sino-Soviet quarrel. During 1963–1964, he tried but failed to round up support for a world Communist conference to expel the Chinese and reassert Soviet hegemony over world communism.

KHRUSHCHEV'S FALL

In October 1964, Khrushchev was suddenly removed from power. The official statement of October 16 in *Pravda* declared:

> The plenum of the Central Committee satisfied the request of N.S. Khrushchev to relieve him of the duties of first secretary of the Central Committee, member of the Presidium of the Central Committee and chairman of the Council of Ministers of the USSR in connection with advanced age and poor health.

Actually, his health was good and many statesmen older than he were directing their countries' destinies. Subsequently, his successors accused Khrushchev of "harebrained schemes," recklessness at home and abroad, fostering a new personality cult, undignified behavior, and dangerous experimentation. His prestige had suffered severely from the Cuban crisis, and between 1960 and 1963 he had almost been toppled on several occasions, but in 1964 his power still had far exceeded that of other Presidium members. Apparently a powerful coalition of interest groups had organized against him. While Khrushchev was on vacation in the Crimea, the Presidium voted him out of office after he had refused to depart gracefully and disregarded his demand to submit the issue to the Central Committee. Having antagonized the military leaders by reducing the size of the ground forces, Khrushchev this time lacked the army support to reverse this verdict. Overnight Khrushchev became emeritus, an unperson rarely mentioned and relegated to obscurity but granted a fine apartment and limousine. The transfer of power, smooth and orderly, to Brezhnev and Kosygin marked a peaceful evolution of the Soviet political system away from Stalinist terror. The Presidium had become a society of relative equals, whose collective weight exceeded that of an individual leader.

A combination of foreign and domestic failures caused Khrushchev's unexpected downfall. His Presidium colleagues blamed him for the Cuban fiasco and setbacks in Berlin. The intensifying conflict with China had split the world Communist movement and encouraged Albania and Romania to assert full or partial independence. The Soviet position in eastern Europe, and with it Soviet security, were imperiled. At home the Soviet economy was stumbling. Industrial growth rates were falling, agriculture had stagnated, and Khrushchev's boasts of soon overtaking the United States sounded hollow. His decision in 1962 to split the party into industrial and agricultural segments had created confusion and antagonized party traditionalists and technocrats. Reduction of Soviet ground forces and efforts to promote détente with the West had alienated influential military men. Khrushchev's hasty reforms and mistakes welded together a potent conservative coalition. However, his basic policies—de-Stalinization, reducing terror, aiding agriculture and the consumer, and increased contacts with the West—apparently were sound. Khrushchev had led the Soviet Union through the difficult post-Stalin transition, ensured the party's predominance, and maintained the Soviet Empire without resort to mass terror.

PROBLEM 7
De-Stalinization—Stalin's Role in the Purges and in World War II

Was Joseph Stalin a "great revolutionary despot" (Deutscher) or a monster worse than Caligula, as his successor, Khrushchev, suggested in 1956? Did Stalin exemplify Soviet communism or represent an aberration from it because of his "cult of personality" after 1934? Why was the Great Purge launched, and what were its results? Was Stalin or his generals to blame for Soviet defeats early in World War II and for eventual victory? Should Stalin be praised for his wartime leadership or should he have been shot for failing to prepare or lead the country adequately? These and similar issues were debated inside and outside the Soviet Union after Khrushchev's "secret speech" in February 1956 at the 20th Party Congress lifted part of the veil that had shrouded Stalin's actions.

STALINIST DEFENSE

The following sources glorify Stalin's leadership, contending that he was a genius and that what he did was necessary and correct. The first is an excerpt from the *History of the All-Union Communist Party (Bolshevik), Short Course*, published orginally in 1938. Approved by Stalin and sometimes attributed at least partly to him personally, this official party history seeks to explain and justify the Great Purge, then underway:

> The successes of socialism in our country gladdened . . . all honorable citizens of the USSR . . . , but infuriated more and more the . . . yesmen of the defeated classes—the miserable remnants of the Bukharinites and Trotskyites. These gentlemen . . . sought revenge upon the party and people for their failures. . . . On December 1, 1934 in Leningrad at Smolny, S. M. Kirov was mostly foully murdered with a shot from a revolver. The murderer, arrested at the scene of the crime, turned out to be a member of an underground counterrevolutionary group which was organized from members of the anti-Soviet Zinovievite group in Leningrad. . . . This group set itself the aim of murdering the leaders of the [Soviet] Communist Party. . . .

From the depositions of the participants . . . it became evident that they were connected with representatives of foreign capitalist states and received money from them. The participants in this organization who were uncovered were sentenced by the Military Tribunal of the Supreme Court of the USSR to the extreme punishment—shooting.

Soon thereafter the existence of an underground counterrevolutionary "Moscow center" was established. Investigation and trial clarified the vile role of Zinoviev, Kamenev, Evdokimov, and other leaders of this organization in arousing among their followers terrorist inclinations and to prepare the murder of members of the Central Committee and the Soviet government. . . . Already then in 1935 it became clear that the Zinovievite group was a hidden White Guardist organization which fully deserved to be dealt with like the White Guardists. . . .

The chief inspirer and organizer of this whole band of murderers and spies was the Judas, Trotskii. Aiding Trotskii and executing his counterrevolutionary instructions were Zinoviev, Kamenev, and their Trotskyist yesmen. They prepared the defeat of the USSR in case of an attack on it by the imperialists, they became defeatists toward the worker-peasant state, they became the despicable servants and agents of the German and Japanese fascists.[5]

The following excerpts from Khrushchev's speech in 1939 show him as the loyal follower of Stalin, praising the dictator and his work slavishly; they are included in a volume of similar speeches dedicated to Stalin:

Today, on the 60th anniversary of Comrade Stalin's birth, all eyes will be turned on our great leader of nations, on our dear friend and father. Working people all over the world will write and speak words of love and gratitude about him. Their enemies will foam at the mouth with rage when . . . speaking on this theme. The working men of the world see in Comrade Stalin their leader, their liberator from the yoke of capitalism. . . . The imperialists of all countries know full well that every word uttered by Comrade Stalin is backed by a people of 183,000,000 strong, that every idea advanced by Comrade Stalin is endorsed by the great and mighty multinational Soviet people. . . .

The biography of Comrade Stalin is the glorious epic of our Bolshevik party. . . . Lenin together with Stalin created the great Bolshevik party. . . . In Comrade Stalin the working class and all toilers possess the greatest man of the present era, a theoretician, leader, and organizer of the struggle and victory of the working class. . . . All nations of the Soviet Union see in Stalin their friend, their father, their leader. . . . Stalin is the father of his people by virtue of the love he bears them. Stalin is the leader of nations for the wisdom with which he guides their struggle. . . . The army and the navy are the

---

[5]*Istoriia VKP(b), Kratkii kurs* (Moscow, 1946), pp. 309–312.

creation of our great Stalin, who increases their might with every day. . . .[6]

KHRUSHCHEV'S CRITIQUE

In his "secret speech" of February 24–25, 1956, Khrushchev detailed Stalin's crimes and blunders while concealing that as Stalin's loyal follower he had participated in them. Khrushchev did not condemn Stalin unconditionally because that would have meant repudiating industrialization, collectivization, and social benefits. While affirming Stalin's contributions in the Revolution and Civil War and in building socialism until 1934, Khrushchev focused on an aberration: the cult of the individual leader and its destructive results. World War II generals led by Marshal Zhukov had pressed Khrushchev to rehabilitate purged military leaders and the Red Army's reputation, partly by discrediting Stalin's wartime leadership. Engaged in a bitter power struggle, Khrushchev may have believed he could undermine conservative opponents such as Molotov by destroying the image of Stalin as an all-wise, all-powerful leader. He glorified Lenin as embodying socialist modesty, comradely behavior, and socialist legality and posed as his true follower. Declared Khrushchev:

> At present we are concerned . . . with how the cult of the person of Stalin gradually grew . . . , the source of a whole series of exceedingly grave perversions of party principles, party democracy, of revolutionary legality. . . . The great harm caused by the violation of collective direction of the party and . . . accumulation of immense and limitless power in the hands of one person, the party Central Committee considers it absolutely necessary to make the material pertaining to this matter available to the 20th Congress. . . .

Marx and Lenin, Khrushchev reminded the delegates, had denounced any cult of an individual leader. Lenin had invariably displayed great modesty while emphasizing the role of the people and party in making history. Instead of dictating to his colleagues, "Lenin never imposed by force his views upon his co-workers. He tried to convince; he patiently explained his opinions to others. . . ." Lenin had realized Stalin's grave character defects, but premature death had prevented him from removing Stalin from office. After Stalin assumed power:

> Grave abuse of power by Stalin caused untold harm to our party. . . . Stalin . . . absolutely did not tolerate collegiality in leadership and work, and

---

[6]Cited in Marin Pundeff, ed., *History in the U.S.S.R.* (San Francisco, 1967), pp. 135–139.

practiced brutal violence. . . . Stalin acted . . . by imposing his concepts and demanding absolute submission to his opinion. Whoever opposed this concept . . . , was doomed to removal from the leading collective and to subsequent moral and physical annihilation. . . . Stalin originated the concept "enemy of the people" . . . which made possible the use of the most cruel repression, violating all norms of revolutionary legality against anyone who in any way disagreed with Stalin. . . .

During the Great Purge, continued Khrushchev:

Stalin . . . used extreme methods and mass repressions at a time when the Revolution was already victorious, . . . when the exploiting classes were already liquidated, . . . when our party was politically consolidated. . . . Stalin showed in a whole series of cases his intolerance, his brutality and his abuse of power. . . . He often chose the path of repression and physical annihilation, not only against actual enemies, but also against individuals who had committed no crimes against the party and the Soviet government.

Generally, the only proof of guilt was a "confession" exorted by force and torture. Such incongruous methods, noted Khrushchev, were employed when the Revolution had already triumphed, the exploiters had been wiped out, and socialism had been firmly established ". . . In the situation of socialist victory there was no basis for mass terror in the country." This terror had been blamed on N. I. Ezhov, chief of the security police, but clearly Stalin had made the decisions and issued the arrest orders.

Khrushchev, seeking to discredit Stalin's role as the chief Soviet leader in World War II, accused Stalin of failing to prepare the USSR for war, of disregarding numerous clear warnings of impending German attack, and of gross incompetence and negligence in directing military operations. Moreover, after victory Stalin had denied the crucial role of his generals and people in achieving victory, taking all the credit for himself. Khrushchev noted the improbable role that many Soviet war novels and films had attributed to Stalin. Supposedly harkening to Stalin's "genius," the Red Army had retreated deliberately, then counterattacked, and smashed the Nazi invaders. Such works ascribed the glorious victory achieved by the heroic Soviet people solely to Stalin's brilliant strategy. Stalin had blamed early severe Soviet defeats on the German surprise attack, though Hitler had announced his intent to destroy communism back in 1933. In the months before the attack, numerous warnings came from the West, Soviet diplomats, and military men that a Nazi invasion was imminent, but Stalin had disregarded them. "Despite these particularly grave warnings, the necessary steps were not taken to prepare the country properly for defense and to prevent it from being caught unaware," said Khrushchev.

Khrushchev was equally critical of Stalin's performance as wartime commander in chief. When the Nazis invaded, Soviet troops had orders not to return fire because Stalin just could not believe that war had really begun. In border areas, much of the Soviet air force and artillery were lost needlessly and the Germans broke through. Believing that the end was near, Stalin declared in panic: "All that Lenin created we have lost forever." For a long time Stalin neither directed operations nor exercised real leadership. He was ignorant of the true situation at the front, which he never visited except for one brief look at a stabilized sector, yet his constant interference with military operations caused huge manpower losses. Exclaimed Khrushchev derisively: ". . . Stalin planned operations on a globe . . . and traced the front line on it!" As a result, early in 1942, the Germans surrounded large Red Army units in the Kharkov area, and hundreds of thousands of soldiers were lost. Yet Stalin believed that he was always right and never made mistakes. "This is Stalin's military genius; this is what it cost us," declared Khrushchev.

Right after Soviet victory, Stalin began unfairly to denigrate the contributions to victory of many top Red Army commanders. "Stalin excluded every possibility that services rendered at the front should be credited to anyone but himself." All Soviet victories, Stalin claimed, had been due solely to his courage and genius. In the postwar Soviet film, *The Fall of Berlin* (1949), only Stalin issued orders; there was no mention of the military commanders, the Politburo, or the government. "Stalin acts for everybody . . . in order to surround Stalin with glory, contrary to the facts and to historical truth.[7]

POST-KHRUSHCHEV DEBATE ON STALIN

On February 16, 1966, at the Institute of Marxism-Leninism in Moscow, a discussion was held of the book by A. M. Nekrich, *June 22, 1941*, which had used the "secret speech" to blame Stalin for Soviet unpreparedness. The debate was wide open by Soviet standards then, though most participants and the audience believed that Nekrich had not gone far enough in criticizing Stalin. Note the critical attitude of Professor G. A. Deborin of the Institute of Marxism-Leninism in Moscow toward the fallen Khrushchev and his partial defense of Stalin.

> **Deborin** Nekrich [a Soviet historian] adopts an erroneous position; he explains everything by the obstinate stupidity of Stalin himself. That is a superficial analysis. . . . Stalin was not the only person involved. . . . It is unnecessary to refer to Khrushchev's declarations which are not objec-

---

[7]N. S. Khrushchev, "The Crimes of the Stalin Era," *The New Leader*, 1956.

tive. . . . Insofar as [Stalin] received false information, Stalin reached false conclusions. He placed too much hope in the German-Soviet pact, . . . but Stalin's estimate of German intentions was endorsed by all those around him. So Stalin cannot be considered solely responsible for his mistakes.

Anfilov (General Staff) And now let us come to the beginning of the war. If all our forces had been completely ready for action, which was entirely Stalin's responsibility, we should not have begun the war with such disasters! And in general the war would not have been so long, so bloody, and so exhausting. . . . Stalin remains the chief culprit.

Dashichev (General Staff) [Nekrich] should have gone deeper. . . . It was [Stalin] who made the situation in which the country then found itself [in 1941]. Stalin's greatest crime was to have eliminated the best cadres of our army and our party. All our leaders understood the international situation, but not one of them was courageous enough to fight to get the necessary measures taken for the defense of the country. . . . The driver of the bus is responsible for every accident that happens through his fault. Stalin assumed the responsibility of sole driver. His guilt is immense. . . .

Vasilenko (Institute of Marxism-Leninism) Objectively, we possessed everything necessary for resisting the German attack. But Stalin ruined everything. And afterwards to explain away his disgraceful defeat, he advanced the ridiculous theory that the aggressor is always better prepared for war.

Slezkin (Institute of History of the Academy of Sciences) I was at the front and took part, at the age of 19, in the June 1941 fighting. There can be no hesitation in saying that Stalin's behavior was criminal. There was a vicious circle of personality cult, provocation and repression. Everyone tried to please his superior by supplying only the information that might gratify him. . . . All this was the cause of immeasurable damage to the country and everyone is guilty in his own way. . . . And the responsibility is heavier in proportion to one's place in the hierarchy. . . . Stalin is the chief culprit. . . .

Peter Yakir (Institute of History of the Academy of Sciences) Some of the speakers . . . have referred to "Comrade Stalin." . . . Stalin was nobody's comrade and above all, not ours. Stalin impeded the development of our armaments by eliminating many eminent technicians, and among them the creators of our artillery. . . . In the concentration camps there were millions of able-bodied men, specialists in every department of the country's economic and military life. And the task of guarding them absorbed considerable forces.

Snegov [who had been imprisoned in one of Stalin's labor camps] Nekrich's book is honest and useful. If a unit is disorganized on the eve of combat, . . . then that unit suffers a defeat. The head of such a unit is generally shot by order of the high command. . . . Stalin was both the supreme commander, and the head of the unit and that unit, in a state of disorganization, was our whole country. Stalin ought to have been shot. Instead of which, people are now trying to whitewash him. . . . How can one be a Communist and speak smoothly about Stalin who betrayed . . . Communists, who eliminated nearly all the delegates of the Eighteenth Congress . . . , and who betrayed the Spanish Republic, Poland, and all Communists in all countries?

Deborin It has not been my task to defend or justify Stalin. What is needed is to examine the personality cult more deeply in all its aspects. . . . It is strange that Snegov should hold the same view [as West German Professor Jacobson]. Comrade Snegov, you ought to tell us which camp you belong to!

Snegov The Kolyma [concentration] camp.

Nekrich . . . It is Stalin who bears the chief responsibility for the heavy defeat and all the tragedy of the first part of the war. All the same, nobody ought to provide his superiors with inexact information because it will give them pleasure. Stalinism began because of us, the small people. Stalin wanted to trick Hitler; but instead of that he got himself into a maze which led to disaster. He knew better than anyone about elimination of the leading cadres and the weaknesses of the army."[8]

RECENT OFFICIAL SOVIET STATEMENTS

President M. S. Gorbachev has continued and in some ways deepened the critique of Stalin that General Secretary Khrushchev began in 1956. Public pressure virtually compelled Gorbachev to address the Stalin issue in his speech of November 2, 1987, but he failed to face it squarely:

> To remain faithful to historical truth we have to see both Stalin's indisputable contribution to the struggle for socialism, to the defense of its gains, as well as the gross political mistakes and the abuses committed by him and his circle, for which our people paid a heavy price and which had grave consequences for society. Sometimes it is said that Stalin did not know about many incidents of lawlessness. The documents at our disposal show that this is not so. The guilt of Stalin and his immediate entourage before the party and the people for wholesale repressive measures and acts of lawlessness is enormous and unforgivable. This is a lesson for all generations.[9]

In his speech of November 25, 1989, Gorbachev returned to this theme, arguing that Stalin's unfortunate legacy—a centralist bureaucratic system—had to be replaced if the USSR were to progress:

---

[8]Selected excerpts reprinted from June 22, 1941, *Soviet Historians and the German Invasion* by Vladimir Petrov, pp. 250–261, by permission of The University of South Carolina Press. Copyright © 1968 by The University of South Carolina Press in cooperation with the Institute for Sino-Soviet Studies, The George Washington University, Washington, D.C.

[9]M. Gorbachev, *October and Perestroika: The Revolution Continues, 1917–1987* (Moscow, 1987), p. 21.

Why did Stalin succeed in imposing on the Party and on all of society his program and his methods? . . . Stalin played cleverly upon the revolutionary impatience of the masses, on the utopian and egalitarian tendencies of any mass movement, on the vanguard's aspiration for the quickest possible achievement of the desired goal. . . . The idea of socialism became equated more and more with an authoritarian command and bureaucratic administrative system.

. . . An ever greater rift [opened] between the theory of Marxism and reality, between the humane ideals and practice. A bureaucratic, extremely centralized economic and political system acted by its own laws. And theory had . . . to create the illusion of the "correctness" of these actions. . . . In the name of the achievement of "the great idea" of socialism were justified the most inhumane means. . . . The 20th Congress, rejecting and condemning the dark sides of the Stalin regime and its extremes, generally left unchanged the bureaucratic system itself. It managed to survive, aided by a new illusion that it was enough to eliminate the extremes of the Stalinist regime—and the liberated energy of socialism in the near future could bring our society to the higher phase of communism. Stalinist distortions led to the loss of the main content of the Marxist and Leninist concept of socialism: an understanding of the individual as the goal, not the means.[10]

A WESTERN EVALUATION

The U.S. scholar Severyn Bialer, in his introduction to Soviet wartime memoirs, seeks to strike a balance between exaggerated praise of Stalin and Khrushchev's one-sided and partisan denunciation. Up to 1953, he points out, Soviet war history had glorified Stalin as an infallible and omnipotent genius. Soon after Stalin's death "war history came to serve the cult of the party," whose infallibility replaced Stalin's. Khrushchev's attack in 1956 had aimed to use Stalin's crimes as a lever to achieve power:

> The singlemindedness with which Khrushchev concentrated on his goal . . . led him to seek not comprehension, not rectification, but destruction of Stalin's role as war leader. . . . Soviet war memoirs testify to Stalin's complete control over the political, industrial, and military aspects of the Soviet war effort. . . . The Soviet dictator personally made every wartime decision of any importance. He alone seems to have possessed the power to impose his will on both civilian and military associates alike. . . .
>
> . . . It appeared to [Western observers] that Stalin had an extraordinary grasp of war goals and major long-range plans for conducting the war and a talent for adjusting the conduct of military operations to political realities. . . . On the second level, that of tactical and technical expertise, Western observers were struck by Stalin's mastery of detail. . . . Their de-

---

[10]*Pravda,* November 26, 1989, pp. 1–3.

scriptions are corroborated in the memoirs of Soviet commanders and industrial managers. . . .

The task of military leadership is located to an overwhelming extent, however . . . in the area of operational leadership which involves planning and control of large-scale military operations—battles and campaigns. In this middle area . . . , Stalin made no real contribution. . . . Stalin's crucial contribution to victory . . . [derived] from his ability to organize and administer the mobilization of manpower and material resources. . . . Stalin . . . regarded his role as that of arbiter and ultimate judge of his generals' strategic plans and operational designs. His major asset as a military leader was the ability to select talented commanders and to permit them to plan operations, while reserving for himself the ultimate power of decision. . . .

Khrushchev recognized Stalin's vulnerability in the crucial operational area and attempted to discredit [his] . . . entire war leadership by demonstrating the weakness of one of its parts. . . . While Soviet generals aired their alleged wartime misgivings about Stalin's judgment and behavior in military matters . . . , the memoirs clearly show that many of them regarded their leader with genuine respect, admiration or awe. . . . Clearly the Soviet generals feared Stalin more than they feared the Germans. . . .

Thus what was crucial to Soviet survival and eventual victory was Stalin's ability to mobilize Soviet manpower and economic resources over a sustained period, his ability to assure the political stability of his armed forces and the population at large despite disastrous initial defeats, and his ability to recognize and reward superior military talent at all levels under his command. . . . It was in just the area of Russia's greatest need that Stalin showed his greatest strength. . . . He was above all an administrator better suited to directing the gigantic military and civilian bureaucracy than to initiating and formulating military plans.[11]

Suggested Additional Reading

BLOOMFIELD, LINCOLN, et al. *Khrushchev and the Arms Race . . . , 1954–1964* (Cambridge, Mass., 1966).

BOFFA, GIUSEPPE. *Inside the Khrushchev Era* (New York, 1963).

BRANT, STEFAN. *The East German Rising* (New York, 1957).

BRESLAUER, G. W. *Khrushchev and Brezhnev as Leaders* (London, 1982).

BRZEZINSKI, ZBIGNIEW. *The Soviet Bloc: Unity and Conflict*, rev. ed. (New York, 1961).

BRUMBERG, A., ed. *Russia Under Khrushchev* (New York, 1962).

[11]*Stalin and His Generals: Soviet Military Memoirs of World War II*, ed. Severyn Bialer (New York, 1969), pp. 34–44.

CHOTINER, B. A. *Khrushchev's Party Reform* (Westport, Conn., 1984).

COHEN, S., ed. *The Soviet Union Since Stalin* (Bloomington, Ind., 1980).

CRANKSHAW, E. *Khrushchev: A Career* (New York, 1966).

DALLIN, D. J. *Soviet Foreign Policy After Stalin* (Philadelphia, 1961).

DINERSTEIN, HERBERT S. *The Making of a Missile Crisis: October 1962* (Baltimore, Md., 1976).

FEIFER, GEORGE. *Justice In Moscow* (New York, 1964).

FRANKLAND, M. *Khrushchev* (New York, 1967).

GITTINGS, J. *Survey of the Sino-Soviet Dispute, 1963–1967* (New York, 1968).

GRIFFITH, W. E. *Albania and the Sino-Soviet Rift* (Cambridge, Mass., 1963).

HILDEBRANDT, R. *The Explosion* (New York, 1955). (Berlin uprising.)

HYLAND, W., and R. SHRYOCK. *The Fall of Khrushchev* (New York, 1969).

KASER, MICHAEL. *Integration Problems of the Planned Economies*, 2d ed. (London, 1965).

KHRUSHCHEV, N. S. *Khrushchev Remembers* (Boston, 1971).

———. *Khrushchev Remembers: The Last Testament* (Boston, 1974).

LEE, WILLIAM, and RICHARD STAAR. *Soviet Military Policy Since World War II* (Stanford, Calif., 1986).

LEONHARD, W. *The Kremlin Since Stalin* (New York, 1962).

LEVINE, IRVING R. *Main Street USSR* (Garden City, N.Y., 1959).

LINDEN, C. A. *Khrushchev and the Soviet Leadership, 1957–1964* (London, 1967).

MacINTOSH, J. M. *Strategy and Tactics of Soviet Foreign Policy* (London, 1963).

MEDVEDEV, R., and ZHORES MEDVEDEV. *Khrushchev: The Years in Power* (New York, 1978).

PETHYBRIDGE, R. W. *A History of Postwar Russia* (New York, 1970).

PISTRAK, L. *The Grand Tactician: Khrushchev's Rise to Power* (New York, 1961).

PLOSS, SIDNEY. *Conflict and Decision-Making Process in Soviet Russia: A Case Study of Agricultural Policy, 1953–1963* (Princeton, N.J., 1965).

ROTHBERG, A. *The Heirs of Stalin. Dissidence and the Soviet Regime, 1953–1970* (Ithaca, N.Y., 1972).

RUSH, MYRON. *Political Succession in the USSR*, 2d ed. (New York, 1965).

SCHOLMER, J. *Vorkuta* (New York, 1955). (Uprising in the labor camp.)

SMOLANSKY, O. *The Soviet Union and the Arab East Under Khrushchev* (Lewisburg, Pa., 1974).

SOBEL, L. A. *Russia's Rulers: The Khrushchev Period* (New York, 1971).

SYROP, K. *Spring in October: The Polish Revolution of 1956* (New York, 1958).

TATU, M. *Power in the Kremlin: From Khrushchev to Kosygin* (New York, 1969).

ULAM, ADAM. *New Face of Soviet Totalitarianism* (New York, 1965).

WOLFE, B. *Khrushchev and Stalin's Ghost* (New York, 1957). (On the secret speech.)

ZAGORIA, D. *The Sino-Soviet Conflict, 1955–1961* (Princeton, N.J., 1962).

———. *Vietnam Triangle: Moscow, Peking, Hanoi* (New York, 1967).

ZINNER, P. *Revolution in Hungary* (Cambridge, Mass., 1961).

CHAPTER SEVENTEEN

SOVIET CULTURE SINCE STALIN, 1953–1990

The death of Stalin ushered in the first of a series of "thaws" in Soviet culture culminating in the Gorbachev revolution. A largely spontaneous outburst of activity in the arts, coupled with Khrushchev's efforts to rid the Soviet Union of the worst aspects of Stalinism, produced a remarkable cultural revival. Soviet cultural policies under Khrushchev and Brezhnev fluctuated between "thaws" and "freezes," but there was no full-scale return to the Stalin-Zhdanov approach. But until the Gorbachev era, socialist realism persisted as the guiding principle in literature and the arts, and the regime intervened decisively to prevent overt expression of dissident viewpoints—as the careers of Alexander Solzhenitsyn, Boris Pasternak, Andrei Amalrik, and Zhores Medvedev revealed.

THE THAW, 1953–1956

An article of May 1953 deploring the lack of human emotion in Soviet films reflected an initial cautious reaction against Zhdanovism. It decried depersonalized "human machines," standard in Soviet films, as untrue to

387

life. A heroine agreeing to marry the hero only if he overfulfilled his production norm was a travesty on human feelings, it claimed. Socialist quotas were important for socialist realism, but individual lives amounted to more than that. Such a view could not have been expressed openly in Stalin's final years. In the new, freer air bold ideas found their way into print. The new collective leadership recognized the utter sterility of Soviet culture under Zhdanovism and permitted freer discussion of alternative approaches.

An article that November by composer Aram Khachaturian, "On Creative Boldness and Imagination," directly attacked bureaucratic interference, which had almost destroyed Soviet musical culture: "We must once and for all reject the worthless interference in musical composition as practiced by the musical establishments. Problems of composition cannot be solved bureaucratically." Without repudiating socialist realism, Khachaturian insisted on artistic integrity. "Let the individual artist be trusted more fully, and not be constantly supervised and suspected."

Others joined the burgeoning criticism. The respected poet Alexander Tvardovskii, editor of the prestigious journal *New World*, denounced Soviet literature as arid, "contrived and unreal." Ilia Ehrenburg, a well-known author and former apologist for Stalin, concluded sadly that Russian classics were more popular with the public than contemporary authors because the older works dealt with human emotions and feelings. Could anyone "imagine ordering Tolstoy to write *Anna Karenina?*"

Not everyone shared these liberal views. Stalinist hard-liners had their spokespersons too, and there was some sharp infighting. But party leaders allowed the artistic intelligentsia freer rein. The mood of the times was captured by Ehrenburg's short novel *The Thaw* (1954), which aptly described these years. Stalinist Russia had been frozen solid, rigid, and sombre. The post-Stalin era was an intellectual spring heralded by melting of ice that had prevented growth. Ehrenburg's novel marked a new path for Soviet culture to follow. Writers of "the thaw" stressed recognition of the gulf between the real and the ideal and emphasized truth in all its complexity, rejected tyranny and fear, and expressed concern for human dignity and the individual; they admitted shortcomings in Soviet life. Ehrenburg believed that these fundamental artistic aims could best be achieved within socialist realism. Great enthusiasm about these issues led to an outburst of literary activity from 1954 to 1956. Poetry annuals and literary almanacs appeared without formal approval by the Writers' Union, and new poetic and prose talents emerged.

Despite high optimism among younger Soviet writers and artists in these years, conservative and Stalinist writers fought hard to defend Zhdanovist principles and retain control of literary institutions. At the Second Congress of Soviet Writers in December 1954, A. Surkov, the

Stalinist Secretary of the Writers' Union, sharply denounced the new mood and trends and demanded a return to Zhdanovist ideological purity. But others at the Congress insisted on even greater freedom, rehabilitation of disgraced writers, recognition of émigré writers, and publication of banned works. Liberals in the Writers' Union looked to Ehrenburg and young writers; conservatives relied on old-line Stalinists who controlled the Union. Because party leaders did not intervene, the two factions fought to a stalemate.

At the 20th Party Congress (February 1956) the pendulum swung toward the liberals. Surkov's hard-line diatribe was answered boldly by Mikhail Sholokhov, who denounced literary bureaucrats and hacks who claimed to speak for all Soviet literature. "A writer can learn nothing from Surkov," he concluded. "Why do we need such leaders?" That Sholokhov said this openly at the 20th Party Congress indicates a climate tolerating intellectual debate. Khrushchev's secret speech had compromised many Stalinist writers, temporarily weakening their influence in the Writers' Union. Thus some works sharply critical of aspects of contemporary Soviet life were published. In 1956, *New World* issued Vladimir Dudintsev's novel *Not by Bread Alone*, which exemplified liberal cultural trends. It castigated the exploitation and victimization of talent by arrogant Soviet bureaucrats, outraging literary bureaucrats like Surkov.

DR. ZHIVAGO AND THE REFREEZE

In this optimistic atmosphere of 1956, Boris Pasternak (1890–1960) submitted his now famous novel *Dr. Zhivago* to *New World*. Pasternak enjoyed the reputation of an outstanding poetic talent even before the Revolution, but had remained largely silent under Stalin, publishing occasional poems, essays, and translations. His extraordinary translations of Shakespeare set a standard for all Soviet translations. Pasternak remained an aloof loner and internal exile, quietly completing his novel in 1955. Revealing his political naiveté, he fully expected *New World* to publish *Dr. Zhivago*. Like Zamiatin and Pilniak 30 years before, he gave a manuscript copy to an Italian publisher, Feltrinelli, for preparation of an Italian edition after the work appeared in the USSR. To Pasternak's dismay, *New World*'s editors politely refused to publish the novel, but Feltrinelli, despite Surkov's protests, published an Italian translation in November 1957. Soon *Dr. Zhivago* appeared in English and an original Russian version was published in the West. It was hailed abroad as a masterpiece, and Pasternak was awarded the Nobel Prize for literature in October 1958, but he was pressured by party authorities to reject it.

Viciously denounced in the Soviet press, he was expelled from the Writers' Union and constantly hounded by the authorities, literally to death in 1960, another victim of the Soviet literary inquisition.

The intensely personal *Dr. Zhivago* traces the story of Yuri Zhivago from prerevolutionary times through the Soviet period. Zhivago's life is a shambles; he never uses his medical training. His life's work is a slender volume of poetry included at the end of the novel, Zhivago's legacy to humankind. Pasternak was proclaiming that though he had produced nothing practical, his poetry, like Zhivago's, could stimulate people to think and act creatively. Zhivago's poems, among Pasternak's most profound creations, contain the novel's essence, affirming the constant renewal of life as suggested by Zhivago's name, meaning "living" (*zhivoi*). Pasternak served as a living bridge from the prerevolutionary Russian literary tradition that stressed human spiritual qualities to contemporary Soviet life. In *Dr. Zhivago* Pasternak's essentially religious conception of the future was based on unwavering faith in resurrection and salvation for Zhivago and Russia itself.

Believing the Soviet public unprepared for such a message, party authorities prevented the novel's publication in the USSR. However, "Lara's Theme" from the 1965 film's score became a hit in Moscow, although the film was banned there.

Even before the Pasternak "affair," the pendulum began swinging back as the screws tightened again on Soviet culture. Soviet armed intervention in Hungary in October 1956 struck at burgeoning de-Stalinization. The more relaxed atmosphere of the thaw ended as Khrushchev moved decisively to halt a headlong race toward liberalization. He warned students of Moscow University to be careful or they would face the full force of his regime. Two hundred students were expelled and the rest intimidated. Stalinism remained fresh in people's minds.

CULTURE UNDER KHRUSHCHEV

Khrushchev's de-Stalinization campaign had loosened the Soviet grip on the Communist Bloc. Hard-pressed by party conservatives, he adopted a more conventional cultural militancy. The abrupt change in official policy caught many off guard. Thus late in 1956 the Soviet poet Evgenii Yevtushenko published a provocative poem proclaiming: "Certainly there have been changes; but behind the speeches/ Some murky game is being played./ We talk and talk about things we didn't mention yesterday;/ We say nothing about the things we did ourselves." This devastating criticism of party leaders and Khrushchev revealed that the more Stalin's actions were discredited, the more present leaders were implicated in his crimes. This could not go unchallenged. Yevtushenko was summarily dismissed from the *Komsomol* (Young Communist League) and stripped of many privileges.

When intellectuals proved slow to respond to Khrushchev's insistence on greater ideological conformity, he personally demanded compliance with his directives. He told Moscow writers at a garden party at his dacha that they were expendable; unless they cooperated, he would use force. Hungary's difficulties in the 1956 revolt could have been avoided, he declared, if intellectuals who had stirred up rebellion had been shot. Khrushchev assured the stunned writers: "My hand will not tremble" (if force were required). The initial post-Stalin thaw had fallen victim to Khrushchev's political requirements and ambition.

Consolidating his personal power by March 1958, Khrushchev cautiously resumed de-Stalinization and built bridges to the West. Some foreign travel was permitted, and cultural exchanges were negotiated with Western countries, including the United States. The literary thaw resumed. Promising and talented young writers published works that focused more on individual concerns in a complex industrial society rather than "building socialism." Writers picked up threads of the earlier thaw and wove them into a new, more sophisticated literature. Despite opposition from party conservatives, fearful of liberal works and cultural rapprochement with the West, the liberals regained their ascendancy. Debate, disagreement, innovation, and experimentation were tolerated within limits. At the Third Congress of Soviet Writers in 1959, Khrushchev expressed satisfaction with the cultural atmosphere. He would be liberal, in Soviet terms, if writers supported the party.

Numerous works appearing in the next years testified to the imaginative power of young, unknown Soviet writers such as Aksionov, Nagibin, Kazakov, Tendryakov, and Voinovich. Discarding the literary didacticism and moralizing of much socialist realist literature, their stories and novels revealed a renewed concern for style, psychology, and human emotions. Attracting much popular attention, their works were avidly read and discussed. Taboo subjects were now openly debated. Thus in 1961 Yevtushenko published his famous *Babi Yar*, an extraordinarily powerful poem about the 33,000 Soviet Jews slaughtered by the Nazis in 1941 in Babi Yar ravine near Kiev. Memorializing the innocent Jews, the poem castigated anti-Semitism, whether in Fascist or Communist guise. Russian anti-Semitism still "rises in the fumes of alcohol and in drunken conversations." The poem was attacked violently by conservatives as slandering the heroic Russian people who had sacrificed so much to destroy Nazism. Liberals lauded Yevtushenko's courage in confronting squarely a problem deeply rooted in the Russian psyche.

Monument at Babi Yar (*Michael Curran*)

The liberal tendency gained ground elsewhere, too. Early in 1962 the respected art critic Mikhail Alpatov published a defense of modern, abstract art. Others followed, suggesting that "the 20th century is becoming an age of triumphant abstractions." Why was the USSR so backward in appreciating modern art? Moscow's venerable Tretiakov Gallery began cautiously opening its vaults to exhibit some innovative early 20th-century Russian artworks, such as those of Kandinskii and Malevich. The poet Bella Akhmadulina proclaimed optimistically in 1961: "I think the time has become happy for us, that it now runs in our favor. Not only can my comrades work, but they are given every encouragement in their endeavor."

During 1962 the liberals pushed their advantage. In October Yevtushenko's poem, "Stalin's Heirs" appeared in *Pravda*. It was a remarkable commentary on the times: "He [Stalin] was scheming./ Had merely dozed off./ And I, appealing to our government, petition them to double/ and treble,/ the sentries guarding this slab,/ and stop Stalin from ever rising again/ and, with Stalin the past." Yevtushenko bluntly confronted the possibility of the revival of Stalinism:

No, Stalin has not given up.
He thinks he can outsmart death.
We carried him from the mausoleum.
But how carry Stalin's heirs away from Stalin?
Some of his retired heirs tend roses thinking in secret
Their enforced leisure will not last . . .

No wonder Stalin's heirs seem to suffer
these days from heart trouble.
They, the former henchmen, hate this era
Of emptied prison camps
And auditoriums full of people listening to poets.[1]

Acknowledging that he had personally authorized publication of Yevtushenko's poem, Khrushchev hinted at a new round of de-Stalinization.

Further confirmation of this came when Khrushchev authorized the unexpurgated publication of Alexander Solzhenitsyn's *One Day in the Life of Ivan Denisovich* in *New World*'s November 1962 issue. Solzhenitsyn's first published work was a powerful portrayal of everyday life in a Stalinist prison camp. Based on his own experiences in the camps, it was understated, dispassionate, and nonpolemical, bringing to life in searing detail one ordinary day in Ivan Denisovich's prison life. It recorded the agony of an inmate reduced to animal level for survival but whose dignity and humanity remained intact. Ivan Denisovich symbolized the indomitable courage of the Russian people in their continuing struggle for freedom and human dignity. *One Day* became an instant sensation, touching millions of Soviet citizens who had experienced years of days like Ivan Denisovich's. Public sentiment about the brutal inhumanity of Stalin's terror was stirred again in apparent preparation for renewed de-Stalinization.

Just as this new campaign began, Khrushchev was immersed in the turbulent political waters of the Cuban missile crisis (October 1962) and an open Sino-Soviet dispute (see Chapter 16). These crises abroad combined with growing economic problems at home again threatened Khrushchev's control of party and state. Sharp consumer price increases that autumn caused outbreaks of violence among workers. All this persuaded Khrushchev to renounce more de-Stalinization.

"Stalin's heirs" prepared a counterattack on the cultural front in November 1962. To a retrospective art exhibition, "Thirty Years of Soviet Art" at the huge Manezh Gallery near the Kremlin were added

---

[1]Cited in Priscilla Johnson, *Khrushchev and the Arts*, trans. G. Reavey (Cambridge, Mass., 1965), pp. 93–95.

about 75 modernistic canvases and sculptures, apparently as an elaborate "provocation" by cultural conservatives. On December 1, Khrushchev and several Presidium members visited the gallery unannounced. He spent most of his time in three small rooms viewing modernistic works of contemporary Soviet artists. His reaction was what conservatives had anticipated—violent and vulgar. Khrushchev's vicious verbal attack startled liberals, then enjoying a heyday. Pausing before an abstract painting, he remarked:

> I would say this is just a mess. . . . Polyanskii [Presidium member] told me a couple of days ago that when his daughter got married she was given a picture of what was supposed to be a lemon. It consisted of some messy yellow lines that looked . . . as though some child had done his business on the canvas when his mother was away and then spread it around with his hands.

Further on, he lashed out against jazz music: "When I hear jazz, it's as if I had gas on the stomach. I used to think it was static when I heard it on the radio." Proceeding through the exhibition, he declared:

> As long as I am chairman of the Council of Ministers, we are going to support a genuine art. We aren't going to give a kopeck for pictures painted by jackasses.

Speaking to one artist but referring to all modernist painters, Khrushchev fulminated:

> You've either got to get out [of the USSR] or paint differently. As you are, there's no future for you on our soil. . . . Gentlemen, we are declaring war on you.[2]

Hours later began a war for "ideological purity." Press editorials demanded that all unions of writers, artists, composers, and cinema workers be amalgamated in order to prevent nonconformity. The message was clear: centralize and control. Some Stalinist bureaucrats ceased "tending roses" and returned to prominent posts. At a meeting between party authorities and cultural leaders to discuss the current situation, Leonid Ilyichev, the Central Committee's chief ideologist, deplored recent demands by intellectuals to end all Soviet censorship and attacked the inexorable advance of Western "bourgeois" influences on Soviet culture. Following his hard-line speech ensued remarkably candid informal exchanges between party officials and writers and artists. Ehrenburg boldly defended the new freedom, insisting that modern art was not a cover for political reaction. Yevtushenko defended abstract painters,

---

[2]Johnson, *Khrushchev and the Arts*, pp. 101–105.

arguing they needed time to straighten out problems in their art. Khrushchev reportedly broke in shouting: "The grave straightens out the hunchback." Unintimidated, Yevtushenko retorted: "Nikita Sergeevich [Khrushchev], we have come a long way since the time when only the grave straightened out hunchbacks." The assembled writers and artists broke into applause with Khrushchev joining in. The intellectuals' unity and sense of common purpose at this meeting provided conservatives with ammunition in the battle against modernism.

The affair of Shostakovich's 13th Symphony further revealed the tense situation. Its first movement was a musical version of Yevtushenko's poem *Babi Yar*. The new symphony was to premiere the evening after the great gathering of party officials and intellectuals. Allegedly, Ilyichev demanded its withdrawal, but Shostakovich refused. The premiere went forward, though many musicians and the choir hesitated, fearing reprisals. After a second performance, further performances were cancelled. As Moscow's frigid winter descended, a new ideological freeze chilled the intellectual community.

It culminated in March 1963 at a gathering of over 600 intellectuals. Ilyichev again attacked writers in general and Ehrenburg in particular. Ehrenburg had argued in his memoirs, *People, Years, Life* (1960–1961), that he and others had known full well what was occurring in the USSR in the 1930s but had to remain silent with "clenched teeth." Ilyichev accused Ehrenburg of enjoying special privileges under Stalin and of having frequently praised him hypocritically whereas he (Ilyichev) and his colleagues had flattered Stalin allegedly out of sincere conviction. Ehrenburg considered that Ilyichev's false remarks made a reply unnecessary.

Khrushchev then delivered a devastating speech partially reaffirming Stalin's straightforward, uncomplicated tastes in art and literature and partially rehabilitating Stalin himself. Khrushchev sought to exonerate Stalin's entourage, and himself, of complicity in his crimes. He then realized the dangers of further de-Stalinization, which might raise questions like "What were you doing during Stalin's criminal rampages?" Ilyichev affirmed he had not known what was happening. Ehrenburg argued that he knew of Stalin's crimes but had remained silent, thus admitting complicity or cowardice. It was clearly better to leave Stalin's ghost alone. De-Stalinization ended as Stalin's conservative heirs used abstract art to dissuade the party from further liberalization. Khrushchev had to yield to mounting pressure within the party, and his personal cultural tastes seemed closer to the conservatives than to the liberals. Anyway, the lid slammed down again. Throughout 1963 at meetings organized by the party, leading cultural figures acknowledged their "errors" and pledged to abide by the party's wise guidance in all matters. Shostakovich, Yevtushenko, Voznesenskii, and many others submitted. Open ferment ended or was submerged. A light frost prevailed with only occasional sunshine.

CULTURE UNDER BREZHNEV

Khrushchev's fall in October 1964 did not herald a new thaw. Brezhnev and Kosygin maintained the status quo: comprehensive cultural controls and inflexible conformity. Writing for "the desk drawer" or painting for "the closet" continued, becoming more widespread after fleeting moments of relative freedom. Literary works in increasing numbers circulated surreptitiously in manuscript copies; artists showed their latest abstract works privately. An organized Soviet counterculture emerged.

New developments in liberal literary circles included *samizdat* and *tamizdat*. *Samizdat*, a play on *Gosizdat*—State Publishing House—meant "self-publication" by authors, not the state. Because individuals lacked access to printing presses, most *samizdat* materials were produced on typewriters or mimeograph machines. Smudged carbon copies circulated from hand to hand; new copies were made when needed. *Tamizdat* referred to materials published abroad—"over there"—that were then smuggled back into the Soviet Union. A considerable body of clandestine literature accumulated in the USSR not subject to official control or censorship.

The Trial of Siniavskii and Daniel

Writing for the desk drawer was often frustrating and unrewarding, so authors sought other means of uncensored expression. Publishing abroad had always been dangerous, as the fate of Zamiatin and Pasternak had shown. Their works had been published abroad out of confusion and misunderstanding, not from conscious intent to evade Soviet censorship. That did not save those authors from vilification and abuse, but neither one was put on trial. Andrei Siniavskii, a distinguished literary critic, and Iuli Daniel, a young writer, consciously evaded party literary controls by smuggling manuscripts out of the USSR for publication abroad under the pseudonyms Abram Tertz (Siniavskii) and Nikolai Arzhak (Daniel), beginning in 1956, when the first thaw ended. For nine years they escaped detection and published stories, short novels, and essays highly critical of Soviet life. These were the first examples of *samizdat* and *tamizdat*.

Siniavskii's publications abroad included a long essay, "On Socialist Realism" (1960), denouncing that doctrine as old-fashioned and inappropriate for the modern USSR. Soviet literature was "a monstrous salad" whose content was distorted by a rigidly imposed form, where bureaucrats regularly interfered. Siniavskii urged abandoning socialist realism and returning to Mayakovskii's literary experimentation of the 1920s. Also published abroad was *The Trial Begins* (1960), a fictional exposé of Soviet justice as fraudulent, cynical, and arbitrary. Other works poked fun at Soviet foibles or satirized Soviet life. All criticized Soviet institutions, but none was directly anti-Soviet.

Daniel's works were, from a Western perspective, rather harmless literary exercises, less sophisticated than Siniavskii's. Of his four stories published abroad, "This Is Moscow Speaking" and "Hands" are the most interesting. The former is a macabre tale about a Public Murder Day supposedly decreed by the Politburo: On August 10, 1961, all citizens over 16 could kill almost anyone they wished between 6 A.M. and midnight. When people failed to use this license to kill, the party condemned it as sabotage, thus implying that mass terror could be reintroduced in the USSR without much public response. The story "Hands" deals with the psychological impact of terror. A former Cheka officer suffers from chronically shaking hands after being ordered as a young secret policeman to shoot priests accused of counterrevolutionary activities. His friends played a joke on him by loading his pistol with blank cartridges. When the priests implored the young officer not to shoot, advancing with outstretched hands, the officer had shot repeatedly as the priests "miraculously" continued to advance. That experience so unnerved the officer that his hands shook constantly.

The KGB (security police) mounted an intense campaign to identify Tertz and Arzhak. (Computers analyzed their writing styles.) Finally, Siniavskii and Daniel were arrested in September 1965, accused under the infamous Article 70 of the criminal code of disseminating "slanderous" and "defamatory" inventions about the Soviet system. After the defendants were convicted in the press, a public trial was held in February 1966. Siniavskii received seven years hard labor (the maximum sentence) and Daniel five years.

The Siniavskii-Daniel trial was unique in Soviet justice. Never before had writers been tried for their writings. Many writers had been publicly denounced and accused of various "crimes"—Zamiatin, Zoshchenko, and Pasternak; many more had disappeared during the purges, but none had been tried in open court. A brilliant young Leningrad poet, and eventual Nobel laureate, Josef Brodskii, had been tried and convicted in 1964, not for his writings, but as a "parasite" lacking gainful employment. (He was a poet but not a member of the Writers' Union.) Unlike defendants in other Soviet public trials, Siniavskii and Daniel defended themselves valiantly.

The harsh sentences shocked Soviet intellectuals. With remarkable unity, liberal intellectuals in the arts and sciences wrote to party authori-

Andrei Siniavskii (right) and Iuli Daniel at their Moscow trial in February 1966 for allegedly slandering the Soviet system with writings published abroad *(SOVFOTO)*

ties to protest the treatment of Siniavskii and Daniel. The only major Soviet writer to support the regime fully over this issue was Mikhail Sholokhov, Nobel Prize laureate, who declared that the sentences were much too mild! Party leaders were unmoved by the storm of protest over the sentences. The trial had aimed to intimidate dissenters. Siniavskii and Daniel were scapegoats for a new "get tough" policy. The trial warned Soviet intellectuals that all works by Soviet citizens were subject to censorship. Succumbing to public pressure would have undermined that aim.

Still, the Siniavskii-Daniel trial backfired, becoming a milestone in a continuing struggle between party leaders and the intellectual elite. From the 1920s onward the literary intelligentsia had been preoccupied with a search for truth based on the conviction that it could be found only in artistic or intellectual freedom. Writers had sought to liberate the creative process from arbitrary party interference. They sought to foster the artistic and moral values of traditional Russian literature: deep concern for the individual, psychological truth, intellectual honesty, and a multifaceted realism. Siniavskii's and Daniel's advocacy of these values led them into direct conflict with the authorities. After their trial, the Soviet intelligentsia realized that the artistic rights they sought could only be achieved with basic political freedoms.

This new consciousness triggered by the Siniavskii-Daniel affair created an unprecedented movement of dissent. Questions were asked about topics previously taboo even in liberal periods of Soviet history. The lack of basic rights, such as freedom from fear and freedoms of speech, press, and assembly—all guaranteed supposedly by the Stalin Constitution—was widely discussed by Soviet intellectuals. The realization grew that Soviet citizens' fundamental rights were violated daily. The Constitution did not authorize censorship. How, then, could the party dictate what writers could or could not write or proscribe peaceful protest? These questions deeply disturbed many intellectuals.

Protesting the harsh sentences in the Siniavskii-Daniel trial, four young intellectuals, led by Alexander Ginzburg, collected extensive materials on the trial, including a verbatim transcript. Their aim was to induce the authorities to reopen the case and review the sentences. In January 1967 copies of these materials were sent to the KGB and Supreme Soviet deputies. The official response was to arrest the four young compilers, but a copy of the "white paper" had reached the West and was published. In January 1968 the four were tried and convicted under the notorious Article 70. The sentences of two, Iuri Galanskov and Ginzburg, were harsher than those of Siniavskii and Daniel. The Galanskov-Ginzburg trial evoked unprecedented public protests and triggered a broader civil rights movement.

Andrei Sakharov, the leading Soviet nuclear physicist and "father of the Soviet H-bomb," organized the Human Rights Movement in 1970. It was designed to protest official policies that violated fundamental individual rights guaranteed by the Soviet Constitution. These freedoms were specified in the UN Declaration of Human Rights, which was signed by the USSR. Prominent Soviet intellectuals joined in the clamor of protest. The regime responded with further unpublicized arrests and repression. The dissenters sought to inform the public of illegal official actions in *The Chronicle of Current Events,* a remarkable *samizdat* account of arrests, harassments, and exiles. The Brezhnev regime found it increasingly difficult to hide behind a veil of secrecy. The Human Rights Movement aimed not to overthrow the regime or alter the basic Soviet legal structure but merely to have existing laws enforced fairly and uniformly. Its patriotic members sought to have Soviet constitutional provisions observed in practice.

Alexander Solzhenitsyn *(United Press International)*

Alexander Solzhenitsyn

Intimately associated with the movement of dissent in the late 1960s and early 1970s was Alexander Solzhenitsyn. His renown grew steadily after publication of his novel *One Day in the Life of Ivan Denisovich* in 1962, though only a few more of his stories were published. Born in 1918, he studied mathematics and physics, became a teacher, and fought valiantly as an artillery officer in World War II. Near the war's end he was arrested and sentenced to the labor camps for referring to Stalin in a personal letter seized by the security police as "the man with the moustache." After eight years in labor camps and three more in exile in Central Asia, Solzhenitsyn in 1956 was considered fully rehabilitated, all charges against him were dismissed as groundless, and his civil rights were restored. *One Day* earned him recognition as a powerful writer and moral authority. Nevertheless, his few published works enraged party conservatives, and under Brezhnev the authorities decided that no more of his works should be published. Despite this decision, Alexander Tvardovskii, editor of *New World,* accepted a major Solzhenitsyn novel, *The Cancer Ward,* for publication there in 1968. The type was already set when the party abruptly ordered Tvardovskii to halt publication. The Galanskov-Ginzburg trial and accompanying protests caused the regime to block publication of a novel dealing with repression, abuse of power, and moral decay. Meanwhile a manuscript copy reached the West and was promptly published over Solzhenitsyn's objections. Nonetheless, the Soviet press orchestrated vicious attacks on the author.

The Cancer Ward deals with the terrifying experiences of Rusanov, a high Soviet official. After discovering he has cancer, Rusanov is unable to use his connections to enter an elite clinic and is confined in an ordinary cancer ward, packed with inconsequential, unsympathetic people whom he despises. Rusanov's antithesis is another cancer patient, Kostoglotov, a veteran of the labor camps and exile. He has suffered and survived, but no longer values life nor fears death. With literally nothing to lose, he has much strength to combat cancer. Rusanov, by contrast, has everything to lose—position, wealth, and family—and fear of death makes him desperate. He cannot accept his condition or combat it rationally.

Another Solzhenitsyn novel, *The First Circle,* an extension on a different level of *One Day,* was published in the West in 1968, but not in Brezhnev's USSR. It depicts a prison housing scholars, scientists, and engineers, all convicted of state crimes. Required to work on state scientific projects, they do not feel the physical anguish of Ivan Denisovich; although well-fed and well-housed, they experience a mental anguish more degrading and destructive than physical suffering. Again Solzhenitsyn deals with a central theme that reappears constantly in his works: the indomitable human spirit triumphant over adversity.

Another of Solzhenitsyn's major works is the broad historical panorama *August 1914,* published in the West in 1971, the first of a series of historical works dealing with Russia's travails in World War I and the Revolutions of 1917. Solzhenitsyn contrasts the Russian people's heroic struggle with the tsarist government's criminal incompetence. A historical parallel between Russia in World War I and the Soviet Union in World War II is evident.

Publication in the West of Solzhenitsyn's works led to a mounting campaign of persecution and public vilification against him. His international reputation and the Brezhnev regime's sensitivity to world opinion provided him a security that other dissenters, except for Sakharov, lacked. Like Kostoglotov in *The Cancer Ward,* Solzhenitsyn had suffered all that the Stalin regime could subject him to, and life held no terrors. Short of physical annihilation, he could not be intimidated or silenced. He spoke out courageously against censorship, repression, and injustice.

"No one can bar the road to truth," he proclaimed in a famous letter circulated at the Fourth Congress of Soviet Writers in 1967, "and to advance its cause I am prepared to accept even death." Solzhenitsyn demanded an end to all censorship, insisting on absolute freedom for writers and artists:

> Literature cannot develop in between the categories of "permitted" and "not permitted," "about this you may write" and "about this you may not." Literature that is not the breath of contemporary society, that does not transmit the pains and fears of that society, that does not warn in time against threatening moral and social dangers—such literature does not deserve the name of literature; it is only a facade. Such literature loses the confidence of its own people, and its published works are used as wastepaper instead of being read.[3]

In 1970, Solzhenitsyn was awarded the Nobel Prize for literature. The anti-Pasternak scenario of 1958–1959 was reenacted as party hacks attacked Solzhenitsyn as a "leper" and had him expelled from the Writers' Union. This public assault failed to intimidate Solzhenitsyn as it had Pasternak. He proudly accepted the Nobel award but declined to go to Stockholm to receive it for fear of being denied reentry to the USSR. His eloquent Nobel lecture was smuggled to the West and published there in 1972. It was a dignified plea for freedom everywhere and reaffirmed strongly the moral responsibility of the writer and artist "to conquer falsehood." Harassment of Solzhenitsyn intensified in 1973. Fearing for his life, he managed to transmit some key manuscripts to friends in the West to prevent his enemies from silencing him even by death. He instructed his friends to publish them if anything happened to him.

In September 1973 the KGB pressured a Solzhenitsyn typist into revealing the whereabouts of a major underground manuscript she had typed. Solzhenitsyn promptly signaled his Western friends to publish the manuscript, previously smuggled abroad. The first volume of the monumental *The Gulag Archipelago, 1918–1956* was published in Paris in December 1973 and in numerous translations, including English, in 1974. Volumes two and three were issued in 1975. *The Gulag*, a powerfully moving history of the Soviet prison camp system, is dedicated "To all those who did not survive." Solzhenitsyn traces the prison camp system back to Lenin, although it developed into a monstrous structure only under Stalin. This remarkable account of man's inhumanity to man was based on Solzhenitsyn's personal experiences in the camps and those of hundreds of former prisoners (*zeks*) who shared their stories with

---

[3]Quoted in *Problems of Communism*, 17, no. 5, p. 38.

Solzhenitsyn. Publication of *The Gulag Archipelago* in the West provoked an unprecedented campaign of slander and abuse of Solzhenitsyn in the USSR and an equally tremendous international outpouring of support for him. The Brezhnev regime hesitated momentarily in the face of world opinion, but in February 1974 had Solzhenitsyn arrested and charged with treason. The next day he was taken to the Moscow airport and put on a plane for West Germany and involuntary exile. Soon his family joined him, and they settled down in the United States, where he has continued to write and denounce tyranny.

In emigration Solzhenitsyn identified himself with Russian Orthodoxy and criticized injustice and corruption not only in the Soviet Union, but also in the West. He denounced détente, arguing that it helped perpetuate the Soviet dictatorship. Solzhenitsyn grew increasingly strident in criticisms of the Soviet Union. Like Alexander Herzen, a 19th-century Russian exile in Europe, Solzhenitsyn continued from a Vermont farm his struggle against tyranny in his native land.

Other Soviet Writers

Under Brezhnev significant changes occurred in Soviet culture. While the state continued to determine what would be published officially, writers and artists achieved greater latitude than under Stalin or even under Khrushchev. During the 1970s some literary and artistic experimentation in form was permitted, producing some excellent results. The best Soviet writers created then a literature with credible characters in real situations. They wrote about personal conflicts and aspirations, not building communism. Renouncing the reformist political writing of the mid-1950s, they stressed concern with self and everyday problems and shifted away from the novel to the novella or short story. In this genre authors focused on isolated incidents, chance occurrences, and private moods and feelings.

The best writers under Brezhnev walked a tightrope between free literary expression and state-defined aesthetics. Iuri Nagibin's stories portray human love and passion on an intimate level. After visiting the United States, he described his impressions with great insight. Iuri Kazakov's characters have received little from Soviet society and are embittered, frustrated rejects. The characters of talented, youthful Vasili Aksionov often reflect dehumanizing aspects of the Soviet regime and closely resembled the drifters and dreamers of American fiction of the 1950s and 1960s. In the 1970s he examined the macabre, pursuing new directions that ultimately proved officially unacceptable.

The *derevenshchiki* ("village writers") favored contemporary rural settings, often in Siberia, for tightly woven, realistic portrayals of the

Kolkhozniki—collective farm workers. The rural heartland reflects the value of the *derevenshchiki* writers. These peasant faces reveal those values. *(Michael Curran)*

peasantry and daily life. Valentin Rasputin explored the pathos of peasant life objectively and clearly. His novella, *Live and Remember,* portrays the tribulations of a peasant deserter from World War II who depends on his wife's wisdom to outwit the authorities. In this simple story of struggle for survival, Rasputin passed no judgments. His gripping tale of rural life, "Money for Maria," describes the problems of a peasant woman managing the village general store. An official audit reveals a large cash shortage for which she is blamed. Respected in the village, she receives much support, but even the entire village cannot cover the shortage. In despair her husband seeks help from a relative in a distant city. Rasputin never reveals whether Maria is exonerated, or if the authorities punish her, but the strength and dignity of the peasant community triumphs. Rasputin's timeless story simply ignored the tenets of socialist realism. In the 1980s, Rasputin spearheaded the drive to save Lake Bacikal from pollution.

Vasili Shukshin's death at age 45 represented a serious loss for Soviet fiction, film, and theater, for he was innovative in all three fields. By his compelling human interest stories, Shukshin epitomized the *derevenshchiki* movement. His novella, *The Red Guelder Rose,* treats the formerly taboo subject of the criminal in Soviet society. After serving his sentence, a convict reforms and resolves to labor honestly in a village as an agricultural worker. His ideal world includes wife, family, and socially useful labor, but he cannot discard his criminal past. Eventually, the criminals from whom he had sought to escape murder him.

Literary innovation and artistic spontaneity also flourished among non-Russians. The popular stories of Fasil Iskander, a Georgian from Abkhazia, possess a remarkable conversational quality. "Something About Myself" (published in English in 1978) begins:

> Let's just talk . . . about things we don't have to talk about, pleasant things. Let's talk about some of the amusing sides of human nature, as embodied in people we know. There is nothing more enjoyable than discussing certain old habits of our acquaintances. Because, you see, talking about them makes us aware of our own healthy normality.

Iskander's "talk" is very incisive and symbolic. In "The Thirteenth Labor of Hercules," a parable about the efficacy of humor in facing reality, Iskander argues:

> It seems to me that ancient Rome perished because its emperors in all their marble magnificence failed to realize how ridiculous they were. If they had got themselves some jesters in time (you must hear the truth, if only from a fool), they might have lasted a little longer. But they just went on hoping that the geese would save Rome, and then the barbarians came and destroyed Rome, the emperors and its geese.

Was this intended for an aging Politburo under a moribund Brezhnev? Whatever Iskander's intent, his tales won him a deserved reputation as a gifted storyteller and subtle critic of the Soviet system. His two major works, *Sandro of Chegem* (1983) and *The Gospel According to Chegem* (1984), published in English translation but not in the USSR until recently, capture the spirit of the patriarchal village succumbing to inexorable modernization and Sovietization:

> In my childhood I caught fleeting glimpses of the patriarchal village of Abkhazia and fell in love with it forever. Have I perhaps idealized the vanishing life? Perhaps. A man cannot help ennobling what he loves. We may not recognize it, but in idealizing a vanishing way of life we are presenting a bell to the future. We are saying, "Here is what we are losing; what are you going to give us in exchange?" Let the future think on that if it is capable of thinking at all.[4]

Iskander portrays the modern history of Abkhazia in the Caucasus in stories featuring Uncle Sandro and many other unforgettable characters from Chegem village. Sandro is a fearless, independent spirit, irreverent toward the Soviet regime.

---

[4]F. Iskander, from Foreword to *Saudro of Chegem* (New York, 1983).

Iskander's digressions as narrator proved unacceptable to Soviet censors. For example:

> With characteristic frankness, Lenin confessed to Gorky . . . that he was humorless. . . . Lenin partially compensated for his deficiency in humor through his magnificent work as an organizer. After Lenin, unfortunately, the Bolsheviks, although they did not possess his genius, decided to follow his lead with respect to humor. . . . They appointed their most unsmiling man [Stalin] to be the country's leader, in the mistaken belief that the most unsmiling man was the most earnest one. This is what revealed the tragedy in the lack of a sense of humor. Yes, he did smile into his moustache with satisfaction, but only later, after 1937 [the Great Purge].[5]

Iuri Trifonov (1925–1981) balanced artistic integrity and political acceptability in his short career. His father, an Old Bolshevik, perished in the purges, but Trifonov adapted to party demands: an early novel of his received a Stalin Prize. In middle age, disdaining party approval, he established his reputation with a series of novellas that probed the past and its influence on the present. The past, he suggested, must be confronted in order to free the future from Stalin's savage legacy. *The House on the Embankment* depicted perceptively the impact of the Stalin era: the problems of growing up, seeking meaning in life, and finding a place in Soviet society from World War II to the mid-1970s. Flashbacks allow Trifonov to explore shifting Soviet values. The successes and failures of Glebov, the main character, are chronicled with nostalgia and resignation, symbolizing the ambiguities of Soviet life: "He dreamed of all the things that later came to him—but which brought him no joy because achieving them used up so much of his strength. . . ." Was that perhaps the fate of Soviet people struggling for small joys only to discover that their struggle merely entailed more travail? Here is no view of a radiant future, nor the party's triumph over adversity, but only the tribulations of an ordinary, unheroic person. One can pity Glebov and his periodic waverings, but the Soviet authorities failed to find Trifonov's work uplifting.

Trifonov's sombre novellas became immensely popular with Soviet readers, who mourned his untimely death in 1981. Trifonov's passing stilled a voice that had spoken appreciatively of ordinary people and everyday experiences, unlike socialist realism's often grandiose portraits, which seemed more and more divorced from Soviet reality. Trifonov's career revealed that genuine talent could flourish to some degree within

---

[5] F. Iskander, *The Gospel According to Chegem* (New York, 1984), pp. 264–265.

narrow Soviet confines. Few others negotiated as successfully the delicate boundary between artistic integrity and party dictates.

From a similar background Vasili Aksionov became an even more famous writer. More politically engaged, he clashed frequently with the authorities until he was forced to emigrate in 1980. Aksionov first won acclaim for his novella *Halfway to the Moon* (1961), recounting experiences of the first generation of Soviet youth to be deeply influenced by the West. His stories, plays, novels, and cinema scripts gained him a reputation as a prolific and outspoken writer.

What triggered Aksionov's expulsion from the USSR (he resides now in the United States) was his leadership in creating the literary anthology *Metropol,* which relentlessly demanded artistic freedom. Defying censorship, it was published in an edition of only 10 copies! Increasingly frustrated with literary censorship, Aksionov had his explosive novel *The Burn* published in Italy (1980) and the United States (1984) without authorization. Depicting Moscow intellectuals' alienation during the post-Stalin thaw, it became an instant success. Deeply influenced by the contemporary West and derived from Aksionov's experiences as a visting lecturer at UCLA in 1975, it is an intense and generally negative portrait of contemporary Soviet society. In style reminiscent of Thomas Pynchon, *The Burn* chronicles the adventures of five men with the same name. The novel has a memorable cast of characters, but the plot is weak and poorly developed.

More interesting is Aksionov's *The Island of Crimea,* a fantasy:

> What if Crimea really were an island? What if, as a result, the White Army had been able to defend Crimea from the Reds in 1920? What if Crimea had developed as a Russian, yet Western, democracy alongside the totalitarian mainland?[6]

Aksionov imagines a Crimea resembling contemporary Taiwan or Hong Kong replete with superhighways, neon lights, designer boutiques, and sun-worshipping bathers on beaches all within sight of the totalitarian mainland. Andrei Luchnikov, the main character and son of a White leader, successfully defends Crimea against the Red Army. Handsome, rich, and powerful, Luchnikov owns a newspaper that leads an unlikely and curious campaign to reunify capitalist Crimea with the Communist mainland. After his emigration, Aksionov's reputation continued to grow both abroad and in the USSR.

---

[6]V. Aksionov, from the Preface to *The Island of Crimea* (New York, 1983).

Other Cultural Areas

Although leaders in music and art under Brezhnev pushed the regime to the limits of the acceptable, little was produced that openly challenged party authority. The cinema remained largely a wasteland, despite a few exceptional works such as Andrei Tarkovskii's excellent and innovative film *Andrei Rublev,* about the great 14th-century Russian iconographer. Because of its religious theme, it could not be shown widely in the USSR, but it received an award at the Cannes Film Festival. The heroism of the Soviet people in World War II still strongly influenced filmmakers, who found in it a virtually inexhaustible supply of themes.

In music Dmitri Shostakovich remained the leading Soviet composer of the Brezhnev era. He continued to produce innovative, rather bitter masterpieces right to his death in 1975. Both his 13th (*Babi Yar*) and 14th symphonies, whose leitmotifs were death, were works of protest. In this period Soviet classical music underwent a slow but inexorable modernistic evolution and increasingly used Western composition techniques. New composers such as Boris Tishchenko and Rodion Shchedrin imitated Western experimentalism. To the unconcealed disgust of second-rate conservatives such as Tikhon Khrennikov, longtime head of the Composers' Union, they moved ever further from socialist realism's hallowed but deadening tenets. However, under Brezhnev none dared challenge ideological orthodoxy directly. During the 1970s the role of regional composers from various national republics grew significantly more important.

CULTURE UNDER GORBACHEV, 1985–1990

At first the new regime moved cautiously in the cultural realm until Gorbachev realized that his program of *perestroika* required endorsement and support from the entire country, especially the cultural elite. Glasnost greatly widened freedom for all the arts; artists' responses were enthusiastic but wary. Decades of cultural conditioning and conformity could not be discarded overnight. Prior experience taught that "thaws" were followed inevitably by "frosts" or even hard "freezes." However, it soon grew evident that Gorbachev was serious about reform and bold individuals decided to test glasnost's limits. The dissidents had already created bases for a Soviet counterculture. Their ideal—an open, freer cultural atmosphere without state-defined norms—fast became reality. The counterculture surfaced rapidly as many radical works, formerly considered unacceptable, now appeared, raising questions about controls

considered unacceptable, now appeared, raising questions about controls and censorship. These works that challenged traditional limits became powerful catalysts promoting truly free expression. Artists and journalists led this remarkable transformation of Soviet culture.

Organizations of writers, artists, and composers grew more important as control over culture shifted from traditional state-dominated organs, such as the Censorship Office and Ministry of Culture, and as the unions won greater influence over culture. But not all unions were dominated by the emerging "liberals." The powerful Writers' Union remained under conservative control, but grew more open and tolerant of various approaches to literature. Innovative leaders prevailed in other unions. Journal editors, historians, and scientists ardently supported glasnost.

An outspoken cultural leader was the Ukrainian writer Vitali Korotich, named editor of the influential journal *Ogonek* (*The Little Flame*) in 1986 and elected to the new Congress of Peoples' Deputies in 1989. He transformed the formerly stodgy, uninteresting journal into a very progressive vehicle of opinion, focusing attention on issues related to glasnost. Korotich stimulated the new national passion of seeking to recapture the past honestly and critically. He published articles critical of Stalin and Stalinism and openly confronted formerly taboo social problems such as prostitution, drug abuse, alcoholism, and the Afghan war. His willingness to push glasnost to its limits made *Ogonek* extremely popular. Nevertheless, Korotich realized that glasnost offered no guarantees: "It's like flying. There's a feeling of exhilaration, but you always have the thought in the back of your mind that the plane might crash."[7]

Gorbachev's political reforms and glasnost's freedom to criticize, speak out, publish, and exhibit sparked a creative renaissance in the USSR. Gorbachev recognized that if his revolution were to succeed it had to enlist the country's most creative minds and free them from party-imposed conformity. The USSR had to be opened to outside influences and its culture reintegrated into world culture. Nonetheless, opposition to glasnost and perestroika persisted, and Gorbachev's critics continued to denounce his policies. At a "conservative" rally in Moscow in February 1988, a Leningrad schoolteacher, Nina Andreeva, warned a wildly cheering crowd that Russia was threatened by a "counterrevolution" that was responsible for grave problems such as strikes, ethnic violence, and moral degradation. These problems, she argued, stemmed from Gorbachev's

---

[7]*Remaking the Revolution: The Soviet Union 70 Years Later* (Los Angeles, 1988), p. 31.

efforts to "westernize" the country and introduce "capitalist exploitation in all our cities."[8]

Literature: New and "Lost" Works

Established authors continued under Gorbachev to publish respectable if unimaginative works with broad appeal. A younger generation of talented, innovative writers emerged, but as of 1990 had not really found its true literary voice. Glasnost produced a major movement to recapture the portion of Soviet literary tradition long repressed by rigid cultural policies. Works that had languished in desk drawers or circulated in tattered manuscripts now were published at a furious rate, straining press capacity. Among long-suppressed classics finally issued in the USSR were Zamiatin's *We*, Pasternak's *Dr. Zhivago*, Akhmatova's *Requiem*, and Solzhenitsyn's *The Cancer Ward*. Even Solzhenitsyn's *The Gulag Archipelago* was being published in 1990. Other long-banned writers were rehabilitated, including Bulgakov, Pilniak, Babel, Mandelshtam, and Siniavskii. (See pages 396–399.) Soviet readers were introduced to long-forbidden émigré authors and Western writers formerly considered decadent. Works by Nobel laureates Josef Brodskii and Vladimir Nabokov were published, as was James Joyce's *Ulysses*. Recent émigré works like Aksionov's *The Burn* and Vladimir Voinovich's *The Life and Extraordinary Adventures of Private Ivan Chonkin* were also issued.

These "lost" works were also analyzed in literary journals and then reintegrated into the USSR's literary legacy. Restrictions on literature brought into the USSR were virtually eliminated. Taboo subjects almost disappeared, as indicated by publication of Anatoli Rybakov's *Children of the Arbat*. Written in the 1960s but set in 1933, this novel records boldly the sinister beginnings of the Great Purges and contains a chilling portrait of Stalin, depicting his callous disregard for human suffering and insatiable lust for power.

An avalanche of works about the Stalin era burst forth, calling attention to the extent of Stalinist repression, which struck the peasantry through collectivization, national minorities by deportation, religious believers through persecution, and the intelligentsia by intimidation. Many of these books had been written decades earlier but were never before published in the USSR. One example is Vasili Grossman's *Life and Fate*, a massive novel about World War II in scale comparable to Tolstoy's *War and Peace*; it was published in the West in 1985 and in the USSR in

---

[8]*New York Times*, February 24, 1988, p. 6. For more on glasnost and perestroika, see Chapter 20.

1988. It portrays with devastating honesty the trauma of war in the Soviet Union, especially in the Battle of Stalingrad, which unleashed Russian venality, prejudice, and suspicion. Grossman holds a mirror to Soviet society, which had glossed over negative aspects of the Soviet Union's wartime role. He draws disturbing parallels between Nazi Germany and Stalin's Russia and holds Lenin responsible for Stalinism and other evils in Soviet society. Completing the novel in 1960, he submitted it to the journal *Znamia* (*The Banner*), which rejected it as "anti-Soviet." The KGB then confiscated the manuscript and harassed Grossman, who died in poverty and isolation in 1964.

Similarly, Vladimir Dudintsev, best known for *Not by Bread Alone* (1956), in 1988 published *White Robes*, a stunning fictional account of the struggle by honest scientists against Trofim Lysenko's perversion of Soviet science under Stalin. (See Chapter 13.) Daniel Granin's curiously titled *Aurochs or Bison* (*Zubr*) depicts the moral dilemma of a Soviet scientist who flees the USSR because of political control of science to pursue his scientific work in Nazi Germany. Such works, questioning the validity of the entire Soviet experience, could not have been published in the USSR prior to Gorbachev.

Recently published officially in the USSR was Fazil Iskander's cycle *Sandro of Chegem* and *The Gospel According to Chegem*, which some critics believe may become a 20th-century Russian classic.[9] Anna Akhmatova's poem "Requiem," recently issued in the USSR, is an impassioned solemn chant for her son arrested during the Great Purges:

> Silent flows the Don
> Yellow moon looks quietly on
> Cap askew, looks in the room,
> Sees a shadow in the gloom.
> Sees the woman, sick, at home,
> Sees the woman, all alone,
> Husband buried, then to see
> Son arrested . . . Pray for me.[10]

Georgi Vladimov's novella *Faithful Ruslan*, published in the USSR in 1989 (1979 in the West) is a frightening parable about a loyal and determined trained guard dog at a Siberian forced labor camp. When the camp is closed, Ruslan cannot understand his new role. When the former prison camp becomes a cellulose factory with free workers, Ruslan and other guard dogs cannot differentiate them from prisoners and harass the

---

[9]Deming Brown, "Literature and Perestroika," *Michigan Quarterly Review*, 27, no. 4 (Fall 1989), p. 769.
[10]In *Selected Poems*, ed. Walter Arndt (Ann Arbor, Mich., 1976), p. 147.

workers as they had harassed the prisoners. Behavior cannot be changed easily after long conditioning, argues Vladimov. Human beings, like dogs, cannot escape their past.

Such literary archives now being opened are helping Soviet citizens come to grips with their brutal totalitarian past. Under Gorbachev literary attention has focused on that past rather than on new, experimental literary works. Noted the critic Georgi Baklanov in 1988:

> Three years ago we would never have dreamed of achieving what we have now achieved in the cultural sphere. Nevertheless, we are still lacking a lot . . . because our society is putting all its energy into convalescing.

However, such "convalescing" is essential if Soviet citizens are to understand massive current changes and place them in accurate context. Another critic, Tatiana Ivanova, wrote in *Ogonek:*

> Our time does not pass in vain. Who can measure the impact of the publication of Grossman's novel [*Life and Fate*] on many thousands of shocked minds? Is it possible for us not to notice the impact of reading *Children of the Arbat,* or *White Robes?* . . . The effect is enormous. . . . We will become different.[11]

A fascinating episode from the Gorbachev era is the national debate over a play not yet produced. The playwright, Mikhail Shatrov, published *On and On and On!* in the journal *Znamia* (The Banner) in 1988 and overnight became a celebrity. Himself a victim of Stalinism, losing his parents and close relatives in the purge, and trained as a mining engineer, Shatrov began writing plays in the early 1950s. Some of the early ones were about Lenin; all were controversial. *The Peace of Brest-Litovsk* (written in 1962, published in 1987) unleashed heated protests. *Pravda* denounced him for "distorting" Soviet history. That was minor compared to the controversy over publication of *On and On and On!,* which raised disturbing questions about the Bolshevik Revolution. His characters ask whether Lenin, had he known the Revolution's outcome, would have led the Bolsheviks in a forceful seizure of power in November 1917. Stalin, portrayed confronting dilemmas, resolves them violently because of his sadistic, paranoid personality. Shatrov wonders if Lenin could have intervened successfully to prevent Stalin's rise to power. Exploring alternatives, Shatrov says that Stalin's rule was not preordained.

Shatrov's irreverent treatment of the great icons of the Bolshevik Revolution and his questioning of its legitimacy ignited vehement protests. Three historians in *Pravda* accused him of "falsifying" history by

---

[11]Tatiana Ivanova, "Who Risks What?," *Ogonek,* no. 24, June 11–18, 1988, p. 12.

portraying Lenin as weak and vacillating. In light of Marxist economic determinism, his critics argued, how could Shatrov suggest that the Bolshevik Revolution was an "accident"? Nina Andreeva castigated Shatrov for spurning socialist realism. Why, she wondered, this obsession with criticizing Stalin? Numerous letters about the play streamed into *Znamia,* mostly praising the play and its publication. A policeman and party member from Irkutsk wrote:

> I want you and Shatrov to know that honest people who value truth and justice are grateful to you for your work which strengthens our belief in the irreversibility of the revolutionary reconstruction of our country.

An unsigned letter from Kiev expressed a very different view:

> Where is your responsibility to the party, your civic honor and simple human dignity when you allow your magazine to publish the vulgarity, anti-Sovietism and political muck produced by Shatrov? . . . Whose mouthpiece have you become?[12]

This debate reflects a continuing dispute in Soviet society over glasnost and perestroika. Shatrov seeks above all to help audiences recapture the past and recognize complex truths. Gorbachev's reforms include an effort to "restructure" the past, and Shatrov has sought to assist him in *On and On and On!*

Art

Soviet artists too have been deeply affected by Gorbachev's reforms. Many artworks hitherto proscribed have emerged from closets and cellars into public view. The rigid confines of socialist realism have shattered, and the distinction between "official" and "unofficial" art has faded. Soviet artists have participated more fully in world art. In July 1989 Sotheby's, a major international art auction house, organized a Moscow auction of 120 contemporary Soviet works. Over 11,000 people attended the preauction exhibition and over 2,000 the auction itself; receipts, far exceeding expectations, yielded $3.4 million. For many previously unknown artists such commercial success has enabled them to pursue creative work full time.

Earlier Soviet artist-émigrés staged successful exhibitions in the USSR. Mikhail Chemiakin, a Leningrad artist who has won international acclaim in Paris and New York, held a major retrospective exhibition in Moscow in 1989. While evading the criteria of socialist realism,

---

[12]"Perestroika and Soviet Culture," *Michigan Quarterly Review, 38,* no. 4 (Fall 1989), p. 589. *Znamia* reported that the letters ran 5:1 for the play.

Chemiakin's art is neither radical nor anti-Soviet. His subject matter comes from traditional Russian culture and history.

Another Soviet artist who recently won critical applause in the West is Ilia Kabakov. His multipaneled works combine images with text. Dubbed "albums" or "portfolios," his works portray lives of ordinary characters moving through life, as he comments on physical and intellectual activity.

Abstract art was long derided in the USSR as decadent, antisocialist, and devoid of social content, but even before glasnost Soviet artists experimented with "unofficial" forms of expression. Under Gorbachev competing styles and forms have been openly accepted. Among well-known Soviet artists who have rejected socialist realism in order to continue the earlier abstract tradition of Malevich, Kandinskii, and Lissitskii are Boris Sveshnikov, Anatoli Zverev, Vladimir Iakovlev, and Vladimir Iankelevskii. Contemporary Soviet abstract painters have won wider acceptance at home and abroad and seek to enter the mainstream of world art. The overwhelming response to the first public auction of contemporary Soviet art indicates how far these pioneers have come in a few years.

Film

The Cinema Workers' and Theater Workers' unions underwent dramatic leadership changes under Gorbachev. The distinguished director Elem Klimov became head of the Cinema Workers, while the liberal Alexander Kamshalov took over Goskino, which supervises the Soviet film industry. Together they opened the film archives and released scores of films repressed over the past 30 years. Among them Klimov's own *Agony,* shown in the West as *Rasputin,* portrays the decadence and depravity of the Russian imperial court in the twilight of tsarism. Alexander Askoldov's film *Commissar* (1968), released for showing in 1988, deals with issues such as anti-Semitism, abortion, and child abandonment. It reveals moral dilemmas confronting a young Red Army "Commissar" in the Civil War who becomes pregnant, considers abortion, has the child in a poor Jewish home, leaves the child with the family, and then returns to the front.

Glasnost's most celebrated film is *Repentance* (1983, released for viewing in 1987), by the Georgian director Tengiz Abuladze. Surrealistic and filled with symbolism that strikes at the heart of totalitarian dictatorship, the film denounces Stalinism and reaffirms human dignity expressed under the greatest adversity. The film was a sensation, viewed by millions who were deeply affected by its humanistic message. The film's final lines of dialogue became the key question for many: "What good is a road that does not lead to a church?" In 1988 Abuladze received the Lenin Prize for *Repentance*, the highest state award for creative work; in 1989 it was recognized likewise at the Cannes Film Festival. Formerly taboo subjects for film such as alcoholism, family conflicts, and environmental problems became acceptable. The film *Little Vera* caused a sensation in 1988 because it dealt with sex, drugs, and for the first time in Soviet cinema featured on-screen nudity.

The Stalinist past provided abundant subject matter for films and documentaries that raised nagging questions about the purges, the betrayals by family and friends, and the issue of responsibility for the past. In documentaries people spoke out about their sufferings in the prison camps, the terror, and people's heroism in combatting it. This examination is part of the vital task of accepting the past.

The most confrontive and controversial film to appear is Stanislav Govorukhin's documentary, *This is No Way to Live*. It is an unrelenting chronicle of more than 70 years of Communist brutality, corruption, criminal activity, and stupidity. To be sure, the film paints everything a uniform "black," just as former socialist realist films painted everything "rosy." It is, however, yet another vehicle designed to help recapture a lost past, not as a novel or as history, but as a documentary virtually all Soviet citizens can relate to based on their personal experiences. It is, therefore, a powerful tool to wrench Soviet citizens out of their apathetic acceptance of authoritarian misrule. Many cannot understand the decision to allow such a devastating indictment of Communist rule to be shown publicly, but Gorbachev reportedly reviewed the film personally and approved its release. Gradually, the Soviet people are regaining their historical memory and this film is an important part of that process.

Music

The cult hero of glasnost is the deceased young balladeer Vladimir Vysotskii, recognized as a symbol of the triumph over repression that had strangled Soviet culture for decades. Officially, Vysotskii, an actor in Iuri Liubimov's famous Taganka Theater in Moscow, also appeared in films. But he was best known as a poet-bard whose bitter, satirical protest songs won him a huge following among youth and members of the intelligentsia. His songs circulated widely in *magnitizdat*, poor quality homemade recordings made at his many concerts and private songfests. Living in the fast lane, Vysotskii died in 1980 as a widely recognized underground hero. Under glasnost he has emerged "above ground" to be acknowl-

Vladimir Vysotskii (1938–1980), popular
Russian poet and balladeer at a concert in
Yaroslavl in February 1979 *(S. Metelitsa/*
SOVFOTO)

edged as a "seer" and "legend." His works have sold hundreds of
thousands of copies, TV documentaries have recorded his life, and he has
achieved huge success in the popular press.

A highly dramatic event associated with musical glasnost was the
triumphant return to Moscow in February 1990 of the distinguished
cellist and conductor Mstislav Rostropovich, who with his wife, the
acclaimed soprano Galina Vishnevskaia, was exiled from the USSR in
1974. They had been accused of "acts harmful to the Soviet Union" for
offering shelter and support to Solzhenitsyn prior to his own expulsion.
Rostropovich's return to the USSR, restoration of his citizenship (re-
voked in 1978), and the return of his Moscow apartment heralded a new
era in Soviet music. The press glorified Rostropovich for his contributions to music and his heroic defense of justice and freedom. Asked about
his view of President Gorbachev, Rostropovich commented that Stalin
had tried in the 1940s to frighten Prokofiev and Shostakovich into writing
more "socialist" music. "I know Gorbachev does not give [music] lessons

Russian-born pianist Vladimir Horowitz triumphantly returned to the USSR for a concert tour in 1986 after 51 years in exile *(AP/Wide World Photos)*

to my friend, Alfred Schnitke."[13] The distinguished, Russian-born pianist Vladimir Horowitz also returned to the Soviet Union for a concert tour in 1986. Glasnost has relaxed controls and provided greater access to the international musical world.

A great artistic revival under Gorbachev has contributed mightily to a cultural catharsis in the USSR. Recapturing the past, artists, along with historians, have liberated the populace from the deception of Stalinism and the stagnation of the Brezhnev era. The strongest support for Gorbachev's restructuring program has come from Soviet artists and writers seeking to energize the nation and generate positive attitudes toward the future.

Alexander Kabakov, a young journalist, published in *Iskusstvo Kino* (*Film Art*) in 1989 a projected script for a science fiction film, *The Non-Returnee*. In this anti-utopian film script, Kabakov portrays a future USSR totally disintegrated and locked in civil war. The country is ruled by roving bands of terrorists, national minorities have all left the Soviet Union, and the economy has sunk to a bare subsistence level. His purpose, stated Kabakov, was to deliver "a stern and sober warning of

---

[13]Cited in the *New York Times*, February 14, 1990, p. B1. Schnitke is considered a leading Soviet contemporary composer.

what could happen if we do not manage to cope with destructive anti-perestroika processes present in our society. Perestroika may be the last chance."[14] Are Kabakov's views prophetic? Soviet culture has often marched ahead of Soviet politics.

Suggested Additional Reading

Most works of literature and literary dissent mentioned in this chapter have been translated into English. Consult your library for the most recent editions and anthologies.

Khrushchev Era

FIELD, ANDREW, ed. *Pages from Tarusa, New Voices in Russian Writing* (London, 1964).

GERSTENMAIER, CORNELIA. *The Voices of the Silent* (New York, 1972).

GIBIAN, GEORGE. *Interval of Freedom: Soviet Literature During the Thaw, 1954–1957* (Minneapolis, 1960).

JOHNSON, PRISCILLA. *Khrushchev and the Arts: The Politics of Soviet Culture, 1962–1964* (Cambridge, Mass., 1965).

LOWE, DAVID. *Russian Writing Since 1953: A Critical Survey* (New York, 1987).

OKUDZHAVA, B. *A Taste of Liberty*, trans. Leo Gruliow (Ann Arbor, Mich., 1986).

PROKOFIEV, SERGEI. *Prokofiev by Prokofiev: A Composer's Memoir*, ed. D. H. Appel, trans. G. Daniels (Garden City, N.Y., 1979).

REAVEY, GEORGE, ed. and trans. *The New Russian Poets, 1953–1966: An Anthology* (New York, 1966).

ROTHBERG, ABRAHAM. *The Heirs of Stalin: Dissidence and the Soviet Regime, 1953–1970* (Ithaca, N.Y., 1972).

SCHWARZ, BORIS. *Music and Musical Life in Soviet Russia, 1917–1981*, enlarged ed. (Bloomington, Ind., 1983).

SJEKLOCHA, PAUL, and IGOR MEAD. *Unofficial Art in the Soviet Union* (Berkeley, Calif., 1967).

Brezhnev Era

AKSYONOV, VASSILY. *The Burn* (New York, 1984).

———. *The Island of Crimea* (New York, 1984).

———, et al., eds. *Metropol* (New York, 1983).

BENYON, MICHAEL. *Life in Russia* (New York, 1983).

BRUMBERG, ABRAHAM, ed. *In Quest of Justice: Protest and Dissent in the Soviet Union Today* (New York, 1970).

---

[14]Cited in *Report on the USSR, Radio Free Europe . . . , 1*, no. 33 (August 18, 1989), p. 9.

DODGE, M., and A. HILTON, eds. *New Art from the Soviet Union* (Washington, D.C., 1977).

DUNLOP, J. B., R. HOUGH, A. KLIMOFF, eds. *Aleksandr Solzhenitsyn: Critical Essays and Documentary Materials* (Belmont, Mass., 1973).

HAYWARD, MAX, ed. *On Trial: The Soviet State Versus "Abram Tertz" and "Nikolai Arzhak"* (New York, 1966).

HOSKING, G. *Beyond Socialist Realism: Soviet Fiction Since Ivan Denisovich* (New York, 1980).

KERBLAY, BASILE. *Modern Soviet Society* (New York, 1983).

KIRK, IRINA. *Profiles in Russian Resistance* (New York, 1975).

MEDVEDEV, ZHORES. *The Medvedev Papers: The Plight of Soviet Science Today* (New York, 1971).

MONONOVA, TATYANA, ed. *Women and Russia: Feminist Writings from the Soviet Union* (Boston, 1984).

OKUDZHAVA, B. *A Taste of Liberty,* trans. Leo Gruliow (Ann Arbor, Mich., 1986).

REDDAWAY, PETER, ed. and trans. *Uncensored Russia: Protest and Dissent in the Soviet Union . . .* (New York, 1972).

ROTHBERG, ABRAHAM. *Aleksandr Solzhenitsyn—The Major Novels, 1953–1970* (Ithaca, N.Y., 1972)

SCAMMELL, MICHAEL. *Solzhenitsyn: A Biography* (New York, 1984).

SHALAMOV, V. *Kolyma Tales,* trans. J. Glad (New York, 1980).

SHIPLER, DAVID. *Russia: Broken Idols, Solemn Dreams,* 2d ed. (New York, 1989).

SOLZHENITSYN, ALEXANDER, et al. *From Under the Rubble: Essays* (New York, 1975).

TOKES, RUDOLF, ed. *Dissent in the USSR: Politics, Ideology and People* (Baltimore, Md., 1975).

TRIFONOV, IURI. *Another Life and House on the Embankment* (New York, 1984).

———. *The Old Man* (New York, 1984).

VOLKOV, SOLOMON, ed. *Testimony: The Memoirs of Dmitri Shostakovich* (New York, 1979).

Gorbachev Era

AITMATOV, CHINGIZ. *The Day Lasts More Than a Hundred Years* (Bloomington, Ind., 1983).

Glasnost: The New Soviet Prose (Ann Arbor, Mich., 1990).

GROSSMAN, VASILI. *Life and Fate* (New York, 1985).

ISKANDER, FAZIL. *Rabbits and Boa Constrictors* (Ann Arbor, Mich., 1989).

"Perestroika and Soviet Culture," *Michigan Quarterly Review,* 1989. (An extremely valuable collection of essays and translations providing a comprehensive account of Soviet culture under Gorbachev.)

Remaking the Revolution: The Soviet Union 70 Years Later. Reprinted from the *Los Angeles Times.* Los Angeles, 1987. (Selections from the *Times'* coverage of the Soviet Union.)

RYBAKOV, ANATOLI. *Children of the Arbat* (Boston, 1988).

———. *Heavy Sand* (New York, 1983).

TAUBMAN, WILLIAM, and JANE TAUBMAN. *Moscow Spring* (New York, 1989).

TUPITSYN, MARGARITA. *Margins of Soviet Art* (Milan, Italy, 1989).

VLADIMOV, GEORGI. *Faithful Ruslan* (New York, 1979).

Journals

Literaturnaia Gazeta, Moscow. (Now available in English as *The Literary Gazette.*)
Moskovskie Novosti. (English language edition is *Moscow News.*)
Ogonek [*The Little Flame*]. (Available only in Russian, ed. Vitali Korotich.)

THE BREZHNEV ERA, 1964–1982

After the Politburo removed Khrushchev from power abruptly in October 1964, a collective leadership assumed control, led by Leonid I. Brezhnev (1906–1982) and Alexei N. Kosygin (1904–1980), both engineers. Following a concealed power struggle with Kosygin and other rivals, Brezhnev gradually accumulated power and by 1971 had established modified one-man rule over the USSR. Despite declining health and vigor after 1975, he dominated the Soviet scene until early 1982. The new leaders, repudiating Khrushchev's risky economic and political experiments at home and his flamboyant foreign policy, acted cautiously, stressing efficiency, order, and stability. Abandoning Khrushchev's de-Stalinization campaign, they returned partially to Stalinism. The new oligarchs tightened controls over intellectuals and dissidents and at first combined industrial and agricultural growth with an impressive military buildup. Abroad, the USSR tightened its control of eastern Europe after invading Czechoslovakia in 1968 while pursuing détente and arms control agreements with the West. China confronted it with ideological and geopolitical challenges that threatened to provoke a Sino-Soviet war. Was the Brezhnev period an "era of stagnation," as M. S. Gorbachev later characterized it, or did it pursue reform? Was genuine stability and consensus achieved, or did resurgent minority peoples, especially Muslims, begin to undermine an apparently solid Soviet Empire? Why did economic growth slow dramatically after 1970? What were the implications of Soviet invasions of Czechoslovakia in 1968 and Afghanistan in 1979 and severe tensions with a liberalizing Poland in 1980–1981?

POLITICS AND DISSENT

After Khrushchev's sudden ouster, an oligarchy in the Presidium (renamed the Politburo in 1966) and Secretariat of the party's Central Committee headed by Brezhnev, Kosygin, N. V. Podgorny, and Mikhail Suslov, assumed power. Right after his removal, *Pravda* castigated Khrushchev's methods rather than his specific policies:

> The Leninist Party is an enemy of subjectivism and drift in communist construction. Wild schemes, half-baked conclusions and hasty decisions and actions divorced from reality; bragging and bluster; attraction to rule by fiat; unwillingness to take into account what science and practical experience have already worked out—these are alien to the Party. The construction of Communism is a living, creative undertaking. It does not tolerate armchair methods, one-man decisions, or disregard for the practical experience of the masses.[1]

Subsequently, Khrushchev was not criticized by name and under Brezhnev was hardly ever mentioned by the press, almost as if he had never ruled the USSR. Consigned to the oblivion of retirement, he was supplied with an apartment and limousine and retained his country dacha. Khrushchev appeared in public only at election times to cast his ballot. As a pensioner, he wrote two volumes of fascinating memoirs and died of heart disease in 1971.[2]

The new leaders, at first insecure, were absorbed in a protracted power struggle that raged beneath a placid surface from the day of Khrushchev's removal. A veil of anonymity, sobriety, and secrecy enveloped them as they jockeyed for position. Group and individual photographs were avoided so as not to reveal the leaders' order of prominence. In the Presidium, which soon reasserted primacy over the Secretariat,

---

[1]*Pravda*, October 17, 1964, quoted in J. Dornberg, *Brezhnev: The Masks of Power* (New York, 1974), p. 184.
[2]*Khrushchev Remembers* (Boston, 1971); and *Khrushchev Remembers: The Last Testament* (New York, 1974).

former Khrushchev supporters at first retained their posts. Some Western observers did not expect this collective leadership to last, but it proved surprisingly durable and effective. Powerful interest groups competed behind the scenes: the party apparatus, high state administrators, "steel-eaters" (heavy industry), and less influential army and police elements. None of these lobbies could dictate to or ignore the interests of the others; clashes among them generally ended in compromise. Whereas the successors of Lenin and Stalin soon had achieved complete or modified one-man rule, this time the top posts of secretary general (Brezhnev) and premier (Kosygin, later N. A. Tikhonov) remained in different hands.

The coup of October 1964 apparently was planned by Mikhail Suslov, chief party ideologist, and executed by opponents of Khrushchev who considered Brezhnev the most acceptable moderate replacement. At the outset Brezhnev's position was highly vulnerable and insecure because he could count on only one sure ally in the Presidium: Andrei Kirilenko. The other members of the Presidium included independent senior figures (Suslov, Kosygin), rivals for his post as first secretary (Podgornyi), Khrushchev protégés or party elders like Shvernik and Mikoian. Brezhnev's status grew even more precarious when Aleksandr Shelepin and Peter Shelest, the Ukrainian party chairman, became full members of the Presidium. The new party first secretary began by wooing elements alienated by Khrushchev's reforms: the party, industrial managers, bureaucrats, and the military. Promptly rescinding Khrushchev's most unpopular policies, the new regime ended his short-lived division of the party and insistence on rotating its leaders. Brezhnev sought to replace conflict and suspicion among powerful interest groups with cooperation and consensus, summed up in the slogan, "trust in cadres." In official life a more relaxed atmosphere prevailed as disagreements were limited to ascertaining the best means to achieve agreed goals. The frenetic administrative reorganizations of the Khrushchev era virtually ceased.

Confounding the skeptics, Brezhnev emerged as a clever and adroit politician and a master of compromise. Within 18 months, after achieving working control of the Secretariat, he had begun to emerge from a pack of contenders as first among equals. A Presidium consensus enabled him to replace followers of Khrushchev with his own adherents. Brezhnev in December 1965 had Podgornyi "promoted" to titular president of the Supreme Soviet. That July Konstantin Chernenko, a faithful personal associate, was named to a key post in the Central Committee. The following April Presidium member Kirilenko, a senior supporter, was appointed to the Secretariat, where he acted as Brezhnev's watchdog for personnel matters. A leading rival, A. Shelepin, who had boasted outside the Kremlin that Brezhnev soon would be replaced by "a man with a little more dynamism and authority," was undermined; he and Podgornyi lost their seats in the Secretariat.[3] The 23rd Party Congress (March–April 1966), naming Brezhnev secretary general of the party, confirmed his superior power. A Western diplomat admitted having underestimated Brezhnev's acumen: "We just didn't give him enough credit. . . . Everybody wrote him off as a party hack, as a colorless *apparatchik*, as a compromise candidate."

Leonid Brezhnev had risen from lowly origins by hard, persistent work, mainly in the party apparatus. Born in 1906 in the Ukraine of Russian worker parents, he was graduated from a classical gymnasium and later obtained a degree as a metallurgical engineer. From 1938 on, his career was linked closely with Khrushchev's. Serving as a political commissar in World War II, Brezhnev became a major general, and once in power his military career was inflated beyond measure. Leaving the military service in 1946, Brezhnev, as a chosen member of Khrushchev's entourage, became party chief in Zaporozhe and a member of the Ukrainian Politburo. In the early 1950s, he served as party chief in Moldavia, then in Kazakhstan. Under Khrushchev he became a secretary of the Central Committee and a member of the Politburo. Kicked upstairs in 1960 as titular president of the USSR, he returned from that political graveyard to true power. After Kozlov's stroke in April 1963 (a stroke of fortune for Brezhnev!), he was restored to the Secretariat and became Khrushchev's heir apparent. In the brutal world of Soviet politics, Brezhnev succeeded through patronage, manipulation, and maneuver. He built a strong political machine—the so-called Dnieper Mafia—of officials from his home region. Brezhnev won the reputation of being efficient, quiet, sensible, and of keeping a low profile—a man of experience and moderation.

Soviet leaders under Brezhnev operated as an exclusive, self-renewing elite, or *nomenklatura*, living in a very private world. The roughly 25 members of the Politburo (Presidium until 1966) and Secretariat, stressing stability and order, had defined rules of conduct that none could disregard with impunity. They acted purposefully to prevent Politburo disputes being aired in the much larger Central Committee by manipulating its semiannual plenums. If agreement could not be achieved, the plenum would be delayed. Politburo members who violated these procedures would be punished, often by losing their posts. If a *non*-Politburo member criticized the leaders' policies at a plenum, he would normally be dismissed. The oligarchs jealously guarded special decision-making powers that separated them from lower party bodies, which merely executed Politburo decisions. Even junior members of the Secretariat or candidate

---

[3]Harry Gelman, *The Brezhnev Politburo* (Ithaca, N.Y., 1984), pp. 74–79.

members of the Politburo belonged to this privileged elite. Under Brezhnev, four or five top men were included: the premier, titular president, and the top three party secretaries. The Secretariat, normally chaired by Brezhnev, managed the party machine and appointed candidates to all senior posts. Moscow-based Politburo members possessed advantages over party leaders of Leningrad, Ukraine, or Kazakhstan, who normally could not attend weekly Politburo meetings.[4]

Powerful Politburo members representing major interest groups blocked Brezhnev's initial efforts at supremacy. However, between 1966 and 1971 Brezhnev removed or isolated leading rivals, and accumulated power without dictating to the Politburo. His authority spread outward from the party base to include foreign policy, state affairs, and agriculture. In 1967 he ousted his main rivals from the Secretariat, and the 24th Party Congress in 1971 confirmed his personal ascendancy as he enlarged the Politburo to include his cronies. Brezhnev's summit diplomacy with Western leaders reaffirmed his authority. During 1973, leading representatives of important interest groups entered the Politburo: Marshal Andrei Grechko (defense minister), Iuri Andropov (KGB chief), and Andrei Gromyko (foreign minister). In May 1975, Alexander Shelepin, his only remaining major rival, was removed from the Politburo; and the July 1975 Helsinki Security Conference vindicated his policy of détente. Changes announced by the 25th Party Congress of 1976 confirmed Brezhnev's supremacy. Ten of 16 full Politburo members by then were his appointees, and his rivals had been weakened and isolated. In 1977, asserting that the USSR had entered the phase of "developed socialism," Brezhnev assumed the title President of the Soviet Union. Despite repeated bouts of illness beginning in 1975, which sharply reduced his capacity to work, Brezhnev remained in command, repeatedly removing younger men who might aspire to replace him. In October 1980, Premier Kosygin retired and died two months later. He was replaced as premier by Nikolai A. Tikhonov, an elderly Brezhnev crony. Careful not to groom a dynamic successor, Brezhnev placed his stamp firmly on an entire era of Soviet history and retained preeminent authority until 1982, his final year of life. His legacy was stability, orderly procedure, and stagnation.

Under Brezhnev the role of the party was further enhanced, and tenure at all levels became more secure. After 1964, there were some abrupt removals from the Politburo, but few changes in the Central Committee or lower. In 1977 only 2 percent of party members failed to retain membership. Party congresses after 1971 were to convene every

---

[4]Gelman, *The Brezhnev Politburo*, pp. 51–58.

five years to coincide with five-year plans. Losing some of its power, the Central Committee was expanded to 241 full members and 155 nonvoting candidates, 90 percent of whom were reelected in 1976. The party continued to grow, reaching 17.4 million members in 1983. Now almost 10 percent of the adult population, it was losing its Leninist vanguard character; its apparatus of full-time, paid workers exceeded 250,000. Meanwhile the educational level and technical expertise of party members had risen sharply. About 25 percent of them were women, but few held important positions and none were in top party agencies. Under "developed socialism" the party was to initiate major reforms, coordinate a complex socioeconomic system, and push forward a cautious bureaucracy. The theme of party control over the ministries was emphasized. Party spirit (*partiinost*), declared Brezhnev, must be combined with expertise.

Western scholars wondered whether the Brezhnev regime represented a stable oligarchy or a modified one-man rule. Was it reverting to Stalinist autocracy or permitting freer debate? Concealing its rivalries from the public, the Brezhnev leadership projected an image of harmony and unity. One Western scholar, Zbigniew Brzezinski, called the Brezhnev regime a "government of clerks" that, seeking to preserve its power and privileges, had repudiated social change. With a decaying ideology, its leaders presided over a petrifying political order. However, Robert Daniels stressed institutional pluralism in which the chief agencies—party, state, army, and police—shared power. Brezhnev adopted no major policies that would endanger the influence of any of them. Stalin's "permanent purge" of top officials had yielded to a remarkably stable leadership. With wider ranging debate in the Soviet press, important decisions were reached after extensive debate and compromise. The party became a "political broker," reconciling and mediating differences among several bureaucracies.

Khrushchev's removal by a large Politburo majority served as a deterrent to a potential dictator. Totalitarian discipline, pointed out French Sovietologist Michel Tatu, could be reimposed only by a massive purge, which party leaders scrupulously avoided. In some ways Brezhnev had fewer prerogatives than democratic chief executives. Lacking sole decision-making authority, he could have policies imposed on him by a Politburo majority that could dismiss or retire him any time. He required his colleagues' consent to alter the composition of the Politburo or Secretariat.

After a brief, relatively liberal interlude, the Brezhnev regime cracked down on political dissent, which was enforced by the KGB under the able direction of Iurii V. Andropov, Brezhnev's eventual successor. De-Stalinization ended abruptly. Beginning in 1965, memoirs by leading

Soviet generals of World War II praised Stalin's wartime leadership, which Khrushchev had castigated. Stalin and the party, went the new line, fully aware of the Nazi danger in 1941, had taken essential precautions, then had guided the heroic Soviet people to victory. A prominent neo-Stalinist intimate of Brezhnev, S. Trapeznikov, described the Stalin era in *Pravda* in October 1965 as "one of the most brilliant in the history of the party and the Soviet state." Brezhnev agreed with powerful party conservatives that discussion of Stalin's crimes and forced labor camps must cease. Official treatment of Stalin grew increasingly positive with only perfunctory criticism of his cult of personality. In an abortive attempt to rehabilitate Stalin completely, Devi Sturua, ideological secretary of the Georgian Communist Party, declared in October 1966:

> I am a Stalinist because the name of Stalin is linked with the victories of our people in the years of collectivization and industrialization. I am a Stalinist because the name of Stalin is linked with the victories of our people in the Great Patriotic War [World War II]. I am a Stalinist because the name of Stalin is linked with the victories of our people in the postwar reconstruction of our economy.[5]

A closed nationwide "seminar" of party ideological officials applauded.

NATIONALISM AND DISSENT

During the Brezhnev era nationalism revived in various parts of the USSR. "Of all the problems facing Moscow the most urgent and the most stubborn is the one raised by the national minorities," wrote Hélène d'Encausse prophetically.[6] Brezhnev's official goal of a "fusion of the nations" was resisted by non-Slavic elements seeking genuine Soviet federalism and autonomy. Efforts at Great Russian linguistic and educational assimilation, effective with smaller ethnic groups, failed in the Caucasus, Lithuania, and Central Asia where religion (Catholicism or Islam) reinforced a local sense of historic and national identity. The Soviet regime provided few mosques for its large Muslim minority, but many worshipped unofficially. Muslim leaders, affirmed d'Encausse, were making communism a by-product of Islam. (For statistics on the ethnic problem see Tables 18.1 and 18.2.)

---

[5]Stephen F. Cohen, ed., *An End to Silence* (New York, 1982), p. 158.
[6]Hélène Carrère d'Encausse, *Decline of an Empire: The Soviet Socialist Republics in Revolt* (New York, 1979), pp. 231, 274.

Table 18.1 *Percentage of Ethnic Groups Compared with Total Population (percent)*

Ethnic Groups	1897	1926	1959	1970	1989
Russians	44.4	47.5	54.6	53.4	50.8
Ukrainians	19.4	21.4	17.8	16.9	15.4
Byelorussians	4.5	3.6	3.8	3.7	3.5
Tatars	1.9	1.7	2.4	2.5	—
Turko-Moslems	12.1	10.1	10.3	12.9	15.4
Jews	3.5	2.4	1.1	0.9	0.7
Europeans (Georgians, Armenians, Latvians, Estonians)	3.9	3.6	3.8	3.8	3.8
Lithuanians	1.3	1.2	1.1	1.1	1.1
Finnish	2.3	2.2	1.5	1.4	1.4
Moldavians (Romanians)	1.0	1.2	1.1	1.2	1.2

The Brezhnev regime persecuted "bourgeois nationalism," especially in the Ukraine. In April 1966, two Ukrainian literary critics were accused of smuggling "nationalist" verses to the West. V. Chornovil, who reported their trial to the world and denounced KGB tactics, was sentenced to forced labor. That fall Articles 190/1 and 190/3, making it a crime to spread "slanderous inventions about the Soviet state and social system," or to "disturb public order," were added to the Soviet criminal code and were used frequently against nationalists and other dissidents. In 1972, Peter Shelest, the Ukraine's political boss, was removed partly for glorifying Ukrainian history and culture and seeking to re-Ukrainize its political apparatus. The Brezhnev regime reacted harshly to efforts by national minorities to assert their rights or complaints of Russian domination. (See Map 18.1.) While declining as a percentage of the total Soviet population, Great Russians remained dominant and privileged, holding with other Slavic elements most top political positions. In the socioeconomic realm, most non-Russians lost ground relative to Great Russians. Industrial development and urbanization centered in Slavic republics with a low rate of population increase and rising labor shortages. On the other hand, Turkic-Muslim areas suffered from economic underdevelopment, growing labor surpluses, and rapid population increases. In Muslim urban centers with only 21 percent of the total Muslim population in 1970, non-Muslims frequently took the best jobs. A 44 percent increase in the Turkic-Muslim population from 1959 to 1970 revealed

Table 18.2 *Population of USSR, 1950 to 2000 (in thousands) (Russia, Central Asia, Transcaucasia)*

	1950		1960		1970		1980		1990		2000	
	Total	Percent	Total	Percent	Total	Percent	Total	Percent	Total	Percent	Total	Percent
USSR	180,075	100	214,329	100	242,756	100	267,057	100	292,324	100	312,215	100
RSFSR	102,191	56.7	119,906	55.9	130,360	53.7	138,842	52	145,686	49.8	147,335	47.2
CENTRAL ASIA	17,499	9.7	24,402	11.4	33,187	13.7	42,449	15.9	55,742	19.1	71,903	23
Kazakhstan	6,628	3.7	9,850	4.6	13,116	5.4	15,710	5.9	19,038	6.5	22,328	7.1
Kirghizia	1,740	1	2,172	1	2,968	1.2						
Tadzhikistan	1,532	0.9	2,082	1	2,943	1.2						
Turkmenia	1,210	0.7	1,594	0.7	2,190	0.9	26,739	10	36,704	12.6	49,575	15.9
Uzbekistan	6,383	3.5	8,704	4.1	11,970	4.9						
CAUCASIA	7,777	4.3	9,921	4.6	12,393	5.1	14,649	5.5	17,660	6	20,671	6.6
Armenia	1,354	0.8	1,867	0.9	2,518	1						
Azerbaidzhan	2,896	1.6	3,894	1.8	5,166	2.2	14,649	5.5	17,660	6	20,671	6.6
Georgia	3,527	2	4,160	1.9	4,709	1.9						

(In the 1980, 1990, and 2000 columns the figures for Tadzhikistan, Turkmenia, and Uzbekistan are bracketed together as a single combined value, as are those for Armenia, Azerbaidzhan, and Georgia.)

Source: H. C. d'Encausse, *Decline of an Empire* (New York, 1979), p. 89.

Map 18.1 *The Soviet Political Units in 1970*

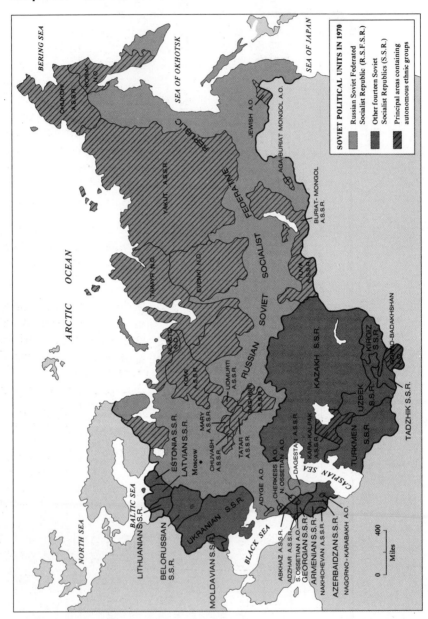

SOVIET POLITICAL UNITS IN 1970

Russian Soviet Federated Socialist Republic (R.S.F.S.R.)

Other fourteen Soviet Socialist Republics (S.S.R.)

Principal areas containing autonomous ethnic groups

powerful demographic pressures in Central Asia, where there was a large rural surplus and intensified pressures on agriculture.[7]

Frequently the Brezhnev regime imprisoned dissidents in psychiatric hospitals. In 1966, the writer Valeri Tarsis, exiled to England, published *Ward Seven,* which described compulsory treatment in a Moscow psychiatric hospital. "I believe in God and I cannot live in a country where one cannot be an honest man," wrote Tarsis. The USSR "is not a democratic country; this is Fascism." The Politburo declared Tarsis insane and a traitor and deprived him of Soviet citizenship! In 1967, former major general Peter Grigorenko, campaigning for the right of Crimean Tatars to return home from exile, was arrested, committed to a hospital for the criminally insane, and beaten by the KGB. Explained another dissident, Vladimir Bukovskii:

> The inmates are prisoners, people who committed actions considered crimes from the point of view of the authorities . . . but not . . . of the law. And in order to isolate them and punish them somehow, these people are declared insane and kept in the ward of the psychiatric hospital.[8]

Andrei Amalrik, a young historian, compared dissident trials under Brezhnev with medieval heresy trials. "Recognizing their ideological hopelessness, they [the leaders] cling in fear to criminal codes, to prison camps, and psychiatric hospitals." Losing his job, Amalrik was convicted of "parasitism" and served 16 months in Siberia at hard labor.

Many scientists and intellectuals joined the dissident Human Rights Movement. Its leading statement was the *Sakharov Memorandum* published abroad in 1968 by the outstanding scientist, Andrei Sakharov. His protest reflected growing support by Soviet scientists for civil liberties and democratization. Citing the deadly danger to humankind of nuclear war, overpopulation, bureaucracy, and environmental pollution, Sakharov urged Soviet-American cooperation to save civilization. The Soviet and American systems, borrowing from each other, were converging toward democratic socialism, he argued. Castigating Stalinism and its vestiges, Sakharov urged democratic freedoms for the USSR and denounced collectivization as an "almost serflike enslavement of the peasantry." He demanded rehabilitation of all Stalin's victims: "Only the most meticulous analysis of the [Stalinist] past and its consequences will now enable us to wash off the blood and dirt that befouled our banner." In May 1970, Sakharov warned Brezhnev that unless secrecy were removed from

---

[7]Robert Lewis et al., *Nationality and Population Change in Russia and the USSR* (New York, 1976), pp. 350 ff.

[8]Quoted in A. Rothberg, *The Heirs of Stalin* (Ithaca, N.Y., 1972), p. 301.

science, culture, and technology, the USSR would soon become a second-rate provincial country.

Despite a severe crackdown by the Brezhnev regime, Soviet dissent during the 1970s, wrote Robert Sharlet, expanded as one component of an emerging "contrasystem" with a flourishing illegal "second economy," and a major system of underground religious belief and *samizdat*.[9] Under Brezhnev, Soviet dissent acquired a history, heroes, and martyrs. According to Amnesty International, over 400 Soviet dissidents were imprisoned or restricted in their movements after 1975, notably before important events such as the Moscow Olympics of 1980. A steadily growing volume of dissident information kept Soviet repression in the world spotlight and gave visibility to dissatisfied national and religious groups. From late 1976, the regime reacted vigorously, often applying Article 190/1. Particular targets were dissidents monitoring Soviet violations of the Helsinki Accords; several political trials of these leaders were staged in 1977–1978. Another police offensive of 1979–1980 brought arrests of nine Helsinki monitors and the internal exile of Andrei Sakharov to Gorkii. KGB tactics included trumped-up criminal charges against dissidents, increased use of psychiatric terror, and the employment of official hooligans to beat up dissidents or burglarize their homes. There was a major increase in forced deportations of prominent opponents of the regime. Nonetheless, the strength of the Soviet counterculture and information about its activities in the West increased.

ECONOMY AND SOCIETY

After a decade of moderate growth and relative prosperity, the Brezhnev regime faced declining economic growth rates and increasing demands on limited Soviet resources. Weather conditions caused the situation in agriculture to fluctuate, but the general trend was slower growth. Some Soviet economists affirmed that the Stalinist model was holding back economic development. Reformers urged drastic changes: eliminating much central planning of prices and introducing competitive bidding between the State Planning Commission (Gosplan) and individual plants. However, the party apparatus and the bureaucracy refused to dismantle the central planning empire, relax controls, or move toward market socialism. Conservative ideologists opposed any concessions to capitalism.

---

[9]Robert Sharlet, "Growing Soviet Dissidence," *Current History, 79* (October 1980), pp. 96–100.

Premier Kosygin, supporting reform, backed many suggestions of Professor Evsei Liberman of Kharkov University, who advocated that state enterprises must show a profit and sell their goods (concept of profitability). Liberman also rejected Stalinist economics based on commands from above and absolute obedience from below and the stress on quantity regardless of cost or quality. He wished to free the individual enterprise from outside controls, except for overall production and delivery goals. Wage increases and bonuses for managers and workers would depend on profitability, that is, on the sale of products, not on fulfilling centrally decided production norms. Using supply and demand, suppliers and manufacturers would deal directly with one another rather than going through central economic ministries. In July 1964, Khrushchev authorized an experiment with aspects of Libermanism in two clothing combines. Profits and sales increased sufficiently to encourage the new leadership to try Liberman's theories on a modified basis in some 400 consumer enterprises. Greater ability to adjust to consumer demand and more emphasis on quality resulted.

This experiment was underway when Kosygin's proposals for general economic reform, heralded as "a new system of planning and incentives," were approved in September 1965. That April Kosygin had challenged the party's role in planning:

> We have to free ourselves completely . . . from everything that used to tie down the planning officials and obliged them to draft plans otherwise than in accordance with the interests of the economy. . . . We often find ourselves prisoners of laws we ourselves have made.[10]

The September 1965 reforms included Liberman's managerial economics and profit ideas, but Kosygin also restored the central economic ministries, often under their Stalinist bosses. Khrushchev's *sovnarkhozy*, defended chiefly by local party officials anxious to retain control of regional industry, were scrapped. The Moscow technocrats regained all of their pre-1957 powers: The new head of Gosplan, N. K. Baibakov, had been removed from that post by Khrushchev in 1957!

Opposition from conservative party elements and Stalinist managers first watered down the Kosygin reforms, then halted their implementation. By January 1967 some 2,500 enterprises had adopted the new incentive system; by 1970 the reforms supposedly applied to all firms, but plant managers' authority was reduced as the ministers determined daily operations more and more. Gross value of output, not profit, remained the key index. Conservatives realized that to free managers from central

---

[10]Cited in Michel Tatu, *Power in the Kremlin* (New York, 1968), p. 447.

tutelage would reduce bureaucratic powers over industry. To orthodox party members, Libermanism was "goulash communism"; to allow market forces to prevail over central planning would be "unscientific." Many managers, fearing responsibility, acted in the old Stalinist manner. Thus the 1965 reforms eventually failed: rather than implementing Libermanism, they merely temporarily took up slack in the old system. A Soviet economist lamented: "I thought they [the leaders] understood from their experience that repressive measures would never achieve results and that they were therefore ready to employ purely economic tools. Now I see there was nothing to it."[11]

As industrial growth rates under Brezhnev declined, Soviet planners were faced with a clear need to improve productivity and quality. (See Figure 18.1.) The traditional Soviet economic policy of concentrating on heavy and defense-related industries and on quantity produced great imbalances and backward light industry and service sectors. Huge investments were required to maintain even lower levels of growth; bottlenecks were promoted by overexpansion of key industries. The centralized Soviet system's economic inefficiencies, wrote George Feiwel, included wasting capital in ill-conceived, protracted construction projects, underutilized capacity, mismanagement of human resources, overcentralization, inertia, lack of initiative, and excessive bureaucracy.[12] Key goals of the Ninth (1971–1975) and Tenth (1976–1980) Five Year Plans were not fulfilled, even though scaled well below levels of previous plans and consumption was slated to grow about as fast as accumulation. Complicating the picture in the 1980s were high labor turnover, labor shortages, and rising consumer demand. Therefore at the 25th Party Congress of 1976 Brezhnev urged a rapid increase in productivity, a sharp cutback in manual labor, increased automation, and improved quantity and quality of consumer goods. However, such exhortations had little effect.

Although output rose during Brezhnev's early years, agriculture remained a weak link in the Soviet economy. Unfavorable weather and inefficient, oversized farms caused the USSR to suffer seven bad grain harvests in a row beginning in 1979. Soviet grain exports shrank; during the 1970s the USSR imported more grain than any other country. In *Letter to the Soviet Leaders* (1973), Solzhenitsyn urged scrapping the entire collective farming system. Soviet agriculture remained subservient to

---

[11]Cited in R. Conquest, "A New Russia? A New World?," *Foreign Affairs*, 54 (April 1975), p. 487.

[12]G. Feiwel, "Economic Performance and Reforms in the Soviet Union," in D. R. Kelley, ed., *Soviet Politics in the Brezhnev Era* (New York, 1980), pp. 70–101.

Figure 18.1 *Soviet Economic Growth Under Brezhnev: Planned Versus Actual*

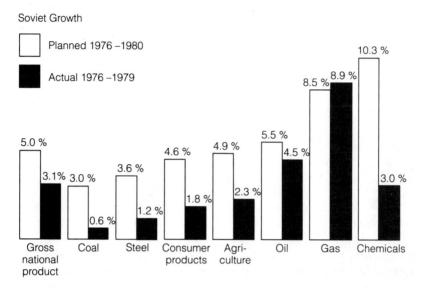

Soviet Growth

☐ Planned 1976–1980

■ Actual 1976–1979

ideology, and under tight central bureaucratic control. Despite higher investments, agricultural growth slowed: a roughly 26 percent increase during Brezhnev's first decade compared with a 41 percent increase under Khrushchev. Fluctuating grain yields—for example, a record 237.2 million metric tons in 1978 falling to 179 million in 1979—prompted Brezhnev to conclude long-term import agreements with the United States and Argentina. Although costs were high, in 1975 Soviet storage capacity was increased to 40 million metric tons. Brezhnev emphasized extension of irrigated lands and undertook a vast land-improvement program for the northwest. With agricultural production roughly 80–85 percent of U.S. output, the Soviet population received enough total calories and proteins, but lacked variety and quality.

Under Brezhnev the trend away from collective farms (kolkhozy) to state farms (sovkhozy) continued. (See Table 18.3.) Soviet farms became huge, impersonal rural factories whose farmers were controlled as strictly as by the estate manager under serfdom. Soviet farmers tilled about 70 percent more land area than did farmers in the United States, with more than seven times the manpower, but with only about one third the tractors and trucks and 60 percent of the grain combines. The Brezhnev regime did establish a minimum wage for collective farmers and raised the income of all farm workers. In 1980 the average collective farmer

Table 18.3 *Collective and State Farms*

	1940	1960	1976
KOLKHOZY			
Total number	235,000	44,900	27,300
Workers per farm	110	445	542
Sown area per farm	500 hectares	2,746	3,597
Livestock	297 head	3,031	4,509
Tractors	4.4	14.4	39
SOVKHOZY			
Total number	4,200	7,400	19,617
Workers per farm	381	783	559
Sown area per farm	2,750	9,081	5,680
Tractors	20	54	57

Source: D. R. Kelley, ed., *Soviet Politics in the Brezhnev Era* (New York, 1980), p. 57.

received 116 rubles per month compared to 170 rubles for an urban worker; state farmers' income fell in between. Despite these improvements, in 1977 about 15 million private plots, averaging about one acre, produced 27 percent of all Soviet agricultural products, 34 percent of livestock products, and almost half of its vegetables and potatoes.[13] Private crop yields per acre and livestock output per animal exceeded substantially those on collective and state farms. These superior results reveal the stronger incentives to produce on private farms than on collective and state farms. More than 50 million people worked on private plots at least part time. Whereas Khrushchev had taken steps to curtail and restrict private plots, Brezhnev promised to foster them. Small garden machines began to be manufactured for sale to private farmers.

Soviet foreign trade in the 1970s rose sharply, spurred by imports of Western technology and grain and exports of oil and natural gas. In a marked departure from traditional Soviet policies of autarchy, the USSR was opened more to foreign technology, especially to increase its output of energy. Besides military equipment and gold, about 85 percent of all Soviet hard currency exports were in raw materials; more than half of these earnings came from petroleum. Soviet oil exports rose from 96 million tons in 1970 to about 125 million in 1975, mostly to Europe and

---

[13]Karl-Eugene Wädekin, *The Private Sector in Soviet Agriculture* (Berkeley, Calif., 1973); Roy Laird, "The Political Economy of Soviet Agriculture Under Brezhnev," in Kelley, *Soviet Politics . . .*, pp. 55 ff.

Table 18.4 *Selected Consumer Goods per Thousand*

Item	1965	1970	1975	1977
Watches, clocks	885	1,193	1,319	1,408
TV sets	68	143	215	229
Refrigerators	29	89	178	210
Washing machines	59	141	189	200

Source: D. Kelley, ed., *Soviet Politics in the Brezhnev Era* (New York, 1980), p. 116.

Cuba. However, Soviet oil output then peaked at 12–13 million barrels per day. Output in older Soviet oil fields in the Caucasus fell rapidly, partly because of technological bottlenecks, while exploitation of newer Siberian fields required advanced and expensive foreign technology.

Soviet living standards, having risen markedly during the early Brezhnev years, leveled off during the 1970s and remained the lowest of major industrial countries. (See Table 18.4.) The average citizen obtained an adequate but uninspiring diet featuring potatoes and cabbage complicated by chronic meat and milk shortages and lived in shabby, overcrowded housing. Consumption in 1970 amounted to about 57 percent of total output (GNP), considerably less than in the United States and other industrial countries. Strong consumer pressure spurred the Brezhnev regime, anxious to avoid strikes like those in neighboring Poland, to provide more and improved consumer goods and services. A more selective urban populace demanded quality products, especially automobiles, motorcycles, and carpets. But for such "high demand" goods no credit was available: The purchase price had to be paid in cash before delivery. Considerable resources were devoted to producing private cars, providing repair facilities, and building decent roads. Five-year plans under Brezhnev channeled much more state investment into consumer products than ever before. Brezhnev's speech to the 26th Party Congress in 1981 stressed the political significance of improving consumption:

> The problem is to create a really modern sector producing consumer goods and services for the population, which meets their demands. . . . The store, the cafeteria, the laundry, the dry cleaners are places people visit every day. What can they buy? How are they treated? . . . The people will judge our work in large measure by how these questions are solved.[14]

---

[14]Quoted in Robert F. Byrnes, ed., *After Brezhnev: Sources of Soviet Conduct in the 1980s* (Bloomington, Ind., 1983), p. 74.

Table 18.5 *Cost of Living: New York City Versus Moscow, 1980*

	Cost of Living	
	New York City	*Moscow*
Hours worked per week	39.7	42
Manufacturing worker's earnings per week	$ 265.60	$ 56.54
Monthly rental three-room apt.	1,000.00	37.00
Heat and electricity per month	82.00	4.50
Bus or subway per ride	.50	.08
Car (Citation/Zhiguli)	6,200.00	10,000.00
Gallon of gasoline	1.35	1.25
Vodka (1 liter)	6.00	11.00
Dental checkup	32.00	Free
Ballpoint pen	.29	1.50
Chicken (1 lb.)	.66	2.55
Pack of cigarettes	.75	.52
Loaf of bread (1 lb.)	.62	.24
Jeans	18.50	45.00
Man's leather shoes	42.00	45.00
Vacation (2 weeks per person)*	910.00	120.00
Woman's dress	90.00	60.00
Sofa	600.00	260.00
Gold wedding ring	75.00	225.00
Hard-cover novel	12.95	3.00
Color television**	710.00	1,094.00
Pantyhose	1.50	10.00
Newspaper (*Daily News/Izvestiya*)	.25	.05
Woman's leather shoes	33.00	40.00

Note: All figures are typical 1980 prices.
*Vacations: The New York figure represents a peak season cost with meals at a major Florida resort city; 70 percent of the Moscow figure is paid by the worker's union.
**25-in. screen in New York, 24-in. screen in Moscow.

Nonetheless, compared with earnings, Soviet consumer goods remained very highly priced. (See Table 18.5.)

Under Brezhnev there was growing official concern over crime and corruption, symptoms of social malaise. A new gun control law of February 1974 prescribed up to five years' imprisonment for unauthorized possession of firearms. As crimes of violence increased, notably in southern areas, severe penalties were imposed for drug abuse, especially involving hashish and marijuana. Juvenile delinquency increased sharply. As the food situation outside of major cities deteriorated, parts of the USSR instituted rationing and even Muscovites searched for food and other consumer goods. As items of real commercial value disappeared from state stores into illegal or semilegal channels, the black and gray markets became crucial for most Russians. Old values and restraints broke down, as cheating and stealing from the state increased. As Russians lost faith that things would improve and regarded the promise of communism as a cynical joke, public morale plummeted. Many Russians told George Feifer, an American journalist: The whole country is sick and getting sicker.[15]

That seemed to be literally true. Whereas earlier the USSR was in the forefront of improving public health, raising life expectancy, and reducing infant mortality, after 1960 an astounding reversal occurred marked by rampant alcoholism, burgeoning infant mortality, and declining life expectancy. Measured by its public health, noted Nick Eberstadt in 1980, the USSR was no longer a developed nation.[16] In no other European country, not even primitive Albania, were lives so short or the infant death rate so high. Western accounts emphasized the devastating effects of alcoholism, especially on Russian men, but also on women and even children. In the early 1970s, the Soviet per capita consumption of hard liquor was over twice the American or Swedish levels. Despite sharp increases in state vodka prices, consumption rose, and almost as much moonshine (*samogon*) was consumed as legally purchased liquor. Alcohol purchases accounted, noted Feifer, for almost one third of consumer spending in food stores. Christopher Davis and Murray Feshbach, leading Western experts on Soviet society, attributed the Soviet health crisis to various factors, including poor quality baby foods and nursing formulas, rising illegitimacy and abortion (averaging six to eight per woman during childbearing years), alcoholism, high accident rates, pollution of the air and soil, and a breakdown in the health-care system. The Brezhnev regime, busily building up its military forces, economized at the expense of public health: The Soviet Union devoted a declining percentage of total output to combating illness.[17] Another Western scholar suggested that the Soviet system itself might be wearing down from a combination of inefficiency, corruption, and rampant cynicism.[18]

Nor, despite official claims, did women's equality exist in the USSR.

---

[15]George Feifer, "Russian Disorders," *Harper's*, February 1981, pp. 41–55.

[16]Nick Eberstadt, "The Health Crisis in the USSR," *New York Review of Books*, February 19, 1981.

[17]In 1955 the USSR spent about 9.8 percent of GNP on health care but only 7.5 percent in 1977; in the United States, largely due to Medicare and Medicaid, the percentage rose from 8 to 11. Eberstadt, "The Health Crisis," p. 25.

[18]Robert Wesson, *The Aging of Communism* (New York, 1980).

The Soviet leadership pursued the goal of sexual equality until it conflicted with economic or military priorities. Under Brezhnev males continued to dominate the higher ranks of all scientific disciplines and most other branches of the economy. However, Soviet women finally had achieved equal pay for equal work and equal entry into most professions.[19] In 1970, women represented 53.9 percent of the Soviet population and 51 percent of the work force. However, women comprised only 22.6 percent of party members, and just 14 of some 300 were full or candidate members of the Central Committee. The USSR had a higher percentage of women doctors, lawyers, and machine operators than any Western country, but women had only token representation in top economic, cultural, and political bodies. That situation partly reflected traditional Russian male predominance. Women were channeled mainly into low-skilled, low-income, physical labor job categories. Lingering traditional concepts of women's role in the home and at work promoted their dual exploitation. The Brezhnev regime, while admitting problems, promoted legal equality of women but permitted economic, cultural, and political inequality to persist.

Soviet society under Brezhnev, despite reduced wage differentials, remained one of concealed privilege and inequality. The "new class," an elite of party, police, state, and military leaders, had established itself as an hereditary aristocracy. This Communist aristocracy without manners, taste, or real competence, passed position and wealth on to its offspring and seemed mainly concerned with its creature comforts. It possessed limousines, special luxury apartment blocks, country estates (dachas), and sanatoria closed to ordinary citizens. It utilized special shops with quantities of otherwise unobtainable goods at heavily subsidized prices. The elevated status of this privileged minority, as in tsarist Russia, separated it from a resentful mass of ordinary workers and peasants. Industrial workers still enjoyed high status in Soviet media, but their wages and pensions remained low. Collective farmers, their position improved by wage and pension increases under Brezhnev, remained at the bottom of the social ladder. "Developed socialism" in Brezhnev's USSR seemed a far cry from the Marxist ideals.

FOREIGN AFFAIRS AND ARMED FORCES

Abroad, a generally prudent Brezhnev regime, carrying a bigger military stick, avoided Khrushchev's dramatic initiatives, threats, and violent reversals. Until 1968, Soviet foreign policy seemed to lack self-

---

[19]D. Atkinson et al., eds., *Women in Russia* (Stanford, Calif., 1977), pp. 219, 224, 355.

confidence. Successful military intervention in Czechoslovakia, halting the erosion of Soviet control over eastern Europe, reversed this picture. Brezhnev thereafter became more decisive and self-assured. As the Sino-Soviet quarrel continued to rage, détente with the West produced important agreements with West Germany and the United States.

Détente and Defense Spending

The new leaders' initial approach abroad was conciliatory, with this message: We are not angry with anyone. They sought to mend their fences with China, but from 1965 on Sino-Soviet competition sharpened over influence in Asia; the gap widened between the bellicose Chinese stance and the moderate Soviet position in the Vietnam War. Exploiting this quarrel to enhance its autonomy, Romania established warm relations with China and increased its trade with the West. In 1966, as the so-called Cultural Revolution began in China, the Chinese boycotted the Soviet 23rd Party Congress, and Russians in China were abused and beaten up. Chinese students left the USSR, and Sino-Soviet trade shrank almost to zero. In January 1969, *Pravda* called Maoism "a great power adventurist policy based on a petty bourgeois nationalistic ideology alien to Marxism-Leninism." As friction mounted along the 4,000 mile Sino-Soviet frontier, the Soviet writer Evgeni Yevtushenko compared the Chinese unflatteringly with the Mongols of Chingis-khan. War between the Communist giants seemed a real possibility, despite the contrary assertions of Marxist-Leninist doctrine. In March 1969 began six months of intermittent but bloody frontier skirmishes over their disputed Ussuri River frontier. According to the dissident historian Roy Medvedev, Brezhnev, who was rabidly anti-Chinese, personally ordered a massive artillery assault and a deep penetration into Chinese territory that killed several thousand Chinese soldiers and poisoned Sino-Soviet relations for years. Rumors circulated that the Soviet military was considering a preemptive nuclear strike against China. In any case, the Chinese were intimidated and agreed not to patrol in areas claimed by the USSR. Meanwhile, the USSR began a major buildup of ground forces along the Chinese border.

Faced with this rising menace in the East, Soviet leaders scrupulously avoided trouble in the West while increasing the USSR's military strength. The Soviets stepped up trade with western Europe, and during Charles de Gaulle's presidency sought to exploit Franco-American coolness in order to split NATO. The similarly independent roles of Romania and France suggested the weakening hold by the two blocs over their members, as contacts increased between eastern and western European countries. The Cuban missile crisis of 1962 had altered Soviet-

American relations considerably. Both sides, noted Hans Morgenthau, an American political scientist, renounced active use of nuclear weapons but retained them as deterrents; both sides aimed at a balance of power and realized that neither could achieve true predominance. Their rivalry in the Third World began to cool as they discovered that neutral countries would not commit themelves totally to either side. In their relations, the United States and the USSR deemphasized ideology and stressed pragmatic power considerations. During the late 1960s, heavy American involvement in Vietnam poisoned their relations; its subsequent decline fostered détente.

In the late 1960s and early 1970s, Soviet policy in the Third World produced both setbacks and successes. Several pro-Soviet regimes collapsed, notably those of Nkrumah in Ghana in 1966 and Sukarno in Indonesia in 1965; anti-Communist military governments replaced them. The Brezhnev regime shifted to practical economic assistance and military aid. Seeking to build up India as a bulwark against China, Moscow viewed the Indo-Pakistan War of 1965 with dismay. Premier Kosygin met with Pakistani and Indian heads of state in Tashkent early in 1966, and the resulting settlement enhanced the USSR's image as a peacemaker in Asia. India's dependence upon Soviet industrial, military, and diplomatic support increased, trade between the two nations expanded, and Soviet naval vessels in the Indian Ocean challenged the former Western monopoly. In the Middle East the USSR supplied major economic and military aid to Egypt and Syria to undermine the Western position and win political influence. Their defeat by Israel in the June 1967 war was a costly setback to Soviet policy, but it increased Arab distrust of the West and dependence on Moscow. After the war, the Soviets rebuilt their clients' military forces, and thousands of Soviet advisers trained Egyptians to use more sophisticated equipment. Iraq, the Sudan, and Algeria also relied heavily on Soviet arms. Soviet influence in the Middle East reached unprecedented proportions only to decline considerably during the early 1970s. President Anwar Sadat of Egypt in 1972 expelled all Soviet military advisers. Then in October 1973 Israel, with which the USSR had severed diplomatic ties, again defeated Egypt and Syria.

A crucial turning point in Brezhnev's foreign policy was the Soviet invasion of Czechoslovakia in August 1968. (See Problem 8.) Earlier that year Czechoslovakia, under Premier Alexander Dubček, had moved rapidly toward democratic socialism, virtually ended domestic censorship, and increased ties with the West. Soviet intervention followed months of hesitation and an apparent agreement with the Czechoslovak Politburo at Čierna-nad-Tisou. Large Soviet forces and token contingents from several Warsaw Pact countries met only moral resistance, and

Moscow disregarded Yugoslav and Romanian objections and Western denunciations. This move, successful from the Soviet viewpoint, revealed that the Brezhnev-Kosygin collective leadership could act decisively. Without hindrance from the United States, the USSR placed six Soviet divisions in Czechoslovakia, altering the strategic balance in central Europe. The Soviet press even echoed Bismarck's famous statement: "Whoever rules Bohemia holds the key to Europe." The subsequent so-called Brezhnev Doctrine warned that the USSR would tolerate neither internal nor external challenges to its hegemony in eastern Europe and that it would use force if necessary to prevent the overthrow of a fellow Communist regime. The Yugoslavs and Romanians wondered whether Brezhnev might apply his "doctrine" against them, but their clear determination to resist apparently dissuaded Moscow. Nonetheless, the Czech intervention reconsolidated the Soviet Bloc in eastern Europe and muted the Yugoslav and Romanian challenge of national communism.

After this major success, the USSR early in 1969 adopted a flexible foreign policy and tried to improve relations with the West. To accelerate Soviet economic growth, Brezhnev sought increased trade with the West and American technology. The replacement of Konrad Adenauer's hard-line rule in West Germany with that of Willy Brandt, a Social Democrat who favored reconciliation with the USSR, weakened NATO and helped Brezhnev heighten his influence in Europe. During 1970 landmark treaties were concluded among the USSR, Poland, and West Germany confirming their post–World War II boundaries and undercutting U.S. bridge building with east European countries. Next the Soviets sought a general European security conference, again to weaken NATO and relax tensions on their western frontiers. But the Soviet hold over eastern Europe remained insecure because of persistent nationalism and the waning force of Marxist ideology. Riots in Poland in 1971 forced the conservative Gomulka to resign and brought the more flexible regime of Edward Gierek to power.

Major increases in military strength enhanced Soviet power and prestige under Brezhnev and created a new world balance of forces. Thus by 1979 the USSR spent an estimated $165 billion on defense, with armed forces totaling some 3.65 million men and women, nearly twice the personnel of the United States' forces. The Red Army, with about 160 divisions, had some 30 percent of its strength along the tense Sino-Soviet border. Possessing huge numbers of tanks and supporting aircraft, the Red Army proved its efficiency and power in the invasion of Czechoslovakia. Whereas during the Cuban missile crisis of 1962 the United States held at least a 3 to 1 advantage in strategic nuclear weapons, by 1969 the USSR had equalled the United States in intercontinental missiles and a decade later was well ahead in ICBMs and submarine-launched missiles.

The achievement of approximate nuclear parity and the growing expense of nuclear armament encouraged the two superpowers to reach significant agreements to limit nuclear weapons, such as the first Strategic Arms Limitation Treaty (SALT I). Until April 1971, the Soviet commitment to SALT remained tentative, but then Brezhnev apparently accepted the concept of strategic parity and championed détente. To Brezhnev this meant developing a working relationship with the United States although Soviet ideology required him to regard the leading capitalist power as an adversary. Explained a Soviet publication of 1972:

> Peaceful coexistence is a principle of relations between states which does not extend to relations between the exploited and the exploiters, the oppressed peoples and the colonialists. . . . Marxist-Leninists see in peaceful coexistence a special form of the class struggle between socialism and capitalism in the world, a principle whose implementation ensures the most favorable conditions for the world revolutionary process.[20]

At their Moscow summit meeting of 1972, President Nixon and General Secretary Brezhnev agreed to limit construction of antiballistic missile defense systems and reached an interim accord on offensive missiles. Additional modest steps toward limitation were taken at meetings in Moscow and Vladivostok in 1974, which set a ceiling on the number of offensive missiles for both sides. This slowed the arms race and inaugurated better relations between the two superpowers. At the European Security Conference, which included all European countries except Albania, plus the United States and Canada, the Helsinki Declaration of August 1975 was signed. The nearest thing to a peace conference ending World War II, it announced: "The participating states regard as inviolable all one another's frontiers . . . and therefore they will refrain now and in the future from assaulting those frontiers." The signatories, including the USSR, pledged to respect human rights.[21]

During a Soviet-American détente lasting until 1980, the Brezhnev regime moderated Soviet policies to permit large-scale Jewish emigration, more contacts with the outside world, and limited diplomatic cooperation to end the Vietnam War. As Robert Kaiser pointed out, during eight years of détente the Soviet Union became a more open society than it had been since the 1920s, and the West learned much more about its internal workings—political, economic, and military—than

---

[20]Shalva Sanakeev, *The World Socialist System* (Moscow, 1972), pp. 289–290.
[21]J. Nogee and R. Donaldson, eds., *Soviet Foreign Policy Since World War II* (Elmsford, N.Y., 1988), p. 263.

before.[22] Tens of millions of Soviet citizens listened regularly to Western radio broadcasts, which undercut the official Soviet version of the truth. The Soviet economy, no longer seeking self-sufficiency as under Stalin, became inextricably linked with the world capitalist system and dependent on Western technology and credits; the eastern European states were increasingly dependent on Western markets and credits. Soviet political controls over the east European Bloc relaxed somewhat, but its members relied more on Soviet energy sources.

Improving Soviet-American relations failed to halt an ominous Soviet military buildup. After the mid-1960s, the Soviet navy was greatly strengthened, becoming second only to the American. The Soviets established a naval presence in all oceans, especially the Mediterranean Sea, to support their Middle East policies. *Red Star,* the Soviet army newspaper, declared in 1970: "The age-old dreams of our people have become reality. The pennants of Soviet ships now flutter in the most remote corners of the seas and oceans." Russia's voice must be heard the world over, declared Foreign Minister Gromyko. Russia's merchant fleet became one of the world's largest. A new, more technically trained generation of Soviet army and navy officers took command of these growing forces from retiring World War II commanders. The armed forces' role in Soviet politics, however, remained stable. Military representation in the Politburo and Central Committee stayed small, and the military did not wish to disrupt a regime that supplied its forces so generously.

The War in Afghanistan

Détente ended in 1980 after growing disillusionment with its fruits on both sides. In December 1979, the USSR, partly to prevent collapse of a Communist regime, abruptly invaded neighboring Afghanistan, a primitive country of warring Muslim tribesmen, where British and Russian imperial interests had clashed in the 19th century. During 1977, under apparent Soviet pressure, the Afghan Communists, divided between a Khalq faction led by Nur Mohammed Taraki and the Parcham group under Babrak Karmal, reunited. In April 1978, army officers and Communists seized power in a bloody coup from the unpopular republic led by elderly President Daoud. Taraki promptly set up a one-man dictatorship—"the People's Democratic Republic of Afghanistan"—and aligned it closely with the USSR. His regime carried out large-scale purges and executions of opponents and removed army leaders and

---

[22]Robert Kaiser, "U.S.-Soviet Relations: Goodbye to Détente," *Foreign Affairs, 59,* no. 3 (1981), pp. 500–521.

A Tadzhik, Soviet Central Asia (© *J. Allan Cash*)

members of the Parcham faction. Babrak Karmal, the Parcham leader, took refuge in Moscow. Khalq leaders, headed by H. Amin, sought overnight to implement socialism in a backward tribal society, violating every Afghan cultural and religious norm. The new regime's blatant brutality and its identification with atheism and the USSR alienated much of the Afghan population.

In August 1978 Afghans from every province rose in revolt against the Taraki-Amin regime under Muslim leaders who proclaimed a jihad (holy war) against godless communism; parts of the Afghan army defected to the rebels. Originally delighted by the Communist takeover, Moscow was now appalled at the new regime's unwise and hasty policies. "The revolutionary transformations [were] . . . accompanied by gross errors and extremist exaggerations on the left, which failed to give due consideration to religious and tribal trends . . . ," declared a Soviet spokesman. Initially, Moscow supported Taraki, but in September 1979, after a shootout in the palace, Amin removed Taraki and ruled as dictator. As the popular revolt against him intensified, the Soviets escalated their role until by November there were some 4,500 Soviet "advisers" backing Amin in Afghanistan; Soviet pilots were bombing rebel positions. (See Map 18.2.) Moscow was being sucked gradually into an Afghan civil war much as the United States had earlier been drawn into the Vietnam imbroglio.

Meanwhile, as he had done in Czechoslovakia in 1968, General I. G. Pavlovskii surveyed the situation in Kabul and concentrated Soviet troops and equipment. On December 24, 1979, regular Soviet units invaded Afghanistan; three days later, a special Soviet assault force attacked the palace in Kabul and killed Amin and his family. As in Czechoslovakia, the Soviet incursion was massive and militarily efficient, but again the political and propaganda aspects were handled with incredible clumsiness. The Afghan "request" for military "assistance" arrived in Moscow three days *after* the invasion began! Only hours after a Soviet minister had called on President Amin, Moscow announced that Amin had been executed for crimes "against the noble people of Afghanistan." Babrak Karmal, installed as the new Afghan leader, arrived from Moscow four days later in the baggage-train of the Soviet army. Then Moscow proclaimed that its army had intervened, overthrown the government, and killed the president in order to forestall "foreign intervention," adding the absurd charge that Amin had plotted with the CIA and Muslim fanatics to destroy Afghan socialism! Yet that September Brezhnev had congratulated Amin upon his becoming president.

The Soviet invasion produced counteraction by the United States. President Carter declared that this Soviet action "has made a more drastic change in my own opinion of what the Soviets' ultimate goals are than anything they've done in the previous time I've been in office." Washington proclaimed the Persian Gulf vital to American security, imposed partial embargoes for awhile on shipments of grain and technology to the USSR, and organized a partially successful Western boycott of the 1980 Moscow Olympics. The United Nations urged the "immediate and unconditional withdrawal of foreign troops from Afghanistan," but Moscow paid no attention.

Was the Soviet incursion part of an aggressive design to dominate the Persian Gulf region or a defensive move under the Brezhnev Doctrine to prevent the fall of a client Communist regime to Muslim fundamentalism? Was this action unprecedented, as some Western observers believed, and thus a dangerous turning point in Soviet foreign policy or merely the Asian counterpart of the Czech intervention? Even before the invasion, Afghanistan had been within the Soviet sphere of influence,

Map 18.2 *Contempory Afghanistan*

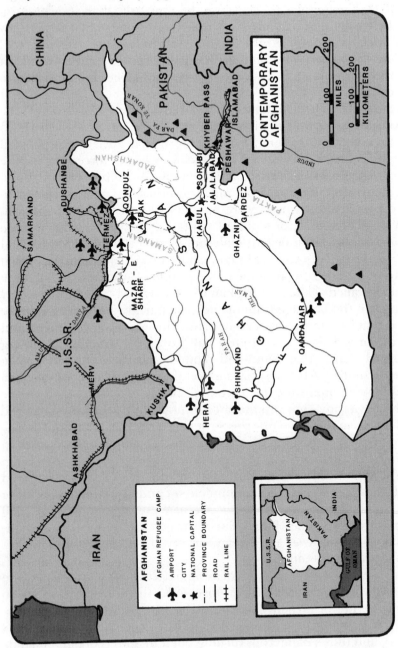

affirmed Thomas Hammond, an American scholar.[23] So the Soviet move thus was really nothing new: Consistent with earlier actions by Moscow in the Third World, the invasion sought to secure Soviet frontiers by surrounding them with friendly and subservient clients and to prevent the fall of any Communist regime. Contributory causes included Soviet fears of Muslim fanaticism spreading into Soviet Central Asia and the Soviet desire to demonstrate effective support of its allies. The invasion of Afghanistan also continued traditional Russian imperialism in the area and aimed to create a more effective and obedient regime.

Babrak Karmal assumed the top posts in the new Soviet-installed government and named token non-Communists to his cabinet while protesting his patriotism and sincere support for Islam. He failed to win much public support because he was known to be an atheist, a Communist, and a Moscow puppet surrounded and controlled by Russian advisers, who carried through progressive Sovietization of Afghanistan. Feuding Afghan tribal factions achieved unprecedented unity in a national liberation struggle and holy war against Russians whom they hated and despised. The rebels (*mujaheddin*) soon controlled most of the country despite the influx of some 115,000 Soviet troops. The strength of the unreliable Afghan army fell sharply. Soviet forces used massive firepower, indiscriminate bombing, and, apparently, chemical weapons in abortive efforts to root out the rebels. By 1984, some 3 million Afghans, or 20 percent of the total population, had fled their increasingly devastated and impoverished homeland; most went to neighboring Pakistan. The Soviet invasion and brutal conduct of the war undermined the influence of the USSR in Muslim lands of the Third World, hastened American rearmament, and severely drained Soviet resources.

Problems with Poland

During 1980, another and potentially even graver threat to the Soviet Bloc developed in Poland on the Soviet Union's western flank. Beginning in 1970, Edward Gierek, succeeding Gomulka as chief of the Polish Communist Party, had pushed a program of rapid industrialization, fueled with Western technology purchased on credit. After a boom period (1971–1975) and rising living standards, severe recession gripped Poland. Skyrocketing energy costs, delays in completing large industrial projects, and rising consumer demand produced alarming deficits in Poland's balance of payments with the West. In the summer of 1980 a series of worker strikes triggered formation of an independent trade

---

[23]Thomas Hammond, *Red Flag over Afghanistan* (Boulder, Colo., 1984).

union movement, Solidarity, which soon obtained the support of most Polish workers. Gierek was forced from office, but his replacement, Stanislaw Kania, failed to stem the workers' campaign for benefits and freedom. As the Polish economy neared collapse and farmers and students also began to organize, party control was threatened. Reports multiplied of a massive Soviet military buildup on Poland's frontiers and veiled threats of intervention from Moscow were designed to restore the Polish Workers' Party's monopoly of power.

The Soviets confronted an acute dilemma: Military intervention might provoke Polish armed resistance and complete Poland's economic ruin, but inaction would imperil fragile Communist regimes in East Germany and Czechoslovakia, and possibly foment discontent within the Soviet Union. Solidarity demanded the virtual replacement of communism with democracy; Polish farmers followed suit by organizing "Rural Solidarity." The Poles sought not merely free trade unions but also elimination of censorship, establishment of independent courts, removal of the police from party control, and institution of free elections. Wisely shunning any demand to withdraw Poland from the Warsaw Pact, the Poles urged reducing its military forces. Clearly, the USSR could not tolerate such a program any more than it could approve the "Prague Spring." (See p. 452.) But instead of resorting to direct military intervention, which could cause a blood bath, Moscow encouraged the Polish army under a moderate, General Wojciech Jaruzelski, to take power and proclaim martial law (December 1981). Poland's military regime forced Solidarity underground and promised decentralizing economic reforms, like those in Hungary. However, Jaruzelski failed to remedy a desperate economic situation.

The 26th Party Congress (February 23 to March 3, 1981) in Moscow brought no real solutions to these difficult problems in Europe and Asia. Secretary Brezhnev, aged but still ascendant, sounded a conciliatory note by proposing a summit conference and renewed arms talks with President Ronald Reagan; otherwise there was complete reaffirmation of the status quo. Indeed, for the first time every full and alternate member of the Politburo and every member of the Secretariat was "reelected." The 5,002 delegates, who included 12 cosmonauts, heard endless speeches praising the "titanic labors" and "colossal life experience" of Leonid Brezhnev. Premier Tikhonov appealed for more efficiency and higher labor productivity; he promised more food and better consumer goods. The goals of the new Eleventh Five Year Plan (1981–1985) announced at the Congress reflected continuing deceleration of Soviet economic growth.

PROBLEM 8
Soviet Intervention in Czechoslovakia, 1968, and Its Repudiation, 1989

The armed invasion of Czechoslovakia on August 21, 1968, by the Red Army and smaller contingents from four Warsaw Pact allies shocked many in the Soviet Bloc and Communists and others in the West. Soviet intervention occurred only weeks after apparent agreement between Soviet and Czechoslovak leaders at Čierna-nad-Tisou just inside Czechoslovakia. Condemning the action, only Romania refused to participate in the massive Warsaw Pact invasion. The military operation was smooth, unopposed, and revealed Soviet military efficiency, but the Czechoslovak passive resistance surprised Soviet leaders and military personnel. Why did the Soviet Politburo decide suddenly, even if reluctantly, to invade an ally still ruled by the Communist party? Was it Czechoslovak domestic liberalization under Alexander Dubček or the danger that the movement would spread to the rest of the Soviet bloc that proved decisive? And why did the Soviet Union and its allies 21 years later repudiate their intervention as mistaken and unjustified?

Soviet invasion followed almost a year of liberalization in Czechoslovakia (the so-called Prague Spring), hitherto one of the most conservative Stalinist members of the Soviet Bloc. Profound change followed the downfall in January 1968 of the unpopular Stalinist leadership headed by Antonín Novotný despite Soviet objections and half-hearted support. Although before World War II Czechoslovakia had been the most democratic and economically advanced east European country, since 1963 it had suffered a grievous economic decline. Early in 1968 much of the rigid, overcentralized Stalinist economic system was dismantled. Under Dubček, the first Slovak to govern Czechoslovakia, liberal Communists instituted far-reaching economic and political reforms, wide freedom of the press, equality for the Slovaks, thorough party reform, and efforts to increase trade and improve relations with the West. Previous Soviet interference in Czechoslovak domestic affairs was denounced publicly by party members and intellectuals. This provoked alarm and fear by conservative Communist regimes in East Germany and Poland and among Soviet leaders that the Czech liberal fever might infect the Ukraine and other Soviet republics. Initially, Dubček apparently convinced Soviet leaders that he could control liberalization and restrict it to Czechoslovakia; he assured Moscow that his country would remain in the Warsaw Pact as a Soviet ally and that the Czechoslovak Communist Party (KSS or CCP) would retain its power monopoly.

Defiant Czech youth waves national flag before a
Soviet tank after the Red Army's unpopular
occupation of Prague, Czechoslovakia, in August
1968 (*AP/Wide World Photos*)

The following excerpts depict the Soviet intervention from several
contrasting viewpoints. Included are official Soviet explanations and
justifications, Soviet dissident reactions, Czechoslovak protests and refu-
tations of Soviet assertions, a Western view, and the 1989 Soviet repudiation.

OFFICIAL SOVIET VIEWS

The following excerpts from the Soviet Communist Party newspaper,
Pravda, one before the invasion and the other after, emphasize the deadly
peril to socialism in Czechoslovakia and the Bloc posed by alleged Czech
reactionaries aided by American and West German agents. *Pravda*
asserted that Soviet forces were invited into Czechoslovakia by elements
loyal to socialism and that the Soviet Union and other Warsaw Pact

countries had the right and duty to act forcefully in the face of such blatant threats to the entire socialist world.

1. *"To the Czechoslovak Communist Party Central Committee,"* Pravda, *July 15, 1968.*

    On behalf of the Central Committtees of the Communist and Workers Parties of Bulgaria, Hungary, the G.D.R. [East Germany], Poland, and the Soviet Union we send you this letter, which is dictated by sincere friendship based on the principles of Marxism-Leninism and proletarian internationalism and by concern . . . for strengthening the positions of socialism and the . . . socialist commonwealth of the peoples.

    The developments in your country have aroused profound anxiety among us. The reactionaries' offensive, supported by imperialism, against your party and the foundations of the Czechoslovak Socialist Republic's social system . . . threatens to push your country off the path of socialism and, consequently, imperils the interests of the entire socialist system. . . . We have not had and do not have any intention of interfering in affairs that are purely the internal affairs of your party and your state or of violating the principles of respect, autonomy and equality in relations among Communist Parties and socialist countries. . . .

    . . . It is the common affair of our countries, which have united in the Warsaw Pact to safeguard their independence, peace and security in Europe and to place an insurmountable barrier in front of the schemes of imperialist forces, aggression and revanche. . . .

    The forces of reaction, taking advantage of the weakening of party leadership in Czechoslovakia and demagogically abusing the slogan of "democratization," unleashed a campaign against the C.C.P. . . . with the clear intention of liquidating the party's guiding role, undermining the socialist system and pitting Czechoslovakia against the other socialist countries. The political organizations and clubs that have cropped up lately outside the framework of the National Front have in essence become headquarters for the forces of reaction. The social democrats persistently seek to create their own party . . . and are attempting to split the workers' movement in Czechoslovakia and to secure leadership of the country so as to restore the bourgeois system. Antisocialist and revisionist forces have taken over the press, radio and television and have turned them into platforms for attacking the Communist party, for disorienting the working class . . . , for carrying out unchecked antisocialist demagoguery and for subverting the friendly relations between the Č. S. R. and the other socialist countries. . . . The reactionaries appeared publicly before the whole country and published their political platform, entitled "The 2,000 Words." . . .

2. *"Sovereignty and the International Duties of Socialist Countries,"* Pravda, *September 26, 1968, by Serge Kovalev.*

    The question of the correlation and interdependence of the national interests of the socialist countries and their international duties has acquired particular topical and great importance in connection with the events in Czechoslovakia. The measures taken by the Soviet Union, jointly with other socialist countries, in defending the socialist gains of the Czechoslovak people, are of great importance for strengthening the socialist community. . . .

The peoples of the socialist countries and the Communist Parties certainly do have and should have freedom to determine the roads of advance for their respective countries. However, none of their decisions should do harm either to socialism in their own country or to the fundamental interests of other socialist countries. . . . This means that each Communist Party is responsible not only to its own people but also to all socialist countries and to the entire communist movement. . . .

. . . When a socialist country seeks to adopt a "non-affiliated" attitude, it . . . retains its national independence precisely thanks to the strength of the socialist community, and above all the Soviet Union as its central force, which also includes the might of its armed forces. The weakening of any of the links in the world socialist system directly affects all the socialist countries, which cannot look on indifferently when this happens. Thus, with talk about the right of nations to self-determination the antisocialist elements in Czechoslovakia actually covered up a demand for so-called neutrality and Czechoslovakia's withdrawal from the socialist community. . . . In discharging their internationalist duty to the fraternal peoples of Czechoslovakia and defending their own socialist gains, the USSR and the other socialist states had to act decisively, and they did act, against the anti-socialist forces in Czechoslovakia. . . .

. . . The troops of the allied socialist countries who are now in Czechoslovakia . . . are not interfering in the country's internal affairs; they are fighting for the principles of the self-determination of the peoples of Czechoslovakia.[24]

This Soviet rationale for armed intervention in other Bloc countries was called the "Brezhnev Doctrine."

PROTESTS BY SOVIET INTELLECTUALS

The invasion of Czechoslovakia soon produced a protest movement by many Soviet intellectuals and a development of the dissident movement in the USSR. Among some courageous objections was this one by a leading Soviet poet, Evgenii Yevtushenko, who telegraphed Chairman Brezhnev:

I cannot sleep. . . . I understand only one thing, that it is my moral duty to express my opinion to you. I am profoundly convinced that our action in

---

[24]A. Rubinstein, *The Foreign Policy of the Soviet Union*, 3d ed. (New York, 1972), pp. 302–304 excerpts.

Czechoslovakia is a tragic mistake. It is a cruel blow to Czechoslovak-Soviet friendship and to the world Communist movement. This action detracts from our prestige in the eyes of the world and in our own. For me this is also a personal tragedy because I have many friends in Czechoslovakia, and I do not know how I will be able to look them in the eye. . . . I tell myself that what has happened is a great gift to all the reactionary forces in the world, that we cannot foresee the overall consequences of this act. . . .[25]

1. *Roy Medvedev, "Was the Invasion a Defense of Socialism?"* . . . *Pravda* writes that the Soviet Communist Party has had an "understanding attitude" toward the decisions made by the CPC at the January 1968 plenum of its Central Committee. But *Pravda* says nothing about the mistakes and crimes of the Novotný group, which brought Czechoslovakia to its present state of political crisis. *Pravda* asserts that the Soviet Communist Party leadership has no desire to impose its views on the CPC concerning forms and methods of social control or the road to socialism. But the facts testify to the opposite.

During the past six months we have tried to impose on the CPC our false understanding of events in that country, and when our point of view was rejected, we resorted to military action. *Pravda* admits that the Czechoslovak leaders insisted that they were in full control of the situation in their country. But the Soviet Party leadership [concluded] that "the course of events was such that it could lead to a counterrevolutionary coup." This was a totally wrong conclusion, based . . . on hysterical appeals by the Novotnýites . . . and by their obvious allies in the Soviet embassy in Czechoslovakia. There was no danger of a counterrevolutionary coup either in the spring of 1968 or later. . . .

. . . By violating Czechoslovak sovereignty, affronting the government of the CSSR and the leadership of the CPC, and offending the national sensibilities of the Czechs and Slovaks, we have weakened, not strengthened, the position of socialism in that country. Our action in Czechoslovakia was not the "defense of socialism" but a blow against socialism in Czechoslovakia and throughout the world.[26]

2. *Aleksandr Ivanov, "Russia's Shame"*

. . . So here we see the Stalinists of our huge country, frightened to death, trying to drown out with the clatter of tank treads the voice of those Communists who in tiny Czechoslovakia were a bit too hasty in trying to cleanse the *human face* of socialism of the trappings of pseudo socialism. . . . With the blow of the iron fist they have, for the moment, saved themselves and the Czech Stalinists—ridiculously small in numbers!—from the irreversible forward march of socialism.

---

[25]From *An End to Silence: Uncensored Opinion in the Soviet Union.* Edited by Stephen F. Cohen, Copyright © 1982 by W. W. Norton.
[26]Cohen, *An End to Silence,* pp. 281–284.

. . . August 1968 was a blow at the *practical reality* of socialism and at the Communist movement throughout the world. It was a blow against the ideas of socialism, against genuine Marxism, against the prestige of Communists in the eyes of all progressive humanity, because this blow was struck in the name of socialism and its ideas. . . . But it was our own "young and green" soldiers who carried out this reactionary deed. They did it without knowing or asking *who* they were going after, *who* they were crushing—whether it was a counterrevolution or a revolution. This blind and obedient willingness to follow any order, this unwillingness to consider the significance of one's own actions . . . —that is our national shame, the national disgrace of our times! . . . We are responsible for the enormous harm done to Czechoslovakia's development toward Communism, for all the consequences of our reactionary intervention. . . .[27]

A CZECH REACTION TO THE INVASION

In the first weeks after the Soviet invasion of August 21, the Czechoslovak people were mobilized in a movement of massive passive resistance by their press, radio, and television, freed from Stalinist controls earlier that year. Here are excerpts from "Commentary of the Day" from *Reportér*, no. 35 of August 26, 1968:

A country that does not need to be saved from anything or freed from anything, that is not asking for it and is actually rejecting it for weeks in advance as an absurdity—such a country cannot be "liberated." Such a country can only be occupied—unlawfully, brutally, recklessly. . . . These are unpleasant truths, and one cannot be surprised that the occupiers do not want to read them on the asphalt of the roads, on the walls of houses, . . . on millions of posters throughout the country. . . . But they cannot do away with these truths, least of all by driving the "natives" into the streets under their automatics and forcing them to tear down the posters. . . . Are they not acting "in the interests of socialism," have they not come as "class brethren" performing their "noble internationalist duty"? It is totally inconceivable to them that they should be compared with those who subjugated this country in an equally brutal manner three decades ago. . . . They did not come to liberate socialist Czechoslovakia on the 21st of August, but to trample it down; they did not come to save the Czechs and Slovaks, but to enslave them. . . .

. . . Stealthily, not like a government of a decent country, but like medieval conspirators, behind the backs of all the legal organs of this country, they joined in a compact with a handful of discredited political corpses and stool pigeons who feared punishment for their participation in the crimes of the 1950's and while still pretending to conduct a dialog in their formal contacts,

---

[27]Cohen, pp. 293—295.

they forcibly invaded the country. Like gangsters, they abducted the Premier of the legal government of a sovereign country, the Chairman of the legal parliament of that country, the First Secretary of the leading political party, and they restricted the movement and action of the head of state, the President of the Republic, a bearer of the highest medals of their own country.[28]

They trampled upon all agreements that had bound them with that country and yet they had enough arrogance to claim that they were doing so precisely on the basis of those agreements. They brutally surrounded the parliament of that country with their tanks and machine guns. . . . Within three days, they flooded that small country with 26 military divisions and 500,000 soldiers, with thousands of tanks and even rocket weapons, which they aimed against our capital city. They drove the voices of this country, its press, radio, and television, underground, and they tried to replace them with their disgusting prattle disseminated out of [East] Berlin in an insulting distortion of our language. . . .

Encountering the calm of the people, a country that fails to offer a single proof in support of their nonsensical pretext for aggression, they started a futile barrage from all their weapons in the middle of the night—perhaps to be able to pretend to themselves that there is, after all, a need to fight. . . .

Can all this be called a rescue, can all this be called a liberation? How does it actually differ from 15 March 1939?[29] Is this not a replica of all that we already went through once? Of *Wehrmacht* and Gestapo, of blood and iron? Of injustice and arrogance, cruelty and recklessness? Is anything changed by the fact that all this is being perpetrated not by enemies but by "friends," not by recognized aggressors but by allies, not by those of whom we might have expected it but by those whom we would never have thought capable of it?[30]

A WESTERN EVALUATION

In a scholarly study, Galia Golan, lecturer in political science at the Hebrew University of Jerusalem, ends with an examination of factors leading to the Soviet invasion of August 1968. She emphasizes the dangers to the Kremlin posed by the "Czechoslovak road to socialism":

While Czechoslovakia's reforms did not lead her to demand genuine independence from the Soviet Union, the growing pressures upon her did prompt more and more frequent references to sovereignty, equality, and a

---

[28]President Ludvik Svoboda was one of very few foreigners to receive the highest Soviet military decoration: Hero of the Soviet Union.

[29]On that date the Nazi armies of Hitler occupied Prague and the remainder of Czechoslovakia.

[30]Czechoslovak "Black Book," in R. Remington, ed., *Winter in Prague* (Cambridge, Mass., 1969), pp. 407–409.

"Czechoslovak" road to socialism. The sources of these pressures, specifically Gomulka, Ulbricht, and the Kremlin, may well have believed that the reform movement would, eventually, lead Czechoslovakia out of the bloc. But subsequent actions—and revelations—suggested that what worried them most was this "Czechoslovak road to socialism," i.e., the threat it presented for socialism as the Soviets conceived it, both in Czechoslovakia and in the other countries of the Soviet bloc. . . . This issue was certainly used by both the East Germans and the Soviets in their accusations against Prague (*viz.* their efforts to link the reform movement with Bonn, revanchism, and the Sudeten Deutsche), but the Soviets never brought to bear all the means at their disposal to forestall such relations. Rather it would seem that something much more serious was deemed to warrant a full-scale invasion: . . . the threat to the continued rule of the party, the threat of pluralism, and the dangers of freedom of expression—all considered incompatible in Soviet eyes with the continuation or building of socialism. Thus Soviet and subsequent conservative Czechoslovak attacks focused on the abolition of censorship, the criticism of the militia (read security organs), and the tentatives towards pluralism, specifically the clubs, of the 1968 revival. . . .

The Soviets made every effort publicly to create the impression that their fear was that Czechoslovakia was falling into the hands of persons who wished to take her out of the socialist alliance, defy the Soviet Union and move towards the West. . . . Moscow's concerns focused on Czechoslovakia's traditional tendencies to democratic socialism, with all its implications for Eastern Europe and the Soviet Union. Like the Comintern and Cominform before them, Moscow, Warsaw, and Pankow were unwilling to accept or believe that this type of socialism could lead to and preserve communism. Specifically, the concept of the leading role of the party . . . had become so intricately connected with the concept of communist rule that Moscow could not conceive of a communist party's remaining in power if it were to abandon its leading role. . . . The implications of this danger were clear: pluralism in Prague . . . might well spread to other countries. . . . The fall of the communist regime in Prague would mean the loss of Czechoslovakia as a reliable ally or even friendly neighbor. . . . It was the democratic nature and content of the Czechoslovak experiment, rather than some fabricated "neutralism" or pro-western tendency, which precipitated the invasion.[31]

THE REPUDIATION OF 1989

In November 1989, encouraged by dramatic political change in neighboring Poland, Hungary, and East Germany, the hard-line Communist regime of Czechoslovakia led by Miloš Jakes fell before a massive but

---

[31]Galia Golan, *The Czechoslovak Reform Movement: Communism in Crisis, 1962–1968* (Cambridge, Eng., 1971), pp. 316, 327–328.

peaceful popular revolution. On December 4, 1989, in Moscow the USSR and the four Warsaw Pact allies that had joined in the 1968 intervention in Czechoslovakia jointly condemned that action. Furthermore, Soviet leaders agreed to discuss with the new Czechoslovak regime the withdrawal of Soviet troops that had been garrisoned in Czechoslovakia ever since August 1968. Here are the texts of the Soviet and Warsaw Pact repudiations of the intervention.

Soviet Statement

The Czechoslovak society is at the stage of a critical reassessment of the experience of its political and economic development.

This is a natural process. Many countries undergo it in one way or another.

Regrettably, the need for constant socialist self-renewal and realistic appraisal of the events has not always been taken for granted, particularly in situations when such events intertwined in a contradictory way and required bold answers to the challenges of times.

In 1968, the Soviet leadership of that time supported the stand of one side in an internal dispute in Czechoslovakia regarding objective pressing tasks.

The justification for such an unbalanced, inadequate approach, an interference in the affairs of a friendly country, was then seen in an acute East-West confrontation.

We share the view of the Presidium of the Central Committee of the Communist Party of Czechoslovakia and the Czechoslovak Government that the bringing of armies of five socialist countries into Czechoslovak territory in 1968 was unfounded, and that that decision, in the light of all the presently known facts, was erroneous.

Warsaw Pact Statement

Leaders of Bulgaria, Hungary, the German Democratic Republic, Poland and the Soviet Union, who gathered for a meeting in Moscow on Dec. 4, stated that the bringing of troops of their countries into Czechoslovakia in 1968 was an interference in internal affairs of sovereign Czechoslovakia and should be condemned.

Disrupting the process of democratic renewal in Czechoslovakia, those illegal actions had long-term negative consequences.

History showed how important it is, even in the most complex international situation, to use political means for the solution of any problems, strictly to observe the principles of sovereignty, independence and noninterference in internal affairs in relations among states, which is in keeping with the provisions of the Warsaw Treaty.

Two days earlier on December 3 the newly formed Czechoslovak government issued the following statement, which apparently provoked the publication of the two preceding statements:

The Government of the Czechoslovak Socialist Republic considers the entry into Czechoslovakia of the armies of the five states of the Warsaw Treaty in 1968 as an infringement to the norms of relations amongst sovereign states. The federal Government entrusts its chairman, Ladislav Adamec, to inform the Soviet Government of this position.

The federal Government proposes, at the same time, to the Government of the Soviet Union to open negotiations on an inter-government agreement which concerns the temporary stay of the Soviet troops on the territory of the Czechoslovak Socialist Republic. It entrusts the Minister of Foreign Affairs, Jaromir Johanes, to conduct the negotiations. It premises that the question of the departure of the Soviet troops must be settled in conformity with the advance of the European disarmament process.

The Government of the Czechoslovak Socialist Republic is prepared, together with the other countries involved, to create a group of historians who would consider, from all angles, the context of the events of August 1968. . . .[32]

CONCLUSION

Explaining their invasion of Czechoslovakia in 1968, Soviet spokesmen had emphasized that a powerful "reactionary movement" had sought to overturn socialism there, allied with West German militarists and revanchists. Moscow claimed the right to intervene anywhere in the "socialist world" to prevent the collapse of socialism and a consequent reversion to capitalism or feudalism. However, they failed to convince even their own intellectuals, to say nothing of foreign Communists, that such threats existed. Both groups deplored an invasion that tarnished Soviet prestige and undermined the world Communist movement. Faced with overwhelming Czechoslovak opposition to the invasion, the Soviets found few citizens who would welcome them into the country. By the intervention the Brezhnev regime regained its self-confidence, reconsolidating its hold over eastern Europe. However, the costs proved high: recementing the NATO alliance, alienating Eurocommunism, and exposing the USSR as a blatant violator of international law and national self-determination.

The east European revolutions of 1989 induced the Soviet regime to reassess drastically the 1968 invasion of Czechoslovakia. M. S. Gorbachev, the Soviet president, had clearly encouraged the popular revolt in Prague, which was preceded by the appearance on Soviet television of Alexander Dubček, leader of the "Prague Spring" of 1968. Moscow hailed that movement as the harbinger of the Gorbachev reforms in the

---

[32]*New York Times,* December 5 and December 3, 1989.

USSR. Soviet support for the removal of the Stalinist Czechoslovak regime confirmed Gorbachev's earlier repudiation of the interventionist Brezhnev Doctrine.

Suggested Additional Reading

Problem 8

GOLAN, GALIA. *The Czechoslovak Reform Movement: Communism in Crisis, 1962– 1968* (Cambridge, Eng., 1971).

HOFFMANN, E. P., and F. J. FLERON, JR. *The Conduct of Soviet Foreign Policy*, 2d ed. (New York, 1980).

LITTELL, ROBERT, ed. *The Czech Black Book* (New York, 1969).

REMINGTON, ROBIN A., ed. *Winter in Prague: Documents on Czechoslovak Communism in Crisis* (Cambridge, Mass., 1969).

VALENTA, JIRI. *Soviet Intervention on Czechoslovakia, 1968: Anatomy of a Decision* (Baltimore, Md., 1979).

ZARTMAN, I. WILLIAM, ed. *Czechoslovakia: Intervention and Impact* (New York, 1970).

Chapter 18

AMALRIK, A. *Will the Soviet Union Survive Until 1984?* (New York, 1970).

BENNIGSEN, A. *The Islamic Threat to the Soviet State* (New York, 1983).

BERMAN, R. P. *Soviet Strategic Forces* (Washington, D. C., 1982).

BESANCON, A. *The Soviet Syndrome*, trans. P. Ranum (New York, 1978).

BIALER, S., ed. *The Domestic Context of Soviet Foreign Policy* (Boulder, Colo., 1981).

———. *Stalin's Successors: Leadership, Stability and Change in the Soviet Union* (Cambridge, Eng., 1981).

BORNSTEIN, MORRIS, ed. *The Soviet Economy: Continuity & Change* (Boulder, Colo., 1981).

BRADSHER, H. S. *Afghanistan and the Soviet Union* (Durham, N.C., 1983).

BREZHNEV, LEONID. *Peace, Détente and Soviet-American Relations* (New York, 1979).

BROWN, A., and KASER, M., eds. *The Soviet Union Since the Fall of Khrushchev* (New York, 1978).

COLTON, T. J. *Commissars, Commanders, and Civilian Authority: The Structure of Soviet Military Politics* (Cambridge, Mass., 1979).

DORNBERG, JOHN. *Brezhnev: The Masks of Power* (New York, 1974).

EDMONDS, R. *Soviet Foreign Policy: The Brezhnev Years* (Oxford, 1983).

ELLISON, H., ed. *The Sino-Soviet Conflict: A Global Perspective* (Seattle, 1982).

D'ENCAUSSE, H. C. *Decline of an Empire: The Soviet Socialist Republics in Revolt* (New York, 1979).

FRANCISCO, R., et al., eds. *Agricultural Policies in the USSR and Eastern Europe* (Boulder, Colo., 1980).

FREEDMAN, R. U. *Soviet Jewry in the Decisive Decade 1971–1980* (Durham, N.C., 1984).

FRIEDGUT, T. *Political Participation in the USSR* (Princeton, N. J., 1979).

GELMAN, HARRY. *The Brezhnev Politburo . . .* (Ithaca, N.Y., 1984).

HAMMOND, THOMAS. *Red Flag over Afghanistan* (Boulder, Colo., 1984).

HOUGH, JERRY. *Soviet Leadership in Transition* (Washington, D.C., 1980).

————, and M. FAINSOD. *How the Soviet Union Is Governed* (Cambridge, Mass., 1979).

HUNTER, H. *The Future of the Soviet Economy, 1978–1985* (Boulder, Colo., 1978).

HUTCHINGS, R. L. *Soviet-East European Relations: Consolidation and Conflict, 1968–1980* (Madison, Wis., 1983).

KAISER, R. G. *Russia: The People and the Power* (New York, 1976, 1984).

KANET, ROGER. *The Soviet Union and the Developing Nations* (Baltimore, Md., 1974).

KELLEY, D. R. *The Solzhenitsyn-Sakharov Dialogue* (New York, 1982).

————, ed. *Soviet Politics in the Brezhnev Era* (New York, 1980).

KUSHNIRSKY, F. I. *Soviet Economic Planning, 1965–1980* (Boulder, Colo., 1982).

LAIRD, ROY, et al., eds. *The Future of Agriculture in the Soviet Union and Eastern Europe* (Boulder, Colo., 1977).

LEWIS, R., et al., eds. *Nationality and Population Change in Russia and the USSR . . .* (New York, 1976).

LITVINOV, P., ed. *The Demonstration on Pushkin Square* (Boston, 1969).

LÖWENHARDT, J. *The Soviet Politburo* (New York, 1982).

MARCHENKO, A. *My Testimony* (New York, 1969).

MEDVEDEV, ROY. *A Question of Madness* (New York, 1971).

MORTON, H., and TÖKES, R. *Soviet Politics & Society in the 1970s* (New York, 1974).

PIPES, RICHARD. *US-Soviet Relations in the Era of Détente* (Boulder, Colo., 1981).

ROTHBERG, A. *The Heirs of Stalin . . .* (Ithaca, N.Y., 1972).

RYAVEC, K., ed. *Soviet Society and the Communist Party* (Amherst, Mass., 1978).

RYWKIN, M. *Moscow's Muslim Challenge* (New York, 1982).

SAKHAROV, ANDREI. *Sakharov Speaks* (New York, 1974).

SINGLETON, FRED, ed. *Environmental Misuse in the Soviet Union* (New York, 1976).

SMITH, HEDRICK. *The Russians* (New York, 1975, 1984).

ULAM, A. B. *Dangerous Relations: The Soviet Union in World Politics, 1970–1982* (Oxford, Eng., 1984).

WESSON, R. *The Aging of Communism* (New York, 1980).

YANOV, A. *Détente After Brezhnev: The Domestic Roots of Soviet Foreign Policy* (Berkeley, Calif., 1977).

CHAPTER NINETEEN

THE SOVIET GERONTOCRACY, 1982 – 1985

In a desperate holding action by the old men of the Politburo, for a decade beginning in 1975, the Soviet Union was ruled by the aged and the infirm. What a far cry from the revolutionary vigor and optimism of 1917, exemplified by Lenin and Trotskii! The Bolshevik Revolution of November 1917 had ushered in a Soviet regime led by dedicated, cosmopolitan revolutionaries with a vision of the socialist future and intellectually the equals of any leadership in the world. Only 60 years later Soviet rule had degenerated into a stagnant bureaucratic regime based on blatant privilege for an elite minority and endemic corruption. Deadly afraid of basic political, social, or economic reform, all long overdue, this conservative oligarchy proved unable or unwilling to tackle a formidable agenda of problems, which Marx had never envisioned for a developed socialist state: A stagnating economy, dissatisfied and restive national minorities, and the embers of resurgent religion amidst the ashes of Leninist ideology. The average age of Politburo leaders by 1982 was almost 70. With the general secretary often unable to mount unaided the

Carter and Brezhnev at 1979 meeting to sign SALT II *(United Press International)*

steps of Lenin's Mausoleum, the Soviet Union at Brezhnev's death was drifting. The Stalinist economic system, consolidated under Brezhnev, once an attractive model for underdeveloped countries, was being repudiated even by some members of the Soviet Bloc as they sought to cast off the confining shackles of centralized planning and overemphasis on heavy industry. One of the elderly rulers, Iurii Andropov, inaugurated significant reforms but died before much progress could be made in implementing them.

DOMESTIC POLITICS

Brezhnev: 1982, the Last Gasps

Evidence mounted during 1982 that Leonid Brezhnev, the consensus politician, was no longer in real command. The struggle for succession apparently began back in 1975 when Brezhnev had suffered a stroke, which removed him from political activity for several months. During that time Mikhail Suslov and Andrei Kirilenko shared leadership of the party. In 1978, Brezhnev's health weakened again, and from then on he relied increasingly upon Konstantin Chernenko, promoting this faithful follower by 1979 to party secretary and full member of the Politburo. Chernenko became Brezhnev's clear choice to be his successor. Economic failures and scandals affecting Brezhnev's cronies and family damaged Chernenko's prospects, however, as Brezhnev's power eroded. First breaking late in 1981, corruption scandals compromised General Semen Tsvigun, Brezhnev's main ally in the KGB. In January 1982, the KGB chief, Iurii Andropov, who had directed the investigations, informed Suslov, the powerful "kingmaker" and chief ideologist, of the general's involvement. After a showdown between them, Tsvigun apparently committed suicide and Suslov died of a stroke a few days later. Early in March, foreign correspondents in Moscow reported that Brezhnev's daughter, Galina, had been involved in a diamond smuggling ring through her intimate friend, Boris Buriata, nicknamed "the Gypsy." Apparently, Andropov had leaked this information in an effort to discredit Brezhnev and undermine Chernenko.[1]

The death of Suslov in January 1982 paved the way for the other political changes of that year destroying the stability and balance of the ruling oligarchy and removing the guardian of proper behavior in the Politburo. Indirect attacks on Brezhnev by the Andropov group were directed against his protection of corrupt cronies. On his return flight from Tashkent in March Brezhnev suffered another stroke and was taken near death to the Kremlin hospital where he remained speechless for several weeks. During this illness, Andropov consolidated control over Suslov's vacant ideological fief, delivered the main speech on Lenin's birthday (April 22), and spent most of his time in the Central Committee. (See Figure 19.1 for a chart of the hierarchy of power.) In May, at a crucial Politburo meeting, Andropov was chosen to succeed Suslov as chief ideologist over the opposition of Brezhnev and Chernenko. In this dress rehearsal for the Brezhnev succession, Andropov moved back into the Secretariat as its second ranking secretary while his candidate, Vitaly Fedorchuk, replaced him as KGB chief. That summer, with the ailing Brezhnev on vacation in the Crimea, Andropov took charge of the Secretariat and arranged the dismissal of two corrupt Brezhnev stalwarts, who were regional party secretaries. Returning to Moscow that fall, Brezhnev, in an address to military leaders, sought to demonstrate that he was still in charge. However, Andropov's supporters then leaked rumors that Brezhnev would resign at the end of the year for reasons of health. That might indeed have occurred had Brezhnev not died of natural causes in November, after clinging to power to the end.

[1]Zhores Medvedev, *Andropov* (New York, 1983), pp. 93–96; Harry Gelman, *The Brezhnev Politburo* . . . (Ithaca, N.Y., 1984), pp. 183–186.

Figure 19.1 *Top Soviet Power Centers, 1980s*

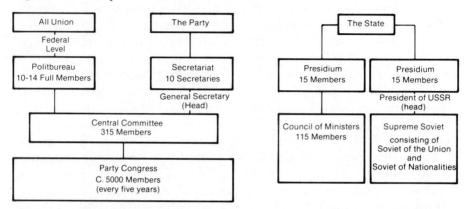

Republic Level (15 Soviet Socialist republics of which by far the largest is the Russian Republic)

Provincial Level

District Level

Local Level

Andropov: The Sick Reformer

In Moscow, the first hint that a top Soviet leader had died came the evening of November 10, 1982. Instead of a scheduled pop concert, a film on Lenin was televised. At 9 P.M., the appearance of a newscaster in formal dress suggested that someone had died, but who? Next morning, more than a day after his actual demise, came simultaneous announcements by Soviet radio and television:

> The Central Committee of the Communist Party of the Soviet Union, the Presidium of the Supreme Soviet of the USSR and the Council of Ministers of the USSR inform with deep sorrow the party and the entire Soviet people that L. I. Brezhnev, General Secretary of the CPSU and President of the Supreme Soviet, died a sudden death at 8:30 A.M. on November 10th.

Like all Soviet leaders except Khrushchev, Brezhnev had died in office. His death was probably hastened by an appearance three days earlier at the frigid celebration in Red Square of the anniversary of the November Revolution. Brezhnev had held the key post of general secretary of the CPSU for 18 years, longer than anyone but Joseph Stalin; he had dealt with five American presidents and four British prime ministers.

Thus the transfer of power to a new leader loomed as an apparent turning point in Soviet history. The swift and smooth transition that then elevated Iurii Andropov to the post of general secretary concealed the

Iurii V. Andropov, general secretary of the CPSU 1982–1984 (right), conferring with Andrei A. Gromyko, Soviet foreign minister 1975–1985 *(AP/Wide World)*

lengthy power struggle described above. The 300-odd members of the Central Committee who filed solemnly into the Council of Ministers building November 12 knew they were merely to ratify the decision made on November 10 by an enlarged Politburo (including candidate members, marshals, and key Central Committee members). That Andropov would be selected had been foreshadowed by his appointment as chairman of Brezhnev's funeral committee. Andropov spoke briefly extolling Brezhnev's services, then Chernenko rose to nominate Andropov, who had outmaneuvered him in the competition for succession. After the Central Committee's unanimous approval was registered, the official power transfer was over. Commented a Soviet engineer: "We used to complain some . . . and tell jokes about the old man. But now that Brezhnev is dead, I feel sad because he conveyed a sense of security and stability."[2] Whereas after Stalin's death 30 years earlier there had been

---

[2]Myron Rush, "Succeeding Brezhnev," *Problems of Communism, 32* (January–February 1983); "Changing the Guard," *Time,* November 22, 1982; Medvedev, *Andropov.*

fear and near panic, now the Moscow public remained calm, hopeful of reform.

Iurii V. Andropov's rise through the party ranks was speeded by Stalin's purges. Born in the village of Nagutskoe in the north Caucasus in June 1914, the son of a railway worker, Andropov left school at 16 to work as a Volga boatman and a telegraph operator. At age 22, he had begun his political career as an organizer for the Komsomol, the Communist youth organization. Later, he resumed his education at a technical college but lacked a university degree. Andropov rose rapidly in Komsomol ranks in the short-lived Karelo-Finnish Republic, where he won the valuable support of Otto Kuusinen, later a Politburo member. During World War II, as a political commissar, he had organized guerrilla forces behind German lines during their occupation of that region. Afterward, he became a party official in Petrozavodsk near Leningrad, and in 1951 he was transferred to Moscow where he joined the staff of the Central Committee Secretariat. From 1954 to 1957 Andropov served as ambassador to Hungary, playing a significant role in the Soviet suppression of the Hungarian Revolution of 1956 and elevation of János Kádár to head the Hungarian Communist Party. During his stay in Hungary, Andropov grew more sophisticated about east European problems. In 1957, he returned to Moscow to direct the foreign affairs department of the Central Committee dealing with Bloc countries. At the 22nd Party Congress (1961), Andropov became a Central Committee secretary, serving under Khrushchev and Brezhnev and traveling to various east European countries. Then in 1967, he became head of the KGB and candidate member of the Politburo. Serving longer than any other KGB chief, Andropov proved very adept at suppressing the dissident movement while giving that dread agency a better public image. Andropov was the only head of the KGB to date to survive that job while increasing his own power and influence. Eliminating remnants of arbitrary terror of the Stalin era, he combated corruption in the party and state apparatuses; he also inaugurated more flexible, sophisticated methods of control and more carefully prepared political cases. He acquired a reputation as a strong, just guardian of the Soviet system.

Andropov's return to the Secretariat in May 1982 had proven crucial in his becoming general secretary of the CPSU six months later. He had obtained the backing of the powerful Soviet military establishment, represented in the Politburo by Marshal Dmitrii Ustinov, and the influential elder statesman Foreign Minister Andrei Gromyko. Andropov, at 68, was the oldest man to rule the party to date. His age and ill health—he suffered from diabetes and kidney disease—may have been the reason for his haste to implement changes and make a mark on the Soviet system. Contrary to some earlier predictions, Andropov swiftly consolidated his power. Within eight months he had become president of the Supreme Soviet and chairman of the Defense Council, posts that Brezhnev had acquired only after many years. Unlike previous Soviet successions, this time there was no prolonged power struggle as the new leader moved smoothly into a position of dominance.

However, Andropov found it harder to accumulate sufficient power to force political change than it was to acquire titular positions. Having achieved power without the support of the network of regional party secretaries who had backed Khrushchev and Brezhnev, he found it hard to move trusted supporters into key positions in the Politburo and Secretariat. Until the end of 1983, the only addition to full membership on the Politburo was the former Azerbaijan party secretary Geidar Aliyev, seemingly a consensus candidate. The coalition that had elevated Andropov to power proved reluctant to allow him to reshape and dominate the Politburo, and he was opposed there by a Brezhnevite "old guard" headed by his defeated rival, Chernenko, and including the elderly premier, Tikhonov. To be sure, Aliyev's designation as deputy premier made him the second most powerful figure in the state apparatus and put him in a position to inherit Tikhonov's position. Two other former subordinates of Andropov soon obtained key posts: Fedorchuk became Interior Minister, being replaced as KGB chief by his deputy, Viktor Chebrikov; and N. I. Ryzhkov was named junior member of the Secretariat. Nonetheless, in his first year in office, wrote the American Sovietologist Harry Gelman late in 1983, Andropov had failed to impart new dynamism or give new flexibility to Soviet policies. Instead the formidable weight of bureaucratic inertia impeded substantive changes. Only Andropov's political style was different: He needed fewer aides and advisers than the senile Brezhnev and made it clear that his speeches would be brief, frank, and infrequent. A key adviser was Iurii Arbatov, head of the Institute of the USA and Canada, a leading Soviet intellectual.

Between June and December 1983 Andropov, while losing a battle against kidney disease, managed to implement significant personnel and political changes. The Central Committee plenum in June confirmed the replacement of retiring A. Kirilenko with the former Leningrad party secretary Grigorii Romanov as a Central Committee secretary. The death of aged Arvid Pelshe enabled Andropov to replace him with Mikhail Solomentsev, who became a candidate member of the Politburo. Returning to Moscow from vacation in October, Andropov apparently realized he had only a few months to live and stepped up his campaign. Although too ill to attend the December plenum, Andropov nonetheless persuaded the Politburo to promote Solomentsev and Vitalii Vorotnikov to full Politburo membership and make Egor Ligachev, another KGB protégé, a Central Committee secretary.

He was greatly aided in these moves by a key ally in the Politburo, Mikhail S. Gorbachev, who was also in the Secretariat. Andropov rewarded Gorbachev, the youngest and best educated of the ruling oligarchy, with additional power over personnel changes in the Secretariat. Gorbachev, sharing Andropov's reformist sentiments, was one of only two men who conferred regularly with the leader following his return to Moscow and had become his choice as successor. They and Andropov's doctors perpetrated a deliberate deception by issuing reports of Andropov's imminent recovery and return to public view to enable him to retain full power until the end of his life. Acting through Gorbachev and Ligachev, Andropov, between November 1983 and January 1984, replaced almost one fifth of all regional party secretaries, the greatest turnover in 20 years. Finally, claims Zhores Medvedev, Andropov enhanced and regularized the status of the second secretary of the Central Committee who would chair Politburo meetings in the absence of the secretary general.[3] Chernenko, who held that post, favored this step, which received Politburo approval, but which would strengthen Gorbachev's position after Andropov's death. Also approved was Andropov's proposal to reduce administrative personnel in central and local organizations and the number of party and state officials in the Supreme Soviet while increasing the proportion of workers, farmers, and engineers. Having taken steps to undermine the power of the "old guard," Andropov died of kidney disease on February 9, 1984.

The Chernenko Succession: The "Old Guard" Hangs On

An emergency Politburo meeting was convened the evening after Andropov's death, but failed to choose a successor. Indeed, not until Monday, February 13, was Chernenko selected. The delay suggests a power struggle between the Brezhnevite "old guard" favoring Chernenko, and the Andropov group, whose candidate was M. S. Gorbachev. Would an old, loyal party hack or a dynamic, sophisticated younger man be selected? If the Politburo were to remain deadlocked, the choice under party rules would devolve upon the 319-member Central Committee, which favored Chernenko. Thus Gorbachev's supporters in the Politburo, affirms Medvedev, agreed to support Chernenko's nomination as new party leader, and keep the decision in the Politburo. In exchange, the Politburo would approve all of Andropov's recent suggestions on political reform. Gorbachev received the newly formalized post of second secretary, becoming the heir apparent

---

[3]Medvedev, *Andropov*, pp. 217 ff.

behind the elderly Chernenko. This arrangement apparently was confirmed by the emergency Central Committee meeting of February 13 at which Premier Tikhonov nominated Chernenko as general secretary. Chernenko's previous appointment as chairman of Andropov's funeral commission suggested this outcome.

Andropov's funeral was smooth, efficiently organized, with a sense of continuity and propriety, and a total absence of grief. Recent party chiefs had been absent due to illness almost as much as they had been present and seemingly had become more a symbolic than an active force. About Andropov one Muscovite commented: "It is a pity. He was just, but he didn't have enough time." Those leaders closest to Andropov during his brief rule—Defense Minister Ustinov and Mikhail Gorbachev—lingered to pay their respects to his bereaved widow, Tatiana. E. M. Chazov, Andropov's chief physician, confirmed that the leader's kidneys had ceased functioning in February 1983, and that he had been on a dialysis machine after that.[4]

At age 72, Konstantin Ustinovich Chernenko succeeded Andropov as the oldest man ever chosen to lead the Soviet Union. Short and white-haired with slightly hunched shoulders, he delivered a lengthy, rambling, and stumbling acceptance speech, frequently mentioning Andropov and pledging to follow his reform initiatives. Significantly, there was no reference to his long-time mentor, Leonid Brezhnev. The old guard in party and state greeted Chernenko's accession jubilantly, believing that it would allow them to prolong their tenure of power. Chernenko's triumph represented a remarkable political comeback for this peasant's son from Siberia with little formal education. However one might assess his intelligence and ability—and there were numerous scornful comments from Russians and foreigners—this man from the people deserved respect for loyalty, toughness, and persistence. An ideologue who emphasized old-fashioned party slogans and virtues, his style was derived from many years working in *agitprop* (agitation and propaganda) in Siberia and Moldavia and for the Central Committee. In the introduction to a collection of his speeches and articles, Chernenko wrote:

> I was born into a large and poor peasant family in the Krasnoiarsk region of Siberia in 1911. I left my mother when I was a young boy. At 12 I went to work for a wealthy master to earn my living. New Soviet life was just coming into its own and I felt its fresh winds when I joined the Young Communist League [Komsomol]. That was back in 1926. We studied and held down our jobs at the same time. We were underfed and poorly clothed, but the dreams of a radiant future for all fascinated us and made us happy.

---

[4]John Burns, "Reporter's Notebook," *New York Times*, February 13, 1984.

Konstantin U. Chernenko, general secretary of the CPSU
1984–1985 *(APN/Liaison-Gamma)*

Chernenko stood forth proudly as a self-made Soviet man by dint of hard work, loyalty, and dedication to Leninist ideals, who had climbed steadfastly to the top of the Soviet pyramid.[5] During a 50-year party career, Chernenko never initiated projects nor enunciated original ideas. As an ideologist, carped Medvedev, he was even duller than his predecessor, Suslov. A pure product of the party apparatus, Chernenko remained an obscure provincial official until meeting Brezhnev in Moldavia in 1948. He followed his mentor upward through the party ranks, becoming a full member of the Central Committee in 1971. In 1976, Chernenko replaced Kirilenko as Brezhnev's closest colleague and heir apparent, being promoted with almost indecent haste as a party secretary in 1976 and full member of the Politburo in 1978. His philosophy was profoundly conservative: All problems could be solved with Leninist ideology, propaganda, and party discipline. Chernenko's short-lived regime, representing a holding action by the gerontocrats, was a throwback to Brezhnev's final years. Visibly feeble when he succeeded Andropov, Chernenko, like his two predecessors, was frequently out of public view,

---

[5]Serge Schmemann, "A Bolshevik of Old Mold Rises to the Top," *New York Times,* February 14, 1984.

laid low by emphysema. As the torpor of the last Brezhnev years resumed, Andropov's 15 months in power stood out by contrast as an interlude of dynamism, initiative, and forward movement.

By early 1985, signs multiplied that the Chernenko era would be brief. Behind the scenes in the Kremlin, the dynamic Mikhail S. Gorbachev positioned himself for the succession. In December 1984, Marshal Dmitri Ustinov, defense minister and a powerful force in the Politburo, died and received a massive funeral. Chernenko appeared at the marshal's bier, pale and unsteady, but was absent from the burial ceremony conducted in bitter cold. Instead, Gorbachev led the way in escorting the burial urn, followed by his rival, Grigori Romanov. The replacement of Ustinov by his deputy, Marshal Sergei Sokolov, suggested the aged leaders' reluctance to yield authority to the younger generation. During January 1985, as Chernenko failed to reappear, Soviet spokesmen admitted that he was gravely ill; rumors circulated that he would soon resign as general secretary. In late February he made two brief appearances on Soviet television, looking very feeble. However, contrary to initial fears, Chernenko, instead of undoing Andropov's reforms, continued them more gradually. One Moscow intellectual noted: "We have come to peace with Chernenko. He has contributed nothing new, the pace has slowed, the results are humble, but at least he has not turned back the clock."[6]

ECONOMY AND SOCIETY

"The Soviet Union simply does not have the resources to invest in all the necessary sectors. The leadership is going to have to make tough decisions on allocations of capital, raw materials, and labor," stated Robert Legvold of the Council on Foreign Relations. "The probable loser in the short term will be the Soviet consumer, accustomed since the 1950s to a steady, if unspectacular, rise in living standards. With Brezhnev's legacy of declining economic growth rates, Soviet citizens clearly would have to settle for minimal improvements during the 1980s," declared the American Sovietologist Walter Laqueur. Such statements reflected economic policies under Brezhnev's successors.

At Brezhnev's death, wrote Marshall Goldman, the USSR faced a severe economic crisis. The country had failed to adapt the rigid, highly centralized Stalinist planning model, which emphasized production of iron and steel to meet radically new economic needs. Whereas Khrushchev had predicted confidently in 1958 that the USSR by 1980 would

---

[6]"Chernenko's Status Shrouded in Rumor," *New York Times,* January 31, 1985.

surpass levels of production of the United States and enjoy abundance, Soviet GNP (gross national product) during the early 1980s hovered between 55 and 60 percent of the American figure. The Stalinist system had developed a momentum of its own, continuing to churn out steel when food and consumer goods were required. As Khrushchev himself once stated:

> The production of steel is like a well-traveled road with deep ruts; here even blind horses will not turn off because the wheels will break. Similarly, some officials have put on steel blinkers; they do everything as they were taught in their day.[7]

With fulfillment of the central plan becoming an end in itself, with managers and planners rewarded for gross output and value of production, many resources were wasted by being diverted to needless increases in the capital intensity of industry and producing large, expensive, and useless commodities. The Stalinist economic system neither rewards intelligent decisions nor punishes stupid ones. The obsolete cannot readily be discarded, nor can innovation and technological change readily be fostered. Well-suited only to heavy industry and most difficult to restructure, the Stalinist model builds up powerful political and economic vested interest groups resistant to basic changes. Reforms, when instituted, tend to get out of control, making the leadership loath to overhaul an outmoded system as long as it shows even minimal growth. Avoided far too long, economic change became more difficult with each passing year.

Yet by 1982 something clearly needed to be done. In 1981, Soviet steel production, previously a source of great pride for outpacing that of the United States, fell below the 1978 level; coal and oil output apparently had peaked, having become increasingly difficult and expensive to extract from remote regions. With almost a quarter of its own crop rotting in the fields or failing to be transported to markets, the USSR had become the world's largest importer of grain. The Soviet worker, with few incentives to produce or conserve and with few desirable consumer goods to buy, was suffering from falling morale and discipline. Beginning in 1980, strikes, demonstrations, and riots broke out in various cities; food rationing had to be reintroduced in major centers for the first time since the 1940s. Meanwhile, Soviet leaders remained committed to a steadily rising military budget and an empire costing over $20 billion per year in subsidies. How little the economy was serving consumer needs was

---

[7]Marshall I. Goldman, *USSR in Crisis: The Failure of an Economic System* (New York, 1983), p. 36.

revealed by a huge and growing volume of savings (from 91 billion rubles in 1975 to 156.6 billion in 1980), as consumers awaited desirable goods. This had stimulated development of a vast black market estimated at almost 25 percent of GNP, but even that failed to close the gap between supply and demand.[8] Any sudden decontrol could trigger panic, huge inflationary pressure, and unemployment. Economic distortions had become too massive to be rectified quickly. A bold leader undertaking basic reform, predicted Goldman, must deal with prolonged inflation, severe unemployment, shortages of desirable capital, surpluses of outmoded capital, profiteering, and severe balance of payments deficits—evils from which only capitalist countries were supposed to suffer. Could the Soviet political system survive such severe strains? No aged or infirm interim leader would take such risks.

How then did Brezhnev's successors deal with these grave economic problems? Andropov began with harsh criticisms of the existing system's shortcomings, rather than with Brezhnev's ritualistic praise of past economic achievements; he bluntly distributed responsibility for current inadequate performance equally among government, workers, and farmers. His aim was not to introduce drastic reform of the economic system, which he feared, but to improve management and worker efficiency, reduce waste, and ensure that everything produced or harvested be made available. His priorities included raising productivity with harder work and better discipline, use of new planning methods, and accelerating introduction of new technology. Thus Andropov sought to make the old Stalinist system function more efficiently. In December 1982, he reorganized the Ministry of Railways and suggested improving coordination of all forms of transport. Lacking a new solution for agriculture, he echoed Brezhnev's expensive Food Program of May 1982 and campaigned for a reduction in food wastage and better storage facilities for farmers. Tougher policies were instituted to promote better work discipline. The police cracked down on loafing and absenteeism; they even corralled slackers in Moscow bathhouses! However, the regime's efforts to stifle the "second economy" by prohibiting unregistered, free-lance work proved premature and counterproductive and were soon abandoned.

Amidst Western speculation that Andropov would institute economic reforms like those in Hungary (decentralization and more scope for market forces, for example), Soviet economic measures of early 1983, noted Medvedev, resembled those of General Wojciech Jaruzelski's mar-

---

[8]Gregory Grossman, "The Second Economy of the USSR," *Problems of Communism, 26* (September–October 1977), p. 25.

tial law regime in Poland. The government raised food prices by rapidly expanding "commercial" trade by cooperatives, diverting more food into that system where prices and quality were far higher than in state shops. At a well-publicized meeting with workers and engineers at a Moscow machine tool plant that January, Andropov stressed better work discipline, stricter observance of the plan, and reduction of absenteeism and deliberately slow work if workers were to obtain more and better goods.[9]

Andropov also accelerated the anticorruption drive, which he had used earlier to undermine and discredit Brezhnev. Reports of high-level corruption and peculation appeared in the Soviet press. Penalties against embezzlement and bribery were increased by a decree in January 1983. So readers would know the source of this campaign, Soviet newspapers published an unusual report entitled "In the Politburo of the CPSU," revealing that the Politburo had discussed numerous letters from workers and farmers complaining of shoddy work, false statistics, poor use of materials, and embezzlement of funds:

> The Politburo drew the attention of the Procurator General of the USSR and Ministry of Internal Affairs to the fact that it is necessary to take proper measures to improve socialist legality in towns and villages taking into consideration the fact that these problems are very frequently the cause of complaints in letters which are sent to the central Party organs.[10]

As Andropov intensified the anticorruption drive, millions of letters from citizens complaining about local abuses flooded into top agencies, which party leaders could not afford to ignore. Corruption at all levels had grown so widespread that the public believed that shortages of food and consumer goods resulted from officials diverting better quality goods into their closed shops and distribution centers.

British journalist Jonathan Steele and TV writer Eric Abraham claim Andropov supported the approach of M. S. Gorbachev, the Politburo's expert on agriculture, in encouraging decentralization and local initiative to stimulate the economy; both men favored fostering greater production of private peasant plots to supplement Brezhnev's Food Program.[11] An industrial reform program of July 1983 reduced the number of centrally imposed economic indicators and gave local managers more autonomy. Reintroducing some aspects of Premier Kosygin's 1965 reforms, it fell far short of the Hungarian economic reforms; there was no attempt to move away from the system of centrally administered prices.

---

[9]Medvedev, *Andropov*, pp. 127–134.
[10]*Pravda*, December 11, 1982, quoted in Medvedev, *Andropov*, p. 142.
[11]Jonathan Steele and Eric Abraham, *Andropov in Power*, pp. 162–165.

Andropov was merely willing to tolerate some experiments and limited decentralization to foster lower level initiative, coupling these with greater social and industrial discipline. His economic reforms may have been limited by opposition within the Politburo, Gosplan, and the party bureaucracy. In his message to the December 1983 Central Committee plenum, Andropov warned: "The most important thing now is not to lose the tempo and the general positive mood for action." That became his legacy.[12]

Under Chernenko there was little apparent progress in remedying grave economic shortcomings. Observed one skeptical intellectual:

> The wheels are still turning from momentum. But they are beginning to slow down. And rot is setting in. But it will take a long time for anything conclusive to happen. It won't happen in my lifetime.

At least economic problems were being discussed more candidly in the Soviet press, noted Robert Kaiser, an American journalist.[13] Dr. Abel Aganbegyan of the Siberian department of the Academy of Sciences noted that too few people were entering the work force. Raw materials and energy sources were disappearing from European Russia where most industry still centered. Siberia and the Soviet Far East accounted for 88 percent of raw material and energy resources, which were becoming increasingly difficult and expensive to extract. Aganbegyan advocated radical reforms to prevent central industrial ministries from interfering with individual enterprises. He complained that Andropov's experimental reforms had been too tentative and limited.

A significant debate over economic policy proceeded under Chernenko between the Brezhnev "old guard" and reformers led by Gorbachev. While noting Andropov's "clear creative mind" and "keen sense for the new," Chernenko pleaded for caution and relied on proven old methods. Younger Politburo members (Gorbachev, Vorotnikov) and Central Committee secretaries (Ligachev, Ryzhkov) promoted by Andropov, taking positions contrary to Chernenko in their election speeches, credited Andropov personally for successes in 1983 in raising output and urged continuing his policies and accelerating the tempo. Gorbachev became the chief advocate of innovation, presenting himself as Andropov's standard bearer and Chernenko's main challenger. Thus in Stavropol in February 1984, Gorbachev interpreted the party's task as to "consolidate and develop the positive trends, and bolster and augment

---

[12]Ernest Kux, "Contradictions in Soviet Socialism," *Problems of Communism*, 33 (November–December 1984), pp. 1–4.
[13]Robert Kaiser in *Boston Sunday Globe*, September 30, 1984.

everything new and progressive that has become part of our social life recently." He advocated "the acceleration of the development of the national economy and the improvement of its efficiency, . . . a profound reorientation of social production toward increasing the people's well-being." In sharp contrast with Chernenko, Gorbachev called for training "cadres capable of thinking and acting in a modern way." Their divergent attitudes and proposals revealed major contradictions at the top level between "conservatives" and modernists, suggesting an ongoing power struggle between Brezhnev's "old guard" and Andropov's "Young Turks."[14]

Despite the absence of basic reforms, the Soviet economy showed signs of an upturn. In the wake of an encouraging trend during 1983, there was a 4.2 percent increase in industrial output and a 3.8 percent improvement in labor productivity in 1984. However, agriculture failed to advance and there was a disquieting decrease in oil production.[15]

FOREIGN POLICY

At Brezhnev's death the Soviet Union faced major and intractable problems abroad in a number of areas. A virtually bankrupt and resentful Poland drained Soviet resources and typified increasing Soviet difficulties in eastern Europe. East Germany, Romania, and even Hungary were only slightly less in debt to western banks than unfortunate Poland. A second set of problems related to Sino-Soviet relations, which had remained generally bad under Brezhnev. The Chinese had been alienated not only by the border conflict of 1969–1970 but also later by the Soviet invasion of Afghanistan and predominance in neighboring Vietnam. Finally, Beijing was still worried by large Soviet military forces stationed along China's frontiers. Thirdly, the USSR appeared deeply mired in Afghanistan, seemingly committed to a military and political victory, regardless of the costs in money, men, and prestige. Meanwhile, Soviet-American relations had plumbed depths of tension and acrimony not equalled since the worst period of the "Cold War." Apparently despairing of reaching positive agreements with a fiercely conservative Republican administration whose chief, Reagan, had denounced the USSR as an "evil empire," Soviet leaders realized that American hostility might well deny them the high technology and equipment they needed to modernize their economy as well as driving up military expenditures to keep pace with a wealthier United States in a new arms race.

---

[14]Kux, "Contradictions in Soviet Socialism."
[15]Serge Schmemann, "Chernenko's Status . . . ," *New York Times,* January 31, 1985.

Changes in Soviet foreign policy under Andropov seemed limited primarily to style, greater flexibility, and personal command. Such new trends followed immediately after Brezhnev's death. His funeral brought an unprecedented number of high-level foreign delegations to Moscow—Andropov talked at length in friendly fashion with the Chinese foreign minister and President Zia of Pakistan. His meeting with Vice President Bush of the United States revealed an intelligence and flexibility in spontaneous exchanges on a variety of issues. Andropov made it clear to some 100 foreign delegations that he would direct Soviet foreign policy firmly and reasonably; the period of diplomatic stagnation was over.

A distinct improvement in Soviet relations with China occurred under Andropov and continued under Chernenko. Brezhnev's speeches during 1982 revealed that Moscow had decided to improve Sino-Soviet relations. Andropov promptly initiated a conciliatory policy toward China: Articles critical of China ceased to appear in the Soviet Union and the Chinese found it much easier to deal with Andropov than they had with Brezhnev. Nonetheless, normalization of Sino-Soviet relations proceeded slowly, hampered by continuing friction over Afghanistan and Vietnam. Under Chernenko progress continued—marked by the visit of an important Soviet official, Ivan Arkhipov, to Beijing and agreements to expand trade and cultural relations.

No significant change in Soviet relations with eastern Europe was evident under Andropov and Chernenko, both of whom considered preservation of Soviet preeminence there of the highest importance. In his November 1982 speech, Andropov declared that the USSR should make better use of the experience of friendly socialist countries, perhaps an allusion to the successful Hungarian economic reforms. Meanwhile, both he and Chernenko welcomed General Jaruzelski's political success in controlling ferment in Poland by martial law and continued to supply some economic aid. Despite the lifting of martial law by 1984, the Polish economy continued to decline. The Polish economic plight adversely affected neighboring Communist countries as well as the USSR.

As to dealings with the West, Andropov from the outset possessed the distinct advantage of knowing more about the United States than Reagan did about the Soviet Union and employed more competent advisers on American affairs (notably Professor Iurii Arbatov, a close friend) than Reagan did on Soviet affairs. By late November 1982, the Western press alluded to Andropov's "peace offensive," which began in earnest with a speech in December 1982. By mid-January 1983, the West was considering some 20 new Soviet proposals in military fields. This offensive was provoked by the imminent installation in western Europe of 572 Cruise and Pershing II missiles and some divergence about them between western European NATO countries and the United States. When the Reagan administration failed to respond very positively to this Soviet initiative, negotiations stalled.

Late in 1983 a tragic incident caused Soviet-American relations to deteriorate sharply. On September 1 a Korean commercial airliner, KAL-007, on a regular flight from the United States to Japan flew far off course into Soviet airspace over Kamchatka Peninsula and was shot down by a Soviet missile off Sakhalin Island, killing all 269 passengers and crew. At first Moscow denied any responsibility for the plane's destruction, claiming that while Soviet pilots were tracking it, the plane suddenly disappeared from their radar screens. Five days later, faced with aroused world opinion, Moscow admitted that one of its pilots had indeed destroyed the plane, but claimed that it had been performing a secret surveillance mission for U.S. intelligence. (See Map 19.1.) In a dramatic nationwide address President Reagan asserted that the destruction of KAL-007 was a deliberate, brutal, and unjustifiable murder.[16]

The Soviet government responded that the Korean airliner had been mistaken for an RC-135 American spy plane that had been flying a parallel course. Soviet defense forces had merely exercised the right to protect Soviet airspace from unwarranted intrusion into a sensitive military area. American leaders, affirmed the Soviet statement, had staged this provocation precisely when ways of preventing a nuclear war were being discussed with the United States. Belatedly Moscow declared:

> The Soviet government expresses regret over the death of innocent people and shares the sorrow of their bereaved relatives and friends. The entire responsibility for this tragedy rests wholly and fully with the leaders of the USA.[17]

The KAL-007 incident of September 1, 1983, brought a measured response from the Reagan administration, which left his right-wing supporters dissatisfied. An order of 1981 denying Aeroflot, the Soviet airline, the right to land in the United States was reaffirmed. Reagan asked the U.S. Congress to pass a joint resolution denouncing the Soviet action. The United States suspended negotiations on several bilateral matters and demanded compensation to relatives of the victims; the Soviets refused. The affair effectively torpedoed nuclear arms negotiations on the basis proposed by Andropov and ended any plans for an Andropov-Reagan summit. The incident also raised disturbing questions about Soviet military confusion and bureaucratic rigidity. Secretary Gen-

---

[16]*New York Times,* September 6, 1983.
[17]*New York Times,* September 7, 1983, p. 16.

Map 19.1 *Confusion and Mistakes Doom KAL Flight 007*

1 An American RC-135 reconnaissance aircraft is spotted on radar at a Soviet air-defense station on Kamchatka peninsula. It is a routine flight that provokes no Soviet reaction.

2 Another blip appears on the Soviet radar, and the Kamchatka command, suspecting it is a second spy plane, scrambles fighters to intercept the plane.

3 The 747 re-enters international airspace over the Sea of Okhotsk. The Kamchatka pilots observe it once again veering into Soviet airspace over Sakhalin. Low on fuel, they break off the chase and alert Sakhalin air defense of the incoming aircraft.

4 The American RC-135 lands at its base on Shemya island.

5 Three Sakhalin island interceptors, two Su-15s and one MiG-23 catch up with the mystery plane. One Su-15 pilot makes eye contact with the plane from a distance of 1.2 miles.

6 Flight 007 has only seconds left inside Soviet airspace. The Su-15 pilot falls back behind the passenger plane and fires air-to-air missiles.

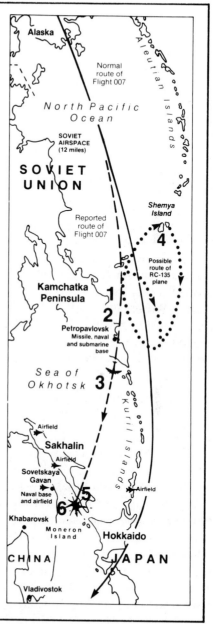

Soviet observers apparently mistook KAL Flight 007, an unarmed passenger plane, for an American RC-135 spy plane. The Soviets claimed they had tried to warn the KAL plane before they shot it down, but transcripts of the pursuit pilot's talk cast serious doubt on this. This incident imperilled Soviet-American relations. *(Newsweek, September 8, 1983)*

eral Andropov apparently played no direct role in the Soviet decision to shoot down the plane.

In a thorough, balanced analysis of the KAL-007 affair, R. W. Johnson, a leading English scholar, discussed the four chief explanations for shooting down the plane: (1) the flight had strayed off course by accident, (2) the pilots had deliberately sought to shorten their route to save fuel, (3) the Soviets had attempted deliberately to lure the plane off course by electronic interference with its navigational equipment, and (4) the plane was involved in an American surveillance mission. Dismissing the first three as virtually impossible, Johnson concluded that the flight had been a risky attempt by the American military to obtain information about the newly discovered Krasnoiarsk radar installation in Siberia.[18] Interviewed July 19, 1984, Ernest Volkman, editor of *Defense Science*, stated:

> As a result of the KAL incident US intelligence received a bonanza the likes of which they have never received in their lives. . . . It managed to turn on just about every single Soviet electromagnetic transmission over a period of about four hours over about 7,000 square miles.[19]

Afghanistan remained a stumbling block in the path of improving Soviet relations with both China and the United States. Under Brezhnev the Soviet media remained overwhelmingly silent about the war there except to make ritual accusations against both powers for "intervening" in Afghanistan's internal affairs. Under Andropov, who was inclined to greater frankness and realism, this attitude began to change. Finally, after almost five years of downplaying Russia's first war since World War II, the Soviet press discovered a war hero, a Byelorussian farm youth named Nikolai Chepik. In February 1984, Chepik reportedly sacrificed his own life to save his comrades while taking 30 of the enemy with him. Wrote *Literaturnaia Gazeta* in January 1985: "The last thing he could see was the peaks of the Hindu Kush, and above them the huge, bright sky, a sky stretching all the way to his motherland." The official creation of a Soviet war hero was part of increasing coverage of the Afghan conflict. Soon a song was composed about the exploits of Chepik, and many schools set up "Chepik corners" where the pupils could study his heroic deeds. Chepik was even awarded posthumously the coveted decoration Hero of the Soviet Union. Increasing parallels were drawn between the Soviet struggle in Afghanistan against the allegedly murderous and

---

[18]R. W. Johnson, *Shootdown: Flight 007 and the American Connection* (New York, 1987), pp. 310 ff.

[19]Johnson, *Shootdown*, p. 339.

brutal rebels and the Nazi invasion of the USSR.[20] The Afghan war continued to drain the Soviet economy and to complicate Soviet foreign relations.

Suggested Additional Reading

ARBATOV, G. A. *The Soviet Viewpoint (New York, 1983).*

BERGSON, A., and H. LEVINE, eds. *The Soviet Economy* (Winchester, Mass., 1983).

BINYON, M. *Life in Russia* (New York, 1984).

BONNER, ELENA. *Alone Together,* trans. A. Cook (New York, 1986). (By Andrei Sakharov's wife about their internal exile.)

BROWN, ARCHIE, AND M. KASER. "Gorbachev: New Man in the Kremlin," *Problems of Communism, 34* (May–June 1985), pp. 1–23.

———, eds. *Soviet Policy for the 1980s* (Bloomington, Ind., 1982).

BRUCAN, SILVIO. *The Post-Brezhnev Era: An Insider's View* (New York, 1983).

BYRNES, R. F., ed. *After Brezhnev: Sources of Soviet Conduct in the 1980s* (Bloomington, Ind., 1983).

CHERNENKO, K. U. *Selected Speeches and Writings* (Elmsford, N. Y., 1982).

DUNLOP, J. B. *The Faces of Contemporary Russian Nationalism* (Princeton, N.J., 1983).

FREEDMAN, R. O. *Soviet Policy Toward the Middle East Since 1970,* 3d ed. (New York, 1982).

GOLDBERG, B. Z. *The Jewish Problem in the Soviet Union* (New York, 1982).

GOLDMAN, M. I. *USSR in Crisis* (New York, 1983).

GROMYKO, A. A. *Peace Now, Peace for the Future* (New York, 1984).

HAZAN, BARUCH. *From Brezhnev to Gorbachev: Infighting in the Kremlin* (Boulder, Colo., 1987).

HILL R. J. *The Soviet Communist Party* (London, 1983).

HOLLOWAY, DAVID. *The Soviet Union and the Arms Race* (New Haven, Conn., 1983).

HUTCHINGS, R. *Soviet Economic Development* (New York, 1982).

———. *Structural Origins of Soviet Industrial Expansion* (New York, 1984).

JOHNSON, D. G., and K. McBROOKS. *Prospects for Soviet Agriculture in the 1980s* (Bloomington, Ind., 1983).

KEEBLE, C., ed. *The Soviet State: The Domestic Roots of Soviet Foreign Policy* (Aldershot, Eng., 1985).

KELLEY, DONALD R. *Soviet Politics from Brezhnev to Gorbachev* (New York, 1987).

KERBLAY, B. H. *Modern Soviet Society* (New York, 1983).

---

[20]Seth Mydans, "An Afghan Footnote: Legend of a Soviet Farm Boy," *New York Times,* January 16, 1985, p. 2.

LAIRD, ROBBIN, AND E. HOFFMAN, eds. *Soviet Policy in a Changing World* (New York, 1986).

McCAULEY, M., et al., eds. *The Soviet Union After Brezhnev* (New York, 1983).

MEDVEDEV, ZHORES A. *Andropov* (New York, 1983).

MILLAR, JAMES R., ed. *Politics, Work, and Daily Life in the USSR: A Survey of Former Soviet Citizens* (Cambridge, Eng., 1987).

PARKS, J. D. *Culture, Conflict and Coexistence* (Jefferson, N.C., 1983).

RUBINSTEIN, A. Z. *Soviet Policy Toward Turkey, Iran and Afghanistan* (New York, 1982).

SHEVCHENKO, ARKADY N. *Breaking with Moscow* (New York, 1985).

SHIPLER, D. K. *Russia: Broken Idols, Solemn Dreams* (New York, 1983).

TREML, VLADIMIR G. *Alcohol in the USSR: A Statistical Study* (Durham, N.C., 1982).

ZEMSTOV, ILYA. *Andropov: Policy Dilemmas and the Struggle for Power* (Jerusalem, 1983).

CHAPTER TWENTY

THE GORBACHEV REVOLUTION, 1985–1990

The succession of Mikhail Sergeevich Gorbachev as Soviet leader in March 1985 marked a major turning point in Soviet history both at home and abroad. Taking power after a decade of gerontocracy, stagnation, and growing demoralization of Soviet society and intelligentsia, Gorbachev faced daunting problems, resembling those facing the reforming emperor, Alexander II, and the reforming first secretary, Nikita Khrushchev. Succeeding Nicholas I and his undiluted autocracy under which the Russian Empire lagged further behind western Europe economically, technologically, and politically, Alexander II had instituted Great Reforms, which brought much change but remained incomplete. (See Chapter 2.) The heir of Stalin's brutal dictatorship, Khrushchev had attempted to liberalize the Soviet system and provide a better life for its people. All three reform leaders have sought to improve the position of Russia or the USSR in the world by ending some of their predecessors' many restrictions or "iron curtain" on contacts with Europe. Aiming to preserve basic institutions and ideologies, all three have sought to rule over a sprawling empire by making it function more efficiently and humanely. The sad experience of his predecessors has made the ultimate fate of Gorbachev's new thinking and domestic reforms dubious: Alexander II was assassinated by leftist extremists and many of his reforms were halted; Khrushchev was removed by his Politburo colleagues and succeeded by Brezhnev's conservative regime.

THE LEADER AND THE SUCCESSION

At his accession to power Gorbachev seemingly possessed a sophistication and political skill greater than either Alexander II or Khrushchev. He was born March 2, 1931, of Russian peasant stock in a village in Stavropol province of the north Caucasus. Only 10 when Hitler invaded the Soviet Union, he was too young to fight in that conflict (though his father did) which left his native village devastated. Young Gorbachev worked summers on the local collective farm, driving a combine and assisting his father. Hard physical labor gave him both satisfaction and self-confidence. Interested in a wide variety of subjects, Gorbachev received a silver medal when he completed secondary school in 1950. At age 18, for excellence in political work in the Komsomol (Young Communist League) and physical labor on the kolkhoz, he was given the Order of the Red Banner of Labor.

Those honors facilitated Gorbachev's acceptance by the law faculty of prestigious Moscow State University in 1951. There he met his future wife, Raisa Titorenko; they married in 1954 in a simple wedding. As a student he served as secretary of the law faculty's Komsomol organization and at age 21 joined the Communist Party. Graduated with honors in 1955, Gorbachev returned to Stavropol as a full-time Komsomol official. For his intelligence, dedication, and hard work, he was promoted rapidly, shifting to the party in 1962 and four years later becoming first secretary of the Stavropol Party committee. In 1971 he was named to the Central Committee of the All-Union Communist Party, the youngest official to be so honored. He cultivated useful ties with several Politburo members and won their support. In September 1978 Gorbachev held crucial meetings with Brezhnev, Chernenko, and Andropov (his three predecessors as party chief) during their visits to Stavropol and the north Caucasus. Two months later he was called to Moscow as Central Committee secretary for agriculture, and in 1980 at 49 he became a full member of the Politburo.

Following Brezhnev's death in 1982, Gorbachev rose swiftly to the top of the Soviet power pyramid. With some younger Central Committee members, he backed Andropov's successful drive to succeed Brezhnev; he then served as his spokesman in the Politburo after the ill Andropov could no longer attend meetings. Checked temporarily when the old

Raisa and Mikhail Gorbachev arrive at Reykjavik,
Iceland, in October 1986 for summit talks with U.S.
President Reagan *(UPI/Bettmann Newsphotos)*

guard selected Chernenko as party leader in 1984, Gorbachev as de facto
second party secretary controlled many power levers, including responsibility for ideology and personnel. His trip to Britain that summer and his
well-publicized meeting with British Prime Minister Thatcher enhanced
his position as evident successor to the ill Chernenko.

On March 11, 1985, the Kremlin announced Chernenko's death after
only 13 months as general secretary and Gorbachev's appointment as
chairman of the funeral commission. Only hours later Moscow confirmed
that the Central Committee had named Gorbachev first party secretary.
Pravda's front page featured Gorbachev and his reform program;
Chernenko's obituary was relegated to page two. Gorbachev's accession
confirmed a decision evidently reached earlier. During Chernenko's
illness he had apparently presided over Politburo meetings. As the eighth
paramount Soviet political leader, Gorbachev at 54 was the youngest
since Stalin to assume control, younger than anyone else in the Politburo

or Secretariat. Foreign Minister Andrei Gromyko, the older generation's most respected leader, had nominated him warmly as first secretary. Mourning was minimal at Chernenko's funeral as a self-confident Gorbachev talked with the many world leaders who attended. Gorbachev's acceptance speech revealed his eager impatience to begin work: "We are to achieve a decisive turn in transferring the national economy to the tracks of intensive development."

Gorbachev's succession of a pathetic and aged leader facilitated his swift consolidation of power. The Soviet public greeted its youthful, energetic new leader with unconcealed enthusiasm, hopeful that their manifold problems would now finally be tackled. "After ten years of gerontocracy," commented a young Soviet writer, "it is like spring. Since Khrushchev we have had nothing done for the people, only repression and rhetoric. Now that generation has come to an end. . . ." Leaving foreign policy initially in the capable although inflexible hands of Gromyko, Gorbachev focused on domestic problems.

At Gorbachev's accession 4 of 10 full Politburo members clearly opposed him: Grishin, Kunaev, Romanov, and Tikhonov. Apparently, it had been the Secretariat and perhaps the Central Committee rather than the Politburo that had elevated Gorbachev to power. In any case he transformed these top party bodies with unprecedented speed. Two party secretaries allied with him soon received full Politburo membership. Egor K. Ligachev assumed control over personnel and ideology; Nikolai I. Ryzhkov was to plan economic reforms. KGB chief Viktor Chebrikov, another Gorbachev ally, became a full Politburo member. In July 1985 Gorbachev abruptly removed his leading rival, Grigori V. Romanov, from the Politburo and Secretariat for "reasons of health" and nudged his own elderly sponsor, Gromyko, "upstairs" into the titular post of Soviet president. Replacing him as foreign minister was a Gorbachev man with minimal experience in foreign affairs, Edvard A. Shevarnadze, former first secretary of the Georgian party. In September Nikolai Ryzhkov succeeded Tikhonov as premier, confirming the passage of leadership to a new generation.

Early in 1986 Gorbachev consolidated his hold. In March conservative Moscow party chief, Viktor Grishin, was replaced on the Politburo and in Moscow by Boris N. Eltsin, a radical reformer. During Gorbachev's first year as party chief, five new full members entered the Politburo. The Secretariat too was transformed with seven of its nine secretaries selected in that time span.[1] The 27th Party Congress of March

---

[1]Jerry Hough, *Russia and the West: Gorbachev and the Politics of Reform* (New York, 1988), pp. 168–170.

1986 brought 125 new members, mostly Gorbachev partisans, into the 307-person Central Committee. And in the executive branch 38 of the 100 ministers were removed and 8 more received new posts.

Gorbachev selected mostly leaders recently arrived in Moscow not identified with the Brezhnev regime. At Brezhnev's death most of these men had relatively low status and less seniority than Gorbachev. They owed their subsequent promotions to him. A majority of those elevated into key power positions had worked with Gorbachev either in Stavropol or elsewhere in the Caucasus, had been Komsomol leaders, or were graduates of Moscow University in the 1950s. By August 1987 almost three fourths of republic and regional first secretaries had been selected since Brezhnev's death while Gorbachev was either personnel chief or first party secretary, which gave him unprecedented control over the party apparatus. At the June 1987 Central Committee plenum Gorbachev made three party secretaries who were his personal supporters full Politburo members: Viktor Nikonov, Nikolai Sliunkov, and Alexander Iakovlev.[2] (See Table 20.1.)

GLASNOST AND POLITICAL REFORM

While consolidating control that first year, Gorbachev enjoyed a remarkable political honeymoon. Helpful to him were his youthfulness, vigor, openness, and skill at public relations revealed in a series of bold, frank speeches, radically different from previous stilted party pronouncements. Repeatedly Gorbachev waded into friendly crowds of ordinary Soviet citizens and workers to exchange banter like the populist Khrushchev. Gorbachev, his highly educated and attractive wife, Raisa, and their children resembled the Kennedys and were featured at receptions, parades, and official gatherings in a drastic departure from Soviet traditions of secrecy. Gorbachev's restless activity, intellectual grasp, and directness contrasted completely with Chernenko's standpat and secretive regime. At first avoiding major controversial reforms that might alienate important groups, Gorbachev emphasized that the Soviet Union must emerge swiftly from political and economic stagnation or face inevitable decline. Enthralled with his style, the Soviet public and Western media overlooked the fact that Gorbachev had reached supreme power after a 30-year political apprenticeship in the Komsomol and party apparatus.

Before undertaking major economic reform, or *perestroika* (restructuring), Gorbachev sought to build support for essential changes among

---

[2]Hough, *Russia and the West*, pp. 170–172.

Table 20.1 *Membership in Politburo of the*
Party Central Committee, 1989

Full Members	Year of Birth	Elected Full Member	Current Position and When Assumed
M. S. Gorbachev	1931	1980	General Secretary, Central Committee (1985)
V. M. Chebrikov	1923	1985	Chairman KGB (1983)
E. G. Ligachev	1921	1985	Agriculture Secretary of Central Committee
N. I. Ryzhkov	1929	1985	Premier (1985)
E. A. Shevarnadze	1928	1985	Foreign Minister USSR (1985)
V. I. Vorotnikov	1926	1983	Chairman Russian Republic Council of Ministers (1983)
A. N. Iakovlev	1923	1987	A Central Committee Secretary
V. A. Medvedev	1929	1989	A Central Committee Secretary
N. N. Sliunkov	1929	1987	A Central Committee Secretary
L. N. Zaikov	1923	1986	A Central Committee Secretary
V. V. Shcherbitskii*	1918	1971	First Secretary, Ukraine (1972)
V. P. Nikonov	1929	1987	

*Removed during 1989.

the Soviet intelligentsia with far greater openness—*glasnost*—in the public media. This *glasnost* would be a spotlight exposing problems. Soviet and Western reporters received freedom comparable to that in other world capitals to cover stories, interview Soviet officials, and reveal facts formerly shrouded in secrecy. The Soviet press began publishing sensitive statistics and reports of crimes and disasters previously only whispered about furtively by individuals. Growing Western fascination with Gorbachev and his policies soon made him and his Soviet Union a leading news story. *Glasnost* also involved efforts by the Gorbachev regime to educate Soviet citizens from above in new traditions of freedom and tolerance. Inevitably, this provoked unsuccessful efforts by conservatives to block or curtail *glasnost*, especially in sensitive areas of culture and history. Party control over the media remained firm, but *glasnost* gathered force rapidly as a formerly dull press now captivated Soviet readers with amazing revelations. In the Baltic republics the official press became so outspoken that conservative Moscow newspapers accused it of being anti-Soviet.

Glasnost was severely tested and the Gorbachev regime embarrassed by technological and natural disasters. Late in April 1986 a near meltdown occurred at the Chernobyl nuclear energy station near Kiev, spewing radiation north and west into Byelorussia, Poland, and Scandinavia. Although Soviet authorities, including Gorbachev, were informed immediately and reacted swiftly, in an apparent repudiation of *glasnost,* the outside world was not told that anything was wrong until three days later. Apparently, Soviet authorities hoped to conceal the whole disaster as had been done in the past. Only 18 days later did Gorbachev speak publicly about Chernobyl, seeking to counter a public relations disaster. Chernobyl cast grave doubt on the future of nuclear power in the USSR and provided live ammunition to the growing environmental movement.[3] After this came a series of railroad accidents, coal-mine disasters, and ship and submarine mishaps that severely bruised Gorbachev's popularity. Then on December 7, 1988, while Gorbachev was visiting the United States, a massive earthquake in Soviet Armenia killed about 25,000 people and left over half a million homeless. Costs of cleaning up and rebuilding the Chernobyl plant and devastated Armenia together exceeded 8 billion rubles. However, the unprecedented openness of Soviet authorities following the Armenian earthquake and massive American and worldwide aid to its victims confirmed the reality of *glasnost,* and enhanced Gorbachev's reputation and Soviet-Western relations.

As Gorbachev encouraged the press "to fill in the blank spots" in Soviet history, *glasnost* exposed the monstrous crimes of the Stalin era in an extension of Khrushchev's de-Stalinization. While attacking Stalin and Stalinism, the media generally defended Lenin's policies and ideology. Novelists, playwrights, and journalists pioneered in historical reevaluation as professional historians hung back cautiously. Reexamining Soviet history, declared Iurii Afanasiev, new liberal rector of the Moscow State Historical-Archival Institute, resembled "awakening from a prolonged mythological dream." As Soviet citizens learned more about their past, "to many in the USSR it has become obvious that there is no people and no country with a history as falsified as Soviet history." In 1989 Afanasiev elaborated on that theme:

---

[3]See Nigel Hawkes, ed., *Chernobyl: The End of the Nuclear Dream* (New York, 1986).

. . . To give a legal foundation to the Soviet regime in the USSR is, it seems to me, a hopeless task. To give a legal foundation to a regime which was brought into being through bloodshed with the aid of mass murders and crimes against humanity, is only possible by resorting to falsification and lies—as has been done up till now. It must be admitted that the whole of Soviet history is not fit to serve as a legal basis for the Soviet regime. By admitting this, we would be taking a step toward the creation of a democratic society.[4]

At a Central Committee plenum of January 1987 Gorbachev urged accelerating the application of *glasnost* to Soviet historical scholarship. After Stalin had been depicted very negatively in film and literature, Gorbachev's speech in November 1987 referred openly to Stalin's crimes. Abel Aganbegyan, Gorbachev's chief economic adviser, described "the misery and brutality of rural life" under forced collectivization. Lacking basic human rights, collective farmers had been paid less than subsistence wages.[5] The critique of forced collectivization under Gorbachev went far beyond anything revealed during Khrushchev's regime. Its beginning was described as a negative turning point in Soviet history when Lenin's NEP was discarded in favor of Stalin's bureaucratic socialism.

Along with efforts to refurbish NEP as a truly Leninist model of reform came political rehabilitation of Stalin's opponents. In January 1988, Moscow's Central Lenin Museum displayed photographs of Bukharin, Zinoviev, Kamenev, and Trotskii—victims of Stalin's Great Purge. Bukharin's full civic rehabilitation in February 1988 contrasted his conciliatory, moderate rural program and political policies with Stalin's terror and "revolution from above." Khrushchev too was partially rehabilitated as Gorbachev described his beneficial reforms and praised his efforts to free the USSR from negative aspects of Stalinism, decentralize the economy, and democratize Soviet politics somewhat. However, Khrushchev was criticized for capricious behavior and unstable policies and for fostering his own personality cult.[6] Positive reassessment of Khrushchev's period coincided with a multifaceted critique of the Brezhnev era (1964–1982) as "the period of stagnation." Gorbachev blamed Brezhnev's failure to institute timely political and economic changes for the USSR's loss of momentum and declining economic growth after 1975.[7] Brezhnev became a convenient scapegoat for most ills of Soviet society, politics, and foreign policy.

---

[4]Iurii Afanasiev at the Kennan Institute, Washington, D.C., October 6, 1988; "Soviet Rule Questioned," *Radio Free Europe*, 6, no. 30, July 20, 1989.
[5]Abel Aganbegyan, *The Economic Challenge of Perestroika* (Bloomington, Ind., 1988).
[6]M. S. Gorbachev, *Perestroika* (New York, 1987), p. 43.
[7]Gorbachev speech of January 26, 1987; *Pravda*, March 1, 1987.

Historical *glasnost* even began to invade the formerly sacrosanct preserves of Leninism and Soviet foreign policy. Stalin, affirmed one article, for personal political reasons had grossly exaggerated the danger of a capitalist-sponsored and French-led invasion of the USSR in 1928–1929.[8] Stalin's policy of "social Fascism," alleged another, had split the German working class and contributed to Hitler's seizure of power and eventually to World War II. One scholar denounced the Nazi-Soviet Pact of August 1939 as a cynical act.[9] In the Baltic republics that pact was denounced as the basis for their forced incorporation into the Soviet Union in 1940. Efforts to uncover the roots of Stalinism led to scattered criticisms of Leninism, chiefly in literature. Marxism-Leninism, suggested Vasili Seliunin, had played a destructive role by denigrating the principle of economic self-interest.[10] Unwittingly, Gorbachev had opened a Pandora's box of revelations that threatened to undermine the entire Soviet system and its ideology.

Beginning in 1986 shocking revelations appeared in the Soviet press about a deteriorating Soviet social system. Statistics were published on infant mortality, incidence of disease, and numerous deaths from suicide and alcohol poisoning. Soviet commentators demanded open reporting of party affairs, even Politburo meetings; the 19th Party Conference in 1989 advocated more publicity in those areas. However, *glasnost* did not imply an independent or free press but rather instructions from above combined with frequent reminders by the leadership of limits and a continued need for controls. Inevitably *glasnost* provoked conservative efforts to curtail liberal probing of sensitive areas of culture, history, and foreign policy.

An offshoot of *glasnost* was the dramatic reappearance in the USSR for the first time since the 1920s of informal, voluntary organizations. Early "informals" were often devoted to the preservation of threatened historic monuments such as churches or to protection of the environment. *Pamiat* (Memory), a right-wing nationalist Russian organization with anti-Semitic overtones and an incipient political party, began as a preservationist group. By late 1985 informals had spread throughout the country, and in August 1987 their representatives meeting in Moscow's Hall of Columns called for creating a federation of informals and establishing a dialogue with the party. In 1988 the regime invited them to help defend *perestroika*. Their number doubled from an estimated 30,000 such organizations in 1988 to 60,000 in 1989. During 1989 many of these

---

[8]*Komsomolskaia Pravda*, June 19, 1988.
[9]Dmitry Volkogonov, *Pravda*, June 20, 1988. See Chapter 14.
[10]V. Seliunin, *Novyi mir*, no. 5, 1988.

groups put forward political goals and planned to operate as political parties and establish foundations for genuine political democracy in the USSR. Popular fronts, first set up in the Baltic republics during 1988, by 1989 were successfully challenging the leadership of the party and electing deputies to the Congress of People's Deputies. From the Baltic republics this popular front movement spread to other minority republics. One free-lance Soviet journalist, Liudmila Alekseevna, concluded in October 1988 that informals had made Gorbachev's program of democratization irreversible. By then some 70 percent of Soviet youth aged 14 to 17 belonged to informals concerned with popular music.[11]

By 1990 Gorbachev's USSR had progressed much further toward political reform than toward economic transformation. At an early stage Gorbachev realized that implementation of essential economic change depended on political reforms. Expressing impatience at the slow pace of reform to the Central Committee in February 1988, Gorbachev attacked opponents of change and urged accelerating the "process of democratization" by restructuring the Soviet political system. He singled out the soviets as the place to start. In February 1987 a limited experiment of competitive elections to some local soviets was launched. In June 1987 elections about 5 percent of deputies were so chosen in scattered districts, but the results were heartening. Deputies to local soviets were to be limited to two five-year terms. Elected representatives began to achieve some power over the bureaucrats. In June 1988 Gorbachev told the 19th Party Conference that prescribed quotas in the soviets of women, collective farmers, and workers were no longer necessary:

> We should not be afraid of the disproportionate representation of various strata of the population. . . . All that needs to be done is to create a well-adjusted competitive mechanism ensuring that voters choose the best possible people out of this group. Then all the basic groups of the population and their interests will be reflected in the make-up of the soviets.[12]

At the 19th Conference significant political reforms were announced, including a new legislature—the Congress of People's Deputies—that was to be more freely elected and the new and powerful post of President of the Supreme Soviet for Gorbachev. (See Figure 20.1.) Officeholders were to be limited to two five-year terms, and local elections were to be contested. Meanwhile, debate escalated between radical reformers like Boris Eltsin and conservatives led by Egor Ligachev, whose stance was

---

[11]L. Alekseevna, "Informal Associations in the USSR," Kennan Institute, October 24, 1988; Fred Starr, "Informal Groups and Political Culture," at the Kennan Institute, December 9, 1988.

[12]Gorbachev to the 19th Party Conference, June 1988, p. 15.

Figure 20.1 *Soviet Political Structure, June 1990*

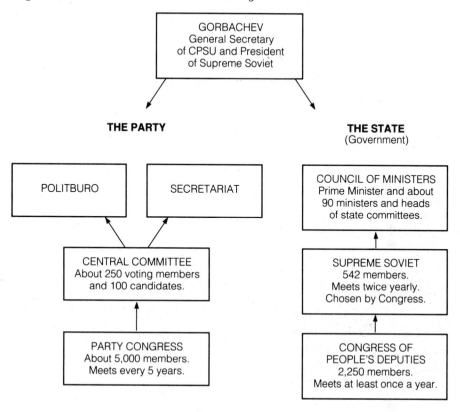

buttressed by a neo-Stalinist letter of a Leningrad schoolteacher, Nina Andreeva.[13] Following animated Politburo discussion, on April 5, 1988, *Pravda* issued a sharp rebuttal, approved by Gorbachev and defending the reforms. The 19th Conference engineered a more reformist Central Committee than that elected in March 1986 without awaiting the 28th Party Congress scheduled for 1991.[14] However, in the United States former dissident Andrei Sakharov criticized Gorbachev's attempt to implement "democratic reform through undemocratic means." Elections to the new 2,250-member Congress, he predicted, would be controlled by the state administrative apparatus. By holding power as both

---

[13]In *Sovetskaia Rossiia*, March 13, 1988.
[14]Michel Tatu, "19th Party Conference," *Problems of Communism*, 37 (May–August 1988), pp. 1–15.

party general secretary and Soviet president, Gorbachev or a successor might abuse it.[15]

Nonetheless, the March 1989 elections came as a welcome surprise to supporters of democratization. "For all their unfairness, fraud, undemocratic framework and stage-managing," wrote a Gorbachev critic, "the present elections will go down in history as the most democratic elections the Soviet people have seen in the whole period of Communist rule."[16] After balloting for 1,500 territorial deputies was completed, one Muscovite exclaimed: "It was as exciting as . . . when we celebrated the defeat of Nazi Germany." As party conservatives withdrew, stunned by their almost universal repudiation, 90 percent of Muscovites voted for Boris N. Eltsin, a leading spokesman for radical political change. In one Moscow district Arkadi Murashov—a young engineer advocating a multiparty political system—triumphed. In Leningrad the five highest party officials met defeat when over half the voters crossed out their names! However, more or less free elections were held in only 200 to 300 districts out of thousands; in most others handpicked party candidates ran unopposed. Despite their deficiencies, the March 1989 elections opened the way for a rapid peaceful evolution toward democracy.[17] Soon thereafter Gorbachev was elected president of the new Supreme Soviet, which at its initial sessions in spring and fall 1989 subjected him and other leaders to unprecedentedly frank questioning. Containing a growing liberal opposition, that body was no rubber stamp.

The ouster and subsequent resurrection of Boris Eltsin throws an interesting light on politics under Gorbachev. An ardent reformer, he was named a Central Committee secretary in July 1985 and first secretary of the Moscow city committee in December, replacing Grishin. He issued emotional appeals for social justice and denounced privileges of the party elite (*nomenklatura*). But after a Central Committee plenum of October 1987, Eltsin, denounced by conservatives and criticized by Gorbachev, was fired abruptly as Moscow party chief and removed from the Politburo soon thereafter. Receiving a modest post in the construction industry but soon named to the Council of Ministers, Eltsin made a rapid comeback as spokesman for the Moscow intelligentsia and electoral reform.[18] Overwhelmingly elected to the Supreme Soviet over a conservative, Eltsin took a leading role among its liberal opposition. During 1989 he emerged as

---

[15]Sakharov at the Kennan Institute, November 14, 1988.
[16]Alexander Amerisov, *Soviet-American Review*, 4, no. 2, February 1989.
[17]Amerisov, *Soviet-American Review*, 4, no. 3, March 1989.
[18]Timothy Colton, "Moscow Politics and the Eltsin Affair," *The Harriman Institute Forum, 1*, no. 6, Columbia University, June 1988.

Boris Eltsin (1931–), maverick Soviet politician, meets the public in Moscow. In 1990 Eltsin was elected President of the Russian Republic (*AP/Wide World Photos*)

Gorbachev's chief left-wing critic, protesting that Gorbachev's reforms were proceeding too slowly. On the right Ligachev claimed that the pace of reform was too rapid. Gorbachev continued to hold the middle ground in Soviet politics.

The dramatic and sudden east European democratic revolutions of 1989–1990, encouraged by Gorbachev's evident unwillingness to repress them forcibly, accelerated Soviet political democratization. In the spring of 1989 Gorbachev had told Hungarian party leaders that he sought "pluralism within a single party system" for the USSR. He told Soviet workers in February that a multiparty system in the Soviet Union was "rubbish." In November, reassuring worried Moscow conservatives, Gorbachev insisted that Marxism would be revived by the party and that the party would continue to lead Soviet society. He defended Article 6 of the Soviet Constitution, which prescribed a leading political role for the party, and headed off efforts by reformers to debate that issue in the Supreme Soviet.

However, in the face of an east European democratic tide and the fading popularity of the Soviet Communist Party, President Gorbachev had to reverse his position. In December 1989 the Lithuanian parliament voted overwhelmingly to abolish the party's power monopoly. In January

1990, confronted in Vilnius, Lithuania, by huge crowds chanting for democracy, Gorbachev declared that he saw "no tragedy" in a multiparty system for the USSR. At a dramatic party plenum in February, he advocated revoking Article 6 and this was then implemented in a vote by the Congress of Peoples' Deputies. In republic elections from December 1989 to June 1990 the public repudiated most party-sponsored candidates. A multiparty system began to emerge as thousands of Communist Party members resigned. The opposition took over the governments of the USSR's three largest cities—Moscow, Leningrad, and Kiev. Power was shifting swiftly from a largely discredited Communist Party to the soviets. Gorbachev was losing control of the political system; his prestige was declining while that of Eltsin and other radical reformers increased. In June 1990 a separate party organization dominated by conservatives was formed for the Russian Republic. Early in July the 28th Party Congress convened in Moscow in an effort to reorganize the party and halt its precipitous decline.

NATIONALITIES AND NATIONALISM

Under Gorbachev the Soviet nationalities emerged swiftly from apparent obedience to assert long-repressed aspirations to autonomy and even independence. This movement was spearheaded by the three Baltic republics, the most westernized portion of the USSR. (See Map 20.1.) In some areas, notably the Caucasus and Central Asia, ethnic unrest led to widespread violence that threatened the entire fabric of Soviet federalism. Meanwhile, Russian predominance declined further. According to the 1989 Soviet census, Russians composed barely over 50 percent of the Soviet population. The USSR's 53 million Muslims, the second largest group, were increasing four times as fast as the overall Soviet population.

In July 1988 a large crowd gathered in a soccer stadium in Vilnius to celebrate a reborn Lithuanian national identity repressed since 1940 when Lithuania, Latvia, and Estonia were annexed forcibly to the Soviet Union. Participants bore pre-Soviet Lithuanian flags, demanded self-rule, and sang their long-banned national anthem. Algirdas Brazauskas, Lithuania's first party secretary, endorsed "economic sovereignty" for Lithuania. Moscow permitted this, and a popular front dominated Lithuania's March 1989 elections. Such leniency stemmed partly from Baltic leadership in implementing *perestroika*, which lagged elsewhere.[19] How-

---

[19]Robert Cullen, "Human Rights: A Millenial Year, *The Harriman Institute Forum, 1,* no. 12, December 1988.

Map 20.1 *Soviet Union Republics, June 1990*

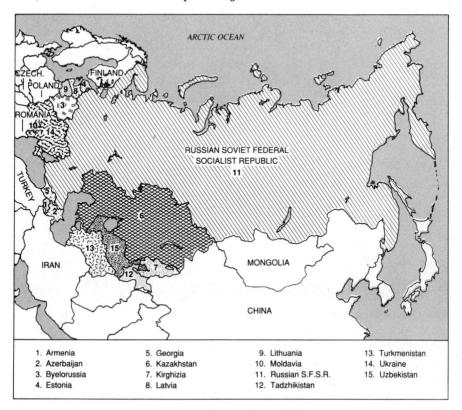

1. Armenia	5. Georgia	9. Lithuania	13. Turkmenistan
2. Azerbaijan	6. Kazakhstan	10. Moldavia	14. Ukraine
3. Byelorussia	7. Kirghizia	11. Russian S.F.S.R.	15. Uzbekistan
4. Estonia	8. Latvia	12. Tadzhikistan	

Source: Forbes, February 19, 1990, p. 107. Map by Robert Mansfield.

ever, Lithuania's declaration of independence in March 1990 provoked Moscow to cut off industrial and fuel supplies to the republic. In July that conflict was settled temporarily when the Lithuanians agreed to postpone independence and Moscow lifted its sanctions. However, all three Baltic republics remain committed to eventual independence.

Beginning in 1988 Gorbachev faced an explosive and bloody ethnic and religious dispute between Armenians (Christians) and Azeris (Muslims) over the Armenian enclave of Nagorno-Karabakh inside the republic of Azerbaijan. (See Map 20.2.) In February 1988 hundreds of thousands of Armenians went on strike, demonstrated, and demanded control over Nagorno-Karabakh. In ethnically mixed Sumgait, Azeris reacted by killing over 30 Armenians. Moscow responded mildly at first,

Lithuanians demonstrate in their capital, Vilnius, for independence January 1990. Signs call for "Independence for Lithuania" and "Leave Lithuania" *(AP/ Wide World Photos)*

then used troops to suppress rioting in Sumgait. Armenians and Azeris emigrated en masse from areas where they comprised minorities. While rejecting Armenian demands to annex Nagorno-Karabakh, Moscow made some minor concessions. In November 1988 Gorbachev expressed deep concern over ethnic unrest:

> . . . We live in a multi-ethnic state, the Soviet Union is our common home. When drawing up and implementing plans of revolutionary perestroika . . . , we cannot count on success if the work for the transformation of society does not take into account the interests of all the nations inhabiting our vast country. . . . Our future is not in weakening ties among the republics but in strengthening them. . . .[20]

Such soothing statements were combined with some repression, including arrests of some Armenian nationalist leaders. In January 1989

---

[20]Philip Taubman, "Gorbachev Says Ethnic Unrest Could Destroy Restructuring Effort," *New York Times*, November 28, 1988.

Map 20.2 *The Southern Caucasus Region*

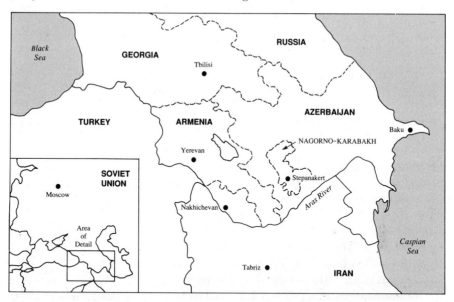

After the Soviet assault in Baku, Nakhichevan proclaimed independence. Nagorno-Karabakh, an Armenian-inhabited region inside Azerbaijan, has been a focus of conflict between Armenians and Azerbaijanis.
Source: New York Times, January 21, 1990.
Copyright © 1990 by The New York Times Company. Reprinted by permission.

Moscow imposed "special situation status" in Nagorno-Karabakh, resembling actions taken by the government of India in handling ethnic conflict. For the first time Soviet leaders recognized that the USSR shared common ethnic problems with various foreign countries and could learn from them. Further decentralization, warned Gorbachev, might lead to disastrous results in the USSR as in Yugoslavia.[21]

As feuding continued, Moscow issued a decree in mid-January 1990 declaring a state of emergency in Nagorno-Karabakh and surrounding areas. Later that month as the Azerbaijan Popular Front sought to assume power from a weakening Azerbaijani party, Gorbachev ordered Soviet troops into Baku, the Azerbaijani capital, where a general strike had brought industry to a halt. Armed Azeri resistance was broken, but no solution emerged to the Armenian-Azeri quarrel. However, Latvia in-

---

[21]Paul Goble at the Kennan Institute, January 23, 1989.

vited Armenian and Azeri leaders to Riga to work out a compromise, by-passing the federal government in Moscow. This was another dramatic demonstration of the growing power of popular front movements.

During 1989 ethnic violence erupted also in Central Asia between Uzbeks and Meshketians, a small population in the Caucasus deported to Uzbekistan by Stalin, inducing Soviet authorities to remove many of the latter to European Russia. Commented Soviet émigré Valeri Chalidze:

> Separatism . . . is far from being the main problem of nationality relations in the USSR. The majority of people of non-Russian nationality has not even considered the possibility of separation from the Soviet Union. I believe these people do want though free development of their national culture and protection of their national uniqueness from unification . . . and a voice in solutions to their own problems.[22]

Chalidze cited past denial of political autonomy and massive persecutions of most Soviet nationalities, and even falsifying their histories to claim that they had joined the USSR voluntarily, massive corruption (especially in Central Asia), and ecological problems as causes of friction. There was an increasing tendency in virtually all Soviet republics to assert their rights—political, cultural, and linguistic—against the Russian center.

During the first half of 1990 the disintegration of the Soviet Union accelerated dangerously as the country appeared to be spinning out of control. Following Lithuania's lead, other Baltic and Caucasian republics asserted their sovereignty. Potentially most serious was a decision by the legislature of the Russian Republic (RSFSR) under its new president, Boris Eltsin, that its laws would take precedence over those of the USSR. A nationalist tide was rising throughout the Soviet empire threatening its continued existence. In June President Gorbachev promised the Soviet Union would be reformed to accord broad sovereignty to the individual republics, but some of them continued to press for full independence. As public order began to break down, numerous Russian refugees poured into Moscow seeking to escape ethnic violence in the Caucasus and Central Asia.

Under Gorbachev, emigration from the USSR of Germans, Jews, and Armenians was liberalized partly because of *glasnost* and partly to win foreign approval and induce the United States to lift trade restrictions. Relaxing restrictions on emigration reflected a trend toward loosening central controls, recognizing more human rights, and promoting a rule of law. Starting in 1986 considerable numbers of Jews, especially "re-

---

[22]Valeri Chalidze, "Nationalities in the USSR," *Commission on Security and Cooperation in Europe Digest* (October–November 1988).

Figure 20.2 *Emigration of Soviet Jews*

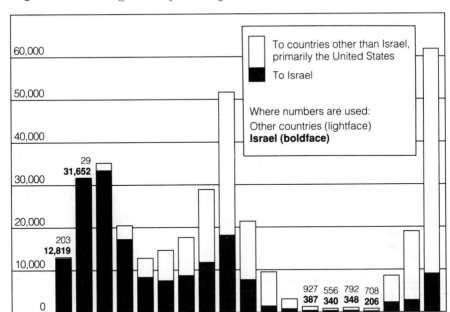

Source: Statistics from National Conference on Soviet Jewry. *New York Times;* December 14, 1989. Copyright © 1989 by the New York Times Company. Reprinted by permission.

fusniks," emigrated, but even more Soviet Germans departed. (See Figure 20.2.) However, there was little emigration of Russians or other nationalities.[23]

Russian nationalism was rekindled under Gorbachev as a backlash against Russophobic agitation outside the Russian Republic and as an outgrowth of an intraparty struggle between radical reformers and conservatives. Initially, Russian nationalism aimed to protect historic monuments and the environment. Nationalists successfully opposed a vast project designed to shift the course of Russian rivers to irrigate arid areas of Central Asia; it was abandoned in August 1986.[24] As Gorbachev's reform plans matured during 1987, neo-Stalinists and conservative Rus-

[23]Laurie Salitan, "The Dynamics of Emigration and Nationality in the Soviet Union," *The Harriman Institute Forum,* 2, no. 2 (February 1989).
[24]Nicolae Petro, "The Project of the Century," *Studies in Comparative Communism* (Fall 1987), pp. 235–252.

sian nationalists allied against *perestroika;* they objected especially to official encouragement of Western "mass culture," which appealed to Soviet youth. However, many Russian nationalists hailed Gorbachev's initiative to celebrate in June 1988 the millenium of the Christianization of Rus, including his well-publicized meeting with Patriarch Pimen. *Pamiat,* the leading Russian nationalist group, whose members wear black military shirts or army greatcoats, advocated "a great undivided Russia" free of Jews. By 1990 this Russian nationalism represented a significant, potentially dangerous force, but its fragmentation into several subgroups reduced its political strength.[25]

PERESTROIKA'S IMPACT ON THE ECONOMY AND SOCIETY

Political democratization and opening the public media under Gorbachev were designed to buttress a radical overhaul of the Soviet economy, or *perestroika.* The chief problem—a monumental one—was to shift a huge economy from a state-owned and -managed system, highly centralized and bureaucratized, to a semimarket economy in which some degree of individual initiative and local decision making would prevail. Another formidable problem was to transform a totally unrealistic price structure into one in which prices and costs would reflect market forces. In short, Gorbachev aimed to move from state to market socialism by using capitalist techniques without restoring a capitalist system.

Under Gorbachev economic reform in 1985–1986 featured traditional approaches such as tightening work discipline and shifting investment. A second stage beginning early in 1987 aimed to overhaul the state economic sector and create a socialist market economy. Richard Ericson dubbed a third phase, beginning in 1988, "the privatization of Soviet socialism" in a desperate effort to overcome stagnation; its reforms included a law on individual labor activity and a law on cooperatives, granting long-term leases to private producers, especially in agriculture. The purpose was "to rescue *perestroika* for the Soviet consumer" by creating institutions promoting genuine competition and removing excessive central coordination and planning. But without steps to legalize essential middlemen, these changes remained ineffective. Legal, bureaucratic, and even public opposition and foot-dragging crippled the new private sector.[26]

---

[25]John Dunlop, "The Contemporary Russian Nationalist Spectrum," *Radio Liberty Research Bulletin,* December 19, 1988.
[26]Richard Ericson, "The Privatization of Soviet Socialism," *The Harriman Institute Forum 2,* no. 9, Columbia University.

Table 20.2 *A Century of Soviet Grain Harvests*

Year	Grain Harvest*	Year	Grain Harvest*	Year	Grain Harvest*
1886–1890	36**	1937	96	1969	162
1900	56	1940	96	1970	187
1910	74	1945	47	1971	181
1913	80	1950	81	1972	168
1916	64	1953	82	1973	222
1920	46	1954	86	1974	195
1921	38	1955	104	1975	140
1922	50	1956	125	1976	224 *BREZHNEV*
1923	57	1957	103	1977	196
1924	51	1958	135	1978	237
1925	73	1959	120	1979	179
1926	77	1960	126	1980	189
1928	73	1961	131	1981	150
1929	72	1962	140	1982	180
1930	84	1963	108	1983	190
1931	70	1964	152	1984	170
1932	70	1965	121	1985	192
1933	68	1966	171	1986	210
1934	68	1967	148	1987	211
1935	75	1968	170	1988	215†

Note: Population figures were 125 million in 1897 and 275 million in 1985.
*In million tons.
**Average annual production in European Russia.
†Projected yield.
Source: Joan F. Crowley and Dan Vaillancourt, *Lenin to Gorbachev* . . . (Arlington Heights, Ill., 1989), p. 165.

Attempts at Agricultural Reform

Nowhere was reform more urgently required than in agriculture, which remained in the paralyzing grip of roughly 50,000 huge state farms (sovkhozy) and somewhat smaller but still large collectives (kolkhozy). On these grossly inefficient units that absorbed vast state subsidies, farmers still had few inducements to work hard or produce much. (See Table 20.2.) Meanwhile, small individual garden plots, strictly limited in size by law, produced roughly one third of Soviet vegetables, fruits, and other consumer staples. Gorbachev's initial response to this dilemma was to create Gosagroprom, an agricultural superagency, in November 1985, while continuing to provide huge state subsidies, especially for meat and milk production.

When this traditional approach failed to overcome the agricultural crisis, Gorbachev in October 1988 proposed leasing substantial amounts of land for up to 50 years to small groups of farmers with the state retaining overall land ownership. Teams of farmers were to purchase agricultural machinery, feed, seed grain, and fertilizers. After fulfilling annual delivery quotas to the state, they could dispose at will of any remaining surplus. Urging adoption of this leasing system throughout Soviet agriculture, Gorbachev by implication condemned Soviet forced collectivization: "What has happened is that people have been alienated from the soil. . . . Comrades, the most important thing today is to make people full-fledged masters of the land again."[27] At a Central Committee plenum early in 1989, Gorbachev urged a radical reversal of 60 years of centralized farming. The superagency Gosagroprom was to be dismantled and free markets introduced gradually. After a transition period, farmers should receive "complete freedom" to market their products. Previous efforts at agricultural reform, such as Premier Kosygin's program of 1965 (see p. 434), had failed, noted Gorbachev, because they had not been radical enough: "The essence of economic change in the countryside should be to grant farmers broad opportunities for displaying independence, enterprise, and initiative." At that March 1989 plenum Gorbachev spoke more frankly than any previous Soviet leader had about the shortcomings of collectivized agriculture. The most inefficient farms, he urged, should be allowed to go bankrupt, then broken up and leased out to farmers or merged with more successful neighboring collectives. However, Egor Ligachev, leading the party conservatives, advocated supplying even larger state subsidies to bolster state farms. That policy, retorted Gorbachev, had proven its utter failure under Brezhnev.[28]

During a month-long tour of Soviet collectives in 1989, Mark Kramer, an American journalist, was told by a Soviet agronomist: "Our farms are disaster areas." Locally, the old failed system remained deeply entrenched. "Even if a collective farm earns money with honest labor," lamented a leading agrarian reformer, "in order to spend the rubles, to build a barn, you still need 1,000 signatures." Lack of incentives and a stifling bureaucracy meant that most collectives lost money. "There are still 200,000 orders, decrees, official instructions, and ministerial instructions. Our economy is tied by all these like a bound child."[29] Even if freed

---

[27]"Gorbachev's Proposal to Lease Farms . . . ," *Radio Free Europe,* 6, no. 4 (November 1, 1988).
[28]Bill Keller, "Gorbachev Urges New Farm Policy," *New York Times,* March 16, 1989.
[29]Mark Kramer, "Can Gorbachev Feed Russia?" *New York Times Magazine,* April 9, 1989.

from controls imposed by a million bureaucrats, were there enough genuine Soviet farmers left to rescue the country from agricultural disaster?

Fiscal Crisis Hampers Industrial Production

Gorbachev inherited an economy in the midst of a grave financial crisis. For years the USSR had been running up huge, carefully concealed budget deficits, amounting in 1985 to almost 20 percent of GNP, roughly twice the U.S. figure. Defense expenditures in the 1980s had continued to increase roughly 3 percent annually to pay for strategic weapons, missiles, and submarines. Soviet state banks had automatically loaned vast sums to inefficient state enterprises. These deficit rubles paid workers but produced no goods for them to buy. Thus from 1970 to 1986 personal deposits in Soviet savings banks rose fivefold because of endemic shortages and low-quality consumer goods. Meanwhile, the ruble remained unconvertible inside the Soviet Union and worthless outside; currency black markets flourished. The USSR owed huge financial obligations to its citizens that it could not meet.[30]

Revamping Soviet finances and the economy proved far more difficult for Gorbachev to achieve than political reform. More radical economic reformers, for a time converting Gorbachev, urged abandoning centralized state planning and artificial prices set by the state for a system in which market forces would allocate most goods, services, and prices. They redefined socialism to embrace rules of the marketplace and private ownership of land. For a time Gorbachev envisioned speedy price reform by 1990–1991 to establish a realistic system; he backed away from such reform when faced with negative reactions from Soviet consumers and workers accustomed to state subsidies to keep prices low. Creating a market economy, realized Gorbachev, would be very difficult technically and dangerous politically.

Abel Aganbegyan, typifying such radical reformist views and a chief Gorbachev economic adviser, advocated rapid and drastic price reform with sharp price increases.[31] Confirming what Western economists had long affirmed, Aganbegyan admitted that in 1981–1985 there had been virtually no Soviet economic growth. Centrally dictated prices, he argued, should be retained "only for the most essential products in order to

---

[30]Judy Shelton, *Gorbachev's Desperate Pursuit of Credit in Western Financial Markets* (New York, 1989).

[31]Abel Aganbegyan, *The Challenge: Economics of Perestroika*, ed. N. Browne (Bridgeport, Conn., 1988).

Pizza prepared by cooks from Trenton, New Jersey, being served to Muscovites at the start of a joint Soviet-American enterprise in 1988 *(SOVFOTO)*

control their rate of growth and stave off inflation." Soviet economic reformers, noted Ed Hewitt, created difficulties for themselves by allocating broad decision-making powers to individual enterprises before instituting price reforms. That allowed them to operate for several years "with distorted prices arbitrarily giving profits to new enterprises and losses to others." For the Soviet economy to become competitive and market oriented, argued Hewitt, it would have to integrate more fully into the world economy. Gorbachev attempted this by abolishing the Ministry of Foreign Trade's monopoly and encouraging joint ventures with Bloc countries and capitalist companies, reflecting a dramatic change in Soviet attitudes.[32]

Early efforts by the Gorbachev regime to reform Soviet industry mostly failed. A party plenum in June 1987 approved the complex law on state enterprise (LSE), which aimed to discard Stalinist economic practices and make Soviet enterprises into autonomous, democratic,

---

[32]Ed Hewitt, *Reforming the Soviet Economy* . . . (Washington, D.C., 1988).

financially independent producers. Individual firms were to exercise initiative, be fully accountable financially, and receive no guaranteed state financial support. That would require overhauling the banking and credit systems and implementing a price reform at the start of the Thirteenth Five Year Plan in 1991. (Later that measure was deferred until 1995.) Indirect economic levers were to replace the former central command mechanism.[33] In January 1988 implementation of this radical industrial reform began, but soon it grew evident that the scheme was simply not working. "*Perestroika* has lost its first decisive battle," lamented a Soviet legal specialist. A major purpose of the LSE was to restrict the power of the ministerial bureaucracy by letting enterprises set their own annual and five-year plans partly through contracts freely negotiated with customers and suppliers. However, enterprise directors, used to receiving orders from above, ensured that state orders would still represent 80 to 90 percent of their output, rather than the intended maximum of 50 to 70 percent. Factory managers remained bound to the ministries, obeying their orders as before and regularly ignoring decisions reached by workers and their elected councils. That resulted partly from the vaguely phrased LSE. The centralized Stalinist industrial system and its vast bureaucracy revealed an amazing capacity to survive.[34]

Despite Gorbachev's exhortations for drastic economic changes, during his first five years they failed to take root. (See Table 20.3 and Figure 20.3.) Growth rates in 1987 and 1988 were only about 1.5 percent, and agricultural output actually fell in 1988. Only about two thirds of the state's priority projects scheduled to be commissioned were actually completed. The backlog of unfinished and abandoned construction grew steadily. Reduced state revenues—combined with rising expenditures for investment, defense, subsidies to unprofitable factories, and Armenian earthquake relief—swelled budget deficits and inflationary pressures. Modernization of industry and real price reforms were postponed, and the USSR lagged technologically behind the West and Japan even more, especially in advanced microcircuits and mainframe computers.[35]

Consumer Complaints Increase

Faced with rising consumer dissatisfaction and bureaucratic obstruction, Gorbachev revised his economic policies in the realization that he could

---

[33]Jerry Hough, *Opening Up the Soviet Economy* (Washington, D.C., 1988).
[34]"Economic Reform Stalled in the USSR," *Radio Free Europe*, 6, no. 8 (December 10, 1988).
[35]Michael Gordon, "Slow Growth Seen in Soviet Economy," *New York Times*, April 23, 1989.

Table 20.3 *Industrial Production Figures*

January–February Production as a Percentage of Preceding January–February

Product	Brezhnev 1982 1981	Andropov 1983 1982	Chernenko 1985 1984	Gorbachev 1986 1985
Electricity	103.4%	103.0%	103.3%	104%
Petroleum (inc. gas condensate)	99.8	102.0	96.3	101
Natural gas	106.4	108.0	109.1	107
Coal	99.3	100.5	98.4	106
Steel	95.6	104.0	92.2	111
Fertilizer	97.7	111.0	98.0	116
Metal-cutting tools	101.5	104.0	103.6	114
Robots	—	147.0	100.0	142
Computer technology	76.8	109.0	110.0	123
Tractors	99.6	102.0	104.0	105
Paper	93.3	108.0	93.7	113
Cement	88.3	113.0	93.7	111
Meat	93.6	106.0	106.3	113
Margarine	100.0	110.0	92.6	108
Watches	100.0	105.0	96.4	108
Radios	98.9	111.0	93.0	106
Television sets	99.9	108.0	100.0	106

Source: Marshall Goldman, *Gorbachev's Challenge* (New York, 1987), p. 70.

not achieve his goals as quickly as he had hoped. The 1989 plan stressed consumption, cut state investment for the first time since 1945, promised a major reduction in defense outlays, and deferred retail price reforms. Priority went to retooling Soviet plants, proceeding with land leasing, and encouraging the private sector.[36] In 1985 *perestroika* had been launched with a barrage of new regulations, slogans, and resolutions, which often proved contradictory and remained mere verbiage. In several key areas the leadership's efforts to decentralize the economy were emasculated by

---

[36]Report by CIA and Defense Intelligence Agency of April 1989, *The Soviet Economy in 1988: Gorbachev Changes Course* (Washington, D.C., 1989).

Figure 20.3 *Growth Rate of USSR Industrial Output, 1961–1990*

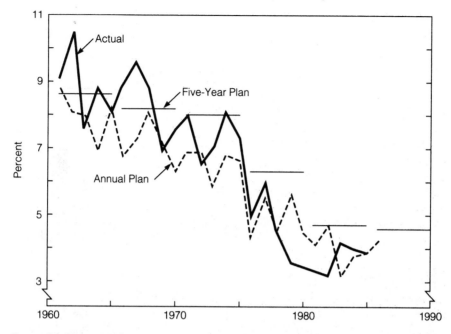

Source: Ed. Hewett, *Reforming the Soviet Economy* (Washington, D.C., 1988), p. 64.

the bureaucracy or simply abandoned. In November 1989 the government set new production quotas for factories and limited some exports. Although Deputy Premier Leonid Abalkin called such measures "temporary," clearly perestroika had stalled as had the Kosygin reforms of 1965. Meeting with economists, Gorbachev conceded: "We have a long way to go from formulating a concept to obtaining the goals we have set and changing the quality of our society."[37]

Problems plaguing a Soviet economy being reformed from above were exemplified by the soap crisis of late 1989–1990. At the slightest hint that soap, detergent, or washing powder might be sold, Russians lined up for hours outside stores. On the black market such items fetched several times the official state price. Nor was soap the only consumer product in short supply: 1,000 of 1,200 everyday items were hard to obtain, noted official figures. Dangerous public dissatisfaction induced the government in 1989 to spend a whopping $16 billion on emergency

---

[37]Peter Gumbel, *Wall Street Journal*, November 21, 1989, pp. 1–2.

Figure 20.4 *Perestroika's Troubled Start*

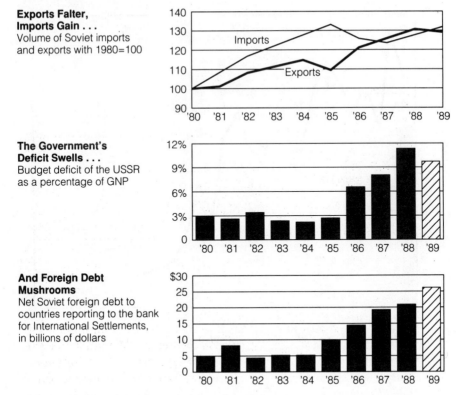

Exports Falter, Imports Gain . . .
Volume of Soviet imports and exports with 1980=100

The Government's Deficit Swells . . .
Budget deficit of the USSR as a percentage of GNP

And Foreign Debt Mushrooms
Net Soviet foreign debt to countries reporting to the bank for International Settlements, in billions of dollars

Source: All data from PlanEcon Inc.
Copyright © Dow Jones & Company, Inc. All rights reserved worldwide.

imports of consumer goods. While preparing even more radical reforms, Gorbachev's economic team admitted it had underestimated the difficulties of reform. Gorbachev told Soviet economists in October 1989: "We can neither return to the beginning nor can we stop half way."[38] The graphs in Figures 20.4 and 20.5 reveal the Soviet dilemma.

Gorbachev relied heavily on the "human factor" to spur the lagging economy. Many corrupt officials were fired, drastic measures were adopted in 1985 to curb alcohol consumption, and Soviet workers were

---

[38]Gumbel, *Wall Street Journal.*

Figure 20.5 *The Plight of Soviet Consumers in the 1980s*

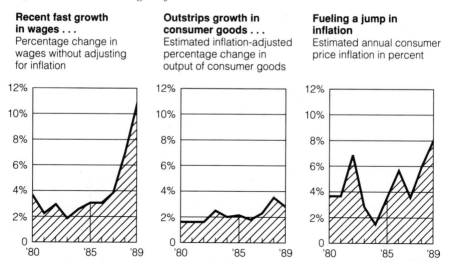

Recent fast growth in wages . . .
Percentage change in wages without adjusting for inflation

Outstrips growth in consumer goods . . .
Estimated inflation-adjusted percentage change in output of consumer goods

Fueling a jump in inflation
Estimated annual consumer price inflation in percent

Source: PlanEcon Inc.

exhorted to abandon casual attitudes toward work. In September 1988 Gorbachev told representatives of the Soviet media: "We must free the social consciousness from such harmful complexes as the faith in 'a good tsar,' in an omnipotent center, in the idea that someone will impose order and organize perestroika from above." Seventy years of Soviet socialism, noted a journalist, had produced a psychology of social dependency: "Give me a free house, cheap meat, and get rid of my neighbor who is working on his own and lives better than I do." Many Soviet citizens responded to Gorbachev's pleas by forming "young peoples' residential complexes," competing to build their own apartment houses with money and materials provided by the state. Cooperatives proliferated—there were over 32,000 by July 1988—to provide consumer services, formerly sadly lacking, such as repair facilities and private restaurants. However, they encountered the "red-eye" disease of envy by those unwilling to see their fellow citizens prosper and many cooperatives were burned down.[39] During 1988 Gorbachev retreated, criticizing cooperatives; he rescinded tough anti-alcohol measures after a surge in illegal production (*samogon*) caused losses of state revenue and sugar shortages.

---

[39]*Radio Free Europe,* "Gorbachev Calls for New 'New Soviet Man'" 6, no. 6 (November 20, 1988).

Consumer dissatisfaction during Gorbachev's first five years was understandable. Per capita consumption remained virtually stagnant. Reduced farm output, inadequate storage facilities, and processing and distribution problems produced serious shortages of some foods. With supplies of meat, fruit, and vegetables sporadic in state stores, prices at collective farm markets rose considerably as did those of manufactured goods. Unsatisfied consumer demand for goods in 1988, noted Premier Ryzhkov, totaled over 90 billion rubles, or 20 percent of consumer purchases.[40] Soviet citizens continued to enjoy free health care and education while housing and necessities remained heavily subsidized, but overall living standards lagged far behind those of the West. "In terms of per capita consumption of goods," wrote Alexander Zaichenko, a Soviet economist, "the USSR . . . occupies between 50th and 60th place in the world." In 1985 almost two thirds of United States' GNP went for wages compared to only 37 percent in the USSR, and the United States was outspending the USSR in education, health care, and social security. In 1985 a typical Soviet family of four with two wage earners spent 59 percent of income on food compared with only 15 percent for an American family. Soviet meat consumption per capita was less than city dwellers had consumed in tsarist Russia. Zaichenko's figures provoked consternation among Soviet officials who questioned those on tsarist meat consumption.[41]

Rapid urbanization added to consumer woes. Since 1917 Soviet cities have been transformed, noted an American geographer. Urban growth rates have approximated 5 percent annually as the percentage of Soviet people living in cities has risen from 18 in 1917 to 66 percent in 1985. Whereas in 1926 only Moscow and Leningrad exceeded 1 million people, in 1985 there were 21 such cities and 292 over 100,000. Whereas advanced rural and urban planning prevailed in the Baltic states, cities in the Urals and Siberia could not provide nearly adequate services.[42] A sharp rise in drug abuse occurred. Under Gorbachev the media published many revealing accounts of a drug scourge formerly dismissed as nonexistent in the USSR. "Concealing an illness will not make it go away . . . ," wrote one newpaper. "We have come to realize that openness is needed in the struggle against drug addiction. . . . "[43]

[40]CIA Report, *The Soviet Economy in 1988* (Washington, D.C., 1989).

[41]"USSR Living Standards Far Below Those of the West," *Radio Free Europe*, 6, no. 17.

[42]George Demko at the Kennan Institute, October 3, 1988.

[43]John Kramer, "Drug Abuse in the Soviet Union," *Problems of Communism, 37*, (March–April 1988), pp. 28–40. In 1988 52,000 persons reportedly were officially registered in the USSR as drug addicts.

The first lawyer to run the party since Lenin, Gorbachev fostered major improvements in human rights and advances toward a genuine rule of law. Nearly all political prisoners were freed and rehabilitated. Gorbachev's report to the 27th Congress in 1986 outlined desired legal changes, and the 19th Party Conference of June 1988 reiterated this theme. Henceforth laws were to be applied in a democratic, evenhanded manner. Moves were made to abolish or dramatically curtail capital punishment, involuntary exile, and forced incarceration in mental institutions. The Conference recommended that "presumption of innocence" be incorporated in a new Soviet law code. The Central Committee decreed in November 1986 that defense counsel be admitted to preliminary investigations in all criminal cases. Endorsing many proposed legal reforms, the 19th Party Conference gave this laudable campaign new momentum.[44]

NATIONAL SECURITY AND FOREIGN AFFAIRS

Introducing dramatic changes in Soviet foreign policy, Gorbachev elaborated a sharply altered view of military power and security. In superpower negotiations the Soviet Union agreed to drastic arms cuts and unprecedentedly intrusive measures of verification. Gorbachev downgraded the military's public role, encouraging civilian defense analysts to propose radical revisions of Soviet military policies. Replacing most of the high command he had inherited, he brought in the obedient General Dmitri Iazov as defense minister and appointed liberal-minded civilians to oversee important aspects of security policy. Most foreign observers viewed Gorbachev's "new political thinking" as constituting a revolution in Soviet security policy.[45]

Some of Gorbachev's statements before 1985 suggest that he had been a defender of Brezhnev's 1970s strategy that expanded military power, combined with arms control and diplomatic negotiations, would enhance Soviet security. However, beginning in 1983 Gorbachev opposed increased defense spending and expressed mounting concern over the USSR's industrial lag.[46] Once in power he urged "civilized relations" with the West, unveiling in January 1986 a proposal for phased but sweeping arms reductions. At the 27th Congress that followed, he

---

[44]William Butler, "Legal Reform in the Soviet Union," *The Harriman Institute Forum*, 1, no. 9 (September 1988).

[45]Raymond Garthoff, "New Thinking in Soviet Military Doctrine," *Washington Quarterly*, Summer 1988, pp. 131–158.

[46]Bruce Parrott, *The Soviet Union and Ballistic Missile Defense* (Boulder, Colo., 1987), pp. 55–56.

declared that growing East-West interdependence required radical improvements in their relations.[47]

At Gorbachev's accession the Soviet Union remained a garrison state with enormous military forces built up over the previous 15 years at high economic and social cost. The USSR under Brezhnev had relied on military might to provide security at home and to serve as its primary instrument of foreign policy. Under Gorbachev this approach was revised substantially. Even in the early 1980s Soviet marshals had wondered whether a creaking economy could support the highly technological armed forces of the future. Policy changes under Gorbachev proved more far reaching than at any other time in Soviet history. His "new thinking" rejected the Brezhnev military buildup as economically prohibitive and politically disastrous. Meanwhile, there was growing public criticism of the Soviet military as bloated, expensive, and even morally corrupt. By 1988 some military men questioned the need for a huge standing army.[48]

When two Soviet officers chained themselves to a lamppost outside the Defense Ministry in April 1989, they drew attention to the miseries of Red Army life. To their amazement, the next day they were sitting in Defense Minister Dmitri Iazov's office complaining about poor living conditions, scandalous health care, and insensitive political indoctrination. Although soon discharged from service, they revealed how *glasnost* had uncovered widespread discontent and caused unsettled times in the Soviet military, which were exacerbated by the unpopular war in Afghanistan.[49]

The Soviet economy had been grievously distorted and overstretched by Brezhnev's military buildup. A weak technological base, warned Marshal Nikolai Ogarkov, could not produce new sophisticated weaponry. Advances in high technology elsewhere, he noted, threatened to make obsolete 20 years of Soviet military growth. Discerning Soviet military men realized that problems of high technology could only be solved if the Soviet economy were redirected away from defense.[50] Gorbachev's team viewed Brezhnev's foreign policy, dependent on military power, as a disaster. The invasion of Afghanistan had triggered enormous American rearmament while alienating Japan and China from the USSR. Rejecting Brezhnev's idea of deploying forces that could

---

[47]Bruce Parrott, "Soviet National Security under Gorbachev," *Problems of Communism*, 37 (November–December 1988), pp. 1–35.
[48]As at a roundtable of June 1988 sponsored by *Literaturnaia gazeta*, a leading Soviet daily.
[49]Bill Keller, "Restlessness in Soviet Ranks," *New York Times*, April 21, 1989.
[50]Report for the Joint Economic Committee, *Allocation of Resources in the Soviet Union and China—1986* (Washington, D.C., 1989).

defeat any combination of foes, Gorbachev accepted the American "zero option" proposal for Intermediate Range Ballistic Missiles even though it required the Soviets to destroy about four warheads for every American one. Gorbachev's United Nations speech of December 1988, in which he offered to cut Soviet forces unilaterally by 10 percent, reflected this new approach. Discussion on creating a smaller professional Soviet army also proceeded in Moscow.[51]

Supporters of *perestroika* sharply criticized the swollen Soviet military in 1988–1990 as blocking substantive progress on basic economic reforms. Attacks on the military as an institution multiplied. An article by Andrei Sakharov, the dissident scientist, virtually accused the Soviet military of genocide in Afghanistan. Some Red Army officers favored eliminating conscription. An army that had expanded by a million men from 1970 to 1985 was proving too costly to maintain, especially since its traditional Russian core was shrinking. Over one third of Soviet soldiers now were Muslims, speaking little Russian; this created severe ethnic tensions within the armed forces. A smaller, chiefly Slavic professional army would alleviate such problems.[52]

In a wide-ranging debate in 1989 on national security issues, "new thinkers" advocated a permanent shift away from military means of ensuring security; they proposed channeling most resources into economic development. "Technocrats" favored a short-term shift of resources to militarily relevant sectors of the civilian economy to develop advanced weaponry. "Old thinkers" continued to urge heavy military spending. The "new thinkers," who included Gorbachev, generally prevailed and urged an evolution of Soviet foreign policy toward cooperation; they argued that overall economic strength was fundamental to national security. "If we become stronger, more solid economically . . . , the interest of the capitalist world in normal relations with us will grow."[53] This victorious view represented a fundamental shift away from the rigid and militaristic thinking of the Brezhnev era.

Soviet foreign policy under Gorbachev was transformed and apparently was inspired by an urgent desire to create a peaceful international environment to encourage realization of major domestic reforms without sacrificing the USSR's status as a superpower. Gorbachev faced painful decisions over Afghanistan, eastern Europe, and German re-

---

[51]Condoleeza Rice, "Gorbachev and the Military: A Revolution in Security Policy Too?", *The Harriman Institute Forum*, 2, no. 4 (April 1989), pp. 1–8.
[52]*Radio Free Europe*, 6, no. 13 (February 1, 1989).
[53]Matthew Evangelista, "Economic Reform and Military Technology in Soviet Security Policy," *The Harriman Institute Forum*, 2, no. 1 (January 1989).

unification. Almost immediately he sought to improve Soviet-American relations and mend fences with China so he could trim military expenditures and concentrate on domestic reform. Similarly, Alexander II had sought to maintain Russia's role as a leading European power while achieving major domestic change. Repudiating Brezhnev's policies, Gorbachev blamed his regime for the USSR's declining growth and power. Seeking to demilitarize and stabilize East-West relations, Gorbachev integrated the Soviet Union increasingly into the world capitalist economic order.[54]

Gorbachev's bold policies prompted George F. Kennan, a veteran American diplomat and an architect of the American post–World War II policy of containing the USSR, to urge Washington to negotiate reductions of nuclear and conventional weapons with a liberalizing USSR as steps toward normal relations. Kennan told the Senate Foreign Relations Committee in April 1989:

> What we are witnessing today in Russia is the break-up of much, if not all of the system of power by which that country has been held together and governed since 1917 . . . [especially] in precisely those aspects of Soviet power that have been the most troublesome from the standpoint of Soviet-American relations, namely: the world-revolutionary ideology, rhetoric and political efforts of the early Soviet leadership, . . . [and] the morbid extremism of Stalinist political oppression . . . [whose] remnants are now being dismantled at a pace that renders it no longer a serious impediment to a normal Soviet-American relationship. . . .

Kennan cited three factors that still troubled U.S.-Soviet relations: swollen Soviet armed forces, continued Soviet hegemony over eastern Europe, and the arms race, but he discerned a changing Soviet security policy, military cuts, and a weakening Soviet hold over the Bloc. Declared Kennan prophetically: "So tenuous is the Soviet hold over these [east European] countries today that I personally doubt that military intervention . . . would now be a realistic option of Soviet policy. . . ." Praising Gorbachev's initiatives on arms control, Kennan concluded that the USSR should no longer be viewed in the United States as an enemy:

> That country should now be regarded essentially as another great power . . . whose aspirations are conditioned outstandingly by its own geographic situation, history and traditions. . . . It ought now to be our purpose to

---

[54]George Breslauer, "Linking Gorbachev's Domestic and Foreign Policies," *Journal of International Affairs*, Spring 1989, pp. 267–282.

eliminate as soon as possible by amicable negotiations the elements of military tension that have recently dominated Soviet-American relations.[55]

The course of Soviet-American relations from 1985 to 1990 provided a basis for Kennan's optimism. Already in April 1985 Gorbachev in a *Pravda* interview repudiated the former Soviet policy of confrontation. Citing President Reagan's apparent pursuit of military superiority through the Strategic Defense Initiative (SDI), dubbed "Star Wars,"[56] as the chief obstacle to rapprochement with the United States, Gorbachev urged achieving a breakthrough through arms control agreements. In a *Time* magazine interview in August 1985, Gorbachev reiterated the crucial importance of a Soviet-American accord to limit nuclear weapons and ban weapons in outer space. At their Geneva summit meeting that November, after extensive private talks, Reagan and Gorbachev issued a positive joint statement. Soviet newspapers, which previously had depicted Reagan as a trigger-happy cowboy, now described him talking amicably with Gorbachev. Later, Gorbachev told the press that their talks, the first between an American and a Soviet leader in over six years, had been "unquestionably a significant event in international life."

After Geneva, both sides moderated their hostile rhetoric. However, Reagan's continued insistence on SDI and his refusal to join with Moscow in a nuclear test ban moratorium slowed progress. Then Gorbachev proposed another summit, and he met with Reagan in Reykjavik, Iceland, in October 1986. They had almost reached agreement to ban all nuclear weapons within a definite time span only to stumble over the issue of testing Reagan's SDI. With Reagan becoming absorbed in the Iran-Contra scandal, Soviet leaders doubted that meaningful agreements could be reached with his administration.

But during 1987 Soviet-American relations moved forward as Reagan moderated his former anti-Soviet stance. In December in Washington he and Gorbachev achieved a major breakthrough by signing a treaty to eliminate medium- and short-range missiles. Scoring a great triumph with the American media and public, Gorbachev announced that the two sides had "emerged from protracted confrontation." The final two Gorbachev-Reagan meetings in 1988 produced no major new agreements but deepened their personal relationship. At the largely

---

[55]George F. Kennan to the Senate Foreign Relations Committee, April 4, 1989, cited in the *New York Times*, April 5, 1989.

[56]On this see R. W. Johnson, *Shootdown: Flight 007 and the American Connection* (New York, 1986), pp. 109–110. Johnson describes how Reagan's National Security Adviser, William Clark, converted the President to the "Star Wars" scheme, keeping this a secret for a month from the secretaries of state and defense.

Soviet President Mikhail Gorbachev smiles as U.S. President George Bush tries on a headphone during their joint press conference at Malta summit meeting, December 1989 *(Reuters/Bettmann)*

ceremonial Moscow summit of May 1988, Reagan, who earlier had dubbed the Soviet Union an "evil empire," chatted happily with Soviet citizens and lectured Soviet intellectuals on democracy. Gorbachev's brief meeting with Reagan and President-elect George Bush in New York that December reinforced their rapport and fostered its continuation under the Bush administration.[57] Conferring in Malta in November 1989 against the backdrop of the east European democratic revolution, Gorbachev confirmed his resolve not to intervene against it and to continue efforts at arms reduction and unifying Europe. Bush and Gorbachev reached substantial agreement on the difficult issue of German reunification, which proceeded more rapidly than either of them anticipated.

Fundamental changes in Soviet relations with eastern Europe after 1985 supported Kennan's predictions and fostered improved Soviet-U.S. ties. Late in 1988 as Hungary and Poland liberalized their political and

---

[57]Gordon Livermore, ed., *Soviet Foreign Policy Today: Reports and Commentaries from the Soviet Union,* 3d ed., (Columbus, Ohio, 1989), pp. 42–73.

economic policies, Iurii Afanasiev, a liberal Soviet reformer, declared eastern Europe should be free to choose its own path even if that meant abandoning socialism. On a June 1989 visit to France, President Gorbachev expressly repudiated the Brezhnev Doctrine, used earlier to justify the intervention in Czechoslovakia, as outmoded. Instead Soviet officials espoused the "Frank Sinatra Doctrine," or "do it your own way." Praising varying east European responses to popular demands for greater freedom, Gorbachev intimated that they were merely implementing *glasnost* and *perestroika* in their own manner.

This major shift in Soviet policy toward the Bloc reflected further development of Khrushchev's theme enunciated 30 years earlier of "separate roads to socialism" and of a "socialist commonwealth." However, neither Khrushchev nor Brezhnev would allow Communist regimes to fall as interventions in Hungary, Czechoslovakia, and Afghanistan confirmed. By contrast, under Gorbachev ideology was largely repudiated in the conduct of Soviet foreign policy. That permitted Gorbachev to allow eastern Europe to go its own way and to withdraw from Afghanistan. By downplaying ideology, Gorbachev enhanced the USSR's image abroad and at first Soviet prestige. Meanwhile, eastern Europe had lost much of its strategic importance for the USSR because under Communist rule it was draining Soviet resources. Gorbachev, the realist, became willing to cooperate with the West to stabilize eastern Europe on a new basis, although surely he did not anticipate how fast events would move there. During 1988–1989 Communist power was undermined first in Poland and Hungary, then popular movements overturned conservative Communist regimes that lacked popular support in East Germany, Czechoslovakia, Bulgaria, and Romania. This dramatic movement toward political democracy and market economies left only tiny Albania, where the USSR had little influence and no troops, under a Stalinist regime in June 1990. The collapse of the East German Communist regime accelerated the process of German unification and left the Soviet occupation army in East Germany isolated.

Another remarkable shift in Soviet foreign policy was the Soviet military withdrawal from Afghanistan early in 1989. The Communist-led Afghan regime of Najibullah remained to face divided Afghan rebels, but was buttressed with generous Soviet military aid. Soviet withdrawal produced many compensations to the USSR. It helped improve Soviet-American relations, so crucial for Gorbachev. It undermined arguments of American "hawks" that the Afghan intervention had proved the aggressiveness of "Russian imperialism towards the Persian Gulf." Soviet retirement seemed to vindicate those who viewed the Soviet invasion as a product of miscalculation and circumstances.[58] It also allowed relaxation of Soviet tensions with China and a reduction of Soviet forces on China's frontiers and improved the Soviet image in the Muslim world, especially in Iran. Although the war had grown highly unpopular inside the Soviet Union, returning Soviet troops were welcomed home by brass bands and assurances they had accomplished their "international mission."

The Gorbachev regime blamed the Afghan intervention on a small hawkish group in the Politburo surrounding the moribund Brezhnev. Very ill at the time of intervention, Brezhnev reportedly had signed the decision slipped to him hastily by Defense Minister Dmitri Ustinov. The Soviets, affirmed Joseph Collins, had "habitually attempted to pursue their interests in Afghanistan by using the lowest level of resources possible . . . , but each rung in this ladder of escalation brought the Soviets into deeper involvement with the Afghan problem."[59] In October 1989 the Kremlin issued a formal apology to the world for the invasion of Afghanistan:

> When more than 100 U.N. members for a number of years were con-demning our action, what other evidence did we need to realize that we had set ourselves against all of humanity, violated norms of behavior, ignored universal human values? I am referring of course to our military engage-ment in Afghanistan. It should teach us a lesson that in this case gross violations of our own laws, intraparty and civil norms and ethics were allowed.[60]

A close parallel was evident between American policies in Vietnam and Soviet intervention in Afghanistan ending in similar discomfiture for both superpowers. Both cases confirmed the strength of resistance by nationalist guerrillas even against a superpower.

After the Afghan withdrawal, Gorbachev charted a new and promising course in northeast Asia with arms control initiatives and overtures to China, Japan, and South Korea. Moscow sought to alleviate tensions there to permit the USSR to reduce its military forces and outlays, end confrontation with China, and encourage Japanese invest-ment in the Soviet economy. From 1981 to 1988, as Soviet leaders strove to end conflict with China, Sino-Soviet trade increased tenfold. Among the troop reductions announced in Gorbachev's U.N. speech of Decem-ber 1988 were 200,000 to be cut from Soviet forces in Asia.[61]

[58]Mark Urban, *War in Afghanistan* (New York, 1988); Joseph Collins, *The Soviet Invasion of Afghanistan* (Lexington, Mass., 1986).
[59]Collins, *The Soviet Invasion . . .* , pp. 124–125.
[60]Eduard Shevarnadze's speech as quoted in the *New York Times,* October 25, 1989.
[61]Rajan Menon at the Kennan Institute, April 3, 1989.

Finally, Gorbachev transformed Soviet policy toward the United Nations, reflecting multifaceted efforts to restore the USSR to the civilized world. His article in *Pravda* of September 17, 1988, contained a remarkable agenda: to enhance the secretary general's role in preventive diplomacy, greater use of U.N. peacekeeping forces in regional conflicts, mandatory acceptance of decisions of the International Court of Justice, a global strategy for environmental protection, and negotiations to make national laws conform to international human rights standards. Previous Soviet leaders had opposed efforts of any secretary general to strengthen U.N. influence and refused to consider third party arbitration of bilateral disputes. Some Western observers dismissed the new Soviet rhetoric about the United Nations as propaganda and an attempt to make the United States, which under Reagan often failed to pay its dues, look bad. Was Gorbachev, needing many years of external stability to implement *perestroika,* seeking to use the United Nations to help extricate the USSR from overextension abroad? Apparently, Gorbachev aimed through the United Nations to make the USSR a major player in world diplomacy, having abandoned class warfare in favor of a new philosophy of international relations to achieve global interdependence and cooperation.[62]

CONCLUSION

The Soviet Union in 1990 was a country and economy in crisis and turmoil. Politically, Gorbachev was seeking to lead a perilous transition from Stalin's brutal totalitarianism toward pluralism and even political democracy. He had moved far beyond Khrushchev by encouraging a pitiless examination of previous Soviet history, which induced some to question the very bases and legitimacy of the Soviet regime. He had fostered a degree of political debate and change unparalleled since Lenin, which threw the party into turmoil, even disintegration. In the economic realm Gorbachev strove against entrenched and powerful opposition to move away from a highly centralized, Stalinist, state-directed economy to market socialism with elements of private capitalism.

Meanwhile, in structure the Soviet Union was shifting rapidly from a Russian-dominated fake federation run centrally from Moscow to a decentralized federation or confederation in which each republic would largely determine its own political and economic policies. Would the Soviet Union survive even in such attenuated form? At least 12 of its 15 republics, led by obstreperous Lithuania and Estonia, already aspired to

---

[62]Richard Gardner at the Harriman Institute, March 23, 1989: "The Soviet Union and the United Nations," *The Harriman Institute Forum 1,* no. 12.

partial or full independence. In national security Gorbachev attempted a shift from huge military forces and a militarized economy based on Cold War ideology to greatly reduced military forces that an indebted nation could afford.

Finally, abroad Gorbachev had revolutionized Soviet policies by rejecting an ideologically hostile, aggressive, and expansionist Soviet posture for one of accommodation, concessions, apologies, and cooperation with democratic nations. He had allowed and even encouraged the dismantling of Soviet hegemony and of the Warsaw Pact in eastern Europe. Eschewing compulsion, Gorbachev encouraged Soviet citizens to contribute voluntarily to a freer, potentially more prosperous and pluralistic society and polity. Could Gorbachev retain power and succeed in these vital and monumental endeavors?

THE GORBACHEV ERA IN DOCUMENTS

The following excerpts from several key statements by President Gorbachev and Foreign Minister Shevarnadze reflect the regime's "new thinking" and provide clues to recent Soviet aims and policies.

1. *Gorbachev on Perestroika (Restructuring)* In his best-selling book, originally published in November 1987 then revised in 1988 for an American edition, President Gorbachev set forth his ideas on problems of domestic reform and on revamping Soviet foreign policy:

> *To the Reader:* . . . My desire is to address directly the peoples of the USSR, the United States, indeed every country . . . , to talk without intermediaries to the citizens of the whole world about things that, without exception, concern us all. . . . We must meet and discuss. We must tackle problems in a spirit of cooperation. . . . It is a book about our plans and about the ways we are going to carry them through, and . . . an invitation to dialogue. . . .
>
> Perestroika has been largely stimulated by our dissatisfaction with the way things have been going in our country in recent years. But it has to a far greater extent been prompted by an awareness that the potential of socialism had been underutilized. . . . I would say from the start that perestroika has proved more difficult then we at first imagined. We have had to reassess many things. . . . Some people say that the ambitious goals set forth by . . . perestroika . . . have prompted the peace proposals we have lately made in the international arena. . . . True, we need normal international conditions for our internal progress. But we want a world free of war, without arms races, nuclear weapons and violence. . . . We are all passengers aboard one ship, the Earth, and we must not allow it to be wrecked. . . . We genuinely seek to improve Soviet-American relations and attain at least that minimum of mutual understanding needed to resolve issues crucial to the world's

future. . . . But we want to cooperate on the basis of equality, mutual understanding and reciprocity [pp. xi–xv].

. . . In the latter 1970s the country [USSR] began to lose momentum. Economic failures became more frequent. Difficulties began to accumulate . . . , unresolved problems to multiply. Elements of what we call stagnation . . . began to appear in the life of society. . . . A gradual erosion of the ideological and moral values of our people began. . . . The economy . . . remains our main concern. But at the same time we have set about changing the moral and psychological situation in society. . . . An uncompromising struggle was launched against violations of the principles of socialist justice. . . . A policy of openness was proclaimed. . . . Unless we activate the human factor . . . and draw [the people] into active, constructive endeavor, we cannot accomplish any of the tasks set, or to change the situation in the country. . . . Perestroika itself can only come through democracy. . . . More glasnost, genuine control from "below," and greater initiative and enterprise at work are now part and parcel of our life. . . . The aim of this reform is to ensure within the next two or three years the transition from an excessively centralized management system relying on orders, to a democratic one based on the combination of democratic centralism and self-management" [pp. 3–20, excerpts].[63]

2. *Gorbachev's Speech to the United Nations General Assembly, December 7, 1988* In this speech Gorbachev set forth an agenda emphasizing Soviet cooperation with the United Nations to achieve a peaceful world, to continue to improve relations with the United States, and to press for military reductions, especially in nuclear weapons, by mutual agreement:

We have come here to show our respect for the United Nations which increasingly has been manifesting its ability to act as a unique international center in the service of peace and security. . . . It is obvious . . . that the use or threat of force no longer can or must be an instrument of foreign policy. This applies above all to nuclear arms. . . . All of us . . . must exercise self-restraint and totally rule out any outward-oriented use of force. . . . The new phase also requires de-ideologizing relations among states. . . . Let everyone show the advantages of their social system, way of life or values . . . by real deeds. . . . International economic security is inconceivable unless related not only to disarmament but also to the elimination of the threat to the world's environment. . . .

. . . We have initiated a radical economic reform. We have gained experience. At the start of next year the entire national economy will be redirected to new forms and methods of operation. This also means profoundly

---

[63]Mikhail S. Gorbachev, *Perestroika: New Thinking for our Country and the World* (New York, updated edition, 1988). © 1987 by Mikhail Gorbachev. Reprinted by permission of Harper & Row Publishers, Inc.

reorganizing relations of production and releasing the tremendous potential inherent in socialist property. . . . But the guarantee that the overall process of perestroika will move steadily forward and gain strength lies in a profound democratic reform of the entire system of power and administration.

. . . We have become deeply involved in building a socialist state based on the rule of law. . . . Soviet democracy will be placed on a solid normative base. I am referring, in particular, to laws on the freedom of conscience, glasnost, public associations and organizations, and many others. In places of confinement there are no persons convicted for their political or religious beliefs. Additional guarantees are to be included in the new draft laws that rule out any form of persecution on those grounds.

. . . Today, I can report to you that the Soviet Union has taken a decision to reduce its armed forces. Within the next two years their numerical strength will be reduced by 500,000 men. The numbers of conventional armaments will also be reduced substantially. This will be done unilaterally. . . .

. . . In the last few years the entire world could breathe a sigh of relief thanks to the changes for the better in the substance and the atmosphere of the relationship between Moscow and Washington. No one intends to underestimate the seriousness of our differences and the toughness of outstanding problems. We have, however, already graduated from the primary school of learning to understand each other and seek solutions to both our own and common interests. . . .

The next U.S. administration, headed by President-elect George Bush, will find in us a partner who is ready . . . to continue the dialogue in a spirit of realism, openness and good will. . . . I have in mind . . . consistent movement toward a treaty on 50 percent reductions in strategic offensive arms while preserving the ABM treaty; working out a convention on the elimination of chemical weapons . . . , and negotiations on the reduction of conventional arms and armed forces in Europe. I also have in mind economic, environmental and humanistic problems in their broadest sense. I would like to believe that our hopes will be matched by our joint efforts to put an end to an era of wars, confrontation and regional conflicts, to aggressions against nature, to the terror of hunger and poverty as well as to political terrorism. This is our common goal and we can only reach it together.[64]

3. *The Kremlin Apology* On October 22, 1989, Soviet Foreign Minister Eduard Shevarnadze delivered a speech to the Supreme Soviet containing apologies over the Krasnoiarsk radar station in Siberia and invasion of Afghanistan (see p. 522 for the apology on Afghanistan):

The power of perestroika does not in itself insure us against mistakes. It is important not to hide them, to admit them and correct them. In this respect,

---

[64]*The New York Times*, December 8, 1988, p. 16.

the Krasnoiarsk radar installation is very significant. It took us four years to get to the bottom of it. We were charged with violation of the ABM [Anti-Ballistic Missile] Treaty because of the station. . . . Finally, we saw it clearly: the station had been built on the wrong site. . . . There stood the station, the size of an Egyptian pyramid, representing to put it bluntly, a violation of the ABM Treaty. At last we resolved this issue and announced we would dismantle the station. . . . We are saving the ABM Treaty and opening the way to the conclusion of the treaty on strategic weapons. . . .

In regard to the transformation of the Warsaw Pact, resulting from the east European democratic revolutions, Shevarnadze declared:

Here, there have been historic, qualitative changes. We are building our relations with them [Warsaw Pact nations] on the basis of sovereign equality, the impermissibility of any intervention and the recognition of each country's absolute freedom of choice. In some of them, new, alternative [democratic] forces are entering the political arena. No one is leading them there. They are coming because that is what the people want. And these states do not cease to be our neighbors, our allies, our friends. . . .

For the first time in many years, not a single Soviet soldier is participating . . . in military actions anywhere in the world. We have now put forth the initiative of curtailing all of our military bases abroad as well as our military presence there by the year 2,000. We are prepared to head toward the dissolution of the military-political blocs in Europe on a mutual basis.[65]

4. Gorbachev's Speech of December 9, 1989, to the Party's Central Committee on the Bloc

Comrades, implementation of the long-term course of perestroika exerts not only a revolutionary influence on all the spheres of life of Soviet society, but also influences other socialist countries and developments in the world. At the same time, perestroika itself comes under the influence of the world, and needs favorable international conditions. . . .

What is taking place in socialist countries is the logical outcome of a certain stage of development which made the peoples of those countries aware of the need for change . . . . They proceed in the same mainstream as our perestroika, although we in no way encouraged these processes. . . . Fraternal parties are no longer ruling in Poland and Hungary. Our friends in the German Democratic Republic and Czechoslovakia have largely lost their positions. New political forces have emerged on the arena. . . .

The Soviet Union is building its relations with east European countries . . . on a single position of respect for sovereignty, noninterference and recognition of freedom of choice. We proceed from the fact that any nation has the right to decide its fate itself, including the choice of a system, ways, the pace and methods of development. . . .

---

[65]*The New York Times,* October 25, 1989.

We are carrying out perestroika on the basis of our own, socialist principles. . . . While refining our society and enriching our economic and social
instruments by new methods and forms, we by no means depart from our
values . . . but seek to fill them with a realistic, humanistic and democratic
content.[66]

5. *Gorbachev's Televised Address to the USSR on Azerbaijan Fighting*   On
January 20, 1990, President Gorbachev addressed his country about
bloody fighting between Armenians and Azeris in the Caucasus and
the dispatch of Soviet troops to Baku, capital of Azerbaijan:

Comrades, we are all witnessing a protracted inter-ethnic conflict between
Azerbaijan and Armenia. We are all seriously concerned over the fact that
the tension that arose there not only fails to subside, but becomes aggravated
from time to time, leading to serious consequences. Over the past two years
central authorities have sought to act . . . patiently and in a thoughtful
manner, trying to solve difficult problems exclusively by peaceful, political
means.

. . . The events assumed a particularly tragic character in Baku: rampages, killings, and the driving of innocent people out of their homes and to
beyond the republic. Extremist [nationalist] forces' actions in Azerbaijan
assumed an increasingly overt anti-state, anti-constitutional and anti-popu-
lar character. The legitimate authorities were forcibly debarred from performing their functions and Government structures were disrupted in a
number of areas. . . . The aim of a forcible seizure of power in the republic
was not practically concealed. It could no longer continue so. . . . Soviet
people demanded from the country's leadership resolute measures to restore law and order, to ensure safety for people. . . . The decree of the
Presidium of the USSR Supreme Soviet has imposed a state of emergency in
Baku, units of the Interior Ministry and the Soviet Army have moved into the
city. . . .

The state is duty-bound to return peace and security to people and the
possibility to develop in a free and democratic way. . . . Today as never
before we need national accord, close cooperation and assistance to each
other in the name of better life for all peoples of our state.[67]

Suggested Additional Reading

ASLUND, ANDERS. *Gorbachev's Struggle for Economic Reform . . . 1985–88* (Ithaca,
N.Y., 1989).
BECKER, ABRAHAM. *Ogarkov's Complaint and Gorbachev's Dilemma* (Santa Monica,
Calif., 1987).

---

[66]*New York Times*, December 12, 1989.
[67]*New York Times*, January 21, 1990, p. 10.

BIALER, SEWERYN, ed. *Politics, Society and Nationality Inside Gorbachev's Russia.* Boulder, Colo., 1989).

———. *The Soviet Paradox: External Expansion, Internal Decline* (New York, 1986).

———, and M. MANDELBAUM, eds. *Gorbachev's Russia and American Foreign Policy* (Boulder, Colo., 1988).

BONNER, ARTHUR. *Among the Afghans* (Durham, N.C., 1987).

BROWN, J. F. *Eastern Europe and Communist Rule* (Durham, N.C., 1988).

BRZEZINSKI, ZBIGNIEW. *The Grand Failure: The Birth and Death of Communism in the Twentieth Century* (New York, 1989).

BUTLER, WILLIAM. *Soviet Law,* 2d ed. (London, 1988).

COHEN, STEPHEN. *Rethinking the Soviet Experience* (New York, 1985).

COLLINS, JOSEPH. *The Soviet Invasion of Afghanistan* (Cambridge, Eng., 1986).

CONQUEST, ROBERT. *Tyrants and Typewriters* . . . (Lexington, Mass., 1989).

CROUCH, MARTIN. *Revolution and Evolution: Gorbachev and Soviet Politics* (New York, 1989).

DALLIN, ALEX, and C. RICE, eds. *The Gorbachev Era* (Stanford, Calif., 1986).

DAVIES, R. W. *Soviet History in the Gorbachev Revolution* (Birmingham, Eng., 1987, and Bloomington, Ind., 1989).

DESAI, PADMA. *Perestroika in Perspective: The Design and Dilemma of Soviet Reform* (Princeton, N.J., 1989).

DZIAK, JOHN. *Chekisty: A History of the KGB* (New York, 1988).

EKLOF, BEN. *Soviet Briefing: Gorbachev and the Reform Period* (Boulder, Colo., 1989).

FRIEDBERG, MAURICE, and H. ISHAM, eds. *Soviet Society Under Gorbachev* . . . (Armonk, N.Y., 1987).

GOLDMAN, MARSHALL. *Gorbachev's Challenge: Economic Reform in the Age of High Technology* (New York, 1987).

GORBACHEV, MIKHAIL S. *Perestroika: New Thinking for Our Country and the World* (New York, 1987,1988).

———. *Selected Speeches and Articles,* 2d ed. (Moscow, 1987).

HOSKING, GEOFFREY. *The Awakening of the Soviet Union* (Cambridge, Mass., 1990).

HOUGH, JERRY. *Russia and the West: Gorbachev and the Politics of Reform* (New York, 1988).

ITO, TAKAYUKI, ed. *Facing Up to the Past: Soviet Historiography and Perestroika* (Sapporo, Japan, 1989).

JACOBSEN, CARL G., ed. *Soviet Foreign Policy: New Dynamics, New Themes* (New York, 1989).

Joint Economic Comittee. *Gorbachev's Economic Plans* (Washington, D.C., 1987).

JONES, T. ANTHONY. *Perestroika: Gorbachev's Social Revolution* (Westview, Conn., 1990).

JOYCE, WALTER, et al., eds. *Gorbachev and Gorbachevism* (New York, 1989).

KITTRIE, NICHOLAS, and I. VOLGYES, eds. *The Uncertain Future: Gorbachev's Eastern Bloc* (New York, 1988).

KNIGHT, AMY. *The KGB: Police and Politics in the Soviet Union* (Boston, 1988).

LAIRD, ROY. *The Politburo: Demographic Trends, Gorbachev and the Future* (Boulder, Colo., 1986).

LAPIDUS, GAIL. *State and Society in the Soviet Union* (Boulder, Colo., 1989).

LEWIN, MOSHE. *The Gorbachev Phenomenon* (Berkeley, Calif., 1988).

MARPLES, DAVID. *Chernobyl and Nuclear Power in the USSR* (New York, 1987).

McCAULEY, MARTIN, ed. *The Soviet Union Under Gorbachev* (New York, 1987).

MEDVEDEV, ZHORES. *Soviet Agriculture* (New York, 1987).

MELVILLE, ANDREI, and GAIL LAPIDUS. *The Glasnost Papers: Voices on Reform from Moscow* (Boulder, Colo., 1990).

MORRISON, DONALD, ed. *Mikhail S. Gorbachev: An Intimate Biography* (New York, 1988).

MOTYL, ALEX J. *Will the Non-Russians Rebel?* . . . (Ithaca, N. Y., 1987).

NOVE, ALEC. *Glasnost in Action: Cultural Renaissance in Russia* (Boston, 1989).

OLIVIER, ROY. *Islam and Resistance in Afghanistan* (Cambridge, Eng., 1986).

DU PLESSIX, FRANCINE. *Soviet Women* (New York, 1990).

ROWEN, H. S., and C. WOLF, eds. *The Future of the Soviet Empire* (New York, 1987).

RYWKIN, MICHAEL. *Soviet Society Today* (Armonk, N.Y., 1989).

SAIVETZ, CAROL R. *The Soviet Union and the Gulf in the 1980s* (Boulder, Colo., 1989).

SHANSAB, NASIR. *Soviet Expansion in the Third World* (Silver Spring, Md., 1986).

SHCHERBAK, IURII. *Chernobyl: A Documentary Story,* trans. Ian Press (New York, 1989).

SINGLETON, FRED, ed. *Environmental Problems in the Soviet Union and Eastern Europe* (Boulder, Colo., 1987).

SMITH, GORDON. *Soviet Politics: Continuity and Contradiction* (New York, 1987).

TARASULO, ISAAC, ed. *Gorbachev and Glasnost: Viewpoints from the Soviet Press* (Wilmington, Del., 1989).

TIMMERMANN, HEINZ. *The Decline of the World Communist Movement* . . . , trans. J. Friend (Boulder, Colo., 1987).

URBAN, MARK. *War in Afghanistan* (New York, 1988).

WOODBY, SYLVIA. *Gorbachev and the Decline of Ideology in Soviet Foreign Policy* (Boulder, Colo., 1989).

YANOV, ALEXANDER. *The Russian Challenge and the Year 2000,* trans. J. Rosenthal (New York, 1987).

ZACEK, JANE S. *The Gorbachev Generation: Issues in Soviet Foreign Policy* (New York, 1988).

ADDITIONAL BIBLIOGRAPHY

The following brief bibliography contains only major reference works relating to Russian and Soviet history and some key general histories in English emphasizing the modern period. For works on specific periods and topics, see the selected bibliographies at the end of each chapter of this text.

Reference Works

ALLWORTH, E., ed. *Soviet Asia-Bibliographies: The Iranian, Mongolian and Turkic Nationalities* (New York, 1973).

American Bibliography of Russian and East European Studies (Bloomington, Ind., annually since 1957).

BENNIGSEN, ALEXANDRE, and S. ENDERS WIMBUSH. *Muslims of the Soviet Empire: A Guide* (Bloomington, Ind. 1986).

BEZER, C., ed. *Russian and Soviet Studies: A Handbook* (Columbus, Ohio, 1973).

CARPENTER, K. E., comp. *Russian Revolutionary Literature Collection* (New Haven, Conn., 1976).

CLARKE, R. A., and D. J. Matko. *Soviet Economic Facts, 1917–1981* (London, 1983).

CRUMMEY, ROBERT, ed. *Reform in Russia and the U.S.S.R.: Past and Prospects* (Champaign, Ill., 1990).

DMYTRYSHYN, BASIL, and FREDERICK COX. *The Soviet Union and the Middle East: A Documentary Record of Afghanistan, Iran and Turkey, 1917–1985* (Princeton, N.J., 1985).

EGAN, DAVID, and M. A. EGAN. *Russian Autocrats from Ivan the Great to the Fall of the Romanov Dynasty: An Annotated Bibliography of English Language Sources to 1985* (Metuchen, N.J., 1987).

The Europa-World Yearbook 1989, 2 vols. (London, 1989).

FLORINSKY, M. T., ed. *McGraw-Hill Encyclopedia of Russia and the Soviet Union* (New York, 1961).

Great Soviet Encyclopedia: A Translation of the Third Edition, 10 vols. (New York, 1973).

HAMMOND, T., ed. *Soviet Foreign Relations and World Communism: A Selected Annotated Bibliography of 7,000 Books in 30 Languages* (Princeton, N.J., 1965).

HORAK, S. M. *Junior Slavica: A Selected Annotated Bibliography of Books in English on Russia and Eastern Europe* (Rochester, N.Y., 1968).

HORECKY, P., ed. *Basic Russian Publications: A Selected and Annotated Bibliography on Russia and the Soviet Union* (Chicago, 1962).

———. *Russia and the Soviet Union: A Bibliographic Guide to Western Language Publications* (Chicago, 1965).

KATZ, Z., et al., eds. *Handbook of Major Soviet Nationalities* (New York, 1975).

KEEFE, E. *Area Handbook for the Soviet Union* (Washington, D.C., 1971).

KERNIG, C., ed. *Marxism, Communism and Western Society: A Comparative Encyclopedia*, 8 vols. (New York, 1972).

KUBIJOVYC, et al., eds. *Ukraine: A Concise Encyclopedia*, 2 vols. (Ottawa, 1971).

LEVIN, NORA. *The Jews in the Soviet Union Since 1917: Paradox of Survival*, 2 vols. (New York and London, 1988).

MAGOCSI, PAUL R. *Ukraine: A Historical Atlas* (Toronto, 1985).

MAICHEL, K. *Guide to Russian Reference Books* (Stanford, Calif., 1962).

———. *Guide to Russian Reference Books II: History, Auxiliary Sciences, Ethnography and Geography* (Stanford, Calif., 1964).

MARTIANOV, N. N. *Books Available in English by Russians and on Russia* (New York, 1960).

NERHOOD, H., comp. *To Russia and Return: An Annotated Bibliography of Travelers' English Language Accounts of Russia from the Ninth Century to the Present* (Columbus, Ohio, 1968).

PEARSON, RAYMOND, ed. *Russia and Eastern Europe: A Bibliographic Guide* (Manchester, Eng., 1989).

PIERCE, R. *Soviet Central Asia: A Bibliography*, 3 vols. (Berkeley, Calif., 1966).

PUSHKAREV, S. G. *A Source Book for Russian History from Early Times to 1917*, ed. A. Ferguson et al., 3 vols. (New Haven, Conn., 1972).

SCHÖPFLIN, G., ed. *The Soviet Union and Eastern Europe: A Handbook* (New York, 1970).

SCHULTHEISS, T., ed. *Russian Studies, 1941–1958: A Cumulation of the Annual Bibliographies from the Russian Review* (Ann Arbor, Mich., 1972).

SHAPIRO, D. *A Selected Bibliography of Works in English on Russian History, 1801–1917* (New York and London, 1962).

SHUKMAN, HAROLD, ed. *The Blackwell Encyclopedia of the Russian Revolution* (Oxford, Eng., 1988).

SHTEPPA, K. F. *Russian Historians and the Soviet State* (New Brunswick, N.J., 1962).

STEEVES, PAUL D., ed. *The Modern Encyclopedia of Religions in Russia and the Soviet Union* (Gulf Breeze, Fla., 1988–).

SZEFTEL, M. "Russia Before 1917," in *Bibliographical Introduction to Legal History and Ethnology*, ed. J. Glissen (Brussels, Bel., 1966).

UTECHIN, S. V. *Everyman's Concise Encyclopedia of Russia* (New York, 1961).

WHITING, K. *The Soviet Union Today*, rev. ed. (New York, 1966).

WIECZYNSKI, JOSEPH L., ed. *The Modern Encyclopedia of Russian and Soviet History*, 52 vols. to date (Gulf Breeze, Fla., 1976–). (Extremely useful.)

WOZNIUK, VLADIMIR. *Understanding Soviet Foreign Policy: Readings and Documents* (New York, 1990).

General Histories

BLACK, CYRIL E. *Understanding Soviet Politics: The Perspective of Russian History* (Boulder, Colo., 1986).

DANIELS, ROBERT. *Russia: The Roots of Confrontation* (Cambridge, Mass., 1985). (General treatment of Russian and Soviet history.)

DMYTRYSHYN, BASIL. *USSR: A Concise History*, 4th ed. (New York, 1984).

DVORNIK, F. *The Slavs in European History and Civilization* (New Brunswick, N.J., 1975).

DZIEWANOWSKI, M. K. *A History of Soviet Russia*, 3d ed. (Englewood Cliffs, N.J., 1989).

ELLIS, JANE. *The Russian Orthodox Church: A Contemporary History* (Bloomington, Ind., 1986).

FLORINSKY, M. T. *Russia: A History and an Interpretation*, 2 vols. (New York, 1953).

———. *Russia: A Short History*, 2d ed. (New York, 1969).

GADDIS, JOHN L. *Russia, the Soviet Union, and the United States: An Interpretive History*, 2d ed. (New York, 1990).

GRAHAM, LOREN. *Science, Philosophy, and Human Behavior in the Soviet Union* (New York, 1987).

HELLER, MIKHAIL, and A. M. NEKRICH. *Utopia in Power: The History of the Soviet Union from 1917 to the Present* (New York, 1986).

HINGLEY, R. *A Concise History of Russia* (New York, 1972).

KOCHAN, LIONEL. *The Making of Modern Russia* (New York, 1983).

KORT, M. G. *Soviet Colossus: A History of the USSR* (New York, 1985).

MCNEAL, ROBERT H. *Tsar and Cossack: 1855–1914* (New York, 1987).

MEDISH, VADIM. *The Soviet Union*, 3d ed. (Englewood Cliffs, N.J., 1987).

MILIUKOV, PAUL, et al. *History of Russia*, trans. C. Markmann, 3 vols. (New York, 1968).

RAEFF, MARC. *Understanding Imperial Russia: State and Society in the Old Regime* (New York, 1984).

RAUCH, GEORG VON. *A History of Soviet Russia,* 6th ed. (New York, 1972).

RIASANOVSKY, N. V. *A History of Russia,* 4th ed. (New York, 1984).

RIHA, T. *Readings in Russian Civilization,* 2d ed., 3 vols. (Chicago, 1969).

ROGGER, HANS. *Russia in the Age of Modernization and Revolution, 1881–1917* (London and New York, 1983, 1988).

SPECTOR, I. *An Introduction to Russian History and Culture,* 5th ed. (Princeton, N.J., 1969).

SUMNER, B. H. *A Short History of Russia* (New York, 1949, 1962).

TREADGOLD, D. W. *Twentieth Century Russia,* 5th ed. (Boston, 1981).

ULAM, ADAM. *A History of Soviet Russia* (New York, 1976).

WESTWOOD, J. N. *Endurance and Endeavour: Russian History 1812–1981,* 2d ed. (New York, 1981).

WREN, M. C. *The Course of Russian History,* 4th ed. (New York, 1979).

RUSSIAN AND SOVIET LEADERS, 1801-1990

1. Russian Tsars:

Alexander I	1801–25	Alexander III	1881–94
Nicholas I	1825–55	Nicholas II	1894–17
Alexander II	1855–81		

2. Soviet leaders (all except Lenin were general or first secretaries of the Communist Party of the Soviet Union):

V. I. Lenin	1917–24	L. I. Brezhnev	1964–82
J. V. Stalin	1924–53	Iu. V. Andropov	1982–84
G. M. Malenkov	1953	K. V. Chernenko	1984–85
N. S. Khrushchev	1953–64	M. S. Gorbachev	1985–

3. Chairmen of the Council of People's Commissars (Prime Ministers after 1946):

V. I. Lenin	1917–24	N. A. Bulganin	1955–58
A. I. Rykov	1924–30	N. S. Khrushchev	1958–64
V. M. Molotov	1930–41	A. N. Kosygin	1964–80
J. V. Stalin	1941–53	N. A. Tikhonov	1980–85
G. M. Malenkov	1953–55	N. I. Ryzhkov	1985–

4. Full Members of Politburo (Presidium, 1952–66) of the Soviet
Communist Party:

V. I. Lenin	1919–24	N. M. Shvernik	1952–53,
L. D. Trotskii	1919–26		1957–66
J. V. Stalin	1919–53	M. A. Suslov	1955–82
L. B. Kamenev	1919–25	D. I. Chesnokov	1952–53
N. N. Krestinskii	1919–21	M. F. Shkiriatov	1952–53
G. E. Zinoviev	1921–26	A. I. Kirichenko	1955–60
A. I. Rykov	1922–30	L. I. Brezhnev	1957–82
M. P. Tomskii	1922–30	G. K. Zhukov	June–Oct. 1957
N. I. Bukharin	1924–29	E. A. Furtseva	1957–61
V. M. Molotov	1926–57	N. I. Beliaev	1957–60
K. E. Voroshilov	1926–60	N. G. Ignatov	1957–61
M. I. Kalinin	1926–46	F. R. Kozlov	1957–64
Ia. E. Rudzutak	1926–32	N. A. Mukhitdinov	1957–61
V. V. Kuibyshev	1927–35	N. V. Podgorny	1960–77
L. M. Kaganovich	1930–57	D. S. Polianskii	1960–76
S. M. Kirov	1930–34	G. I. Voronov	1961–73
S. V. Kosior	1930–38	A. P. Kirilenko	1962–81
G. K. Ordzhonikidze	1930–37	G. V. Romanov	1976–85
A. A. Andreyev	1932–52	K. V. Chernenko	1977–85
V. Ia. Chubar	1935–38	A. N. Shelepin	1964–75
A. I. Mikoyan	1935–66	P. E. Shelest	1964–73
A. A. Zhdanov	1939–48	K. T. Mazurov	1965–78
N. S. Khrushchev	1939–64	A. Ia. Pelshe	1966–83
L. P. Beria	1946–53	V. V. Grishin	1971–85
G. M. Malenkov	1946–57	F. D. Kulakov	1971–78
N. A. Voznesenskii	1947–49	D. A. Kunaev	1971–89
N. A. Bulganin	1948–58	V. V. Shcherbitskii	1971–89
A. N. Kosygin	1949–50,	Iu. V. Andropov	1973–84
	1960–80	A. A. Gromyko	1973–88
		D. F. Ustinov	1973–84
V. M. Andrianov	1952–53	A. A. Grechko	1973–76
A. B. Aristov	1952–53,	N. A. Tikhonov	1979–85
	1957–61	M. S. Gorbachev	1980–
S. D. Ignatiev	1952–53	G. A. Aliyev	1982–87
D. S. Korochenko	1952–53	M. S. Solomentsev	1983–88
O. V. Kuusinen	1952–53,	V. I. Vorotnikov	1983–87
	1957–64	V. M. Chebrikov	1985–
V. V. Kuznetsov	1952–53	E. G. Ligachev	1985–
V. A. Malyshev	1952–53	E. A. Shevarnadze	1985–
L. G. Melnikov	1952–53	N. I. Ryzhkov	1985–
N. A. Mikhailov	1952–53	L. N. Zaikov	1987–
M. G. Pervukhin	1952–57	V. P. Nikonov	1987–
P. K. Ponomarenko	1952–53	N. I. Sliunkov	1987–
M. Z. Saburov	1952–57	A. N. Iakovlev	1987–

APPENDIX B

AREA AND POPULATION OF UNION REPUBLICS

(JANUARY 1989)

Name of Republic	Area (in 1,000 square miles)	Population (in thousands)	Capital	Population (in thousands)
Armenian SSR	11.5	3,830	Erevan	1,199
Azerbaijan SSR	33.4	7,029	Baku	1,757
Byelorussian SSR	80.2	10,200	Minsk	1,589
Estonian SSR	17.4	1,573	Talinn	454*
Georgian SSR	26.9	5,449	Tbilisi	1,260
Kazakh SSR	1,049.2	16,538	Alma Ata	1,128
Kirghiz SSR	76.6	4,291	Frunze	616
Latvian SSR	24.9	2,680	Riga	915
Lithuanian SSR	25.2	3,690	Vilnius	582
Moldavian SSR	13.0	4,341	Kishinev	665
Russian SFSR	6,592.8	147,386	Moscow	8,769
Tadzhik SSR	55.3	5,112	Dushanbe	595
Turkmen SSR	188.5	3,534	Ashkhabad	339*
Ukrainian SSR	233.1	51,704	Kiev	2,587
Uzbek SSR	172.7	19,906	Tashkent	2,073
USSR	8,649,540 sq. miles (22,402,200 sq. kms.)	286,717	Moscow	

* 1984 figure.
Source: The Europa World Yearbook, 1989: A World Survey (London, 1989).

POPULATION OF THE LARGEST CITIES OF THE USSR, 1989 (ESTIMATED)

1.	Moscow	8,769,000	11.	Tbilisi	1,260,000
2.	Leningrad	4,456,000	12.	Kuibyshev	1,257,000
3.	Kiev	2,587,000	13.	Erevan	1,199,000
4.	Tashkent	2,073,000	14.	Dniepropetrovsk	1,179,000
5.	Baku	1,757,000	15.	Omsk	1,148,000
6.	Kharkov	1,611,000	16.	Cheliabinsk	1,143,000
7.	Minsk	1,589,000	17.	Odessa	1,115,000
8.	Gorkii	1,438,000	18.	Kazan	1,094,000
9.	Novosibirsk	1,436,000	19.	Perm	1,091,000
10.	Sverdlovsk	1,367,000	20.	Ufa	1,083,000

Source: The Europa World Yearbook, 1989.

APPENDIX D

SOVIET PRODUCTION OF SELECTED INDUSTRIAL ITEMS

Item	1913	1940	1958	1975	1988
Pig iron	4.2	14.9	39.6	99.9	112 million tons
Steel (crude)	4.3	18.3	54.9	136	163 million tons
Coal	29.2	165.9	496.1	684	772 million tons
Petroleum	10.3	31.1	113.2	459	624 million tons
Electric power	2.0	48.3	235.4	975	1,705 billion kilowatts
Automobiles (1910–1915)	.45	5.5	107.8	1,119	1,300 thousands

Source: The Europa World Yearbook, 1989.

INDEX

Abalkin, Leonid (economist), 511
Academy of Arts (1758), 120
Academy of Sciences, 279, 283–284
"Address from the Throne" (1906), 86
Aehrenthal, Alois von (Austrian Foreign Minister), 96
Afanasev, Iuri (Soviet historian), 491–492, 520
Aganbegyan, Abel (Soviet economist), 477, 492, 507
Akhmadulina, Bella (poetess), 392
Akhmatova, Anna (1888–1966, poetess), 293–295, 410
Akselrod, Paul (Russian Marxist), 67, 70–71, 139
Aksionov, Vasili (Soviet writer), 391, 403, 407
Aleksandrovich, Vladimir (grand duke), 79
Alekseev, M. V. (Russian general), 134, 161, 184
Alekseevna, Liudmila (Soviet journalist), 494
Alexander I (tsar, 1801–1825), 4, 19, 20, 325
Alexander II (tsar, 1855–1881), 4, 21, 27–33,

36–39, 41, 55, 56, 59, 62, 63, 518
Reforms of, 28–30, 107, 485–486.
Alexander III (tsar, 1881–1894), 38, 39, 41, 46, 47, 64, 69, 115
Alexandra of Hesse (empress, 1894–1917), 39, 137–138
Alexis I (tsar, 1645–1676), 54
Algeciras Conference (1906), 96
Aliyev, Geidar (Soviet party leader), 469
Allilueva, Nadezhda (Stalin's second wife), 222
All-Russian Union of Soviet Writers, 287, 303
First Congress of, 288–289, 302
Alpatov, Mikhail (art critic), 392
Amalrik, Andrei (Soviet dissident writer), 387, 431
Amin, H. (Afghan Communist), 446, 448
Andropov, Iuri V. (KGB chief, party first secretary), 486
career of, 468
economic policies of, 475–478
foreign policies of, 479–482

politics and, 468–470
rise to power, 464, 466
Anglo-Russian Convention (1907), 47, 96
Anti-Comintern Pact (1936), 323
"Anti-Party Group" (1957), 362–365, 374
"April Theses" (1917), 157
Arbatov, Iurii (Soviet scholar), 469, 479
Arkhipov, Ivan (Soviet official), 479
Armand, Inessa (friend of Lenin), 188–189, 199
Association for Contemporary Music (ASM), 269–270
"August Bloc" (1912), 89
Austro-Russian agreements (1897, 1903), 47
Averbakh, Leopold (Soviet writer), 287
Azev, Evno (terrorist), 73, 89

Bagdad Railway, 98
Baibakov, N. K. (head of Gosplan), 433
Bakst, Leon (designer), 118, 122
Baku Congress (1920), 318
Bakunin, Mikhail (socialist), 59–61, 63

Purge – see great Purge

TAAN — 387

263 War Communism (1917–1921)
263 NEP (1921–28)

FIRST FIVE YR PLAN 1928/29
GREAT PURGE 1935–38

WRITERS ENGINEERS OF HUMAN SOUL pg 302

PERSONALITY CULT – (MARXIST TERMINOLOGY) – A DELIBERATE,
ORGANIZED PROCESS OF PERSUADING A
COMMUNITY THAT ITS LEADER HAS A
SUPREME EXCELLENCE IN HIS PERSONAL
QUALITIES WHICH ENTITLES HIM TO
CHARACTERISTICS
UNQUESTIONING LOYALTY.